INTERFERENCE

BOOKS BY DAN E. MOLDEA

The Hoffa Wars:
Teamsters, Rebels, Politicians and the Mob
1978

The Hunting of Cain:
A True Story of Money, Greed and Fratricide
1983

Dark Victory:
Ronald Reagan, MCA and the Mob
1986

Interference:
How Organized Crime Influences Professional Football
1989

Interference

How Organized Crime Influences Professional Football

Dan E. Moldea

William Morrow and Company, Inc.
New York

Library of Congress Cataloging in Publication Data

Moldea, Dan E., 1950–
Interference : how organized crime influences professional football / Dan E. Moldea.
p. cm.
Bibliography: p.
Includes index.
ISBN 0-688-08303-X
1. Sports—United States—Corrupt practices. 2. Football—United States. 3. Organized crime—United States. I. Title.
GV718.2U6M65 1989
796'.0973—dc20 89-12268
CIP

Printed in the United States of America

2 3 4 5 6 7 8 9 10

BOOK DESIGN BY NICOLA MAZZELLA

To Mimi

Acknowledgments

THIS WORK COULD NOT have been completed without the assistance of my associate, Washington journalist William Scott Malone, who encouraged me to write this book. Malone was the chief investigator and an associate producer of the January 1983 *Frontline* program on public television, "An Unauthorized History of the NFL." His research, interviews, and advice have been invaluable to me.

I would also like to express my gratitude to Thomas Mechling, the executive director of the National Center for Gambling Information, who conceived of the *Frontline* program. He also has done research on behalf of the National Football League Players Association.

Also essential were the help and guidance of Professor G. Robert Blakey of Notre Dame University; Ledra Brady of the Drug Enforcement Administration; Ronald Goldstock, the executive director of the New York Task Force Against Organized Crime; Patrick Healy, former Chicago Crime Commission executive director, and Jerry Gladdin, the commission's chief investigator; Aaron Kohn, the former executive director of the Metropolitan Crime Commission of New Orleans; Phil Manuel, former chief investigator of the U.S. Senate Permanent Subcommittee on Investigations; Joe Nellis, former deputy chief counsel of the Kefauver Committee; Leroy Orozco of the Los Angeles Police Department; Vincent Piersante, former chief of the Michigan attorney general's division on organized crime; Ralph

Salerno, the former supervisor of detectives for the New York Police Department; U.S. Senate investigator and author Walter Sheridan; Washington, D.C., police detectives Carl Shoffler and Joe Quantrille; Frank Silby, former chief investigator of the U.S. Senate Labor Commission; John Sopko, deputy chief counsel of the U.S. Senate Permanent Subcommittee on Investigations; enforcement attorney Tom von Stein of the Securities and Exchange Committee; investigator Joseph J. Theis of the U.S. Department of Labor; and Joseph Yablonsky, the former chief of the Las Vegas FBI office.

I would also like to thank those additional confidential sources of information with the Alameda County (California) District Attorney's Office, the U.S. Department of Labor, the Detroit Police Department, the Federal Bureau of Investigation, the Florida Department of Law Enforcement, the U.S. General Accounting Office, the Internal Revenue Service, the Los Angeles Police Department, the Miami Crime Commission, the Nevada Gambling Commission, the Nevada Gaming Control Board, the New Jersey Casino Control Commission, the New Jersey State Police Intelligence Division, the Organized Crime and Racketeering Section of the U.S. Justice Department and its Strike Force field offices, the Pennsylvania Crime Commission, the San Diego Police Department, the U.S. Securities and Exchange Commission, and the Washington, D.C., Metropolitan Police Department.

I am also grateful to several members of the sports-gambling community whose experiences and insights were extremely valuable, especially: oddsmakers Bobby Martin of New York and Michael Roxborough of Las Vegas; handicapper Mort Olshan of *The Gold Sheet,* which is based in Los Angeles; and professional gamblers Ed Curd of Miami, Donald Dawson of Detroit, Lem Banker and Marty Kane of Las Vegas, and Gene Nolan of Baton Rouge.

I would also like to thank several members of the press, including: independent investigative reporters Mike Acoca, Jack Anderson, Dick Brenneman, David Fisher, Seymour Hersh, Jonathan Kwitny, Larry Leamer, Hank Messick, Jim Neff, and Robert Pack; Lowell Bergman of CBS News; Chris Blatchford of KCBS-TV in Los Angeles; Bill Brubaker and Charles Trueheart of *The Washington Post;* Pat Clawson of *Radio & Records;* William K. Knoedelseder, Jr., of *The Los Angeles Times;* Peter Noyes of KNBC-TV in Los Angeles; Richard O'Connell and Betty Bosarge of the Washington Crime News Service; John Oravecz of *The Pittsburgh Press;* David Robb of *Daily Variety;* Ira Rosen of ABC News; and Denny Walsh of *The Sacramento Bee.* Special thanks are given to John Hanrahan, executive director of the Fund for Investigative Journalism, who provided me with a research grant.

Deep appreciation is also extended to the Reporters Committee for Freedom of the Press, especially executive director Jane Kirtley and attorney Warren W. Faulk of Camden, New Jersey, for their efforts on my behalf after I was subpoenaed as a defense witness—in the midst of my work on this book—in a 1988 federal racketeering trial and ordered to reveal a source who was quoted in my last book, *Dark Victory: Ronald Reagan, MCA and the Mob.* I refused to reveal the source and was defended by Faulk and the committee. The subpoena was eventually quashed, saving me considerable time and expense.

Sincere gratitude is further expressed to *Regardie's* magazine and its publisher Bill Regardie, editor in chief Brian Kelly, and managing editor Bob Vassilak, who played important roles in the publication of my February 1988 cover story, "The NFL and the Mob: Pro Football's Dirty Secret."

And my additional thanks are extended to the members of my family, as well as Cindy Abrams, Merilou Baker, Ed Becker, Leonard Bertsch, Dick and Linda Billings, John Boslough, Peter Bourne, Howard Bray, Gervais Brekke, John Burns, Cristine Candela, Mark Carson, Buddy and Guta Carter, Judy and Tor Carlsson, Gene Cesar, Isolde Chapin, Mae Churchill, Kay Constantine, Chuck Conconi, Donn Cory, David Cross, Bob and Kaye Davis, Nancy Davis, Tim Davis, Michael deBlois, Chuck DeCaro, Vivian DeWitt, David and Penny Dial, John Dinges, Trina Duncan, Michael Ewing, Debbie Farris, Lou Farris, Rachel Fershko, Bob Fink, Arthur Fox, Gordon Freedman, John Friedman, Mike Gale, Ted and Françoise Gianoutsos, Jeff Goldberg, Angie Graves, Frank Greco, Jim Gross, Anne Grower, Robin Beasley Herbst, Bob Hirasuna, Jim Hougan, Pam Johnson, Walter and Helen Johnston, Lance Karkruff, Myrna Khalid, Mary King, Larry Kramer, Frank Kuznik, Chris Lancianese, Todd Lane, Bob Lawrence, Paul Levy, Neil and Susan Livingstone, Bob Loomis, Myra MacPherson, Matt Mahurin, Bob and Jan Manning, Don and Kathy Marteny, Tom Matuk, Lisa McCormick, Phil Melanson, Janet Michaud, Ethelbert and Denise Miller, Kristy Miller,

Luree Miller, Marsha Moldea, Mary Moldea, Larry Momchilov, Harry Moore, Rich Munsey, Don Murdock, Pam and Joe Nargie, Gary and Helen Nesbitt, Jo Nicholson, Noodles, Don North, Katie Oana, Jean O'Neil, Tom and Stephanie O'Neill, Ken Paff, David Pecchia, Mark and Nina Perry, Mike Pilgrim, Dan Porter, Susan Raehn, Peter Range, Barbara Raskin, Jere Real, Bob Reiss, Jim Retter, Vic Reynemer, Joan Rice, Rigo, Nick Roetzel, Stu Rose, Bryan Ross, Wayne Rosso, Tricia Rubacky, Richard Rymlin, Judith Saks, David Scheim, Curtis Seltzer, Frank Selzer, Jeff Stein, Greg Stone, Charles Sutherland, Joel and Margery Swerdlow, Jim Switzer, Marge Tabankin, Bill and Belle Thomas, Rhys Thomas, Jonathan and Margie Toth, Shelly Tromberg, Dawn Trouard, Judith and Les Turner, Merilou Vierheller, Jeff Wachtel, Jimmy Warner, Garland Weber, Herbert Wechsler, Danny Wexler, Herb White, Peter and Rebecca Whitmore, Marjorie Williams, Lee Wilson, Dick and Jean Wolford, Richard Wright, Cathy Wyler, Abe Zaidan, Bob Zangrando, and Anne Zill.

Also, in memory of my father, Mary Chima, Sue Davies, Jean Kisbac, Joe and Betty Madigan, Egberto Miller, Sam Pistrui, Earl Popa, Eli Utan, and George Vocar.

Finally, I would like to thank attorney Ronald Goldfarb of Washington, D.C.; Mel Berger of the William Morris Agency; my booking agents Bob Katz, Jodi Solomon, Karin Hauch, and Ellie Deegan, of K & S Speakers in Cambridge, Massachusetts; my personal attorneys, George L. Farris of Akron, Ohio, and John Sikorski of Northampton, Massachusetts; Janet Donovan of Creative Enterprises; my writing coach, Mrs. Nancy Nolte of Boulder, Colorado; William Morrow's Lori Ames, Thomas A. Bisdale, and Bob Shuman; and my patient editor at Morrow, Lisa Drew, who believed in and fought for this project from the outset.

Contents

Glossary

Action: Betting.
Bagman: An intermediary who picks up and delivers money.
Bank: The financial backer of a gambling operation.
Beard: A proxy bettor, a front man.
Betting cards: A system of betting in which gamblers must pick between three to twenty winners from a list of upcoming games.
Betting line: The posted list of upcoming games and their point spreads.
Black Book: The list of undesirable people who are forbidden to enter any casino in Nevada.
Blue box: A device used by some bookmakers to make illegal long-distance calls.
Bookmaker: A broker who accepts wagers from gamblers, usually taking a commission on losing bets booked.
Bottom sheet: A bookmaker's accounting of gambling debts.
Circled game: A contest in which only limited action is accepted.
Closing line: The final list of point spreads offered before game time.
Covering the spread: Beating the posted point spread.
Edge: An advantage that one believes might improve one's ability to predict the outcome of a game.
11–10: The traditional bet with a bookmaker in which the gambler puts up $11 to win $10.
Fall guy: A guilty or innocent person who accepts the full blame for a crime in order to protect others.
Favorite: The predicted winning team in a particular contest.

Fixed game: A game in which one or more participants willfully manipulate the final outcome of a game.
Flip: To turn state's evidence.
Front man: One who has a façade of legitimacy but secretly represents the interests of his underworld backers.
Grease: A bribe.
Hack: A sportswriter who provides unconditional loyalty to a particular team or sport in order to maintain his access and sources.
Handicapper: One who determines the conditions and sets the odds that will equalize two teams in an upcoming game.
Handle: The total amount of money bet on a particular game or series of contests.
Hedge: The covering of a bet with a second bet; a layoff.
High roller: A high-stakes gambler.
House: The operator of any gambling business.
Injury report: A description of the status of an injured player, which is frequently used as a variable in betting equations.
Inside information: The data obtained on a particular team or its players and/or staff that may impact upon the final outcome of a game.
Juice: The money owed to a bookmaker or a loan shark.
Juice collector: One who collects the juice.
Lay: To bet.
Layoff: A bookmaker's bet with another bookmaker made in order to help equalize the excess action he has accepted from his customers.
Line: The posted list of games and their point spreads.
Loan shark: One, usually mob-connected, who loans money at a high weekly interest rate.
Lock: A sure winner.
Man-to-man betting: Gambling without either party taking a commission for the bet made.
Marker: An IOU.
Middling: Betting on both teams in a game at different point spreads, in the hope that the final score comes in between so that both bets can be won.
Moving the line: Making alterations in the line based on the volume of betting or other factors, such as injuries.
Odds: The ratio of money that may be won versus the amount of money bet.
Oddsmaker: A person who sets the line.

Off the boards: A situation in which bookmakers will accept no further action.

Opening line: The initial list of point spreads for upcoming games.

Outlaw line: The early, private line set by professional gamblers, which is financed, distributed, and enforced by the organized-crime syndicate.

Over/under the total: Betting that the combined score of two teams in a particular game will be over/under a predicted number.

Pari-mutuel: A betting system in which the amount of money paid out to winners is based upon the total pool of bets.

Parlay: Betting on a combination of two or more games.

Pen register: A device attached to a telephone line that maintains a record of each number dialed.

Pigeon: An uneducated, naïve, or unsophisticated gambler.

Player: A gambler.

Point spread: A form of handicapping in which oddsmakers predict how many points one team needs against another in order to even out the public betting on a particular game.

Power rating: A number created by a handicapper on the basis of the strength of a particular team.

Press: To increase one's bet.

Price: Point spread.

Pricemaker: An oddsmaker.

Push: A bet that falls right on the point spread; a tie in terms of a money decision.

Runner: A messenger.

Scalping: Selling tickets to a contest at a price above their face value.

Shaving points: The act of one or more participants in a contest manipulating the outcome of a game so that the final score does not cover the spread.

Skim: The cash siphoned off from an operation before it is reported.

Spike mike: An electronic-surveillance device.

Sports book: A legal sports-bookmaking business.

Stand off a bet: To tie or push.

Straw man: A front man.

Taking a lead: An early bet with a favorable price in anticipation of a subsequent movement in the line.

Thrown game: A game lost intentionally by a participant.

Title III: The section of the 1968 Omnibus Crime Control and Safe Streets Act that permits court-authorized electronic surveillance if certain conditions are met.
Tote board: A device that posts teams, contests, and either the odds or the line.
Tout: An individual of questionable credentials who sells his predictions of the outcomes of games.
Underdog: The predicted losing team in a particular contest.
Unnatural money: Large wagers that suddenly appear against the conventional wisdom of the oddsmakers and handicappers.
Vigorish: The bookmaker's commission.
Wagering stamp: A federal occupational tax for gamblers.
Welsh: To refuse to pay off a bet already made and lost.

Among the types of conduct detrimental to the NFL and professional football that call for serious penalties are the following:

1. Accepting a bribe or agreeing to throw or fix a game or to illegally influence its outcome.

2. Failing to promptly report any bribe offer or any attempt to throw or fix a game or to illegally influence its outcome.

3. Betting on any NFL game.

4. Associating with gamblers or with gambling activities in a manner tending to bring discredit to the NFL.

Any such conduct may result in severe penalties, up to and including a fine and/or suspension from the NFL for life.

NFL COMMISSIONER PETE ROZELLE

Prologue: Dealing with Myths

YEARS BEFORE HE BECAME president of the United States, actor Ronald Reagan portrayed Notre Dame's George Gipp in the 1940 Warner Brothers movie *Knute Rockne—All-American.* Gipp had died of pneumonia in December 1920 after an illustrious college football career. His purported deathbed request to Rockne, "Win just one for the Gipper," was used during a locker room pep talk and helped to inspire Rockne's 1928 team in its upset victory against Army. And, as the Gipper incarnate, Reagan used the line to inspire voters to elect him to the California governor's mansion and later the White House. To those who saw the movie and listened to Reagan utter those now-famous words, Gipp epitomized the virtues of good character, sportsmanship, and "the right way of living."

History, however, now shows that Gipp, a man of truly questionable moral values, probably never made any such request on or off his deathbed; that Rockne, who was known for grasping at anything to incite his players, had fabricated the incident; and that Reagan's movie further embellished the Gipp/Rockne charade.

Hollywood, which is notorious for cooking up such fantasies as the Gipp/Rockne story, realizes that most Americans view sports as a vehicle of inspiration and entertainment. Thus, sports history is routinely manipulated. Left unquestioned, stories like that of the Gipper become permanent fixtures of Americana. Regardless of the facts, the American public continues to believe the legend of George Gipp's deathbed request to Knute Rockne.

The difficulties in debunking the myth about one college coach and one of his players is an indication of the problems in dispelling the legends about an entire institution, particularly one as popular as football. Powerful forces in America have built empires around these myths; and the preservation of these empires and the personal wealth of those who own them depend upon the maintenance of the legends.

In the Reagan movie myth of the lives of Rockne and Gipp, there is one scene in which Rockne chases away a gambler who is looking for an edge. Rockne, played by actor Pat O'Brien, tells him, "We haven't got any use for gamblers around here. You've done your best to ruin baseball and horse racing. This is one game that's clean and it's going to stay clean."

Considering that Gipp, with the knowledge of Rockne, was a notorious sports gambler, the O'Brien quote perhaps best illustrates my point.[1]

To a large degree, the National Football League (the NFL) has become the embodiment of the Gipp/Rockne myth. It has wrapped itself around the American flag and strutted into America's homes to the thrilling stir of brass and percussion music as the choreography of bone-crushing tackles in dramatic slow motion flashes across the nation's television screens. Based upon the illusion, the country's love affair with professional football has given sports fans confidence that the NFL is an institution unencumbered by corruption.

However, the greatest threat to professional football is also institutionalized: It is the institution of organized crime in America—and its control of illegal gambling and illicit drugs.

At least twenty-five million people bet a total of over $25 billion each year on National Football League games. Bobby Martin, the nation's premier oddsmaker, told me, "Nobody really knows how much is bet. It could be twenty-five billion. It could be a hundred billion. Nobody knows for sure."

Jack Danahy, the former security chief for the NFL, told me, "It was a joke trying to estimate the dollar figure. I remember I once got a call and was asked to provide a figure on how many bookies there were in New York. I made a fast call to the New York Liquor Authority, and I found out the number of licensed bars in the city. I multiplied it times two. I called back and said that I had it on an authoritative source that there were 14,756 bookmakers. Even though it was bullshit, he bought it. I figured that every decent bar in New York had at least two bookies."

Indeed, betting on pro football games has become a veritable American institution—with individual gamblers averaging wagers of between $100 to $500 on a single sporting event. And of all the money that is wagered on NFL games, only a small percentage of that amount is placed in Nevada, the only state where sports gambling and bookmaking are legal.

The situation has been further exacerbated by the media. Newspapers insist on printing the line, for upcoming games. The television networks have hired oddsmakers to predict the outcomes of games. Law-enforcement officials estimate that each time an NFL game is nationally televised, the volume of legal and illegal gambling increases by an estimated 600 percent. The dollars wagered increase dramatically during the play-offs. And bets skyrocket for the Super Bowl. More money is bet on pro football in a single month than on major-league baseball in an entire year.

Politicians and the media have failed to educate the public about the dangers of gambling, causing massive public insensitivity to the issue. During the spring of 1989, charges were filed against baseball great Pete Rose, the manager of the Cincinnati Reds, alleging that he had bet heavily on baseball games. In citing a *Washington Post* poll taken during the Rose investigation, sports columinst Thomas Boswell marveled that the survey showed "strong national support for Rose, even if he's bet on baseball and, more amazing, even if he's bet on the Reds. . . . In other words, almost half of all people who identified themselves as serious fans fundamentally disagree with the game's long-standing rules [against baseball personnel gambling] that have not changed since the Black Sox scandal of 1919."

"The only thing that keeps the NFL going is gambling," former all-pro defensive lineman Alex Karras, who was suspended from the NFL for gambling in 1963, told me, "and I have objected to the hypocrisy within the NFL for not facing up to that." Karras is probably right. Gambling has made football more interesting for millions of Americans. But gambling has also brought Mafia figures, bookmakers, layoff operators, loan sharks, and juice collectors into the game. Law-enforcement authorities say that the largest source of revenue in organized crime's gambling operations comes from wagers on NFL games.

Donald Dawson of Detroit, a convicted sports gambler, told me, "The NFL turns their collars around and pretends that they're holier than thou. They say, 'Oh, we can't have gambling on football games.' And up in the stands there are eighty thousand people who have money down on their favorite teams. Betting has made football, and the NFL knows it. It's the bettors who made bookmakers. The bookmakers didn't make bettors out of people who didn't want to gamble. People like to bet on sports, and the NFL has profited from it."

As all gamblers know, bookmakers are not too concerned with which team wins or loses a particular game. They are concerned only with balancing their books, hoping that an equal amount of money is wagered on both teams in any given contest. Bookmakers collect a 10 percent commission on the losing bets they book. Consequently, all a bookmaker wants out of life is a volume business and a balanced book.

The effective manipulation of the point spread—a form of handicapping in which oddsmakers predict how many points one team needs against another in order to even out the public betting on a game—will help ensure the bookmakers' vigorish, or commission. The total pool of bets—and how those bets have been placed—will cause the point spread to be adjusted, up or down, before a game is played.

Ronald Goldstock, the chief of the New York Organized Crime Task Force, told me, "If a bookmaker can't balance his books and suffers a major loss he can't cover, he will be forced to go to some Mafia loan shark and borrow the money at a five percent weekly interest rate. If he loses the following week, too, he'll be forced to borrow again. Sooner or later, he'll have to pay—one way or the other. Bookmakers, like gamblers who bet borrowed money, dread that visit from the mob's juice collector, who will break their legs or worse if they don't pay up." Thus, the idea that gambling and bookmaking are victimless crimes is another myth.

There is also a myth that today most bookmakers in the major cities are independent contractors. Special agent Charlie Parsons, formerly of the Las Vegas FBI office, told me, "It's difficult to find any truly independent bookmakers in New York, Chicago, Detroit, and in the other big cities who operate without the permission of the mob. There are actual members of the LCN [La Cosa Nostra] who are bookmakers themselves—and that's their major source of revenue. They take the layoff action themselves, while others [who are independent] pay a percentage to the mob to do the same thing."

To ensure its investments, the underworld has infiltrated every level of the NFL—from the players' locker rooms to the owners' luxury boxes. For years, mobsters, bookmakers, and big-money gamblers have maintained relationships with NFL team owners, coaches, players, trainers, and game officials—relationships that have threatened the integrity of professional football. And these associations pose more far-reaching dangers to the game than the specter of a fixed game.

At present, the NFL confirms that there have been only two attempts to fix NFL games. The first was in 1946 when gamblers tried to bribe two New York Giants players to throw the NFL championship game. The other was in 1971 when a player with the Houston Oilers was allegedly approached and offered money by a former teammate to shave points. According to the NFL, neither attempt was successful.

However, this is also a myth. This book will provide evidence that there have been many other attempts to compromise the integrity of the game—with far greater success.

Today, NFL games are rarely, if ever, fixed. The mechanics of bribing a team member or a referee who can guarantee the outcome of a game without raising suspicion are so intricate that the risk far outweighs the return. Seemingly everyone, from the NFL commissioner's office to the highest echelon of the organized-crime syndicate, appears to be concerned about maintaining the integrity of the game.

When I asked Jack Danahy whether there had been attempts to fix NFL games while he headed the league's security unit from 1968 to 1980, he replied, "I'm sure there were. I think that in ninety percent of the cases, the ballplayer didn't even bother to report it. He didn't want to go through the hassle. It's a lot easier to say, 'Look, you bastard, I'll hit you in the mouth if you don't get lost.'

"Approaches are very, very subtle. A guy isn't going to walk right up to a player, and say, 'Here's ten grand. And I want you to drop that key pass at the crucial moment in the game on Sunday.' In some instances, the player probably didn't even realize that he was being approached.

"That's the danger of drugs. They can potentially compromise the players. Thomas 'Hollywood' Henderson [a former Dallas Cowboys star linebacker] would've been an ideal situation. There's a guy who played a hell of a Super Bowl. Of course, he was a colorful guy. He was attracting as much attention as the rest of the team put together. Within a year after that, he confessed that he had a terrible habit, and that he had shot something like a hundred and sixty thousand dollars on cocaine. That's a dangerous situation—because the potential was there for him to be compromised by his dealer."

Despite the fact that organized crime has always enjoyed a financial bonanza through its control of gambling on NFL football games, local, state, and federal governments have done little to stop it. Professional football has become a sacred cow, seemingly immune to anything more than incomplete probes by law-enforcement agencies. This book will document numerous examples of collapsed and even suppressed investigations.

Much of this material has never before been published. With the help of my associate, William Scott Malone, I have uncovered a wealth of government documents and conducted dozens of public records searches, as well as over two hundred interviews. Because former NFL commissioner Pete Rozelle and the NFL team owners refused to be interviewed for this book, I have been forced to use selected statements made by them that have been obtained by other reporters with whom they have cooperated. In those cases in which previous reporting has been done, I have been scrupulous in crediting those who were responsible for it. And when describing a previously reported situation, I have attempted to advance the current state of evidence.

I am a crime reporter, not a sportswriter. My job is not contingent on maintaining access to and the goodwill of the personnel of any particular team or sports institution. Friends of mine who do write about sports have expressed the need "to behave" and admit that they have willingly become a part of the NFL's sophisticated public-relations machine on occasion in order to maintain their sources of information. I believe that the need for this professional access and goodwill has prevented a fair and responsible analysis of the relationship between professional sports and organized crime by all forms of the sports media.

Punitive action has been the norm against those who cover sports and are critical of their local team management. One close friend, Washington reporter and author Robert Pack, wrote an article critical of Washington Redskins owner Jack Kent Cooke and was banned from the Redskins' front office, locker room, and even the stadium, which is paid for by public funds.

Further, this story doesn't presume criminal guilt by association—although associations between NFL personnel and gamblers clearly violate the NFL's own rules. Yet, organized crime is "enterprise crime," crime by association, and operates accordingly. The leaders of the underworld have developed conspiracies that have resulted in criminal empires. And the NFL has often fallen prey to them.

What this book does is outline the patterns of association that have been tolerated by the NFL while the league and the federal government were claiming to take a hard line against organized crime and its influence on professional sports. In fact, the NFL has too often been lax in the enforcement of its own rules, and law-enforcement agencies have permitted the NFL to get away with it. This sweetheart relationship has greatly contributed to the myth about the integrity of the NFL.

Consequently, the NFL is sure to attempt to discredit this book, which strikes at the heart of the business of professional football, in any way it can—just as it did with an article I wrote about this subject after the 1987 regular season. An unnamed league spokesman said that the story "was a cut-and-paste job and not very factual. It was filled with inaccuracies, gossip and innuendo."[2] But that response was a complete turnabout.

In fact, I read my article to the current NFL Security director, Warren Welsh, prior to publication to solicit whatever changes he felt were required. And, because of Welsh's expertise and inside information, I trusted him and made several necessary modifications upon his advice. In the end, he told me that it was a "fair and accurate" report. However, the NFL, for reasons only its unnamed spokesman can explain, changed its tune after the story was made public. But no one from the league would meet me face-to-face in a public forum to explain what its specific objections were, even after having been invited to do so on two national television programs on which I appeared.

Predictably, with the publication of this book, the league's now-familiar tactic will be to remain aloof from the charges, deny them from afar, and then send its front line of defense, the loyal sportswriters, to attack the messenger. But, once again, in good faith and asking only for confidentiality, I offered this manuscript to Welsh for his review. But neither he nor anyone else from the NFL responded.

For the record, this book, just like my article, has been fact-checked extensively, read by sports and law-enforcement experts, and closely reviewed by attorneys. Sooner or later, the fans of honest football will be forced to enter this or a similar fray and finally demand accountability from the NFL.

—DAN E. MOLDEA
Washington, D.C.

1 On Fixing Games and Inside Information

I ONCE ASKED PRO Football Hall of Fame quarterback Len Dawson of the Kansas City Chiefs whether the fact that his team's games had been taken off the betting boards by bookmakers across the country during the late 1960s was an indication that they were fixed. Dawson replied, "It would be a dangerous thing to fix a game. To me, a player would be branded for life if he did that. His teammates would express shock and anger. I don't know how one guy could do it, even a quarterback. In our system, we ran the ball a lot. Even when I wasn't in there, it didn't make much difference who was quarterback, because the defense scored points to help win games.

"I suppose the quarterback could put the ball on the ground, with turnovers in crucial situations. It would certainly have a bearing on the game. Hell, a kicker could have as much to do with it just by missing. He has more control over it than sometimes the quarterback does."

Defensive back Dick "Night Train" Lane, formerly of the Detroit Lions and also a member of the Hall of Fame, told me that while he was a player he was once approached by Donald Dawson, the Detroit gambler who was later linked in a federal probe with Len Dawson, who was no relation. Recalling the incident, which he did not report to the NFL, Lane says, "Don told me, 'Quarterbacks do a lot of betting themselves. Did you know that?' I said [laughing], 'Get out of here.' He said, 'You know it can be done, Night Train. You're the only man between the goalpost and a receiver. You can slip and fall and let the guy score.' "

When I asked Lane whether Don Dawson was really suggesting that he throw a game, Lane replied that that was clearly his impression. He added that he had known Dawson for years and worked for his cousin, a Detroit car dealer, during the off-season. Lane also said that Dawson talked about the other players with whom he did business—a fact confirmed by agents for the FBI, the U.S. Strike Forces Against Organized Crime, and the IRS, among other federal agencies.

Don Dawson admitted to me that he had made that statement to Lane, whom he described as "a good friend of mine." Dawson says, "I'm sure I said that to him. Not that I was trying to bribe him, but he was probably trying to feel me out, too. Over the years, there were a lot of players I bet for, but they weren't necessarily doing any business [participating in a fix]. But some of them were prepared to do it. They came to me. I was a wealthy guy. I had money. The players weren't making any money. The owners were making all the money."

Former all-pro defensive back Bernie Parrish, an author of a 1971 book critical of the NFL and whose playing career spanned from 1959 to 1966, told me, "Sure, there were players who participated in shaving points in games and that sort of thing. Yeah, I played in them. But I always heard about it after the game was over."

Don Dawson confessed to me that during the 1950s and 1960s he had been personally involved in the fixing of no fewer than thirty-two NFL games.

That was the fear during the 1980s when, according to law-enforcement officials, no fewer than nine NFL teams—the Cleveland Browns, Dallas Cowboys, Denver Broncos, Miami Dolphins, New England Patriots, New Orleans Saints, San Diego Chargers, San Francisco 49ers, and Washington Redskins—found themselves the targets of investigations in which players had been allegedly given drugs by gamblers who were looking for an on-field edge. And, particularly in 1988, numerous other NFL teams found their players being disciplined by the league for using, buying, and/or selling drugs, which along with gambling are the two most lucrative enterprises of organized crime.

Don Dawson's shocking admission is a first. No one has ever stepped forward and claimed to have actually been involved in fixed games. Although such charges have occasionally been made through the years of the NFL's existence, they have traditionally been hard to prove. "They are cases where it's difficult to discover hard evidence as to who is involved," says Brian Gettings, a former Strike Force attorney in Miami who was responsible for prosecuting Gilbert Lee Beckley, the Mafia's onetime top layoff bookmaker. "You have to have an individual directly involved in the sports bribe or the fix to get a successful prosecution. And that is quite difficult."

Marty Kane, one of Beckley's top associates, told me, "If I wanted to fix a game, there're three players I'd get: the quarterback, the offensive center, and a defensive back. Then I would bet as much money as I could. I would have beards. I would have people all over the country trying to bet for me on this game."

Oddsmaker Bobby Martin remembers, "There were a lot of fixed games during the 1950s, but there's nothing like that anymore. Years ago, players bet, mostly on their own teams. They'd say, 'Oh, I see we're six-point favorites or four-point underdogs. We'll win this game. We know much better than the people who post the odds about what we can do.' And then they'd bet a hundred or two hundred dollars.

"But, now, the players are paid too much money. There's too much of a spotlight on them. Oddsmakers want honest football. We don't want anything dishonest. It interferes with our handicapping if the games are fixed. I can't get a true picture of the value of the teams."

Mort Olshan, perhaps the most renowned football handicapper in the United States and the publisher of the widely read *Gold Sheet,* agrees and told me, "The tip-off on any fix is manifested in the movement of the odds and the appearance of 'unnatural' money. To orchestrate a fix would require the cooperation of a coach and one or more of his top players; no nonessential player or underpaid sub is in a position to affect the outcome. Even then there is no guarantee the culprits could pull it off. There are too many outside factors.

"To make the risk worthwhile, the high-salaried athlete would expect a sizable payoff. But the chief deterrent to a setup is that virtually the only source one can place a substantial bet with is a bookie. And just as soon as the first plunge is made, the odds will move dramatically. Since this would be no penny-ante venture, more bets would follow. To avoid instant suspicion, 'unnatural' money would be spread all over the nation's betting marts. Since bookmakers have telephones, word would spread faster than news of a nuclear attack. If the jackpot got too big the game would be taken off the board. The skullduggery would be spotted in no time."

Olshan also added that sporting contests have been fixed. "Sure, that kind of foul was going in college basketball during the 1950s. Games were fixed, and points were shaved. For the handicappers and the bookmakers, it was corrupt and costly. Bookmakers were burned financially and the handicappers' figures became irrelevant. If you look at the college basketball fixes during the early 1950s, it had the effect of putting a lot of bookmakers out of business. When a game is fixed, they are the first ones to suffer the consequences."

A star of the 1969 Super Bowl, Jim Hudson, a former defensive back with the New York Jets, told me, "My theory always was: If somebody was going to buy me to fall down on a pass play, I would want to know when that son of a bitch was going to pay me. Now, if you're a gambler, would you pay me before the game? No. Would you pay me at halftime? No. You would say you'll pay me after the game. Now, I'm the player, and I'm going to say, 'Do you think I'm going to wait until after the game when I'm never going to see your ass again?'

"How are you going to bribe someone? Every bookie in the world is going to know about it. And that line is going to go crazy. I don't believe that things like that went on then or now."

Nevertheless, some argue that it doesn't make any difference whether a game is fixed to anyone who doesn't know that it is. Given the economics of bookmaking, which will be discussed at length in this book, the uninvolved and innocent bettor still has a fifty-fifty chance of winning, whether or not the game is fixed. The only people a fixed game means anything to are those who know about it. They know they have a winner. And their large bets, strategically placed around the country to avoid suspicion, simply become a part of the multibillion-dollar pool of wagers booked on every NFL game.

To them, a fixed game is like insider trading on Wall Street. Every day, there are a handful of people who know a sure thing is going to happen before it happens. Yet, even when it does happen, the investment markets in America somehow manage to survive—and usually no one outside of the fix ever finds out about it.

There is also the contention that it has been extremely rare that a member of the organized-crime gambling syndicate ordered a member of a team to throw a game or to shave points. History shows that fixers are prosecuted, and they go to jail. When a sporting event has been fixed, the public becomes disillusioned and loses confidence in the sport in which the fix occurred. That means less bookmaking volume from those who gamble and less vigorish for those who book their bets.

When I asked Baton Rouge bookmaker Gene Nolan whether he had ever known anyone who ordered a fix, he replied, "I don't know that anybody ever told anyone what to do. I think someone just found out what a member of a team was going to do—on the basis of whether the player or the coach thought he could or couldn't win. I don't think anyone ever told someone to lie down—like a fighter."

Consequently, it is naïve to think that the only litmus test of honest NFL football is whether or not its games are fixed. It is not. There are far more important considerations in making this determination. And those considerations must encompass the associations of NFL personnel with the underworld and, most important, the backgrounds and business relationships of those who rule professional football: the NFL team owners.

The organized-crime gambling syndicate believes that inside information is necessary in order to discover what a member of a team is doing or might be doing. Aside from the rare fix, inside information is the commodity that professional gamblers will bank on. The mob wants to learn everything it can about the players' health, their marital problems, deaths in their families, drug dependencies, internal team problems, and anything else that might affect on-field performances, especially those situations that are not immediately reported in a public forum.

Los Angeles mobster-turned-government-informant Jimmy Fratianno told my associate, William Scott Malone, that from personal experience inside information is key for organized-crime figures and their associates. "They get information, like, a person might know the coach, and some guy might have gotten hurt on Monday in practice, a key player. They [the team] won't reveal that until probably later on in the week, because they don't want the opposite team to get prepared for it. They get hurt on Monday; they reveal it on Thursday. Somebody finds out about it, and they bet on the game. Well, as soon as it is revealed that this person is hurt, then the odds will change. The guy that had the information already is in with maybe three or four points to the best of it."

On the importance of injury reports, Mort Olshan only partially agrees with Fratianno. "Ninety-five percent of the rumors [about injuries] are baloney and wouldn't have a bearing on the game even if they were true," Olshan says. "The most meaningful reports are those where multiple injuries occur on the same team, thereby wrecking the club's cohesiveness and causing either the defense or the offense to overwork."

Organized-crime expert G. Robert Blakey, a former top Justice Department lawyer who is now a professor of law at Notre Dame, told me, "The Mafia wants an honest game because they know they have the contacts within the NFL teams to determine how to bet as accurately as possible. That's the only edge they need. Providing inside information happens every week of the season. And that's what goes to the heart of the integrity of the NFL."

Another top crime expert, Vincent Piersante, who headed the organized-crime unit of the Michigan attorney general's office, explained to me, "The Mafia wants ace-rock information so that they can set a realistic point spread. They just want the public to bet. They make their ten percent commission on losing bets, so, as long as their bookmakers balance their books, what the hell do they care which team wins or loses. The old-line mob guys recognize the danger of trying to fix one game and destroying the whole structure. They just want the inside information that can help predict a player's performance."

Al Davis, the owner of the Los Angeles Raiders, also appears to agree with Fratianno and the others about the importance of inside information: "They [bookmakers] have contacts with every owner in the league."[1]

Gene Klein, the former owner of the San Diego Chargers, told me, "I've heard rumors [about fixed games], but I probably closed my mind to it. I have had people come up to me and say, 'How could the gamblers hit the points so well?' But I am convinced that most owners are goddamn decent people.

"Yet, everybody is looking for inside information. Everyone wants the edge. That's the great thing about [the NFL's] publishing the injury reports. That's the source of information. The league is very, very forceful on that point so that everyone has the same information."

The league's former commissioner, Pete Rozelle, strongly opposed legalizing sports gambling. He has said that "gambling is more serious than drugs because it goes to the integrity of the game." Rozelle knew this better than anyone. He was forced to deal with a gambling problem of one kind or another every year since he was elected the NFL's chief executive officer in 1960. The fact that most fans can't recall much about the NFL's gambling scandals is testimony to his ability to enhance the league's public image while he policed the conduct of its personnel.

"We have a basic rule in the NFL," says a former law-enforcement official who advises the NFL on security matters. "It is to keep it upbeat and keep it positive. But, above all, they want to keep everything quiet."

Rozelle's ability to keep things quiet earned him criticism, as well as admiration, in some quarters. A top NFL official is adamant in his defense of Rozelle. "Why should the NFL publicize hearsay and innuendo? If the commissioner publicized a matter under investigation, that would be irresponsible. It's our policy not to create a problem that might not be there. And if it is a problem, we handle it ourselves. And if the problem hits the newspapers, then we respond publicly."

The security consultant replies, "Rozelle's job [was] that of the protector of the *appearance* of integrity within the NFL. To Rozelle, a problem with a player's gambling or an owner's having some Mafia associations [didn't] really become a major problem until the situation received publicity. Then he [was] forced to act in a public way.

"Rozelle is an honest guy. He [had] a long-term contract and a half-a-million-dollar-a-year salary to guarantee that. But his job [was] really dependent on the goodwill of the twenty-eight owners in the NFL to whom he [was] accountable . . . And when you consider the investments they have in their teams, none of them wants bad publicity. It's bad for business."

Since the underworld's attempt to fix the NFL's 1946 championship game—after which two New York Giants players, Frank Filchock and Merle Hapes, were suspended—the league has become especially conscious of occasional maneuvers by organized-crime figures, bookmakers, and gamblers to guarantee the outcomes of football games. When Bert Bell was the league's commissioner from 1946 to 1959, he maintained close contacts with members of the nation's gambling community in order to monitor unusual fluctuations in the betting line and unusually large, suspicious bets that were placed on games.

Because of the concerns of Bell and Rozelle, a notice in bold letters now hangs in every locker room to warn NFL personnel of the league's rules on gambling. The league prohibits players from betting on NFL games, from accepting bribes or agreeing to throw or fix games, from failing to promptly report offers of bribes or attempts to throw or fix games, and from associating with gamblers or with gambling activities in a manner that would discredit the NFL. "Any such conduct," reads the sign, "may result in severe penalties, up to and including a fine and/or suspension from the NFL for life."[2]

Rozelle's antigambling policy has been publicly supported by the NFL's team managements. During my interview with Steve Guttman, the president of the New York Jets, he said, "My views about gambling are precisely those of the league. I wouldn't want to characterize them in any way to deviate from that. And I would want to stand on that."

As is well known, defensive tackle Alex Karras of the Detroit Lions and running back Paul Hornung of the Green Bay Packers each received one-year suspensions from the NFL in 1963 because of their admitted gambling activities. Since then, only one other person has been suspended for gambling: Art Schlichter, a rookie quarterback with the Baltimore Colts. In 1983, he admitted to associating with gamblers and losing more than $700,000 in bets on NFL games and other sporting events.

As a result of the 1963 players betting scandal, Rozelle created NFL Security and selected Jim Hamilton, the former chief of intelligence with the Los Angeles Police Department (LAPD), as its first chief. In 1966, Hamilton, who died after a long illness, was replaced by William Hundley, the chief of Robert F. Kennedy's organized-crime division in the Justice Department. Hundley was succeeded by Jack Danahy, a New York FBI agent, in 1968. Danahy held the position until 1980, when he was followed by the current director of NFL Security, Warren Welsh, a former Miami-based FBI agent.

The directors of NFL Security have attempted to safeguard the league against the corruption of its players, trainers, coaches, owners, and referees, all of whom are potential targets for blackmail and payoffs in exchange for inside information and other favors. NFL Security is supported by a network of private investigators, mostly former officials with the Justice Department and other law-enforcement agencies, who are stationed in the twenty-six cities where the twenty-eight NFL teams are based (New York and Los Angeles each support two teams).

"These representatives are on retainer to the league, and they specifically report to the league," Warren Welsh told me. "In addition to their game-day coverage and their liaison with the local law-enforcement community, they would also do background investigations that we might have for game officials, an ownership group, impersonations, misrepresentations, whatever it might be, as opposed to just working for the local team."

The NFL, under Rozelle, followed Bert Bell's policy of maintaining regular contacts with members of the gambling underworld in order to monitor the betting on NFL games.

Warren Welsh explains, "We're very cognizant that the early line comes out on Sunday, and we have somebody in Vegas that follows that for us. And then we have our security reps all over the country report in to us and give us the opening line. And then if there are changes in the line that are over two points, they report that immediately. If not, then the security reps report to us on Friday at about noon. And then we are able to disseminate the line and any changes to our key executives so that they are aware of the information and any changes."

Monitoring NFL personnel, as well as the line, may be unpalatable, but it is necessary. Two years before the Schlichter suspension, several members of the Denver Broncos were quietly disciplined by the league for receiving cocaine from gambling figures. And, in 1986, the league began an investigation of Irving Fryar, a wide receiver for the New England Patriots who was accused of betting on NFL games. Fryar had been named by his team's officials as one of six Patriots players who used illegal drugs. The investigation remains open.

The conditions under which players may be compromised are clear and present in the NFL today. "Our worst case would be the athlete who is strung out on drugs and has a line of credit with his drug dealer and can't pay the bill," says Welsh. "Then he gets that knock on the door. And [the player] says, 'Hey, I told you. I can't pay the bill.' And then [the dealer] says, 'Hey, I don't want your money, but now you're going to work for us.' "

A major West Coast bookmaker agrees. "A lot of players have gotten involved in cocaine and are well over their heads—

as much as ten thousand to twenty thousand dollars a month in cocaine. There is a very real danger that if they can't pay their debt, they give information and do make some mistakes in a ball game so that the dealer can make a bet and even out. And that's a great opportunity for a bookmaker, too: to set up something for a cocaine dealer and find out information that way."

Michael Roxborough of Las Vegas, who has succeeded Bobby Martin as the nation's most influential oddsmaker on NFL games, told me, "The NFL is not doing a very good job in the area of drug enforcement. But people just don't think that there is a problem with the manipulation of the outcome of NFL games. Most people think that drugs aren't a very serious problem. Until the public demands that it gets cleaned up, the NFL isn't going to feel that it has to do very much."

Former Olympic gold medalist Bob Hayes, who was also a receiver for the Dallas Cowboys and pleaded guilty to setting up a cocaine deal after he retired from football, told me, "It goes a lot further than just saying no to drugs. And the NFL has been unrealistic about that because they treat drug abuse as a problem, not a disease. The use of drugs is a disease. And when you have a disease, you are a sick person and you need to get well. Until then, people are going to try to take advantage of you."

Criticism of the NFL's security system is generally not targeted at the commissioner or the security director. Instead, it's directed at the NFL owners, who establish the league's policies.

Aaron Kohn, the former executive director of the Metropolitan Crime Commission of New Orleans, told me, "They [the NFL owners] have a tendency to employ as security people former FBI agents and other people of confidence who do competent investigations and do accumulate adverse information. But at the policy-making level, the decisions are not made consistent with the fact-finding.

"I know that the NFL can't go too far. They are going to do whatever they have to to prevent the problems of their owners and players and their overall profits from becoming subjects of public scrutiny."

Some critics say that the league enforces its rules selectively. "Rozelle [couldn't] enforce the rules against the owners because he [worked] for them," Gene Upshaw, the executive director of the NFL Players Association (NFLPA) and a former all-pro guard for the Oakland Raiders, told me. "There's no way he [could] say,

'I'm going to punish you because you own a racetrack, because you're involved in Las Vegas, or because you do business with people who are involved in gambling.' But I would like to think that the rules of suspension and banishment should also apply to the owners."

One top NFL official says, "We've had owners that have supposedly been friends or associates of mobsters, and when we looked into it they had dinner in a restaurant, maybe four or five times in a year." Nevertheless, the NFL did nothing about these owners who socialized with underworld figures.

Another football insider says that many investigations of NFL owners have ended up in "a black hole" and were never disclosed. "To me," he says, "NFL Security is a special police force that monitors the players but protects the owners. It's one thing to monitor the activities of the players, because they come and go. It's quite another to monitor the activities of the owners. They seem to last forever."

Patrick Healy, the former executive director of the Chicago Crime Commission, told me, "The NFL tries to give you the public Kiwanis Club talk: 'We have very little gambling; we have very little drugs. We have everything under control. We have FBI agents working for us, and whenever any rumor comes out they pounce on it. They discover it. They investigate it.' Actually, the whole thing is really just a witch tale."

Former Senate investigator Phil Manuel, another critic of the NFL security system, told me, "The oldest trick in the world is to hire old Justice Department officials and then make them understand that the security they are to protect is the security of the NFL owners.

"These retired law-enforcement guys maintain their ties to their old agencies, and they can then tell which investigations are being done and whether they might be troublesome. When some wrongdoing is ready to go public, the NFL Security people can go to their old fellow workers and say, 'We can handle this ourselves. Give us a chance to straighten the mess out without all the attention your public investigation will bring.' "

Ralph Salerno, the former supervisor of detectives for the New York Police Department, goes even further. "How does the NFL protect itself with one guy in each NFL city? They do it illegally. The local NFL Security guy takes the local police commissioner, the chief of detectives, and any other important law-enforcement official and gives him season tickets and box seats. They get wined and dined and taken out to play golf.

"And then these public employees who are paid with public funds come up with criminal information and turn it over to profit-making corporations, like the New York Giants, the Cincinnati Bengals, and so on. And that is illegal. Do the police do that for every trucking company or every furniture manufacturer? Of course not. It would be illegal for them to do it with anyone. But they do it for the NFL. That whole NFL Security operation that Rozelle [bragged] about is simply an illegal operation."

Welsh defends the current system. He insists that he is a "fact finder" and has never been asked to halt an investigation of any NFL personnel. "And there have never been any roadblocks put up in my path in terms of investigating anything that would have to do with a member club—whether it was a player, coach, or an owner."

That might be true: Warren Welsh and his predecessors have all been men of high integrity. But they have had no final decision-making powers. Thus, the real question is: What have their bosses, the NFL owners, done once they received the results of their investigations? The evidence is clear that they have protected themselves and their investments—sometimes to the detriment of the sport they represent.

2 Getting Organized

EARLY PROFESSIONAL FOOTBALL POSSESSED little finesse and only basic strategies. The public's draw to the game was based upon its display of legal violence. During his eight-year tenure as president, Theodore Roosevelt had actively tried to ban the game because of its inherent brutality. For the most part, the players—who looked like faces on a post office wall—were picked for their size and toughness rather than their agility, intelligence, and speed. Many of them carried railroad ties, chopped wood, and cow-poked during the rest of the week. Fans came to football games to see dogfights—and to gamble.

The only known successful bribery incident in the pre-NFL period took place back in November 1906, in the midst of an early attempt to organize a professional football league. During a two-game series between the Canton Bulldogs and the Massillon Tigers in Ohio, Blondy Wallace, the head coach of the Canton team, and Walter R. East, a key Massillon player, made a deal in which Canton was to win the first game and Massillon was to win the second, forcing a third game—with the biggest gate—to be played legitimately. Several gamblers involved with Wallace and East had also offered a $5,000 bribe to the Massillon coach and members of his team, but without success.

When the rumors of the attempted bribery became widespread, East, who had boasted of fixing a college football game the year before, as well as a baseball game that same year, was fired from the Massillon team. The Canton-Massillon incident became the first known case of professional gamblers' attempting to fix a professional sport.

Professional football had emerged during the early part of the twentieth century in small towns and cities without major colleges. In the large cities, college football was still king. The American Professional Football Association (APFA) was officially formed on August 20, 1920, during a meeting at the brick, three-story Odd Fellows building that housed the Hupmobile and Jordan automobile dealership of Ralph Hay, the general manager of the Canton Bulldogs in Canton, Ohio. By the beginning of its first season, the association consisted of fourteen teams from five states.[1] Each owner was required to pay $100 for his franchise.

Among those initial teams created in 1920 were the Racine (Avenue in Chicago) Cardinals, organized in 1899 by South Side Chicago contractor Chris O'Brien. Another was the Decatur Staleys, sponsored by a manufacturing company and represented by twenty-five-year-old ex-sailor George Halas. Formerly a New York Yankees right fielder, Halas's baseball career had been cut short by a hip injury. Later, after receiving loans from his mother and Chicago businessman Charles Bidwill, an associate of the Al Capone mob, Halas bought the football team from his employer, A. E. Staley. In 1921, Halas moved his team to Cubs Park in Chicago where it became the Chicago Bears.

The legendary Jim Thorpe, whose mentor had been coach Glenn "Pop" Warner, was elected the first president of the association. Four years earlier, while Thorpe was playing for the Canton Bulldogs, he and a fan of the rival Massillon Tigers had a heated exchange about which team was better. Just hours before a game between the two teams, Thorpe slapped down a blank check and filled it out for $2,500, challenging the fan, a wealthy local businessman, to respond in kind.

A local newspaper, which reported the betting incident, took the matter in stride. "Massillon had plenty of money to stake on the outcome of the game," the paper reported, "while many of the Canton bugs were rather shy. They evidently feared the hoodoo which Massillon has been in former years. Now that the jinx has been chased the wagering in years to come is likely to be more lively."

One of Thorpe's star Bulldog players, Joe Guyon, recalled, "Gamblers tried to buy us off. They would approach us at the hotel, where we stayed on the weekend . . . They didn't fool with me . . . But there were guys who took their money . . . We had one guy. Oh, he was a high traveler. A halfback. We saw his contacts at the hotel. Then we saw his play. He was detailed to cover a man, and when he didn't, why, we said it was an accident. But the second time, it was too obvious. I said, 'What the hell is going on?' I went over to the bench and said, 'He didn't cover his man, Jim. This guy is not covering his man.' Jim braced him right there. He fired him."[2]

Thorpe was replaced as the president of the professional football league in 1921 by Joe Carr of Columbus, Ohio, a highly respected sports reporter and promoter. Perhaps his greatest contribution was his crusade to prevent NFL teams from snagging college players for pro ball until they had graduated.[3]

In 1922—the year that the APFA changed its name to the National Football League—a scandal involving the year-old Green Bay Packers erupted. The team's owner was disciplined by Carr for hiring college athletes who used aliases and were paid for playing in NFL games during the 1921 season.[4]

With the Packers' ownership in deep financial trouble in the wake of the scandal, local businessmen in Green Bay purchased the team for $2,500 and made it a public, nonprofit corporation in 1923. Citizens purchased stock in the team for $5 a share. Today, the Green Bay Packers are still the only team owned by the citizens of the city that it represents.

Most of the early owners were viewed as "sportsmen" who gambled heavily on horse racing, baseball, and any other sporting events available. Gambling was widely practiced and accepted, particularly in those early days of professional football when the fledgling sport wasn't thought to be in the same league as professional baseball.

Wagering at baseball games had become a part of the ballpark spectacle. It was common knowledge that bookmakers usually operated in the right-field bleachers of nearly every stadium in the country.

Halas said, "Fans bet heavily, but I forbade my players to gamble on any of our games. Betting on one's own team to win may not be harmful, because one player cannot make a team win.

"One player can make a team lose, however, by fumbling or missing a pass or failing a tackle. Although players have a sixth sense for detecting when a teammate is not doing his best, there is a terrible temptation to bet against the team. No gambler has ever approached me. Perhaps the word got around that gamblers would, at best, be wasting their time."[5]

In the early days of professional football, an NFL owner had to have what was then an enormous cash flow, over $100,000 a season. Generally, only gamblers and robber barons had that kind of money. Unfortunately, the names of the sports gamblers and bookmakers with whom the "sportsmen" did business were unknown to most sports fans—whose loyalty to the home team was usually backed up with their wagered cash.

"You always used to hear this game or that was fixed," a longtime amateur sports gambler told me. "If a name like Al Capone or Arnold Rothstein or even some big-name player wasn't involved, it really wasn't something you'd worry about. You might wait and watch, but when things blew over you placed your bet on the next game."

Feared by the public and protected by Tammany Hall, Rothstein had been the most successful bookmaker in the country during the early part of the century. Along the way, he was thought to have committed numerous other crimes, including extortion and murder. During his career, Rothstein gambled and did business with, among others, Julius Fleischmann, the heir to U.S. Steel; Canadian distiller Joseph Seagram; U.S. Senator Edward Wolcott of Colorado; and Percival H. Hill of the American Tobacco Company.

With the advent of Prohibition in 1919, Rothstein had already solidified his power and served as an intermediary for the new Mafia families emerging in New York. Bootleggers crawled out from under every rock and began to make their fortunes. And organized-crime figures who engaged in the illegal liquor business, like Rothstein, also became involved in other rackets, including sports gambling.

By allegedly fixing the 1919 World Series in the Chicago "Black Sox" scandal, Rothstein established himself as the all-time king of notorious sports gamblers. A larger than life American figure in the eyes of some, Rothstein was the inspiration for the character Meyer Wolfsheim in F. Scott Fitzgerald's *The Great Gatsby*.

Ralph Salerno, New York's former supervisor of detectives, told me, "It was the White Sox players' idea to do the fixing, but Rothstein was behind the fix. There's no doubt about that. Everyone was coming to him, trying to get him to finance the whole deal. But Arnold, who didn't want to have direct responsibility, sat back and sent out his beard, who met the players and made the deals. It was no wonder that the players were cheated out of their money, and Rothstein made an untraceable fortune. And, best of all, Rothstein could deny any involvement.

"His beard was indicted. But being the only man who could implicate Rothstein, he left the country. As the case was coming to court, the prosecution's evidence just disappeared while its witnesses developed amnesia or simply vanished."

The case was eventually dropped—with no official court record that the 1919 World Series had ever been fixed. Nevertheless, Rothstein became even a larger legend. But he, too, overestimated his own power and invulnerability. In 1928, he was shot to death upon the orders of a rival mobster.

The 1919 scandal forced baseball team owners to hire an outsider to administer league policy and to police baseball personnel. He was Judge Kenesaw Mountain Landis, who was honest, distinguished, and grandfatherly. Judge Landis's job was to clean up the image of baseball and bring wholesome family entertainment back to the game.

Landis decreed, "No player that throws a game, no player that entertains proposals or promises to throw a game, no player that sits in a conference with a bunch of crooks where the ways and means of throwing games are discussed, and does not promptly tell his club about it, will ever play professional baseball."

As major-league baseball had, the NFL added a rule to its charter prohibiting gambling by any owner, coach, or player. But, as in baseball, gambling in football would continue to flourish.

Meantime, in September 1931, three years after Rothstein's murder, the traditional Sicilian Mafia became Americanized; thus, disorganized crime became organized crime, which included a cadre of Jewish gangsters. A national crime syndicate was established by twenty-nine-year-old Meyer Lansky of New York and Chicago mobster Johnny Torrio. As part of the plan, the United States was divided into twenty-four subdivisions, each controlled by the most powerful Mafia families in these various geographic areas. Nine of the leaders of these twenty-four crime groups were selected to sit on a national crime commission that would settle jurisdictional disputes.

The crime syndicate was created to stop the infighting among the crime families, which interfered with the mob's primary goals—to make money and to stay out of jail. With the increased stability and decreased exposure, mob financiers like Lansky were free to find legal and illegal moneymaking ventures, raise the necessary capital from participating crime families, launder funds through "friendly" banks, buy political protection, and oversee the fair distribution of profits from these activities.

Professional sports, particularly the NFL, would be among the underworld's biggest money-makers.

3 The Old Days with the Old Gang

INHERITING ARNOLD ROTHSTEIN'S BOOKMAKING empire—with the approval of Meyer Lansky and New York Mafia figure Frank Costello—fell to New York's Frank Erickson. Ralph Salerno told me, "Erickson met Costello and Lansky through Rothstein. The estate Rothstein left his family was peanuts, but the empire he left his criminal friends was enormous and taken up by the guys who worked for him. Rothstein had recruited Erickson. And after Rothstein was murdered, Lansky and Costello went to Erickson and said, 'We'll be partners, but you run the bookmaking on the day-to-day basis.' Meanwhile, Lansky and Costello were running the casinos in upstate New York, Miami, and New Orleans. They were all partners in all of their gambling operations."

Born in 1895, the pudgy Erickson maintained his headquarters in New Jersey while continuing to live in New York. He had his gambling contacts in all forty-eight states. Federal investigators estimated that he handled between $20,000 and $40,000 a day in betting action. In the ten-year period between 1933 and 1943—while serving as a banker for other gamblers as well—Erickson netted an estimated $22 million, and split it with Costello, Lansky, and other mobsters in the growing national crime syndicate.

It was during Erickson's reign that fast-money sports rigging became widespread, particularly at the racetrack. Because thoroughbred horses couldn't testify before federal grand juries, they were often the targets of illegal doping. Heroin, in fact, received its street name, "horse" because it was the early drug of choice by corrupt horsefixers.

Soon after George Halas bought the Chicago Bears, a large and tough New York bookmaker and boxing promoter with close ties to Erickson and the Tammany Democratic machine, bought an NFL franchise. Thirty-nine-year-old Tim Mara paid $500 for the New York Giants in August 1925. His team played its games at the Polo Grounds, the home of major-league baseball's New York Giants.

Mara's gambling operations were semilegal, and he was known for having booked bets beneath a striped umbrella at New York racetracks. After dropping out of school when he was thirteen, he became a runner of Rothstein associate Thomas "Chicago" O'Brien, a major New York gambler. Mara delivered newspapers and worked in a book bindery by day; by night he made pickups and deliveries for O'Brien. He later opened up his own book bindery company, which fronted for his own bookmaking operation. Soon, Mara worked his way up to his own enclosed space at Belmont Park and became a member of the local racing association. He handled as much as $30,000 in wagers in a single day.

"Mara was a bookmaker when it was legal at the racetrack to be a bookmaker," says Salerno. "The law prohibited betting away from the track, but you could go there and bet with a bookmaker. They actually had slate chalkboards on which they would post and change the odds. Gamblers would be running from one bookmaker to the next, trying to get the best odds."

At the time Mara bought the Giants, he had never even seen a football game. "But the promoters of the [NFL] knew that bookmakers were a type extremely susceptible to new forms of investment," according to one report. "They offered Mr. Mara the franchise."[1]

During the Giants' first season, Mara was already facing financial difficulties and his team was verging on collapse. But all was well after seventy-three thousand fans jammed the Polo Grounds to see New York lose, 19–7, to the Chicago Bears, who had signed running sensation Red Grange earlier that year.[2] Gate receipts produced enough money to help the Giants' franchise to survive. The team won its first NFL championship in 1927.

Active in politics, Mara, a Roman Catholic, was a major supporter of the 1928 presidential campaign of Democratic nominee Al Smith, the first Catholic to seek the presidency.

Mara's office was later raided by agents from the U.S. attorney's office in New York, which alleged that Mara and his employees had been scalping tickets to the Giants games. But Mara, who still had good political contacts, was not indicted. He insisted that the sale of thousands of tickets at the higher price was "nothing worse than an error in making change."

The passage of the Beer-Wine Revenue Act in March 1933—which amended the Volstead Act to legalize beer and wine—served as the prelude to the Twenty-first Amendment and the repeal of Prohibition on December 5, 1933. According to the FBI, "The resulting end of their bonanza caught mob leaders with large hordes of wealth, vast fleets of trucks, and whole armies of trained gunmen at their disposal. Most branched out into other fields of criminal endeavor (such as gambling, loan sharking, narcotics, labor racketeering, etc.), whereas quite a few added to their flow of illicit wealth by investing their funds in legitimate investments, ranging from real estate and manufacturing plants to hospitals and theatrical agencies. It was also at this time that many racket leaders tried to play down their past histories and adopt an air of pseudorespectability in their local communities." Through front men and associates, the mob's influence also moved in to sports.

Charles W. Bidwill, a bootlegger, gambler, racetrack owner, and an associate of the Al Capone mob in Chicago, bought the Chicago Cardinals in 1933 for $2,000 in cash.[3] In order to purchase the team, he had to give up his minority interest in the Chicago Bears, where he also served as a vice president under Halas.

Among Bidwill's holdings were the majority interest in Hawthorne racetrack in Chicago, dog tracks in Jacksonville, Miami Beach, and Tampa, as well as a string of Chicago apartment houses. He also owned stock in a large printing company that published the programs and eventually the pari-mutuel tickets of America's racetracks.

Another new owner entered the league in July 1933. Thirty-two-year-old ex-amateur boxer Arthur J. Rooney bought the Pittsburgh Pirates—renamed the Steelers in 1940—for $2,500. The team was operated out of the Fort Pitt Hotel in downtown

Pittsburgh.[4] Like Halas, the quiet and stocky Rooney was a former baseball player who turned to football after a career-ending injury.

Born in 1901 in Coulterville, Pennsylvania, Rooney came from a family of steelworkers and coal miners. The Rooney family had moved to Pittsburgh in 1903 and opened Rooney's Saloon on the city's North Side. The Rooneys' tavern became a renowned hangout for sports fanatics and those who booked their bets. The bar also became a favorite retreat for local politicians and led to young Rooney's flirtation with politics. A staunch Republican who attended Duquesne and Georgetown universities, he once ran for local registrar of wills and lost.

Another big-time gambler who allegedly became the most powerful layoff man in Pittsburgh, Art Rooney once hired a coach for the Steelers because he owed Rooney money from gambling. The coaching job was to help work off the debt. Remaining a heavy gambler while an NFL owner, Rooney, like Bidwill, later purchased several horse- and dog-racing tracks.

Rooney reportedly once won $256,000 after two days of betting at Empire City and Saratoga racetracks. Recounting the story of that now-legendary day of gambling, Rooney once told columnist Red Smith, "I had Tim Mara's figures but sometimes I'd see something the charts didn't see, like a change of jockeys or post position, and I'd use my own judgement [*sic*]. I was betting with Peter Blong, who was working in the ring for Frank Erickson that day . . . If Erickson had been there I'm sure he would have kept taking my action. Anyway, I came close to sweeping the card."[5]

So close were Art Rooney and Tim Mara that Rooney and his wife named one of their sons Timothy in honor of Mara.

"Bookmakers in those days were such a different brand of people from what they are today," Rooney told reporter Myron Cope. "They were great people. They had class."[6]

On July 9, 1933, the day after Rooney purchased the Steelers, his close friend deBenneville "Bert" Bell, another racetrack gambler with ties to the Erickson gambling syndicate, bought the Frankford Yellow Jackets in Philadelphia and changed the name to the Philadelphia Eagles. Bell and his partner, Lud Wray, paid $4,000 for the club; Bell became the team's coach.

Five feet eight and 195 pounds, Bert Bell was a star quarterback for the University of Pennsylvania in 1916 and 1917 before leaving school to work in an army hospital in France during World War I. He returned to Penn after the war and became the captain of his college team. He remained on as the backfield coach at Penn after graduating with a bachelor's degree in English. He served under head coach John Heisman, for whom the Heisman Trophy—the annual award for the best college football player—is named.

Bell coached at Penn until 1928. He then operated the family-owned Ritz-Carlton Hotel in Philadelphia for two years before leaving to resume coaching at Temple University. While at Temple, Bell and Wray got together and decided to buy a professional football franchise in 1933. Bell had already married Francis Upton, a popular musical-comedy star and member of the Ziegfeld Follies, who gave him the money to buy the Eagles.

"Bert Bell was born to great wealth," his son Upton Bell told me. "But he chose both sides of the track. He was just as comfortable with Alfred Vanderbilt as he was with Al Capone. Oh, sure, he knew Al Capone.[7] He knew all the gamblers because he was a gambler himself at one time. He was a young man during Prohibition. All the rich people in those days knew all the gangsters. He knew those people, and they trusted him.

"Before he married my mother, he was engaged to a society woman. My grandfather, who was extremely wealthy, tried to talk him into settling down with this woman and gave him fifty thousand dollars. My father took the money and lost it all in one day at Saratoga racetrack. When my father came back, he said that he was sorry that he had lost the money, and that he was not going to marry the woman. My grandfather banished him from the house and cut him out of the will."

In June 1934, the NFL team, the Portsmouth Spartans, was sold for $21,500 to Detroit investor George "Dick" Richards, a former automobile dealer and another heavy gambler, who then moved the team to his hometown and renamed it the Detroit Lions. Although it was against the league rules for any member of the NFL—owner, coach, or player—to gamble, Harry Wismer, a radio announcer and onetime part owner of the Lions, wrote, "Everyone knew Richards gambled, as did many of the other owners. They always bet on their own team, and in those days odds, not points, were used to indicate the difference between the teams. In the letters he had foolishly written . . . Richards revealed that he had bet heavily on a number of the Lions' games and called for everyone's best efforts to win for him."[8] He once claimed to have bet $50,000 on a single NFL game.

The famed Earl "Dutch" Clark, one of Richards's star players, talked about the owner's gambling habits. "[Richards] liked to bet on the Lions and he would get some of the players to go in with him . . . Richards figured they'd play twice as hard to win twenty-five bucks, or maybe fifty bucks. So he got them going along with him."[9]

Richards sold the Lions in 1940, after he was caught paying off a college player to play on his professional team. He sold out for $225,000 to Fred Mandel, who owned a Chicago department store.

Three years earlier, in 1937, a group of investors organized the Cleveland Rams, selling the team in 1941 for $100,000 to twenty-nine-year-old New York businessman Dan F. Reeves, a very slight and fine-boned little man who was the son of the founder of a chain of grocery stores based in New York. Young Reeves became the heir to the family business, which sold its six hundred stores to Safeway in 1940 for $11 million. An officer in the Army Air Force in World War II, Reeves suspended play by the Rams in 1943 while he was in the service. When Reeves returned from the war, he bought a seat on the New York Stock Exchange.

Later, in 1946, Reeves moved his stock brokerage firm to Beverly Hills and, with his NFL team in tow, created the Los Angeles Rams. After suffering losses of over $200,000 from his football investment the following year, he took on four partners, one of whom was entertainer Bob Hope.[10] Each of the partners bought in for a mere $1—with the proviso that they share in the losses of the team. It would be one of the worst deals Reeves ever made because the Rams rarely lost money after that. Meantime, he had given away two thirds of the team for a total of $4.

When Rooney sold his Pittsburgh team in 1940 to Alexis Thompson, a New York drug manufacturer, he became Bell's partner in the Philadelphia franchise. Rooney and Bell then swapped teams with Thompson the following year—with Rooney regaining the Steelers. And then, because of the war, the Pittsburgh and Philadelphia teams merged and became the Phil-Pitt Steagles. This hybrid team played together only for the 1943 season.[11] However, Bell remained with Pittsburgh, serving as the team's president and general manager.

4 The Baugh Surveillance

IN THE LATE FALL of 1943, rumors began to circulate that members of the Washington Redskins—particularly Sammy Baugh, the Redskins' quarterback sensation—were associating with Washington gamblers who were linked to Frank Erickson's gambling syndicate. Talk of game fixing had already begun after a November contest between the Redskins and the Phil-Pitt Steagles.

The Redskins' "Slingin" Sammy Baugh was one of the greatest quarterbacks to ever play the game of football. He was an all-American at Texas Christian University in 1936 and signed with Washington the following year. In his first season as a pro, Baugh electrified fans with a spectacular passing offense and led the once-failing Redskins to their first NFL championship.

The next year, after threatening to quit football if he didn't receive more money, Baugh negotiated a three-year contract for $25,000 with Redskins owner George Preston Marshall. A West Virginia-born laundry owner in Washington who had bought the Boston Braves football team in July 1932, Marshall had moved the team to Washington, D.C., forming the Washington Redskins in February 1937. Marshall, a onetime horse-racing enthusiast and gambler, had reformed himself and begun beating a tambourine in his efforts to prevent sports gambling. Always a showman, Marshall was determined to make professional football respectable.

Although the Chicago Bears had destroyed the Redskins, 73–0, in the 1940 NFL championship game, it took Baugh only two years to avenge the Redskins and take the title back from the Bears. "I guess this kinda makes up for that thing in 1940, don't it?" cowboy Baugh told newsmen after the game.

The Bears' running sensation, former all-American George "One-Play" McAfee, a 9.8 sprinter in the hundred on a cinder track back, told me about the 1940 game, saying, "The funny thing about that game was that two or three weeks earlier, the Redskins had beaten us, seven to three. We left there with some hard feelings because we thought we had gotten some bad calls from the officials. And when we came back to play them, we wanted to get even. But ol' Sammy, he was a great quarterback. We played both ways in those days—so I was in the backfield offensively and played in the secondary on defense. I remember on one play I felt someone bumping me. When I turned around, it was Sammy blocking me downfield. And he was the quarterback. Sammy always played full out." McAfee intercepted a pass and ran thirty-four yards for a touchdown during the Bears' rout of the Redskins.

Baugh also remembers the 1940 rivalry with the Bears, especially the championship game. Baugh told me, "We played the Bears on the last day of the regular season that year, and we beat them, seven to three. In fact, McAfee ran the ball down to the one yard line. And before they could score, the officials said that the game was over. That left a real bad taste in their mouth.

"But there was no doubt in my mind that the Bears were the best team in the league that year, game in and game out. We had more good players that year than I could ever remember playing with. But I doubt that we were as good as they were. We might have been a little lucky to have beaten them in that seven-to-three game. But when they left that field they were madder than hell. They just couldn't believe that we beat them.

"On the day of the championship, we were a damn tired team. We were practicing really hard the week before the game. We would have been better off had we not worked quite so hard."

In 1943, Baugh had led the Redskins to sixteen consecutive games over two seasons without a defeat. Then, Washington was beaten by the Steagles on November 28. Earlier that month, the Steagles had tied the Redskins, 14–14, ending Washington's consecutive victory streak at thirteen. Prior to the loss to the Steagles, the Redskins were 6–0–1 and in first place in the NFL's Eastern Division. The Steagles were 4–3–1 and in second place.

Baugh entered the November 28 game with a knee injury he had received in a game two weeks earlier. The Steagles had held the Redskins scoreless until the final seconds of the third quarter when Baugh threw a touchdown pass. With the score 14–7 in the fourth quarter, Baugh led the Redskins downfield hoping to tie the game. However, a Baugh pass was intercepted, which led to another Steagles touchdown. When the Redskins got the ball back, Baugh attempted a quick kick (a surprise punt before fourth down) that was blocked and recovered by the Steagles on the Redskins one yard line. The Steagles then plunged in for another score. Baugh, who was twice booed by the Redskins fans because of his performance, threw a second touchdown pass in the final seconds of the fourth quarter. Too little too late, the Steagles won, 27–14.

In early December, two sportswriters for *The Washington Times-Herald,* Vincent X. Flaherty and Dick O'Brien, began reporting on the rumors circulating in Washington about Baugh and the Redskins. Although dismissing such talk as "pool hall gossip," Elmer Layden—a member of the legendary Four Horsemen of Notre Dame who had become the first commissioner of the NFL in 1941[1]—reported, "So far I have not been able to find the slightest bit of factual evidence of collusion between anyone in the league and gamblers."

Infuriated over Flaherty and O'Brien's report, Redskins owner Marshall denied that members of his team had been gambling and said defiantly, "Anyone connected with professional football who is gambling or has gambled on a game in our league should be thrown out immediately." Marshall then offered a $5,000 reward for any proof of any gambling by any member of the Redskins. *The Times-Herald* could not advance their case further and dropped the story.

"We heard those rumors weeks ago," Baugh told the two reporters during their investigation. "The boys on our team just laughed at them."

I asked Baugh about the charges of gambling against the Redskins players. He explained that the entire team had first been confronted prior to its game with the Detroit Lions earlier in the 1943 season. "The first time we heard about it was in our dressing room before the game," Baugh says. "someone came in and said that there was a rumor going around that we were throwing the game that day. I remember that shocked everybody, and we just made up our minds to beat the hell out of

Detroit if we could." The Redskins ran up the score and won, 42–20.

After the allegations of team associations with bookmakers were first made public, Baugh continues, "someone was talking about Mr. Marshall taking us down to the newspaper office and make the sons of bitches prove it. Some said not to pay that much attention to it—just let the damn thing go. I told them that I'd rather make them prove it—if they had any proof. 'Let us see it.' "

However, Baugh did not know that George Marshall had secretly recorded the quarterback's conversations with known bookmakers during the week Flaherty and O'Brien had broken their initial story. The surveillance was arranged through a D.C. police officer, Joe Shimon, who had been hired by Marshall via publisher William K. Hutchison.

"Hutchison ran a news service in Washington and was very close to Marshall," Shimon told me. "Hutchison had some newsreel cameramen who filmed Redskins games. Then he and Marshall would invite some friends to see the films.

"Hutchison called me and asked how to wire a room for sound. When I asked why, he told me that Marshall suspected that some of his players were fixing games and wanted to prove it. So I arranged for Hutchison to get the equipment he needed to do the job.

"I didn't hear anything more about it until several years later when Hutchison died. He had left me some of his personal effects and included was a stack of the recordings of Baugh, some other players, and bookmakers talking about the Redskins games."

The surveillance of the conversations, recorded on old seventy-eight phonograph records, has been obtained for this book. They include conversations in which Baugh and other players were heard discussing point spreads, player injuries, inside information, bets, and their bookmaker friends.

In 1943, most of the Redskins from the 1942 NFL championship team had been drafted into the military and gone to war. Baugh, who had joined the team in 1937, was not among them. He had received a deferment because he was the sole source of support for five people, including his wife and two children. He also was a rancher and in 1941 had purchased a sixty-five-hundred-acre cattle ranch in Rotan, Texas, an hour north of Sweetwater and at the foot of Double Mountain in East Texas. The government wanted ranchers ranching and providing food for the troops overseas. Later, Baugh developed his property into a twenty-one-thousand-acre spread. During the recorded conversations, Baugh told those present, "I wish I had [the] ranch in Texas paid for."

Baugh brought Pete Gianaris's name into one of the discussions. Gianaris was a Washington gambler who had been convicted of bookmaking in 1938 and once owned a 25 percent interest in boxer Rocky Marciano. He was the personal Washington representative of Frank Erickson on the local gambling scene. In an earlier taped conversation, Gianaris had been recorded telling a Redskins player from whom he'd been receiving inside information and placing bets, "I'm the only one that books football. . . . The story is out that I've been fixing the [Steagles] game."

Gianaris was alleged to have bet $40,000 against the Redskins at 4 to 1 odds and won $160,000 on the game. Gianaris guarded his words during the discussion and never admitted during the recording to have paid off any Redskins players. When he was asked by another person in the room, "Don't you understand that people think you're fixing Baugh?" Gianaris flat out denied it. "I am not," Gianaris said. "I've never given him a nickel in my life."

When Gianaris's name was brought up at a subsequent conversation, Baugh asked, "You know what I'm worried about?" "I do know Pete Gianaris. See, he's been down that [road with Marshall]—just like [Baugh then recites the names of three gamblers/bookmakers] and all us boys."

"What's the difference, Sam?" someone asked.

"Well, that's the only gamblers I know, see? . . . Well, people know I know Pete, and they see me with Pete, see? And there's talk come of it that makes it look bad."

"Well, when they come and ask you, I'd say, 'I certainly know him,' I wouldn't try to deny it."

"I don't try and deny it," Baugh replied.

"So what the hell's the difference? You're going out with a gambler. You know a gambler. So [why] the hell are three gamblers owning three clubs in the league? . . . How about Charlie Bidwill? . . . And you've got Tim Mara. And you've got Art Rooney. So what the hell, 'Why sure I know gamblers. They're friends of mine.' Goddamnit, they don't own our club, though."

Although there is no evidence on the recordings that Baugh or any other Redskins player ever threw a game in 1943, the evidence is clear that Baugh and perhaps as many as four other players had personal and/or financial relationships with gamblers and bookmakers.

Nevertheless, even with the evidence in hand, Elmer Layden and George Marshall issued a joint statement—simply declaring that their investigation of Redskins' associating with gamblers had "turned up absolutely nothing." Later that year, the Redskins became the Eastern Division champions but lost the NFL championship game to the Chicago Bears, 41–21.

I told Baugh that his room had been ordered to be bugged by Marshall, and I read him a portion of the transcripts of the recordings in his hotel room. Baugh became furious and replied, "Now wait just a goddamn minute! There wasn't anybody in that room beside football players! I never knew any bookmakers! I never made a damn bet in my life, and I won't today!"

When I specifically asked him about Pete Gianaris, Baugh explained, "You know what I remember about Pete Gianaris? One of the boys [a Redskins player], I don't remember who it was, asked me if I wanted to go have dinner at a fan's house one night. It was Pete Gianaris. I never knew Pete Gianaris was a gambler. I never knew what Pete Gianaris did. I won't deny that I knew Pete Gianaris . . .

"I never made one damn bet in my life on a football game. I made one bet in my life on a horse race. It lost, and I [vowed] that I was never going to bet again. The horse didn't get the call."

Reflecting on his life playing football, Baugh says, "I enjoyed it all my damn life. Money wasn't that important then. You did it because you enjoyed the game."

5 The Big Fix

ALTHOUGH BASEBALL WAS STILL king among sports gamblers, gambling on college and professional football games had increased in popularity after World War II, giving Bert Bell, the new NFL commissioner, more and larger headaches.

Bell had replaced Elmer Layden on January 11, 1946. Bell—who received a three-year contract at $20,000 a year—sold his interest in the Pittsburgh Steelers to Art Rooney so that he could accept the position. However, he later moved the NFL's headquarters from Chicago to One Bala Avenue in Bala-Cynwyd, just outside Philadelphia. Action had always seemed to follow Bell, and his role with the NFL would be no different.

On December 15, 1946, just hours before the NFL championship game between the New York Giants and the Chicago Bears, New York mayor William O'Dwyer, district attorney Frank S. Hogan, and NFL officials announced that there had been an attempt to fix the game. Gambler Alvin J. Paris of Elizabeth, New Jersey, was immediately arraigned for his attempt to bribe Giants players Merle Hapes and Frank Filchock, the former backup quarterback for Sammy Baugh in Washington.

Baugh told me, "Filchock was a real good football player. We got him on a trade from Pittsburgh. He was a good passer and a smart quarterback. I remember Mr. Marshall was talking about trading him [to the Giants in 1946]. I told him that, no matter what they did, they should never trade Filchock because he was as good a quarterback as anybody in the league at that time."

Baugh said that Filchock's role in the attempted fix "surprised" him. "Filchock never got into any trouble at all at Washington as far as I knew. I remember both Filchock and Hapes. We heard they were offered the money and didn't report it."

During my interview with Merle Hapes, he told me, "On the day of the championship game, Bell came with some people and picked us up. They put us into a private room. We told them we were innocent, but their announcement had already been made [that an attempt had been made to tamper with the game]. We had been blackballed, and they had to do something. They didn't want to hear what we had to say.

"Sure, I knew the man [Alvin Paris], and I couldn't lie about that. His father [Sidney Paris, who had served four years for mail fraud] was a member of the Elks in New York, and I was a member in Mississippi. The son asked me if I would throw the game, and I laughed at him. I said, 'I could never do anything like that. Forget about me.' Bell asked me if I took any money, and I told him, 'I had nothing to do with it.' "

The attempted fix had been discovered through a wiretap on Paris's telephone. Paris was held on a $25,000 bond and was later convicted for his role in the attempted fix.

Paris had actually fronted for three partners who were associates of Frank Erickson and had bet at least $20,000 on the Bears to win by ten points. Even after the attempted fix had been uncovered, the Bears still won the game, 24–14.

Hapes, a fullback, was benched before the game by order of Commissioner Bell. Only Hapes's name appeared in wiretapped conversations conducted by New York law-enforcement officials. The wiretaps indicated that past NFL games, as well as several college basketball games, also may have been successfully fixed. It was known that underworld figures had been wining and dining professional and college athletes at cocktail parties and in local nightclubs.

Filchock—who denied being approached and thus was permitted to play nearly the entire game—threw two touchdown passes and six interceptions in the Giants' losing effort, in which the bookmakers' bets were covered. Hapes told me, "I still can't figure out why they didn't let me play. They let Frank play because they needed a quarterback. I was their sucker, and I'm still damn bitter about it." Later, Filchock admitted that he had been made the bribe offer.

Each player was to receive $2,500 to throw the game, in addition to $2,000 in bets that would have been placed on their behalf. They were also offered off-season jobs. The situation became the biggest public sports scandal since the fixing of the 1919 World Series.

On the basis of Paris's statements to the district attorney, East Coast gamblers David Krakauer, Harvey Stemmer, and Jerome Zarowitz were also indicted and later convicted. At their sentencing, the trial judge scolded them, saying that they had "attempted to destroy the faith and confidence of the public in American sport."

Stemmer had been previously convicted for offering bribes to members of the Brooklyn College basketball team.

Within twenty-four hours of the sentencing of the conspirators, both Hapes and Filchock were suspended indefinitely by the NFL commissioner. Bell said that the two players were "guilty of actions detrimental to the welfare of the National League and of professional football." Both Filchock and Hapes went to play in the Canadian Football League.

Hapes says, "I'm not putting the blame on anybody. It was a screwup. Bell gave us a reprieve, but we were already going to Canada. He told us that we could go to any club we wanted. I went on to Canada anyway to play for five years."

In the wake of the bribery scandal, Bell received a five-year contract as commissioner from the NFL team owners, which increased his salary to $30,000 a year; and in 1954 it was extended twelve more years. Bell, who realized that gamblers had taken a major interest in the NFL, said, "Let them bet. That's their privilege. My job is to keep it from having an influence on our game."

On January 23, 1947, at the NFL owners' meeting in Chicago, Bell was given dictatorial powers designed to crush all future attempts to corrupt professional football. Specifically, Bell ordered that anyone in the league who receives "an offer directly or indirectly, by insinuation or by implication, to control or fix or accepts or bets anything of value on a professional football game in any manner whatsoever" must report to his club officials or the commissioner. Those who failed to comply with Bell's directive could be barred from the game for life.

He also ordered all NFL owners and personnel to stay out of gambling casinos in Las Vegas and elsewhere. Bell said that NFL personnel "must be not only absolutely honest; they must be above suspicion." To ensure this, Bell later hired former law-enforcement officials as consultants in several NFL cities to monitor the behavior of the league's players.

But gambling continued and had already become more sophisticated.

According to sportswriter William Barry Furlong, the point spread was invented during the early 1940s by University of Chicago-trained mathematical wizard Charles K. McNeil, who was also an obsessive sports fan.[1] This new method of handicapping attempted to attract an equal amount of betting on teams playing uncompetitive games that would otherwise draw little public interest and low-betting volume. Under this system of pricemaking, gamblers could bet on the favorite team and give points to the underdog—or take the underdog and the designated points.

Prior to this, bookmakers simply gave odds, like 3 to 2 or 7 to 5, on upcoming games. This traditional practice of making the odds rather than setting the point spreads continues to be used for betting on several sports, including baseball.

However, the best evidence is that the point spread began before McNeil. Frank Costello's personal bookmaker, Ed Curd, who was also an influential Kentucky oddsmaker and a close friend of McNeil, told me that McNeil did not invent the point spread. "I don't know of anyone who can take credit for that. McNeil fell into line like everyone else. But in my estimation he was the best handicapper who ever lived. He operated out of the Gym Club in Chicago. While he was there, he was a very active player [gambler]. He was probably more of a player than a bookmaker. He was his own service. Back then, people made out their own prices [point spreads]. There were different prices all over the country."

Mort Olshan, who later became one of the most respected sports handicappers in America, told me, "McNeil might not have invented the point spread, but he certainly refined it. There were scattered but reliable reports that point spreads had preceded McNeil in various regions of the country. They were based on regional games, particularly in the South, rather than on national projections. I understand that the point spread was used during the 1930s—before McNeil came along."

There were at least two oddsmakers who were using the point spread form of handicapping during the early 1930s in Minneapolis: Darby Hicks and Karl Ersin. During my interview with Ersin, he told me, "It was the Depression, and I needed something to do. I always liked sports very much and used to read everything I could. I kept book after book about football. It just got to be a habit. There was already a handicapper at *The Minneapolis Journal* named Darby Hicks. So, during the early 1930s, I went down to the other newspaper, *The Minneapolis Star Tribune,* and said, 'Can you use a handicapper?' And they hired me. I put an article in there every week. Darby and I used the point spread as our way of handicapping, and we had a contest to see who could do better [in picking the games]."

Ersin's oddsmaking career did not end there. "Billy Hecht owned a liquor store I used to go in, and we got to talking. He had just started something called the Minneapolis Gorham Press. He didn't know anything about setting a line, and so he hired me and a couple of other guys. I liked handicapping on football best; it's the best betting sport, particularly with the use of the point spread."

The Minneapolis Gorham Press, which was created by Hecht in or about 1937, became the first national oddsmaking institution. Many considered its newsletter to be a bible for gamblers, the first national "service" for bookmakers to set and distribute the line—a list of point spreads on sporting events. Its subscribers, who numbered only a few hundred, were also invited to telephone in during the week and receive the latest adjustments to the line on the upcoming games.

Speaking of the hazards of "suspicious" games, Ersin says, "We suspected that games were fixed in the thirties and forties, but we could never find out for sure. So the games we didn't want much action on we just circled. We always knew what was going on when we got loaded up with bets on them: unnatural money. We were scared of pro games because we didn't know what was going on with them. There were too many winners. We thought the fix was in often enough. Our clients complained that they wanted a line on the pro games, but we wouldn't give it to them very often—because we just didn't trust the games."

Five-feet-six Leo Hirschfield—who had lost the hearing in his right ear after a bout with influenza while in the Marine Corps during World War I—bought into the Gorham Press in 1940 and became Hecht's partner. Hirschfield changed the name of the company to Athletic Publications, Inc.; and its newsletter, *Weekly Gridiron Record*, became better known as simply *The Green Sheet*. The whole operation consisted of only eighteen full-time employees but, at its height, annually grossed nearly $10 million.

Mort Olshan, who was like a "surrogate son" to Hirschfield, worked on *The Green Sheet* along with Karl Ersin, Jimmy Harris, and Joe Katzman, who was the senior handicapper. Olshan told me, "There were four handicappers with Leo Herschfield, who was the active partner with a one-third interest and ran the service operation. I never met Billy Hecht in my whole life; he was never around. He had another partner [Joe Numero] in the separate bookmaking part of the operation. They were bookmakers and took the action. They had separate jobs and separate offices from the service activity.

"Leo was a totally honest man, and he avoided all the shady associations. He had a mind that worked like a computer. Even though he wasn't a sports fanatic who followed the games religiously, and he didn't have anything to do with the actual handicapping of the games, he knew instinctively when a wrong line was set."

Born in 1926, Olshan is a Buffalo native and a Marine combat veteran who saw action in Okinawa in World War II. He attended the University of Buffalo for one year, hoping to become either a sports reporter or play-by-play announcer. He says that he, too, has been collecting newspaper and magazine clippings about football since he was seven years old.

"I read an article entitled 'The Wizard of Odds' about Leo and the Minneapolis line in *Collier's* magazine, and on an impulse I went to Minneapolis to ask Leo for a job. I thought that there was excitement in betting and handicapping, and that there might be a future in it for me. Athletic Publications, Inc., also published player statistics and the schedules for all the games in the entire country, including the rotation of the games—which was crucial to the industry and really united it.

"I started working at *The Green Sheet* in 1948 making ninety dollars a week as a statistician. By the end of my first month, my salary was increased to a hundred. And after a couple more months, I was raised to a hundred and fifteen dollars. I had tears in my eyes when they gave me those raises, because that was big money for a twenty-two-year-old man at the time. When I got there, we expanded *The Green Sheet* with different features and write-ups, so that it became more of a full-service, multidimensional publication with interesting stories and analyses of games."

Olshan says that each of *The Green Sheet* handicappers worked independently of one another. "We would read everything we could get our hands on—maybe as many as forty daily newspapers each day. Most of our work was done on Saturday and Sunday after we analyzed the college and professional games. On the basis of our information, we would set our own lines.

"Every Monday morning, the four of us then went into Leo's office with our own numbers. Because we were trying to equalize or balance the public's money on each game, we would have to carefully assess the strengths and weaknesses of the two teams and the public's perception of the games and then anticipate how the public would bet. It was rare, if ever, that we could achieve a totally even distribution of the betting, but we worked hard to get as close as possible. Joe Katzman would compare our individual point spreads, and we would often argue over the numbers. Joe would arbitrate the differences and would make his own adjustments based on the discussion. He would then set the ultimate line that would then be distributed around the country. The whole idea was to come up with a line that our subscribers could use and profit by."[2]

As NFL commissioner, Bert Bell began the process of calling cooperative bookmakers and gamblers, particularly those associated with the Minneapolis line, during the week before NFL games were played. His intent was to discover if there were any unusual fluctuations in the betting line.

"He took to the grave with him the names of his contacts in the underworld," Bell's son Upton told me. "My father had three phones. One was for regular use. Another was for the players who could call him at any time. And there was a third phone that he used for the gamblers and the people who were feeding him information about the odds or about a player's behavior. All of these guys had a code name. And Bert Bell was the only one who had these names.

"There was a certain honor among them. They wanted the games on the up-and-up because if they placed a bet they wanted to know that some guy down the line wasn't fixing the game. They knew if they told Bert Bell, they could get to the bottom of it. If he saw any great fluctuations from Monday right up to game time on Sunday, he was right on the phone to the team involved."

Among other bookmakers Bell kept in touch with were those controlled by Meyer Lansky, Frank Costello, and the then-boss of the New Orleans Mafia, Sylvester Carolla. The three syndicate figures had agreed in 1947 to create "a national communications center in New Orleans to transmit financial information. Such a clearinghouse would, for instance, make it possible for the bookmaking syndicate in New York to know instantly if a horse, ball team, or what have you was being heavily wagered elsewhere in the nation. Any break in the betting patterns would indicate a fix or an attempt to swindle the syndicate."[3]

Ed Curd, Costello's personal bookmaker, set a major national line on sporting events during the late 1940s that rivaled that published by *The Green Sheet.* Curd told me that he had met Costello in 1946. "Costello said that he could handicap his own horses and his baseball games, but he wanted me to give him a football team or two. What was I going to say? No? He told me that if I ever needed anything in New York, that I shouldn't hesitate to call on him.

"There wasn't anything he wouldn't do for me. And we did business together for several years. Later on, he wanted me to go to Vegas, and he would see that I was taken care of. But I turned him down. I always thought that staying in the middle of the road was best for me. I wanted to do my own thing. I didn't want any partners."[4]

Operating with two Teletype machines, three telephones strictly for long-distance business, and four secretaries, Curd ran his line out of Kentucky and distributed it across the country. He also was responsible for a new innovation in gambling: 11–10, the bookmaker's standard 10 percent vigorish on all losing bets.

"We had so much business on football that we had two ways of dealing," Curd recalls. "We had nine to ten odds for up to fourteen points, that's ninety cents on the dollar. And we had six to five for fourteen and over. And then we had an outcome price on every game—sometimes as ridiculous as one to twenty and fifteen to one. We had a price on every game. Well, we had control of the business. But it was getting awkward handling everything.

"So one Monday morning, just before we sent out the line, I said, 'We're going to change things, and see if we can get away with it.' What I wanted to do was get rid of the outcome prices. I wanted to eliminate them altogether. But they were being dealt all over the country. So I knew I had to give the operators around the country something better to work with, more money. So I made up my mind that regardless whether there was a bet on a four-point game or a twenty-point game, I'd put it right on the spot. Let them lay eleven to ten [put up $11 to make $10], and that would be our commission.

"When we came out that Monday, each place saw it the way we saw it. Eleven to ten looked more inviting and less trouble for the operator. It was accepted because they could keep their businesses together a lot easier. And eleven to ten has been the standard ever since."

Curd also became known for his sixth sense about how the injuries of players would affect the point spreads of the games their teams played.

Meantime, when Frank Filchock's NFL suspension was lifted, he joined the Baltimore Colts, which was part of a new, rival football league called the All-American Football Conference (AAFC), which had been founded in June 1944. The new league, fielding eight teams, had been dreamed up by influential *Chicago Tribune* sports editor Arch Ward. Twice offered the position as NFL commissioner in 1940 and 1941, Ward turned it down both times. Instead he had recommended Elmer Layden for the job.

Several early team owners in the AAFC were high-stakes gamblers, including trucking executive John L. Keeshin, who had bought the Chicago Rockets; Indiana oil company president Ray Ryan, who had petitioned for a New York team with the widow of baseball star Lou Gehrig; New York Yankees owner Dan Topping and his minority partner, developer Del E. Webb; racetrack owner Ben Lindheimer of Chicago, who bought the Los Angeles Dons along with actor Don Ameche, who had tried but failed to obtain an NFL team; and cab company owner Mickey McBride, who founded the Cleveland Browns, named after his head coach, Paul Brown.[5]

The owner of a Chicago trucking company, Keeshin was known to have made a direct cash "loan" to James R. Hoffa, then the head of the Central Conference of Teamsters.[6] Government investigators later viewed the loan as nothing more than the price for labor peace with the Teamsters. Also a racetrack owner, Keeshin did business with Allen M. Dorfman, Hoffa's handpicked fiduciary manager of the Teamsters' Central States Health and Welfare Fund—and later the Central States, Southeast and Southwest Areas Pension Fund. Dorfman's stepfather, Paul "Red" Dorfman, had been the head of the corrupt Chicago Wastehandlers Union and was responsible for introducing Hoffa to numerous Midwestern underworld figures. Although both Keeshin and the Dorfmans principally lived in Chicago, they each had second houses in Eagle River, Wisconsin, and were close friends.

Ray Ryan proudly proclaimed himself as one of the biggest gamblers in the country, particularly on professional football games. A close associate of Frank Erickson and Texas oil tycoons H. L. Hunt and Jack Davis, Ryan was the co-owner of the Mount Kenya Safari Club in Africa, along with actor William Holden.[7] Members included Erickson, as well as East Coast Mafia figures Gerardo Catena and Tommy and Pasquale Eboli.

Ryan had also been a partner in the syndicate that purchased RKO Pictures Corporation from Howard Hughes in 1952. However, after *The Wall Street Journal* reported that Ryan and his partners had all been involved with "organized crime, fraudulent mail-order schemes, and big-time gambling," and Ryan was specifically linked to mobster Frank Costello, the RKO deal collapsed. The studio's ownership reverted back to Hughes—who kept the $1.5 million down payment put up by Ryan and his partners.

A onetime associate of Hughes told me, "Howard Hughes knew the kind of people he was dealing with; he always did. He knew their backgrounds, and he knew their associations. That was the way he operated . . . He took their down payment and then waited. At the right time, he leaked the story to the press."

Ryan was later shaken down for $60,000 by Chicago mobster Marshall Caifano. Ryan testified against him in court and helped send him to jail for ten years. Ryan was later killed in Evansville, Indiana, when his car was bombed. Caifano was suspected of ordering the murder but was never prosecuted.

Ryan and Mrs. Gehrig had withdrawn their interests in the AAFC franchise before league play began. The New York franchise then went to Dan Topping, the president of the New York

Yankees baseball team. Topping had owned the Brooklyn Dodgers franchise of the NFL but switched to the AAFC, also calling his new team the New York Yankees.

Topping's partner in the Yankees baseball and football franchises was Del E. Webb, an associate of numerous organized-crime figures. A builder from Phoenix, Webb was the contractor selected by gangster Bugsy Siegel to build the Flamingo, the first major hotel/casino in Las Vegas. Along with his building contract, Webb also received a 10 percent interest in Siegel's hotel. Later, Webb built and owned the Sahara hotel/casino and had other casino holdings in Las Vegas, Reno, and Lake Tahoe.

Ben Lindheimer bought the Los Angeles franchise and called it the Los Angeles Dons, named after his partner, actor Don Ameche. Lindheimer was the overlord of Chicago's racetracks. He was closely associated with the Chicago underworld. His personal attorney was Sidney Korshak, a young mouthpiece for the old Capone mob, who had also been hired by Ray Ryan to handle labor negotiations for RKO before the deal with Hughes collapsed.

Through political favors and payoffs, Lindheimer was principally responsible for the creation of the Illinois Racing Commission and was appointed as the chairman of the Illinois Commerce Commission. In an attempt to legalize the state's three thousand bookmakers, Lindheimer later led the lobby to legalize offtrack betting. He was supported by the state attorney general Otto Kerner.[8] However, the governor vetoed the bill.

6 The Wire Services

ANOTHER TEAM IN THE All-American Football Conference was the Cleveland Browns, formed by a crime-syndicate bookmaker, Arthur "Mickey" McBride. At the time he owned the Browns, McBride was the head of the Continental Racing Wire, the mob's gambling news service—which the Special Senate Committee to Investigate Organized Crime in Interstate Commerce, better known as the Kefauver Committee—later described as "Public Enemy Number One."[1] McBride's partner was James M. Ragen, Sr., of Chicago.

Born in Chicago in 1888, McBride was selling newspapers on the street at age six and became the circulation manager of William Randolph Hearst's *Chicago American* in 1911. Two years later, he was sent to Cleveland by Hearst and held the same position for *The Cleveland News,* an afternoon paper. McBride became the newspaper's point man in its rough-and-tumble circulation wars against *The Cleveland Plain Dealer.* Ragen was the circulation manager of *The Cleveland Leader,* the *News*-owned morning paper. In the midst of the battles, trucks were hijacked and people were beaten, stabbed, and shot.

Through these wars, McBride recruited Morris Dalitz and his Cleveland-based Mayfield Road Gang for the rough stuff. McBride remained in the newspaper business until 1930 when he purchased his first taxicab company and parlayed it into the only cab company in the metropolitan Cleveland area.[2]

A shrewd businessman with a wide variety of investments in

Cleveland, Chicago, and the Miami area, the quiet McBride once said, "Nobody ever got rich on a salary."

McBride had founded the Continental Racing Wire in the wake of the collapse of the Nationwide News Service, which had been operated out of Chicago by Moses L. Annenberg, who like McBride and Ragen had started his career as a circulation manager for the Hearst newspaper chain. After Annenberg's August 1939 indictment for criminal tax fraud, he made a deal with the government that provided that similar charges be dropped against his son Walter Annenberg and two of their associates in Nationwide. In return, Annenberg pleaded guilty, paid $9.5 million in back taxes and penalties, and went to prison in 1940.[3] Walter Annenberg closed down Nationwide and took over his father's publishing empire, which included *The Philadelphia Inquirer* and *The Daily Racing Form,* which the elder Annenberg had bought in 1922.[4]

Among those sent by the Chicago mob to work for the elder Annenberg on his wire service had been Johnny Rosselli. After the collapse of Nationwide, Rosselli went to Hollywood to work for the Motion Picture Producers Association. Within three years, he and six other Chicago mobsters—who had taken over the International Alliance of Theatrical Stage Employees, the largest union in Hollywood—were indicted and convicted for selling labor peace to the major movie studios.[5]

While the Mafia was busy shaking down Hollywood, Nationwide's Chicago manager, Tom Kelly, persuaded his brother-in-law, Mickey McBride, to create Continental in November 1939, in the wake of Nationwide's collapse, with a mere $20,000 investment. McBride was also encouraged to do so by James Ragen, who was indicted with Annenberg for his role in the Nationwide scheme and pleaded guilty.

The intent of the wire service had been to provide every bookmaker in the country with needed information on all aspects of sports gambling, particularly horse racing. Sports results were transmitted over both the telephone and telegraph to twenty-four large "distributors" throughout the United States. The gambling information was then printed and delivered to subscribers to the service.

Former Chicago FBI agent Aaron Kohn, who investigated the wire service, told me, "One of the mob's major sources of income was their operation of the wire service systems and the layoff network for gambling on football. Among the clever devices they used for reaching out to the largest possible mass of consumers were football-betting parlay cards. By the 1950s, they were widespread.

"The mob had to do everything they could to control the outcome of these games in order to control the level of their profits. You found them manipulating and corrupting in football, as they sometimes did in basketball. They would corrupt players and move into ownership control of teams whenever they could. Once the mob found the market for illegal gambling, corruption became an inseparable part of their operation."

Within two years of creating Continental, McBride sold it to Ragen, with whom he had been involved in some real estate deals after the newspaper wars. Because Ragen needed McBride's contacts, he asked the Cleveland businessman to stay on and become his minority partner. McBride agreed and kept a one-third interest in the wire service—but he placed his investment in the name of his son Edward McBride who was away at college at the time of the purchase.

The Chicago Mafia viewed Continental as potentially a multimillion-dollar business and a vehicle through which it could control sports bookmaking in the United States. In 1946, Chicago Mafia boss Tony Accardo, the Chicago mob's political fixer Jake "Greasy Thumb" Guzik, and syndicate member Murray "the Camel" Humphreys offered to buy Continental from Ragen. Despite the underworld's promise to keep Ragen as a partner, Ragen refused because he foresaw the obvious problem: Sooner or later, he would lose his independence.

When the Chicago mobsters refused to relent, Ragen went to the FBI and signed a ninety-eight-page affidavit informing the bureau that Accardo, Guzik, and Humphreys were trying to take over his business. He also told the bureau that his own wire service had paid out over $600,000 to numerous unnamed politicians throughout the country for protection.

The Chicago Mafia responded by setting up a rival wire service, Trans-American Press Service. Accardo-hired leg breakers attempted to muscle Continental's subscribers to cancel their contracts. When that ploy failed, Ragen, although supposedly under police protection, was ambushed and shot while driving in rush hour on a Chicago street on June 24, 1946. He died from his wounds seven weeks later.

Indicted for the Ragen murder were David Yaras and Leonard Patrick. Yaras, a non-Italian/Sicilian member of the Chicago Mafia, was a henchman for Chicago Mafia chiefs Accardo and Sam Giancana. However, the two key witnesses against Yaras and Patrick were murdered; two others then refused to testify. Consequently, the case was dropped.[6] Yaras, who was among the first Chicago mobsters to "discover" Florida after Al Capone went to prison, was a key figure in the Continental Racing Wire and an ally of Mickey McBride.

Soon after, McBride, again in his son's name, bought out Ragen's two-thirds interest from Ragen's son. Trans-American immediately folded, and its customers were given to Continental, clearly indicating Accardo's approval of McBride.

Joe Nellis, the assistant counsel of the Kefauver Committee, told me that there was high drama when McBride was called to testify. "It took me two days to tear his ass apart," Nellis says. "The McBride situation was a very serious matter. Here was a guy who owned the Cleveland Browns, who was in bed with a lot of gamblers and hoodlums. And he was a man people respected. They took off their hats when he came around.

"He tried to tell us that Continental Press was supplying racing wire information. That was simply not true. In the end, we undid Continental. It went out of business shortly after we exposed McBride as a supplier of illegal information to bookmakers all over the country about all sports."

McBride was indeed the embodiment of the connection between organized crime and professional sports. In its final report, the Kefauver Committee charged that McBride was "making a gift to the Mafia-affiliated Capone mob in Chicago of about $4,000 a week." The committee also concluded that as a result of the national network created by McBride, "the Capone affiliates and the Mafia are now in control of the distribution of racing wire news with a resultant source of enormous profits and power over bookmaking."

Another target of the Kefauver investigation was Chicago Cardinals owner Charles Bidwill, who had died in April 1947 of bronchial pneumonia in Chicago's St. George's Hospital.[7] Aside from his interest in the Cardinals, the fifty-one-year-old Bidwill was also president of the National Jockey Club, which operated the Sportsmen's Park racetrack, and was the managing director of the Hawthorne racetrack. Both were located in Cicero, a Chicago suburb.

Bidwill's partner at Sportsmen's Park was William H. Johnston, who was identified by the select committee as an operative in the Capone syndicate; Bidwill and Johnston had bought out Jack Keeshin, a founding member of the All-American Football Conference and the owner of the Chicago Rockets. The attorney for the two partners was Edward O'Hare, who had also represented Capone and was the business manager of the Cardinals team. O'Hare was murdered in 1939. Another investor at Sportsmen's Park was Frank Erickson.

During testimony before the Kefauver Committee, racetrack operator John Patton—a Chicago Mafia associate and business partner of Frank Erickson—said that he, Bidwill, and Johnston had operated Sportsmen's Park together until Bidwill died.

After his purchase of the Chicago Cardinals NFL franchise in 1933, Bidwill had also become the president of Bentley-Murray Printing Company, which was one of Moses Annenberg's subsidiaries. The NFL owner and the mob-connected wire-service tycoon had been close friends for years. Still, Bidwill continued to do business with McBride and the wire-service operations after Annenberg was sent to prison.

When I asked Nellis what danger is posed to professional sports when underworld associates like McBride and Bidwill were involved, he replied, "The shaving of points, the fixing of games, and any of the illegal activities that you can think of related to organized sports is made much easier by those people who know the characters and the tricks of organized crime."

The Kefauver Committee also crippled another Bidwill business partner, bookmaker Frank Erickson, by exposing his gambling empire. In the wake of the hearings, Erickson was indicted and convicted for sixty counts of bookmaking and conspiracy. He was sentenced to two years at Riker's Island Penitentiary.[8] After another conviction for criminal tax fraud, Erickson moved from New York to Miami where he mentored a young gambler named Gilbert Lee Beckley who also maintained strong ties with the Mafia. Beckley would soon become the major figure in sports gambling in America.

The Kefauver Committee's clear evidence of a concentrated national syndicate of crime that controlled the bulk of the nation's gambling operations forced Congress to pass two pieces of legislation. It banned wire-service operations while imposing a 10 percent excise tax on legal bets and forcing legal and illegal bookmakers to pay $50 a year for a gambling stamp, which was considered an "occupation tax."

The new laws had the immediate effect of driving Continental and the wire services out of business.

Although both pieces of legislation were important, the overall response by Congress was wimpish. The Kefauver Committee's request to legalize wiretapping and electronic surveillance by federal law-enforcement officials was rejected, as was a proposal to provide immunity to those within the underworld who were willing to testify against their more dangerous bosses.

Congress's weak response to the work of the Kefauver Committee was among the reasons for the eventual institutionalization of organized crime in, among other groups, professional sports and America's political system.[9]

Meantime, the NFL's new, Bell-inspired rules on corruption covered owners, players, coaches, and other team personnel—but did not include officials. Discussing who would be the ideal person on the field to fix, Harry Wismer said, "Too many situations arise over which the players or coach have no control . . . The person I would go to would be an official . . . They are underpaid and overcriticized. They are a perfect target for a player or a coach who is anxious to alibi on poor performance."[10]

At the beginning of the 1951 NFL season, Los Angeles mobster Jimmy Fratianno was $35,000 in debt and looking for a way out of his financial problems. "It just happened to be that this friend of mine called me [one] night and told me that they had this referee for the [Los Angeles] Rams, and to start betting on the Rams," Fratianno told my associate, William Scott Malone. "And so I started betting all over the country. And I bet between eighty thousand and ninety thousand dollars, I'm not sure." Fratianno added that he gave the information to friends in the Cleveland Mafia.

The game Fratianno claimed was fixed was between the Rams and the now-extinct New York Yanks NFL football team on September 28, 1951.[11] The Rams won, 54–14.

"Then, the next game we had was the San Francisco–Rams game [on October 28, 1951]," Fratianno continued. "And we had a loser there. We bet on the Rams and the Forty-niners won the game, [44–17]."

Because the Rams played so poorly, the alleged fixed referee could not help them win their bets. "Everything they [the Rams] did went wrong," Fratianno told UPI reporter Gregory Gordon. However, Fratianno said that they bet only $15,000 on that game.

Fratianno also said that there was a third game, the Rams versus the Green Bay Packers [on December 16, 1951], which he and his partners bet on and won. The Rams won, 42–14. "We won two and lost one. But then . . . the attorney general or somebody started investigating it. The bookmakers complained [about] all the money they lost, that there was something wrong. So [the referee] quit. That was the end of that with this referee."

Describing the mechanics of the relationship with their referee, Fratianno said that he and his partners had laid down only $2,500 in bets for him on each game. In return, "He just called penalties, you know."

Giving credence to Fratianno's story was the 1951 Rams star quarterback Bob Waterfield, who told Los Angeles reporter Bob Hunter that "at the end of the season, two officials were fired" by Bert Bell. Waterfield recalled seeing a referee arrive early for the Rams' workouts. After a period of time, the referee would talk to someone who would then make a telephone call. "I told [Rams owner] Dan Reeves about it," Waterfield said. "He reported it to the NFL office, which had the official tailed. It turns out the calls were made to Las Vegas. The official was fired."

All the games named by Fratianno were officiated by the same game officials, a crew headed by Rawson Bowen. Lawrence Houston was the field judge for the Bowen crew in 1951. A longtime college referee from UCLA, Houston, who was born in 1906, was asked to become an NFL official in the late 1940s.

When I found Houston and asked him about Fratianno's charges, he told me that he was part of the crew that officiated the three games cited by Fratianno. He added that he had known Waterfield since his days as a star quarterback with Van Nuys High School while Houston was coaching at the rival Eagle Rock High School. However, Houston denied knowing anything about fixed games or the dismissal of any official for gambling.

"In all the time I was associated with the professional football program, no one ever approached me, suggested it, or talked about it," Houston says. "I never knew of any referees, owners, coaches, or players who gambled. The crew I worked with were very, very fine people. Nothing of that nature was ever discussed."

Discussing his job as an official, Houston says, "We had to go out an hour before game time to inspect the field for markings and all of that. We would visit the dressing rooms and examine whether any player had any special protection. We had to examine whether there was a hard surface that might be injurious to someone else if they contacted it. After we got that, we went into our own dressing room, and we would chat about the mechanics of the game, just to be sure we were prepared and in the right frame of mind. We had a job to do.

"There were observers up there watching us. I understand that the commissioner of officials would have someone up there, and he might even come out himself and watch us work. The crew never got together socially at any time. The only times we were together were on the days we worked games or if Hugh 'Shorty' Ray, who was in charge of officials for the NFL, would come out in the late summer or early fall for a day or two and have a meeting with us and go over things, like rules changes and things like that. We would actually be tested to make sure that we knew the right answers about any given situation that might arise during a game. Those were the only times we got together.

"I never knew of anyone who had a vested interest in the outcome of a game."

Houston remained with the NFL until 1953 when he was knocked to the ground and injured by a player after he had blown a play dead. "He hit me between my shoulders and knocked me about fifteen feet away from the ball. The crowd loved it, of course. But I could hardly shave or comb my hair for about three weeks. That ended my career."

The world of sports expanded, seemingly unaffected by the revelations of the Kefauver Committee, which had been shoved off the front pages by the Red-baiting hearings of the U.S. House UnAmerican Activities Committee and Senator Joseph McCarthy's witch-hunt. To most people, Godless communism was a bigger threat to America's national security than the organized-crime syndicate was. With this public attitude to its advantage, the underworld fueled the fires of the Red scare and almost became perceived as acceptable citizens in the process.

7 Boss Colt

THE CLEVELAND BROWNS, BALTIMORE Colts, and San Francisco 49ers were the only three teams from the defunct AAFC that were merged into the NFL in 1950.[1] The deal was cinched by Mickey McBride and his two close NFL friends Tim Mara and Art Rooney, who had been convinced by Bert Bell to warmly welcome the AAFC teams into the NFL—so as to avoid potential antitrust problems with the federal government.

However, the Colts folded at the end of the 1950 season after team owner Abraham Watner had lost $760,000. Part of the void left by the Colts was filled by the new Dallas Texans. But the owners of the Dallas team found themselves in even worse financial shape than Watner had been and gave up their franchise during the 1952 midseason. The Texans then went into a receivership controlled by Bert Bell and the NFL. The final five games of the Dallas Texans season were played in Hershey, Pennsylvania.

The city of Baltimore desperately wanted the return of its NFL franchise. And commissioner Bell was happy to accommodate the Baltimore sports fans. But his major concern was finding an owner who had enough money to carry the team beyond a single season.

Carroll Rosenbloom had all the looks of a winner. Born on March 5, 1907, in Baltimore, he was handsome, charming, witty, and frequently generous. But friends and associates have also said that his generosity sometimes carried a price, and that he could be thin-skinned, condescending, and meanspirited. Because his ego was as big as his financial portfolio, he seemed to enjoy keeping people guessing.

Totally unpredictable, he was the kind of guy who could slap a newspaper boy around for throwing the morning edition in the bushes—and then the next day offer to put the same boy through college. One NFL team owner said, "Carroll always gave you the feeling that if you crossed him, he was capable of slitting your throat, then donating your blood to the Red Cross blood drive."[2]

Of course, those who crossed him were rarely forgiven. If he was in the midst of a war with someone and discovered that he had been wrong, he would rarely apologize. Instead, he would simply send flowers with a funny note attached and pretend that nothing had happened. His tone was slow and deliberate, as he switched between his Ivy League speech and racier, "mothah-fuckah" street talk. He was intensely competitive and also a heavy gambler.

A ruthless businessman, he was the son of Solomon Rosenbloom, a manufacturer of denim work clothes. Carroll Rosenbloom's older brother Ben Rosenbloom told me, "When our father came over from Russia, he couldn't speak English. In about 1888, he became a partner in the Standard Overall Company in Baltimore. But, as his sons got older, he decided to start a business that they could participate in. He sold out to his partners in Standard and then founded S. Rosenbloom, Inc. We manufactured all kinds of denims and sportswear. And everything just evolved from there.

"When another overall company, [which eventually became] Blue Ridge Manufacturers of Roanoke, Virginia, went up for sale, we bought it [in or about 1900]. Soon, we had plants all over the country. We sold our products to all the big chains, like Sears and Montgomery Ward."

The athletic, five-feet-eleven Carroll Rosenbloom grew up on Hollins Street—near the home of writer H. L. Mencken—before the family moved into a large home on Auchentroly Terrace, across from Druid Hill Park in northeastern Baltimore. A psychology major at Baltimore City College, he transferred to the University of Pennsylvania.

There were nine children in the family, six boys and three girls.[3] All the boys were raised to work in the family business; the girls were brought up to be good wives. Carroll went to work for his father when he graduated from college.

But Carroll wanted more responsibility and soon helped expand the family business, creating new companies and opening new plants. During the mid-1930s, he became the head of Blue Ridge and its subsidiaries—which, at the time, had eighty employees and included the Imperial Shirt Company.

"Carroll's father was a genius," said another member of the Rosenbloom family. "Although his oldest son, Isadore, was the obvious heir, and he ran another Rosenbloom company, Marlboro Shirts, while Solomon was alive, really none of the sons were very ambitious, with the exception of Carroll. He was special. He was dynamic but totally self-centered and gruff. He wasn't a very classy man, and despite his education, he didn't appear to be well educated."

When Solomon died in 1942, Carroll Rosenbloom assumed control of all the family's business interests, as directed by the elder Rosenbloom's will. "Upon my father's death, Carroll consolidated all our family's holdings under Blue Ridge," says Ben Rosenbloom. "Carroll did a hell of a job for all of us. He was the man who made it tick. He was a terrific guy."

Solomon had named Carroll as the executor of his estate, passing over all the other, older sons. A member of the Rosenbloom family recalls, "Although there was a lot of trouble over the will, all the children received enough money to retire on after Blue Ridge and Marlboro were later sold. No one ever had to work again. Carroll was really the only member of the family to remain active and in business for himself."

Ben Rosenbloom explains, "I had a sister Rose and she objected to some of the things in the will. We went to court, and it was settled. She basically challenged Carroll's authority over the estate. But everyone else was on Carroll's side because we knew he was doing the right thing."

According to a close friend of the family, Rose had contended that her brother had handled the corporate affairs in a manner to enhance the family's wealth at her expense. She charged that she lost $700,000 as a result of Rosenbloom's actions. Rosenbloom claimed that he had increased the worth of the family's businesses tenfold. He ended up settling with his sister for $500,000. As part of the final agreement, the paperwork in the case was sealed by court order.

After taking over the family business, Carroll quickly became known as the "Overalls King of America" during World War II. Doing work for the Philadelphia Quartermaster Depot, he built upon the family fortune by cornering the market on the blue-green battle fatigues and parachutes for American soldiers. He had also expanded the business to include the manufacturing of industrial garments, leather jackets, children's play clothes, and various adult sportswear, which included matched sets of shirts and slacks.

Two years after the war ended, Rosenbloom bought the twenty-one-year-old, eight-hundred-employee Blue Buckle Overall Company of Lynchburg, Virginia, and Marshall, Texas, for $2 million. The takeover of Blue Buckle, one of the largest producers of work clothes and sportswear in the United States, had the effect of merging three of the top brand names in overalls—Blue Ridge, Blue Buckle, and Blue Jay—under the control of Rosenbloom and his management team. The entire company employed nearly seven thousand workers.[4]

Carroll Rosenbloom, a former second-string halfback at the University of Pennsylvania, had caught the eye of his old college football backfield coach, Bert Bell. Witnessing the collapse of the Baltimore Colts and the Dallas Texans, Bell approached Rosenbloom. Rosenbloom told *Los Angeles Times* reporter Charles Maher, "Bert had a home near me in Margate, New Jersey. He kept telling me I ought to come into the league and I kept saying I didn't have time. Finally, to get away from him, I took the family to my home in Palm Beach and shut off the phones. But one of my brothers flew down and said, 'Carroll, you're really in a hell of [a] jam. Bert Bell has told the press the only way Baltimore can keep the franchise is if you will come in as owner.' So Bert had me on the spot. If I didn't take the team, they'd 'hang the Jew bastard.' But I got the franchise for nothing, really."

Bell offered Rosenbloom membership in the National Football League, which was "a very private club," and the Colts franchise at a bargain price: $13,000 as a down payment for majority ownership. Rosenbloom bought his 52 percent interest in the Colts on January 23, 1953.[5] His four partners each laid down $3,000 as their down payments.[6] If that wasn't attractive enough, Bell even offered to guarantee his investment if the Colts continued to lose money.

"Bert Bell was very anxious to get someone to take over the Colts," Ben Rosenbloom explains. "Carroll was doing him a favor by taking it over. But it turned out to be a very good favor."

In 1953, his first season as the Colts' owner, the team sold

15,755 season tickets, worth nearly $300,000, to Baltimore fans. Rosenbloom had banked $1.5 million at the time of his purchase and vowed that when this money had been spent then he'd pull out of the NFL. But the Colts were so successful that Rosenbloom never had to touch his reserve funds.

At first, Rosenbloom was a passive owner until he saw one particular play. The Colts' great halfback George Taliaferro told me, "We were playing the Green Bay Packers in Green Bay in 1953 and the game, for all intents and purposes, had been decided. We were getting beaten badly. When Green Bay kicked off to us after one of their many touchdowns, I took the ball and just took off. I went down the sideline and took a big hit. Rosenbloom later asked me why I just didn't go out of bounds. And I told him, 'Because you can't make a touchdown if you go out of bounds.' To me, it was just playing football.

"Rosenbloom said that it was that kind of determination that helped him make his decision. If I wanted to play that badly and wanted to go that extra yard, he wanted to put together an organization that would challenge the champions in the National Football League."

After witnessing Taliaferro's unbridled devotion to the game of football, Rosenbloom decided to become more active in team matters, and he promised the city of Baltimore a championship team within five years. Before long, season ticket holders numbered over fifty thousand.

8 Growing Pains

THE NFL GREW REMARKABLY between 1953 and 1958. Television began taking an active interest in broadcasting games across the league. The now-defunct DuMont Network bought the rights to the NFL championship game beginning in 1951 for $75,000. In 1955, DuMont was outbid by NBC, which paid $100,000 to broadcast the title game. The following year, CBS began airing some regular season games.

On December 28, 1956, professional football players organized the NFL Players Association, a guild founded along the lines of the players' union of major-league baseball, which had been organized in 1946. Every NFL team, with the exception of George Halas's Chicago Bears, joined immediately. For years, Halas's players were among the lowest-paid in the league.

The NFL players were concerned about several issues, which had led to the formation of the union. Among them were the simple questions of who was going to pick up the players' expenses during training camp and whether the players should be paid for the exhibition season. A player representative was selected from each participating NFL team to discuss these and other problems. The player reps then selected two players, Norm van Brocklin of the Los Angeles Rams and Kyle Rote of the New York Giants, to be their spokesmen during a meeting with Bert Bell.

Although the NFL owners refused to recognize the players' union, they agreed to begin paying the players for their training camp expenses and through the exhibition season. Carroll Rosenbloom took the lead among the NFL owners to grant these concessions to the players. After this initial peace, Bell decreed, "It is submitted that if any problems now exist or hereafter arise, the player or players on each club should meet with their individual owners for the purpose of discussing and resolving their particular grievances."

Bell's declaration didn't hold for very long. On February 25, 1957, the U.S. Supreme Court ruled, 6–3, to reinforce a decision that, unlike major-league baseball, the NFL was subject to federal antitrust laws. This landmark decision against the NFL resulted from a suit filed by William "Squato" Radovich, a guard from the University of Southern California who had played with the Detroit Lions from 1938 to 1941 and in 1945 after the war. Radovich then jumped leagues and began playing with the Los Angeles Dons of the AAFC until 1947. When Radovich tried to return to the NFL, he couldn't find a team that would take him.

Radovich claimed that he had been blacklisted by the NFL owners. He filed suit, charging that they had tied players to one particular team and prevented them, by the use of the NFL's reserve clause, from becoming free agents. The U.S. Justice Department under President Dwight D. Eisenhower intervened in the case on behalf of Radovich; he won his case but never played professional football again.

Even after the Radovich decision—which would haunt the league for years to come—the NFL owners still refused to formally recognize the NFLPA as the official bargaining agent for all NFL players, granting only minor concessions after another confrontation between the owners and the players in December 1957.

Meantime, during the 1950s, gambling had become a major problem within the NFL but little was made of it publicly. Mobster Mickey McBride had sold the Cleveland Browns in 1953 for $600,000 to a partnership headed by Ohio businessmen David R. Jones and Saul Silberman who personally bought half of McBride's interest. Silberman was the colorful president of Tropical Park, Randall Raceway, and Painesville's Commodore Downs.

A business associate of several well-known bookmakers, Silberman was forced to sell his interest in the team after the 1953 season because of his gambling activities. "[H]e used to call me for information on our upcoming games," wrote Browns head coach Paul Brown, "and I never understood why until I found out that he was betting on football games, forbidden for all owners by the NFL constitution. I reported these calls to Bert Bell, as required by the rules, and a short time later, Silberman was ordered by Bell to sell his Browns stock because of conduct detrimental to football."[1]

Silberman sold out for $575,000, almost doubling his initial investment. This is the only known case in which an NFL majority or minority owner was forced to sell his interest in a team because of his gambling activities.

Nevertheless, gambling in the NFL continued. Vincent Piersante, the former head of the organized-crime unit of the Michigan attorney general's office, told me, "There was alleged to have been some pretty heavy betting going on by the Detroit Lions players on a game-to-game basis with a Detroit bookmaker named Dice Dawson. But it never became public. None of the games I investigated were ever proven to be thrown. But there were situations of shaving points or working with the point spread, particularly when the bookies were working with the players who had bet on the games."

Born in 1921, Donald "Dice" Dawson was a popular figure in the Detroit gambling world and well known among sports figures in the Motor City. Former Detroit Lions star Dick "Night Train" Lane, who says that Dawson was a friend of his, told me, "Don is a good operator. He hung around gamblers all of his life, and that's what he wanted to be. But he is a very likable guy and always fun to be around."

Dawson is the son of a wealthy and respected Detroit Chevrolet car dealer. When young Dawson was thirteen, he was the water boy for the Detroit Lions, then owned by gambler Dick Richards. Dawson began gambling at an early age and in high school earned his nickname, Dice, because of his crap-shooting abilities. He attended Holy Cross, through which he became acquainted with other alumni, including attorney Edward Bennett Williams who would later become president of the Washington Redskins. Dawson also was in the Marine Corps and served in the South Pacific during World War II.

Upon his release from military service, Dawson went to work for his father, selling Chevrolets. He also started betting heavily on sporting events. During my interview with Dawson, he said, "I wasn't an actual bookmaker. But I used to get the guys from the country club where I belonged in Detroit. They used to bet through a guy with me. I bankrolled it. I booked it all—but indirectly. I gave the booker twenty-five percent of what we won."

Dawson admitted to me that he did business with Lions quarterback Bobby Layne. "It was Bobby Layne who was the bettor, who I bet for," Dawson says. "I knew him better than [I knew] my own brothers. And he did plenty. He'd be playing in his own game, and he'd be betting all over the board. He'd bet five, six, seven games on a Sunday."

Like Night Train Lane, quarterback Bobby Layne is a member of the Pro Football Hall of Fame. He is viewed as being among the best pressure players ever to play the game of football. Layne was born in Santa Ana, Texas, and grew up in the Dallas–Fort Worth area. A graduate of Texas University, he played his first year in the NFL with the Chicago Bears and with the defunct New York Bulldogs, which was owned by singer Kate Smith, in his second. In 1950, he joined the Detroit Lions and led his team to three NFL championships.

Layne was thought to have shaved points or participated in the fixing of several NFL games, according to several bookmakers and law-enforcement officials. One was the final game of the 1956 season in which the 9–2 Lions played the 8–2–1 Chicago Bears on December 16. Layne left the game in the second quarter supposedly with a concussion. The Bears won the game, 38–21, and the Western Division title.

Lions receiver and 1955 Heisman Trophy winner Howard "Hopalong" Cassidy told author Bernie Parrish of the Cleveland Browns that Layne "had faked his injury" during the 1956 Bears game. However, Parrish added that "other players discounted the story because of the enmity between Hoppy and Bobby Layne."[2]

Don Dawson told me, "I wasn't involved in that game. He [Layne] was then with a bookmaker in Odessa, Texas. Bobby was whacked pretty good in the 1956 Bears game. He really was. If he was doing anything, like betting against himself, the last thing he would've wanted to do was get injured. He would've wanted to continue in the game to control it. I would say that Bobby did not throw that particular game. It was not fixed."

However, Layne did fix games and shave points on other occasions. "I used to go down and play golf with Bobby in a tournament and would stay at his house," Dawson recalls. "Bobby was shaving, and he was doing all the betting. When I got to know Bobby, he blew the other guy [in Odessa] off. And then he started betting with me. He came to me. He bought a couple of cars from me when I first met him."[3]

When I asked Dawson what the mechanics of the fixes were, Dawson replied, "Layne would come to me and say, 'I need some bread.' Then he'd ask me to make a bet for him and myself. If the Lions were ten-point favorites, he'd say, 'Well, we'll probably win by six or seven. We won't cover the spread.'"

Dawson adds that Layne had fixed games or shaved points in no fewer than seven games over a period of four years—while Layne played with Detroit Lions and later the Pittsburgh Steelers.[4]

On the subject of whether there were other players who fixed games and shaved points, Dawson told me, "There were a lot of players who did business. That's all I can say. I wouldn't want to say anything else because they are still alive and have families. Bobby was one of several players I knew. Naturally, I wanted to do business with the quarterback because he handles the ball on every play. And a lot of quarterbacks were shaving points. Sure, it happened. The players didn't make any money [from playing football], and so they bet. In those days, they were barely getting by. They were getting their brains beaten out for almost nothing.

"I was involved with players in at least thirty-two NFL games that were dumped or where points were shaved. I knew a lot of players and then through them I got acquainted with other players and then did business with them."[5]

Within the organized-crime syndicate, troubles were brewing as the U.S. Senate created yet another select committee to investigate corrupt union and management practices. In January 1957, the Senate Rackets Committee, as it became known, was created and chaired by Senator John McClellan of Arkansas. His chief counsel was a tough, young attorney Robert F. Kennedy, whose brother John Kennedy, the junior senator from Massachusetts, was a member of the panel. The Kennedy brothers were the sons of Joseph P. Kennedy, the former ambassador to Great Britain, who, in his past life, had been a Prohibition bootlegger and an associate of Frank Costello.

But the Kennedy brothers, especially Robert, were not their

father and did not share his enthusiasm for the dark side of American business. To the contrary, their driving passion was to shed some light on it.

The underworld was so concerned over this investigation that it became a main topic of discussion the following November when over a hundred reputed mobsters from around the country gathered in Apalachin, New York, at the home of mob boss Joseph M. Barbara, for the largest-known meeting of organized-crime figures. However, through brilliant police work, the state police discovered the Apalachin Conference and raided it, arresting fifty-eight of those in attendance, many of whom had been convicted for illegal gambling. Several of these gangsters were marched in front of a national television audience after being subpoenaed to testify before the McClellan Committee.

The committee would operate until March 1960 after conducting 270 days of hearings and receiving testimony from 1,526 witnesses who filled 46,150 transcript pages. Congress was finally going to war with the organized-crime syndicate.

While the Senate Rackets Committee conducted its investigation, the organized-crime syndicate's gambling operations went further underground.

Handicapper William Kaplan, a chunky man with a ruddy complexion, born in 1897, had created the Kaplan Sports Service during the 1930s. He put out football line information to his subscribers in a scratch sheet called *Handicapped.* A bachelor, he operated out of Chicago's Croydon Hotel. In the Chicago yellow pages, his business was listed under "Football Service."

Kaplan was also a close associate of Sidney Wyman, a former St. Louis bookmaker and a known front man for mob casino operations in Las Vegas. Among other jobs, Wyman had worked at the Flamingo and the Riviera.

Kaplan paid protection to Ralph Pierce, a former personal adviser to Al Capone. Pierce operated out of Chicago's Fifth Ward, which was represented by Sidney Korshak's brother Marshall, and answered to Chicago mob boss Sam Giancana. Pierce—who had been acquitted of shaking down several Hollywood studios—was a top suspect in several gangland murders. He had earlier controlled John Scanlan, who had owned Mid-West News, a Chicago-based racing wire service, which had been run out of business by the Kefauver Committee.

In 1957, Pierce—along with two other Chicago mobsters,

Gus Alex, who had taken the Fifth thirty-nine times before the McClellan Committee, and Alfred Frabotta—leaned on the sixty-year-old Kaplan and allegedly forced him to accept a partner, local mob soldier Donald Angelini, also known as Don Angel.

Already starting to burn out, Kaplan, who wanted to make the partnership look voluntary, told oddsmaker Bobby Martin, "I'd like to come to Miami for three or four months a year. So I'm going to bring someone in with me." Kaplan moved into the Peter Miller Hotel in Miami Beach when winter began to approach.

I asked Angelini whether Gus Alex had forced him on Kaplan. Angelini replied, "That's not true. But I don't want to go into that. Bill and I had similar interests. He was a helluva guy. We got along fine. He was like a father to me."

Born in December 1926, Angelini had had several scrapes with the law. Between 1946 and 1949, he was arrested four times for disorderly conduct and twice for traffic violations. Between 1950 and 1954, he was arrested four times for gambling violations—while using the alias Marc Schwartz.

When Angelini joined Kaplan, their handicapping service became Angel-Kaplan Sports News, Inc. Angelini and Kaplan contracted with Sam Minkus, the owner of National Publications of Miami, the largest producer of football betting cards in the United States—fifty thousand a week. Government prosecutors estimated that the underworld kept 80 percent of the take through its use of betting cards—in which gamblers picked no fewer than three and as many as twenty winners from a choice of thirty college and pro football games. A three-winner bet paid 4 to 1; a twenty-winner game paid 5,000 to 1.

"Angelini was a genius at sports handicapping," a Chicago authority on the local underworld told me. "He had the best track record around for helping the bookmakers balance their books. He knew how to set a line. He was also responsible for bringing others into the business as well."

Martin adds that after hiring Angelini, Kaplan told him that the Angel-Kaplan line was going great guns. Kaplan told Martin, "That was the best thing I ever did. I'm making more money and have more free time than ever before." The Chicago Crime Commission proved that Kaplan grossed "between ninety thousand and a hundred thousand dollars during the football season." But that figure was considered quite low.

There were consequences to his newly expanded partnership, mainly exposure. Kaplan was subpoenaed before a federal grand jury in August 1958 in Indianapolis, Indiana, that was investigating a Terre Haute gambling syndicate. Several arrests had already been made of bookmakers Kaplan acknowledged doing business with. "Sure," Kaplan told prosecutors, "I traded information, such as handicapping, with the Terre Haute fellows. I paid them seventy-five dollars for their information, and they paid me seven hundred and twenty dollars during the football season for my service."

Of course, these sums were small potatoes. But Kaplan had never been anything but. However, his partner, Don Angelini, had become a man to watch.

9 Winning Some and Losing Some

ON DECEMBER 28, 1958, nationally televised professional football came of age when Carroll Rosenbloom's Baltimore Colts defeated the New York Giants, 23–17, for the NFL championship. After missing an earlier attempt, Colts placekicker Steve Myhra booted a twenty-yard field goal with seven seconds left to play in regulation, tying the game at 17–17.

The game then went into the first sudden-death play-off in postseason play. The Giants won the toss and chose to receive. However, they failed to make a first down and were forced to punt. The Colts received the Giants' punt and marched eighty yards downfield in thirteen plays. The Colts' Johnny Unitas—a quarterback drafted and released by the Pittsburgh Steelers whom Rosenbloom signed for a mere $7,000 in 1956—completed four passes during the drive. Halfback Alan Ameche also tore off a twenty-three-yard run on a trap play.

A few plays later, with second down and goal-to-go on the Giants eight yard line—easy field goal range—the Colts gambled and elected to pass, with Unitas throwing to Jim Mutscheller who was downed on the one yard line. On third down, the Colts' bench again refused to send in kicker Myhra to end the game. Instead, Unitas gave the ball to Ameche, who plunged in for the touchdown and the championship with eight minutes and fifteen seconds elapsed in the sudden-death period.

A fourth down decision never had to be made. But, for years, rumors have circulated that the betting line influenced the final play.

Johnny Unitas told me that no one had ever told him about any bets on the game. "I called all the plays," he says. "If there were any audibles to be done, I did those at the line of scrimmage. I was responsible for calling for the pass and for calling Ameche's number for the winning touchdown.

"Any time there is a field goal situation, the field goal team would be sent in from the bench. But they never sent the field goal team in, so my job was to go for the touchdown."

Recalling the final moments of the game, the Colts' head coach, Weeb Ewbank, told me, "We had missed one field goal, and we had luckily gotten one to tie the game to put it in overtime. We did not have a great placekicker. I made the decision not to send the field goal team out there.

"In the closing minutes of the game, there was a time-out. John came over and asked, 'What are you thinking?' And I said, 'Alan is a fine ball carrier, and he doesn't fumble the ball.' But the one thing we needed was to have the ball in front of the goalposts because we wanted an opportunity to kick if we had to.

"When John faded back to pass, I was afraid that somebody would hook his arm. I have seen too many times where somebody hooks an arm, misses an assignment, or just falls down. Too many things could happen. When anyone asks me why we passed, I tell them, 'Ask John. He was the one who called it.' "[1]

According to author Kay Iselin Gilman, "There was gossip among so-called Football Insiders that owner Carroll Rosenbloom had placed a mammoth bet on the game and that Weeb called for a touchdown to ensure that the Colts would beat the point spread. Weeb termed these innuendos 'So much nonsense, I had no idea what the point spread was and I couldn't have cared less.' "[2]

During my interview with Ewbank, he said, "I was with the Colts for nine years, and I never talked to Carroll Rosenbloom or any of his friends during a ball game. I wasn't even conscious of what the line on the game was. Carroll never told me anything like that. He never gambled around me."

However, later in the interview, Ewbank complained that he did have trouble with Rosenbloom because of his attempts to interfere with his on-field coaching decisions. But Rosenbloom didn't deal with Ewbank directly in these instances. "He would say it to the general manager, Don Keller. And then Keller would come to me. And I'd say to Keller, 'Do you feel that way?'

And Keller would say, 'No, but I have to sit up there with Carroll.'

"Of course, I would do what Carroll wanted. And then I'd get in trouble with the players because they thought I had made the decision."

However, Ewbank insists that Rosenbloom did not use Keller as his messenger during the final minutes of the 1958 championship game.

Nevertheless, according to numerous figures in sports gambling, the decision by the Colts' management to go for the touchdown instead of the field goal was "no decision." One major bookmaker told me, "You have to understand that a week before the game, the Colts were favored by three and a half points. So much money was coming in on them that the point spread in some places really went up to four and a half, five, and even five and a half points. The talk was that Rosenbloom and some big-time gambling buddy of his had taken the Colts and given the points and bet a million bucks. That's some serious money. If it were your team and you had that kind of money at stake, would you go for the field goal and win the game but lose the bet? Or would you risk everything, go for the touchdown to win it all?"

Once and for all, Rosenbloom did indeed bet on the game, and it was for a million dollars, which he split with a friend.

Oddsmaker Bobby Martin confirmed the wager to me. "We knew that there was unnatural money showing up and driving the spread up," Martin says. "We ascertained that Lou Chesler and another guy were making bets for and with Carroll Rosenbloom. Chesler was known as a big gambler."

Ed Curd also knew about the Rosenbloom bet. "[Bookmaker] Gil Beckley was one of my best friends, and he always wanted to get my opinion on things. He told me about the 1958 championship game. Carroll had done his business with Gil. And Carroll was quite a player."

Gene Nolan of Baton Rouge, another major bookmaker and close associate of Beckley, confirmed, "Gil handled that overtime game bet."

Also, an official with the NFL told me that Bert Bell knew about the bet and had scolded Rosenbloom for his gambling activities.

The Colts repeated as NFL champions in 1959, again defeating the Giants, this time, 31–16. It is not known whether Rosenbloom bet heavily or not on that game. No unnatural money appeared—although, as any gambler knows, Rosenbloom could have learned his lesson and had his bookmaker lay off his large bet in small increments all over the country. Numerous people who knew Rosenbloom also knew that he gambled heavily with Chesler, his business partner.

Lou Chesler, a three-hundred-pound Toronto financier, was also a business associate of and occasional bagman for crime-syndicate financier Meyer Lansky of Florida. Chesler made his millions by purchasing Canadian mining stocks, especially Loredo Uranium Mines—through which he had met Lansky and, later, New York mobster "Trigger" Mike Coppola, a major banker in the Mafia's national bookmaking operations.

Chesler had met Coppola through Gil Beckley, who had succeeded Frank Erickson as the crime syndicate's top layoff bookmaker during the 1950s after Erickson went to prison. Chesler and Beckley had met while Beckley was operating out of New York; Chesler also made bets with Beckley's bookmaker friends Max Courtney and Frank Ritter, the founders of the Courtney-Reed Sports Service of New York and later Montreal.[3]

Courtney and Ritter, both former associates of Erickson and New York underworld figure Dutch Schultz, were later expelled from Canada and returned to the United States where they were joined by a third bookmaker, Charles Brudner. Everyone in the Montreal crowd worked alongside Charles Gordon, formerly of the Louisiana/Texas Gulf Coast region, who was described by the Kefauver Committee as "a main cog in a national football betting syndicate."

In 1956, Chesler, who was then operating in the United States, became part of the investment syndicate that took over the Florida-based Chemical Research Company and renamed it the General Development Corporation, a home-building and financing firm that developed three small Florida communities.[4] Carroll Rosenbloom was among the major stockholders in General Development, along with publisher Gardner Cowles and investment banker John Weinberg. Another big stockholder was Miami businessman Max Orovitz, also a longtime associate of Meyer Lansky.

Public-relations man John Reagan "Tex" McCrary, a business partner of Rosenbloom and Chesler, told me, "I knew Carroll very well. I first met him through Chesler. He was Chesler's best friend. And they were clients of my PR firm. We handled public relations for the General Development Corporation."

Another associate of Chesler and Rosenbloom explains, "Chesler didn't control General Development, but he brought the company the money with which it could go forward and develop these various parts of Florida. Chesler was way ahead of that parade. The trouble with Chesler was that he loved to get drunk at night, and that was dangerous."

That same year, Chesler began to purchase failed companies and use them to obtain millions of dollars in bank loans. Along with Carroll Rosenbloom and New York attorney Morris Mac Schwebel, he rebuilt one of these companies, Universal Products, and renamed it Universal Controls—a company then listed on the New York Stock Exchange that specialized in the leasing of pari-mutuel equipment for racetracks through its American Totalizator subsidiary.

Schwebel told me, "Carroll was an extremely competent businessman. He was a man of his word. Chesler brought Carroll along as an additional investor [in Universal Controls]. I was Carroll's guest on many occasions in his box at the Colts games."

In 1956—through another shell company renamed Associated Artists—the Chesler-Rosenbloom-Schwebel group moved into show business. Schwebel continues, "The motion picture studios did not want to invite the wrath of the theater operators if they gave movies to that horrible thing called 'television.' There were simply no movies around for television. Through negotiations that took place between Lou Chesler, Eliot Hyman, myself, and the Warner people, we were able to buy the pre-1948 library from Warner Brothers for twenty-one million dollars. Once we got those pictures—all the Bogart and Sidney Greenstreet films—in no time did we pay off the debt incurred. And all of the shareholders made substantial profits. That was the beginning of any decent pictures for television."[5]

Along with board chairman Chesler, Schwebel credits Associated Artists president Eliot Hyman with finalizing the deal. "He ended up with Seven Arts, the company that showed the cartoons on television."

Seven Arts was founded in 1958 by Hyman and another Associated Artists board member, film producer Ray Stark. It became a motion picture production and distribution firm. The new company then purchased the rights to several movies and cartoons from the Canadian-based Globe Film Productions—in return for nearly 350,000 shares of Seven Arts stock.

Soon after, the Chesler-Rosenbloom-Schwebel group purchased Globe's interest in Seven Arts and took control of the company. Chesler became chairman of the board of Seven Arts and its largest stockholder, the second and third largest being directors Mac Schwebel and Carroll Rosenbloom, respectively.

Other directors of Seven Arts included Tex McCrary and Maxwell M. Raab, a former Wall Street attorney who, from 1953 to 1958, had served as President Eisenhower's secretary to the Cabinet and a special assistant to Sherman Adams, Eisenhower's political mentor and a Washington powerbroker.[6]

Rosenbloom had been a close friend of Florida gambler Michael J. McLaney, a former deputy sheriff in New Orleans who had become a professional golf gambler. McLaney had first introduced the Colts' owner to Chesler, with whom McLaney had owned L'Aiglon, a supper club in Surfside, Miami. In return for that introduction, McLaney was given five thousand shares of stock in Universal Controls as an "introduction fee."

"Rosenbloom and Chesler were both criticized for making Christmas presents and birthday presents of stock in General Development and Universal Controls," says McCrary. "And they were accused of touting the stocks [through] the football players on the Colts." McCrary was a regular in Rosenbloom's owner's box during Colts home games; McCrary's son had been the team's water boy.

Former Baltimore Colts offensive tackle George Preas, who described Rosenbloom "a super man, top-drawer," told me that he had met both McLaney and Chesler through Rosenbloom. Although he says that he met McLaney only once, "Chesler traveled with the team on occasion. He was a close friend of Carroll." Upton Bell, who later became the Colts' personnel director, says, "When I first went to the Colts' training camp, Lou Chesler and his kids were there." Weeb Ewbank told me that he became acquainted with Chesler through Rosenbloom, too.

In September 1958, mobster Morris Dalitz and the Mayfield Road Gang offered to sell their interest in the luxurious, fortress-like, 450-room Hotel Nacional casino in Havana.[7] The sale price was $800,000. McLaney was interested and he immediately went to Rosenbloom and Chesler for financing. Rosenbloom personally gave McLaney $240,000 for his share of the Nacional. To pay for his own interest in the hotel, McLaney sold his stock in Universal for $116,000. After the sale, both Chesler and Rosenbloom began making frequent trips to Cuba.[8]

According to numerous government officials, McLaney had sought out and received Lansky's approval to purchase the Nacional. The casino operators enjoyed the cooperation of President Fulgencio Batista, who was nothing more than a Lansky puppet.[9] The Nacional had been the regular meeting place for the Chicago and New York crime syndicates.

However, within three months after the sale of the Nacional, Fidel Castro swept down from the Sierra Maestras and overthrew the oppressive, Mafia-controlled Batista regime. After Castro's victory, the underworld—which had hedged its bet and provided support to both sides in the Cuban revolution—believed its investments in Cuba to be safe. However, Castro double-crossed the Mafia the following April. He shut down the gambling and narcotics operations and exiled Lansky; he boarded up the casinos and imprisoned other mobsters.[10] Among the biggest losers in the wake of the Castro betrayal were McLaney, who was one of those imprisoned in Cuba, and his partners, Rosenbloom and Chesler, who were safe in the United States.

Also in April 1959, within days after Castro shut down the casinos, Rosenbloom suddenly sold off the bulk of his family's clothing businesses for $7 million in cash and $20 million in stock to the Philadelphia & Reading Corporation, which was a diversified management and holding company with subsidiaries in the apparel, toy, and electrical component industries.[11]

10 A New Commissioner

ON AUGUST 14, 1959, twenty-seven-year-old Texas oilman Lamar Hunt announced that what soon became known as the American Football League (AFL) had been created to rival the NFL. Hunt was the owner of the new Dallas Texans and one of three sons of H. L. Hunt, Jr., an oil-rich tycoon who was also a big-money sports gambler and a close friend of Mafia bookmaker Frank Erickson. Lamar Hunt had earlier tried and failed to buy both the Chicago Cardinals and a new Dallas franchise for the NFL but was rejected. Consequently, he decided to form his own league.

Harry Wismer—who had been part owner of the Washington Redskins and became the majority owner of the New York Titans, another AFL team—wrote that he had first met Lamar Hunt when the AFL was being formed.[1] However, Wismer had previously known Hunt's father. "I first met the [elder] Hunt at a party given by Ray Ryan, an old friend of mine. Ryan [was] one of the biggest gamblers in the country and called the senior Hunt his 'pigeon.' There was nothing phony about Hunt. He made his fortune by borrowing fifty dollars and betting he could find oil on land where the geologists said there wasn't any. H. L. Hunt's philosophy of life was that a man would succeed if he kept plugging and was willing to gamble. Ryan told me [Wismer] he thought that H.L. bet close to a million dollars a week during the football season. That's a staggering sum to most but a drop in the bucket to him."[2]

Author Don Kowet reported, "Hunt's only use for money, outside of making more money, was to wager it. He employed a graduate of MIT as a full-time statistician, to compute the odds on his various bets. He placed those bets through a special communications system, installed in his office, which connected him with the major horse tracks and bookmakers around the country."[3]

Bookmaker Marty Kane told me, "H. L. Hunt stiffed about four or five bookmakers for a lot of money, including Gil Beckley. Hunt just told them he wasn't going to pay. He was really a greasy son of a bitch."

The Hunt family contained serious gamblers. However, there is no evidence that the low-key Lamar Hunt was ever a sports gambler. Yet, it is difficult to believe that he did not, wittingly or unwittingly, pass along inside information about his team to members of his family. There is little in his father's background to suggest that he was above gaining such an edge.

Another AFL team owner was Barron Hilton. He purchased the Los Angeles Chargers and moved the team to San Diego in 1961. A longtime gambler, Hilton was a top executive of the Hilton Hotel chain. He was the son of Conrad Hilton, who had built the first Hilton Hotel in 1919.[4] Barron's older brother, Nicky, had been the first husband of actress Elizabeth Taylor.[5]

Barron Hilton, a college dropout, resisted the hotel business at first, turning down an offer at age nineteen to work for his father. Instead, he bought interests in other companies. By 1960, he had sold off his own business and returned to the family fold. He was immediately appointed by his father as a vice president for the hotel chain. While taking an active role in Hilton affairs, he helped to create the Carte Blanche credit card company and bought the Chargers of the AFL.[6]

Hilton told *The Wall Street Journal* that he was called into his father's office when his businesses appeared to be in trouble. "I've been reviewing the operations of the football club and I've noticed that you have a very substantial loss of about $900,000," Conrad Hilton told his son. "And the credit card business looks to me like it's going to lose about $1.5 million. What kind of record are you trying to establish?"[7] Barron Hilton later sold his interest in Carte Blanche, but he kept the Chargers.

Hilton had maintained a long-term personal and business relationship with Los Angeles attorney Sidney Korshak, according to an official statement made by Korshak to the New Jersey Division of Gaming Enforcement. Korshak has also been described by law-enforcement agencies as "the link between the legitimate business world and organized crime." He had been active in Hollywood since the early 1940s but had moved to Los Angeles in January 1948, beginning a new and more sophisticated era of the crime syndicate's penetration of the film industry.[8]

Korshak had done legal work for Hilton. He had been recommended to Hilton by Patrick Hoy, a mutual friend and a top executive with General Dynamics, the military hardware firm.

The other members of the AFL—all of whom put up $25,000 for their charter franchises, as well as "performance bonds" of $100,000—were

- Philips Petroleum heir and the AFL's cofounder Kenneth Stanley "Bud" Adams of the Houston Oilers, a close friend of the Hunt family, who owned Texas Adams Oil which distributed Philips Petroleum's products;
- minor-league baseball team owner Bob Howsam of Colorado, who purchased the Denver Broncos and immediately named Frank Filchock as his head coach;[9] and
- Austrian-born Max Winter, an ex-boxing promoter and vending machine operator, who bought the Minnesota Vikings. Winter was the former owner of the Minneapolis Lakers of the National Basketball Association. The team moved to Los Angeles in 1957 and became the Los Angeles Lakers.

Two other AFL franchises were purchased in the fall of 1959.

- Detroit trucking executive and thoroughbred race horse stable owner Ralph C. Wilson, the owner of Ralph C. Wilson Industries and a onetime minority owner of the Detroit Lions, created the Buffalo Bills after unsuccessfully attempting to gain the use of the Orange Bowl for a Miami franchise.
- Pittston Corporation executive William H. "Billy" Sullivan, Jr., organized the Boston Patriots.[10]

World War II pilot and Congressional Medal of Honor recipient Joe Foss, the former governor of South Dakota, was selected as the AFL's commissioner. League play was slated to begin in 1960.

The owners of the AFL were nicknamed the Foolish Club. Professional football experts and the media gave the new league little chance of long-term survival.

However, there was good news for the upstart AFL in July 1960. Giving the new league a showcase, ABC bought the five-year television rights to AFL games for $10.65 million. The AFL proved its worth, producing a new, wide-open style of football featuring exciting passers and pass-receivers, as well as high-scoring contests, which caused oddsmakers to take notice and to begin setting lines on the new league's games.

On October 11, 1959, two months after the formation of the AFL, sixty-five-year-old Bert Bell died of a heart attack with six years left on his contract as NFL commissioner. Also, earlier in the year, seventy-one-year-old Tim Mara, the founder of the New York Giants, had a heart attack and died too. His team was taken over by his sons, Wellington and Jack Mara.[11]

Bell had actually been supportive of the entry of the AFL into the ranks of professional football and provided the new league's management with considerable advice and support. Although he may have done so for altruistic purposes, Bell was also fully aware that in Washington, D.C., Congress was in the midst of its preliminary investigation into possible antitrust violations within the professional sports world. By encouraging the AFL, Bell and the NFL had hedged their bet.

After Bell's death, NFL treasurer Austin Gunsel became the acting chief executive officer of the league. Gunsel, a former FBI agent, wanted to maintain Bell's ritual of keeping in touch with mobsters and bookmakers in order to monitor the betting line. "When my father died," Upton Bell told me, "Austin Gunsel asked my older brother [Bert Bell, Jr.] who these people were. My brother said, 'I don't know, and I wouldn't tell you if I did.' Bert Bell promised that as long as they gave him the information every week, he would take their names to his grave—which he did." Consequently, Gunsel had to develop his own sources.

On January 26, 1960, thirty-three-year-old Alvin "Pete" Rozelle, who had served as the general manager of the Los Angeles Rams, was tapped to succeed the seemingly irreplaceable Bell at a meeting of the NFL owners at the Kenilworth Hotel in Miami.

Rozelle was selected as a compromise candidate on the twenty-third ballot of voting.[12] He was strongly supported by New York Giants owner Wellington Mara, head coach Paul Brown of the Cleveland Browns, and Carroll Rosenbloom, who placed Rozelle's name in nomination. Rozelle left the room while the vote was taken. A few minutes later, Rosenbloom came out alone and gave Rozelle the good news.

Tall and lanky, Rozelle, who was born in South Gate, a Los Angeles suburb, was a former high school basketball player and teammate of the future Brooklyn Dodgers baseball star Duke Snider. After graduation, he spent two years in the Navy, serving in the South Pacific during World War II. When the war ended, he studied at Compton Junior College and then landed a job as a stringer for the sports page at *The Long Beach Press Telegram* before receiving his undergraduate degree. He also worked as Compton's athletic publicity director. That same year, the Cleveland Rams moved to Los Angeles and set up training camp at Compton. Rozelle began working part-time for the Rams.

Encouraged by the Rams' public relations director, Maxwell Styles, Rozelle returned to college and received his degree in English in 1950 from the University of San Francisco, where he also served as athletic news director. Through his association with the university and his past contacts, Rozelle met the Rams general manager, Tex Schramm, who offered him a post as head of the team's newly vacant public relations office. Rozelle worked with the Rams until 1955 when he left the team to take a job with P. K. Macker Public Relations and Advertising in San Francisco. However, urged by Bert Bell, Rozelle returned to the Rams in 1957 to become the team's general manager, replacing Schramm, who had left in the midst of a dispute among the Rams' owners.[13]

As Rams manager, Rozelle was criticized in 1959 for signing Heisman Trophy winner Billy Cannon of Louisiana State University before he was eligible. Rozelle had slickly persuaded Cannon to sign an undated contract. However, just after Rozelle became NFL commissioner, a judge voided the contract between Cannon and the Rams and chided Rozelle for his actions. Cannon eventually signed with Bud Adams and the Houston Oilers of the AFL.

The new commissioner, who was married and had a sixteen-month-old daughter, was given a three-year contract that paid him $50,000 a year—$20,000 more than the league's highest-paid player. After he moved the league's front office from Philadelphia to New York, Rozelle's initial problems with managing the NFL had to do with questions of expansion and the league's own television rights.

Rozelle advocated that the NFL sell its television rights to a single network, and that the money from these rights be evenly divided among the NFL teams. Rozelle's attempts to make such a deal with CBS were struck down by two federal court decisions. However, after Congress passed and President Kennedy signed the Sports Broadcasting Act in September 1961, permitting these kinds of single network arrangements, the NFL signed the first such deal with CBS the following year. The NFL received $9.3 million for two years; each team received nearly $332,000.

"It was like fate," said Art Rooney. "I don't know of any commissioner in sports who could have done a better job with television and the league as a whole."[14]

Rozelle's popularity was well deserved. He was making the NFL owners extremely wealthy as he embarked upon a plan to share the wealth among all the teams. According to Rozelle's "revenue-sharing" program, which was loosely based on the AFL's policy, the NFL owners divided television revenues and league promotional activities evenly; gate receipts for preseason games were split fifty-fifty; revenues for play-off games were equally shared; and gate receipts of regular season games were divided sixty-forty between the home and visiting teams.[15]

The result of this was that a team with a losing record would still make nearly the same money as the league champion made.

Acting quickly on rumors of corruption in the NFL, Rozelle had investigators probe a 1960 game between the Pittsburgh Steelers and the Washington Redskins—because of a reported sudden and dramatic change in the point spread. The week before the game, the Steelers were favored by seven points and then suddenly dropped to only one point, forcing bookmakers to take the game off the boards. The game, played in Washington, ended in a 27–27 tie. Those who had placed money on the Redskins and had been given one or more points won their bets.

The results of Rozelle's investigation showed that during the week prior to the game a photograph had been published across the country of Steelers quarterback Bobby Layne—who was holding up his injured passing arm. It was determined that

Layne's well-publicized injury had caused the line to change so dramatically.

The incident contributed to the institutionalization of a new NFL policy—initially begun informally under Bert Bell—which forced NFL teams to file injury reports to the league's front office every Tuesday and Thursday during the football season. As soon as these reports were collected and organized, they were released to the public. Later, NFL teams were required to describe player injuries under one of four categories: probable, questionable, doubtful, and out.

A top NFL official told me, "It's just a matter of making sure that the gamblers and the bookmakers don't have a monopoly on this kind of information. We publish the injury reports so that it becomes common knowledge, taking the edge away from the professional gamblers."

Also two days after Rozelle became commissioner, the NFL admitted two new teams, the Dallas Cowboys and the Minnesota Vikings, the latter of which had earlier been slated to become an AFL franchise but withdrew when the NFL slot was offered.

In response to the Vikings' action, the new league immediately filed a $10 million antitrust suit against the NFL, which the AFL later lost. Also in 1960 the AFL sold a new franchise, the Oakland Raiders, to an eight-man partnership headed by Y. Chet Soda.[16]

11 Murchison, Modell, and Ford Buy In

THE FOUNDER OF THE Dallas Cowboys, Clint Murchison, Jr., who wore a crew cut and spectacles, paid $550,000 for the team and selected former Rams general manager Tex Schramm as the architect and general manager of the new franchise. The Cowboys' owner was the son of another wealthy and outspoken Texas oilman.

Murchison's father had been expelled from Trinity College for gambling. Soon after, he became a wildcatter who struck it rich during the Texas oil boom of the 1920s. Murchison Sr. is famous for his observation: "Money is like manure. If you spread it around, it does a lot of good. But if you pile it up in one place, it stinks like hell." He once bet a million dollars on a single flip of a coin—and lost.

The Murchisons were enthusiastic supporters of Senator Joseph McCarthy's witch-hunt and major backers of Vice President Richard Nixon in his 1960 presidential campaign against John Kennedy. After Nixon lost the election, he bought a lot from the Murchisons in Beverly Hills for the bargain price of $35,000.

The Nixon property was a part of the exclusive Trousdale Estates, which had been developed by the Murchisons—with the help of a $6.7 million loan from the Teamsters' Central States, Southeast and Southwest Areas Pension Fund on February 26, 1959.[1]

A successful businessman like his father, Clint Murchison, Jr., was also a heavy gambler. The Murchisons operated the Del Mar racetrack in Southern California. In 1954, profits from the track were diverted to Boys, Inc., a nonprofit corporation to help homeless boys which had been created by the Murchisons and their business associate Sid W. Richardson, another high-stakes gambler.

In 1959, the Murchisons and Richardson were investigated by the California state legislature for allegedly using Boys, Inc. as a vehicle for the racetrack owners to evade taxes. When the investigation was concluded, both the state and the IRS began to levy taxes against Boys, Inc. Later, a federal court overturned the rulings and Boys, Inc. was again exempted from federal taxes.

An annual guest of the Murchisons' nearby Hotel Del Charro in La Jolla, California, was J. Edgar Hoover. A horse-racing fan and another big gambler, Hoover had made a ritual of checking into the Del Charro during the racing season at Del Mar. When the Murchisons and Richardson found themselves in trouble over Boys, Inc., Hoover stepped forward in the midst of the controversy and said, "I know Clint Murchison quite well and I think he would be the last person in the country to use such a plan as a clever tax or business subterfuge. In fact, I spoke to Murchison about ten years ago about devoting some time and help to youth work and the charitable corporation of Del Mar is one of his answers. This work helps directly in making the nation sturdy, for communist penetration is currently directed mainly at labor organizations and youth organizations." Hoover also described Murchison as "the type of rugged individualist that made this country great."[2]

Young Murchison had been a short but tough, 120-pound halfback at a New Jersey prep school. He did his undergraduate work in electrical engineering at Duke, where he was a Phi Beta Kappa scholar, and received his master's degree in mathematics from MIT. By the time he bought the Cowboys, the personal wealth of his family was estimated as being more than $2 billion—which, in Texas, was second only to their longtime rivals, the Hunt family.

The owner of a labyrinth of businesses, the highly secretive Murchison was investigated by no fewer than nine federal agencies and two congressional committees during a ten-year period beginning in 1955. The Senate Commerce Committee wrote that Gerardo Catena of New Jersey, a top-ranking member of the

Vito Genovese crime family, "allegedly owned almost 20% of all the production of Murchison Oil Lease [Company], Oklahoma" during the early 1950s.

Murchison was also involved in business partnerships with numerous associates of Carlos Marcello of New Orleans, the most feared Mafia boss in the South. And Murchison personally had real estate and banking ties with Marcello. Although Murchison had always denied knowing Marcello, he did admit that he occasionally had dinner at the Plantation, Marcello's New Orleans restaurant.[3]

Joseph Campisi was a close friend of Murchison. Campisi, the owner of the Egyptian Lounge in Dallas, was associated with numerous underworld figures, particularly Joseph Civello, the head of the Marcello-controlled Dallas Mafia. Campisi has never been convicted of any crime but was arrested in 1944 for murder. The case was dismissed when the county grand jury determined that he had acted in self-defense. However, he has been linked by law-enforcement agencies to Marcello and "with both gambling and bookmaking activities in the Dallas area."[4]

An employee of the Dallas Cowboys told my associate, William Scott Malone, "Joe Campisi comes by the office on a regular basis. And whenever he does enter the [headquarters] of the Dallas Cowboys, everyone seems to bow to him . . . He can go in and out of any office he wants. And everyone is just sort of thrilled to see him . . .

"During draft time, he brings by dinner because everyone works late getting ready for the draft. He supplies pizza and so forth for the general office staff. He is considered part of the Cowboy family."

Murchison also hired Washington lobbyist I. Irving Davidson to handle public relations for one of his companies. Davidson had often boasted that he was a "door opener and arranger" for Marcello.[5]

Prior to buying the Cowboys, Murchison had considered buying the San Francisco 49ers and, when that failed, made George Marshall a bid for the Redskins. Marshall opposed Murchison's attempt to purchase any NFL team. But he relented after Murchison bought the rights to the Redskins' fight song, which had been obtained by Marshall's ex-wife as part of their divorce settlement. Consequently, Murchison refused to give Marshall the right to use the song. Soon after, Murchison bought the Cowboys with no opposition—and Marshall got his fight song back.

Featured, along with his brother, on the cover of the June 16, 1961, issue of *Time,* Murchison told the magazine, "Some people say we are gamblers, but that isn't true. In gambling, you are betting on Lady Luck; in speculating, you have your mind to help you, and you are betting on yourself."

Also in March 1961, thirty-five-year-old Arthur B. Modell bought the controlling interest in the Cleveland Browns. Born and raised in Brooklyn, Modell quit school in the tenth grade to get a job and help his family through the Depression. He later finished high school at night and then joined the Army Air Force in 1943. After the war, he studied broadcasting in New York and became a producer/director for a daytime television program.

In 1954, he slid out of television and into the advertising game, joining the L. H. Hartmann Company, which had primarily handled ads for liquor companies since the repeal of Prohibition. Because of his business savvy, Modell soon became a partner in the firm. One of the companies with which Hartmann did business was Tele King Corporation, a television company founded and owned by syndicate figure Meyer Lansky.

L. H. Hartmann also introduced Modell to Ben Marden, a former bootlegger and casino operator in Havana who was associated with Lansky. "He was a great friend," Modell said of Marden in an interview with reporter Peter Phipps of the *Akron Beacon Journal.* "He had one of the first casinos ever in Fort Lee [New Jersey] in the 30s . . . I was a friend of his long after it closed down."

Modell also had ties to several bookmakers and gamblers. For instance, after buying the Browns, he became a partner in a horse-racing stable with Youngstown native Morris "Mushy" Wexler, who had been named by the Kefauver Committee as one of the "leading hoodlums" in McBride's national wire service.[6] A truck driver for McBride during the Cleveland newspaper wars, Wexler, who was linked to Dalitz's Mayfield Road Gang, ran the Empire News Service and was one of McBride's twenty-four "distributors," handling business throughout the states of Ohio and West Virginia. During Wexler's tenure as the head of Empire News, Youngstown, which experienced considerable political corruption, became a safe haven for bookmakers, gamblers, and the mobsters with whom they did business. He had been arrested no fewer than four times for gambling and bookmaking—but each time the charges were dismissed.

The way the bookmaking worked at Empire was described by Eliot Ness, who had become the director of Cleveland's Department of Public Safety after his racket-busting days with "the Untouchables" in Chicago. Ness wrote in 1940, "The entries, odds and results of the races come to the Empire News Service Company via teletype over the Western Union Telegraph lines and are then sent out over Ohio Bell Telephone Company's lines to the numerous bookmaking establishments by a party operating a switchboard in the offices of the Empire News Service Company."

Joe Nellis, the assistant counsel of the Kefauver Committee, told me, "Mushy Wexler was Mickey McBride's man. Wexler owned a restaurant called the Theatrical Grille in Cleveland where all the 'boys' used to gather. Wexler was an inveterate gambler, and he had even been in business in Covington, Kentucky, with bad guys like [Cleveland Mafia figures] Al Polizzi and Jimmy Licavoli. Wexler was a bookmaker, and his restaurant was a known hangout for the Cleveland gambling and bookmaking crowd." Among Wexler's most frequent patrons was his old friend Art Modell.

Bernie Parrish, a former Browns defensive back, wrote in his autobiography that Louis "Babe" Triscaro, a Cleveland Teamsters official and underworld figure, had told him that Modell had paid Triscaro $1,900 to steal "a police file investigation of Arthur B. Modell's background and possible connection with old-time Mafia figures." Modell has admitted to having been a friend of Triscaro but described Parrish's charge as "unadulterated garbage." Parrish also described Modell as "a rabid sports-fan gambler."[7]

When Modell married actress Patricia Breslin, the ceremony was held at the Las Vegas home of William Weinberger, who owned a restaurant near Wexler's saloon. Weinberger also was one of Modell's closest friends and became the president of Caesars Palace in Las Vegas. One of Weinberger's top executives at Caesars was Jerome Zarowitz, who was convicted for attempting to fix the 1946 NFL championship game.

Before his marriage to Breslin, Modell reportedly dated the daughter of Carroll Rosenbloom's business and gambling partner

Lou Chesler. Modell has denied this and insisted that he had met Lou Chesler only once. However, according to Tex McCrary, "Art was a great friend of both Carroll Rosenbloom and Lou Chesler. His advertising firm represented the General Development Corporation," which was run by Chesler.

Modell left the Hartmann agency and joined Kastor, Hilton, Chesley, Clifford & Atherton, which was where he was employed when he bought the Cleveland team. The firm was the source of his seed money to buy the Browns. Modell and his partner Rudy Schaefer of New York, the owner of Schaefer Beer Company, purchased the team for $3,925,000, splitting the stock and with Modell holding the controlling interest. The two men reportedly had been total strangers before the Browns deal. Modell and Schaefer raised $1.4 million in cash with the help of a dozen smaller investors, including a group from the Atlantic City Racing Association. Prodded by department store tycoon Robert Hays Gries, who had been McBride's onetime partner in the Browns, Cleveland's Union Commerce Bank lent the group $2.5 million. Gries and his heirs later became Modell's principal partners.[8]

After buying the Browns, Modell, who had been viewed by local fans as a carpetbagger, said, "I came to Cleveland as an out of towner and purchased one of the great loves of this community. I think I understand that responsibility and I'm thankful for the support the people of this area have given me and my family." Within three years of his purchase, Modell shocked the Cleveland fans by firing the team's longtime coach and namesake Paul Brown.

A third management change occurred in 1961. The new president of the Detroit Lions, William Clay Ford, was the vice president of product design for the Ford Motor Company and a member of its board of directors. He was also the son of the company's founder, Henry Ford. In 1964, Bill Ford bought the Lions for $6.5 million.[9]

Although Ford's older brother, Henry Ford II, became involved in casino gambling operations on St. Maarten island, there is no evidence that his gambling ties or Henry Sr.'s little-known underworld contacts were handed down to William Clay Ford.[10] The NFL has never disclosed any investigation it has done on Ford or his family's gambling businesses.

12 The Gambling Scandal Erupts

CARROLL ROSENBLOOM WAS FLYING high. By 1962, he, Morris Mac Schwebel, and Lou Chesler were still the three largest stockholders in Seven Arts, which had already purchased the film libraries of Warner Brothers and Twentieth Century-Fox. Also that year, Seven Arts purchased the film library of MCA/Universal Pictures for $21.5 million with a down payment of $7.5 million.[1]

Since the back-to-back NFL championship seasons in 1958 and 1959, Rosenbloom and his Baltimore Colts had barely played .500 ball but were doing so in front of large, enthusiastic crowds. Rosenbloom was making a fortune on his team.

Three of the members of that Colts team—Alan Ameche, Joe Campanella, and Gino Marchetti—had come to Rosenbloom to borrow $100,000 to help them finance a local small restaurant. Without flinching, Rosenbloom loaned them the money. It was another good bet. The little restaurant became the first of the Gino's national fast-food franchises. Seeing how successful the experiment was, Rosenbloom continued to loan his players money when they wanted to start their own businesses. Of course, Rosenbloom became a major stockholder in their companies.

"Our objective is to help all our players invest their money well," Rosenbloom told reporter Bob Oates. "I don't believe the bromide: 'The only good ball player is a hungry ballplayer.' I don't want any hungry athletes around me. The way to win games and titles is with 40 players who are free to give their undivided attention to football because they don't have a worry in the world." He also saw to it that his players were perennially among the highest-paid in the NFL.

Rosenbloom was a close friend of Ambassador Joseph Kennedy and his son Senator John Kennedy of Massachusetts, a member of the Senate Rackets Committee who had become the President of the United States in 1961. Young Kennedy was one of Rosenbloom's golf partners.

According to author Doris Kearns Goodwin, on the day Kennedy was elected, Rosenbloom was out on the lawn of the Kennedy compound in Hyannis Port, playing touch football with Kennedy friends and family. At dinner on election night, Rosenbloom was one of only three friends present and had flown in a bushel of hard-shell crabs from the Chesapeake Bay for the occasion.[2]

Kennedy family spokesman, Steve Smith, who was also present at the election night dinner, told me that he did not recall Rosenbloom's being there. He did, however, say that Rosenbloom and Joe Kennedy had been members of the same country club in Palm Beach, Florida. "There was never any business relationship between Rosenbloom and any member of the Kennedy family that I'm aware of. He was a friend, and the family liked him," Smith said.

Rosenbloom had given Robert F. Kennedy a game ball signed by the members of the 1958 World Champion Colts. Kennedy kept the ball in his office when he became U.S. attorney general under his brother.

"Rosenbloom was a great, great friend of Joe Kennedy," says Rosenbloom's longtime friend and business partner Tex McCrary. "And he was a great friend of Jack Kennedy. Carroll worshipped Jack Kennedy. And he used to love quoting old Joe. He used to love telling a joke Joe Kennedy used to tell him: 'Never trust an Irishman with a bottle of booze or a Jew with a pack of matches.' "

Ironically, in April 1962, four insurance companies initiated lawsuits against Rosenbloom, charging that he had filed false reports about a fire at his Margate, New Jersey, house on September 5, 1950. The companies hired a Miami private investigator, Sam Benton, to look into the charges that Rosenbloom had hired an arsonist to burn down his house in order to collect the fire insurance. The companies charged that Rosenbloom had received $152,529 on the basis of the false reports. The companies accused Rosenbloom of making "false statements intending to deceive and defraud" them. The suit demanded repayment of the amount given to Rosenbloom, along with 6 percent interest and $500,000 in punitive damages.

And that was only the beginning.

Rosenbloom's old friend Mike McLaney still had been experiencing severe financial troubles a year after Castro took over Cuba and closed down the casinos, which cost McLaney and his two partners, Rosenbloom and Chesler, a fortune. Rosenbloom and Chesler could afford it, but McLaney could not.

In the wake of the fall of Cuba, McLaney claimed that Rosenbloom had reneged on a deal to permit him to repurchase his stock in Universal Controls at the original sale price. Consequently, McLaney sued Rosenbloom in September 1960 for $4.25 million. U.S. District Judge Joseph Lieb of Miami dismissed McLaney's suit and sealed all the evidence in the case, which included a series of damaging affidavits and depositions filed against Rosenbloom.

In October 1962, private investigator Benton, a close friend of McLaney, went to Rozelle with a new, reconstructed version of the sealed material against Rosenbloom. The documents had been obtained while Benton was working for the insurance companies that had accused Rosenbloom of fraud.

On December 6, 1962, in the midst of Rozelle's cursory investigation of Rosenbloom, the Colts' owner authorized his attorneys to turn over the remaining sealed documents in the case to Rozelle for a private review. However, Rosenbloom's attorneys warned that the public release of the documents "would be scandalous in nature." Rosenbloom threatened a $7.5 million lawsuit if they were revealed. The figure was based on the 1963 estimated worth of the Colts. Rosenbloom believed that McLaney's charges could jeopardize his ownership of the franchise.

Nevertheless, believing that Rozelle was not taking the evidence seriously, and in defiance of Rosenbloom's threat, Benton and McLaney then circulated forty copies of the affidavits and depositions at the annual meeting of the NFL owners at the Kenilworth Hotel in Bal Harbour in January 1963.[3]

Among these depositions was one filed by Miami restaurant owner Charles Schwartz, who had known Rosenbloom for twenty years and had been McLaney's operating partner in the

Havana casino. Schwartz stated that he had received a telephone call from Beldon Katleman, the owner of the El Rancho Vegas, a casino in Las Vegas. Katleman had won "a lot of money" from Rosenbloom playing gin rummy and had called Schwartz to complain that Rosenbloom had been avoiding him. When Schwartz called Rosenbloom and gave him Katleman's message, Rosenbloom replied, "Oh, I was playing gin, and I had to make a plane, and we never finished the game. It's an unfinished game, and we are supposed to continue it."

Eventually, the two men settled the debt. Rosenbloom in his 1960 deposition confirmed that he had owed the money to Katleman and that McLaney and Schwartz had served as intermediaries. He said that he settled with Katleman for $25,000 and added that the original debt was $600,000—but that they had been playing "for fun."

McLaney, who was having additional financial difficulties at the time of his suit against Rosenbloom and was claiming nearly $164,000 in debts, also filed more serious charges against Rosenbloom, alleging that the Colts' owner had bet against his own team in a 1953 game between Baltimore and the San Francisco 49ers.

In a pretrial deposition in his case against Rosenbloom, McLaney said of his business relationship with the Colts' owner, "One of the other transactions was my betting knowledge and background, and a business relationship was formed for the purpose of betting large sums of money on football games . . . On some occasions we would not be equal partners because Mr. Rosenbloom had much more money than I had and was able to bet higher. On one occasion, for instance, he bet as high as fifty-five thousand dollars against his own team, the Baltimore Colts, against the [San Francisco 49ers]."[4]

How credible was McLaney's statement? Robert J. McGarvey was an eleven-year veteran of the Philadelphia Police Department and Rosenbloom's personal aide from 1951 to 1954. McGarvey claimed, "After Mr. Rosenbloom purchased the Baltimore Colts . . . one of the services I performed for him during 1953–54 was placing his bets, or assisting in the placing of his bets on professional football games. During this period Mr. Rosenbloom bet frequently and in large amounts . . . Mr. Rosenbloom wagered to win and, when he felt his own team would not win, bet against the Colts on such occasions.

"I remember that in the last game in the 1953 season, when

his Colts were playing the Forty-niners on the West Coast, Mr. Rosenbloom bet a large sum of money against his own team and won."

In another affidavit, Larry E. Murphy, a former caddy who had met Rosenbloom and McGarvey at the LaGorce Country Club in Miami Beach, confirmed this and also stated, "I know that he frequently bet on professional football games and many times bet against his own team."

In still another affidavit, Florida businessman Richard Melvin, a golfing partner of Rosenbloom and the husband of bandleader Tommy Dorsey's widow, said, "I distinctly remember that during one professional football season he made nine straight winning bets on professional football games."

The Colts and the 49ers game in question was played on December 13, 1953, at San Francisco's Kezar Stadium. The Colts, who were twenty-three-point underdogs, lost the game, 45–14. It was the last game of the regular season for both teams. The Colts' record that year—Rosenbloom's first in the NFL—was three wins and nine losses.

In the Colts' first possession of the game, Buddy Young, fielding a punt, ran ninety-two yards for what appeared to be the first score of the game. But the play was called back because Baltimore had too many men on the field. The twelfth man was not identified by officials. In its report on the game, *The San Francisco Examiner* wrote: "That delay by the Colts' unidentified twelfth man in clearing the premises, and the loss of the squirming [*sic*] touchdown could have altered the course of the game. It might have set the Colts afire for an upset.

"However, that was only a longshot possibility because of the Colts' lack of man power." The Colts racked up only two yards passing and twenty-two yards rushing in the first half. Down 31–7 at halftime—and 31–30 against the spread—the Colts totaled only 136 yards for the entire game. The 49ers completely outmanned the Colts and dominated the contest.

McLaney had charged that Rosenbloom had intentionally "decided to leave several of his fine players at home."

In fact, the Colts played the game without their starting quarterback, Fred Enke, and their best running back, George Taliaferro, as well as other starters.

However, in Rosenbloom's defense, Taliaferro told me, "There was Fred Enke, Dick Flowers, and Jack DelBello. Those were the quarterbacks. They couldn't play. Each of them was injured. That prompted Keith Molesworth, the Colts' head coach, to ask me if I could play quarterback. But I had never taken a snap directly from the center—where I had to put my hands right under his hind end.

"So I played quarterback when the Colts played the Los Angeles Rams in Baltimore, two weeks before the Forty-niners game. We lost that one, twenty-one to thirteen. The week before the Forty-niners game, we played the Rams again—this time in Los Angeles. During that game, I snapped the cartilage in the interior portion of my right knee.[5] There was no way that I could play in the Forty-niners game. Fred Enke was not able to play either.

"Molesworth was so desperate for a quarterback that he just asked everyone, 'Is there anyone on this team who can throw a football?' So we had a small halfback. He was the guy who played quarterback in the San Francisco game. He had never played quarterback in his life. But we didn't have anyone else."

Under oath in 1960, Rosenbloom denied all charges of gambling on or against the Colts. The Colts' owner added that although he was a gambler and had made numerous wagers on the golf course with McLaney, he had never made a bet on a professional football game since buying the Colts in 1953. To say or do anything to the contrary would have violated NFL rules and could have cost him his franchise.

After Benton had circulated the documents, Rozelle was asked by reporters why the case had lain dormant for so long. Rozelle simply replied, "We are exploring the allegations. We do not comment publicly on specific matters we are exploring." Rozelle also said that there had been a time problem—because the 1962 football season had just ended and other investigations were being carried on.

In the midst of the Rosenbloom investigation, another unrelated betting scandal suddenly went public. On January 4, 1963, Chicago Bears owner George Halas, a friend of Rosenbloom, was quoted in *The Chicago Tribune,* saying that the NFL was investigating the possible gambling activities by "a member of a Midwest team." Halas added that he had given the information to Rozelle, who was investigating the charges.[6]

Rumors about possible widespread gambling among NFL players had begun early in the 1962 season after the heavily favored Green Bay Packers did not cover the spread in its 9–7 defeat of the Detroit Lions in a contest played in Green Bay. Large bets and unnatural money had appeared on this game, which had been placed by beards who had received money from supposedly untraceable sources. Consequently, East Coast bookmakers took several subsequent NFL games off the boards.

After Halas made his statement, Rozelle confirmed that several members of the Bears team, along with players from as many as four other teams, were being investigated—because they "associated with undesirable types." Rozelle added, "We haven't found any fire, but anytime we see any smoke we look fast." He also said that the NFL looked into at least fifteen such cases each year. "Normally the only thing they produce is misjudgment on the part of players who are seen in the wrong places talking perhaps with the wrong kinds of people. We have not found a basis for any criminal prosecution. Usually the players are warned, and they immediately get back into line."

Reportedly, Halas had been miffed because similar charges had been made against the Bears' star fullback, thirty-one-year-old Rick Casares. Supposedly cleared in a probe of his associations with a gambler by passing two polygraph tests, Casares, who liked to gamble in Las Vegas, had admitted a relationship with a Chicago gambler, known only as Zaza, which continued after the Bears and the NFL had instructed him to end it. The first lie detector test had been administered after Casares fumbled twice in a game between the Bears and the Los Angeles Rams in October 1961. He took the second test only a few weeks before the 1963 betting scandal had flared up—in the midst of dramatic changes in the point spreads of recent games.

During the polygraph examination, Casares was specifically asked: "Did you ever attempt to shave points?" "Did you deliberately fumble?" "Have you ever been offered money to shave points?" Casares answered no to all three questions and passed. However, when he answered no to the fourth question, "Is there anything in your personal life for which you could be pressured?" the needle of the polygraph jumped off the page. Casares explained that he had been the driver of a car in 1953 that crashed head-on into another vehicle. His female companion had been killed.

After Casares passed the second test, Halas declared, "The investigation can end right now because I'm convinced not a single one of the Bears has ever tried to shave points or otherwise fix an NFL game."

What was not publicly known at the time was that Casares's "godfather" was Florida Mafia boss Santos Trafficante of Tampa, according to two of the player's close friends.

One of these friends alleged, "Rick Casares bet. I remember in one particular game. All of the players, the water boys, everybody was standing on the sideline, totally involved with the game, except Rick—who was sitting alone on the bench with his eye on the scoreboard and the clock. He wasn't paying a bit of attention to the game. He was a total character, and he loved to gamble. He loved to gamble!"

Also investigated was Bob St. Clair, a star tackle for the San Francisco 49ers, who in 1956 had been loaned $6,000 against his salary and, along with several unknown people, had invested in a failed oil project that cost the player $7,000. St. Clair insisted that he had not known that several of those involved in the deal were heavy gamblers with ties to major underworld figures. Reporter Bob Curran wrote, "St. Clair, Rozelle's friend when they were undergraduates at San Francisco, phoned Rozelle and said, 'They're crucifying me in the papers out here, calling me a crook and rat without even benefit of a trial. You've got to announce your findings that I'm not guilty.'

"Rozelle told him, 'Sorry, Bob, we're going to have to make one announcement that will cover every case we've investigated that has been made public.' "[7]

AFL commissioner Joe Foss told reporters that his league was not the target of any investigations. "I'm not so naïve, however, to think that in any league of this kind, with so many players, there may not be a few boys who would have some contact or association with people who might be considered tainted."

Meantime, yet another NFL investigation concentrated on Detroit Lions star defensive tackle Alex Karras, who was accused of being seen with several Detroit gamblers in a front-page report in *The Detroit News* on January 7, 1963. Karras initially had become a target because of his part ownership in the Lindell Bar with a known gambler and the gambler's brother. The all-pro tackle simply announced that he would quit football before selling his interest in the bar, and his colorful defiance brought him even more attention.

Karras told me, "The NFL asked me to leave the bar because of the unsavory characters who walked into the bar. I said, 'Fine, I'll do that, just as long as you don't let the unsavory characters come into the stadium.' The NFL did not reply to that. I never worried about whether the league gave me permission or not. I was making nine thousand dollars a year playing football and eighteen thousand with the bar. It didn't make much sense to leave the bar to go play football."

Then, Karras was interviewed by NBC reporter David Burke on January 13. Early in the interview, Karras stated, "I enjoy betting . . . I assume that there is betting going on in the league."

During later questioning, Karras was asked, "Have you ever bet on a game in which you were playing?"

"Yes, I have," Karras replied.

Karras's indiscretion forced the scandal to explode when the interview was aired on January 16 on NBC's evening news program, *The Huntley-Brinkley Report.*

When told of Karras's appearance on the news program, Rozelle said, "If Karras said that, he may have a real problem."

13 The Party Bus

DESPITE ALL THE PUBLICITY the 1963 NFL gambling scandal produced, the full story behind the Lions' role in the affair has never been told. In Detroit, the investigation began in the early-morning hours of Saturday, August 18, 1962. Later that night, the Lions were to play the Dallas Cowboys as part of an NFL preseason doubleheader in Cleveland. Detroit police officers were conducting surveillance at the Grecian Gardens, a popular Detroit restaurant in the city's Greektown section. The café was located only a block south of police headquarters.

The police had been tipped off that Detroit's top Mafia figures were present at the restaurant that night, including: Anthony Zerilli, the son of the boss of the Detroit mob, Joseph Zerilli, and an officer of the Hazel Park Racing Association; Peter Vitale, a narcotics trafficker; Sam Giordano, who had been twice convicted of gambling; Anthony Corrado and Dominic Corrado, the sons of the "enforcer" of the Detroit Mafia, Peter Corrado; Anthony Cimini, a lieutenant in the local underworld; Anthony Giacalone, who was convicted of bribing a police officer in an effort to end the department's gambling surveillance and arrests; Vito Giacalone, Tony's brother and a convicted gambler; and Anthony Thomas, a convicted murderer.

Also identified in the police reports as being with the group was Wayne Walker, a linebacker for the Detroit Lions.

At 4:10 A.M., the police observed Vito Giacalone drive out of the parking lot in a 1947 twin-bus containing several men and women. The bus—painted in blue and silver, the Lions' team colors—was registered to Odus Tincher, a three-time-convicted gambler who was part of the group. The police report stated that Walker left the restaurant with the group and climbed into his 1961 Oldsmobile station wagon with Idaho tags and followed the bus.

The "party bus," as it was known to the Detroit police, was a frequent sight on the city's streets. When in use, the bus was always loaded with mobsters, their women, and booze. There was even a bar and some bunk beds built in. So many Detroit gangsters were seen in the bus at the same time that one police officer joked that a simple speeding violation could lead to the biggest arrest since the 1957 Apalachin Conference.

At 5:50 A.M., both the bus and Walker's car arrived at the Bunk House Cafe in Toledo, which was described in the police reports as being "connected in gambling operations in the Toledo area." The police looked into the café through a window and observed nine Detroit men and four women sitting and talking together. A half hour later, both the bus and the station wagon left the café and continued on to Cleveland. Also, three other people, who had not been present in Detroit, were now in Walker's car. Among them was Raymond Gentile, the owner of the Bunk House, who was identified by police as "a well-known hoodlum in that area." In all, there were now sixteen people in the Detroit group.

At 7:39 A.M., according to police reports, the Ohio Highway Patrol "stopped the bus and the station wagon but got only the names of the drivers of the vehicles—Vito Giacalone was driving the bus and Wayne Walker was driving the 1961 Olds station wagon." The cars proceeded to Cleveland without further interruption.

A few days later, the Detroit police decided to discuss the matter with the Lions' head coach, George Wilson. An appointment was made at a surburban restaurant, the Fox & Hounds Inn, which was part-owned by Donald Dawson, the Detroit gambler. During their conversation, Wilson said that he knew nothing about Walker's reported drive to Cleveland, but that several of his players—Walker, Alex Karras, guard John Gordy, and defensive end Darris McCord—had requested to return to Detroit apart from the rest of the team. Wilson said that all but Walker were to be traveling on a bus. Walker wanted to return in his own car—which was going to be driven to Cleveland by Jimmy Butsicaris, a weekend gambler and Karras's partner in the Lindell Bar.

Pete Rozelle had ruled the Lindell off limits to NFL personnel because Detroit gamblers and Mafia figures often went there. However, Rozelle, according to Wilson, had lifted the ban when Karras told him that he wanted to become a partner in the Lindell with Butsicaris and the gambler's brother. Karras had paid the Butsicarises $40,000 for his one-third interest. Lions president, William Clay Ford, supported Karras's Lindell partnership.

The police report continued that Wilson had said, "Karras was a gambler and he [Wilson] didn't believe that he would ever stop gambling." Wilson told the police that he would talk to Karras and Walker—as well as make the Grecian Gardens off limits to his players.

On January 4, 1963, as revelations about NFL gambling started to become public, the Detroit police interviewed Jim Butsicaris. In generally confirming the police surveillance reports, Butsicaris added that he and another Detroit gambler had sat on the Lions bench during the game as guests of Karras and Walker. Although Butsicaris was not identified in any police reports as being among the Detroit group traveling to Cleveland the previous August, he told the police that he, not Walker, had driven Walker's station wagon to Cleveland. The police did not confront him with the fact that the Ohio Highway Patrol had identified Walker as the driver.

After the game, Butsicaris said, the Detroit group went to Captain Frank's restaurant near Cleveland Stadium for dinner. Although Walker was not listed as being in attendance, the Detroit group was joined by players Gordy and Karras. Vito Giacalone picked up the check for everyone, according to Butsicaris, who added that Gordy and Karras then stayed with the group at the Shaker House Hotel in Cleveland. They all returned together on the bus the following afternoon as Giacalone's guests.

Detroit Police Commissioner George Edwards reportedly gave Rozelle a written report on December 27, 1962. However, Lions president Ford said that he wasn't notified of the police investigation until December 31. He learned of the probe from the Lions' general counsel. Apparently, head coach Wilson had failed to report his August meeting with the Detroit police to his superiors.

On January 6, 1963, after the NFL betting probe was revealed, the Miami police, at the request of Detroit police officials, placed Vito Giacalone and another Detroit mobster, Mike "the Enforcer" Rubino, under physical surveillance while they were present at the Lions–Pittsburgh Steelers play-off game at the Orange Bowl in Miami Beach. They were accompanied by Tony Zerilli and Tony Corrado. The Lions won the game, 17–10.

The Miami police had learned that the four Mafia figures were registered at a local hotel under assumed names. However, while tailing them in traffic, the police twice lost the mobsters' rented Cadillac. Although there were no known contacts between the Mafia figures and Lions players during that trip, the Detroit gangsters were observed meeting with Joseph Massei, the gambling overlord of the Miami area.

On the Sunday before the game, Rozelle—who had been notified of the surveillance prior to the mobsters' arrival in Miami—met with NFL player representatives and reportedly gave them a stern lecture about associating with gamblers and betting on NFL games. The Lions' representative and cocaptain, Joe Schmidt, did not attend. Asked by reporters about the continuing gambling investigation, Schmidt replied, "I don't think there's any foundation to it at all."

On January 7, the day after the Lions-Steelers play-off game, the Detroit police interviewed Wayne Walker. Specifically, he was questioned about any knowledge he had about "shaving points, gambling on football games, or throwing ball games." According to the police report, Walker replied that he had "no knowledge of any extensive gambling engaged in by members of the Detroit Lions." He added that he personally "occasionally played a football card" and had bet on a football game on only one occasion—on a game between the Green Bay Packers and the New York Giants. He said that he had made the bet with "a close personal friend" who played with the Packers. Walker did not identify the player.

Walker admitted to having become acquainted with mobsters Tony and Vito Giacalone, Dominic and Tony Corrado, Peter Vitale, and Odus Tincher through bar owner Butsicaris. Walker said that even after learning that these men were "gamblers," he did not stay away from them. He insisted that he simply "would run into them at the Grecian Gardens."

The Lions, Walker said, occasionally "had a 'spirit party' in the back hall of the Grecian Gardens which was hosted by Dominic Corrado" at which all food and drinks were free. Walker described the "spirit parties" as being like "pep rallies" and said that they had been arranged by Karras. Walker added that he once had a drink alone with Vito Giacalone at another bar but denied any other association with him. He reported that a former member of the Lions, Howard "Hopalong" Cassidy, was a business associate of the Giacalones, which was confirmed through an independent police investigation.

Walker also admitted that he had been on Odus Tincher's bus en route from Chicago to Detroit after a 1961 game between the Lions and the Bears. He added that he had been on the bus that one time because Jimmy Butsicaris had taken Walker's father along as a guest. Others on the bus during this trip included Vito Giacalone, Dominic, Peter, and Tony Corrado, as well as Karras and Lions end Glenn Davis.

However, Walker denied to the police that he had been either at the Grecian Gardens or driving his station wagon during the August 18 trip to Cleveland. Upon hearing that, the police report continued, "Walker was confronted by the following officers who had observed him during the early morning hours of August 18, 1962: Sergeants William DePugh and Joseph Areeda who had observed him at the Grecian Gardens and Patrolman Eugene Caviston who had observed him at the Bunk House Cafe.

"After the confrontation, Walker stated that it could be possible that he was at the Grecian Gardens on the above-mentioned date, but that he could not have been at the Bunk House Restaurant." Walker offered to take a polygraph test, insisting that he had loaned his car to Butsicaris.

Walker was not confronted with the fact that he had been identified as the driver of the station wagon by the Ohio Highway Patrol. The reason? The Ohio patrolman who had stopped the bus and the station wagon on August 18 had developed amnesia when questioned by the Detroit police and could not remember the identity of the driver of Walker's car. Also, their notepads containing the information had been lost. And the dispatcher who had received the information from the officers had since been fired "because of inefficiency."

Even though the Detroit police officers refused to retract their earlier reports, Rozelle and the NFL believed Walker. In his final report on the matter, Rozelle made no specific mention of the details of the Lions' associations with members of the Detroit Mafia or whether Walker or any of the Lions players were ever polygraphed.

How widespread had gambling been within the Lions team? Vincent Piersante, then a top official in the Detroit Police Department who was directly involved in the Lions betting case, told me, "I recall an incident in which a bunch of Lions players got their noses out of joint because they were winning the game by one point but had given the three-point spread. There were less than thirty seconds left in the game, and they had an opportunity to score. But instead of driving for the touchdown or field goal, the quarterback Milt Plum decided, 'We've got the game won. There's no sense in taking a chance.' So instead of going for the score, he just sat on the ball to secure the game. Plum was obviously not betting. One of the reasons Milt Plum was not the effective leader some thought he could've been was because he didn't care about the point spread and that wasn't in the tradition of some previous Lions quarterbacks."

Rozelle's probe concluded that Alex Karras had made no fewer than "six significant bets" since 1958, including $100 on his own team in 1962 in a game with the Packers—and another $100 on the Packers that same year in its title game with the New York Giants. In the wake of these revelations, Karras said, "I haven't done anything I'm ashamed of, and I am not guilty of anything."

During my interview with Karras, I asked him about the players' associations with the Detroit mobsters. Karras replied, "Games were never mentioned. They never tried to get inside information or any edge on the field. I never heard anyone get out of line and ask me any of those stupid questions 'Who's going to win and by how much?'

"I'm from Gary, Indiana. And I know what betting is. I've been betting all my life. My association with those guys I hung around with was, number one, they were my age, and, number two, we hung around the same places, like the Grecian Gardens, and we met each other socially at the places where we hung around. It wasn't a heavy relationship. It was a 'same-age' relationship. We had a lot in common. So I never had any problem with them; and they didn't have any problem with me."

Karras added that the Lions' management was fully aware of these associations between the players and the mobsters—and never did anything about them.

Rozelle's investigation also showed that running back Paul Hornung of the Green Bay Packers, the 1956 Heisman Trophy winner from Notre Dame, had associated with lumber company owner Abe Samuels, a West Coast gambler who was part owner of the Tropicana, a Las Vegas hotel/casino. The two men had met in San Francisco prior to the 1956 East-West college football game. They struck up a social relationship and later Hornung, who personally bet as much as $300 a game, provided him with "inside information" about the Packers team.

According to a report made public by the NFL, Samuels, who wasn't named, had "developed the habit of querying Hornung by telephone regarding his opinion of the outcome of various games." In one season, Hornung won $1,500 from his gambling on NFL games. Samuels admitted to betting nearly $100,000 each season.

Also implicated with Samuels were both Rick Casares and Bears line coach Phil Handler, who had worked for the gambler as a salesman at his lumber company for fifteen years during the off-season. Samuels had also offered Hornung a job with his Louisville printing company. "This is a business deal and has nothing to do with Hornung as a football player," Samuels told *The Chicago American.*

Casares told the newspaper, "I've met Abe Samuels a few times, but I knew him as a businessman. When you meet a man in a group and he is identified as a businessman, you can't very well ask him if he gambles on football games."

In his attempt to defend his Packers teammate, defensive end Bill Quinlan told UPI, "Take Samuels. Sure I know the man. And so does Paul and a lot of other players. But understand this—never once did the man so much as ask any of us how we thought we were going to do in a ball game.

"It's ridiculous. A man like Samuels, with his money, needs a Hornung or a Quinlan or a Dan Currie [a Packers linebacker] like he needs a hole in the head."

Rozelle said that he had heard rumors about Hornung and began his investigation during the spring of 1962. It is not known whether Quinlan or Currie were also targets of the probe. However, it is clear that Hornung was not actually questioned until January 1963.

Why the long delay? "I didn't want to confront him until we had absolute proof," Rozelle told reporters, "and we didn't get that proof until this past January . . . When I told Hornung of the charges, he admitted them."

On April 17, 1963, commissioner Rozelle indefinitely suspended Hornung and Karras. Five other Detroit players—guard John Gordy,[1] running back Gary Lowe, linebacker Joe Schmidt, linebacker/placekicker Wayne Walker, and defensive end Sam Williams—were fined $2,000 each for betting on NFL games in which they were not playing. Each had bet $50 on the December 30, 1962, NFL championship game between the Green Bay Packers and the New York Giants. The Packers won, 16–7.

Dick "Night Train" Lane remembers when the bets were made. "There was a place where we met," he told me. "I was there and little Archie Stone [a close friend of Jim Butsicaris] said, 'The guys are talking about who they're going to bet on; they're going to bet on the Giants.' I told him that I thought Green Bay was going to win. I told him, 'They can bet anything they want. I'm going to the golf course.' "

Lane insists that he did not, per se, make a bet. Instead, he told Stone, " 'Archie, if you want to bet fifty dollars, I'll put it up for you.' I gave him the fifty, and I left. I don't know whether he bet it or not. I never got anything, and I wasn't looking for anything."

During the NFL's investigation of Karras, Lane says Karras had fingered him as being among those who bet. "Alex told Pete Rozelle, 'Night Train was there, and you don't have him down.' So I told Alex, 'What are you mentioning my name for? You're drowning, and you want to pull people down with you?'

"Rozelle asked me to take a lie detector test. I took it, and I passed. They asked me about a couple of guys in Las Vegas, and I told him that I hadn't been in Vegas for years. In my earlier days, I was a gambler. I'd gamble on anything. But I never bet on pro football while I was playing." Lane, who also admitted to knowing Detroit gambler Don Dawson and the Giacalone brothers, was not accused of any wrongdoing.

However, the Detroit team was also fined $4,000 because its head coach, George Wilson, although not personally fined, had failed to report "certain associations by members of the Detroit team," according to the NFL.

Rozelle also announced that he had received evidence that several other players around the league had been playing football betting cards. The players involved, who were not named, were reprimanded but not fined. Neither Rick Casares nor Bob St. Clair was charged with any wrongdoing. Those other players and coaches who had also admitted relationships with Abe Samuels were not fined or reprimanded either.

After the penalties were handed down, Rozelle wrote in his final report, "There is no evidence that any NFL player has given less than his best in playing any game. There is no evidence that any player has ever bet against his own team. There is no evidence that any NFL player has sold information to gamblers." Rozelle interviewed fifty-two people "relating to individuals connected with eight different clubs" during his probe of the players.

Karras remains defiant about the whole matter and told me, "I put myself on the line by saying that I gambled on the *Huntley-Brinkley Report,* which was totally edited [and taken out of context]. I went on to say how I gambled and what I gambled on. 'Do you gamble?' I said, 'Yes.' 'That's Alex Karras of the Detroit Lions saying that he gambles.' That to me was a total setup. I don't know who set me up, but whoever it was—it worked. It was probably Carroll Rosenbloom and George Halas. Because it took a lot of heat off the NFL by putting Paul Hornung and me on suspension."

However, Hornung was completely repentant. "I made a terrible mistake," he told reporters. "I realize this now. I am truly sorry."[2] The suspensions of both players were lifted after one year. They were reinstated to their teams.

Meantime, NFL Players Association president Pete Retzlaff, a star end for the Philadelphia Eagles, announced that the NFL players will "police our own ranks. If the league advises us that a player is frequenting a shady establishment, we'll have three or four of the club leaders attempt to straighten him out." Retzlaff, who also owned a cocktail lounge, asked, "How do you recognize these creeps [gamblers who frequent bars owned by NFL personnel]? They seek us out, we don't seek them out. If the league or the owners know who they are, let them tell us."

After announcing the players' punishments, Rozelle added that his investigation of Rosenbloom was continuing but, "Carroll Rosenbloom has denied the charges [of betting against the Colts in 1953] in a sworn affidavit given to the commissioner and each of the individuals making such charges has since repudiated or withdrawn the allegations in affidavits or signed statements."[3]

In fact, of all those signing statements against Rosenbloom, only Robert McGarvey, the former Philadelphia police officer and Rosenbloom aide, actually recanted. In a complete turnabout, McGarvey said, "I did all the betting on football games. Rosenbloom to my knowledge never bet on a pro game. I thought Rosenbloom would seek me out and offer me a job or something . . . I therefore repudiate my affidavit."

Richard Melvin and Larry Murphy—the two other Rosenbloom associates who had signed affidavits against him—never repudiated their stories in their subsequent statements to Rozelle. Larry E. Murphy added, "My statement doesn't back down on a thing."

McGarvey refused to be questioned about any pressure he had received to sign the repudiation—or who had applied it.

14 Rosenbloom in the Bahamas

INCREDIBLY ENOUGH, THE PERSON responsible for supplying the affidavits that appeared to clear Carroll Rosenbloom was Mike McLaney! Pete Rozelle told reporters McLaney "refuted the affidavits, all of them . . . Mr. McLaney is the one who obtained the other affidavits, and he was the one who came to me and gave me a written statement that all of them were wrong."

And then, suddenly, after providing the NFL with evidence of Rosenbloom's innocence, McLaney, who claimed to be $164,000 in debt when he first filed his charges against Rosenbloom, was able to buy a half interest in a private club/casino on Cat Cay in the Bahamas, where Rosenbloom and Chesler had already been making substantial investments through their partnerships. In fact, they were opening a casino of their own—with the help of several top organized-crime figures.

After the loss of Cuba and the clampdown on the Mafia by the Kennedy Justice Department, Meyer Lansky and the organized-crime syndicate had targeted the Bahamas as its new off-shore gambling and narcotics empire. Gambling was illegal in the Bahamas without a "certificate of exemption" which permitted gambling under certain conditions. A faltering Bahamian economy opened the door for such exemptions to a small group of investors. With the help of the Bahamian Batista, Sir Stafford Sands, the minister of finance and tourism and the leader of the "Bay Street Boys"—the all-white United Bahamian Party (UBP)—Lansky's partners entered the gambling scene.

The 1939 law providing for the exemption, which had been proposed by Sands, gave official approval to two casinos that had been operating illegally. One was the casino on Cat Cay—one of the small Bahamian Out islands, fifty miles off Florida's eastern coast—and the other was the Bahamian Club, which was on the western outskirts of Nassau. The exemption for the Cat Cay Club expired in 1961 and was not renewed—until McLaney came along with his newfound cash.

Sands, who had a glass left eye and, like Chesler, weighed over three hundred pounds, had been bought by Lansky and the underworld with the payment of $1.8 million in bribes disguised as legal fees laundered through Bahamian land owner Wallace Groves. Interestingly, Sands was considered a lawyer, even though he had never graduated from any college.

Born in 1902, Groves was a Baltimore businessman and Wall Street broker who had studied law at Georgetown University in Washington, D.C. In 1941, he had been indicted, convicted, and sentenced to two years in prison for his role in a $750,000 stock fraud scandal. He served only five months of his two-year sentence at Danbury.

Soon after his release, Groves, with nearly $10 million in personal assets, moved to one of his houses on Little Whale Cay in the Bahamas—he had been given his own fiefdom by Bahamian government officials with whom he was friendly. He was also paying them off. Groves received 150,000 acres of land for $2.80 an acre and the rights to lease a large share of the 530-acre Grand Bahama Island. He founded the Grand Bahama Port Authority in 1955 and sectioned off over 200 acres of land, calling the area Freeport—a place where there were no taxes of any kind levied on personal or business income. However, by 1960, the Port Authority had fallen on hard times and was not attracting the tourism Groves had hoped for.

Underworld leaders had been dealing with Bahamian politicians since the Prohibition era. Among those who had been receiving payoffs for their cooperation was Sir Roland Symonette, who, at the time of Lansky and the mob's entry into the Bahamas in the early 1960s, was the Bahamian premier.

On April 1, 1963, Groves and his Port Authority, operating through Bahamas Amusements, Ltd., were granted a certificate of exemption by Sands and the Bahamian government, which they had applied for in March. They received clearance to build and operate a hotel/casino in Freeport. Without delay, Groves then struck a deal with Lou Chesler, whom he had known since 1955. Soon, Carroll Rosenbloom and the Seven Arts film company were involved as well.

"In the beginning, it was all kind of a joke," according to Seven Arts vice president and director Tex McCrary. "I was originally trying to get Chesler into Cuba. I owned *The Havana Times* under Batista. I wanted to take General Development into Cuba and do a job on housing under Batista. When Castro came in, we left. We had an idea, but we needed an island. And that's when we went to the Bahamas.

"I put together the Grand Bahama Development Company [Devco] for Groves and Chesler and everyone else. We ran the campaign to legalize gambling in the Bahamas—which meant dealing with the white government. And the deal I had with Stafford Sands and the white government was I wanted to build an international shopping bazaar for the development company."[1]

The initial $12 million for the hotel/casino, which planned to hire a 103-member staff, had been raised principally by Chesler and Rosenbloom—through Seven Arts, which held nearly 21 percent of the stock in Devco, an offshoot of Chesler's General Development Corporation which had developed three Florida communities.[2] Because he held the certificate of exemption and owned the land, Groves received a 50 percent interest in Devco. Seven Arts and other investors owned 41.5 percent. Chesler held the remaining stock in his own name.

The legal paperwork securing another $5 million of Devco stock was listed in the name of S. Rosenbloom.[3] Carroll Rosenbloom, whose family corporation had been named S. Rosenbloom, Inc., was as involved in the construction of the hotel/casino as were Chesler, Groves, and Sands. And the latter three were working in concert with Meyer Lansky, according to both the U.S. Justice Department and an official Bahamian inquiry.

Chesler's partners included Lansky associate Max Orovitz, who was later indicted because of a General Development stock fraud scheme,[4] and New York lawyer Morris Mac Schwebel, who was indicted in a separate securities case in February 1961 while president of Universal Controls.[5] Schwebel resigned his post in the wake of his indictment, and Chesler resigned as Universal's board chairman to concentrate on his Bahamian interests.

Consequently, Rosenbloom became the chairman of the board and the president of Universal Controls. During his tenure on the board, Rosenbloom had sold a great deal of stock in the pari-mutuel tote board company to Colts head coach Weeb Ewbank and to Colts players. Ewbank told me, "I had some money in it. Carroll recommended we go into it. In fact, he guaranteed my investment."

As part of their $23 million total investment in the Bahamas, Chesler, Rosenbloom, and their syndicate built the Bahamas' first casino, the Monte Carlo, at the 250-room Lucayan Beach Hotel in Freeport on Grand Bahama, which opened in January 1964. Chesler personally put up the casino's initial $600,000 gambling stake. The casino staffed six roulette tables, six crap tables, and six blackjack tables.

Airline junkets from south Florida carried gamblers, who paid $18 for a round-trip ticket, to Grand Bahama Island on eighteen flights each day; charter flights were also arranged from Chicago and New York at equally rock-bottom prices. The casino was an immediate success.

Chesler had promised that there would be "no invasion of Grand Bahama Island by the underworld. No North American personnel will be used as croupiers or as supervisory personnel." However, Lansky and his associates were permitted to skim 30 percent of the net profits from travel packages, as well as their portion of the skim from the casino. The Justice Department estimated that the Lansky group illegally received no less than $6 million from the Monte Carlo in its first year.[6]

Also, Chesler and his partners immediately hired three of the syndicate's top sports bookmakers—Charles Brudner, Max Courtney, and Frank Ritter—to operate the Monte Carlo. All three had fled the United States to escape prosecution in New York, but of all America's high rollers they had the best credit records in the country. The Miami Crime Commission had described the three men as the "biggest, heaviest bookmakers and sports bookmakers in the country." Chesler referred to them as "my bookmakers in the United States. That's how I happened to hire them. I had a great deal of experience with them." Chesler admitted that he had been gambling with Ritter since 1946.

Chesler was later described by a Bahamian investigative panel as "a compulsive gambler . . . not confined to casinos. He bet on horses, football, base-ball, jai alai—almost anything."[7] The panel also noted that Chesler had "lost as much as $200,000 at one time to the casino. Indeed, he told us he had lost 'much more.' "

McCrary agreed, saying, "Chesler bet like hell on everything."

Casino records showed that two other big-money losers were Mafia capo Mike Coppola and Carroll Rosenbloom. Both lost at least $100,000 each. Another NFL owner with a $100,000 line of credit was Art Modell of the Cleveland Browns. However, Modell drew only $5,000 against his account in February 1964.[8]

Mike McLaney, the engineer of the gambling charges against Rosenbloom, found himself with a half interest in the Cat Cay Club, operating under a similar certificate of exemption as Chesler and Rosenbloom were. The Cat Cay had been a nongambling resort since the 1961 death of its owner, Louis R. Wasey. In the midst of the NFL's investigation of Rosenbloom, McLaney suddenly and inexplicably obtained a 50 percent interest in the casino with Wasey's daughter and came up with enough money for the casino's gambling bankroll—just days before McLaney told Rozelle that Robert McGarvey and others had recanted their affidavits against Rosenbloom.

While the preparations for the opening of the Monte Carlo were being made, the NFL's gambling investigation had reached its climax with the suspensions of Karras and Hornung. The investigation of Rosenbloom's gambling activities was still continuing.

On July 16, 1963—three months after the players' suspensions—Rozelle officially cleared Rosenbloom, saying that there was "no proof whatever" against him. "In light of all available information, the investigation of Mr. Rosenbloom's case has been completed and the commissioner concludes that the charges were unfounded." Regarding charges that Rosenbloom was a heavy gambler who bet on sports other than professional football, Rozelle proclaimed that Rosenbloom had "ceased such practices."

Upon hearing the news that he had been cleared for betting against his own team, Rosenbloom said, "I'm pleased. It [was] a long time coming, but it was a thorough job. I'm happy with it not only for myself but for the Baltimore club as well."

In an unpublished interview, reporter Jessica Savitch asked Rozelle about his view of Rosenbloom's dealings with Chesler.

Rozelle replied, "It wasn't just his relationship with Lou Chesler. It was, I believe, his involvement with Mr. Chesler in an entertainment company [Seven Arts]. And when the entertainment company contemplated expanding into the Bahamas and starting a gambling casino, I talked to Mr. Rosenbloom.

"And I said that the entertainment company is one thing, but I think that the type of operation that the company is expanding to could hurt you and the reputation of the league. And Mr. Rosenbloom did not participate in that. He ensured that that was spun off from the company he had invested in."

Rozelle serenely gave reporter Bob Curran a less-guarded explanation. "Yes, I could have said, 'He goes or I go,' and I would still have the job, but I would be ruining a man's life—and the Colts are his life—just to prove that I really am 'a strong commissioner.' I could not do that. I had to make a decision on whether there was proof there or not. The proof was not there."[9]

Upton Bell told me there was no question about Rosenbloom's guilt in the matter. "One of the NFL team owners told me that everyone knew he was guilty. And there's no question in my mind that Rozelle knew he was guilty. And if my father had been commissioner, even though Rosenbloom was a friend, he would have thrown him out of the league. They had him dead to rights."

Ralph Salerno, New York City's supervisor of detectives, agreed. "I know as a fact that the NFL knew that Rosenbloom was a notorious gambler. And they knew that he gambled with bad people. And they just worried that he might need money bad enough to be not adverse to a fix or a shave."

As the NFL gambling scandal wound down, Senator John L. McClellan, chairman of the U.S. Senate Permanent Subcommittee on Investigations, announced that he was going to look into other suspicious NFL activities, including a possible fixed game between the Chicago Bears and the San Francisco 49ers in September 1962. Reports had been received by the Senate panel that three unnamed 49ers players had been paid off by gamblers for the fix. The six-point-underdog Bears won the game, 30–14. However, no players were ever charged with any wrongdoing.

In a speech about sports, gambling, and narcotics to the Chicago Crime Commission on April 24, McClellan said that the threat of organized crime in America "transcends and exceeds any immediate danger of infiltration or subversion by the Communist international conspiracy." To combat the problem, he called for court-authorized wiretaps on mobsters and the creation of a national crime commission with subpoena power and the authority to investigate all aspects of crime.

However, after the investigation and its hearings were announced, the subcommittee, claiming insufficient evidence, dropped the inquiry. McClellan himself began referring questions about gambling and professional football to Pete Rozelle.

What happened? Attorney General Robert Kennedy, an unabashed football fan, stepped in. A top Kennedy aide told me, "Bobby quietly told Rozelle and the NFL owners that the league was going to have to get tough with NFL people who violated league rules, as well as federal gambling laws. When Kennedy saw the firm action Rozelle took on the gambling matter, he was convinced that the NFL could handle these matters internally. Kennedy [who had been McClellan's chief counsel during the days of the Senate Rackets Committee] simply told the old man to back off. McClellan trusted Bobby and did just that."

Rozelle and the NFL responded to Kennedy's demands at the NFL owners meeting in St. Louis on May 22, 1963, by creating a new arm of the NFL: NFL Security. Previously, such investigations had been handled informally under both Bert Bell and Rozelle. Specifically under Bell, the NFL had established a loose-knit network of private investigators around the country.

Selected to head NFL Security and streamline the NFL security network was fifty-three-year-old Captain James Hamilton, a tall, well-built man who was the chief of the Organized Crime Intelligence Division of the Los Angeles Police Department. A police officer for twenty-six years, Hamilton was to serve as the liaison among the NFL headquarters, various law-enforcement agencies, and the private investigators hired by the NFL in each of the cities where professional football was played.

"It's largely a preventive measure," Rozelle told reporters. "He [Hamilton] will also be available for consultation by the players." Using the Detroit Lions as an example of how Hamilton would be used, Rozelle said that if there were rumors that players would be on a bus with known gamblers, "a trip like that will have to be checked out and clarified." He added that if NFL Security had existed the previous year, the entire NFL gambling scandal probably would not have occurred.

Hamilton had been recommended by Bob Kennedy and *Los*

Angeles Times ace crime reporter Jack Tobin, who each cited Hamilton's contributions to the Senate Rackets Committee. Hamilton had also received high praise for his investigations of the underworld from the Special Crime Study Commission on Organized Crime in California, which had worked in concert with the Kefauver Committee.[10]

15 Football and Hollywood

IN MAY 1963, AFTER archrival Clint Murchison had verbally threatened to run him out of Dallas, Lamar Hunt moved his Dallas Texans to Kansas City, where the team became the Kansas City Chiefs. Soon after, Hunt proposed a world championship game between the winners of the NFL and the AFL. The NFL laughed off the proposal.

That same year, Harry Wismer, who had filed for bankruptcy, sold his New York Titans for $1 million to a five-man investment group headed by David A. "Sonny" Werblin, who was also a director of Monmouth Park Jockey Club in Oceanport, New Jersey.[1] Werblin immediately renamed his team the New York Jets.

Werblin was a top executive of MCA, Inc., a major entertainment conglomerate and the most powerful force in the motion picture industry. MCA (Music Corporation of America) was the parent company of Universal Pictures, Universal Television, and Decca Records (which later became MCA Records). MCA executives, including Werblin, had maintained close personal and business ties with Chicago mob attorney Sidney Korshak who represented the underworld's interests in Hollywood.

The Brooklyn-born Werblin was a short but ruggedly good-looking former Rutgers football player. He had studied journalism and worked as a copyboy for *The New York Times.* At MCA, he started with a part-time job, working as an errand boy for Billy Goodheart, who, along with Jules Stein, had founded MCA in

1924. Goodheart referred to Werblin as Sonny boy, and the nickname Sonny stuck. Werblin also became the band boy for Guy Lombardo's orchestra, which MCA represented. Werblin moved up quickly within the company and, just prior to World War II, replaced Goodheart as the head of MCA's New York office. A close friend of Carroll Rosenbloom, Werblin had snatched up former Baltimore Colts head coach Weeb Ewbank for the Jets in April 1963 after Rosenbloom had fired him because of a 7–7 1962 season.

Ewbank told me, "The only problem with Carroll was that he thought money could buy everything. Because we didn't win another championship, he got antsy. He was a good friend of the Kennedys, and he thought youth was the thing." Rosenbloom replaced Ewbank as head coach with Detroit Lions defensive coach Don Shula, who was only thirty-three and had played under Ewbank at Cleveland and Baltimore.

In January 1964, the AFL celebrated the signing of a $36 million-, five-year television package with NBC, which guaranteed the long-term success of the new league. Each AFL team received nearly $900,000 a year from the deal. Prior AFL contracts had been negotiated by MCA, which had enjoyed a sweetheart relationship with NBC.

The association was so cozy that it had earlier become a target of a federal investigation during the Justice Department's 1962 antitrust probe of MCA. Werblin, who handled MCA's television sales, was a close friend of Robert Kintner, who was the president of NBC at the time of the 1964 negotiations with the AFL.

In one document, the Justice Department described NBC as a "captive market for MCA's television shows," primarily because of the relationship between Werblin and NBC's Sarnoff family and Kintner.[2]

Carroll Rosenbloom confirmed that Werblin's clout with NBC won the day for the AFL. "Sonny Werblin pulled a coup," Rosenbloom said. "He [was] a top man for the Music Corporation of America and very close to [Robert] Sarnoff of NBC. All Sonny had to do was say, 'Look, I want a television contract for the AFL' and he would get it. NBC agreed to pay that league $36 million over five years. That was about $900,000 a year per club."[3]

As the 1964 AFL television deal was being negotiated with NBC, Rosenbloom, who lived next door to Werblin on Ocean

Highway in Golden Beach, Florida, became the sole owner of the Baltimore Colts by buying out his two partners on January 20. One of them, Zanvyl Kreiger, told Alan Greenberg and Mike Goodman of *The Los Angeles Times,* "He [Rosenbloom] took advantage of me. There isn't any question he let us have it with both barrels right between the eyes. He gave us the sob story . . . He pleaded that he wanted the team for his [son]. The day after we signed the contract, I saw the headlines that the [multi] million [dollar] CBS contract [for television rights to NFL games] had been announced. We knew nothing." Rosenbloom paid his partners $11 million for their shares of the Colts.

During the summer of 1965, the Atlanta Falcons and the Miami Dolphins were each given franchises in the NFL and the AFL, respectively. Insurance executive Rankin M. Smith was the new owner of the Falcons for $8.5 million; entertainer Danny Thomas and Minneapolis attorney Joe Robbie became the Dolphins' owners. They bought the team for $7.5 million.

Smith had worked his way up through the family-owned business, Life Insurance Company of Georgia, starting as a filing clerk and becoming senior vice president at the time he bought the Falcons. He later became president and chairman of the board.[4]

Upon entering the league, Smith immediately aroused controversy when he attempted to depreciate and deduct his players' contracts—which he viewed as capital investments—on his income-tax returns. In the past, an owner depreciated only tangible items such as the players' equipment. The IRS quickly denied the deductions. However, Smith appealed and won in federal court, which approved the depreciation of his Falcons. "The court recognizes that there is a value to the players," Smith said after the decision.

Another innovator took control of the Miami Dolphins. Lifelong Democrat Joe Robbie of the Dolphins grew up in South Dakota, where he served as a representative to the state legislature along with Republican Joe Foss, the future AFL commissioner. Foss and Robbie were longtime friends and had attended the University of South Dakota together. Robbie ran for Congress twice but lost and ran once and lost as a candidate for governor. Soon after his defeat, Robbie moved his law practice to Minneapolis.

Robbie met Danny Thomas while serving as a member of the

board of directors of Thomas's St. Jude Children's Research Hospital in Memphis. Robbie was responsible for bringing Thomas into the football deal. Robbie was the president and managing general partner.[5] Selected as the Dolphins' first coach was George Wilson, the former head coach of the Detroit Lions during the 1963 gambling scandal. Wilson had left the Lions in 1964.

Robbie was the poorest owner in the NFL and had never made over $30,000 in a single year from his law practice. His thrifty ways incited Bud Adams of the Houston Oilers to charge that he was "running a multimillion-dollar-a-year business like a fruit stand." In the end, Robbie would have the last laugh; his players would become the highest paid in the NFL.

On January 2, 1965, Sonny Werblin of the New York Jets announced that he had paid $427,000, mostly in bonus money, for a three-year $25,000-a-year contract with Alabama quarterback Joe Namath. The Jets of the AFL had outbid the St. Louis Cardinals of the NFL for the rights to Namath. At the time that Namath signed the contract, Werblin found him a roommate, Joe Hirsch, who wrote a betting line and an inside information sheet on professional sports. Namath wrote in his autobiography, "I met Joe at his place of business, the race track. No, he doesn't book bets; at least, he's never booked any of my bets. Joe writes for the *Morning Telegraph,* which is read by known gamblers. We met because Mr. Werblin, who was then president of the Jets, suggested that Joe, an old friend of his, look me up and show me around."[6]

Werblin's signing of Namath—promoting the "star system" he had learned while with MCA and all the publicity it produced—helped guarantee the Jets' future success. Because of the tremendous amount of publicity generated by the Namath deal, the Jets sold nearly three thousand season tickets within a week of the announcement. Further, the big-money deal completely changed the face of professional football forever. Even though the grunt in the NFL trenches was still making a yeoman's wages, the public's perception of player salaries would never be the same.

In April 1966, as the war between the NFL and the AFL reached its height with bids for college draft picks forcing skyrocketing salaries and bonuses, AFL commissioner Joe Foss resigned and was immediately replaced by thirty-six-year-old interim chief Allen M. Davis, the head coach and general manager of the Oakland Raiders. The appointment of street fighter Davis signaled that the AFL was taking off the gloves.

Davis was Brooklyn-raised and the son of a children's clothing manufacturer. He was an athlete and loved all sports, particularly football. Upon graduation from college in 1950, Davis coached at New York's Adelphi College. He then served in the military, coaching football at Fort Belvoir in Virginia.

In June 1954, at age twenty-four, Davis became an unpaid, expenses-only scout for Carroll Rosenbloom and the Baltimore Colts. He served the next two years as line coach at the Citadel, where he worked under General Mark Clark, the president of the college. From 1957 to 1959, after his success at the Citadel, he coached at the University of Southern California. Davis headed up the defensive unit in his final year but developed problems with the NCAA over his aggressive recruiting practices. USC's head coach, Don Clark, resigned in the midst of the NCAA's sanctions against the university. Davis was passed over as the new head coach; instead, the job went to John McKay, who didn't ask Davis to remain with the team. In 1960, Davis signed as an assistant coach for Sid Gillman and the new Los Angeles Chargers of the AFL.

When Davis, only thirty-three years old, accepted the job as head coach of the Oakland Raiders in January 1963, he took over a team that was 9–33 over its three-year history in the AFL. A genius in football strategy, Davis turned the Raiders around to 10–4 in his first season.

According to legend, Davis and Pete Rozelle had met, by telephone, back in 1953 while Rozelle was with the Los Angeles Rams and Davis was head coach at Fort Belvoir. Rozelle was scouting talent and said in one report, "I developed a phone relationship with Al, calling him to ask about players in his team. He said he wanted to be paid for any information, and for delivering players to the Rams." Davis, who acknowledged receiving money from the Rams for some scouting work, replied, "It's possible, but [Rozelle] was just a PR man."

In mid-May 1966, during his four-month tenure as AFL commissioner, Davis opposed the merger of the two leagues. He declared war on the NFL after the New York Giants signed Pete Gogolak, the Buffalo Bills' soccer-style kicking star, as a free agent. The Gogolak contract signaled the beginning of the high-priced raids on veteran players between the two leagues and almost scuttled the growing goodwill between them. And the stratospheric salaries being paid to the players were threatening the fundamental financial structure of professional football. In 1966 alone, the two leagues spent $7 million for their draft choices, including $1 million for two players: Donny Anderson and Jim Grabowski, who received $600,000 and $400,000, respectively, from the Green Bay Packers.

Davis recalled in a 1980 deposition that after the Gogolak deal, "[o]ur entire focus shifted from the progressive atmosphere of the American Football League into an all-out confrontation with the National Football League . . ." Davis's declaration of war made everyone in both leagues take pause. The relentless Davis was known to take no prisoners.

On June 8, 1966, with the money war hurting both leagues and field marshal Davis readying his blitzkrieg, Rozelle announced that the teams of the NFL and the AFL had agreed to merge—a move Rosenbloom and Werblin had been plotting for nearly three years. The deal was made between Tex Schramm, general manager of the Dallas Cowboys, and Lamar Hunt during a now-famous meeting in April 1966 in the airport lobby of Love Field near Dallas. Hunt had delayed his flight to Houston so that he could discuss the matter with Schramm. The two men, through a convincing series of talks with others in their respective leagues, brought about another meeting.

"In 1966," Rosenbloom later recalled, "owners of the two leagues [had] spent $7 million to sign draft choices. This could not go on. The AFL resumed negotiations [with the NFL owners]. This time there were Hunt, Wilson, and Sullivan. With me were Modell and Tex Schramm. Pete Rozelle acted as arbitrator. Late in the evening we came to an agreement. All nine AFL teams would come into our League, making twenty-six [after two more teams were added]."[7]

The expanded NFL would begin regular season play in 1970. Until then, the leagues were to remain separate with the champions of each to face off in an AFL–NFL world championship game—first proposed by Lamar Hunt—which later became known as the Super Bowl.[8]

To Davis's chagrin, Rozelle was selected to head the newly merged National Football League. Davis, who purchased a 10 percent interest in the Raiders for only $18,500, returned to Oakland as the managing general partner.

Congress approved the AFL–NFL merger on October 21,

1966, exempting the agreement from federal antitrust laws. According to several sources, the deal with Congress was greased when the powerful Senate Finance Committee chairman, Russell Long of Louisiana, was guaranteed that the next NFL franchise would be in Long's home state.

During the merger negotiations between the two leagues, commissioner Rozelle began to establish "ownership rules," described in David Harris's book *The League* as including

- a prohibition of corporate ownership. "While entities like Anheuser-Busch, Ralston Purina Corp., and CBS owned franchises in other sports leagues, such were not allowed in the NFL";
- a prohibition of "public ownership of NFL franchises, either through purchase by governmental entities or through the issuance of publicly traded stock";
- "the fifty-one percent rule," which would "require all franchises' ownership to include someone with at least a bare majority, so that franchise control was vested in a single individual"; and
- the prohibition of "cross-ownership," which was "by far the most controversial. At issue was the ownership of other sports businesses by NFL members. The League's 'traditional position' was that 'no person having an operating control of a franchise in the National Football League may acquire control of, directly or indirectly, any other team sports enterprise or business.'"[9]

Of course, Rozelle's cross ownership rule did not apply to those team owners who also owned racetracks since horse racing was not a team sport. Nevertheless, there were several owners in violation of the ownership rules. For instance, the Green Bay Packers were still a publicly held corporation. The Dallas Cowboys, New York Giants, and St. Louis Cardinals were owned by families with no single member owning a clear 51 percent majority interest; and the Sullivan family, the largest owners of the Boston Patriots, could not combine its interests for a clear majority. Bud Adams of the Houston Oilers, Bill Bidwill of the St. Louis Cardinals, minority owner Jack Kent Cooke of the Washington Redskins, George Halas of the Chicago Bears, Lamar Hunt of the

Kansas City Chiefs, and Art Rooney of the Pittsburgh Steelers—all had interests in other professional sports teams.

The NFL solved the dilemma by opting to exempt current owners from these rules and make them applicable only to future owners.

Meantime, in the Bahamas, Lou Chesler attempted but failed to purchase the stock of his partner Wallace Groves in Devco. In fact, Chesler's plan completely backfired, and he was bought out by Groves instead—with the blessing of Meyer Lansky.

In the wake of Chesler's ouster, according to Morris Mac Schwebel, Rosenbloom emerged as the second-largest individual stockholder in the Seven Arts film company. Only Schwebel owned more.

When Chesler left the Bahamas in 1964, so, too, did Mike McLaney, who then went to Las Vegas where he and his brother William operated the Carousel Club casino until 1966.[10] However, McLaney returned to the Bahamas later that year and announced that he was going to open another casino. Chesler, who was also forced to resign as the head of General Development Corporation in 1966, returned that same year to develop the Great Harbor Cay.

Among those attending the opening of Chesler's development were Sonny Werblin and Joe Namath of the New York Jets. Author Bernie Parrish reported that Edward Bennett Williams, the president of the Washington Redskins, had been "a frequent guest at Chesler's quaint little hideaway hotel in Jamaica, and the Redskins star quarterback, Sonny Jurgensen, spent two weeks at the Sunset Lodge Hotel and Beach Club on Montego Bay at host Lou Chesler's expense . . . [Cleveland Browns owner] Arthur Modell 'used to lose at blackjack to Chesler while courting one of Lou's daughters.' "[11]

Rosenbloom, who was rarely, if ever, mentioned in any news reports about his Bahamian gambling investments, was in the midst of getting a divorce from his first wife, Velma, in June 1966. The couple had had three children—Steve, Suzanne, and Daniel—all of whom were grown. Details of Carroll and Velma's divorce were sealed by court order, hiding the extent of Rosenbloom's personal wealth and his gambling interests in the Bahamas. Within a month, he was married again. This time the fifty-five-year-old Rosenbloom married thirty-eight-year-old Georgia Hayes. The wedding took place in London.

The divorce from Velma was a formality. Rosenbloom and Hayes had been living together since 1958. They later had two children of their own—Chip and Lucia.[12]

16 "The Quarterback"

AFTER THE AFL–NFL MERGER agreement, the joint league agreed to add two more teams to its roster: the New Orleans Saints in 1966 and the Cincinnati Bengals in 1967.

The Bengals were purchased by a group headed by longtime Cleveland Browns head coach Paul Brown, who was already a legend in professional football. Among the greatest coaches of all time, Brown had been fired in January 1963 by Art Modell over a dispute on how the team should be operated. A strict disciplinarian, Brown had become unpopular with some of the players, including fullback Jim Brown, who was enjoying his superstar status and was defiant of Brown's team rules. Modell fired Paul Brown in the midst of a Cleveland newspaper strike. "The announcement was timed to take advantage of this news blackout," Brown later wrote, "and Modell had organized a full-scale publicity force to back him up. He had hired out-of-work sportswriters from the struck newspapers, and they put out a pamphlet that was supposed to present all sides of the story. It was nothing but a thirty-two-page justification for Modell."[1]

The creation of the Saints was controversial because of its owner, twenty-seven-year-old John W. Mecom, Jr., a Houston businessman from an oil-rich Texas family. A close friend and neighbor of Bud Adams, the owner of the Houston Oilers, Mecom, along with twenty-one minority stockholders, paid $8.5 million for the franchise. His father, John Mecom, Sr., held a 15 percent interest in the team.

While in college at the University of Oklahoma, young

Mecom met his future wife, Katsy Mullendore, the sister of E. C. Mullendore III, one of the largest ranchers in the United States and the owner of Oklahoma's Cross Bell Ranch. Subsequent to their marriage and in the midst of his own financial difficulties, E.C. was later found shot between the eyes with a .38.

For help, Mullendore had turned to New Orleans Mafia boss Carlos Marcello and Leon Cohen, a convicted rapist and con man. Cohen and Mecom had been business associates. Cohen and his partner in United Family Life Insurance Company had written $22 million worth of insurance policies for members and associates of the Mecom family, as well as players on the Saints team.

"[T]he New Orleans Saints were scheduled to play the Falcons at Atlanta," according to author Jonathan Kwitny, "and the Mullendores and Mecoms decided to make a weekend of it, [culminating with] a lavish bash in Cohen's house honoring the owner of the Falcons [Rankin Smith] and the owner of the Saints and many of their acquaintances . . . Among them, according to law enforcement sources, was a New Orleans football fan named Carlos Marcello. Cohen kept the reputed Mafia boss's telephone number in his pocket secretary."[2]

The title to the Mullendore empire was later given to Mecom and his wife. The murder was never solved. The Mecoms cooperated fully with the police investigation and were under no suspicion.

However, Mecom Jr. had close ties with the New Orleans underworld. He was also heavily involved in horse racing and associated with the sons of ex-boxer and convicted bootlegger James Brocato, aka Diamond Jim Moran, who was a bodyguard for Senator Huey Long on the day he was murdered. Brocato, who died in 1958, had been deeply implicated with the New Orleans Mafia, particularly with Marcello. Brocato was also named with mobster Frank Costello in a scheme to embezzle $500,000 in state funds.

Brocato owned what became known as La Louisiane restaurant in the French Quarter. It was a popular meeting place for the city's top underworld figures, including Marcello's brothers, Sammy and Vincent Marcello, who headed the Marcello family's bookmaking operations. The restaurant was taken over by Brocato's four sons, three of whom had changed their names to Moran.

A former top executive with the New Orleans Saints says, "I

know Jimmy Moran [Jr.], and he had a restaurant in the Quarter that was sports-oriented. He had all the helmets on the wall. He knows many of the players, and the players know him. He's always been, with me and other people, an up-front, straight-out kind of guy, and I can respect that. He's helped some of our players here. He would give those who liked to do a little hunting and fishing, for example, a little direction in that respect."

Former FBI agent Aaron Kohn, who was managing director of the Metropolitan Crime Commission of New Orleans, told me, "La Louisiane was a hangout for Mecom and his players. Sammy Marcello, Carlos's youngest brother, who ran the city's layoff bookmaking activity, had a table where he sat by a telephone constantly. When the sons got into trouble with the financing of the restaurant, they turned to the Marcellos, who ended up taking over the restaurant."

The fourth son, Dr. Robert Brocato, who had not changed his name, became the Saints' dentist after Mecom purchased the team. Brocato had access to all the Saints' injury information. Known for his hot temper, Dr. Brocato was later charged with attempting to murder a New Orleans police officer who had ticketed his car for a parking violation. The district attorney, Jim Garrison, another close associate of Marcello, refused to prosecute. Garrison had once declared that there was "no evidence of organized crime" in New Orleans.

Speaking of Mecom's relationship with Marcello's associates, Aaron Kohn says, "It was an exposure to a criminal influence. That's what was wrong with hiring an organized-crime-connected dentist for the New Orleans Saints or when Mecom would bring his key players to La Louisiane to be met by the owners of the restaurant. Friends do favors for friends. That's a normal, and certainly not undesirable, quality. As a result, an NFL owner, coach, or player cannot tolerate the development of such friendships, especially when they are financial ones with people who have an intent to use it to their personal advantage and to the disadvantage of the integrity of sports, in this case professional football."

The five-feet-two Marcello, whose real name is Calogero Minacore, is one of the most notorious men in American history. Quite simply, he has wielded incredible control over Louisiana—its politicians, law-enforcement authorities, business leaders, and union officials—as well as in its neighboring states. He has been known to use the Ku Klux Klan as occasional enforcers.

Known as "the Quarterback" by many, Marcello, who became the Mafia boss in New Orleans in 1950 and then built himself a multibillion-dollar empire, has owned numerous politicians and has been immune from legal pressures by most state and local law-enforcement agencies. He was a student of Frank Costello, who came to Louisiana in 1934 at the invitation of Huey Long, whose son, U.S. Senator Russell Long of Louisiana, enjoyed the full support of Marcello and his organization during his political career.[3]

Born in Tunis, Africa, in 1910 and a grade school dropout, Marcello—who enjoyed describing himself as "a tomato salesman" before he became a "real estate investor"—robbed his first bank in 1929. It wasn't until four years later that he was charged with attempting to kill a New Orleans police officer and convicted for the robbery of a grocery store. He spent four years in Louisiana State Penitentiary and was released after he received a pardon from Louisiana governor O. K. Allen. In 1938, he pleaded guilty to possession of marijuana and served another ten months. During the 1940s and 1950s, he was operating a string of gambling houses throughout the South. Marcello, through his Nola Printing Company, was also the New Orleans distributor of the Continental Racing Wire under Cleveland Browns owner Mickey McBride.

Marcello and his partner and alter ego in Florida, Santos Trafficante, the boss of Tampa and the protégé of Meyer Lansky, were the principal narcotics traffickers in the southern United States and Latin America. When Cuba became a satellite nation of the American underworld, Marcello personally controlled one third of its narcotics trade while Trafficante was Lansky's peacekeeper in Havana's gambling and casino operations.

An associate of Marcello alleges that whether or not Mecom knew it, he had been selected by Marcello to buy the Saints. "There were a bunch of doctors who had a chance to own an NFL team," he alleges. "But they ended up not wanting it. They had already gone to Marcello and discussed possible financing with him. Carlos got ahold of Mecom's [people] to see if he was interested in owning the team, and he was. [There was a meeting] at Marcello's fishing camp. And then there was another meeting at Marcello's house on [Clifford] Drive in Metairie at about one in the morning. That's where they did the firming up of it. Mecom dealt with all the other people."

The associate claims that one of the middlemen in the arrangement between Marcello and Mecom was Lou Gale, the owner of a major construction firm in Houston, Mecom's hometown. Gale, the source alleges, was also one of the top layoff bookmakers in the Houston area and connected with a nationwide gambling syndicate operated by Gil Beckley, which was protected by Mafia figures Mike Coppola and Tony Salerno of New York.

There was a subsequent dispute over the location of the Saints' stadium, the Louisiana Superdome. Marcello's associate says, "They built it downtown, which was the worst thing they could've ever done. Carlos had offered to donate two hundred acres of land. He wanted the stadium out in Jefferson Parrish, on his property. He was hurt, really dumbfoundedly hurt, because they turned down the site. But Carlos was really proud of the fact that they got the football team there."

The source also alleges that Mecom was gambling on NFL games—and that Marcello was upset about it. "You know those Louisiana people, they love their ball teams," the source says.[4]

Aaron Kohn confirms that Marcello had offered to donate his land for the stadium site—in return for the multimillion-dollar parking concession. However, Kohn says that he had no knowledge of Mecom's alleged gambling or about Marcello's selecting Mecom for the team's ownership. "I thought Marcello was probably supporting Lou Roussel, Jr.," says Kohn. "There was a former FBI agent, who, when an NFL franchise for New Orleans developed, became the investigator to review the applications. He was viewed as the best FBI agent ever in the New Orleans office. One of the applicants was Roussel. He was the owner of banks, insurance companies, and politicians. He was a very wealthy man. When the FBI came to me for information about the people who had applied for the team, I was able to supply him with information that Roussel had corrupted judges, including two in our state supreme court. And he later admitted his personal and financial relationship with Marcello."

Numerous attempts to interview the Houston-based Mecom for this book were unsuccessful. However, Mecom has vehemently insisted that he had never knowingly done business with Marcello or his associates. Marcello is currently in Texarkana Federal Penitentiary.

17 Gil Beckley and the Layoff

ATTORNEY GENERAL ROBERT KENNEDY had wreaked havoc on the underworld, particularly the organized gambling syndicate. While eating mobsters for breakfast, Kennedy said in 1961, "It is quite evident that modern organized crime's commercial gambling operations are so completely intertwined with the nation's communications systems that denial of their use to the gambling fraternity would be a mortal blow to their operations."[1]

Prodded by Kennedy, Congress began to act. In September 1961, Senator John McClellan and his Permanent Subcommittee on Investigations conducted hearings into gambling and organized crime. Among those called to testify during the so-called family-sports stage of the investigation were Don Angelini and Bill Kaplan—both of whom were associated with the Chicago-based handicapping service Angel-Kaplan Sports News, Inc.

Prior to his testimony, old man Kaplan was asked with whom he was doing business. He replied, "Somebody might drop a ton of bricks on my head if I start talking about my customers." However, Kaplan did say that Angel-Kaplan serviced only thirty-six customers in Chicago, Montreal, Miami, and New York.

Angelini and Kaplan—along with two other associates, Sam Minkus, the owner of the Angel-Kaplan football betting card business, and Angel-Kaplan oddsmaker Frank "Lefty" Rosenthal—took the Fifth during their testimonies before the subcommittee. Rosenthal had stood accused at the hearings of fixing both basketball and football games.

At the time of the hearings, the Chicago Crime Commission stated in a confidential memorandum, "Kaplan is now about the age of 64 years and the firm employs three office clerks plus correspondents who attend college [and professional games] throughout the United States and who pass on information as to health and personal affairs of athletes. The publication is printed by a Minneapolis firm. As a sideline, Donald Angelini, alias Don Angel, sells insurance."

The subcommittee concluded that, even though the initial line on football and other sporting events was probably based upon honest estimates, the final line was regularly manipulated through "regular consultation" with the gambling syndicate's top layoff bookmakers.

As a result of the McClellan hearings, Attorney General Kennedy, with the support of the committee, had rammed legislation through Congress that supplemented an earlier law passed in the wake of the Kefauver hearings.

A top assistant to Kennedy told me, "By simply making the transmission of the betting line, wagers, and gambling paraphernalia across interstate borders illegal—as well as personal travel from state to state for the purpose of gambling—bookmakers had to operate completely underground. And the FBI now had jurisdiction in these cases. That was a big victory." Those violating the new antiracketeering acts faced a $10,000 fine and two years in prison.

Don Angelini told me that the new law seriously crippled his business. "The Angel-Kaplan sports service went out of business in 1968 when the government passed a law saying that the transmission of gambling information was illegal," he said. When I reminded him that the law was passed in 1961, not 1968, he replied, "Well, they may have passed that in 1961, but we went out of business in 1968."

Another bookmaker lamented, "Kennedy made it illegal to make a phone call."[2]

Later, Congress passed the Federal Sports Bribery Act of 1964.[3] New York Senator Kenneth Keating said during the debate over the legislation, "This bill would provide the authority our law-enforcement agencies need to prevent gamblers from corrupting college and professional sports. It would halt the contamination of sports by organized gambling syndicates by punishing any players or officials, as well as gamblers, who attempt to corrupt these games for personal gain. It would cover schemes to affect the point spread in a contest, as well as to throw the game entirely, and would apply to every case in which interstate facilities—such as the telephone or the mail—have been used to carry out the conspiracy."

Because of Kennedy's war on organized crime and gambling, bookmakers had to become increasingly creative in the operations of their businesses in order to continue making money and staying out of jail.

The basic economics of bookmaking dictate that every bookmaker will occasionally have to place a layoff wager with another bookmaker to create a more favorable balance in the bets he books and thereby reduce his risk. For example, if a Washington bookmaker has collected too much money on the Washington Redskins for an upcoming game against the San Francisco 49ers, he must either change the line in order to attract more balanced betting or lay off some of the money with a regional or national layoff bookmaker—so that he has as much money bet on the 49ers as he does on the Redskins.

"Arnold Rothstein created the first national layoff system," Ralph Salerno told me. "He had some bookmaker friends in Baltimore, with whom he'd opened up a racetrack. He also knew bookmakers in Boston and Philadelphia and elsewhere. And they were all sitting around talking, and one of them said, 'I had to turn down some heavy action because I was lopsided the other way. I didn't want to be loaded on one team over the other.' Rothstein told them, 'Schmucks, the next time something like that happens, you go through me. And I'll take some of your Boston excess, and I'll match it against your Philadelphia excess. And we'll all make money.' "

As initiated by Ed Curd, gamblers generally put up $11 to win $10 from bookmakers, who are simply interested in the 10 percent commission, or vigorish, they receive from the losing bets they book.[4] Without the layoff man, the local bookmaker could be forced out of business after a single, one-sided, big-betting game.

There are devices local bookmakers can utilize to maximize their winnings and minimize their losses. They can make individual adjustments in the line, knowing that most hometown fans will generally bet with the hometown team regardless of the spread. They can insist on winning all bets in which the spread between two teams ends in a tie. They can also circle games or take them off the boards, indicating dramatic changes in the conditions of particular games or outright suspicions of unnatural money showing up. When games are circled or taken off the boards, bookmakers can limit or completely stop accepting money on them.

The major regional and national layoff bookmakers have long been controlled and financed by the Mafia. In the 1960s, the biggest layoff bookmaker in the United States was Gilbert Lee "the Brain" Beckley, who was also called to testify before the McClellan Committee in 1961 and took the Fifth twenty-five times. "He had accounts with just about every significant bookmaker in every significant city and in every little hamlet throughout the United States—approximately a hundred and twenty of these accounts," says Brian Gettings, a former U.S. attorney who prosecuted Beckley. "He might move or take a half a million dollars in bets from just one of these gamblers a week."

Born in 1912 in New Orleans, Beckley was raised by foster parents. "He was extremely sensitive about the fact that he was a bastard," one of his top associates told me. "He was adopted out of an orphanage. But he later found his mother and got to know her." Beckley's unhappy childhood was a constant topic of conversation when the bookmaker spoke to his closest friends. Characteristically, several say, he would often go into deep depressions over his mother; he would weep openly and uncontrollably.

Beckley moved to St. Louis after he dropped out of high school and began to lay off bets on horse races for Louis "Murph" Calcatera, a St. Louis mobster. He then became a protégé of New York's Frank Erickson, who was rendered ineffective after his bouts with the Kefauver Committee and his two-year imprisonment.[5]

Curd, who was one of Beckley's partners in Kentucky and one of the top oddsmakers in the country, told me, "I did a lot of business with Frank Erickson. But he was strictly a bookmaker. Erickson didn't have an opinion on the [oddsmaking of] ball games.

"Beckley was like Erickson. He operated on other people's opinions. There was a long period that he relied on what I was doing. Beckley didn't know if a game should be six or twenty points. He wasn't a pricemaker. He was a bookmaker who got some prices. And he was a good businessman."

Gene Nolan, another Beckley associate, told me, "Gil worked

with the oddsmakers. He didn't fix the line on all games, just occasional ones that he wanted, that he was interested in, or the ones he had [his clients] on. And he would set the line in such a way that he would entice the bettors to bet on a certain ball team. Now, once in a while, when he fouled up or couldn't produce, he found out about it ahead of time. Say, he fixed the line at three, and it ended up going to four, four and a half, then his deal fell off. Then he'd try to recoup. Now Gil would go with the team that was giving the points, instead of the team that was taking them. Of course, his answer to the changing of the line was that 'the money did it.' Well, sure, but it was *his* money that did it."

Beckley initiated the underworld's gambling operations in the Midwest, eventually setting up his layoff headquarters in the Newport/Covington region of Kentucky after a brief stay in Indianapolis.[6] In Newport, one of Beckley's top associates, Tito Carinci—a onetime football star at Cincinnati's Xavier University—was later implicated in the frame-up of Newport's reform sheriff candidate George Ratterman, who was drugged by syndicate figures and photographed in bed with a known prostitute in 1961. Ratterman had been a pro quarterback with, among other teams, the Cleveland Browns. With the help of Attorney General Kennedy, Ratterman was elected and cleaned up the town.

Beckley also became active in the mob's casino operations in pre-Castro Cuba. He was directed, supported, and protected in Cuba, as well as in Newport, by Genovese crime family capo Michael "Trigger Mike" Coppola, who managed the New York underworld's interests in Cuba and south Florida.[7] According to federal investigators, Beckley split his winnings fifty-fifty with Coppola and the Genovese group.[8]

When Castro assumed power, Beckley was expelled from Cuba and moved to Canada. While he worked in Montreal, he was protected by the syndicate of "French Connection" heroin traffickers, Antonio d'Agostino and his partners, Vinnie and Pepe Cotroni.[9] However, the Royal Canadian Mounted Police (RCMP) busted up the operation.

Beckley then moved to Miami and picked up a junior partner, Marty Sklaroff. Beckley moved into a condominium in Miami's plush, Teamsters-pension-fund-built Blair House, where Jimmy Hoffa also maintained his Florida residence.

No fewer than ten people would regularly give Beckley $25,000 or more a week to bet for them. According to his associates, Baltimore Colts owner Carroll Rosenbloom and Dallas Cowboys owner Clint Murchison were among his biggest clients. Beckley had been introduced to Rosenbloom by Lou Chesler. Rosenbloom and Chesler had placed their million-dollar bet on the 1958 NFL championship game through Beckley.

"Rosenbloom's numbers were in the hundreds of thousands of dollars," says another former Beckley associate. "Murchison was very discreet. There was a lot of action from him, too. He bet big, and, sometimes, one of his partners would call and bet for him."

The associate alleged that Art Modell of the Cleveland Browns even came to them to bet. "Modell was not discreet. He didn't give a shit, and I don't think he gives a shit today. Everybody in the country knows he's a bettor."

Detroit gambler Donald Dawson told me, "Most of the owners played [bet on games]. The NFL owners are in there because they're competitive. They like sports. And everyone gambles on sports."

Marty Kane, who was indicted and convicted with Beckley for bookmaking, said that when Beckley bet on someone's behalf Beckley would make a great deal of money. "Say, one of the clients would call Gil and say, 'What do you see on the Miami-Cleveland game?' And Gil would say, 'I see five [points].' The client would say, 'I want to lay the five for thirty thousand dollars.' So Gil would start calling bookmakers all over the country, and he'd start to bet for the client. He might go to one bookmaker and find that game for four. He would move fifteen thousand dollars at four. The client would stand off his bet, and Gil would pick up whatever money he moved on four. That would belong to him.

"It was just a matter of finding enough bookmakers around the country where he could get different prices. Really, Gil was more like a broker than a bookmaker. I saw him in situations where he wouldn't actually be making the bet, but he actually acted as somebody's beard."

By betting heavily on one team, Beckley was able to manipulate the point spread and create a differential as much as six points. He would then bet on the other team with another bookmaker at a more favorable spread. Beckley hoped to "catch a middle"; that is, he hoped that the final score would come down the middle, so that he would win both bets.

"Let's say a team received one and a half [points]," Beckley's associate explains. "He loved those one and a half games. This was his big money because he ended up playing the middle. Let's say Gil had two hundred thousand dollars from the New England area, say, from Raymond Patriarca [the boss of the New England Mafia] or his man. Patriarca would call Gil and say, 'I got two hundred thousand dollars minus one and a half on Washington.' So Gil would say, 'I'll get right back with you.' Then he'd call San Francisco or some other end of the country, and say, 'I can get you a half a point.' Then he would try to sell that new line.

"So Gil would have at least a point. Now this was great when the Los Angeles Rams played a New York team. At both ends of the country, the bookmakers would be betting in opposite ways. So Gil would take one and a half from the guy who just laid it off to him, to laying a half a point the other way, or more if he could get it. Gil didn't care who won, plus he got the ten percent on the one who lost. Middling. He sometimes got up to two and three points, particularly if the spread was big, like fourteen. He got a lot of the big spreads there. When he laid that line, he was forcing people to bet against the winner.

"But Gil didn't rip off the smaller bookmakers. He was accepting their action, because they were loaded up. They got to balance their books with the layoff to Gil and keep their ten percent on the losers."

Speaking of "catching a middle," another bookmaker says, "Bookmakers cannot afford to move a game two or three points. They're apt to get middled when they go across a key number. When you open a game at six, and you go to seven and a half, you're only moving it a point and a half, but you're moving it across a key number, which is seven, a touchdown and an extra point. It's the same as when you open a game at two, and then move it to three and a half. That's across a key number, three, a field goal. When we're getting these numbers, a bookmaker will not move from one side of a touchdown and field goal to the other unless he is very financially sound on the game."

Bookmakers view the key betting numbers as: three, six, seven, and ten. These numbers hold the greatest risk and effect for them and their businesses.

To provide some idea of the national scope of Beckley's layoff operation, another member of Beckley's bookmaking network, Elmer Dudley of Atlanta, says, "I had a pool of fifteen people, and

I could get together fifty thousand to seventy thousand dollars in bets [on a single game]. You multiply that by sixteen cities, and it adds up to a lot of money."

According to both underworld and government sources, Beckley often found "cooperative" players to help secure his wagers. They provided him with good inside information or even shaved points and fixed games. Other personnel who were helpful to him included team owners, coaches, and trainers, as well as their families and even the janitors in the locker rooms. Those who cooperated were well paid.

When I asked Gene Nolan whether Beckley was actively fixing games, Nolan replied, "He wouldn't tell me because I was betting too much. But, hell, I'm not blind. I don't know that he did the fix as much as he just found out which way the players were going to go."

On January 8, 1966, Beckley's apartment in Miami Beach was raided by federal agents. They seized his copy of *Bartlett's Familiar Quotations* which was filled with the coded names of some of the most prominent figures in business, entertainment, labor, politics, and sports. Government investigators believed that some of the people whose names were in the book had been Beckley's clients. Among those named were gamblers Frank Erickson and Frank "Lefty" Rosenthal; political fixer Bobby Baker; Carroll Rosenbloom's business partner Lou Chesler; casino operator Wilbur Clark; former boxer Billy Conn; Teamsters boss Jimmy Hoffa; the owner of the San Diego Chargers, Barron Hilton; entertainer and onetime Los Angeles Rams partner Bob Hope; Green Bay Packers star Paul Hornung; oil tycoon H. L. Hunt, Jr.; Florida state senator Richard Fincher; entertainer Ted Lewis; former heavyweight boxing champion Rocky Marciano; actor George Raft; restaurateurs Toots Shor and Sam "Radio" Winer, who was also a bookmaker; entertainer Frank Sinatra; and composer Jules Styne.

"The book itself was not a gambling book," says Brian Gettings, who was the chief prosecutor in the Beckley case. "But by matching the book with the gambling records, we were able to show that the gambling records were accounts for many, many of the people who were in the book. I don't know why [Beckley] did this, but there were people who were listed in the book who there were no accounts for. Why he put them in there, I don't know. Beckley never explained it."

Gene Nolan told me, "When the government got that address book, they found out that Gil kept everybody he ever met in that book—even if there wasn't anything to it. They weren't all just his clients. Some of them were people he just knew."

Marty Kane agrees with Nolan, "Gil was a very complex man. His greatest asset was his charm. He was the most charming man I've ever met. He had more legitimate people who loved him and loved to be around him. He was self-educated. If he had had the opportunity to go to school, he would have ended up a respected businessman."

Beckley's records showed that he had handled more than $250,000 on the day of the federal raid, which came the week after the NFL and AFL championship games were played. Of that sum, $129,000 was profit. Had the raid occurred a week earlier, the haul would have been considerably more.[10]

Significantly, the same year as the raid, Beckley was spotted at the Kentucky Derby as the guest of Paul Hornung, a native of Louisville and in his final year with the Green Bay Packers. Just two years earlier, Hornung's suspension for his association with a West Coast gambler and his own gambling activities had been lifted. "I won't bet, you know that," Hornung told *The Miami Herald.* "I just met him [Beckley] a few times . . . and I took care of his wife when they came up to the [Kentucky] Derby. It was all personal—no business."

Another associate of Beckley's told me, "Paul Hornung and Gil Beckley were good friends. I went to dinner with them one time. Paul was there with twenty-nine gamblers."

Marty Kane says, "Beckley and Hornung were drinking buddies, and they were friends. All the time I knew Gil, we never, ever thought anything strange was going on with a Green Bay game. I think Hornung has gotten a bad rap. He was a fifty-dollar bettor who mostly bet on other people's games." Kane added that he believed that Hornung had been betting for his teammates at Green Bay and had taken the fall for all of them.

Hornung repeatedly refused to be interviewed for this book.

According to several of Beckley's associates, another professional football player with whom the bookmaker was allegedly acquainted was the legendary quarterback/placekicker George Blanda, the number one leading scorer in the history of professional football.[11] A twenty-six-year veteran of several teams—the Chicago Bears, Baltimore Colts, Houston Oilers, and Oakland

Raiders—Blanda angrily told me during a telephone interview, "I'm not going to answer any of your questions when you talk about gambling. I'm not going to be involved pro or con in anything that you might suggest about gambling, period."

When I specifically asked Blanda whether he knew Beckley, the NFL great replied, "You don't have to ask me anything, because I'm not answering. I'm sorry you called." Blanda then hung up.

Beckley was indicted by a Miami grand jury in May 1966, and two days after that he was arrested for violating federal gambling laws. He was later found guilty. Also indicted and convicted were Martin Sklaroff and Marty Kane.

Five months after the release of Beckley's coded address book, Barron Hilton, who was among those listed, sold 70 percent of his ownership in the San Diego Chargers to a twenty-one-man syndicate headed by Eugene Victor Klein, a former used car salesman, for $10 million. Hilton, who became the chief executive officer of Hilton Hotels that year, retained 30 percent of the team. It is not known whether the NFL forced Hilton to give up control of the team because of his alleged association with Beckley.

The new managing general partner, forty-five-year-old, six-feet-five Eugene Klein was a native of the Bronx, who, like Hilton, had dropped out of college after the Japanese attacked Pearl Harbor. He began as an aviation cadet in the ATC—the Air Transport Command, which Klein likes to call the Army of Terrified Civilians—during World War II. He retired from the Army Air Force as a captain in 1946 after flying non-combat missions over India, Africa, China, and the South Pacific.

Klein returned from the war with $2,000 to establish an automobile dealership. In a unique marketing ploy, Klein sold cars by the pound, advertising them as "cheaper than hamburger." By 1959, he had become the first distributor of Volvos in the United States. He later purchased a large amount of stock in National Theatres & Television, Inc., formerly a subsidiary of Twentieth Century-Fox.

In 1961, National Theatres became the National General Corporation. Klein told me, "It was a company whose basic purpose was to enhance the value of the stock and to make money. We ended up making a lot of money. We had the second-largest theater chain in the country. We produced motion pictures and distributed motion pictures for CBS and ourselves."

National General became one of America's first conglomerates, and it attracted considerable controversy. It was fined by the state of New York's insurance department for questionable business practices. *Business Week* wrote that its deals "smacked more of 'cronyism and self-aggrandizement,' as one broker puts it, than of real interest in the stockholders." Klein still denies those charges and says, "Who responds to bullshit?"

At the time of his 1966 purchase of the Chargers, Klein also had ties to the same major organized-crime figure as Hilton had: attorney Sidney Korshak.

Klein told me, "I've known Sidney Korshak for twenty, twenty-five years. I was introduced to him by my late, great friend Gene Wyman [a powerful Los Angeles attorney and the head of California's Democratic party]. He and I were as close as brothers. I hired Sidney Korshak for National General as a labor negotiator. He was terrific. He got things done. I paid him a retainer, fifty thousand dollars a year. Whenever we had any labor problems, I picked up the phone and called Sidney. Whatever he did, it was done."

When I asked Klein whether Korshak had done any work for the Chargers, Klein replied, "Yeah. At the stadium, there was a labor problem with the ushers. That was the only time I used Sidney [with the Chargers], and he handled that problem, too."

18 Bill Hundley and NFL Security

INCREDIBLY ENOUGH, GIL BECKLEY'S conviction was bad news for some top NFL officials. In fact, they did everything they could to keep him out of jail. The reason? Beckley had also been working for the NFL.

As the prelude to Beckley's work with the league, the highly respected NFL Security director Jim Hamilton had died in 1966 after a long illness. Following a lengthy search for his successor, he was replaced by William G. Hundley, another man of impeccable credentials and reputation.

Hundley grew up in the Flatbush section of Brooklyn. After high school, he enlisted in the Army and was decorated with a Bronze Star for heroism during World War II. A 1950 graduate of Fordham Law School, Hundley was recruited by the Justice Department in 1951. Soon after, in the wake of the Kefauver Committee hearings, he was prosecuting alleged Communists for alleged Smith Act violations.

Until September 1966, Hundley had been the head of the Organized Crime and Racketeering Section in the Justice Department. Hundley was the attorney who "handled" Joe Valachi, climaxed by the mobster-turned-informant's sensational televised testimony before the Senate's Permanent Subcommittee on Investigations in the fall of 1963. Kennedy had described Valachi's testimony as "the biggest intelligence breakthrough in organized crime yet in the United States."

When he resigned from the Justice Department in 1966,

Hundley went into private practice. With the death of Jim Hamilton, Rozelle was searching for a replacement. The commissioner then turned to Hundley, and the NFL became his first major client.

"They brought Hundley in for two reasons," Ralph Salerno told me. "One, they needed a replacement for Hamilton. Two, the NFL already had high-priced attorneys, but they needed an attorney with some good Justice Department friends and contacts. The NFL and the AFL were going through a merger, and they didn't want to run afoul of the federal antitrust laws."

On March 8, 1967, the same month as Beckley's federal conviction in Miami, William Cahn, a Nassau County, New York, prosecutor, met privately with Hundley. A few weeks earlier, Cahn had indicted Beckley, Marty Sklaroff, Gene Nolan, and nineteen others. The indictments followed a massive investigation of a $100-million-a-year bookmaking operation in the New York metropolitan area.

The probe began after several unnamed NFL players were found to be living in a Nassau County apartment house in which two known bookmakers also lived. Cahn received wiretap authorizations against the bookmakers and discovered that they had links to gambling syndicates in Canada, Las Vegas, Miami, New Orleans, and on the West Coast. Other top sports figures had been implicated in the bookmaking operation, but none of them was named in the indictment. Cahn said that they had been part of an "information network" for bookmakers.

With Hundley, Cahn wanted to discuss "reports that certain points in at least nineteen [professional football] games . . . were rigged." Pete Rozelle had stated in November 1966 that Hundley "was conducting a general investigation of continuing rumors in the American Football League." Cahn said that he had discovered that Beckley had "picked nineteen out of twenty winners" and had actually picked the point spreads of each winner.

Cahn explained to Hundley that he had been told "bookies took four AFL games 'off the boards' last season, indicating gamblers were suspicious of the games." He had also uncovered evidence that an unnamed, well-known college coach had been working in cooperation with the gamblers and had won $20,000 betting on a single game. "As a result," Cahn told reporters after the indictments, "certain layoff bets were completely switched by all the bookmakers with orders to go heavily on the team backed by this coach." The line had jumped from fourteen to eighteen points after the coach had made his bet.[1]

In the end, Beckley and his coconspirators were permitted to plead guilty to reduced charges—because the courts had begun to question the manner in which intelligence on the case was collected; the wiretaps could not be used as evidence in court.

However, Beckley's indictment and guilty plea had little impact on Beckley or on the NFL's relationship with the bookmaker. Hundley assured Cahn that he had the Beckley situation under control.

Salerno says, "Beckley had gone to Hundley and said, 'I know who you are, and you know who I am. While you were with the Department of Justice, you were on one side of the fence, and I was on the other. And I would never dream of approaching you about anything. But you no longer work for the Justice Department. You now work for the National Football League. And that puts you and me on the same side of the fence. You and me are on the same team.' And Hundley said, 'What the hell are you talking about? I'm not on your team!' And Beckley said, 'Yes, you are—because you want what I want: honest National Football League games.'

"Hundley's interest was to protect the integrity of the game; Beckley wanted to protect the integrity of the bets he booked and the volume of his business. Beckley told Hundley, 'I will be your chief informant, because what I do all week long is exchange bets, take bets, and layoff bets with bookmakers in every NFL city. These guys are sharp, and they know what's going on. And the deal we will have is that instead of just laying bets with me, these smart cookies will tell me everything they hear—a whisper, a rumor, and everything else. And I will convey that to you.'

"That's why, when he was convicted, Beckley went to Hundley and said, 'Look, I've been helpful. I called you and told you what was going on. All I want you to do is tell the judge that I, Gil Beckley, did more to keep the National Football League honest than any human being alive.' And they had that deal."

Marty Kane, who was indicted with Beckley in Miami on the federal bookmaking charges, told me that he was aware of Beckley's relationship with Hundley and the NFL. "Gil was living in New York at the time," Kane says. "Gil would call me on either

Sunday night or Monday morning and asked me what the NFL line was. And I would give it to him. He wanted to know at what price these games opened, at what price they closed, and if there were any unusual moves, and what the reasons for them were. He knew that I would know whether a player was out—which would cause the line to go from three to six.

"Gil told me that he was doing this for Bill Hundley. The reason Gil did this was that he thought Hundley might be able to help us in our case."

In an extraordinary letter on NFL stationery and dated April 20, 1967—sent on Beckley's behalf prior to his sentencing in Miami—Hundley wrote to a federal probation official: "Shortly after I left the Justice Department to join the National Football League, I was contacted by Gil Beckley, who said he knew me by reputation in Justice . . . He offered, on a confidential basis, to furnish any information that came into his possession concerning the possibility of endeavors to corrupt professional football players, [or to] seek unauthorized information about players' conditions, and [to] supply any other information that might reflect adversely on the integrity of professional football.

"During the season, he was most helpful in apprising us of any unusual fluctuations in the betting odds and assisting us in ensuring the integrity of professional football from the influence of undesirable elements."

Hundley added that Beckley had not asked the NFL for any assistance "in connection with his present difficulties with the government."

On April 17, 1967, just three days before Hundley wrote his letter on Beckley's behalf, the Justice Department's Organized Crime and Racketeering Section, which Hundley had just left,[2] wrote an internal report that stated that "Beckley was deeply entrenched with La Cosa Nostra [LCN] elements" and had become "involved with Michael Coppola, a/k/a 'Trigger Mike'—identified by [federal witness] Joseph Valachi . . . as a 'capo regime' of the Vito Genovese family of LCN . . . Trigger Mike was receiving approximately 50% of the profit on Beckley's wagering operation. Trigger Mike died just last year and with his demise Anthony Salerno, a/k/a 'Fat Tony,' took his place as the Mafia's representative."[3]

Hundley was aware of the Justice Department's view of the bookmaker. But, despite Hundley's surprising confidence in

Beckley, which was shared by NFL commissioner Rozelle, the bookmaker received the maximum sentence for his federal bookmaking conviction in Miami. C. L. Williams, Beckley's probation officer, to whom Hundley had sent his letter on April 20, told U.S. District Judge Theodore Cabot of Miami that Beckley should be sentenced to the maximum eight years in prison. In spite of Hundley's letter, Williams wrote that Beckley was "the number one figure in nationwide gambling . . . involved with the Cosa Nostra, and [paid] tribute to that organization . . . The sentencing of Gilbert Lee Beckley would deal a severe blow to organized illegal gambling in the United States."[4]

Beckley appealed and moved his operations from Miami to New York City and then to Atlanta while the federal government pressured him to talk.

Hundley defends the NFL's relationship with Beckley. "Beckley was one of the many contacts in the bookmaking field who used to give us information about point-spread fluctuations, suspicions, and rumors," Hundley told me. "We took his information. We knew who we were dealing with and judged what he told us accordingly." Hundley added that Beckley was never paid by the NFL for anything he did.

Sources inside and outside the NFL say that Beckley was consulted in several NFL Security investigations:

• Just after Hundley became NFL Security chief, an FBI agent in Detroit received information from a Detroit mobster that the second 1966 game between the Chicago Bears and the San Francisco 49ers in Chicago had been fixed for the 49ers. Knowing that the Bears and the 49ers had played to a 30–30 tie in their first game earlier in the season, FBI agents monitored the second game that was played in San Francisco. This time, the 49ers demolished the Bears, 41–14. The 49ers, who were 6–6–2 that year, had also defeated the Detroit Lions in Detroit by the same score later that season.

The FBI reported the matter to the NFL, which approached Beckley. Beckley claimed to know nothing about the game. Without additional evidence, the investigation was dropped.

• Beckley had worked with the NFL on an investigation of "the relationship between a star American Football League quarterback and two bookies, Carmello Coco and Philip Cali of Boston. The inquiries were stepped up after the player's teammates were overheard in the locker room angrily accusing him of 'throwing' the game they had just lost."[5]

• Another investigation involving Beckley's information was of Boston Patriots quarterback, Vito "Babe" Parilli, a former all-American from the University of Kentucky. Parilli and several of his teammates were known to be patronizing Arthur's Farm, a Revere, Massachusetts, bar owned and operated by a convicted gambler. Law-enforcement officials claimed that the bar was a hangout for underworld figures and had linked the Patriots quarterback to Boston mobster Henry Tameleo, a top capo under New England's Mafia head, Raymond Patriarca.[6] Parilli was polygraphed by the NFL, but the results were not made public.

• Beckley was also consulted after several games of two teams—the Kansas City Chiefs and the Washington Redskins—were taken off the board by oddsmakers in Las Vegas and New York in 1967 and 1968.

Washington attorney Edward Bennett Williams had been among those responsible for the selection of Bill Hundley, a close friend of Williams, as NFL Security chief. After Hamilton's death in 1966, Williams, the president and a minority owner of the Redskins, suggested to Rozelle that Hundley be Hamilton's replacement.

Williams had bought 5 percent of the Redskins in 1962 and was credited with finally desegregating the team later that year after obtaining running back Bobby Mitchell in a trade with the Cleveland Browns. Williams was named club president by team owner George Marshall, a longtime client, in 1966.[7]

The senior partner in the powerful Washington, D.C., Williams & Connolly law firm and a major player in the Democratic National Committee, Williams was counsel to the Teamsters Union and had personally represented Jimmy Hoffa in 1957 during the government's unsuccessful attempt to prosecute him on bribery charges. He had also handled important legal cases for Frank Costello, Lou Chesler, Senator Joseph McCarthy, sports oddsmaker Bobby Martin, political fixer Bobby Baker, and former Teamsters president Dave Beck.[8]

Born in Connecticut in 1920 and educated at Holy Cross, Williams served in the Army Air Force in World War II and was the sole survivor of a B-17 crash. Known for his loyalty to his friends, Williams was called by Robert Maheu, who later became the liaison between the CIA and the Mafia in the Castro-assassination plots, when Maheu needed a hotel reservation while he was in Las Vegas to serve a subpoena in 1958. Williams and Maheu had gone to college together, and they served on Holy Cross's debating team.

To accommodate Maheu in Las Vegas, Williams promptly introduced him to Chicago mobster Johnny Rosselli, whom Maheu later enlisted for the CIA to serve as its conduit to the Mafia in the Castro plots. As a favor to Williams, Rosselli booked Maheu into the El Rancho Vegas, which was owned by Beldon Katleman—the man Maheu had come to subpoena and to whom Carroll Rosenbloom had once lost a reported $25,000 in a gin game.

"I had a quick decision to make," Maheu told me during a 1978 interview. "Was I going to be a son of a bitch and serve the subpoena? Or was I going to go back home and explain what happened? To me, it wasn't a big decision. There was no way in the world that I was going to compromise my friendship with Ed Williams, and the man I had just met, Johnny Rosselli, under those circumstances."

Williams gave loyalty to those he trusted—and expected it in return.

In September 1967, after two games played by the Washington Redskins were taken off the boards in New York, the Internal Revenue Service launched "National 125 Baltimore," the reference number for an investigation into gambling—mainly football gambling—in the Washington, D.C., area. The targets of the investigation were several of Beckley's D.C.-based associates, including D.C. crime boss Joseph "the Possum" Nesline, his top D.C. lieutenant, Eugene Corsi, and local bookmakers Richard McCaleb and David McGowan. All were "engaged in conducting a football pool wagering activity and accepting sports wagers over the telephone," according to an IRS memorandum. Nesline had been acquitted of federal gambling violations just the previous year.

A confidential D.C. police report described Nesline as "an internationally known organized crime figure who is affiliated with several infamous syndicate members, including Charles 'The Blade' Tourine and Meyer Lansky . . . Nesline can be characterized as a major force behind illicit gambling activity in the Washington Metropolitan Area with ties to virtually all of the city's major gambling figures." Nesline had also been active in Cuba during its pre-Castro days and worked at the mob-controlled Tropicana, along with Santos Trafficante.

About the same time, an IRS undercover agent reported that Vince Promuto, a veteran Washington Redskins guard and the team's captain, was a friend of McCaleb and was suspected of gambling on sporting events. Promuto was also a close friend and former teammate of Rick Casares of the Chicago Bears, who had been investigated and cleared of gambling charges by the NFL in 1962. Casares played for the Redskins in 1965.

The U.S. attorney in Alexandria, Virginia, convened a federal grand jury on May 7, 1968, after the houses and offices of several of its targets had been raided. Thirty-nine witnesses were called to testify. In addition to several local bar and restaurant owners and a television sports reporter, they included former Washington Redskins quarterback Ralph Guglielmi and tackle Fran O'Brien (then a member of the Pittsburgh Steelers). Informants had characterized O'Brien as "a large gambler," which was more of a reference to the size of his bets than the broadness of his shoulders.

A second set of subpoenas was to be served on Promuto and no fewer than five other NFL players, including Redskins quarterback Sonny Jurgensen and defensive tackle Andy Stynchula. However, none of the subpoenas was executed. According to a classified Senate subcommittee report, an IRS investigator involved in the probe reported that "the subpoenas were never served because his superiors were concerned about the involvement of professional football players and the publicity [they] might trigger."

One of the IRS agents familiar with the probe told my associate, William Scott Malone, "The procedure in federal grand juries is that the praecipes are issued—which is the order for the clerk to draw up the subpoenas to have these people before the grand jury. Between the time we had the praecipes issued and when we walked into the clerk's office for the subpoenas, we were told to turn in the praecipes. The subpoenas would not be issued. We were not told why."

The Senate report concluded, "The agent was ordered to stop his investigation. The IRS agent said he believed that the Department of Justice had limited the scope of the investigation." Another agent involved is even more succinct. "We were had," he says. "It was fixed. Absolutely, the case was fixed."

But federal agents had already reported the IRS intelligence data on Promuto to the NFL, and he had been questioned by NFL Security. Promuto admitted knowing bookmaker McCaleb but denied placing bets through either McCaleb or his partner, McGowan.

Promuto told me that he was friendly with McCaleb, whom he had met through his wife's family, but repeated that he had not gambled with him or anyone else. He also denied having anything to do with McGowan. "I made it a point not to have dinner with the guy. And I never went out socially with him. He was McCaleb's friend. I saw him maybe five times in my life, when he was with McCaleb—and just to say hello. That was the extent of it.

"The reason I would see them was Fran O'Brien, who was the best man in my wedding. He had a restaurant, and I would go down to see him. And in that restaurant there were people they called prostitutes, gamblers, and this and that. But my objective for going down there was seeing Fran O'Brien, whom I had played next to for six or seven years.

"If I knew anyone who was gambling while I was playing, I wouldn't tell you. On the other hand, if I thought somebody was gambling—because I was captain of the Redskins—I would have been very pissed at them. The same thing goes for throwing a game. After years of playing with injured shoulders and two knee operations, I wanted to win. If I'd heard that someone was betting, shaving points, I wouldn't have stood for it. But I would never be a snitch."

Sonny Jurgensen's name had originally come up in the investigation after Jean Bates, an assistant television producer in New York and McCaleb's girlfriend, told federal agents that she "was present on more than one occasion when Sonny settled with McCaleb for the bets that Sonny was bringing in from the Redskins players." Federal agents confronted the star quarterback with this information during a meeting with him in Wilmington, North Carolina, Jurgensen's hometown. Jurgensen denied any wrongdoing.

Jurgensen told me that he had been informed about the gambling probe before the grand jury was convened. "When NFL Security told me what was going on," he says, "the government had already checked my car and my apartment, and they had come up empty. I said, 'Hey, I'd be willing to take a polygraph test any time you want.' I took the test and passed. In other words, in no way was I involved in gambling . . . What it amounted to was that some girl [Bates] had said something: that I had something to do with this gambler. That I was either running or collecting. The talk was that a big red-headed guy was collecting money for Ritchie McCaleb. I knew who that was, but it wasn't up to me to tell them [the IRS] who he was. I knew the guy's name. He was a bartender, and he worked with Ritchie."

On May 3, 1968, Hundley and his former subordinate at Justice, Robert D. Peloquin,[9] then Hundley's partner with NFL Security, sent Rozelle a confidential memorandum about the Redskins matter. The memorandum was signed by Peloquin and included in the confidential Senate report.

Peloquin wrote that he had learned that the grand-jury investigation was going to begin in four days and would primarily concentrate on McCaleb and McGowan, whose houses had been raided by IRS agents in early January. He added that both gamblers were represented by Washington attorney Edward Bennett Williams, then president of the Washington Redskins. According to Peloquin, Williams dropped the case "when he learned of the potential conflict in his interests."

Replacing Williams as counsel was Plato Cacheris, a former chief assistant U.S. attorney in Virginia, who later became Hundley's law partner. Peloquin wrote that Cacheris "will do his best not to embarrass the league."

Peloquin added that "potential witnesses with whom we would have concern are . . ." and then he listed the names of six players, including Promuto and Jurgensen. Promuto and several of the Redskins were also represented by Cacheris during the grand-jury investigation.[10]

Subsequently, Peloquin and Hundley met with Henry Petersen, Hundley's successor as the chief of the Justice Department's Organized Crime and Racketeering Section, who assured them "that no NFL players would be called before the grand jury without [the NFL] being advised beforehand," according to the Senate report. Petersen became an associate in Hundley & Cacheris when he left government service.

Hundley told me that he and Peloquin had simply gone to Petersen to find out whether anyone involved in professional football was a target of the grand-jury investigation. "I told him that if the department needed anything, I would supply it. If they needed information from anyone, I would deliver them."

The NFL, IRS, and the Justice Department investigations stopped dead right there.

"What we've got here," another IRS agent who was also involved in the NFL gambling probe says, "are connections among the Cosa Nostra, the federal government, the big attorneys in the D.C. area, sports figures, and the television news media. And it's still going on. We were getting too close to the people at the top. Nesline was being protected by people within the Justice Department."

Brian Gettings, the former U.S. attorney who prosecuted Beckley, confirms that NFL Security intervened with the U.S. attorney in Alexandria on behalf of the Redskins players and "prevailed upon the prosecutor not to subject them to the embarrassment of the grand-jury process."

"I was convinced that none of the Redskins players was involved in gambling," Hundley told me. "That has been my very firm conviction."

McCaleb, McGowan, and Corsi were convicted on conspiracy and racketeering charges and sentenced to prison. Neither Nesline nor any of the Redskins players was charged.

19 Seven Arts, Bobby Baker, and Mary Carter

IN JUNE 1967, SEVEN Arts bought the forty-four-year-old Warner Brothers studios in Hollywood in an $84-million-cash-and-stock deal. Eliot Hyman—Lou Chesler's onetime partner in Associated Artists, which had purchased Warner's film library in 1956—was selected as the chairman of the board of Warner Brothers-Seven Arts.

Carroll Rosenbloom remained the second-largest individual stockholder in the newly merged company, still behind attorney Morris Mac Schwebel. The fortunes of both men increased considerably.

Within a year of the Seven Arts takeover, Gene Klein, the owner of the San Diego Chargers, attempted to buy the newly merged company through his National General Corporation. But he was thwarted by the federal government when threatened with an antitrust action.

Klein told me, "When I couldn't get it, I helped Steven Ross get it."[1]

Steven Ross was the owner of the National Kinney corporation, a funeral parlor, parking lot, and cleaning services company, which purchased Warner Brothers-Seven Arts for $400 million in 1969.[2] Ross had taken over his father-in-law's New York funeral parlor business and then merged with Kinney Systems, the city's largest parking lot company, in 1962. Ross then consolidated both companies under National Kinney and sold public stock.

Schwebel told me that he was responsible for making the initial arrangement with Ross, after being introduced to him through New York Giants head coach Allie Sherman.

Kinney reorganized in 1970 and officially changed its name to Warner Communications in 1971, with Carroll Rosenbloom remaining as the company's second-largest individual stockholder. Another big winner in the deal was Clint Murchison of the Dallas Cowboys, who had also owned a chunk of Seven Arts stock and had been named as a member of its board of directors.[3] Murchison also owned a large tract of property in the Bahamas.

Murchison had been implicated in the Bobby Baker scandal that rocked Washington during the mid-1960s. A close friend of Gil Beckley, Baker, who hailed from Pickens, South Carolina, was a former Senate aide to and protégé of Senate majority leader Lyndon Johnson, who was elected as John Kennedy's vice president in 1960. Many referred to Baker as "Lyndon Jr." or even the "101st Senator." After the election of the Kennedy-Johnson ticket, Baker became the top aide to Senator Mike Mansfield, Johnson's successor as majority leader. However, Baker remained extremely close to Johnson.

Baker and his associate, lobbyist Fred Black, were found by Attorney General Robert Kennedy to have been go-betweens for Las Vegas underworld figures and their political contacts in Washington during the summer of 1963. Two of Meyer Lansky's operations were directly involved with Baker's Serv-U Vending Corporation, which had received a major contract from NASA. Baker's partners in the venture included Black and Lansky operatives Edward Levinson, a Gil Beckley associate who operated the Fremont Hotel in Las Vegas, and Benjamin Sigelbaum, one of Lansky's bagmen.

Baker resigned from his Senate post the month before the murder of John Kennedy and the ascent of Lyndon Johnson to the presidency. Even with Edward Bennett Williams as his attorney, Baker was convicted in January 1967 on seven counts of fraud, grand larceny, and tax evasion and spent eighteen months in Lewisburg Penitentiary.

Murchison was questioned by a U.S. Senate committee in 1965 about his relationship with Baker, particularly after federal investigators discovered that Murchison paid for Washington parties thrown by Baker, who had arranged for dates between Capitol Hill women and wealthy businessmen. Baker had also owned the Carousel Motel in Ocean City, Maryland, which had been built with loans from the Teamsters' pension fund. Baker used the location as a party spot for his clients. Murchison had offered to buy the motel from Baker for $1.5 million.

After Murchison failed to obtain approval from the Food and Drug Administration (FDA) to import products from his Haitian meat-packing business in Port-au-Prince, Baker intervened on Murchison's behalf and received the necessary FDA approval. Baker had also tried but failed to use his influence on Murchison's behalf to shift the home-mortgage-guarantee business of the Veterans Administration and the Federal Housing Administration to private insurance companies owned by Murchison's associates and other close friends.

When one of Murchison's top assistants was asked where he had met Baker, the assistant replied, "It was in the office of Lyndon Johnson." Baker later claimed that he had made a $25,000 payoff to a top Washington politician to help Murchison secure his Dallas franchise in the NFL.[4]

In 1961, the Mary Carter Paint Company, after being charged with deceptive advertising by the Federal Trade Commission, moved into the Bahamas and eventually purchased thirty-five hundred acres of land on Grand Bahama Island.[5] The property was acquired from Wallace Groves, who later introduced company officials to Sir Stafford Sands when the company became interested in building a casino in the Bahamas.

During 1964 and 1965, Mary Carter paid Sands no less than a $240,000 in legal fees to help the company purchase Paradise Island, a resort across the bay from Nassau, which was owned by A & P chain-store heir Huntington Hartford.

Hartford told me in 1980 that he had purchased Paradise Island in 1959 for $11 million and then spent another $19 million to develop the area. He added that he had "hosted and entertained Richard Nixon at Paradise Island" after Nixon's defeat in the 1962 California gubernatorial election. "Nixon was a charming man, who, along with Jim Crosby [the owner of Mary Carter], ended up giving me the shaft," Hartford says.[6]

Meantime, the government permitted Mary Carter—through Wallace Groves—to construct a gambling casino on Paradise Island. The casino license was placed in the name of Groves's wife. She was to own five ninths of the casino. Hartford was to receive his 20 percent interest out of Mary Carter's four-ninths interest. With Groves assuming control of the Paradise Island casino—through his Bahamas Amusements, Ltd.—the way was paved for Mary Carter to obtain the operating license of the Bahamian Club, which had been open since 1939.[7]

By May 1967, Groves had been crippled by a series of Bahamian Royal Commission hearings on illegal gambling. The scandal had caused the fall of the corrupt all-white Bahamian government and led to the election of black leader Lyndon O. Pindling as the new president of the Bahamas. Subsequently, Mary Carter bought out Groves's interests on Paradise Island.

Meantime, Strike Force prosecutor Robert Peloquin had insisted in a January 1966 memorandum to William Hundley—who was in his final days with the Justice Department, just before he took over NFL Security—that the conditions in the Bahamas provided an "atmosphere ripe for a Lansky skim."[8]

During the Royal Commission of Inquiry's investigation, Chesler, Carroll Rosenbloom's partner, testified that he had contacted Lansky about setting up the Bahamian gambling operations. Chesler admitted that he had gone to Lansky and "consulted him on the staffing of the Monte Carlo casino even before the certificate for that casino was granted." Chesler identified Lansky during his testimony as "the dean of gambling." Representing Chesler was Washington Redskins president Edward Bennett Williams.

According to testimony before the U.S. Senate, a government witness, Louis P. Mastriana, alleged that "Meyer Lansky had given one Michael McLaney one million dollars and Mr. McLaney was to turn this money over to . . . Lyndon O. Pindling for a gambling license."[9]

During an interview on February 9, 1967, McLaney, another former partner of Rosenbloom, told Sargent E. W. McCracken of the Miami police intelligence unit that he had been libeled in a February 3 *Life* magazine piece about his alleged role with Lansky and Pindling in the Bahamas and planned to file suit.[10] In his report of the McLaney interview, McCracken wrote, "Mr. McLaney is in fact negotiating at this time in order to build a gambling casino and hotel in Paradise Island in the Bahamas. He stated that he is definitely not associated with any mobster here or in the Bahamas and that he is opposed to the mobster element. He desires, if and when he is permitted to go into business, to run a legitimate business."

McCracken concluded his report, "Upon my departure it

was noted that his [McLaney's] next-door neighbor is Anthony Salerno." At the time, Salerno was financing the Gil Beckley national layoff syndicate, in which Rosenbloom, Murchison, and other NFL owners were clients.

McLaney—who, like Chesler, was being squeezed out of the Bahamas by Lansky—did not receive his gambling license from the Pindling government. Instead, the Royal Commission declared, "We formed the opinion that Mr. McLaney was an unscrupulous individual who was playing on the worldly inexperience of the Premier [and his political party] with the aim of maneuvering them into a position whereby they would feel obliged to 'do a deal.' There is little doubt that the deal would have involved some sort of gambling concession. We regard Mr. McLaney as a thoroughly dangerous person who is likely to do nothing but harm the Bahamas."[11]

The Royal Commission's report also referred to McLaney's relationship with Rosenbloom—but without actually naming the Colts' owner. The report stated that McLaney "has been associated in business with Mr. Chesler, notably in relation to a restaurant and supper club in Surfside, Miami, in 1955 and 1956. In October, 1958, after prolonged negotiations and with indirect backing from Mr. Chesler he took over the casino in the Hotel Nacionale [*sic*] in Havana using money supplied by friends for the purpose. As with more than one of his enterprises, he arrived on the scene too late for the project to be a success. Fidel Castro on assuming control of Cuba, closed the Havana casinos early in 1959 and Mr. McLaney thereby lost his friends' investments. In 1963 and 1964 with his brother William, he operated the casino at Cat Cay for its short season. He was also concerned in 1963 in Baltimore in gambling on football games which received much newspaper publicity and ended in litigation with a business associate."[12]

By the end of the year, Peloquin left the Justice Department and—along with his new law partner, Bill Hundley—was hired by Mary Carter in October 1967 to provide advice about security in its casino operations in the Bahamas. Also, by that time, Hundley and Peloquin were already working for NFL Security.

It was Bob Peloquin who advised Mary Carter to hire Eddie Cellini to manage its new casino at the $15 million Paradise Island Hotel, which opened in December 1967.[13] The hotel was operated by Loew's Theatres, Inc. Cellini was a longtime associate of Gil Beckley from their days in Newport, Kentucky. Cellini had gone to work at the Monte Carlo in Freeport and then moved to the Bahamian Club in 1967 under the direction of Crosby and Groves. Peloquin knew, probably better than anyone, that Cellini had worked as a dealer for Lansky at Havana's Riviera casino in pre-Castro Cuba and later had operated a London-based croupier school.

Cellini, the brother of Dino Cellini, a longtime business associate of Lansky, was obviously mob-connected, causing immediate challenges to Mary Carter's claims that it had rid the company of the influence of organized crime.

Significantly, Dino Cellini was a close friend and business associate of Washington, D.C., syndicate leader, Joe Nesline, who was the target of the 1967–68 IRS investigation of sports gambling and the Washington Redskins. Nesline told Washington, D.C., reporter Frank Kuznik, "I think what little I know about gamblin' came from Dino. He was very good with figures. He could tell you what a cigarette smoked halfway down was worth. There's nobody I know who ever came close to Dino for being a gentleman and a nice man. He got a lot of bum raps."

However, under public pressure, Eddie Cellini was forced out as the head of the casino, although he remained on payroll, arranging tours of Paradise Island from Crosby's offices in Miami. During his three-year contract with Crosby, Cellini made nearly $500,000. Peloquin later stated that Cellini was ousted because of "guilt by association . . . damned because of the alleged organized-crime involvement of his brother, Dino."

In mid-1968, after selling off its paint division for nearly $10 million, Mary Carter changed its name to Resorts International, with James Crosby as its chairman of the board and I. G. "Jack" Davis, a Harvard M.B.A. and longtime employee of the paint company, as its president. That same month, Resorts opened its second gambling spot, the Paradise Island Casino.

With the murder of Robert Kennedy in 1968,[14] the federal government's war against organized crime, waged so effectively by the Kennedy Justice Department, was over. And two of its best warriors—Bill Hundley and Bob Peloquin—were dressed for war but had no one to fight.

In July 1970, with $2 million from Crosby and Resorts, Peloquin and Hundley cofounded International Intelligence, Inc., or Intertel, a subsidiary of Resorts International. Peloquin became its president; Hundley, the secretary and chief counsel. Intertel was created "to provide unique services to domestic and multinational corporations, their outside law and public accounting firms as well as brokerage firms and investment bankers that support corporate objectives," according to a company brochure.

Peloquin and Hundley hired numerous former top officials and agents in the Strike Force, FBI, IRS, and CIA, among others, as well as officials from Scotland Yard and the Royal Canadian Mounted Police. Among them was William Kolar, the former chief of the intelligence division of the IRS. Intertel was a supersecret, private, Strike Force-type organization hired by corporations "to keep the underworld out of the companies affairs," says Tom McKeon, Intertel's executive director and another respected member of Robert Kennedy's legendary anti–organized-crime staff.

Intertel immediately became the security arm for Resorts International's casino operations, as well as for Howard Hughes's casino empire in Nevada[15] and the St. Maarten's gambling casino of Henry Ford II, the brother of Detroit Lions owner William Clay Ford.

Although Hundley remained as a member of Intertel's board of directors, only Peloquin continued full-time and became a vice president and member of the board of directors of Resorts International.[16] The law partnership of Hundley and Peloquin dissolved in 1970. Soon after, Hundley & Cacheris was formed. Subsequently, Hundley, one of the greatest anti-Mafia prosecutors in history, told a reporter, "My days with Valachi convinced me that the Cosa Nostra was the most overrated thing since the Communist party."

On October 15, 1970, a glimmer of hope in the war against organized crime was revived when the Organized Crime Control Act became law. The new legislation provided for immunity for those who testified against more dangerous criminals, the creation of the Federal Witness Protection Program, and gave the FBI jurisdiction over "major gambling operations and hoodlum infiltration of legitimate business," according to an FBI statement. Most important, Title IX of the act was the Racketeer Influenced and Corrupt Organizations Statute (RICO), which gave federal prosecutors the means by which indictments and convictions could be obtained when a "pattern of racketeering activity" could be proven within a particular crime group. The new law also threatened the underworld's financial base—since convictions could lead to federal seizures of mob assets obtained illegally and even legitimate enterprises if it could be proven that they were purchased with illegally obtained money.

The author of the act was the chief counsel of a subcommittee of the U.S. Senate Judiciary Committee, G. Robert Blakey, who was also responsible for drafting the Omnibus Crime Control and Safe Streets Act of 1968, which approved court-authorized electronic surveillance.[17]

"RICO is to organized-crime prosecutions what Rockne's invention of the forward pass was to football," Blakey told me. "It's a whole new ball game. We used to prosecute individuals and tried to lock them up. Now we could prosecute whole organizations—and not only lock them up but seize their ill-gotten gains."

However, it would not be until almost ten years later that the full impact of RICO would be realized by federal prosecutors.

20 The Kansas City Shuffle

WHEN ASKED WHETHER GIL Beckley had ever influenced the outcomes of professional football games, FBI supervisor Ralph Hill replied, "The records would show that, yes. They would have been manipulated in many ways. One is getting to the ballplayers, to get the coaching staff to manipulate the points down and then ensure that they are within the spread."

Hill added that Beckley and his associates were successful in getting to those team members who could guarantee their bets. "They would have to. If you're going to get to a given football organization, you would have to get to those key people."

Hill cited one government informant who was a part of the Beckley/Sklaroff organization and had claimed to have fixed several players on a particular team. He told my associate, William Scott Malone, "We have this guy . . . who says that on a particular occasion he had at least [three members of one team] sharing in their profits from manipulating a point spread on certain football games. [He] is in a far better position to do that than I am because he was involved; and he was there."

In convicted bookmaker Jimmy "the Greek" Snyder's autobiography, he told of the Kansas City Chiefs being taken off the betting boards in Las Vegas during the 1968 season because " 'unnatural money' had begun to show up on their games. I should say, unnaturally *big* money."[1]

Snyder wrote that he had investigated the situation and discovered that two or three Chiefs players were thought to have been cooperating with gamblers and throwing games.

Mobster Jimmy Fratianno told Malone, "For years, bookmakers were always skeptical about Kansas City. When money starts showing up on a team, there is a reason for it . . . When everybody starts coming in and bets Kansas City—Kansas City or the other side, it doesn't matter. They know something is wrong. Either they have got some information that somebody is hurt or maybe they got a little help in there."

Bookmaker Ed Curd told me, "What was going on with the Kansas City Chiefs was common knowledge all over the country. We took many of those games off the boards."

Marty Kane says, "I used to find out about these Chiefs games because I worked in Las Vegas. Whenever I'd see a Kansas City game go off the board, I'd run to a pay phone and call Marty Sklaroff in Miami and say, 'Listen, bet with whoever is still playing the Chiefs for all you can take.' "

Oddsmaker Bobby Martin agreed and noted that Washington, Detroit, Oakland, San Diego, and Houston also had been taken off the boards on occasion. "It's always hard to find out for sure what's going on," he told me. "I personally believed that there were two players with the Chiefs who were shaving points. They had a mutual friend betting for them, and week after week the bets got bigger and bigger. Sooner or later, the money started showing up."

Discussing the Chiefs, sports reporter Larry Merchant wrote, "I've always had success betting on and against the Chiefs, which is why I have always retained a scintilla of doubt about the exact nature of their alleged misdeeds.

"I believe, absolutely, Bob Martin's revelation about the betting pyramid that resulted in the Chiefs being taken down from the line in 1966. What I'm not so sure about is how the pyramid started."[2]

For years, the rumors about the Kansas City Chiefs have circulated among bookmakers and gamblers. However, the origin and circumstances of this talk have never been explained. A major Mafia-connected gambler in New Orleans told me, "In the case of Kansas City being taken off the boards, it was not because of some vague rumors." And there weren't just gamblers who were hearing these rumors.

During the late 1960s, it was thought by federal and local law-enforcement agencies that members of the Kansas City team had been cooperating with the Beckley/Sklaroff gambling network, particularly through Kansas City mobsters, and were occasionally shaving points and even throwing games in return for a piece of the gambling action.

Throughout the 1966, 1967, and 1968 football seasons odds-makers took several Kansas City Chiefs games off the boards—and no further bets were accepted on them. According to FBI documents, the FBI considered a sports-bribery investigation into an October 1, 1967, game between the Chiefs and the Oakland Raiders, which the Raiders won, 23–21. The heavily edited document, obtained through the Freedom of Information Act, stated, "An investigation was initiated by the Kansas City Office . . . to determine whether a sports bribery violation had occurred involving a member of the Kansas City Chiefs football team, in the Oakland-Kansas City football game."

The following week, the FBI monitored the game between Kansas City and the Miami Dolphins in Miami, which the Chiefs won, 24–0.

After the Chiefs' big victory over the Dolphins, the matter was considered closed because FBI "auxiliary offices [have] failed to reflect any relevant information indicating sports-bribery violation. Information compiled does reflect that bookmakers are generally reluctant to accept bets on the Kansas City Chiefs football games because of their erratic play and alleged squad dissension."

At the time Kansas City was off the boards, two Chiefs players were suspected to have been involved with members of the gambling community: quarterback Len Dawson and defensive back Johnny Robinson. Both players were thought to have been providing inside information to bookmakers, if not shaving points and even fixing games.

Len Dawson is one of the greatest quarterbacks of all time.[3] He grew up in Alliance, Ohio, just about twenty miles from the automobile agency in Canton where the NFL was chartered in 1920. A three-letter man in football, basketball, and baseball at Alliance High School, he starred at Purdue and became an all-American. He was drafted by the Pittsburgh Steelers in 1957. He remained with the team until 1959 when he was traded to Cleveland.

Dawson told me, "I started two games in five years in the NFL, but I never started and finished a game. I don't think I ever played in two games in a row for any amount of time in those five years.

"My first year at Pittsburgh was the year Buddy Parker quit at Detroit, and Art Rooney talked him into coaching the Steelers. Walt Kiesling drafted me. He was the head coach. Walt had some health problems, and Art didn't want to subject him to what was looking like another losing season. So he brought Buddy over. I was the number one draft choice. Teddy Marchibroda and Jack Scarbath were the other quarterbacks. He traded those guys and he got Earl Morrall, who was with the Forty-niners. He also brought Jack Kemp in, who was a rookie, like me. Kemp had been released by the Lions, so Buddy brought him over to the Steelers.[4] So the three quarterbacks in my first year were two rookies, Kemp and I, and Earl Morrall, who was in his second year.

"After the second game of 1958, Buddy traded Earl Morrall to Detroit for Bobby Layne. And he was the quarterback. I was at Pittsburgh for 1958 and 1959, and then I got traded to Cleveland."

In 1962, Dawson jumped leagues to join Lamar Hunt's Dallas Texans, which became the Kansas City Chiefs in 1963.

According to FBI records, nearly twenty games played by the Kansas City Chiefs over a period of two and a half seasons, 1966–68, were the targets of unnatural money. In a vast majority of these games, the side where the unnatural money turned up was the winner.

During that period the Chiefs won the AFL Championship in 1966 with an 11–2–1 record but lost the first AFL–NFL World Championship Game (which became known as the Super Bowl in January 1969) to the NFL's Green Bay Packers, 35–10, on January 15, 1967. During the 1967 regular season, the Kansas City team slipped to 9–5 and did not make the AFL play-offs.[5]

According to NFL Security chief William Hundley, the numerous Kansas City games were taken off the boards because gambling interests in Louisiana had been killing the big bookies by betting on the Chiefs. "A Baton Rouge bookmaker had beat the spread on the Chiefs something like thirteen weeks in a row," Hundley told me.

In 1968, as the bookmakers began to loosen up the freeze on Kansas City's games, the FBI concentrated its investigation of Eugene Nolan, a Baton Rouge bookmaker who was associated with Carlos Marcello of New Orleans, the boss of the Louisiana Mafia.

"We're in the same area," Nolan told me, speaking of Marcello. "One time, there were some kidnappers from Chicago who wanted a piece of my action. And I wasn't going to give it to them. So they were coming to get my daughter, who was then a baby. And my father-in-law found out about it. He sent my wife, my daughter, and me to New York and put off-duty police officers in the house. It cost me six hundred dollars a day. The only people these cops threw off were the FBI and the IRS, who were staking out my house.

"So I called that man [Marcello] and told him what was happening. He called back and said, 'You can come home.' I went to see him. He threw down some pictures of the guys who were after me and said, 'These are the motherfuckers that wanted to do it. They said they wanted some money. I told them, "If you want some money, take mine." ' He told me to go to Chicago and tell them that I already have a partner. 'You tell them it's me,' the man [Marcello] said. 'And I guarantee you that when you leave, they'll be kissing your ass.'

"So I went to Chicago, and I told them just that. And they said, 'If you have him as a partner, you don't need us.' And everything was okay. But I haven't been back to Chicago since."

Nolan was born in 1930 in Baton Rouge. After high school, he tried to get into Yale but did not score well enough on his college boards. He then attended Tulane but ended up at Louisiana State University, where he received his degree with honors in accounting. Through his participation in the ROTC program in college, he became an officer, first in the National Guard, followed by twelve years in the Army Reserves.

"As far back as I can remember, I've been gambling," Nolan told me. "I started shooting craps when I was a child during World War II. When my high school football team had its picture taken, I wasn't there for it. I was dealing blackjack someplace. I gambled forever, and I just got to be good.

"A brother-in-law of mine had dealt with Gil Beckley and introduced me to him right after I graduated from LSU in 1953. Gil, who was about twenty years older than me, got me to come to Newport, Kentucky, to visit with him. We later shared an apartment together in a hotel for six months. I was dealing coast to coast, but I was primarily betting. I would take a bet on occasion, but that wasn't my business."

Nolan had been indicted with Gil Beckley and others for gambling violations in 1967 in New York's Nassau County. He later pleaded guilty and received a one-year suspended sentence. Nolan was also convicted in Oklahoma for conspiring to use a telephone to carry on an illegal gambling operation. His appeals were turned down; his attorney was Washington Redskins president Edward Bennett Williams.[6]

Like Beckley, Nolan also enjoyed a relationship with the NFL. Nolan says, "Gil told me that if anything ever happened to him, he wanted me to call the NFL twice a week to tell them if any unusual money was showing up. Hundley was his man, and I was around Hundley a lot."

Federal agents investigating the Kansas City Chiefs were interested in Gene Nolan because his brother Joseph Lee had been convicted in 1968 for participating in a conspiracy to bribe football players at Louisiana State University to fix four LSU games.[7] The case became the first successful use of the Federal Sports Bribery Act of 1964. "Jo-Jo" Nolan was to have paid the LSU players off in up-front cash—through a middleman—and lay down bets for them.

An FBI source in New Orleans told special agents that Gene Nolan had been doing business with the Kansas City Chiefs, particularly Johnny Robinson, a 1960 LSU graduate and a teammate of the legendary all-American halfback Billy Cannon, who had been playing for the Houston Oilers and later the Oakland Raiders before he joined the Chiefs.[8]

Robinson, who is now the director of Johnny Robinson's Home for Boys in Monroe, Louisiana, denies that he knew Gene Nolan. "We happened to be from the same town [Baton Rouge]," Robinson explained to me. "I just never knew the guy. I only ran into him maybe once or twice someplace. I never knew him on a personal basis."

Dawson told me that he did not know Gene Nolan at all.

Essentially, Nolan agrees with Robinson and Dawson. "I don't think I've been around Johnny more than three times," Nolan told me. "I don't remember speaking to him but once. And, emphatically, I don't know Len Dawson at all."

Nevertheless, the FBI took the New Orleans source particularly seriously because members of the Kansas City Mafia often visited New Orleans to make deals with Marcello. "The New Orleans family is like a big brother to the Kansas City mob," a Strike Force attorney says. "Kansas City won't do anything in a big way without Marcello's permission."

Aaron Kohn, the head of the New Orleans crime commission, was more specific, saying, "There is constant travel back and forth. The Kansas City mob leaders were down here constantly. They always made their first stop at Marcello's office in the Town & Country Motel in Jefferson Parrish to pay their respects to Marcello. One of the sons in the Civella crime family was married to the daughter of a New Orleans family that was in the chicken and egg business—the principal owner of which was the Marcello mob."

The head of the Kansas City Mafia was Nick Civella. Backed by Marcello and his gang, as well as by the Chicago Mafia, Civella took power after the Kefauver Committee hearings had been eclipsed by Senator Joseph McCarthy's red-baiting barrage. Civella's territory covered all of eastern Kansas and western Missouri. He was backed by his ruthless brother Carl Civella. In 1966, the Civellas, through their middlemen, received a $5.5 million loan from the Teamsters' pension fund for the purpose of completing construction of the Landmark hotel/casino in Las Vegas, in which the family had a hidden interest.[9]

Meantime, the New Orleans informant insisted to the FBI that the September 15, 1968, game between the Chiefs and the New York Jets was being fixed for the Jets, and that the big money that would be bet on the Jets was coming from Nolan's Baton Rouge operation.

The FBI immediately opened another sports-bribery investigation with Nolan, Robinson, and Dawson as its targets. Consequently, Nolan and both players were placed under surveillance, according to the FBI. An FBI official says that the investigators received "absolutely no cooperation from the NFL."

The Jets, who were six-point underdogs, won the game, 20–19.

Nolan, Robinson, and Dawson all flatly deny that they had been working together in this or any other game. And evidence I have collected from numerous sources in the gambling underworld and a variety of law-enforcement agencies clearly indicates that there was no conspiracy among Nolan and the two players, all of whom were unaware that the investigation was even going on.

Thus, in this investigation, the FBI was simply off the track. Meantime, the Chiefs continued going off the betting boards.

After defeating the twenty-one-point-underdog Denver Broncos, 34–2, on September 22, the 3–1 Chiefs were preparing to play the 1–3 Buffalo Bills on October 5, 1968. Both teams had been impressive the previous week—with the fourteen-point-favorite Kansas City defeating Miami, 48–3, and Buffalo narrowly defeating the Jets, 37–35. Because the Bills' regular quarterback, Jack Kemp, had been injured and lost for the season, the Bills coaches were experimenting at quarterback and decided to start rookie Dan Darragh against Kansas City. Consequently, the Chiefs, led by veteran Len Dawson, were heavily favored, at first, by as many as eighteen points.

However, according to FBI documents, a tremendous amount of unnatural money again began to pour in on the Bills. The amount was so great that the spread dropped from eighteen to thirteen and even to twelve in some parts of the country. The Chiefs won the game by eleven points, 18–7; those who had bet on the Bills and taken the points won. The small and middle-size bookmakers were reportedly furious because many of the bets were placed at the last minute and could not be laid off.

After the Buffalo game, Kansas City was off the boards again in Las Vegas for its 13–3 victory over the Cincinnati Bengals on October 13. While the Las Vegas bookmakers were conducting their blackout of Kansas City's games, the Chiefs played the Oakland Raiders on October 20. It proved to be another bizarre game, because the Chiefs, led by Dawson, one of the greatest passers of all time, threw the ball only three times, the fewest passing attempts for a single game since 1950. Nevertheless, despite the lack of an aerial attack, the Chiefs won, 24–10, and upped their record to 5–1.

The Chiefs remained off the boards the following week when they defeated San Diego, 27–20. The Chiefs went back on the boards the next week as two-point underdogs against the Raiders. The Chiefs lost that game, 38–21.

Consequently, the Chiefs went off the boards for the next five weeks in their games against Cincinnati, Boston, Houston, San Diego, and Denver. Kansas City won all of these games.

But, back on the boards again on December 22 as three-point favorites in their divisional play-off against the Raiders, the Chiefs were slaughtered, 41–6. Dawson completed seventeen of thirty-six passes for 253 yards and had four interceptions.

The NFL concluded that the Chiefs' games had been taken off the boards because the team was "too unpredictable" in 1968. NFL executives failed to note that during the 1968 season, the

Chiefs had compiled a 12–2 record, which was the best in the AFL that year.[10]

Hundley denies that the NFL ever attempted to influence the government's investigation of the Chiefs and says that his own investigation had cleared Len Dawson and Johnny Robinson. Hundley told me, "I was convinced that neither Dawson nor Robinson had ever fixed a game or shaved points." However, Hundley does describe Dawson as "the most controversial man ever to play the game of professional football."

At Hundley's request, Dawson and Robinson were questioned and passed polygraph examinations in which they denied having any associations with bookmakers.[11]

Recalling the experience, Dawson told me, "It happened after practice one day. It wasn't like I knew three days in advance that these people were coming. Hank [Stram, the Chiefs' head coach] just said, 'There're some people from the league office down there, and they want to discuss something. I don't know what it's about. A commercial or something. You're supposed to meet them at seven.' I really didn't ask any questions. Little did I know how it was going to end up.

"We met downtown at the President Hotel. And we drove out to the Best Western motel out in Overland Park on the Kansas side. When I got there, Johnny Robinson was there. And I said to myself, 'Something's going on here.' The NFL people were talking about somebody [Gene Nolan] whom Johnny had known in college. I had never heard the guy's name; Johnny never mentioned him.

"They put me in a motel room with a guy with the [polygraph] machine. I was very apprehensive when they wired me up. I'd never been attached to one of those things before. He apparently had the questions written down. He asked me my name and basic questions. 'Now are you familiar with [Nolan]? Did you ever meet him? Did you ever talk to him? Did you shave points? Did you try to fix games?' I passed the test. I never bet on anything but cards or a golf game in my entire life."

Dawson adds, "Up to that time, I had no idea that there was an investigation going on. I was pissed because it was just thrown on me. I was upset with Stram because he didn't give me a hint as to what was going on."

When I asked Stram for his explanation of the suspicions revolving around the Chiefs, he replied, "I never paid any attention to it. I didn't know if we were off the boards or on the boards. The first time I heard about this off-the-boards thing, a very dear friend of mine, Tony Zoppi, who worked in Las Vegas, called me and said, 'Hey, coach, there's a guy here in town, a bookmaker, who really hates your team. He said that a couple of guys on your team were gambling and throwing games.' " Stram told me that Zoppi had identified the bookmaker as Jimmy "the Greek" Snyder.

Stram added, "Later, after I started broadcasting games and Jimmy was with CBS, he mentioned to me, 'You had two guys on your team who were throwing games: Johnny Robinson and Lenny Dawson.' I said, 'Jimmy, how can you so irresponsibly make those kinds of statements about these two kids. I recruited Lenny as a kid at Purdue. I know his moral, social, and athletic fiber. There is just no way in the world that Lenny Dawson would be involved in something like that, nor would Johnny Robinson.' "

In December 1968, Bill Hundley resigned as the director of NFL Security and was succeeded by Jack Danahy, a Columbia law school graduate and a former FBI special agent who had headed the New York office's organized-crime division. A man with a history of military-intelligence experience, he had monitored German intelligence for the FBI during World War II, and he later became an expert on Soviet espionage.

"I became the director of NFL Security through Bill Hundley," Danahy told me. "Before he was head of the Organized Crime and Labor Racketeering Section, he was a special assistant to the attorney general, prosecuting espionage matters. And I was the supervisor of the Soviet-espionage squad in New York. So we knew each other from back in that era.

"Then Bill switched over to organized crime in the Justice Department. At about the same time, in 1961, I was transferred to Washington. And then, just three months later, I was sent back to New York to take over the organized-crime squad there. So we were running on parallel tracks again.

"About the time Bill's law practice began to pick up in Washington, Pete Rozelle wanted to have his security chief in the NFL office in New York. Bill was reluctant to leave his practice, so he told Pete he was going to have to give up the job.

"Pete asked him to recommend someone, and he recommended me. I came in on December 13, 1968. I had retired from the FBI that Friday and came to work to my new job the following Monday morning. Actually, Hundley and I overlapped a little. Pete asked me if I would come aboard for a transition period. The Super Bowl was in Miami that year, and I went down there about a week before the game to meet with Hundley and all the security representatives. In effect, Hundley broke me in. He taught me the ropes. Hundley stayed on, as counsel to security, for a year or two after that. That ended after Hundley and Peloquin split up."

A week after Danahy's arrival, the NFL hired Bernie Jackson as Danahy's assistant chief. Well-qualified for the job, attorney Jackson had been a New York City police officer and later an assistant U.S. attorney.

Like his predecessors, Danahy watched the fluctuations in the line carefully. "We all deal with bookmakers to monitor the line," Danahy says. "I dealt with bookmakers whom I had known when I was with the FBI—my own private sources in New York."

Danahy's office conducted about 50 investigations a year at first and as many as 150 by the end of his tenure in 1980. Most were background checks on prospective business partners for players, prospective new owners, and candidates to become NFL referees. Danahy and Jackson also continued a program that Hamilton had begun, which consisted of traveling from team to team during the preseason and discussing the problems of gambling and associations with the NFL players and staff.

Most players think beyond football and plan for their futures—and they attempt to make the contacts in the outside world necessary for players to achieve their postfootball goals. "Players are in the public eye," Danahy says. "They are naturally going to attract con men. First of all, they are young men who have come right out of college. They have had a minimum amount of business experience. So they're potential bait for business sharpies.

"We initiated a program to assist the ballplayers in business opportunities. We would investigate the individuals who were offering these deals to them to see if they were legitimate. We would give them the results of our investigations, without recommendations. And then they would have to make up their own minds."[12]

21 The Outlaw Line

WARREN WELSH, A TOP NFL Security official, told me that the betting line is still one of the biggest problems that faces the NFL today. "The thing that really hurts us," he says, "is that you go to a game and you have a thrilling contest and the final score is twenty-one to twenty in favor of the home team. And you have people who are really angry when they leave the stadium [because the home team didn't cover the spread]. It's very unhealthy."

Most sports reporters and all professional bookmakers know that, for years, the official betting line was set by Robert "Bobby" Martin, who has been the most influential sports oddsmaker in the United States since the early 1950s. Martin is considered to be something of a genius at his trade. And, like Beckley, he cooperated with the NFL in the mid-1960s. "When Bill Hundley was the head of NFL Security," Martin recalls, "he asked me to give him the opening line, the line in the middle of the week, and how it would close. And then maybe he'd ask for a reason why the line would close as it did."

Born in Brooklyn in 1918, Martin was gambling by the time he was twelve years old. After earning his degree in journalism from New York University and serving in France during World War II, he became a professional gambler, hustling at Fiftieth Street and Broadway in midtown Manhattan. He moved to Washington, D.C., in 1952, after betting on the wrong teams during the 1951 college-basketball point-shaving scandal. Consequently, he was financially wiped out.

"I was brought to Washington by Julius Silverman," Martin recalls. "He had heard that I was good at making prices and predicting winners of fights. I was dead broke, and Julius wanted me to help set the odds on fights and to pick winners. We became the number one fight bookmakers in the United States. Everyone was afraid of fights, because they thought they were fixed. But we were trusted. We had everyone betting with us on the fights."

In 1959, Martin, Silverman, and another associate Meyer "Nutsy" Schwartz were convicted of illegal gambling activities while operating from their office in a Foggy Bottom row house near the State Department. They were fined and sentenced to five years in prison. But the U.S. Supreme Court in the landmark *Silverman* v. *United States* overturned their convictions because the surveillance method that had been used to gather evidence against them was deemed to be illegal—and it was a violation of their Fourth Amendment rights against unreasonable search and seizure.[1] Edward Bennett Williams was their attorney. After the Justice Department renewed the government's case, this time without the surveillance records, all three pleaded guilty to lesser charges. They were fined $5,000 each but were not sentenced to prison.

Martin, who also worked with Gil Beckley, moved to Miami in 1961 but returned to Washington the following year. In 1963, the heat that was being put on gamblers by the Kennedy Justice Department caused him to move to Las Vegas, where he began to set and distribute line information legally. In 1967, he became the chief oddsmaker of the Churchill Downs Sports Book and became the premier oddsmaker in the country.

Here's how Martin created the weekly line on NFL games: "On Sunday night I'd make my own pro line. I'd tell what line I thought the games should be, then I'd consult with a few people. I'd say, 'What do you think of such-and-such game?' And some guys would say, 'Well, I think you're wrong here.' And we would make what we call 'man-to-man' bets.[2] So it's getting a few opinions from people I call professionals, whose opinions I respect. The next morning we'd get a number of opinions, make some wagers, and then make some adjustments in the line [based on the betting]."[3]

Martin calls the end of the process "the opening line." The FBI calls it "the outlaw line."

After Martin created the line, it was posted in the Las Vegas casinos and then received widespread dissemination around the country. Bookmakers would base most of their action on his numbers, hoping they would attract an equal division of betting. The amount and trend of the money wagered, as well as injuries and inside information, caused adjustments in the line throughout the week.

NFL Security chief Jack Danahy told me that the NFL regularly monitors the line. "Our security representatives would start calling in, originally on Monday. And after *Monday Night Football* started, the line moved back to Tuesday. They would start calling us on Tuesday and give us the line in their particular city. And we would chart and monitor it. If there was any significant change during the course of the week, they would call it in to us, and we would seek an explanation for it. In most instances, there was an obvious explanation. Say, a key player had been injured the previous week or in practice, and the problem was more serious than originally thought. He would not be available. So we followed the line right up to game time."

Martin was principally responsible for making the Baltimore Colts a seventeen-point favorite over the New York Jets in Super Bowl III on January 12, 1969. When the Jets upset the Colts, 16–7, Martin became the butt of jokes. Naïve football fans thought that he had badly misjudged the strengths of the teams.

But picking a winner wasn't Martin's job. "Our opening line was seventeen," he explains. "The money that came in on Baltimore drove the price up to nineteen. Quite a few people thought that was too many points, and they bet on the Jets. Eventually, the line came back to the original price. That was one of the better prices I ever made because it threw money both ways."

In the 1969 Super Bowl, the Jets' head coach since 1963, Weeb Ewbank, had been the Colts' head coach from 1954 to 1962. Don Shula, the Colts' head coach, had also played for the Colts under Ewbank. Sonny Werblin, one of Rosenbloom's closest friends and the man responsible for building the Jets into an AFL powerhouse, had sold his 23.4 percent interest in the team to his four partners in May 1968.

Werblin was replaced as president of the club by Donald Lillis, who died two months later and was succeeded by Philip Iselin.[4]

For years, there have been questions as to whether Super Bowl III was fixed. Bubba Smith, a defensive lineman for the

Colts, has charged that the game had been "set up" for the Jets in an effort to give the AFL legitimacy.[5] Smith claimed that he had heard this charge from a bookmaker in New York and members of the NFL Players Association. He wrote in his autobiography that he had been told about "the Rosenbloom bet . . . East Coast say [*sic*] it was a cool million on the Jets to win."[6] Smith believed that Carroll Rosenbloom had actually bet $1 million on the Jets.

In a subsequent interview with *Playboy,* Smith provided a little more detail. "A bookie in New York and members of the N.F.L. Players Association told me that the game was set up, because if the old AFL didn't establish credibility with the NFL by a certain year, the merger would never take place. That Super Bowl game, which we lost by nine points, was the critical year. The game just seemed too odd to me. Everything was out of place. I tried to rationalize that our coach, Don Shula, got outcoached, but that wasn't the case.[7] I don't know if any of my teammates were in on the fix."

Danahy told me that Smith's charges are "bullshit." He adds, "I would not deny the fact that Carroll Rosenbloom bet occasionally. He was a betting man. And he wasn't the only owner who did. But the situation was investigated.

"It started with an article by the late Ed Sullivan. He wrote the story the day after the Super Bowl. In effect, he said that Carroll Rosenbloom had not only lost the Super Bowl but that he had lost something like a hundred thousand dollars in bets he had made on the game.

"Pete [Rozelle] had seen the Sullivan story and called me, telling me to get on it. I knew Ed Sullivan, and I finally got ahold of him. He was very ill and many times didn't get to write his own column. He had an assistant. On the night of the Super Bowl, Sullivan was in a restaurant in New York. In general conversation at the bar, somebody made a remark to the effect that Carroll Rosenbloom must have lost a bundle on the game. Sullivan asked how much he lost. And the guy replied that he must have had a hundred grand on the game. He implied that the bet had been made through Las Vegas. So Sullivan wrote a note to himself. Sullivan's assistant picked up his notes and wrote the column."

Upton Bell, who served as the Colts' personnel director from 1965 to 1971, told me, "After the game, I rode down in the elevator with Rosenbloom. I know an actor when I see one, and

I could tell when he was play-acting. He was so bitter about that loss. He said to me, 'They will never forget this day: that I was the one who lost the Super Bowl.' "

According to published reports, Rosenbloom was totally distraught after the Colts' loss. He felt disgraced. Dave Anderson of *The New York Times* wrote, "When he [Rosenbloom] returned to his Golden Beach home, he was consoled by Senator Edward Kennedy, a long-time friend . . . Senator Kennedy persuaded him to go for a swim in the surf before the players, coaches, front office and friends arrived for what had been planned as the Colts' victory party. When everybody arrived, Carroll Rosenbloom was there to greet them with a smile—a forced smile. That night a six-piece band played, everyone had a few drinks and Carroll Rosenbloom was out where they could see him. He did not hide."

A member of the Colts told me that immediately after the loss, "there was a closed-door meeting with Rosenbloom, Shula, and the organization. Nothing was discussed with the players. They were very shocked that we had lost the Super Bowl. Rosenbloom was very depressed. He didn't speak to anybody before their meeting."

Despite the fact that there is no evidence that Rosenbloom had bet against his own team, some football insiders, aside from Smith, have continued to allege that there was something fishy about Super Bowl III.

Bernie Parrish, a former defensive back for the Cleveland Browns, has speculated that Jets quarterback Joe Namath had been given the Colts' defensive signals prior to the game. "Namath's most difficult job as quarterback is to recognize and read the opposition's defenses," Parrish wrote. "With this problem solved before he came to the line of scrimmage on every play, the Colts wouldn't have had a chance."[8]

In the NFL's official video highlights of the game, the narrator marvels at the manner in which Namath picked apart the Colts' defense, which is described as the finest defensive team in the history of the NFL.[9] Namath boasted after the game, "Some people were saying that the Jets'd be scared of the Colts defense. Scared, hell—the only thing that scared me was that they might change their defense."[10]

The story from Jets representatives is that the team's defensive coach, Walt Michaels, also a former star linebacker with the Cleveland Browns, had figured out the Colts' defense and tutored Namath on passing options when the Colts were aligned in a zone defense with a possible linebacker blitz. However, according to sports reporter Lou Sahadi, neither Michaels nor even Weeb Ewbank had been responsible for spotting the weakness in the Colts' defense. Instead, according to Sahadi, it was Namath and his roommate, Jim Hudson, the Jets' safety.

"Namath and Hudson began to study films of the Baltimore-Los Angeles game," Sahadi wrote. "They were viewing a part of the game in which the Rams were on offense. One particular Ram pass pattern caught Joe's eye. He kept running the sequence through over and over . . . Namath, who can read films as well as anyone in the business, detected a flaw in the Colts' pass coverage on a particular type of pass pattern. It would provide at least one approach for him to pick the Colts' pass defense apart."[11]

Namath refused to be interviewed for this book, but Hudson told me that he disagrees with Sahadi. "Lou [Sahadi] hung around the Jets. A lot of the stuff he wrote about, well, we may have been pulling his leg. And he probably didn't even know it. Joe would say, 'Yeah, we had their signals. We got them from the films.' But nobody had their signals. I don't remember anything that complicated. The Colts were a blitzing team, and a lot of times they showed the blitz. That leaves certain pass patterns open."

Namath has written that he called over one third of the Jets' offensive plays in audibles from the line of scrimmage, depending on the Colts' defensive alignment. "[W]hen I saw Lou Michaels come on the field, I knew positively that the Colts were going into a tight five-one defense . . . [T]he first play with Michaels on the field, I said, 'We'll go on the first sound.' I called a 19-straight, a handoff to [Matt] Snell, and Matt bounced around the left side and scored."[12] Namath said that he picked up on Michaels's tip-off of the five-one defense from watching films of the Colts.

The Colts' premier placekicker, Lou Michaels, who was Walt's brother and a backup defensive lineman, told me, "Namath is full of baloney. Whenever I came in, we were in a goal-line defense—to stop the short yardage. A goal-line defense is never a five-man line. I came in as a defensive tackle on the inside, and they ran outside around the end when they scored their one touchdown. Everything else, we stopped. They had to kick three field goals."

Those who still insist that something about the game was suspicious call attention to a meeting between Namath and Lou Michaels at a restaurant in Fort Lauderdale on January 5, 1969, a week before the big game.

Michaels told me that the meeting at a Miami bar/restaurant was quite accidental and even confrontational. "I was with Danny Sullivan [a Colts offensive lineman and Michaels's roommate] at a table in the back, and he saw Namath and Jim Hudson come in. Namath was wearing his big, full-length fur coat. So I said to Danny, 'Let me go up and get another drink for us.' I walked up to the bar. I wanted to shake hands with Joe. But he pointed his finger at me and said, 'We're going to kick the shit out of you, and I'm going to do it.' And he pointed to himself. And that got me very upset. He caught me off guard, and it put me in a different mood. He tried to aggravate me. We would have gotten along fine had he just come up to me and said, 'Hi, I'm Joe Namath. I recognize you. You're Walt's brother.' I had heard that he was a nice guy.[13]

"I told Namath, 'We got Unitas. We got Morrall.' He told me that they were 'over the hill. We don't have to worry about them.' I said to him, 'What happens if we beat you?' And he said, 'I'll sit right in the middle of the field and cry.' We went back and forth, exchanging words. At one point, I told him, 'I'd like to have you outside, just for one minute.' After that, we calmed down and relaxed.

"I went back to Danny and told him what happened. Then, after a while, Hudson came over to our table and started talking and then Joe came over, too. We sat there for about an hour or so. We had about two or three drinks. I don't remember.

"Joe paid for the whole tab. He threw a hundred-dollar bill down and gave us a ride back to our hotel in his rented car. Nothing particular was discussed on the way back. What we talked about had no relationship to the game."

Hudson agrees with Michaels that "nothing technical" about the game was discussed. "Everybody had been drinking—and maybe Lou more than others. Joe didn't start it. I remember Lou talking about how they were going to kick our asses."

Soon after the incident between Namath and Michaels took place, Namath came out publicly and guaranteed the game. "We're going to win Sunday," Namath boasted. "I'll guarantee you."

Recalling Namath's guarantee, Weeb Ewbank told me, "When we went down there, I told the whole squad that we were seventeen-point underdogs. And I told them that if I could, I'd make it twenty-one. I told the players to be careful what they said and not light any fires under the Colts. When Joe said that he could guarantee the game, I could've shot him. I told Joe to watch what he was saying." Ewbank added that Namath, even in private, was absolutely positive that the Jets were going to win.

Did Michaels, while boasting of his team's strengths, tip Namath and Hudson off to the Colts' defense? "I don't think it's likely," Michaels told me. "We did have a few drinks, but I would never do anything to hurt my team."

Namath completed seventeen of twenty-eight passes for 206 yards and no interceptions during the 16–7 Jets victory. Shaken up at one point during the contest, he missed only one series of downs and was replaced by the Jets' backup quarterback, Vito "Babe" Parilli. Namath was selected as the game's most valuable player.

Ewbank told me that his victory over the Colts was particularly sweet after his 1963 firing by Carroll Rosenbloom. "Before the game, Carroll walked around the field with me. While we were talking, he invited me and my wife, Lucy, to a party at his place at Golden Beach after the game. But I told him, 'We are planning to have a party of our own.' "

Pressing too hard, Michaels had missed two field goals of twenty-seven and forty-six yards during Super Bowl III. Michaels says, "On the first one I really thought, deep down, that it was good. I kicked it. It was going straight between the bars. But, no alibis, I missed. I kicked for the middle of the bars, and I should have kicked for the left. It was close. It blew right over the top of the bar. It just drifted away. Naturally, I was a little depressed.

"The second one was about a forty-six yarder. And I just kicked a lot of dirt. I guess my mind was on the last field goal that I missed, because I thought that I should've had it. I just topped the ball. I might have pressed for that one.

"The only trouble is: For the rest of my life, this is the only game they'll remember about me. They block every other game out. They don't remember the two field goals I kicked against Cleveland two weeks earlier for the NFL championship that helped get us into that Super Bowl."[14]

Danahy concludes, "We checked it all out backward and

forward. First of all, if Rosenbloom or anyone else had made a large bet, there would have been a lot of noise about it. We checked all over Las Vegas, and there was no heavy movement. But I guess that Rosenbloom could have spread the money through beards all over the United States."

Bobby Martin agrees that there was no fix and cites as evidence the fact that no unnatural money was bet on the game.

However, in documents that were obtained for this book, a top convicted-bookmaker-turned-federal-witness said that Rosenbloom had indeed bet on the game—but that he had bet on his own team, the Colts. The government informant claimed that he had handled a portion of Rosenbloom's money while he served as a member of the Mafia's gambling network that was operated by Gil Beckley and Marty Sklaroff.

"Carroll Rosenbloom bet a million dollars with us on the Colts against the Jets," the informant said. "Because of the size of the bet, Marty Sklaroff and Gil Beckley had to lay it off around the country. I laid off two hundred thousand dollars of it, and they laid off the rest of it."

22 Broadway Joe

JOE NAMATH WAS BORN and raised in Beaver Falls, Pennsylvania, also the hometown of quarterback Babe Parilli. As a boy, Namath was a runner for local bookmakers. After his all-American playing days at the University of Alabama and his $427,000 contract with Sonny Werblin and the Jets, Namath became the symbol of the new-wave professional athlete of the late 1960s. With his trend-setting clothes, Fu Manchu mustache, expensive shag carpeting, white football shoes, and his overall demeanor, Namath became the Frank Sinatra of his generation—another hip, swingin' kind of guy with a "fuck off" attitude. Namath appealed to America's youth—and to just about every gambler and bookmaker in New York.

Although Namath has insisted that he never bet with a bookmaker on a football game, the Jets quarterback wrote in his autobiography, "I'm a known gambler, and I don't just mean on third down. Anyone who's ever seen me in Las Vegas knows I'm a gambler. I don't go out there to look at the sand. My last three trips to Vegas, I've lost $2,500, $2,500, and $5,000 in the casinos, a total of $10,000, not really much for a gambler . . . I'm friendly with known gamblers, too. Like, I'm friendly with my mother."[1]

Namath's associations with gamblers became a major controversy later on in 1969 after his big Super Bowl win. In late 1968, Namath—along with his partners, Ray Abruzzese[2] and Bobby Van—opened Bachelors III, a New York restaurant at Sixty-second Street and Lexington Avenue.

Recalling Namath and Bachelors III, Jack Danahy told me, "Joe was a naïve young guy who enjoyed fun and games. Unfortunately, he bought into this bar. And it became a fantastic hangout for bad guys. A bookmaker had established himself in the basement of the place and was using the telephone. The New York Police Department had an undercover guy in the place.

"Just before the 1969 Super Bowl, I got a call from a friend of mine, a very high-ranking NYPD official. He said, 'Jack, don't worry about the game, but when you get back we have to talk to you about something involving one of your Jets.' When I got back, they gave me the whole story. And we called in Joe."

Namath was told that "undesirables"—mobsters and gamblers—had been frequenting his establishment. Specifically, notorious New York Mafia figures such as Carmine Tramunti, Carmine Persico, and Thomas Mancuso, as well as New Jersey's Joseph Zicarelli, were regular customers. It was also known that besides the basement telephone in Bachelors III, Namath's personal line in his private office had also been used to place bets. Namath simply shrugged the information off. Months passed and nothing more was said.

The NYPD's supervisor of detectives, Ralph Salerno, told me, "Bachelors Three was the big hangout. When it would close at four, most of the hot contenders and the drawing cards hanging around there would then go to an after-hours joint that was mob-run. The guy who owned the after-hours place was Carmine Trumanti, who succeeded Three-Finger Brown [New York Mafia boss Thomas Lucchese].[3]

"There was a bug that picked up a conversation between Trumanti and Namath during which Trumanti said, 'Hey, kid, you're sitting on top of the goddamn world. You're a big football star. You're making a lot of money. You shouldn't hang out with these creepy bastards. They're no good for you.'

"I give Trumanti a lot of credit for that. He told Namath he didn't need mob guys."

On June 3, while appearing at a New York banquet, Namath was contacted again by Danahy, who instructed him to sell his interest in Bachelors III. A meeting was arranged with Namath in Rozelle's office. Rozelle was cool as he explained to Namath the NFL rules on players associating with gamblers and ordered him to sell his interest in the restaurant or be suspended from football.[4] The NFL had also learned that the telephones in Namath's bar had been wiretapped and gambling information was collected.

Danahy says, "I told him, 'Look, I don't care whether you give [your interest in the bar] to your mother or anybody. Just get your name off that license.' "

Weeb Ewbank told me that he discussed the controversy with Namath. "I told him not to get into an argument with the commissioner. Joe had kept saying that he thought the commissioner was being unfair because there were a lot of players who had restaurants. He said that they were trying to say that some bookmaking was going on there. But Joe told me that there hadn't been. He said that whatever was going on was happening on a pay telephone—and that there was nothing he could do about that."

On June 5, Namath agreed to sell.

But, Danahy continues, "Namath ran into sports announcer Howard Cosell, who talked to him. They were drinking, and they wound up at Joe's apartment. And Cosell gave him his best legal knowledge about his rights and privileges as a free American boy. And the next thing, going contrary to the recommendations of his lawyer, Namath decided that he wasn't going to sell. He was going to fight the league. About this time, I was sort of an irritant on the thing, the hard-nosed guy, and so Pete asked me to step aside, which I did."

The twenty-six-year-old Namath called a press conference at Bachelors III to announce his retirement from football. "I'm not selling. I quit," he tearfully told reporters. Namath later said, "I hadn't done anything wrong. I hadn't bet with bookmakers on football games one way or the other. I'd never lost a game on purpose or tried to shave points. I admit I had deliberately given information to gamblers to affect their bets: Before the 1969 Super Bowl, I'd guaranteed that we'd win the game."[5]

Soon after, Rozelle held his own press conference, expressed his regret at Namath's decision, and hung tough. The commissioner said solemnly, "It is obviously impossible for a player to be aware of the background and habits of all persons to whom he is introduced. However, continuation of such associations after learning of a person's undesirable background and habits is a cause for deep concern. Such conduct gives the appearance of evil, whether or not it actually exists, and thereby affects the player's reputation, the reputation of his fellow players, and the integrity of his sport."

Namath said that after refusing to sell, he was accused of fixing games, particularly two games in 1968 in which he threw five interceptions in each and lost both contests. Denying any fix, he wrote, "Hell, you'd have to be an idiot to make it that obvious. If you want to throw a game, you don't have to allow a single pass to be intercepted. You just screw up one or two handoffs, and the running back can't handle them, and he fumbles the ball, and he takes the blame. Then maybe you throw a critical third-down pass a little low, and you let the punter come in and give the ball to the other team. You don't give it away yourself."[6]

On July 18, after a four-hour meeting with Rozelle, Namath relented; he again agreed to sell his interest in Bachelors III and to return to his team. "I'm happy to announce Joe will be back with the Jets," Rozelle said. "He and I have privately reached total accord. He is selling his interest in Bachelors III, and we consider the entire matter closed." Rozelle added that Namath would not be disciplined in any way.

The whole matter dropped. Namath wasn't punished. The wiretap transcripts taken over the telephones at Bachelors III were never released. And the grand-jury investigation of the links between gambling and professional sports never got off the ground.[7]

Danahy disagrees with Bill Hundley that Len Dawson was "the most controversial man ever to play the game of professional football." He says, "Bill was wrong about that. It was Namath. Joe liked hoodlums."

One of the consequences of the Namath situation was felt by the NFL early during the 1969 season—when a Jets game went off the boards on September 26, 1969, because of rumors revolving around Namath. Danahy told me, "In my twelve years with the league, it only happened about four or five times. I remember one specific incident in the fall of 1969. The Jets had won the Super Bowl, and they were scheduled to play the Chargers in San Diego. They were actually in the air, flying out there, when I received a call from one of my security reps in the Midwest. He told me that the San Diego-Jets game had gone off the boards. And that rang all sorts of bells. Then, in a short period of time, I received calls from three or four other reps in other cities, like Chicago, Detroit, and Buffalo. The rumor was spreading.

"They all went to work to find out the reason that the game went off the boards. And they all came up with the same answer:

that Joe Namath would not be playing because he had sprained his thumb in practice on Thursday.

"By the time the Jets' plane landed in San Diego, I had my man right there to see the coach, Weeb Ewbank. We washed the thing right out. The whole thing was strictly b.s. The following day, Pete issued a statement that there had been a false rumor, and that there was no problem. Joe Namath would be playing. The game immediately went back on the boards.

"This is how we attributed it. Somebody was trying to affect a gambling coup by starting a rumor. When the price changed, they tried to middle. And they went a little too far."

Numerous attempts to interview Namath for this book were unsuccessful.

While Namath was in the midst of explaining his gambling associations to NFL officials, Leonard Tose, the owner of Tose Trucking Company of Bridgeport, Pennsylvania, bought the Philadelphia Eagles for $16.1 million from bankrupt developer Jerry Wolman on May 1, 1969. Tose, who had been outbid for the Eagles by Wolman in 1963, borrowed most of the purchase price from banks, using his trucking firm and soda-canning business as collateral.[8]

The dapper Tose had started out as a driver in the family trucking business founded by his Russian immigrant father. A 1937 graduate of Notre Dame with a degree in business, Tose had also served in the Army's military police in Puerto Rico. He had left Tose Trucking in 1956 to go to work as a top executive for Highway Trailer Industries of New York and soon developed K. S. Canning, which manufactured and distributed flattop cans.[9] He returned home after his brother's 1963 death. His father died two years later. Len Tose then took over the firm, brought his fleet up to nearly nine hundred trucks, and began raking in $15 million in annual revenues.

As one of the largest trucking companies on the East Coast, Tose had to deal directly with the Teamsters Union and sat on several negotiating councils with union representatives, including Jimmy Hoffa, who was the subject of some of his most repeated stories. Perhaps by coincidence, Tose's major competitor was hit with a wildcat strike during the mid-1960s, during which time Tose's company reportedly tripled its revenues.

Not surprisingly, Tose was also a heavy gambler, who reportedly bet money on everything from card games and horse races to golf and football. "It was not uncommon for him to bet $10,000 on a gin game or a round of golf. At the racetrack, the Eagles owner was known to lose money hand over fist."[10]

Tose told reporter Barry Rosenberg that he used to gamble on football games but stopped after buying the Eagles. "A thousand [dollars]. Maybe two. Maybe three. But that's all. I guess I wasn't very good at it, I didn't win very often. Besides I've cut all that out."

According to his ex-wife, Tose had bet "between two hundred thousand and three hundred thousand dollars a year" on NFL games.

"We did do an investigation of Tose," insists Danahy. "He admitted that he was a gambler. Several owners have admitted that they had a tendency to gamble. But they all agreed to take the pledge [that they would not gamble while owning NFL teams]. There was no problem about Tose's gambling because that was a pretty well-known fact. Our biggest concern with investigating Tose was establishing that he had the financing. Tose had it."

Tose had really moved into the ground floor of the new NFL. Five months after the 1969 Super Bowl, as the NFL and the AFL began to create divisions in the new merged league, the Baltimore Colts agreed to jump to the new AFL-team-dominated American Football Conference, along with the Cleveland Browns and the Pittsburgh Steelers. The other traditional NFL teams remained in the new National Football Conference. Of course, there was some incentive. The owners of those three defecting teams—Carroll Rosenbloom, Art Modell, and Art Rooney—all received $3 million in indemnity fees for their "sacrifice." It was thought that the three owners would lose at the box office because of the switch. In the end, because of the enthusiastic support for the NFL and all its old and new teams, no one even noticed.

Regarding Rosenbloom's decision to jump conferences, Colts personnel director Upton Bell told me, "Carroll felt that with the merger, he could finagle his team to go over to an easier conference with teams he thought he could beat. He got himself out of the NFL's Western Division, which was the Rams, Lions, Packers, Bears, Vikings, and Forty-niners. There was never a conference that strong."

23 Lenny Dawson on the Brink

DURING THE 1969 NFL season, after four more of the Kansas City Chiefs' games were taken off the boards by Las Vegas bookmakers,[1] Len Dawson became a target of an IRS investigation that concentrated on Detroit gambler Donald Dawson, who was no relation to Len but had supposedly made calls to the Chiefs quarterback.

Len Dawson told me that he suspected that something was going on on January 4, 1970, the day the Chiefs defeated the Oakland Raiders, 17–7, for the AFL crown and the right to play the NFL-champion Minnesota Vikings in Super Bowl IV. "We were staying at the Mark Hopkins Hotel in San Francisco, getting ready to play the Raiders in Oakland," Dawson says. "And there was a note in my box for me to call Pete Rozelle. And I said, 'What the hell does he want to talk to me about?' That Sunday, I got ahold of him, and he said, 'Oh, nothing. I just wanted to wish you luck.' Well, I was thinking about the game, but it struck me kind of funny. Why would he call to wish me luck? That was the first inkling I had that something was going on.

"Then on the flight back to Kansas City after the game, Hank [Stram] said that there might be some sort of inquiry from league officials."

Stram told me that prior to the Chiefs' game with Oakland, "The NFL intercepted me at the airport. Mark Duncan [the assistant supervisor of NFL personnel] took me in his car and said, 'I have some terrible news. Len Dawson's name is being mentioned with Don Dawson, and the story is going to break soon.' " Stram says that he later discussed the matter with his quarterback, who admitted meeting the gambler while he was with the Pittsburgh Steelers. Len Dawson insisted that Don Dawson had called him only twice since those days. Stram was completely satisfied with Dawson's response.

Soon after, Stram was contacted by Duncan again. "Duncan told me, 'Don't worry about it [the gambling probe]. We squelched the story, and everything is fine.' "

But the NFL had "squelched" the story only temporarily.

The roots of the IRS investigation of Don Dawson, who had ties to Gil Beckley, began when federal agents discovered that baseball Hall of Fame pitcher Jerome "Dizzy" Dean, formerly of the St. Louis Cardinals, was a close friend of a high-stakes gambler Howard Sober, a wealthy Michigan trucking executive. At the same time, the agents alleged that Sober, another big-time gambler, had lost nearly a million dollars in bets to Don Dawson, who had introduced Sober to Dean.

In June 1969, Sober was rushing, trying to make a flight connection at an airport and gave an airport employee $50 to make a call for him to place an $800 bet. The employee called the FBI instead. A federal agent told him to make the call while agents listened on an extension. No wiretap was involved.

After the call was made, federal agents determined that Sober's bookmaker was Dawson. Checking Dawson's telephone records, the IRS compiled a list of nineteen hundred calls Dawson had made to gamblers, sports figures, and other bookmakers. During telephone calls monitored—but also not wiretapped—by the IRS,[2] Dawson had once complained that he had lost "a bundle" on the New York Jets' 13–6 loss to the Kansas City Chiefs in their 1969 divisional play-off game.

According to IRS documents, Don Dawson stated that his "man with K.C. had certainly done his job," but that "Namath should have at least tied the game . . . I'm going to contact my man with K.C. and see what he says; we've got to come back after being a big winner. Now, I'm a loser."

The original probable cause for wiretaps stemmed from statements by IRS agents who had witnessed the Detroit gambler giving money to an unnamed former member of the Detroit Lions.

A top IRS official directly involved in the investigation was more specific, saying that the affidavit requesting wiretaps on the telephones of the principal targets of the investigation came after federal investigators discovered Don Dawson meeting and giving money to Dick "Night Train" Lane, formerly of the Detroit Lions, who had been polygraphed and cleared during the 1963 players-gambling scandal.

Lane told me, "Don Dawson had a cousin named Dawson Taylor, who had a Chevrolet dealership. I started working for him in 1962. There were a lot of players who worked for him. I was married to [the popular jazz singer] Dinah Washington, and she had put three songs Taylor wrote to music. He was grateful, so he gave both of us a new car every year.

"We were working on a base salary and percentage of what we sold [at the car dealership]. Don Dawson asked me if I'd sold anything that month. I told him, 'Not too many. One or two.' He said, 'Well, I want to get my daughter a car, and so I'll let you get it for her. I'm going to put a down payment on it, and let her keep it up.' He gave me eighteen hundred dollars in cash.' That's the only money I ever got from him." Lane says that he gave Dawson a receipt for the cash.

Don Dawson insists that he never gave Lane any money. "Why would I go to my cousin to buy a car when my dad was in the same business? I never gave him eighteen hundred dollars. I have given a lot of the other players money, but I never gave Night Train any."

Based on the alleged Dawson/Lane transaction, the IRS special agent in charge of the investigation, Herbert Hinchman, who filed a thirty-page affidavit, wrote, "Donald Dawson of Birmingham, Michigan, is engaged in the business of accepting wagers on sports and horse races; that Dawson also lays-off some of the large wagers accepted by him to other bookmakers in the Detroit area and also to other bookmakers throughout the United States." Dawson was also part owner of the Fox & Hounds Restaurant in Bloomfield Hills, Michigan, a popular spot for local sports figures and celebrities.

Another top IRS official who was involved in the investigation told me, "It was a bookmaking and layoff investigation. We put a request in for wiretaps in June 1969 on Sober, Dawson, and several college coaches. We also had the probable cause for Santa Anita racetrack and some hockey bookmakers in Toronto. We went to the IRS commissioner and requested them. We had the authority for Title Three at the time if the commissioner approved it. He declined after months of negotiations. He wanted us to work with the FBI and bring them into the case.[3]

"We agreed and went to the FBI for the wiretaps. Bill Lynch [the head of the Strike Forces] and his deputy, Ed Joyce, went to the bureau as our liaison. J. Edgar Hoover said, 'Yeah, we'll take the case, but we want all the information and for the IRS to back off.' I told the FBI they'd have to shove it. We wanted their cooperation, a joint effort. I wasn't about to give the FBI the case we'd been working on. So the FBI refused to cooperate.

"We decided to go with the probable cause we had. And we would have to give up the coaches, Santa Anita, and some bookmaking on hockey. Professional football, we had cold. It was clear to us that games had been fixed by players [who were] shaving points in cooperation with several organized-crime-connected bookmakers."

In early January 1970, after an eight-month investigation by the IRS, federal agents arrested fourteen people in a series of raids in Detroit, New York, Las Vegas, Phoenix, and Biloxi against a nationwide sports-betting ring. Among those arrested was the forty-eight-year-old Don Dawson. At the time of his arrest, Dawson, who had been the principal target of the probe, was found with over $450,000 in cashier and business checks in his possession.

James Ritchie, the head of the Detroit Strike Force Against Organized Crime, said at the time of the raids, "Statements made by some of those arrested and seized records indicate a national scheme involving famous figures in baseball and football." Ritchie described Don Dawson as "one of the largest bookmakers in the Midwest."

There was more. NFL players had reportedly received telephone calls from Don Dawson. Besides Len Dawson, others receiving calls included quarterback Bill Munson of the Detroit Lions, quarterback Karl Sweetan of the Los Angeles Rams, and at least four other big-name players.[4]

Munson told me that he had first met Don Dawson in 1967 in Milwaukee while the Rams were preparing to play the Green Bay Packers for the divisional title. "He sort of acted like he was an intermediary for Bill Ford [the Lions' owner], but I think that was bullshit. He was real smooth, and I couldn't figure him out. See, I was playing out my option and trying to get traded, and he seemed like he was laying some groundwork for me to come to Detroit. Anyway, I met him that morning on the Saturday before the game and had coffee with him."

Dawson approached Munson again, this time in Miami, just before the Rams played the Cleveland Browns in the Playoff Bowl, which featured the runners-up in each NFL division. "I still couldn't figure this guy out," Munson continued. "We were talking, and he was trying to get close. I didn't know what he wanted. I think I gave him my phone number because he was coming to California. We decided we'd have dinner.

"Before I was traded to Detroit [in May 1968], he called me, and we had dinner in Beverly Hills. During the dinner, Dawson told me, 'You know, you can make a lot of money in Detroit outside of football.' I just walked away and acted like I didn't know what he was talking about. I didn't say anything."

Munson says that he ran into Dawson one final time at the Red Run Golf Club near Detroit. Munson was playing a round of golf with former teammates Ron Kramer and Dan Currie when they ran into Dawson on the course. Munson insists that he never saw him again, adding that he never bet with him. "I wasn't nuts enough to do something like that and get suspended for a year. And I had no urge to do it."

Munson says that he was never interviewed by federal agents about his relationship with Dawson—but has been audited by the IRS every other year since then.

Speaking of Len Dawson, Don Dawson told me, "When Lenny played for the Cleveland Browns [in 1960–61], I got acquainted with him. He was Milt Plum's backup man. Lenny and I got to be pals and I knew his wife, Jackie. Her father was a car dealer in Shaker Heights [a Cleveland suburb]. I got to be friends with her dad and her mother because I came to Cleveland all the time. Lenny was a very shy young man. It was Jackie and I who got him to get the guts to go in and tell Paul Brown, 'Either start me next year or trade me.' Well, they wound up trading him to the Chiefs."

Don Dawson adds, "When Lenny was at Cleveland, he gave me information, and I made some small bets for him. He was on the bench. Nothing more than a hundred dollars. Just a token bet. Nothing big.

"When he got with the Chiefs, I never heard from him, but I knew he was doing a lot of gambling over there. In Kansas City, the Civellas were betting really big money. Some of these people got ahold of Lenny, and they made a shithouse full of money. I got wind of it through another Detroit bookmaker. But I never contacted Lenny or said, 'Let me in with a play. I know what you're doing.' Who knows? The Civellas might have said, 'Hey, this guy is muscling in on our territory.'[5] So I had not talked to Lenny since 1968–69, when the Chiefs were off the boards."

During my interview with Len Dawson, he flatly denied ever betting with Don Dawson or having any business dealings with the Civella crime family, adding, "I met Don while I was with Pittsburgh. I understood him to be from a wealthy family in Detroit. He was a friend of Bobby Layne, and I met him through Bobby.

"My wife didn't know Don Dawson except through me. Her father worked for Ford for a lot of years. He got tired of traveling, so he bought into a Ford dealership. Then he moved back to Cleveland and got into [another] dealership there."

Len Dawson told me that Don Dawson had nothing to do with his confrontation with the Browns' head coach. "Paul Brown ruled with an iron fist. He could bring a guy to his knees with a few words faster than anybody I'd ever seen. In those days, they didn't have agents. They just sent you a contract and said, 'Sign it.' I hadn't signed it by a certain time, and he wanted to know why. I said, 'I'm not very happy about not getting an opportunity to play.' "

When I specifically asked Len Dawson whether he had ever been approached by Don Dawson to fix a game while he was with either Pittsburgh or Cleveland, the quarterback replied, "No. I don't know why he would. I never played. In Pittsburgh, Bobby Layne played all the time. I think in the five years that I played for Pittsburgh and Cleveland, I think I threw maybe forty-five passes."

IRS agents also said that Don Dawson had called at least two college head coaches: Bob Devaney of the University of Nebraska and Frank Kush of Arizona State University, who had been especially plagued by longtime allegations of associations with gamblers. Kush denied any relationship with Don Dawson, insisting, "I never met Don Dawson. I don't know who he is."

Dawson told me that he had never talked to Devaney, a former coach at Michigan State. "He was a good friend of Howard Sober," Dawson says, adding, "I never met any of them, except Frank Kush. We had dinner together in Phoenix, along with Howard and my wife. But Kush never called me, and I never called him."

Lions coach Joe Schmidt, who had been disciplined by the NFL for gambling in 1963, admitted knowing Don Dawson, but denied having seen him "for years." Alex Karras, who had been suspended for a year for betting, also admitted knowing Dawson—but told reporters that he had advised players, like Munson, to stay away from him.

There were other complications. On January 5, 1970, Bill Matney, a reporter for *NBC News,* broke a story on NBC's *Huntley-Brinkley* nightly news program, announcing that the grand jury was planning to subpoena NFL personnel. Among those to be called before the twenty-three-member federal grand jury in Detroit, according to the report, was the thirty-four-year-old Len Dawson, who was in New Orleans, preparing to play in Super Bowl IV, in which Kansas City was playing the Minnesota Vikings.

Matney told me that the source for his story was an official with the Strike Force in Detroit. After receiving his information about the grand-jury probe, he checked the official out with a respected federal judge in Detroit, who vouched for him. "To be doubly certain," Matney says, "NBC sent one of our top field producers to Detroit to validate my findings. The producer actually met the [Strike Force] source. So he was an additional witness. In fact, we met the source at the Howard Johnson's in downtown Detroit, and he watched the story we filed on *The Huntley-Brinkley Report.* After we watched it, the source said, 'You're right on the money.' "

Len Dawson recalls, "Stram told me that they were going to break a story on *NBC News.* I was up in Hank's suite because he said that the NFL Security people wanted to talk to me. I was trying to rest because I did have a game to play. The NFL people were trying to make a determination as to what to say to the press and what to release. They brought in some sportswriters from Kansas City and other cities. They were trying to get their opinions on what to say to the wolves [news reporters] out there. Finally, I just told them, 'Why don't we just tell the truth. I do know the person. I've only seen him a couple of times in my life. The truth is, I did talk to him on the phone.' "

Dawson remembers, "I thought, 'What the hell is going on?

Why me?'" He adds that he did not see the news report but knew that no specific allegations were made against him or any other player mentioned in Matney's story.

"I'll tell you what happened in Detroit," Jack Danahy says angrily. "There was a Strike Force in Detroit. They were particularly unimpressive, and they were dying for publicity. They got a search warrant on Don Dawson. Len Dawson was probably one of a hundred sports figures whose names were in a telephone directory that Don Dawson had assembled over a period of years. The week before the Super Bowl—the big football event of the year—they made a sneak release to NBC. And that's when it hit the fan.

"I was down in Miami with all my security people, having a security conference the week before the game. I sent the guys from Detroit back to Detroit to get the story there. We sent our representatives out to interview all the NFL players whose names were in the book.

"I flew over to New Orleans, and I met Lenny Dawson at the Fontainebleau. Mark Duncan was with me. I talked to Lenny for about an hour and a half. It was very open. He admitted knowing Don Dawson. He recounted to me the various occasions that he had talked to Dawson. The last time he had talked to him was when Lenny's father died.[6]

"I wrote up a signed statement for [Len] Dawson in longhand. Dawson had had a tough day. He had had practice, and then the press was all over him as a result of this news report. By the time I finished writing up his story, I looked up and Lenny was sound asleep in his chair. So I woke him up. He read the statement and signed it.

"We went back to the Royal Orleans Hotel where Pete Rozelle was, and I gave him the statement. Pete asked me, 'Do you buy it, Jack?' And I said, 'I sure do.' He asked why. And I said, 'I've taken signed statements from a lot of guys—murderers, spies, you name it—but this is the first one who ever went to sleep on me.'

"Dawson had also offered to be polygraphed again, but we decided that there was no basis for it."

The following day, at a crowded press conference, Len Dawson faced reporters and read the statement Danahy had written for him: "My name has been mentioned in regard to an investigation being conducted by the Justice Department. I have not been contacted by any law-enforcement agency or been apprised of the reason my name has been brought up. The only reason I can think of is that I have been a casual acquaintance with Mr. Donald Dawson of Detroit, who I understand has been charged in the investigation. Mr. Dawson is not a relative of mine.

"I have known Mr. Dawson for about ten years and have talked to him on several occasions. My only conversation with him in recent years concerned my knee injuries and the death of my father. On these occasions, he contacted me to offer his sympathy. His calls were among the many I received. Gentlemen, this is all I have to say. I have told you everything I know."

When a reporter immediately asked whether he and the gambler had ever had any personal meetings, Dawson replied, "Are we going to get into all this?"

"Gentlemen," the Chiefs' head coach, Hank Stram, interrupted, "Len has made his statement. Now we would like to discuss the football game with you if you have any questions about that."[7]

Running back Ed Podolak, who was a rookie with the Chiefs at the time of the Super Bowl, told me, "We had a team meeting and coach Stram told us that there was an effort to do anything possible to take our concentration off the game. Here was a chance for the AFL to defeat the NFL two years in a row, and that would absolutely destroy the myth of the NFL's superiority over the AFL. So we were told to put all of this behind us and not to worry about it. Coach Stram said that it didn't affect anybody; that the allegations were untrue."

Pete Rozelle was annoyed that Len Dawson had admitted knowing Don Dawson. The commissioner told *The Detroit News,* "I'm sorry he said it. I'd have preferred it would have come later." Rozelle also called the news reports on the investigation "totally irresponsible . . . While the entire matter has been under investigation by our security department for several days, we have no evidence to even consider disciplinary action against any of those publicly named."

Rozelle chose that moment to reveal that Len Dawson had voluntarily taken the polygraph test in 1968 and passed. "More than a year ago, during the 1968 season, rumors were circulating regarding [Len] Dawson. At that time, Dawson and his attorney cooperated fully with our office and Dawson volunteered to take a polygraph examination to establish his innocence in regard to the rumors. The test and our independent investigation proved to our satisfaction that the rumors were unsubstantiated."

Don Dawson told me that Len Dawson had had an opportunity to get the gambler off the hook with his statement—but didn't. "I drew a lot of criticism," Don Dawson says. "Lenny saw me in the newspapers, and he knew what was going on. He said that he casually knew me, but he's a fucking liar. As far as Lenny goes, yeah, he was doing plenty of gambling. And that was way before my thing ever erupted. I had no connection or further conversation with Lenny after he left the Browns. He wasn't gambling with me anymore. He was then with the Civellas in Kansas City, but I was the one who got all the publicity. And I was the one who got arrested.

"I imagine Lenny said what he said for his own protection—for which I don't blame him. But he should have called me later to apologize, because I was hung out to dry."

NBC, which never interviewed Don Dawson, did not back off its original story. Matney says that he received "complete support" from the network. However, James Ritchie of the Strike Force lambasted the news report, saying, "The peacock is NBC's trademark, and the peacock has turned out to be poppycock." U.S. attorney James Brickley of Detroit angrily said, "There is no federal process against these persons named by NBC, or any other sports figures."

Matney said that soon after his report aired "I got a call from the Washington [NBC] bureau and one of the guys in the office said that Attorney General John Mitchell was 'furious.' Then I got a call from my source. He said two things were happening: One, that Mitchell had ordered an investigation within the department to find out who leaked the information and, two, the [Strike Force] was going to be forced to change its *modus operandi.* Instead of calling the players to testify in person, it was going to dispatch agents to see them, avoiding any appearance in court."[8]

On January 11, 1970, under an overcast sky and on a wet field, the Kansas City Chiefs, who were thirteen-point underdogs, upset the Minnesota Vikings, 23–7. Despite the new NFL gambling scandal, oddsmakers in Las Vegas refused to take the game off the boards.[9] It was the second consecutive year that the AFL champions defeated favored NFL teams.

Before the game, President Richard Nixon, an avid football fan and a longtime gambler, had called Hank Stram and told him,

"Dismiss it [the gambling scandal] from your mind and go out and play like champions. I know there is nothing to the rumors about Dawson. He shouldn't be upset about them. Would you tell him that for me?" Nixon also called after the game to congratulate Len Dawson.

Dawson, who had missed six games during the regular season because of his knee surgery, completed twelve of seventeen passes for 142 yards and one touchdown. Only one of his passes was intercepted. The thirteen-year-veteran quarterback deservedly was selected as the game's most valuable player. Gate revenues from the game were nearly $4 million. Super Bowl IV captured the largest television audience of any prior single-day sporting event.

Len Dawson told me, "After the victory, [CBS sportscaster and former New York Giants star] Frank Gifford was interviewing me. Before the cameras went on, he said, 'Christ, everyone on the Giants team knows that guy [Don Dawson]. He was just one of those guys who seemed to get acquainted with football players.' "

When I asked Len Dawson how he was able to play so well in the Super Bowl under such conditions, he replied, "Throughout the week, once I hit the practice field, I was able to concentrate and focus my attention on what I had to do. On the day of the game, I knew what was there. I knew the pressures on me. My back was against the wall. I was guilty until proven innocent. I was there, and I was the story. I was the center of everything.

"You look for little signs that this might be your day. When I was warming up before the game, my arm felt great. That was one thing I could erase from my mind. The first play was a play pass, and I hit Mike Garrett for a first down. That really helped."

CBS-TV, which broadcast the game, never directly mentioned the gambling charges in its four hours of coverage—and only referred to the "extra strain" Dawson had suffered.

With the investigation blown by the timing of the NBC report and without wiretap authorization or the cooperation of any of the gamblers or players involved, the 1970 probe into sports gambling collapsed. On February 13, federal officials—who had promised "several dozen" more arrests in the gambling case—instead dropped all charges against several of those already arrested in early January.

However, ten more gamblers were indicted on February

24.[10] Don Dawson and Howard Sober were among them. Dizzy Dean was named as an unindicted coconspirator. Don Dawson pleaded guilty and spent nine months at Lewisburg and Allenwood in Pennsylvania. One month after Dawson's release, former attorney general John Mitchell entered Allenwood after his conviction for his role in the Watergate cover-up. Mitchell's attorney was Bill Hundley, the former chief of NFL Security.

After the Super Bowl, the heat on Len Dawson was still not off. The IRS began a lengthy audit of his income-tax returns because he had allegedly failed to report a portion of his income. "Dawson's wife claimed that the omission of his income had been a mistake on her part," an IRS official says. "The revenue agents did not believe this explanation but were forced to accept it because of 'pressure on high.' " The official says that the pressure came from the U.S. Department of Justice.

When I asked Dawson about this charge, he told me that he was not aware of any pressure from the Justice Department for the IRS to back off the investigation. To the contrary, he says that the IRS took a year and a half to conduct its probe of his finances.

"They came in after the Super Bowl," Dawson says. "A guy from Detroit and the guy from the IRS sat down in our family room and told me, 'You better have your lawyer with you.' They were honest. They were looking for some money in a secret bank account I supposedly had that had not been claimed. Really, they were looking for a payoff.

"They went through all the microfilm at the bank. In fact, I was on the board of the bank that I dealt with. They [the bank officers] were telling me the number of man-hours they [the IRS agents] spent going over everything—every deposit, every check. It was unbelievable.

"In the end, my wife was taking care of the books and maybe didn't report a couple of things. It had nothing to do with anything major. We're talking about a few hundred dollars. There was no hidden bank account, and that's what they were looking for. They found virtually nothing, except maybe a couple of hundred bucks from a speaking engagement—but nothing of any wrongful intent."

24 Restaurants and Hotels

WITH THE PUBLIC PRESSURE off the World Champion Kansas City Chiefs, new little-known investigations involving the Chiefs and other NFL personnel were launched.

In December 1970, the Chiefs' Johnny Robinson purchased a swimming and tennis club/restaurant in Kansas City from Edward P. "Eddie Spitz" Osadchey, who had been described in U.S. Senate testimony as a "part of the Kansas City organized-crime structure."[1] However, Robinson was not buying the business straight out. Osadchey was holding a $275,000 promissory note on the sale, which was to be paid in monthly installments until 1980. Also, Robinson's partner in the club was Jim Moran of New Orleans, who had also been described by law-enforcement authorities as a close associate of both Carlos Marcello and New Orleans Saints owner John Mecom.

"We've managed to bring New Orleans cooking to steak and potato country," Robinson told reporter Peter Finney. "In the fall, when our menu is extensive, Jimmy [Moran] comes up on Fridays and Saturdays [from New Orleans] to do the cooking himself."

When the Kansas City Crime Commission began to investigate the transaction, Robinson said that he had bought the business with the permission of the NFL. "I went through the proper channels on this," Robinson told me. "I notified the NFL and told them what I was going to do, and they told me to go ahead."

Reflecting on the Robinson-Osadchey controversy, Aaron Kohn says, "Robinson placed himself in the total financial control of this mob-connected guy because he owed all that money to him. This situation was evidence of the fact that the NFL was not meeting its responsibilities to the public. It demonstrated that they do not accept the high standard of responsibility to keep the sport untouched by compromising influences."

Pete Rozelle, who had been supplied information about the relationship between Marcello and Moran by Kohn's Metropolitan Crime Commission of New Orleans, publicly denounced the Kansas City Crime Commission for its investigation of Robinson and called the transaction a "simple purchase of property."

A similar arrangement was also made in 1970 by New Orleans running back Ernie Wheelright, who had formerly played with the New York Giants. He had opened two clubs in New Orleans. However, the real ownership of Central Park South, one of Wheelright's nightclubs, was traced directly to Carlos Marcello and Marcello's brother and son. The other lounge, the Zodiac Club, was owned by Anthony Glorioso, who had been indicted for his role in an interstate-gambling operation.

Once again, even after the NFL, the Saints, and Wheelright were notified of the underworld involvement in the clubs, the sales were permitted. The Saints' chief of security even helped to arrange them.

Rozelle, though critical of Wheelright's decision to go ahead with the deals, held a hearing on the matter at the NFL's New York offices. "The hearing showed that he wasn't culpable," Jack Danahy told me. "He hadn't violated any rule."

Wheelright quit football at the end of the 1970 season.

The same month that Robinson went to the NFL for permission to buy his restaurant, the FBI raided a Miami restaurant, the Bonfire, a popular hangout owned by fifty-nine-year-old Sam "Radio" Winer, a convicted bookmaker, who was another principal in the Beckley/Sklaroff bookmaking network. An FBI report described Winer as "a well-known Miami hoodlum." Involved in the world of Bahamian gambling, Winer had also been a close friend of Mafia capo Mike Coppola and Lou Chesler. In October 1969, Earl Faircloth, the state attorney general in Florida, charged that the Bonfire was "controlled by Mafia money." One law-enforcement official also said, "Winer was tight with Sklaroff and every O.C. [organized crime] figure on the beach."

FBI supervisor Ralph Hill remembers the Bonfire raid and says, "Among the things we discovered were some sheets reflecting what we refer to as bottom-line figures which bookmakers keep. Coach Hank Stram of the Kansas City Chiefs, his numbers were on these records—private, unlisted telephone numbers at home and his private, unlisted numbers at the field office. As a result, we interviewed Coach Stram about these numbers."

The FBI interviewed forty-six-year-old, Chicago-born Stram in Miami in February 1971. Hill says, "Coach Stram denied any complicity with Sam Winer other than having been a patron of his restaurant when he was in Miami as an assistant coach at the University of Miami [and later] . . . When questions were proffered to [Stram] about the unlisted telephone numbers," says the FBI agent, "his explanation was, 'Well, I felt that he was calling me as a nice person, as a friend, to inquire about the health of ballplayers.'

"When questioned about the bottom-line figures [that were over $10,000] that were named on the sheets, he [Stram] said, 'Well, it must have been a restaurant bill' that he incurred when he was in Miami during the Super Bowl the previous year. And it was explained to him that the Super Bowl was not played in Miami the previous year [rather it was in New Orleans], and the interview was concluded at that point."

Hill added that the federal grand jury investigating Winer's operations had considered a subpoena for Stram to testify—but the Strike Force chief in Miami decided against issuing it.

When I asked Stram how his name ended up in Winer's address book, Stram explained, "Winer was a good friend of the University of Miami when I was an assistant coach there in 1959. Winer was also a great friend of Andy Gustafson, who was the head coach at the time. So anytime we had to entertain visiting players or any dignitaries, Andy would say, 'Take them down to Radio's and have dinner.'

"So this one particular time, my wife, Monsignor Mackey, and I went over to Radio Winer's for dinner. We had a great dinner. And my wife loves stone crabs, and I do too. So during the discussion about the good meal we had, I mentioned to Radio, 'God, I wish we could get stone crabs where we are [in Kansas City], because we like them so much.' He said, 'That's no problem. I'll just send them to you.' I said, 'Can you do that without any trouble? Won't they spoil?' And he said, 'No, I'll package them up and send them to you in Kansas City.' I said, 'How much will they be?' And he said, 'Don't worry about that. I'll send them to you, and then let you know.'

"I gave him the address and phone number at my home and

office. I told him to call me before he sent them so that I knew when to pick them up."

Stram says that he has no idea why his name appeared on Winer's bottom sheets and insists, "I have never gambled on anything in my life." He added that whenever he went to Miami, "I would stop by to say hello to Radio and have dinner."

Chiefs owner Lamar Hunt later pushed out Stram as head coach, saying, "I am determined that the Chiefs are going to be a source of pride. I am confident that this announcement will begin a new era in that respect." Stram, who had been with the Dallas Texans/Kansas City Chiefs since the inception of the AFL, then became the head coach of John Mecom's New Orleans Saints.

In March 1970, San Diego Chargers owner Gene Klein[2] was registered at the twenty-one-room Acapulco Towers in Mexico during a meeting of major underworld figures. The meeting was reported in a confidential memorandum prepared by the Illinois Bureau of Investigation (IBI). Among those in attendance were Meyer Lansky and Morris Dalitz.

A night clerk for the hotel told the IBI that it "was never really run like a hotel." In fact, it was a private club. It was busy for three months during the year and empty the rest of the time; and it didn't attempt to attract guests during the off-season. The IBI report stated that several Hollywood celebrities had stayed there. They included actors Tony Curtis, Cyd Charisse, Tony Martin, Kirk Douglas, and Robert Evans, the producer of *The Godfather.*

The investigation of Acapulco Towers led to the indictment of Lansky, who had been hiding out at the hotel. He had been indicted for conspiracy to defraud the federal government of taxes on income of over $36 million, particularly from money skimmed from the Flamingo hotel/casino in Las Vegas. Lansky later fled to Israel, which, after a twenty-six-month legal fight, refused to accept him as a citizen because of his criminal background.[3]

Danahy told me that the NFL was completely unaware of either Klein's interest in Acapulco Towers or any of the events or principals involved with the hotel. Alexander MacArthur, the chairman of the Illinois Racing Commission, had publicly described Acapulco Towers as "a sunny place for shady people."

Klein was one of twelve stockholders in the hotel, who also

included Sidney Korshak and Moe Morton, a major gambling figure in California.[4] When I asked Klein about Acapulco Towers, he laughed. "That is such bullshit. I was playing tennis with Gene Wyman at my house. He said, "Hey, how would you like to buy ten percent of a hotel in Acapulco?' I asked, 'Who's buying?' He said, 'I'm buying ten percent. Sidney [Korshak] is buying ten percent. Phil Levin's buying ten percent. Greg Bautzer's buying ten percent. Moe Morton, I had never met him.' I said, 'Fine, I'll buy ten percent.' It was for a very insignificant amount of money. He said, 'We'll have a hotel. We'll have a place to go.' I said, 'Super! Let's go.'

"So sometime later, we pack in my jet. I take Gene and his wife. I take my late wife, and we went down to Acapulco. And we see Acapulco Towers. That was when I met Moe Morton. He ran it. He was married to some interior decorator who also had a piece of the hotel. The whole thing was no big deal. I kept it for a while, didn't make any money, and then we sold it to Phil Levin and Gulf and Western.[5] We broke about even."

When I asked Klein whether he was registered at the hotel during the Lansky mobster conference, Klein replied, "I could have been registered at the hotel. We used to go down there. We used to bring our own food. We swam in the pool. We cooked hot dogs and hamburgers. We had a great time. We spent three, four days in the sun. It's not even a real hotel. It's an apartment hotel. And then we went home.

"I spent all of my time at the pool. I've never met Meyer Lansky. I never knew him. I never talked to him. I never corresponded with him. I knew who he was because of the publicity."

A few months later, on September 21, 1970, the betting patterns of America changed dramatically as ABC-TV introduced *Monday Night Football,* an idea promoted by Pete Rozelle. As a result of the extra night of football, bookmakers rearranged their collection and payoff schedules from Mondays to Tuesdays. In the 1970 opener, the Cleveland Browns defeated the New York Jets, 31–21. There were 85,703 fans jammed in Cleveland's Municipal Stadium. The program was a ratings success and became a financial bonanza for the NFL, as well as for America's gambling crime syndicate.

25 The Heir Apparent

IN FEBRUARY 1970, AFTER the latest NFL gambling scandal flamed out and the movement to legalize offtrack betting in New York geared up, fifty-six-year-old Gil Beckley disappeared and was presumed murdered while still out on bond after his most recent gambling conviction.

"It is the opinion of many law-enforcement agencies, including representatives of the Federal Bureau of Investigation," says Nassau County prosecutor William Cahn, "that Beckley was done away with by the top echelon of syndicated organized crime because Beckley might have been cooperating with law-enforcement agencies."

Thought to have been behind Beckley's killing was New York mobster Tony Salerno, who had been Beckley's banker and equal partner in his nationwide bookmaking operation.

"Gil told me that he was going to make a deal with the government," one of Beckley's top associates told me. "Gil was doing poorly before he disappeared and for a long time before that." He adds that Beckley was a little off the wall at the end. Among other things, he was dealing in stolen clothing and airline tickets, as well as bogus credit cards. "In 1969, he couldn't pay off. He owed me over thirty thousand dollars.

"Gil was in bad shape. During the baseball season before he disappeared, Gil told me, 'Let me give you the people who are making the plays [bets] so that I can be sure that they get paid.' In other words, Bettor A was betting with him X amount on games, and he couldn't handle it. He wanted to give me Bettor

A's business so that I could pay and collect from him. But he wanted to be the one who talked to them, to make the deal. He wanted to be my beard. He was falling down bad."

The last known person to see Beckley alive was Elmer Dudley, an Atlanta-based member of Beckley's national bookmaking syndicate. Dudley claims that Beckley decided to flee the country to escape prison, and that Beckley had asked him to drive him to the airport in Montreal. "He had a suitcase with over a million dollars in it," Dudley recalls. "Don't ask me where he got it from." Dudley says that after dropping Beckley off in Montreal, he never saw him again. However, he, too, believes that he was murdered before he got away.

Another Beckley associate Mary Kane told me, "Knowing Gil as well as I did, I think it would have been impossible for him to stay hidden. Somebody would have known where he was. He didn't low-key it."

Taking over a portion of what remained of the Beckley network was his junior partner, the thirty-eight-year-old, five-feet-six Marty Sklaroff.

Sklaroff was an only child. While he was in high school during the late 1940s, he worked as a runner for his father, Jesse Sklaroff, a Philadelphia bookmaker. "In 1948 [while a student at Temple University], I started using heroin and I became addicted," Sklaroff wrote in a letter to his probation officer. "I was arrested in 1949 and convicted in 1950 in Philadelphia and got a one-year suspended sentence."

After Sklaroff moved to Miami, his father opened up the Silver Dollar Bar. Soon after his 1953 marriage, Sklaroff kicked his drug habit and became a professional gambler in his own right. By 1958, Jesse Sklaroff was working for his son, who had taken over the family business. Four years later, Marty was arrested for operating a gambling house and was fined $1,000. In 1964 and again in 1965, he was arrested for failing to have a federal wagering stamp, which identifies gamblers to the IRS for tax purposes.

In 1967, he was indicted and convicted with Beckley for interstate bookmaking and was given a two-year sentence. "At the time," Sklaroff wrote, "I was clerking for Gil Beckley, making phone calls for him in order to bet his information so that I could make bets on my own." Oddsmaker Bobby Martin told me that he was responsible for introducing Sklaroff to Beckley.

Incredibly, a federal judge in Miami, after Sklaroff's 1967 conviction, decided that the bookmaker had been "rehabilitated" and reduced his sentence from two years to six months in an "honor prison." The judge's decision was based on character references provided by several of Miami's top citizens. Sklaroff served only four months at Eglin Air Force Base and was released.

But on March 25, 1970, the month after Beckley's disappearance, the "rehabilitated" Sklaroff and three other men, including his father, were indicted on twenty-three counts of federal gambling violations in Miami, stemming from a series of raids in July 1969, as well as wiretaps placed on Sklaroff's telephones. All those indicted pleaded not guilty.

But the feds didn't just have Sklaroff good; they had him beautiful. Sklaroff's bookmaking operation had been receiving telephone calls at a bank of pay phones at the Miami International Airport. Federal agents found out about the system and received court authorization for wiretaps, which were monitored for six days.

The significance of this case was that, for the first time in American history, the wiretaps used were legal and admissible as evidence in federal court.[1] Unfortunately, all the wiretapping was done during the 1969 baseball, not football, season. Nothing about football betting was even discussed. During the six days of surveillance, the Sklaroff syndicate would make "over two hundred calls and receive and furnish line information, discuss baseball activities about major league pitching, make and accept baseball wagers . . . lay off bets over the telephones with persons in ten major cities located outside the state of Florida," according to the FBI.[2]

On June 1, 1971, a jury found Sklaroff guilty on six counts and sentenced him to four years in prison. He immediately appealed his conviction; his appeals were later rejected.

Sklaroff was indicted again on the same charges in Atlanta, also in June 1971.[3] He was again convicted and received a three-year prison sentence. He appealed, again questioning the legality of the federal wiretaps.

Speaking of the increasing use of electronic surveillance on bookmakers, Sklaroff lamented to reporter Jim Savage of *The Miami Herald*, "It's going to put us out of business. You can't work without a telephone . . . I wouldn't mind going to jail so much if they would let me have a couple of telephones in my cell. You know, so I'd have something to do."

Marty Steinberg, the head of the U.S. Strike Force in Miami, charged that "any small bookmaker can finance his own operation. But once you've reached a certain scale, winning is fine but every bookmaker gets into a streak where he loses and when you have the type of volume that Martin Sklaroff had . . . if you lose, you lose big. You don't have the cash reserves to pay off all the winners. So the financial arrangement is usually made that you split your winnings fifty-fifty with your organized-crime backer and the organized-crime backer will pay all losses."

Steinberg added that Sklaroff had an "interstate connection to obtain information about sports in various states and to obtain odds and to obtain information about teams and players. [It] is also used to fix sporting events so that bookmakers will win a large percentage and in turn split the winnings with the organized-crime figure." Like Beckley, Sklaroff's interstate connection was Tony Salerno, who was the former employer of Sklaroff's assistant, Reuben Goldstein of Las Vegas, according to Strike Force documents. Goldstein became Sklaroff's runner.[4]

During Sklaroff's bookmaking reign, a federal grand jury was impaneled in Cleveland in November 1970 and subpoenaed certain NFL records, as well as those of no fewer than eighteen NFL teams, The grand-jury probe had been prompted by charges made against the league by Walter Beach, a former defensive back for the Cleveland Browns. The grand-jury investigation focused on the possible impingement of players' rights by the NFL team owners.[5]

"I testified before that grand jury," NFL Security chief Jack Danahy told me. "There were charges that NFL Security was used to harass ballplayers, and that we never bothered the owners. It was funny. At the time, I had never given a player a polygraph. But I had polygraphed about five owners for a variety of reasons. I told the grand jury that, and they didn't want to see me anymore. The two Justice Department lawyers who were conducting the grand jury didn't want to hear about that. And so I was excused."

When I asked Danahy whether he had polygraphed any owners for gambling, he replied, "Yeah. One owner owned a chain of restaurants, and he had a bartender who was booking in his bar. I had notified him. I got this information from a police department source in the city in which it was occurring. After consulting with Pete—this was a ten percent owner—I told the owner that he had a bartender who had two jobs. And that he was also working as a bookmaker.

"The dopey owner took the telephone from the bar and put it back in the kitchen. That was his way of curing the situation. Of course, my source was the police officer who was sitting at the bar, listening to the guy. Now the guy was going into the kitchen to make the bets. So we really got pissed off at that.

"The owner came into New York for a game. And I invited him to stay over. And we polygraphed him to determine whether he had guilty knowledge of the guy's bookmaking—and whether he was involved with him. He wasn't. He passed the polygraph.

"Another one was Ralph Wilson from the Buffalo Bills. The general manager of his stables had sold a horse on his behalf to a mob guy in New Jersey. The Thoroughbred Racing Protective Bureau did an investigation. They gave their report to the steward at Saratoga, and the steward suspended Ralph Wilson.

"I went out to the thoroughbred-racing office and read the report. I then called the directors to tell them that the details of the case did not agree with the summary. They were contradictory. Ralph Wilson did not admit or have knowledge as to whom the horse was sold. So they had to retract it. To clear the air, we polygraphed Wilson on a Saturday morning in New York. He passed."

Danahy says that other instances of polygraphing owners involved "tampering" cases—in which one owner was trying to woo either a player or a coach from another team while he was still under contract, a violation of NFL rules.

In early January 1971, in the midst of the grand-jury probe, *The Cleveland Press* reported that three NFL players had been linked to a northeastern Ohio gambling syndicate, headed by, among others, James "Jack White" Licavoli, a top figure in the Cleveland Mafia, and his chief lieutenant, John Calandra. The investigation, being conducted by the U.S. Strike Force, reportedly concentrated on allegations that NFL players were involved in widespread gambling with and the passing of inside information to underworld figures. *The Press* reported that none of the players was a member of the Browns team.

However, the case was simply dropped, with no indictments

and no explanation as to who or what had been under investigation.

In late 1972, Jim Kensil, Rozelle's deputy, announced that an unnamed player had been approached by an unnamed former player and asked to throw a game for $10,000. Kensil said that details of the attempted fix were reported to Florida congressman Claude Pepper, who had chaired the U.S. House Select Committee on Crime's May 1972 hearings on "Organized Crime in Sports."[6] The unnamed player was identified by the committee only as Player X.

It was disclosed at the time that Player X was going to testify at further hearings on the mob's role in sports. "We intend to get into football, baseball, and basketball next year," Joe Phillips, the committee's counsel told *The New York Times* in December 1972. Phillips also charged that the NFL had been circulating a story that it had given the information about the alleged fix attempt to the committee. However, Phillips insisted that the committee had found out about it on its own—with no help from the NFL. Regardless, the hearings were never held.

Danahy explains what happened. "On a Sunday morning I got a call from our security man in Houston. Jerry Sturm [a center with the Houston Oilers] had come in and told his coach about being approached. We had a fast conference, and I called the coach. I also consulted with Rozelle. We agreed to let Jerry play.

"An ex-player for Denver had a company that had gone bad and had lost a lot of money in an investment. And he was looking for a score. They were out drinking, like Thursday night, and that's when the offer was made. We gave the case to the FBI, but I don't think anything came of it."

Specifically, Sturm had been offered $30,000 to help shave points in three 1971 Oilers games. He reported to the NFL that he had been visited by a former teammate Donnie Stone.[7] Stone, who had retired five years earlier, had allegedly introduced Sturm to a gambler who offered him $10,000 a game for his cooperation.

"On field-goal and extra-point situations, they wanted me to snap the ball over the kicker's head," Sturm told reporter Bill Brubaker, who is now with *The Washington Post.* "Then, when we were down on the goal line ready to score, they wanted me to not get the ball to the quarterback."

Sturm, who was making $30,000 a year in salary, told the two men that he would get back to them. He turned the offer down the following day. He then reported the incident to Ed Hughes, the head coach of the Oilers, who told NFL Security. The Oilers won their game against the Pittsburgh Steelers, who had been six-point favorites, the following Sunday, 29–3.

When Stone was confronted with the allegations by the FBI, he denied making the bribe offer. Consequently, it was Sturm's word against Stone's, and the government refused to prosecute.

Soon after, Pete Rozelle received a letter from an unnamed person who charged that he had loaned $10,000 to Stone for the purpose of fixing an NFL game. Stone had allegedly skipped off with the money, and the author of the letter wanted to make a claim against Stone's NFL pension.

The gambler in the Sturm case, who was also investigated but not arrested, was allegedly a part of the Beckley/Sklaroff gambling network operating out of Texas. No wiretaps had been authorized to help confirm Sturm's story.

26 "Points of Contact"

CONGRESSMAN PEPPER'S COMMITTEE ALSO received explosive testimony about an NFL owner on May 31, 1972, supplied by Aaron M. Kohn, the highly respected head of the Metropolitan Crime Commission of New Orleans. Kohn testified, "Many 'points of contact' have been established by gamblers and other racketeers with officials, staff, and players of the New Orleans Saints in the National Football League."

Kohn revealed that, just the previous month, John Mecom, Jr., the owner of the New Orleans Saints, "was a principal in the organization of two corporations at Fort Walton Beach, Florida. Two other principals are a convicted gambler and a developer with ties to the Marcello syndicate."

The two men with whom Mecom was doing business were Sam Presley, Jr., who "was sentenced to serve one year in prison for conspiracy and the use of an interstate facility to promote a gambling enterprise," and Gerald E. Stenner, who "has a considerable record of forming business partnerships with individuals who are also partners of Carlos Marcello or other major members of the Marcello structure."[1]

Kohn added that " 'point of contact' is the need for great concern in talking about the influence of organized crime on professional sports . . . And what do you talk about when you are a football player? You talk about your everyday life, which is football. When you are an owner of a football team, [you] talk about your interests. And nothing is of more interest to people who are 'points of contact' for the gambling fraternity than that kind of relaxed discussion of what is happening before the game, what the anticipations are, the boasting, the criticism, the inner fighting. And it is at that level that these people easily establish 'points of contact.' "[2]

Speaking of Mecom, the New Orleans crime fighter concluded, "When local sports officials, expected to protect sports against corrupting influences, are instead actively participating in organized crime, or economically allied with organized-crime elements, the public interest is endangered and the need for federal checks becomes imperative."

On June 14, two weeks after Kohn's testimony, Commissioner Rozelle announced that the NFL had conducted an investigation of Kohn's charges against Mecom. Rozelle concluded that Mecom's business interests with Presley and Stenner were "simple real estate deals." However, the commissioner did acknowledge that Presley "has an Internal Revenue Service conviction on a gambling charge, but it was not Mr. Mecom who brought him into the transactions and the individual is by no means an associate of the Saints' owner."

Despite the fact that Rozelle had absolved Mecom of any wrongdoing, he added, "[T]o remove all possible suspicion of involvement with alleged undesirable persons, Mr. Mecom has agreed to dispose of his holdings and sever all connections with the investment programs." Rozelle did not say whether the league had forced Mecom to sell.

Mecom—who said the day of Rozelle's announcement that he had cooperated fully with the NFL's investigation—angrily released a statement, saying, "My name was mentioned by Mr. Kohn who thought by insinuation and far-reaching innuendos to make headlines derogatory to my character, business reputation, and the New Orleans Saints. These insinuations and innuendos have no basis whatsoever for the damaging conclusions Mr. Kohn attempted to draw from them . . . It is my firm belief that divesting myself of any interests in the Florida investments will dispel any public doubts concerning this situation."

Kohn is still bitter about the way he was treated by the NFL and told me, "These people have to use the only weapon available to them when they are confronted with the truth: To deny the facts and to attack the messenger."

Earlier in 1972, during a January appearance on CBS-TV's

Face the Nation, Rozelle, referring indirectly to Danahy's work, announced that NFL team owners had been subjected to lie detector tests which asked whether they had been gambling on NFL games. Although no specific case was mentioned, Rozelle left the impression that everyone passed. "If an owner were proven guilty of gambling," he said, "according to the league rules he would be expelled from the NFL."

During his 1972 appearance on the CBS program, Rozelle, a longtime critic of legalized sports gambling, also announced that he was totally opposed to any movement that would expand offtrack betting to football. "I don't ever want to see the day when a whole new generation of fans exists who will sit in a stadium and boo a home team for sitting on a four-point lead and not covering the point spread."

Rozelle then took the opportunity to announce that although some players had been known to take drugs, like "greenies" and "pep pills," before games, the practice of drug abuse within the NFL "was not widespread."

At the time of Rozelle's appearance on CBS, the league was in negotiations for the creation of a new NFL franchise in Seattle, Washington. In June 1972, an investment group headed by Lloyd W. Nordstrom, the owner of a large, eight-state department-store chain that carried his name, and Herman Sarkowsky, the majority owner of the Portland Trail Blazers of the NBA, announced their intention to buy the franchise for $16 million. They were awarded the franchise in 1974.

The partners immediately announced that they were going to build a sixty-five-thousand-seat, indoor stadium called the Kingdome. The team, which didn't begin league play until 1976, was called the Seattle Seahawks. However, before the Seahawks' first game, Nordstrom died of a heart attack, leaving Sarkowsky as the managing general partner.[3]

There was more news on the owners' front. On July 13, 1972, Carroll Rosenbloom stunned the sports world by swapping his Baltimore Colts for the Los Angeles Rams, with no money changing hands. "Actually, the deal was made over a year earlier," a longtime friend of Rosenbloom told me. "When Dan Reeves [the owner of the Rams] died in April 1971, part of his estate, including the team, was put up for sale. Rosenbloom had been unhappy in Baltimore and had been taking a lot of grief from the local media for some time and wanted out. So he bought an option on the Rams. That gave him the ability to approve its next owner."

Forty-nine-year-old, ex-Marine Robert Irsay, the president of a major heating and air-conditioning company based in Skokie, Illinois, was looking for an NFL team to buy and had always been a big fan of Johnny Unitas of the Colts. In 1971, Irsay, who was publicly accused by his wife of being an alcoholic and a heavy gambler, sold his company to Katy Industries and had money to burn.[4]

"Irsay became Carroll's beard," the friend continued. "Irsay went in and bought the Rams for nineteen million dollars. Of course, he had the approval of Rosenbloom, who immediately gave Irsay the Colts in return for the paper on the Rams. Irsay got Unitas and Rosenbloom got to move to the West Coast.[5] Everyone was happy, and the league didn't interfere."

Indeed, Washington Redskins owner Jack Kent Cooke, who was one of Rosenbloom's neighbors in Los Angeles, told sports columnist Shirley Povich of *The Washington Post* that the NFL would approve of the trade. "It was brilliantly conceived by one of our league's finest men. I applaud it."

Also, the even trade permitted Rosenbloom to legally save nearly $4.5 million in capital-gains taxes. "I am the hundred percent owner of the Rams," Rosenbloom said in a statement. "That's the only way I operate. I didn't have any cash in the transaction. It was simply a trade." The 1972 Colts/Rams trade resembled the 1941 swap between the Pittsburgh Steelers and Philadelphia Eagles, which involved Art Rooney, Bert Bell, and Alex Thompson.

Rosenbloom had reportedly grown disillusioned in Baltimore—even after his team had gone fifteen years without a losing season and won three NFL championships, including the 1971 Super Bowl over Dallas, 16–13, with five seconds left in the game. He charged that the Baltimore Orioles major-league baseball team and its owner, Jerry Hoffberger, were receiving preferential treatment over the Colts by the city.

Rosenbloom was also constantly complaining about the condition of Baltimore's Municipal Stadium. Threatening to move the Colts to a nearby Maryland suburb or even to Tampa, Florida—where Rosenbloom had planned to play three exhibition games in 1972—he had felt misled by local politicians who had promised to make improvements.

Also, being the second-largest individual stockholder in Warner Communications,[6] Rosenbloom was looking forward to moving to Southern California and becoming part of the Hollywood set, where he could watch over his massive investment in the corporation.

After his move to Los Angeles, Rosenbloom sold his East Coast houses, including one in Golden Beach, Florida, where he was a neighbor of his old friend Sonny Werblin, the former owner of the New York Jets. Rosenbloom immediately bought a huge mansion in Bel Air and a second house on the Pacific Ocean on Broad Beach Road near Malibu. He soon became a host to the stars he met through Warner Communications.

His son Steve—who had served as club president of the Colts since March 18, 1971, when his father promoted himself to chairman of the board—balked at first about going to the West Coast. Steve had his own business investments and had recently married a woman whom the elder Rosenbloom did not like.

But, after sitting out for the 1972 season, Steve Rosenbloom succumbed and moved to Los Angeles,[7] as did Rosenbloom's general manager, Don Klosterman, who retained Tommy Prothro as the Rams head coach.

Speaking of the former Colts' owner, Klosterman once said, "The most important man on a pro football team is the club owner. That's why I joined Carroll Rosenbloom in Baltimore when I got the chance. The marrow of a football structure is ownership. You win if you have absolute direction, if you have the know-how and if he's willing to pay the price."[8]

Rosenbloom seemed to confirm that at his first press conference in Los Angeles after he bought the Rams. Showing off his Super Bowl ring, Rosenbloom told reporters, "I'm hoping that some of the luck I've had will rub off on the Rams. There's nothing of which I'm more proud than my Super Bowl ring. I'd like to be the first owner to win the Super Bowl in both conferences."

There was only one lingering problem that resulted from the Colts/Rams trade. A Jacksonville attorney, Hugh Culverhouse, had reportedly made a handshake agreement with Dan Reeves—before Reeves's death—to buy the Rams for $17 million. Consequently, Culverhouse filed a $6 million antitrust suit in federal court against the Colts and the Rams. Culverhouse charged that the transaction suppressed competition and would "further monopolize the monopoly power acquired by them in the business of pro football in the territory of Los Angeles and its environs."

The Culverhouse suit was settled with the terms undisclosed. NFL sources have indicated that Culverhouse was promised the inside track on the next available NFL franchise. Pushing the deal, of course, was Carroll Rosenbloom.

Fitting into Los Angeles society like one of his designer suits, Rosenbloom, a major contributor to Richard Nixon's 1972 reelection bid, threw a party and a half for the 1973 Super Bowl VII in which the Miami Dolphins defeated the Washington Redskins, 14–7. Because the game was being played at the Los Angeles Memorial Coliseum, Rosenbloom cheerfully assumed the role of host, taking thirty of his closest pals to the game on a bus after a champagne brunch at Chasen's.

Then, there was an aftergame dinner party at the Bistro restaurant in Beverly Hills, which is owned, in part, by mob attorney Sidney Korshak. Among the guests were MCA's chief executive Lew Wasserman, attorney Eugene Wyman, Ethel Kennedy, NFL owners Gene Klein and Al Davis, astronauts Alan Shepard and Gene Cernan, sports reporter Howard Cosell, ABC sports director Roone Arledge, tycoon Alfred Bloomingdale, former California senator John Tunney, singer Dionne Warwick, former New York Giants star Frank Gifford, filmmaker George Stevens, Jr., and movie stars Henry Fonda, David Janssen, and Darren McGavin.

Carroll and Georgia Rosenbloom had arrived in Los Angeles.

27 Operation Anvil

DURING JUNE AND JULY 1973, in the midst of his appeals, Marty Sklaroff was wiretapped—once again during baseball season. Federal agents discovered that Sklaroff was still bookmaking, but now he was also working in concert with two known drug dealers. According to a confidential Justice Department memorandum, in one operation alone, "surveillance of Sklaroff also indicates that he is associating with Mr. Marty Katz and Mr. Frank Balicchio, both of whom are known to the Strike Force to be heavily involved in narcotics trafficking and loan-sharking. Assistant U.S. Attorney [Marty] Steinberg feels that this is a definite indication that Sklaroff is becoming more deeply entrenched in the machinery of Organized Crime."

Sklaroff was also taped, implicating himself in a $116,000 layoff operation financed by the Mafia. In another Sklaroff enterprise, the Strike Force discovered that his "operation was worth approximately $50,000 a day or $18,000,000 a year."

Although Sklaroff had been rapidly losing his influence in the national gambling syndicate because of his perpetual legal problems, his activities prompted the initiation by the Organized Crime and Racketeering Section (OCRS) of the Justice Department of Operation Anvil, which had begun after Beckley's disappearance. The investigation was directed by William S. Lynch, who had replaced Henry Petersen as the new chief of the OCRS in 1969. Petersen had become the head of the criminal division under John Mitchell.

Lynch wrote, "As a result of the data accumulated during Anvil, we now estimate that a minimum of $29.8 billion a year was bet in 1973: $19.2 billion on sporting events . . . The LCN [La Cosa Nostra] controls 42.9% of the volume of gross wagers placed and 45.9% of the profit thus derived. In addition, they and their associates control most of the line and layoff services used by non-connected bookmakers, thus adding to their profit in this field."

Hoping to inspire his troops, Lynch continued, "I cite these figures to emphasize the importance of gambling enforcement to the overall suppression of organized crime. And while I realize that such activity is tedious and often unrewarding in terms of sentencing, it must be continued. To that end I want you to rework, by means of Title III [the federal wiretap authorization included in the 1968 Omnibus Crime Act] whenever possible, all gambling cases that have been worked in the past five years."[1]

Lynch also codified the OCRS's and the Strike Force's priorities in the war against the national gambling syndicate. "New cases involving major gambling violators should be sought out and prosecuted. For the purposes of this memorandum, an operation is considered major if:

1. It involves an LCN member or any of the more famous LCN associates (i.e., of a stature of Gil Beckley, Frank Rosenthal or Jerome Zarowitz or the equivalent) as an active participant in the operation;
2. It involves line making and dissemination;
3. It involves regional (i.e., three or more states) or national layoffs or a layoff operation essential, in your opinion, to the successful functioning of other bookies in your area;
4. It involves a numbers operation, horse book or sports book of substantial wagering volume;
5. It involves a gambling operation as to which there is substantial likelihood of developing evidence of official corruption."

During my interview with Lynch, he told me, "We viewed the organized-crime syndicate as being the dominate force in the national gambling operations. And we found that some of the top LCN chiefs were working directly with the bookmakers and the layoff artists. Operation Anvil was really the government's full-court press against the organized-crime syndicate. Our targets were the big sports gamblers and the mob chiefs who backed them."

By the time Operation Anvil concluded its work in 1974, Marty Sklaroff was cold coffee. The federal government's effort to shut him down had been completely successful. According to a confidential report from the Strike Force in Miami, "Sklaroff was betting back into his own line of information, unknown to his financial backer, Tony Salerno. When Sklaroff would win, he failed to declare his winnings to Salerno. However, when he lost he declared the [losses] and they were absorbed by Salerno . . . Sklaroff is gradually becoming a 'man on the outside' primarily due to his having attempted to conceal winnings from Tony Salerno. Sklaroff is heavily in debt to Salerno and is also becoming increasingly entangled within the workings of the U.S. Courts."[2]

Another former top Justice Department official told me, "During the Operation Anvil days, the federal government was using about seventy-two percent of its electronic surveillance on gambling connections. But the cost of wiretapping is very high. You need men stationed around the clock, day in and day out, to monitor the target's calls. And that ran us at least a thousand dollars a day and sometimes a lot more. I've known of cases where month-long surveillance jobs were involved that cost us anywhere from three hundred thousand to four hundred thousand dollars.

"So what happens? The target gets indicted using all the evidence we've accumulated. And he's not a Beckley or a Sklaroff. Those kinds of cases don't come in very often. Instead the target is a midlevel bookmaker. So he comes in, plea-bargains his way out, and is, maybe, fined ten thousand dollars for his medium-size, twenty-five-thousand-dollar-a-month operation. I think we just kind of looked at each other and started to ask ourselves whether all of this was worth it."[3]

According to the FBI, the dissemination and enforcement of the outlaw line is a principal function of the organized-crime syndicate. During the 1950s and 1960s, the outlaw line was controlled by the New York Mafia. After Beckley's disappearance and Sklaroff's demise, the responsibility for the outlaw line was assumed by the Chicago Mafia—although other Mafia families received a share of the profits in proportion to their investments in it.

The man responsible for managing the outlaw line for the Chicago Mafia was Frank Larry "Lefty" Rosenthal. Born Norman Rosenthal in Chicago's Albany Park in 1929, he was the son of an owner of thoroughbred racehorses. An impeccably dressed, six-feet-one, trim, handsome man with blue eyes and thinning blond hair, which he fretted over, Lefty Rosenthal is a character out of a Damon Runyon story.

Marty Kane, one of his closest and most loyal friends, told me how he received the "Lefty" tag. "He was living in Miami, and he was getting raided, and he got mad," Kane says. "And he punched through a window with his right hand. The glass cut the nerves in his hand so badly that he had to start learning how to write with his left hand. He's not naturally left-handed. That's when everyone started calling him Lefty." Several Mafia figures had also dubbed Rosenthal as "Pazzo," an Italian word meaning "crazy" or "deranged."

Speaking of Rosenthal, another one of his associates told me, "This is a real dangerous character. He had swindles going on everywhere."

Rosenthal gambled from the age of thirteen and booked bets with classmates while in high school. Rosenthal attended Wright Junior College in Chicago to study business administration but never graduated. Instead, he became a professional gambler. He befriended other famous gamblers, like Minnesota Fats and Nicholas "Nick the Greek" Dandolas, and Chicago mobsters, like Don Angelini, Frank "the Horse" Buccieri, and Joseph "Spa" Spadavecchio.

During his gambling career, Rosenthal has been arrested no fewer than fifteen times—but has never been convicted of a felony. He was first arrested in October 1953 in Evanston, Illinois, for distributing parlay-betting cards. The case was dismissed. The following year, he joined the U.S. Army, later receiving an honorable discharge.

Rosenthal returned to Chicago and opened Mutt and Jeff's, a hot dog stand that was suspected as being a front for his gambling activities. Leaving that behind in early 1957, he went to work for handicapper Bill Kaplan and Chicago Mafia soldier Don Angelini on the Angel-Kaplan Sports News, Inc. He worked as a $150-a-week-handicapper. Angelini, who had been forced on Kaplan in 1957 by Gus Alex and the Chicago Mafia, became Rosenthal's mentor, according to law-enforcement officials.

Investigators from the Chicago Crime Commission interviewed Angelini in January 1961 and asked him about Rosenthal. According to the commission's report, "We were told by [Angelini] that Rosenthal was employed by the Sports Service from early 1957 to late 1959 as a clerk. He left of his own accord and proved to be a capable worker and one 'who liked the work.' "

Rosenthal told reporter Jan Allyson Wilson, "You can't bet the tables (blackjack and craps) because of the PC (percentage) and the limit. The only gambling game you can beat is a game of opinion—the sporting events." It wasn't unusual for Rosenthal to bet $100,000 on a single contest; Rosenthal once boasted of having bet $500,000 on a football game. "For Lefty to have bet that kind of money," says a top Justice Department lawyer, "he had to know the outcome of the game in advance."

Like Beckley, Rosenthal had a long list of team personnel who received money in return for supplying him with inside information. In 1960, while working for Angel-Kaplan in Miami, Rosenthal was charged with conspiring to fix a basketball game between New York University and West Virginia University during the regional finals of the NCAA tournament in Charlotte, North Carolina. He had offered a bribe to one of the NYU players. Rosenthal pleaded nolo contendere and was fined $6,000.

A confidential report states that one of Rosenthal's coconspirators, David Budin, told agents from the North Carolina Bureau of Investigation "that he [Rosenthal] and Gil Beckley were partners and exchanged information."

Budin also told state agents that he "had given [the] New York District Attorney's office enough information to make a similar investigation involving football. That this would be almost as big as basketball, but that New York never did anything about this. Budin further stated that in his opinion fixes had never stopped. That this was especially true in professional football."

"Rosenthal was always trying to fix something," a former associate says. "I'd tell him, 'Lefty, this team can't win.' And he'd say, 'Just watch.' He must have had somebody on the other side. He thinks everything is crooked. He just doesn't breathe clean air."

Two years later he was indicted for attempting to bribe Michael Bruce, a halfback for the University of Oregon, prior to a 1960 football game against the University of Michigan.

On September 23, 1960, according to Bruce, Rosenthal and an associate offered Bruce $5,000 for his help in throwing the game—which was to be played the following day—another $5,000 for successfully soliciting the cooperation of the team's quarterback, and $100 a week for providing Rosenthal with inside information.

Bruce told his coach about the offer; the coach called the police. Fearing for his life, Bruce refused to testify in court against Rosenthal, and so the case was dropped. However, Bruce later testified about the offer before the U.S. Senate Permanent Subcommittee on Investigations in 1961. Confronted with Bruce's charges, Rosenthal took the Fifth, and he was never indicted.

Regardless of the charges, Rosenthal denies ever fixing anyone. He later would tell the Nevada Gaming Commission, "I did not in my entire life corrupt or bribe an athlete or public official. I admit I gambled illegally outside the state of Nevada, and my judgment should have been better in who I associated with . . . The FBI knew I was a top gambler. They wanted me to act as an informant for them—to rat on other gamblers. They said I could call my own shot."

Only a few months after the Bruce incident, in December 1960, Rosenthal was arrested for operating a gambling establishment in his Miami apartment.[4] No action was taken against him on that charge. At the moment of the raid on Rosenthal's apartment, Lefty was speaking on the telephone with Gil Beckley. However, Rosenthal was accused of attempting to bribe a police officer at the time of the arrest.

One of the police officers who had arrested Rosenthal, Martin F. Dardis, reported, "Mr. Rosenthal said he could not understand it [the arrest] because he had been paying off five hundred dollars a month not to be harassed. Mr. Rosenthal then asked me if I had been 'shortchanged' and stated, 'Didn't you get your piece?' . . . I interpret Mr. Rosenthal's comments as indicating that Mr. Rosenthal was paying money to law-enforcement officers to keep them from interfering with his gambling operation."

Consequently, because of his alleged bookmaking activities and his boast of bribing police officials, his license from the Florida Racing Commission was revoked. Labeled as an undesirable, he was also banned from Gulfstream Park and other Florida racetracks.

On May 16, 1962, after nearly a year of being arrest-free, Rosenthal was indicted in New York for being a coconspirator in a scheme "relating to 'fixing' basketball games across the country from November 20, 1957, through March 17, 1961," according to court documents that cited "over 72 overt acts." Rosenthal's alleged coconspirator was convicted; Rosenthal was not.

In early 1963, Rosenthal went to work for Sam Green, the president of Multiple Sports in Miami, which published "a weekly sheet of games and schedules, as well as provided a telephone/line service to its customers, relaying the latest odds as they changed," according to a federal memorandum. "Sometimes those odds would change 2 or 3 times a day . . . Frank Rosenthal was solely responsible for setting the line and its changes."

Soon after, while working with Green and Multiple Sports, Rosenthal was picked up by the Miami Beach police for disorderly conduct. At the time of his arrest, he was in the company of a man named Anthony Spilotro, who had become Rosenthal's young protégé. The case was dismissed against Rosenthal.

The following June, Rosenthal was arrested by Maryland state police officers outside Washington, D.C., along with local gambling czar Joe Nesline, who was investigated in the 1967–68 sports-gambling probe in Washington, and New York mobster Charles "the Blade" Tourine for gambling violations. The charge was later reduced to disorderly conduct. Rosenthal pleaded guilty and forfeited his $100 bond. Interestingly, at the time of the arrest, Rosenthal and Nesline gave the same Washington address as their residence.

Between 1964 and 1966, Rosenthal was arrested four more times for disorderly conduct, failure to make criminal registration, gambling, and "open profanity," but all these charges against him were dismissed. During that same period, he was listed in the U.S. Senate Subcommittee Hearings on Organized Crime and Illicit Traffic in Narcotics as an associate of several top organized-crime figures, including Anthony Joseph DiChiarinte and Spartico Mastro, both of whom were narcotics dealers.

In 1965, Multiple Sports was shut down after the FBI raided its offices. However, neither Rosenthal nor his boss, Sam Green, were prosecuted. That same year, Rosenthal was ejected from Miami's jai-alai gambling community because he was termed to be a "bookmaker, sports fixer, undesirable."

Rosenthal and Green were called to testify before a federal grand jury in Miami in June 1967 but both refused to answer questions. They had been implicated in a series of local bombing attacks. No charges were filed against them.

However, soon after Rosenthal's appearance before the grand jury, he suddenly left Miami and returned to Chicago. He also started spending a great deal of time in Las Vegas. Then, he cited his employment as "personal handicapping." According to a Justice Department memorandum, "While in Chicago, he [Rosenthal] maintained close ties with Tony Spilotro, supposedly assisting him in setting up the bookmaking network which had been [recently] disrupted by law enforcement officials. He also maintained ties with Green, even to the point of calling Green from Spilotro's Chicago phone."

In 1968, Rosenthal officially moved to Las Vegas and received a work permit from the Clark County sheriff's office. He opened and became the general manager of a legal bookmaking business, Rose Bowl Sports Book—although, according to federal records, hidden interests in the Rose Bowl were held by Boston bookmaker Elliot Paul Price, and Price's mentor, Jerome Zarowitz, a former executive at Caesars Palace who was convicted of attempting to fix the 1946 NFL championship game and spent twenty months in prison.

Zarowitz and Price had been present at an October 1965 meeting in Palm Springs, which has become known as the "Little Apalachin Conference." Also present at the meeting were Meyer Lansky's Mafia messenger, Vincent "Jimmy Blue Eyes" Alo, and Tony Salerno. Another convicted Miami bookmaker, "Fat" Ruby Lazarus, was in attendance as well.

Federal prosecutors alleged that among the topics of the meeting was the division of ownership for Caesars Palace, which had been financed in part by a $10.5 million loan from the Teamsters' Central States Pension Fund.[5] Another major topic was the underworld's layoff operations on the East Coast. Lazarus was called to testify before a federal grand jury in Los Angeles and took the Fifth twenty-five times, refusing to answer questions about the meeting.

Caesars Palace was sold to Lum's, Inc., the restaurant chain, in October 1969. Lum's retained Zarowitz, who was making over $300,000 a year, despite his criminal background. In May 1970, after Zarowitz refused to obtain a license through the Nevada Gaming Commission, he was forced to resign by public-relations-minded casino executives. However, investigations of the sale of

Caesars Palace to Lum's yielded Zarowitz $3.5 million of the $58 million purchase price, even though Zarowitz was not listed as owning a single share of stock.[6]

Price, an associate of Boston Mafia boss Raymond Patriarca, had been bankrolled by Beckley after experiencing financial difficulties. Another Beckley associate, Marty Kane, was Rosenthal's chief assistant at the Rose Bowl Sports Book. And former Sklaroff associate Reuben Goldstein later became Kane's runner.

Kane told me that he ran the Rose Bowl in Rosenthal's absence. "I worked there because I was doing Lefty a favor. He was kind of sick. He had ulcers, and he asked me to go in there. I'd get information on games. When Lefty couldn't show up, I would run the place. Otherwise, I was just another clerk."

Apparently, the remnants of the Beckley/Sklaroff network had shifted to the new Rosenthal network. Thus, to all intents and purposes, the entry of Rosenthal, Zarowitz, Price, Kane, and Goldstein into the Rose Bowl's bookmaking business sent a signal to law-enforcement officials that the outlaw line had officially moved from Miami to Las Vegas. It was a move that could not have been accomplished without the consent of the underworld's nine-member national crime commission.

On December 12, 1970, while working at the Rose Bowl Sports Book, Rosenthal, Price, Zarowitz, and several others were arrested for their roles in an interstate-gambling operation. Among the federal raids in twenty-six cities in eleven states—which Attorney General John Mitchell had called "the largest coordinated gambling raids ever"[7]—agents hit both the Rose Bowl Sports Book and Caesars Palace, where more than $1.5 million in hundred-dollar bills was found in lockboxes registered in Zarowitz's name. The money had been the alleged yield from an illegal bookmaking operation.

The government charged that, among other things, Rosenthal had obtained information that would have changed the point spreads of college and professional football games. Instead of releasing this information to the public, Rosenthal gave it to only his favorite customers. Those arrested were indicted in January 1971.

But the indictments against Rosenthal and company were dismissed on November 5, 1975, by U.S. District Judge Roger Foley because the wiretaps that had been used to collect the evidence against them had been obtained before the government had exhausted normal investigative procedures. Also, the authorization for the wiretaps had been botched by the Mitchell Justice Department.[8]

While under indictment, Rosenthal, who had undergone major surgery for the removal of his stomach ulcers, had been hired as the Stardust hotel/casino in Las Vegas as a blackjack floorman. However, the Nevada Gaming Control Board insisted that Rosenthal submit an application to be licensed. Instead, Rosenthal was taken off the casino floor and placed in the hotel's public-relations department, a job that did not require licensing. At the time Rosenthal was hired, the Stardust was owned by a reputed front man for Los Angeles mob attorney Sidney Korshak, who was still the top mouthpiece for the Chicago Mafia.

Meantime, Rosenthal had remained the mentor and the closest friend of Chicago Mafia soldier Anthony Spilotro, who became the enforcer of the outlaw line.

Rosenthal later testified, "I have known Tony Spilotro as his mother conceived him [*sic*], which happens to be the exact truth . . . Tony Spilotro over the many, many years of our junior and adult life has been a very personal, close friend of mine."

In an interview with my associate, William Scott Malone, James Fratianno, a Mafia-boss-turned-federal-witness, said, "Tony Spilotro bets big on football games, and Lefty Rosenthal is his very, very close friend. [Rosenthal] tells him which teams to bet. He bets maybe twenty, thirty thousand [dollars] on a game, maybe more. It all depends what team they are betting on."

Spilotro was a feared and ruthless man who wielded considerable power in Las Vegas and in Southern California. Credited with at least twenty-five brutal gangland murders, including one in which he was said to have crushed his victim's head in a carpenter's vise, Spilotro soon became among the most feared Mafia figures in America.

Spilotro was the fourth of six sons born to Patsy Spilotro (their father), the proprietor of Patsy's, a favorite hangout for members of the Capone mob on Chicago's West Side. The restaurant failed soon after Patsy's death in 1953. Tony Spilotro was a roughneck and a punk in high school; he beat up other students and even teachers with equal indiscretion. He was thrown out of school in 1955 when he was in the tenth grade and never returned.

Spilotro, nicknamed the Ant because of his muscular five-feet-three frame, got started in the business by running errands and collecting money for Chicago mobster Sam DeStefano with whom he was working when he had met Rosenthal. Later, Spilotro became a registered bail bondsman for the Cook County criminal court in Illinois. Soon he was a top juice collector, and he rose in prominence because of his ruthlessness. After he allegedly murdered DeStefano, he went to work for another Chicago Mafia leader, Felix Alderisio, until he moved to Miami to become a runner for Rosenthal.

In 1971, with Rosenthal's help, Spilotro moved to Las Vegas with his wife and son. He quickly became the most feared loan shark on the Strip. At the height of his power, he directed a forty-man goon squad. In the 1970s, it was widely thought that he was behind a string of syndicate slayings in which the victims were killed by several shots to the head from a .22 caliber pistol with a silencer held at close range. At that time, according to law-enforcement officials, Spilotro reported to Joseph Lombardo, a top capo with the Chicago Mafia.

Although Spilotro had been arrested for bookmaking, loan-sharking, and three times for murder, he had never spent more than twenty-four hours in jail. His only conviction was for filing a false mortgage application.

In the NFL, problems were brewing within the Oakland Raiders. Managing general partner Al Davis and the team's major stockholder, Wayne Valley, had gone to war with each other after Raiders wide receiver Warren Wells, already convicted of attempted rape and placed on probation in September 1969, was arrested again in February 1971, this time for driving while intoxicated and illegal possession of a handgun. The following September, he was arrested for a third time after he beat up a woman, who then stabbed him.

Davis went to Valley and asked him to use his influence on the judge, who was a personal friend of Valley, in Wells's case. Wells was released—but not for ten months. Davis reportedly left the clear impression with the other Raiders players that Valley would have acted more promptly had Wells been a white man. Valley was furious with Davis over the rumor and decided not to renew Davis's contract in 1976.[9]

Davis then went to Ed McGah, the third Raiders partner

who had not been a party to the Davis/Valley dispute. Davis convinced McGah to sign him to a twenty-year contract at an annual salary of $100,000. McGah also gave Davis broad powers over the operation of the team. The contract was signed in July 1972, but Valley didn't find out about it until February 1973 and immediately filed suit. However, Valley lost the case and sold his interest in the Oakland team. Consequently, Davis bought another 15 percent of the club.

Embroiled in the struggle to maintain control of the Raiders, Davis might have been surprised to know that his future would soon be intertwined with those of Lefty Rosenthal, Tony Spilotro, and the new man in Las Vegas: Allen R. Glick.

28 Façades of Legitimacy

ALLEN R. GLICK HAD been an unknown thirty-two-year-old, La Jolla-based real estate executive.[1] Overnight, he became the second-largest casino operator in Nevada, behind Howard Hughes's Summa Corporation[2] and would bring the largest hotel sports book to Las Vegas. While Lefty Rosenthal provided the brains for the new legalized sports-bookmaking operation, as well as the outlaw line, Tony Spilotro was poised in the shadows as his muscle.[3] Spilotro was so quiet that Glick told me, "I never dealt with Spilotro, never was he on any of my payrolls. I never met him."[4]

Born in Pittsburgh and the son of a scrap-iron dealer, Glick won a Bronze Star Medal in Vietnam, where he served as an aerial observer and artillery adviser aboard a helicopter. A graduate of Ohio State University and Case Western Reserve University Law School in Cleveland, he never actually practiced law, although he was a member of the bar in Pennsylvania and California.

Out of college, Glick became a close friend of Joseph Philip Balistrieri, the son of Frank Balistrieri, the boss of the Milwaukee Mafia, which is within the Chicago Mafia's sphere of influence. In 1969, Glick and his wife moved to a suburb of San Diego, where he began working as a $750-a-month assistant in multifamily projects with the American Housing Guild.

In mid-1971, Glick went to work for Saratoga Development Corporation of La Jolla. The company had been founded in 1965 by Dennis Wittman, a financial adviser to Carroll Rosenbloom.

By September 1972, Glick had become a 45 percent owner of the business. "I acquired an interest in Saratoga for $25,000 and the obligation of guaranteeing all corporate projects and being an executive of the company," he says. Immediately, Glick became a millionaire since the company was worth an estimated $10.5 million.

After a trip to Las Vegas later that year to negotiate a land deal, he, along with four partners, purchased the Hacienda hotel/casino for $4 million. Glick's four partners were Columbus, Ohio, businessman Gene Fresch; Paul Lowden, and entertainment and real estate executive; Dr. Joe Ingersol, a prominent Las Vegas dentist; and gaming executive Gene Neely. "Fresch found the deal," Glick told me, "and presented it to me for a recreational-vehicle park and the use of its fifty-plus acres on the Strip. The real estate was the key. It was decided later to renovate and operate the hotel for revenue to help the real estate development. The partners later felt the revised numbers on maintaining the hotel and holding the real estate were a more viable approach to obtain a profit on the real estate."

Glick then attempted to buy King's Castle, another hotel/casino near Lake Tahoe, along with Marty Buccieri, who worked at Caesars Palace and was an associate of Meyer Lansky. According to published reports, the deal didn't go through because of Buccieri's background.[5] However, Glick insists there was another reason and told me, "The submitted proposal for financing was deemed not adequate . . . and I was never aware of any other basis for the denial."

In March 1974, Glick was approached by Los Angeles businessman Todd Derlachter,[6] who asked him if he wanted to buy Recrion, formerly known as the Parvin-Dohrmann Company, which had been wracked by problems with the federal government.[7] Among other holdings, Recrion owned the Stardust and the Fremont hotels/casinos in Las Vegas.

Glick indicated that he was interested, so Derlachter introduced him to Delbert Coleman and Recrion's principal stockholders. However, Morris Shenker, a St. Louis criminal attorney who had represented Jimmy Hoffa, was also interested in the purchase.

Nevertheless, Glick, who did not make his offer contingent on being licensed, outbid Shenker, offering $62.5 million for Recrion. Glick managed to pull together $2 million as the down payment. Derlachter was promised and received a $1.26 million finder's fee in return for introducing Glick to Coleman. The fee included a $10,000-a-month consultant's salary for doing little or nothing else.

A federal prosecutor familiar with the sale said, "Allen Glick very much wanted to buy these two hotels and casinos from Del Coleman, so much that in a weekend of hard and fast negotiations a deal was struck between Glick and Coleman for the sale. Glick put up in escrow two million dollars that was based on a pledge backed by [one of Glick's other companies] and a line of credit for the sale, but this was more than sixty million dollars shy of the purchase price."

With less than two months to come up with the rest of the money, Glick went to Frank Balistrieri to discuss his purchase of Recrion. Balistrieri told Glick to hire his two sons, ostensibly as house counsels, and to grant them the first right of refusal to buy a half interest in the multimillion-dollar company for a mere $25,000. Glick was also told to purchase his hotel insurance from Allen Dorfman's Amalgamated Insurance Company[8] and to retain Lefty Rosenthal as a top executive with his casino operations. Glick was under the clear impression that if he did not agree to Balistrieri's conditions, he would not be helped.

In return, Glick, as he understood it, would get a $62.5 million loan from the Teamsters' Central States, Southeast and Southwest Areas Pension Fund. Insurance executive Dorfman, the former fiduciary manager of the fund, had been indicted in 1972 for accepting kickbacks from the recipients of pension-fund loans.

Glick did as Balistrieri suggested and received the purchase price for Recrion and loans for other investments from the Teamsters. The process had been handled by Dorfman and pension-fund trustees Bill Presser, Roy Williams, and Frank Ranney. A Dorfman puppet, Al Baron, who had replaced Dorfman as the fund's manager, was simply rubber-stamping Dorfman's behind-the-scenes decisions. However, Glick was under the impression that Frank Balistrieri, the father of his friend, had made the arrangements for the loan.

Glick then created Argent—a word he selected because it is both French for "money" and "silver" and an acronym for Allen R. Glick Enterprises.

Glick told me, "The time [for obtaining the loan] was over a hundred and twenty days from the start of the paperwork given the fund. There was a $62.5 million loan for Argent on the acquisition, and $25 million for a high rise that was built. There was a $25 million loan for Eastmont Mall Shopping Center, and $7 million at Beverly Summitt for a real estate project in Los Angeles. Many of these loans were partial assumptions of existing debts the fund already had. There also was a $13 million loan on the GSA [General Services Administration] real estate project in Texas that I was ultimately involved in." The latter deal involved several NFL players.

Glick officially took over the Stardust and the Fremont in August 1974.[9] As part of the quid pro quo, Lefty Rosenthal became Glick's process man. Rosenthal, who was named by Glick as his $250,000-a-year "assistant to the president," became the caretaker for the Chicago Mafia's interests in Las Vegas, particularly within Argent.

According to Glick, he was unaware that his project had already become tied to intricate Mafia deals, including an elaborate skimming operation at his casinos. Cleveland Mafia chief Angelo Lonardo later said, "[Organized-crime figure Moshe] Rockman told me that the skim started when Allen Glick approached Frank Balistrieri about Glick's obtaining a Teamsters pension fund loan so that Glick could purchase a Las Vegas casino . . . Balistrieri talked to Nick Civella, boss of the Kansas City family, since he controlled Roy Williams, who was a high official with the Teamsters. Civella told Balistrieri that he would find someone in Cleveland who could talk to Bill Presser. Civella got ahold of Rockman and asked him to talk to Bill Presser about getting a pension loan for Glick. Glick told Balistrieri that in return for the pension loan he, Glick, would give the Milwaukee, Kansas City, and Cleveland families a piece of the casinos."

Nick Civella, who had been convicted in 1970 of operating a sports-bookmaking network, had allegedly made payoffs to members of the Kansas City Chiefs during the 1960s. He was indicted and convicted again in July 1975 for illegal sports bookmaking.

Lonardo continued, "Rockman also told me that Glick received the Teamsters' pension loan and purchased the Stardust [and] Fremont . . . casinos. Lefty Rosenthal ran the skim operation in Las Vegas. Kansas City would get the money from Las Vegas, and cut it up between themselves."

In this way, Glick says, he was kept unaware that the Mafia

had become his silent partner. "Glick did not understand there would be obligations," a federal prosecutor explained. "He didn't understand at the time he got the loan that the partners came with it. The partners understood this, and they understood there were obligations to be paid and dues to be paid."

Nevertheless, there was immediate suspicion about Glick because of his sudden and dominant entry into the Nevada gaming scene. There were also concerns that penetrating questions about Glick's background and associates could kill his chances to be licensed by Nevada gaming authorities. But, against his attorney's advice, Glick agreed to take a polygraph test. The examination took over four hours and was conducted by Chuck Lee, one of the top polygraph operators in the country.

When Glick completed the test—during which he was asked all the major questions that troubled law-enforcement officials—he passed with such flying colors that Lee offered to be a witness for him at his licensing hearing. Soon after, Glick's license was approved.

Quickly, with Rosenthal running the show from behind the scenes, the Stardust became the world's largest legal sports-bookmaking operation when it opened its own sports and race book in September 1975. "The Sports Book was Rosenthal's suggestion," Glick told me, "and he conceived of this before I acquired Recrion and already had outlines and sketches. He handled this project and worked out guidelines with the state for its operation. I can't take any credit for its creation."[10]

With a $2 million project which created a nine-thousand-square-foot wing to the hotel, the Stardust Sports Book seated 250 bettors and featured a twenty-five-foot computerized reader board and a forty-eight-square-foot television screen, which, along with the smaller televisions on the front wall of the lounge, allowed gamblers to watch a variety of sporting events.

In addition to his salary as the chief of Glick's casino operations, Rosenthal also hosted a weekly local television program from the Stardust, "The Frank Rosenthal Show," in which he discussed the upcoming line on NFL football games and other sporting events.

The Stardust became the center for gambling on NFL games. It became the home of the outlaw line. The nation's leading oddsmaker, Bobby Martin, had left the Churchill Downs Sports Book to become the chief oddsmaker at the Union Plaza, which had created the first hotel sports book earlier in 1975. Martin's weekly line served as the basis for the numbers used by legal and illegal bookmakers through the country. The Stardust became among the first casinos to post Martin's line and take action on his prices.

Managing the Stardust Sports Book for Rosenthal was his longtime associate Marty Kane, who had been indicted with Gil Beckley for bookmaking in 1967 and was later convicted. Kane, who served in the Army during World War II and graduated from the University of Alabama, had started gambling during the 1950s in Washington, D.C., and then moved to Miami where he worked with Beckley during the early 1960s.

Kane told me, "I spent two years in jail from 1972 to 1974 for the conviction with Beckley. When I got out, I laid around for a few months. And then I got a call from the Union Plaza. They wanted me to come to work in their sports book. While I was thinking about it, Rosenthal called me and told me to forget about the Union Plaza. He wanted me to come to work at the Stardust and run their sports book. And so I took that job."

Glick's contacts within the NFL were numerous. For example, prior to his purchase of Recrion, he—along with his partner, Dennis Wittman—had operated a variety of partnerships with active NFL players, including Lance Alworth of the San Diego Chargers and later the Dallas Cowboys; Steve DeLong, Sam Gruneisen, John Hadl, Ron Mix, and Walt Sweeney, all of the Chargers; and Jim Hudson of the New York Jets.

Hudson told me, "I never really knew Allen Glick. I met him through Dennis Wittman, who ran Saratoga. I met Wittman through John Hadl. Hadl and I played golf every year with DeLong and Joe Namath. Hadl knew I was building apartments and office buildings in Austin, and Hadl came down and said, 'I have this guy I want you to meet. I'm working for him.' And that's how I met Wittman. So they came down and did some deals with my entity, Hudson Properties."

During my interview with Hadl, he explained, "It was Lance Alworth who introduced me to Wittman for a real estate deal in San Diego. We had a couple of partnerships, and we bought some land there. Glick wasn't even involved at that time. He came later."

Alworth told me, "I was retiring from football. I didn't know what was going on. I was looking for a second career. And I was trying to learn something to make a living. Saratoga had everything I needed. And Allen gave me free rein to run around and learn. I have nothing but good things to say about Allen. He's a friend of mine, and I respect him.

"I really didn't bring anybody into the business. I went to the Dallas Cowboys for a couple of years [for the 1971 and 1972 seasons] and when I returned to California, Hadl and Hudson were working with Dennis [Wittman]. Now, Dennis was a friend of mine, and I had introduced him to Hadl. I met Dennis through a coach on the Chargers, who told me that Dennis had helped him with his financial difficulties. So I went to see him, and he let me hang around.

"Dennis kind of helped me on the side. I never was really involved in the company. I was never on its payroll. I was an investor in one little deal and lost money like everyone else. I probably would've lost a whole lot more—but I had lost everything earlier. I really didn't have any money. I had just gone through a bankruptcy."

Explaining how he was introduced to those sports figures involved, Glick told me, "Wittman hired Lance Alworth and then John Hadl. He gave them assignments at Saratoga. He also met Ron Mix and put together an investment with him in which football people were investors. Wittman did not like gambling at all and always had a fondness for football and football people. He would have liked to have been an owner of a [professional football] team. It was a passion for him. Because of this and a religious disliking for gambling, he would never be involved in Las Vegas.

"Alworth introduced Davis to Wittman and Davis introduced some of the coaches to Wittman for a real estate investment. I had no role in this area as it was Wittman's special area. I never met the coaches and only met Davis when problems came up at Saratoga and in their investment in a project. When I met him [Davis] at this late date, I found him very intelligent and honest to work with."

Later, Mix filed a fraud-and-breach-of-contract suit against Glick and others, claiming that they failed to pay him a $105,000 finder's fee for introducing Al Davis, the managing partner of the Oakland Raiders, to their investment group. The case was later dismissed.

Besides Davis, other business partners in a variety of ventures included Buffalo Bills owner Ralph Wilson, Chuck Knox, the head coach of the Los Angeles Rams; John Ralston, the head coach of the Denver Broncos; Don Shula, the head coach of the Miami Dolphins; Sid Gillman, the general partner and general manager of the Houston Oilers; and even Jay Malkoff, the team doctor of the San Diego Chargers.

Glick insists that Wittman's ties with Carroll Rosenbloom were exclusive, and that he did not share in them. Glick also told me that he was not personally acquainted with all those involved, and that there were never any efforts to compromise the on-field integrity of any NFL personnel.

Although Glick had represented these investments as simple tax shelters, most investors involved with Saratoga lost money. One of the partnerships, Hudson Properties—which included players Hudson, Hadl, and DeLong, among others—immediately lost $3 million, despite the fact that Glick had obtained a $13 million loan from the Teamsters' pension fund to develop Hudson's properties in downtown Austin.

Glick told me, "The [NFL] partners made a small amount of profit, although Saratoga didn't. Hudson Properties was owned by Hudson, and I don't know what it made yearly or lost."

Hudson confirms the $3 million loss, the sum his company had loaned to Saratoga. He adds, "There was bitterness," but said that he preferred not to elaborate. Hadl told me, "We were minority partners in Hudson Properties. But I lost money in that deal, too. That was in 1973 when everybody got killed. Interest rates went to twenty-two percent. They called in all the notes, and they didn't have that kind of money."

Alworth simply told me, "When Saratoga went down, Allen Glick was the only one who stood up and was counted. He tried to get all the investors back their money."

Glick's business ties with the NFL personnel were extremely complicated. Most of his dealings with them were through Saratoga and its twenty-four subsidiaries. In May 1975, to add to the chaos, Glick's Saratoga Development Corporation went bankrupt. When Saratoga went under, its 419 creditors claimed debts totaling $15 million more than Saratoga's actual worth. Dennis Wittman had resigned as Saratoga's president just days before the legal papers were filed.[11]

However, Al Davis, who was involved in one of the Saratoga partnerships, had one sweet deal with Glick that remained intact. In 1974, Davis became Glick's personal business partner after he paid $5,000 for a 25 percent share of the Eastmont Shopping Center, a $25 million mall in Oakland that also had been financed by the Teamsters' pension fund.[12]

Glick describes Davis's role in the project, saying, "Davis received an interest because of his commitment to be involved in the center and to use his good name in Oakland to make the shopping center successful. The project had been in bad shape for the lender, who had foreclosed on it, and our newly formed partnership acquired the project for assumption of the debt. No money was paid up front, so no money was needed from the partners. Davis paid for his shares as I did. The purchase was with a new partnership."

While these deals were being made, the NFL was fully aware of what was going on—but never tried to interfere. In a December 1975 interview with reporter Joe Hughes of *The San Diego Evening Tribune,* NFL Security chief Jack Danahy said, "Mr. Glick is legally licensed to operate hotels and casinos in Las Vegas. The league has found no involvement by Mr. Glick in illegal sports activity." When asked specifically about Davis's relationship with Glick, Danahy replied, "That is the subject of much legal involvement." He refused to say anything more about the subject.

Concerning Glick, Davis stated in a sworn deposition, "The way I understood it, Allen was an attorney. He was a war hero, decorated with honor—and was [a] very bright land developer and tax attorney. Now, whether he was or not, I don't know, but this is what the young people who came to me, who I had coached, recruited, learned to live with, love . . . assured me."

In outlining his business relationship with the casino operator, Davis, who said he, too, had met Glick through players Alworth and Hadl, added, "I formed a limited partnership with several owners in the National Football League. We invested in the deal with Wittman and Glick . . . Then that deal became a very profitable situation for us, so in 1972 we formed another partnership. We invested somewhere between one million and two million dollars. Again I brought in several owners and coaches in the National Football League, and Carroll Rosenbloom was obviously one because one of his players, John Hadl, was working for these people. In fact, Carroll negotiated with them contracts and might have gone into business with them separately. I know the Rams coaches did."

Davis added that in 1974 Glick came to him and asked him to invest in the Eastmont mall. "I thought it was fantastic," Davis testified. "And so I went in with him as a limited partner, with no management affair in the business. They thought by bringing me in in Oakland it would somehow or other bring image or stature to the shopping center . . . It was the most expensive shopping center built in the United States."[13]

Davis said that he had recommended black NFL players to serve as Glick's "unpaid advisers" for the mall to handle occasional community-relations work, like signing autographs and shaking hands. Two of the players involved were Gene Upshaw and Clement Daniels, both of whom played for the Raiders. Upshaw, who owned a bar, Gene Upshaw's Patio, near the mall, had been the NFL's "Man of the Year." He later became the president and then executive director of the NFL Players Association.

Upshaw told me, "Al Davis asked me—as a member of the team and also as a member of the community—if I would participate in the mall as a community-relations guy. And that's what I did. It was myself and Clem Daniels. We shared an office together at the mall.

"The mall was located in a totally black area of town, and it had had a lot of problems. Davis thought that if Clem and I got involved it could add some credibility to it. And we were willing to do it. We weren't being paid for it. We appeared at store openings. We were at security meetings to try to help with things we saw in the area. That mall was very important to East Oakland. It was the only facility in which the blacks could come and shop. And we wanted to see quality stores go in. We didn't want to see it run down and return to the condition it was in when Davis and the others took it over."

Regarding Glick, Upshaw told me, "I knew Allen Glick, but I never invested any money with him. There were no documents signed. My business was not located in the mall. Gene Upshaw's Patio was six blocks away. I had no business in the mall at all."

29 Foreshadowing a Drug Problem

IN JULY 1974, THE NFL notified the New York Giants that the team's orthopedic surgeon since 1964, Dr. Anthony Pisani, was under investigation and could be named in an upcoming indictment, along with two New York bookmakers, Thomas Musto and Michael Astarita. Musto was identified as a soldier in the Vito Genovese crime family.[1] Pisani immediately resigned as team doctor.

On August 20, the forty-count indictment was handed up after a two-year investigation into gambling in New York. The two bookmakers were charged for their roles in a $26-million-a-year bookmaking operation. Pisani was named in the indictment but not charged for agreeing to provide them with inside information on the Giants players' injuries prior to the last four games of the 1973 NFL season—which came in the midst of the Giants' seven-game losing streak. Pisani reportedly cooperated with the Manhattan district attorney's office during the probe. Both of the indicted men had been his patients.

In one telephone conversation on October 4, 1973, cited by law-enforcement authorities, Pisani gave the two bookmakers a detailed description of an injury sustained by the Giants' star running back, Ron Johnson. In another conversation, Musto refused to discuss the line or handle a bet until he received his inside information. "I want to speak to the doctor first to find out what he knows about injuries," Musto said during the monitored conversations.

During the four weeks of communication between Pisani

and the bookmakers, the Giants never covered the point spread. The bookmakers won money from each of the four games by taking the opposing team and giving points to the Giants. The D.A.'s office stated that they handled over $100,000 in gambling action during that period.

New York Times columnist Neil Amdur reflected, "The most painful lessons to emerge from the Tony Pisani case are that team physicians are almost as crucial to the function of a professional football team as a good chef is to the cuisine at a French restaurant, and that doctors, like players and fans, are only human. They bear the same scars and frailties that show up on Sunday afternoon when a cornerback feigns a limp to the bench after having been beaten by a wide receiver for the game-winning touchdown."[2]

Another team doctor had earlier produced a major drug scandal within the San Diego Chargers. The case began when Houston Ridge, a defensive lineman, filed suit against the Chargers, claiming that prior to an injury of his hip in a 1969 game against the Miami Dolphins, he was fed nine pills, including three amphetamines and three muscle relaxants. With the pain deadened by the drugs, Ridge continued to play and was even more severely injured. The injury ended Ridge's career. Doctors determined he had been permanently disabled and was forced to begin walking with a crutch. In his lawsuit, Ridge alleged that the Chargers dispensed as many as ten thousand pills to its players in a single year. Ridge eventually won a $295,000 settlement from the team.[3]

The San Diego County district attorney's office, which also investigated the Ridge case, charged that the team had engaged in the "indiscriminate use" of drugs from 1966 to 1974. The Chargers team, owned by Gene Klein, was fined $20,000 for "supervisory omissions"; head coach Harland Svare was fined $5,000; and eight players were fined $1,000 to $3,000 each.[4] Houston Oilers general manager Sid Gillman, the former Chargers' head coach, was placed on probation by the NFL for forcing his Chargers players to take drugs. Also, punished for prescribing excessive amounts of amphetamines was Dr. Arnold J. Mandell, who was fired as the team psychiatrist but was not charged with any crime.

Mandell, the cochairman of the Department of Psychiatry at the University of California at San Diego, wrote, "I had already been privy to a lot of the players' personal drug information. I had begun to educate them on an individual basis about the use of drugs—their actions and side effects, approximate doses, advantages and disadvantages. It was straight information. As good and fair as I could make it. For some of the veterans with eight-to-ten-year pre-game amphetamine use, I had already given prescriptions. I had begun to negotiate the doses downward and toward stability. Away from weird mixes and street stuff."[5]

In December 1973, a few months before the Chargers' drug scandal exploded, Klein had sold his four hundred thousand shares in National General for a reported $20 million to American Financial Corporation, a Cincinnati-based holding company.[6] "There were two considerations in my decision to sell," Klein told me. "First, I had taken this piece of shit and turned it into a helluva corporation. We were a billion dollars in assets. So I sat down and said to myself, 'Now what are you going to do? Go for two billion dollars? Four billion dollars? What the fuck do you want to do?' I said, 'I want to run my football team.' I thought that would be great fun."

At that point, Klein turned all his attentions to the Chargers. He moved from his Bel Air mansion to the La Costa Country Club in Carlsbad, California.[7] The Chargers' offices are in nearby La Jolla.

But when the San Diego drug case broke open, Klein discovered that operating a football team wasn't as much fun as he thought. Klein told me, "At the time of the depositions [in the Houston Ridge case], charges were made that the Chargers were handing out amphetamines—openly in the locker room. And I put a fucking stop to that. I had absolutely no knowledge of that. I am the most antidrug person around. I said, 'This will stop. We will not give anybody amphetamines.' I told the doctors, the trainers, 'That's out; there's no way.' I changed coaches. I fired Gillman and I hired Svare.

"I talked to my son, whom I have great respect for. I said, 'Mike, what the hell do I do? How do I fight this son of a bitch? It's a bitch of a problem.' He said, 'Why don't you get a shrink?' I said, 'That's not a stupid idea.'

"Well, he knew Dr. Mandell, and he introduced me to Arnie Mandell. And I met with him, and I talked to him about the drug problem. And I said, 'How the hell do we fight this? How do I make sure this never happens again?' And this was all a direct result of the Houston Ridge thing.

"We got friendly. He said, 'Let me hang around the team

and look.' I said, 'All right. You're on your own. You're not on the payroll.' Mandell was also very friendly with Svare. And he got interested in football. So he would come down to training camp. He started giving talks, telling how bad drugs were. I sat through the talks. And that was the way I had hoped to do something constructive.

"Then it turns out that that dirty son of a bitch was prescribing amphetamines. One day I am confronted with evidence that he had written hundreds of prescriptions. I was in shock. I said, 'What the fuck are you doing, Mandell?' And the league found out about it. And the league comes to me, and Rozelle wants a fucking hearing. Mandell says, 'They're out on the black market getting pills. I know the stuff I give them. I know what it is.' I said, 'That's a pretty fucking poor excuse.'

"So I fly in my airplane with Mandell and my lawyer, and we go before Rozelle in New York. And, also at that time, they had some evidence of marijuana smoking at the training camp at Irvine. So we went before Pete and laid the whole thing out. And then Pete meets with me privately. He says that it was gross negligence on the part of Svare for not knowing this, and that Mandell is a disaster. I said, 'Mandell is gone. This is just bullshit with all these prescriptions. He's out.' Pete says, 'I want you to fire Svare.' I said, 'I won't do it. He goofed. He didn't know, and I can't believe he was involved. He's a very honest, legitimate guy. I'm not going to fire him.' Pete says, 'If you don't fire him, I'm going to fine you twenty thousand dollars.' I said, 'Fuck you, fine me twenty thousand dollars!' So I didn't fire him, and I was fined twenty thousand dollars by the NFL. And I paid the fine. The players were fined two thousand dollars each.

"Mandell was not indicted. But some medical board of examiners brought him before a hearing officer of the state pharmacological board, and they took his license away. Then he got a lawyer, and they went to court. The decision to take away his license was revoked. As far as I know, he's still on the staff at the university."

After the fines were handed out, Klein recommended that every NFL player be required to take a urine test after each game—and that anyone failing the test should be suspended.

There had been isolated drug problems in the NFL since May 1963 when Eugene "Big Daddy" Lipscomb, the all-pro defensive tackle of the Baltimore Colts, was found slumped over a chair in the kitchen of a friend's house with a half dozen needle marks in his arms. Lipscomb's death from an overdose of heroin shocked the sports world but appeared to be a completely isolated, as well as a tragic, situation.

After Lipscomb's death, there wasn't another public drug-related problem for years. Somehow, the NFL had managed to get through the late 1960s without a major drug scandal.

"We were getting rumbles on the side that players were socializing with marijuana," NFL Security chief Jack Danahy told me. "They were coming out of the sixties era. We would have been naïve not to think that drugs were not present at that time. But there was never a big scandal. We had individual instances of players being arrested for possession of marijuana, but I don't remember any action being taken by the league. There were no suspensions. The first fines and suspensions for drugs weren't until the San Diego drug case."

But, contrary to Danahy's statement, prior to the 1974 Chargers' revelations there were several incidents involving illegal drugs and drug dealers—and NFL responses and non-responses to those incidents:

- In December 1971, Bob Berry and Randy Marshall of the Atlanta Falcons were found in Marshall's apartment with a couple of joints in an ashtray. A twenty-year-old woman who was with the two players was charged for possession; the two players were not.
- In February 1972, Duane Thomas of the Dallas Cowboys was arrested and later pleaded guilty for possession of marijuana. The Thomas case caused public cries for the automatic suspension for life of any player convicted of any narcotics violations. However, Rozelle refused to ban Thomas from football.
- A year later, Lance Rentzel of the Los Angeles Rams pleaded guilty to possession of marijuana and codeine. He was later suspended from football following a second arrest for indecent exposure for which he pleaded guilty.
- In June 1973, the U.S. House Commerce Committee, at the conclusion of its hearings into drug abuse by professional athletes, called for spot-check urinalyses to determine whether players had been using narcotics. The committee also suggested stronger penalties for those involved with drugs. The NFL Players Association reacted harshly to the committee's conclusions,

blaming the public perception of drugs in sports on sensational newspaper headlines. The players' union also refused to support any program that violated the players' right to privacy.

Ed Garvey, who had become the executive director of the NFLPA in 1971, told me that the association had no choice in the matter. He explained, "The union's responsibility is to its members, to try and get them help, to save their jobs, and get them a fair hearing in the event that there was ever any kind of drug testing."

- Also in June 1973, Commissioner Rozelle announced a new program to combat drug abuse in the NFL by organizing a reporting system within each of the NFL teams. Rozelle said that he would consider harsh penalties and might explore the use of urinalysis.
- Within a month after Rozelle's announcement, controversial Joe Don Looney, a former star running back with several NFL teams, was arrested for possession of a submachine gun. Also arrested with Looney was a man the police described as "a wholesale dealer of cocaine."[8]
- In October 1973, Cleveland Browns owner Art Modell permitted receiver Gloster Richardson to play with the team—even after his conviction for possession of illegal drugs.
- That same month, Mack Herron, a fullback for the New England Patriots, pleaded guilty in a Winnipeg court to possession of marijuana.[9]
- Soon after, center George Burman told Sandy Padwe of *Newsday* that nearly one third of his Washington Redskins teammates regularly used amphetamines prior to playing. Rozelle immediately opened an investigation of Burman's charges and promised a crackdown on amphetamine use. That was Burman's last year in the NFL, and no players were named in the NFL's investigation.
- In February 1974, Levi Johnson of the Detroit Lions was arrested for possession of marijuana, along with three Texas A & I University athletes in Kingsville, Texas.

And after the drug scandals involving Dr. Pisani and San Diego Chargers, incidents of drug abuse continued.

- In August 1974, David Reavis of the Pittsburgh Steelers was arrested for selling marijuana and thirty-five thousand amphetamines to an undercover agent. He pleaded guilty to possession of 250 pounds of marijuana and was placed on probation. He then joined the Tampa Bay Buccaneers in 1976 and played with the team for the next seven years.

- At the same time, NFL Security initiated an investigation of Mike Ernst of the Cincinnati Bengals who had been arrested after a game for possession of cocaine. Within forty-eight hours after the arrest, Ernst was waived by the Bengals and was not picked up by any other NFL team. Ernst pleaded not guilty to the charges.
- In January 1975, a nineteen-year-old woman, Roxie Ann Rice, claimed to have been a go-between for major drug dealers and NFL players after she was arrested in possession of a credit card owned by Ken Houston of the Washington Redskins. When the U.S. Drug Enforcement Administration (DEA) asked for a full-scale investigation of Rice and her charges, she recanted everything—despite her thirty-nine-page statement to police officials. Without their key witness's testimony, DEA agents later declared that there was no evidence that Rice had been involved in a drug ring with any NFL players.
- In March 1975, Bob Maddox of the Cincinnati Bengals was charged with possession of a hallucinogen after a raid on his house in Ohio. The police also found $12,000 worth of hashish. Maddox, who pleaded guilty and received five years' probation, was permitted to continue his football career by Rozelle.
- In August 1975, Shelby Jordan, a lineman for the New England Patriots, was arrested by federal drug agents for selling cocaine in Amherst, Massachusetts. He was found guilty and received a two-year sentence.
- A year later, Pittsburgh Steelers quarterback Joe Gilliam went on trial for possession of heroin. He was found guilty and later sentenced to forty days in jail after a parole violation. Gilliam left the Steelers and tried to make his comeback with the New Orleans Saints—but was cut.

In the midst of the NFL's growing drug problems, Bernie Jackson, the assistant director of NFL Security, left his post to become an assistant to Governor Hugh Carey of New York.[10] Replacing Jackson was Charlie Jackson, who was no relation to his predecessor. Before coming to the NFL, Charlie Jackson, the former assistant city manager of Yonkers, had been serving as the head of the narcotics squad of the Westchester County police department and chief of a tri-state narcotics task force for Connecticut, New Jersey, and New York.

Commenting on the drug situation in professional sports, particularly the NFL, New Orleans crime fighter Aaron Kohn told me, "Those who supply the drugs to the players have an extortionate weapon to hold over their heads. Once players become consumers of drugs of any kind, their suppliers can destroy their source of income, and they can destroy their public acceptance. To the degree that their sources of drugs have communication or are involved with organized crime—which considers the proceeds of gambling a major part of their continuing wealth—players can be extorted to do favors on the playing field."

Another, less tragic, controversy emerged in the NFL when the New York Giants team refused to renew its lease to play in Yankee Stadium after the 1973 season, making arrangements to move to Hackensack Meadows—better known as the Meadowlands—in East Rutherford, New Jersey, just across the Hudson River and west of the Holland Tunnel. The team's new, seventy-six-thousand-seat stadium was financed by bonds placed under the supervision of the New Jersey Sports and Exposition Authority, which was headed by former New York Jets owner Sonny Werblin. As part of the $300 million sports complex, Werblin also built both thoroughbred- and harness-racing tracks.[11]

The New York Giants began to play in New Jersey at the beginning of the 1976 season. There was precedent for the team's move to another municipality. In 1971, the Dallas Cowboys, which had been playing home games in the Cotton Bowl, moved to Texas Stadium in Irving, Texas. That same year, the Boston Patriots moved to Schaefer Stadium in Foxboro, Massachusetts—just across the street from Foxboro Raceway, which was also owned by the Sullivan family—and became the New England Patriots. And in 1975, the Detroit Lions moved to Pontiac, Michigan.

30 The Bad, the Worse, and the Ugly

IN JANUARY 1975, *The New York Times* published a four-part series on sports gambling. Reporter Steve Cady warned, "[T]he *Times* study indicates that the enormous growth of sports betting has multiplied the temptation for betting coups, made bookies ever warier than usual and put the integrity of the games under increasing pressure. Despite assurances from leagues that players do not bet, persons close to the gambling scene suspect that many athletes are at least part-time bettors."

The impact of gambling on American sports was to be addressed by a federal commission, which began a study of the situation in 1974; it had been originally mandated by Congress under the Organized Crime Act of 1970 while Richard Nixon was president. Appointed as the chairman of the fifteen-member commission was Charles H. Morin, a Washington attorney; its executive director was former Justice Department attorney James E. Ritchie, who had headed the U.S. Strike Force in Detroit during the Donald Dawson gambling scandal in early 1970 and had come to the commission from the Strike Force office in San Francisco.

As the National Commission to Review National Policy Toward Gambling was impaneled, Ritchie made it clear that "we are not a crime commission. We are mandated by Congress to make a study of gambling and recommend changes, if necessary."

There were institutional problems with the commission.

First of all, Morin, its chairman, was general counsel to the Teamsters Union; and the union's pension fund had contributed over half a billion dollars to Las Vegas casinos and to those people associated with them. That was significant because during the 1972 presidential campaign, Las Vegas casino operators and their associates had contributed over a million dollars to Nixon's reelection effort.

When the creation of the commission on gambling was announced, Nevada's gaming industry began to sweat and wanted its voice heard inside the commission. Frank Fitzsimmons, then the general president of the Teamsters, obliged, using his sweetheart relationship with the Nixon White House and his union's support for Nixon in the 1972 election as leverage. The writing on the wall was apparent when members and staff of the commission were "comped"—given free room, food, and entertainment—at Caesars Palace during investigative trips to and official hearings in Las Vegas.

Morin had been recommended as the commission's chair by Fitzsimmons's close friend, White House counsel Charles Colson, who had left the White House in March 1973 in the midst of the Watergate scandal and became Morin's law partner at Morin & Shapiro. Colson, who has described Morin as his closest friend, was responsible for Morin being retained by the Teamsters. In order to make room for Morin and Colson, the Teamsters fired its longtime general counsel, Washington Redskins president Edward Bennett Williams—because of his representation of the Democratic National Committee in the Watergate break-in case. Colson was later indicted and pleaded guilty to obstruction of justice, stemming from the break-in of Daniel Ellsberg's psychiatrist's office by the White House "plumbers unit."

On March 10, 1975, soon after the commission began its series of hearings, Thomas Mechling, the executive director of the New York-based National Center for Gambling Information, wrote to Ritchie: "There is a widespread feeling among interested observers that your Commission is not 'reaching out' and soliciting the views of interested parties. Your communications to this pool of potential informational resources have been practically nil. You have not even notified many of the interested press media—let along other potential expert witnesses—of the future schedule of public hearings. It is as if you were trying to conduct your 'public' hearings, privately."

Ritchie replied to Mechling, "Please keep in mind that the total commission staff numbers only eighteen. We have a wide range of activities to carry out and simply cannot conduct a large-scale publicity effort."

The 413-page final report of the commission, which was submitted to Congress in October 1976, indicated that 80 percent of all Americans approved of legalized gambling and 68 percent gambled themselves.[1] Among other recommendations, the commission advocated that all federal gambling laws and regulations be repealed, thus permitting the individual states to determine their own laws and regulations. It also concluded that the influence of organized crime in the state of Nevada had declined since 1966.

Two members of the commission, Sam Steiger of Arizona and Charles Wiggins of California, both Republican congressmen, refused to sign the report and filed a minority opinion distancing themselves from the commission's conclusions. Their particular objection was to another commission recommendation to exempt gamblers and bookmakers from federal excise taxes, which Congress had imposed in 1951 in the aftermath of the Kefauver hearings.

With regard to the sports-gambling business, the commission concluded that the states should become competitive with illegal bookmakers and permit offtrack betting on sporting events. According to a University of Michigan survey contracted by the commission, "Sports betting, popularly thought to be associated with 'organized crime,' is seen by bettors as having little impact on current organized-crime revenue. It is not viewed as likely to attract racketeers."[2]

Among those who provided testimony to the commission and were vehemently opposed to legalized sports gambling were NFL commissioner Rozelle and major-league baseball commissioner Bowie Kuhn. Both warned that the institutionalization of sports gambling would lead to certain disaster.

Specifically, Rozelle issued a position paper stating, "The league believes legalized gambling on professional sports will dramatically change the character of the fan interests in the sports. No longer will sports fans identify their interests with the success or failure of their favorite teams but with the effect of their team's performance in the winning or losing of bets . . . Legalized gambling will greatly multiply the security problems confronting all professional sports."

Interestingly, Las Vegas oddsmaker Bobby Martin told me that Ritchie had sent him early drafts of the commission's report for his review. "Jim Ritchie called me and asked me to do it," Martin said. "Of course, I was glad to. I do have some expertise in this area."

Soon after the commission's hearings ended, Ritchie became legal counsel for, among others, the National Association of Off-Track Betting and the Western Enterprise Political Action Committee. Both of these concerns were progambling-lobbying groups. Ritchie was also placed on retainer by two trade associations—the Nevada Casino Association and the Gaming Industry Association of Nevada—within three weeks after the commission filed its final report. He received an annual retainer of $75,000.

Reporter Robert S. Stokes, who published a critique of the commission in *The Washington Post,* found sources within the commission who alleged that Ritchie had self-serving motives for taking the job. One of those sources told Stokes, "[Ritchie] wanted to drum up clients for his future law practice. He talked about it frequently, how he was going to land the Las Vegas casinos as his clients. His priorities were Nevada casinos, U.S. horse racing and British gambling interests."[3]

Ritchie admitted that while still with the commission, he had discussed the possibility of being retained by a legal English bookmaking firm in the event that it expanded its operations to the United States. "I saw nothing improper in it," Richie told Stokes.

Repeated attempts to interview Ritchie for this book were unsuccessful.

Criminologist Jerome Skolnick of the University of California at Berkeley was quoted by Stokes, saying that the commission's report was "a superficial work that did not require a three-million-dollar effort. The commission went through the motions of holding hearings with the predictable result that its report is shallow, and it certainly doesn't, in any way, challenge the claims of the gambling industry. It could scarcely be called a deep and profound investigation of the role of gambling in the United States."

In August 1976, two months before the commission's final report was delivered to Congress and while fourteen states were considering sports lotteries, the state of Delaware, which had legalized a numbers-formatted lottery in 1974, announced that it was going to be the first to operate a fully state-run sports-gambling lottery.

Two games, played on computerized cards, were going to be offered to bettors. One was called Touchdown, in which a person could pick the winners of three and five games, as well as the point spreads of each. The other game, Football Bonus, contained two slates of seven games each. Gamblers, who could wage between $1 and $10 for each game, could bet on one or both scales. All winning payoffs would be on a pari-mutuel basis.

After the state refused to respond favorably to a written protest by Rozelle against the lottery, the NFL finally filed for a temporary restraining order in federal court to block Delaware's effort, charging that the state's sports lottery could cause "irreparable harm" to the NFL. Rozelle, in his deposition, insisted that "the NFL clubs have established an organization of teams which are highly skilled, well-balanced, and honestly competitive, so that the public has come to expect, in the playing of NFL football, the highest degree of excellence, free from outside influence."

At the time, Rozelle was reminding sports-gambling advocates that just the previous January, during Super Bowl X, the reaction of the fans did not correspond with the outcome of the game. The Pittsburgh Steelers won the championship, defeating the Dallas Cowboys, 21–17. Down 10–7 at the end of the third quarter, the Steelers, who were seven-point favorites, came back in the final quarter, scoring on a Dallas safety and two field goals, making the score 15–10. With just three minutes left in the game, Pittsburgh quarterback Terry Bradshaw connected on a sixty-four-yard touchdown pass to Lynn Swann. Although the extra point failed, the Steelers had covered the spread with a 21–10 lead.

The Steelers' fans were ecstatic. Their team was going to win the Super Bowl, and they were going to win their bets.

Then, with one minute and forty-eight seconds remaining, Dallas marched eighty yards on five plays, climaxed by a thirty-four-yard touchdown pass from Roger Staubach to wide receiver Percy Howard. The extra point was good, and the Steelers won by only four points—and did not cover the spread.

Dallas had lost the Super Bowl, but its fans had solace. They had taken the points and won their bets.

Editorializing on the NFL's suit against Delaware, Mort Olshan of *The Gold Sheet* wrote, "One can only speculate why the NFL initiated legal action so late; too late for the court to adequately consider their argument. The fact is that [neither] the NFL, nor any other sports league for that matter, owns a proprietary interest in the outcome of a sporting event. No court will grant them that right.

"It is just possible legalized betting on the NFL would give [the NFL] a tremendous shot in the arm. According to recent television ratings and the contracts negotiated, viewer interest just might possibly have peaked out. The ancillary rights that could be capitalized on were the sport to gain new fans would be enormous."[4]

Delaware's attorneys insisted that its new betting games were nothing more than a formalization of the betting pools in most offices around the state and country.

On August 27, U.S. District Judge Walter Stapleton rejected the NFL's arguments in a one-and-a-half-page decision, saying that the league had failed to demonstrate how the lottery would result in "irreparable harm." The federal judge gave no other reasons for his ruling.

Meantime, *CBS Sports* blitzed the foes of legalized sports gambling by hiring convicted bookmaker Jimmy "the Greek" Snyder, recently pardoned by President Ford, as a color commentator during a four-minute halftime segment of the televised exhibition game between the Oakland Raiders and the San Francisco 49ers on September 12. "The Greek's Grapevine" was sponsored by Consolidated Cigar Corporation, a subsidiary of Gulf & Western. The company paid $500,000 for the spot.

Anchorman Brent Musburger enthusiastically introduced Snyder, saying, "Jimmy has some pretty good contacts in pro football. You'll be seeing him every Sunday on CBS-TV." Snyder then began sharing his inside information and making his predictions.

Handicapper Mort Olshan told me, "Jimmy the Greek was a creation of television, which wanted a 'dem' and 'doze' guy from Las Vegas, who could talk about football and discreetly discuss the line."

Aaron Kohn, chief of the New Orleans crime commission, says, "The old wire services weren't needed anymore—because television sports reporting and the newspapers were doing the job for them legitimately. So here you have free enterprise protected by the First Amendment and serving as an adjunct to the gambling economy."

Rozelle told reporters that he discussed the matter with CBS, which assured the commissioner that Snyder would not be citing the point spreads of games. Instead, he would simply contribute "general football discussion."

Barry Frank, the head of *CBS Sports,* told Red Smith, "I think Jimmy is more than just a gambling figure. He's kind of a character. He's kind of interesting and has, if you will, a mystique in the minds of people who figure he knows more than they do about something . . . This isn't a case of CBS promoting gambling. I don't think we want to take a position on gambling versus not gambling. We're just trying to offer something different and maybe catch a little bigger share of that Sunday afternoon audience."[5]

In his autobiography, Snyder wrote, "[W]e all have our little identity problems. Mine has been to make people understand that I'm an oddsmaker. I don't pick winners. I'm not a sportswriter trying to match wits in the weekly 'guesspert' competition. I establish favorites, odds, and point spreads—that is, the margin necessary to *equalize* the two teams."[6]

However, the question remains as to whether Snyder, who has denied the existence of organized crime in America,[7] occasionally used his authority as an oddsmaker to pick one team over another to help "equalize" the national betting action accepted by the major bookmakers. Snyder's enormous power to balance the bookmakers' books through his national television appearances was clear and present.

Within a few days of Snyder's first appearance on *CBS Sports,* two million NFL lottery tickets were put up for sale in Delaware, offering the public its Touchdown and Football Bonus betting games. The state expected to net $5 million to $8 million a year from the sports lottery. The second week's sales were 30 percent greater than the first, indicating popular support for this legal, state-run bookmaking operation.

However, disaster struck for the Delaware lottery on Saturday, December 11, when the agency's director, Pete Simmons, voided all betting cards sold for the following day's NFL games. Professional gamblers had gone public, charging that the state's handicappers had picked weaker teams as the favorites in two contests and were too far off on the point spreads of three other games. The gamblers also were quoted in newspaper stories advising bettors how to beat the state's line.

Immediately after the state refused to cover the bets it booked, the Delaware lottery collapsed. Later, however, to prevent a public uprising, the state attorney general's office relented and paid off the winners who had not already thrown away their tickets in disgust—forcing the state to dig into its emergency fund as a consequence of its three-week experiment.

31 Davis's Dilemma

WHILE THE NATIONAL COMMISSION to Review National Policy Toward Gambling was busy advocating legalized sports gambling and insisting the Mafia was no longer a factor in Las Vegas, Allen Glick, the Stardust, and Argent were in trouble with their gambling operations.

Glick had attempted to fire Rosenthal for making personnel decisions without his approval. Upon hearing the news, Rosenthal angrily told Glick, "I think it's about time we had a discussion, Glick. You're not my boss. And when I say you're not my boss, I'm talking not just from an administrative position, but [about] your health. If you interfere with what's going on here, you will never leave this corporation alive."

Glick then called Balistrieri who confirmed Rosenthal's claims and threats. A federal prosecutor explained, "Nick Civella and Frank Balistrieri quarreled over Allen Glick . . . his failure to pay the $1.2 million obligation for getting [the Teamsters'] loan, the hidden costs of doing business [with the mob] of which naïve Allen Glick was not even aware. What a trap this man was in!"

In March 1975, Glick was instructed by Rosenthal to go to Kansas City where he would meet with Nick Civella, the ailing boss of the local Mafia. Glick, who was picked up at the airport by mobster Carl DeLuna, was taken to a hotel room and seated in a chair directly across from Civella, who was wearing dark clothes and dark glasses. A single bright light shone down on

Glick's bald head as the men talked. Glick later described the scene as being "like interrogating a prisoner in a police room." Civella coldly instructed Glick to "cling to every word I say."

Civella growled, "You don't know me, but if it would be my choice, you wouldn't leave this room alive." With Glick's full attention, Civella demanded that Glick give him $1.2 million. He explained that he, not Frank Balistrieri, had been responsible for getting Glick his loans from the Teamsters' pension fund; and that he [Civella] was among Glick's secret partners. Glick said that Balistrieri had not explained that to him.

When Glick replied that he didn't have any untraceable cash for the payoff, Civella told Glick that Rosenthal would take care of it. "You have a commitment to us," Civella said. "You owe us $1.2 million. I want that paid. In addition, we own part of your corporation, and you are to do nothing to interfere with it . . . We will let Mr. Rosenthal continue with the casinos, and you are not to interfere."[1]

According to Glick, when he returned to Las Vegas from Kansas City, he complained to Rosenthal that he had been misled. Rosenthal then informed him, "You are no longer in a position where you control your destiny in this company."

That sounded ominous. But Glick's problems were just beginning—and they would implicate Al Davis.

Tamara Rand had been a $100,000-a-year consultant to the Glick/Davis Eastmont Mall since March 1975—the same month as Glick's meeting with Civella. A San Diego businesswoman and a partner with Glick in several real estate projects, Rand received the consultant's fee as a means of paying off a portion of a $500,000 loan Rand had earlier made to Glick when he purchased Recrion.

After Saratoga went sour in 1975, Rand filed a $560,000 lawsuit against Glick, charging that he had defrauded her in a San Bernadino, California, land deal.

On November 9, 1975, the fifty-four-year-old Mrs. Rand was found shot to death in the kitchen of her Mission Hills house. Her body had been hit with five bullets fired from a high-standard, .22 caliber, semiautomatic pistol with a well-tooled silencer. Holes had been drilled through the barrel of the gun to dissipate sound; and the steel-wool-packed silencer sleeve fit over the barrel to further muzzle the shots. One bullet was found in her back, one entered her brain through her left ear, and three were clearly visible under her chin. All five had been fired at close range.[2] She had been killed between 3:00 P.M. and 5:30 P.M. There were no indications of a forced entry, and nothing of value had been stolen. Her body was found by her husband, Dr. Philip Rand, a prominent San Diego obstetrician.

A homicide officer with the San Diego Police Department told me that when he saw Rand's body, he also saw a message delivered. "The configuration of the wounds made us believe that the murder was a warning as well as an indication of why Mrs. Rand was killed. To me, when somebody gets shot like that, it means that they have been talking too much and were being silenced. According to our information, she was going to expose someone's activities."

On advice of counsel, Glick refused to respond to oral questions about the murder from the San Diego police. Instead, he asked that all questions be submitted in writing through his attorney. His refusal to cooperate raised suspicions and placed him at center stage in the investigation.

Underworld figure Jimmy Fratianno told my associate, William Scott Malone, "Well, Frank Bompensiero [the onetime head of the San Diego Mafia] told me that Spilotro killed Tamara Rand. And Tamara Rand had a lot to do with Glick. I don't know if she was his secretary or whatever it was, but she was very close to him and had a lot of information. And they [the underworld] found out that she was going to tell the FBI or whatever. And they just killed her. They didn't want Glick to get in no trouble. That would mean that they would lose the Stardust."[3]

After the Rand murder, heat started coming down on Glick's partner Al Davis. When challenged about his view about the NFL rule forbidding associations with gamblers, particularly his business relationship with Glick, Al Davis answered in a deposition, "Sometimes there is association with gambling, and sometimes there is the appearance of being associated with gamblers, and I think direct association is wrong." When asked to explain what he meant, Davis responded, "It is what is. You know, when I came into the National Football League, many of our owners owned horses, owned dog tracks, owned all the familiar gambling habitats of gamblers and gambling. We have learned to accept this in the National Football League. We have people, as I say, who own hotels in Las Vegas, and it is not frowned upon. We have learned to accept in our business a differentiation between association and appearance. That is the point I was trying to get across."[4]

Rozelle had become increasingly critical of Davis and advised him to "divorce" himself from his business ties with Glick. However, Rozelle did not force the issue, saying publicly that Davis's investment in the Eastmont Mall was "just a tax shelter."[5]

NFL Security chief Jack Danahy recalls, "Glick was the subject of a big FBI investigation. And he was of interest to us because he shared ownership with some of our people [in the NFL]. There was the shopping center he had with Al Davis, but our people found out a lot about Glick after they bought it. He was just coming under FBI scrutiny. And you couldn't just walk up to Al Davis and say, 'You gotta sell this thing.'

"There were several other people involved, and they bailed out of it. We went to them and said that this guy [Glick] was bad news, and they severed their relationships with him. Al Davis said, 'As far as I know, this guy is a lawyer, and he's my partner.' Pete consulted with the league lawyers, and they said we couldn't do anything. Later on, of course, it developed that Glick was a front man for the mob."

Although NFL coaches Chuck Knox, Don Shula, and John Ralston gave up their interests with Glick's businesses, Davis refused to. As a consequence, he was investigated by the NFL, and his tax returns were mulled over by the IRS.

Reflecting on the Glick matter, a longtime supporter of Davis told me, "I'm not too hard on him for this. Davis appears to truly love professional football, and it is hard for me to believe that he would ever do anything that could jeopardize his ownership of the Raiders. Surely, he understood that his relationship with Glick could do just that. His enemies in the NFL saw this as a means to run him right out of football."

Meantime, Lefty Rosenthal, who was still the director of Argent's Nevada operations, was beating his chest around Las Vegas, boasting that he was the real decision maker behind Argent and that Glick was merely his moneyman. Such indiscreet comments prompted federal and state investigators to believe that Glick was indeed only a front man, wittingly or unwittingly, for Rosenthal, Spilotro, and/or the crime syndicate. And the Rand murder had only heightened their suspicions.

"One of Lefty's biggest problems was that he loved the publicity," Marty Kane, a top Rosenthal associate, told me. "That's when he got into trouble. When the politicians came after him, instead of backing off, he challenged them."

Rosenthal's reapplication for a casino license was rejected in January 1976. The commission cited his criminal record and underworld associations as the reasons for the denial. The panel also noted his 1960 nolo contendere plea in North Carolina for attempting to bribe a college basketball player during the NCAA tournament. The chairman of the gaming commission, Peter Echeverria, said, "In my three-and-a-half-year tenure I have never found an applicant whose background was so repugnant. As far as suitability, Rosenthal would be at the bottom of the list." Consequently, Rosenthal was finally released by Glick.

Surprisingly, Glick had testified on Rosenthal's behalf at the hearing, saying that to deny Rosenthal licensing would "certainly be one of the greatest mistakes ever to take place in the State of Nevada . . . I decided unilaterally—and I want to emphasize unilaterally—that what would be best for Argent would be to have Frank Rosenthal as my personal adviser."

At the time of the commission's decision, *Rouge et Noir News,* a newsletter for the casino gaming community, protested, "Rosenthal's background was well known to the enforcement officials when his services were engaged by Glick. We thought that Rosenthal had an excellent chance of approval because a rejection on the basis of 15-year-old data would make Nevada authorities look ridiculous. They could have acted on the same background data immediately on hearing of Rosenthal's appointment about a year ago. If Rosenthal was not suitable a year ago, why didn't the Nevada authorities act then?

"The Rosenthal case begs the question as to how many undesirable employees continue in their jobs only because the Nevada gaming authorities haven't chosen to classify the position as requiring a key employee designation. And what undesirable employees remain at jobs just below the 'key employee' designation to avoid a thorough investigation of their backgrounds?"

After Rosenthal was ousted from Argent, he was replaced by another Chicago mob associate and former Caesars Palace executive, Carl Thomas, who pinch-hit for Rosenthal and continued to manipulate Glick.[6]

The government's suspicions about Argent were confirmed in June 1976 when the FBI filed an affidavit in federal court charging that the Balistrieri crime family had received over

$100,000 in skimmed casino money from Argent. The affidavit stated that the Balistrieris were "answerable to the Chicago organized crime family which controls Anthony Spilotro's illegal activities in Las Vegas and the Western United States . . . Based upon electronically intercepted conversations demonstrating Anthony Spilotro's . . . influence with various aspects of the Stardust and Fremont Hotel/Casinos, Spilotro and the organized crime figures to whom he reports in the Midwestern United States have an undisclosed control over and proprietary interest in the Argent Corporation, in its operation of the Stardust and Fremont Hotel/Casinos, and that Allen R. Glick is merely a straw party controlled by the organized crime syndicate, and designated by them to be the licensee, on paper, in the State of Nevada."

Ironically, it was the July 1975 disappearance of Jimmy Hoffa[7] that had ignited the federal government's renewed interest in organized-crime investigations, particularly in the areas of pension-fund frauds and general labor racketeering, for the first time since the Kennedy administration.[8] Among the major targets of federal law-enforcement agencies was the Teamsters' Central States Pension Fund.[9]

32 Colonel Culverhouse and Major Realty

ON A SATURDAY AFTERNOON in December 1974, Carroll Rosenbloom, overwhelmed by work and responsibilities, began complaining of flu symptoms and stomach cramps. He was taken to the hospital where it was discovered that he had suffered a heart attack. Although the attack was considered mild, Rosenbloom did not respond well to treatment, and his doctors feared that he could have another. To him, the worst consequence was that he missed the Rams' 1974 divisional championship game against the Washington Redskins, which his team won, 19–10, and the NFC championship game against the Minnesota Vikings, which it lost, 14–10.

Eleven months after his coronary, the sixty-eight-year-old Rosenbloom was admitted to Daniel Freeman Hospital for cardiac bypass surgery. Afterward, Rosenbloom became a new man. Interviewed by *Los Angeles Times* reporter Charles Maher, Rosenbloom told him that after early morning business phone calls, "I'll check with the Ram office to see what they have scheduled for me. Then, before I do anything else, I'll stretch. I'm a great believer in stretching. Then I check the tide in your newspaper so I can get down on the beach and run when the tide is low . . . I'm out there about an hour and fifteen minutes. I call it roving. The dogs go out with me and Chip [his youngest son] does when he's here. We'll run a while, then walk very fast, then jog a little." Rosenbloom also swam, played tennis, had daily rubdowns, ate right, and generally took care of himself. To beat the tension of Los Angeles traffic, he bought a red-and-white Bell 206B2 helicopter. He drove his Mercedes roadster just for fun.

Rosenbloom removed himself from all corporate boards and concentrated on a handful of investments and some oil drilling, particularly in Louisiana. The business meetings he did have away from home were generally held at the Beverly Hills Hotel, which was near his Mediterranean-style Bel Air mansion.

Rosenbloom also owned a two-story "summer house," worth an estimated $2 million, located on three oceanfront lots in Trancas Beach, just north of Malibu. His neighbors included Jack Lemmon, Steve McQueen, Dinah Shore, and Billy Wilder.

Along with his wife, Georgia, the ball club became the center of Rosenbloom's universe, even though he referred to the Rams as "a hobby" and not a full-time job. At Rams games at the Coliseum, there was Carroll's Corner, a vacant broadcasting booth on the stadium's second tier where Rosenbloom's male friends would congregate. "Carroll only felt comfortable with guys in his Corner," said one of his associates. "He wouldn't even leave to go to the bathroom. In front of the guys, he could just take a piss in a Dixie cup."

Georgia Rosenbloom had the nearby Georgia's Grandstand that was high above the crowd in the eastern end zone of the stadium.

Despite his changing life-style, Rosenbloom still enjoyed finding adversaries and going to war with them. His most bitter conflict was with a most unlikely foe: Pete Rozelle. During the mid-1970s, the two men were locked in a bitter feud. It was sparked in 1975 when the commissioner invoked the Rozelle Rule after the Rams signed wide receiver Ron Jessie away from the Detroit Lions. The Rozelle Rule permitted the commissioner to award compensation when two clubs could not agree after one team had signed a veteran as a free agent who had played out his option. As compensation for Jessie, the Rams were forced by Rozelle to give the Lions the Rams' star running back Cullen Bryant.

As a means of revenge, Rosenbloom was thought to have been behind Bryant's subsequent legal action, challenging the Rozelle Rule; Bryant had retained one of Rosenbloom's attorneys. At the time Bryant filed suit, the NFL was locked in another litigation with John Mackey, an all-pro tight end with the Baltimore Colts and the president of the NFLPA, who had earlier challenged the rule and was awaiting a decision.[1]

In the midst of the Mackey trial—and after a Los Angeles federal judge chided the NFL during an initial hearing in the Bryant case—the commissioner relented and permitted Bryant to stay with the Rams but gave the Lions the Rams' first- and second-round draft choices in the next college draft.

Although Rosenbloom won his battle, he became the target of severe criticism, particularly by the Lions' management. The club's head coach, Rick Forzano, described Rosenbloom as being the "most selfish owner in football . . . Rosenbloom wants to win so badly he would really go as far as this—to cheat another team. He is hurting professional football." William Clay Ford, the Lions' owner, wrote to Rosenbloom, expressing similar sentiments. Rosenbloom's replies to both men were predictably acrimonious, and he wanted Rozelle to fine the Lions' ownership for attacking him.

Rozelle refused and again began to feel the wrath of Carroll Rosenbloom, who hired a private investigator to probe Rozelle's past. Rosenbloom's detective came up empty. Author David Harris notes, "Pete Rozelle was an exceedingly difficult person upon whom to find dirt. The commissioner didn't run around with women, and, though he drank, it was rarely to excess. He had nothing to do with Las Vegas, and his only significant involvement with gambling was navy poker games during World War II. He was scrupulous about his personal behavior and seemed to take to the role of Caesar's wife with an almost religious intensity."[2]

In November 1975, the month of his bypass surgery, and still with nothing on Rozelle, Rosenbloom exploded at the commissioner during an owners' meeting, called him "a crook" and actually threatened him. "If I can't get you in this room, I'll get you outside it," Rosenbloom told Rozelle. "I will not return to any meeting while this man is in the chair." Rosenbloom then stormed out of the meeting. The only owner to support Rosenbloom in the aftermath of his tirade was Al Davis of the Oakland Raiders. Rosenbloom had once said of Davis, who had been a frequent houseguest of the Rosenbloom family since the early 1960s, "I like Al Davis because he is a mean, conniving s.o.b., just like I am."

Rosenbloom then began a year-long boycott of the NFL's

owners' meetings. His son Steve attended the meetings in his place.

Rozelle, who appeared to be trying to avoid full-scale war with Rosenbloom, found himself in a dilemma the following month. Bill Bidwill, the owner of the St. Louis Cardinals, had discovered that Rosenbloom, knowingly or unknowingly, had been skimming money from the NFL revenue pool when post-season games were played in the Los Angeles Coliseum. The Rams' owner, like all other NFL owners, was required to forward all monies, after expenses, earned from play-off games to NFL headquarters for equal distribution among all NFL teams.

Rosenbloom had withheld 10 percent of the gross, claiming that it was rent for the Coliseum. However, Bidwill suspected and Rozelle's records confirmed that Rosenbloom owed no further rent to the Coliseum management by the end of the regular season. Thus, the 10 percent sum, deducted as rent—approximately $270,000—wound up in Rosenbloom's pocket.

Confronting Rosenbloom in private, Rozelle gave the Rams' owner the benefit of the doubt and assumed that the apparent skim was simply a bookkeeping error. An NFL committee looked into the matter and concluded that Rosenbloom indeed owed the league the money. The most outspoken of those at the meeting was Tex Schramm of the Dallas Cowboys, who was reportedly relentless in his assault on Rosenbloom—who, in turn, was so outraged by the attack that he didn't speak to Schramm for two years.

Furious with the ruling, Rosenbloom completely severed his relationship with Rozelle and those club owners who supported the commissioner. The embattled Rozelle became philosophical—and a little sarcastic. "I'm sorry Carroll is disturbed," the commissioner said, "but I know he'll grow to love me once again."

Soon after, Rosenbloom may have struck back again. During the spring of 1976, two IRS investigators showed up at the NFL's New York offices. "They wanted to see Pete Rozelle and the League's treasurer," writes Harris, "and it was not a casual visit." The IRS agents read them their Miranda rights and told them that they were under criminal investigation. "The object of the IRS's inquiry was the $300,000 loan at seven percent which the League had given Rozelle in 1974 for the purchase of his new place in Westchester."[3] The IRS investigation continued for two years before finally being dropped. Rozelle was never charged with any wrongdoing.

A tentative peace between Rosenbloom and Rozelle was reached in November 1976 after a three-man committee—Edward Bennett Williams of the Washington Redskins, Leon Hess of the New York Jets, and Charles Sullivan of the New England Patriots—met with Rosenbloom in Los Angeles. "They seemed to have the strange feeling that the league would be better off with me there than without me there," Rosenbloom told reporter Rich Roberts. "Of course, I have strong feelings about how the league should be run. My only dispute with Pete is that I want him to go back to being what he was—the best commissioner in pro sports."

With Rosenbloom's conciliatory tone, a settlement was reached—although the Rosenbloom-Rozelle relationship remained forever strained.

While Rosenbloom was recovering from bypass surgery, Hugh F. Culverhouse of the Tampa Bay Buccaneers officially joined the ranks of NFL owners in 1976 and quickly became the most powerful force in the league. The foundation for Culverhouse's power in the NFL was and is his banking connections, particularly in Florida, and his seemingly unsurpassed knowledge of the U.S. tax laws, which the NFL owners took advantage of whenever necessary.

Originally, Culverhouse had been outbid for the Los Angeles Rams by the Carroll Rosenbloom / Robert Irsay swap deal in 1972. Supposedly a deal had been struck between the NFL and Culverhouse, promising him the edge when the next franchise became available.

But Culverhouse was outbid again in his quest for the new Tampa Bay franchise on October 30, 1974, by developer Thomas D. McCloskey, the son of Philadelphia Democratic power broker Matt McCloskey. However, after the deal appeared secure, McCloskey, who had been outbid by Leonard Tose in an effort to buy the Philadelphia Eagles in 1969, shocked everyone two weeks after his bid for the Buccaneers had been accepted by indicating that he could not raise the $16 million franchise price. Culverhouse then stepped up and slapped down $4 million as his first installment. He was immediately awarded the team.[4]

The delay between Culverhouse's purchase of the Buccaneers in 1974 and its first NFL game in 1976 resulted from the renovation of Tampa Stadium, which increased its seating capacity from 46,500 to 72,000.

According to a member of the Buccaneers, Tampa mob boss Santos Trafficante may have played a key role in the negotiations over the stadium, with or without Culverhouse's knowledge. The player quoted a top member of the Buccaneers' front office as saying, "You can't do anything in this town without Trafficante's approval. In fact, if it wasn't for Trafficante, we wouldn't even have this team."

Trafficante was among the most powerful Mafia figures in America. He controlled Florida's narcotics network and gambling operations, particularly the "bolita lottery," a Cuban numbers game. A protégé of Meyer Lansky, Trafficante was Lansky's principal enforcer in the crime syndicate's Cuban gambling establishments in pre-Castro Cuba. After Castro overthrew the Cuban government and closed the casinos, Trafficante was arrested and held in custody. Soon after his release and return to the United States, he was recruited by the CIA for his participation in the CIA/Mafia plots to assassinate Castro.[5] He was also a close friend and business partner with Carlos Marcello of New Orleans.

Although there is no further evidence of a connection between Trafficante and the Tampa Bay team, there is a strong connection between Trafficante's mentor, Meyer Lansky, and Culverhouse.

Culverhouse, an ex-Golden Gloves boxer, did his undergraduate work at and received his law degree from the University of Alabama. He also served in the Army Air Force during World War II as the head of logistics in the Air Transport Command and retired as a full colonel in the Air Force Reserves. After spending two years as an assistant attorney general in Alabama, he became a top attorney in the Florida office of the Internal Revenue Service. His principal responsibility while with the IRS was investigating tax liabilities of suspected organized-crime figures in the wake of the Kefauver Committee.

Culverhouse, who was appointed by President Kennedy to his White House tax advisory committee, had founded his own law firm—Culverhouse, Tomlinson, Mills, DeCarion and Anderson—based in Jacksonville and Miami in 1956. He represented Bebe Rebozo during the Watergate Hearings. His son, attorney

Hugh Culverhouse, Jr., was on the legal team headed by William Hundley that defended former Attorney General John Mitchell during his prosecution for Watergate-related crimes.

Also a real estate developer in Florida, Indiana, and Ohio, Culverhouse became a director of Major Realty, a Florida-based real estate company. Another director was George Smathers of Florida—who was a member of the U.S. Senate while serving on the board.[6] Major Realty had been a frequent target of federal investigations during the 1960s and 1970s because so many of its investors, attorneys, lenders, and clients had ties to Florida mobsters, especially Meyer Lansky and Santos Trafficante.

A confidential 1978 report prepared by the Florida Department of Law Enforcement (FDLE) emphasized that "Major Realty has had a past history of organized-crime associations." Max Orovitz, who founded Major Realty in 1961, was one of Lansky's closest friends and business associates. He had been a partner of Carroll Rosenbloom and Lou Chesler and had replaced Chesler as the president of the General Development Corporation in 1965. Three years later, Orovitz was convicted in New York for violations of federal stock-registration laws.

Another key player in Major Realty was financier Benjamin Sigelbaum, who was responsible for providing loans to the real estate company and keeping it afloat in 1966. He was also identified in a Florida Department of Law Enforcement report as the "financial investor for Meyer Lansky"; in other words, a bagman. Implicated in the Bobby Baker scandal, Sigelbaum had been convicted of bankruptcy fraud in 1936. Twenty-two years later, President Eisenhower gave him a full pardon. However, the state of Israel subsequently rejected Sigelbaum's application for citizenship—because of his close association with Lansky.

After years of selling Florida land at a loss, Major Realty finally announced a profit in 1968 based on the sale of 175 acres of land for $3,500,000. The news caused its stock to jump from $0.11 a share to $14 a share during a twenty-month period. The SEC moved in to probe the transaction. At the close of its investigation, the agency called the land sale "a mere fiction designed to create the illusion of profits or value as a basis for sale of securities."

Culverhouse was not personally accused of any wrongdoing.

33 On the Principal Subjects List

THE ANNOUNCED BUYER OF Major Realty's land in 1968 was Edward J. DeBartolo, Sr., a major builder of shopping malls around the United States, who was alleged by a variety of law-enforcement agencies to have business ties with top organized-crime figures, including Meyer Lansky, Carlos Marcello, and Santos Trafficante.

In 1970, DeBartolo's name had appeared on the U.S. Justice Department's Organized Crime Principal Subjects List, a catalogue of people who are suspected of having links to organized crime. Later, DeBartolo challenged the listing of his name on the register through his attorney, Charles F. C. Ruff. At the time of this action, DeBartolo was attempting to obtain a license to operate a racetrack in Oklahoma and didn't want the list to prejudice the Oklahoma Horse Racing Commission, which issues the licenses.

In response to this challenge, David Margolis, the chief of the Organized Crime and Racketeering Section, responded to Ruff. Margolis wrote, "The so-called Principal Subjects List was created in the late 1960s and distributed to a number of government agencies in 1971. Individuals whose names appeared in investigative reports were placed on the list, although they were not necessarily the subjects of criminal investigations. Over the years the list became outdated, and persons remained on it even though they were no longer of interest to the Department of Justice, were not the subjects of any investigation or were deceased." Margolis added that the list had not been in use since August 1975—after an order had been issued by Margolis's predecessor that "the list should be destroyed."

DeBartolo was born in the Smoky Hollow section of Youngstown, Ohio, in 1909.[1] He received his degree in civil engineering from Notre Dame and made his fortune in the construction business, primarily as a builder of shopping centers. Between 1952 and 1954, DeBartolo and members of his company were subjected to six bombings of their offices and shopping centers. No one was killed, and the bombing spree was never solved. In 1960, he purchased the Thistledown racetrack near Cleveland, and the following year he bought the nearby Randall Park racetrack. The concessions for these tracks were handled by the Emprise Corporation, a Buffalo-based sports-services conglomerate, which was indicted and convicted in 1972 for racketeering and fronting for several organized-crime figures. In 1973, DeBartolo bought another racetrack, Balmoral, just south of Chicago.

Also during the 1960s, DeBartolo had engaged in a joint development in Florida with Lou Chesler and his General Development Corporation. According to their contract, Chesler and General Development were responsible for building houses in Port Malabar, Port Charlotte, Port St. Lucie, and other locations on both Florida coasts, while DeBartolo handled all commercial construction, such as shopping centers.

By 1965, DeBartolo had begun building shopping malls, beginning with the Summit Mall in Fairlawn, Ohio, near Akron. A 1978 classified report from the Florida Department of Law Enforcement described him as "a very wealthy, powerful, influential person with organized-crime connections in Ohio. Subject deals in land purchases, construction, and development of large shopping centers throughout the United States."

DeBartolo is also an admitted gambler and has had a $100,000 line of credit at Caesars Palace in Las Vegas. Also the owner of the Pittsburgh Penguins of the National Hockey League and the Pittsburgh Civic Arena, DeBartolo had made several unsuccessful attempts to purchase major-league baseball teams during the late 1970s. Among those teams he tried to purchase were the Chicago White Sox (twice), Boston Red Sox, Cleveland Indians, and Seattle Mariners; he also tried to bring a major-league baseball team to New Orleans.

In the end, DeBartolo either withdrew his bid when it became clear that he would be facing stiff opposition, or he was flat out rejected because of his ties to racetracks and gamblers.[2] "My father has too much class for baseball," Edward J. DeBartolo, Jr., told *The New York Times.*

In March 1977, the elder DeBartolo purchased 90 percent of the stock of the San Francisco 49ers for $17.6 million and made it a subsidiary of his corporation. The team was then given to his thirty-year-old son. "Eddie Jr. bought it from me," DeBartolo told *The Pittsburgh Press.* "Everyone thinks I gave it to him, but Eddie financed it and paid for it." However, the senior DeBartolo personally secured his son's purchase.

Tampa Bay owner Hugh Culverhouse was retained as the DeBartolos' tax attorney for the 49ers' sale. At that time, NFL Security reportedly could find nothing in the DeBartolos' background to prevent them from buying the team.

However, when I asked NFL Security chief Jack Danahy about that report, as well as the nature of the senior DeBartolo's background, Danahy replied, "I'm not going to discuss that one." It was the only time during my interviews with Danahy that he refused to answer a question.

Oakland Raiders owner Al Davis stated in a sworn deposition that he, too, was directly involved in the sale of the 49ers to DeBartolo. "The selling group, I guess, was the San Francisco 49ers consisting of the two Morabito women,[3] [and] Lou Spadia, and Frank Mieuli[4] would stay on with his—I think he had ten percent. The DeBartolo family would be buying ninety percent of the 49ers with options from Mieuli if he wants to sell or if he wants to buy another five percent. I think they gave him a right based on his preemptive right not to let them buy."

"And you also represented the buying group and that was the DeBartolos?" asked the attorney questioning Davis.

"I represented the buying group to the DeBartolos. I didn't represent the 49ers group. I kind of brought them all together and kind of advised both of them what I thought was fair and et cetera, like that, yes."[5]

In return for his role as intermediary, Davis reportedly received a "finder's fee" of $100,000, paid by the DeBartolos. However, Davis has been coy about the figure, indicating it was probably much higher.[6]

Soon after the DeBartolos bought the 49ers, an FBI wiretap picked up Los Angeles mobster Jimmy Fratianno discussing a meeting with New Mexico criminal lawyer William Marchiondo to be held in San Francisco. The transcript of the conversation stated:

"Fratianno: Hey don't forget now: when the Miami Dolphins play, you're going to come over here. See, I got it arranged so you're going to sit with this guy, the owner of the 49ers.

"Marchiondo: Well, I want to talk with this guy, but that's a bad time for me to leave . . ."

Fratianno explained the conversation to my associate, William Scott Malone, "I arranged through this friend of mine [Youngstown Mafia figure Ronald Carabbia] for an attorney in New Mexico to sit with DeBartolo in the press box. They wanted to talk some kind of business. I don't know what it was. So I arranged a meeting."

Fratianno added that DeBartolo Sr. was "very friendly" with Carabbia.[7] He also said that the two men "used to go on junkets to the Tropicana [in Las Vegas]. And [DeBartolo] was a pretty heavy gambler. He would lose a lot of money. He had a pretty good line of credit in Vegas."

Ronald J. Parr, a racetrack owner and a respected government informant, who once wore a wire during an investigation of DeBartolo, told Malone that he had come to know the shopping mall king well. "DeBartolo is a heavy, heavy gambler," Parr alleges. "I mean, he bets in the hundreds of thousands of dollars on the outcome of a football game. When you have a guy like that owning a football team, it makes you very nervous."

The DeBartolo racetrack ownership issue also posed a striking difference of the required standards demanded by officials of the NFL and major-league baseball. Jack Danahy told me that racetrack ownership by NFL team owners "didn't bother me. That was a legitimate enterprise. There's no prohibition against owning a racetrack."

Consequently, while DeBartolo was being turned away by professional baseball for his racetrack ties, he was embraced by the NFL. And DeBartolo's situation in the NFL was not unlike that of the Rooney family of Pittsburgh.

In addition to the Steelers—which Art Rooney's son Dan operated—the Rooney family owned Yonkers Raceway in Yonkers, New York, and the Liberty Bell Raceway in northeastern Philadelphia, both of which were harness-racing tracks.[8] The Rooney family also bought the Continental racetrack, a thoroughbred track in Philadelphia, and the Palm Beach Kennel Club, a Florida dog track. And they owned Shamrock Farms, a thoroughbred stable in Winfield, Maryland. The family's sports operations were consolidated under the Ruanaidh Corporation.

Author William Henry Paul notes, "While Art gambled on horses, his sons gamble on the tracks where they race. Art says the family borrowed to the hilt to swing the purchase of Yonkers Raceway in 1972 for $45 million in cash plus assumption of $7 million in liabilities. 'Sometimes I wonder whether we're stretching ourselves too thin,' he says, shaking his head slowly."[9]

At the same time that DeBartolo faced repeated humiliation trying to buy a professional baseball team, the Rooneys purchased another racetrack, Green Mountain in Pownal, Vermont—with no complaints from the NFL, despite evidence of organized crime's past involvement with the track. Raymond Patriarca, the boss of the New England Mafia, had been involved in some of the decisions made by the previous Green Mountain management.[10] The former president of Green Mountain was a close associate of Patriarca, who had a hidden interest in Berkshire Downs, along with New York Mafia chief Thomas Lucchese.

Pownal reporter Helen Renner questioned Art Rooney's son John Rooney, the president of the Vermont track, "as to organized crime at Green Mountain." Rooney replied that he did not "feel major criminal elements had any foothold here. He pointed out that any large enterprise, financially attractive, will have its hangers-on of petty rascals, but there is no evidence of serious problems here."

34 The Quiet Man

MIAMI OLDSMOBILE DEALER AND high-stakes gambler Richard Fincher is a former Florida state senator with ties to major organized-crime figures and narcotics dealers. Federal investigators have identified Fincher as "the center of a major bookmaking ring, which operates through a labyrinth of automobile dealerships [throughout] the country."

Fincher is truly a man of mystery who, somehow, seems to show up everywhere and knows just about everyone. For instance, Fincher has been a longtime friend of Mike McLaney, who had operated a casino in Havana in cooperation with Carroll Rosenbloom and Lou Chesler.[1]

Fincher had also been a business partner of President Nixon's banker/friend Bebe Rebozo, and Michael O'Neil, the owner of General Tire and Rubber Company, in the development of Lummus Island, a subsidiary of Fisher Island, Inc. in south Florida. Responsible for building a causeway between Fisher Island and the Florida mainland was Clint Murchison, the owner of the Dallas Cowboys.

Fincher's name appeared in Gil Beckley's coded address book in 1966, and several law-enforcement authorities say that Fincher fronted for Beckley in his national gambling operation. Fincher has admitted only knowing Beckley and occasionally doing business with him.[2]

"Dick used to bet with us when I was with Gil," a former Beckley associate told me. "If Gil bet on a game, he would put

Dick Fincher down for whatever it was he bet. He would call Dick and tell him, 'You got the Bears minus three for a thousand.' And once in a while Dick would want to bet on a game on his own.

"I feel sorry for Dick. He could've been governor of Florida if he hadn't been screwed up with us."

Another name that appeared in the book was ex-Green Bay Packers star Paul Hornung, and Fincher was close to him too. Both Fincher and Hornung were known associates of Kentucky Governor John Y. Brown—the former owner of Kentucky Fried Chicken and the Kentucky Colonels of the American Basketball Association. Brown was also a heavy gambler and in close contact with numerous bookmakers in his state. Fincher admitted that he was responsible for introducing McLaney to Brown.[3]

An underworld figure in Las Vegas says, "Dick Fincher was moving the money. He was running the sports offices from Miami. He was very, very close to Lefty Rosenthal, and they have been in business together for a long time. In the layoff, Fincher worked for Lefty, just as he had done for Gil Beckley."

During a 1977 investigation of a Florida drug dealer with whom Fincher had been linked, state law-enforcement officials reviewed Fincher's telephone toll records. They show that Fincher called, among others, associates of Carlos Marcello and Santos Trafficante—and numerous car dealers, Las Vegas casino operators, racetrack owners, bookmakers, narcotics traffickers, and arms dealers.

Fincher also called John Y. Brown, who Florida law-enforcement agents described as "an associate of organized crime and heavily involved in gambling," and "James George Synodinos [Snyder], aka Jimmy the Greek."

In the world of football, calls from Fincher's phone went to New Orleans Saints head coach Hank Stram, former University of Texas head football coach Darrell Royal, and University of Alabama head football coach Paul "Bear" Bryant, as well as three former members of the Green Bay Packers: Paul Hornung,[4] tight end Ron Kramer, and Max McGee, a wide receiver who was the Most Valuable Player in Super Bowl I between the Packers and the Kansas City Chiefs. The report also notes that Billy Quinlan, another former Packer, was Fincher's frequent houseguest.

Explaining his relationship with Fincher, Stram told me, "Dick was a great friend of mine through the University of

Miami." The coach added that, as was the case with Radio Winer, he was completely unaware of Fincher's gambling activities. "I met Dick through Andy Gustafson [the head coach of the university's football team] while I was an assistant coach there in 1959. Fincher would provide a car for Andy and his coaching staff on occasion."

In 1977, Fincher was implicated in a federal and state investigation of the WFC Corporation, a shady investment company founded by a Cuban refugee. The investigation of WFC began when Fincher, who was also the co-owner of a Miami pest control company, was probed for being involved in the trafficking of millions of dollars of marijuana and cocaine. According to a confidential report by the Florida Department of Law Enforcement, "WFC Corporation is a cover for the largest narcotics operation in the world." Law-enforcement agency documents also stated that WFC had been heavily influenced by Florida Mafia boss Santos Trafficante.

A 1979 report of the FDLE states that the Florida comptroller's office was investigating "what appears to be spurious loans made by the WFC Corporation from its Grand Cayman Island subsidiary, through the Metropolitan Bank and Trust Company of Tampa, a banking institution whose majority stockholder is Edward J. DeBartolo [senior]."[5] According to bank sources, the law firm of Tampa Bay Buccaneers owner Hugh Culverhouse represented Metropolitan.

While Fincher faced government probes, NFL owners DeBartolo and Culverhouse could laugh their problems off because no one, especially the NFL, was going to lay a glove on them. However, Dallas Cowboys owner Clint Murchison was not so carefree. He, like Fincher, was either a subject or the actual target of several federal probes.

In a report of an investigation being conducted by the Bureau of Alcohol, Tobacco and Firearms (ATF) of the Department of the Treasury, special agents had learned "that Murchison was 'fronting' for O/C [organized crime] out of Florida at Tony Roma's Place for Ribs in Dallas."

The ATF reported that "Murchison is indeed partners with Tony Roma, real name Anthony LoPresti, and past manager of Playboy Clubs in Chicago and Montreal, Canada." Roma had been registered at Acapulco Towers at the same time that the 1970 mobster conference was being held there. The report also linked Murchison with Ettore Zappi, a capo in the Carlo Gambino crime family in New York.

"From data presently available," the ATF report concluded, "it appears that Murchison is firmly entrenched with individuals who are proven national Mafia figures."

Murchison's name was also dragged into a major financial scam in which $2 million in Teamsters' insurance premiums were diverted to several organized-crime operations. Among those insurance companies implicated in the scheme was National American Life Insurance Company. The owner of the firm was a close business associate of Carlos Marcello.

Murchison was later named as a member of National American's board of directors, along with Joseph Hauser, a convicted insurance swindler who was trying to secure a major insurance contract with the Teamsters' Central State Health and Welfare Fund. Also implicated in the scheme was Washington lobbyist and Marcello associate I. Irving Davidson. On October 31, 1977, Davidson gave a sworn deposition in the case. His attorney was Plato Cacheris, the law partner of former NFL Security chief Bill Hundley.

Davidson explained that he and Murchison, with whom he had been a good friend for "about twenty years," were partners in Burbank International, along with Thomas Webb, a former FBI agent and administrative assistant to J. Edgar Hoover, who had originally introduced Davidson to Murchison. Explaining the connection between Hauser and Murchison, Davidson said: "I was going to try and get Mr. Hauser's computer business for a firm owned by Mr. Clint Murchison called Optimum Systems."

Davidson added, "I called Clint and told him Tom [Webb] was standing with me, and that we had been working with this man Hauser, who we thought could get a lot a business for several companies that Mr. Murchison owned, ran, and operated. And we thought it would be a good idea if he got on the board of this new company. Clint says, 'What do you know about Hauser?' We said, 'We think he is okay.' He says, 'Let me talk to Tom.' Tom said that same thing to Clint. He [Murchison] said okay. And that's the way it ended. He is a very short man on the telephone . . ."

However, when the federal investigation was completed, Hauser was indicted for his role in the operation.

As part of a secret plea-bargaining arrangement, Hauser

agreed to become a federal witness and wear a wire against several organized-crime figures, including Marcello. For cover, Hauser and two FBI undercover agents created a dummy insurance company in Beverly Hills.

Davidson needed a favor and asked Hauser to help—not knowing that Hauser had been flipped by the government. Hauser responded by bringing the two undercover agents to the meeting, and they asked Davidson to introduce them to Marcello. They explained that they needed the underworld boss in order to obtain major insurance contracts in Louisiana.

In addition to wiring Hauser, an electronics surveillance device had been placed in the ceiling above Marcello's desk. During the conversations, according to federal agents, Murchison's name was picked up numerous times on tape because Davidson had served as a go-between for the NFL team owner and Marcello. Murchison and Marcello were involved in negotiations for the sale of a portion of Marcello's estate, Churchill Farms.

In the midst of Hauser's tapings of Marcello—in which he made a thinly veiled admission that he had arranged the 1963 murder of President John Kennedy—Murchison's name was brought up several times in connection with a wide range of business deals. The tapes detailed Davidson's role as a go-between for Marcello and Murchison on a land deal and a bank purchase the two men were negotiating. The FBI sting operation became known as Brilab, which had broadened into an investigation of bribery of labor union officials and politicians in Arkansas, Kansas, Louisiana, Oklahoma, and Texas.

Davidson—who was indicted in the Brilab case along with Marcello and three others—admitted that he had introduced FBI sting man Hauser to Marcello and vouched for him. However, Davidson was acquitted.

Marcello was later convicted and finally sent back to prison. At the mob boss's sentencing hearing, a federal judge told Marcello, "You've led a life of crime. The record shows that. By any evaluation, I think it's fair to say you're a bad man."

Murchison was neither prosecuted nor investigated further. There also was no known investigation of Murchison by the NFL.

Another NFL owner had proven that he could maintain a direct link to a major organized-crime figure without any reprisals from the league.

35 More Players and Bookmakers

WHILE NFL OWNERS MAINTAINED their close connections with members of the organized-crime syndicate with little or no exposure from law-enforcement agencies, the league, or even the sports media, several incidents involving NFL players did receive considerable attention.

After a widely publicized 1977 investigation of ten Miami Dolphins players, the team's all-pro quarterback Bob Griese was threatened by the NFL with a stiff fine "for associating with a suspected bookmaker," thirty-seven-year-old J. Lance Cooper, a former golf pro and Miami real estate broker.[1] Cooper had been arrested in November 1976 with four other bookmakers who were charged with illegal gambling.

After reading about the arrest, Dolphins coach Don Shula notified the NFL that some of his players knew Cooper. Shula cooperated fully with the probe—which included wiretaps on Cooper's house and office that were authorized by the local district attorney. A big team booster who had bought carpeting for the Dolphins' clubhouse, Cooper had enjoyed free access to the Dolphins' locker room and practice field for seven years up to the time of his arrest.

Shula told reporters, "When I first came down here, I met him [Cooper] as a friend of some of the players who were on the 1970 Dolphins. I accepted him as a friend of theirs . . . He was welcome at practice. There were times when I saw him in the locker room, talking to some of the players he knew pretty well."

The names of Shula and three players—Griese, backup quarterback Earl Morrall, and defensive end Bill Stanfill—were found in Cooper's address book, according to the Miami police.

NFL Security chief Jack Danahy explained that there were "people in the Dolphins organization who were aware that Cooper had some interest in gambling." Cooper reportedly swore that he had "never used any of the ballplayers for . . . gambling purposes." However, he later admitted during a polygraph examination that he had passed on information about the Dolphins to organized-crime figures. He pleaded guilty to the gambling charges and was sentenced to two years probation and fined $1,500.

"I've probably known Lance longer than any of the other players," Griese told Edwin Pope of *The Miami Herald.* "I got to know him through Jack Clancy [an ex-Dolphin receiver]. I met Lance through Jack, and then I went to work in the real estate business and eventually so did Lance and Jack. Lance was a golfer. We probably played golf once or twice together way back when. He's been coming around our practices for a long time, maybe as far back as the late 1960s."

No fines were leveled against any NFL personnel. "We have found no evidence of wrongdoing and found no reason to fine anyone," said Jim Kensil, Commissioner Rozelle's deputy.

Also investigated by NFL Security in a separate incident was Craig Morton, the quarterback of the American Football Conference champions, the Denver Broncos, who, in early January 1978, was found to have been in serious financial trouble just prior to Super Bowl XII—despite his $150,000-a-year salary. Like Len Dawson in 1970, Morton was besieged by reporters during the week before the game and asked embarrassing questions about a $38,000 bank loan and a $34,635 IRS lien against him. The obvious concern was whether Morton was considering shortcutting his money problems, placing some bets, and then taking a dive in the Super Bowl.

Advised by the Broncos' quarterback coach, Babe Parilli, Morton refused to dignify most questions with an answer and took the high road, denying that he really had any financial problems.

When finally confronted during a press conference, he told reporters, "Everyone come in close. I'm going to talk about this once and then I'm not going to discuss it anymore. It's all being taken care of. We've talked to the Internal Revenue Service, and the matter will be settled. I've paid the taxes I thought I owed, and then another amount was added on. That's about it. It's really not important. It's not on my mind. Now, any more questions?"

When asked about his money problems again later, Morton repeated, "Everything is being taken care of . . . I've already paid the IRS about sixty thousand dollars. They didn't accept some of the things I claimed [as deductions]. And now they want some more money."

Denver's opponent in the Super Bowl was the Dallas Cowboys, with whom Morton had played from 1965 to 1974. Morton had been the Cowboys' quarterback in Super Bowl V in 1971, completing only twelve of twenty-six passes for a mere 127 yards and one touchdown. He also threw three interceptions as Dallas lost to the Baltimore Colts with five seconds left in the game, 16–13. In Super Bowl VI the following year, Morton was benched in favor of Roger Staubach, who led the Cowboys to a 24–3 win over the Miami Dolphins.

While with the Dallas team, Morton also ran into financial difficulties and filed for bankruptcy. Although he recovered after opening a Dallas discotheque, he nearly lost everything again when another business venture, a Dallas restaurant, collapsed.[2] Morton was traded to the New York Giants in 1974 and remained there until 1976. During those three years, the Giants' records were 2–12 in 1974, 5–9 in 1975, and 3–11 in 1976.

However, after being traded to Denver in 1977, Morton, who had become a born-again Christian, experienced a resurrection, leading the Broncos to a 12–2 season, the best record in the NFL. In one of the two games Denver lost—that against Dallas in the last game of the regular season—Morton played only one series of downs. Dallas, which was a five-point favorite, won, 14–6. After stunning victories against Pittsburgh in the divisional play-off game and against Oakland for the AFC championship, Denver, although still five-point underdogs, went to the 1978 Super Bowl in Miami to face Dallas brimming with confidence.

However, unlike Len Dawson in 1970, Morton could not rise to the occasion under all the pressure he was under in the Super Bowl. In the first half alone, he threw four interceptions and his teammates gave away three fumbles. After completing only four of fifteen passes for a game total of nineteen net yards, Morton was replaced by Norris Weese early in the fourth quarter. The

Broncos lost to Dallas, 27–10. Morton said after the game, "They beat us at our own game—taking turnovers. So many times this season, other teams gave us all those turnovers. Today it was just our turn."

Later that year, on December 18, 1978, yet another incident involving a bookmaker and active NFL players occurred—but this matter was hushed up for nearly four years, even after a state law-enforcement agency notified the NFL, in writing, of the problem.

On that December day, Georgia state law-enforcement officials raided the house of convicted bookmaker Bennie R. Fuqua, who was operating a $500,000-a-year gambling operation. Inside the house, agents found two NFL players present: all-pro safety Jake Scott of the Washington Redskins, and Craig T. Hertwig, a former offensive tackle for the Detroit Lions. Scott was a life-long friend of Fuqua.[3] Neither player was charged during the raid.

During my interview with Fuqua, who was the target of wiretaps, he told me, "I've lived here at the same house since 1962. I wasn't doing any gambling out of here. I have my business somewhere else. And the police just came here. They searched the place but didn't find anything. Really, they just came here to arrest me and lock me up for bookmaking. See, I had someone else working for me. And he called me one day at home and said, 'Twenty-six [a bettor's code] made a bet with you on some team at five and a half.' And I said to him, 'Stupid, why are you calling me here?' So that was the basis for the arrest.

"Jake and Craig were here visiting. Scott was living here at the time. But it's not a gambling house."

Fuqua denies that he ever received any inside information from either player. "Anyone who ever gave me inside information were usually the biggest losers—and that goes for coaches, football players, and radio announcers. What I do, I do. And that is separate from any relationship I have with Jake and Hertwig."

The raid occurred two days after the Redskins were upset by the four-and-a-half-point underdog Chicago Bears, 14–10, in Washington. Fuqua reportedly won $1,700 betting against the Redskins.

Fuqua told me that he doesn't remember betting on that particular game. "I very seldom bet. If I bet anything, it's only a hundred or two hundred dollars. If they [Scott and Hertwig] ever bet, they bet with someone else. I told them that they were stupid if they do. And I wouldn't have anything to do with it."

Hertwig, an all-American from the University of Georgia and a two-year starter with the Lions, had been released by Detroit during the 1978 preseason. He was picked up by the Bills for the last game of the season—the week before the raid on Fuqua's house—but did not play. The Bills, who were three-point underdogs, lost that game to the Baltimore Colts, 21–14. Hertwig was later accused by the Georgia Bureau of Investigations of being a payoff man for Fuqua. Both Fuqua and Hertwig denied the charge.

Despite being notified about the raid, the NFL did not even question the two players. Scott played in the 1979 preseason with the Minnesota Vikings before being released, and Hertwig played his preseason with the Buffalo Bills before being cut.

When I asked Scott about the incident, he replied, "We're just simple people who like to have fun."

While violations of NFL rules regarding the association between NFL personnel and bookmakers continued, the league's drug problems intensified as well. In May 1977, Randy Crowder and Don Reese of the Miami Dolphins were arrested for selling a pound of cocaine to an undercover agent for $233,000. Dolphins owner Joe Robbie immediately suspended both players.

After Robbie suspended them, Crowder and Reese filed a grievance with the NFL Players Association, charging that Robbie had assumed their guilt before their trial. A subsequent hearing ruled in the players' favor, with Robbie being ordered to reinstate or trade them.

Robbie angrily replied, "What will happen if two players are arrested for fixing a football game? Will their owner be prohibited from suspending them until they are tried in court so that they can play under indictment? What happens in the case of a player who bets against his own team?" The Dolphins' owner then released the two players and announced that he was going to file suit against both the NFL and the NFLPA.

Also implicated in the Dolphins drug scandal was an Eastern Airlines stewardess Camille Richardson, who cooperated with law-enforcement officials. She testified that she had done cocaine with nine NFL players, including six members of the Dolphins. With Richardson's testimony, Crowder and Reese decided to plead guilty. However, no other players were named or indicted. Richardson received a suspended sentence. The two players each received a one-year prison sentence. Soon after, Robbie dropped his suit against the league and the players' union.

"There is this incredible ability by the American public and even the NFL to distinguish drug dealers and bookmakers from organized crime," a top Strike Force attorney told me. "When a player has been doing drugs, he has been associating with a dealer who has ties to the underworld. That is a fact of life. Although there are gamblers and bookmakers who will have nothing to do with drugs and drug dealing on principle, I really doubt that there are many drug dealers who are principled enough to refuse to gamble on NFL games and to exploit those players whom they are supplying."

36 Car Dealers' Bonanza

SINCE THE ALLEGED FIXES in 1951 by a crooked referee, game officials in the NFL have become targets of close scrutiny by the league. A thorough background check is conducted on all potential candidates for these crucial positions on the football field. This is necessary because most referees accept their jobs on a part-time basis. When not in striped shirts and knickers, with whistles around their necks, they are wearing tailored suits and running businesses, practicing law, selling insurance, or teaching school, among other full-time professions.

Football referees, like umpires in baseball, are the most unpopular people in the sport for which they officiate. They remain silent, receive little credit for their good work, and get immediate and long-lasting blame when they perform poorly. And, the NFL holds them accountable for their actions.

Each crew is responsible for submitting written responses to criticisms they receive from NFL team managements. NFL representatives are assigned to each game specifically to monitor the performances of the officials and then hand out weekly grades on the basis of their work. Those who score the highest grades week after week are invited to officiate during the divisional play-offs and the Super Bowl.

Referees and game officials can completely shift the momentum of a game with a timely penalty. For instance, very few plays are completed without someone on the offensive line holding on to a charging defender—especially when the quarterback is in the pocket and needs time to find an open receiver. Not a blatant, obvious infraction, like pass interference or clipping, offensive holding is among the most common penalties called and costs the offensive team ten yards. It can also negate a touchdown pass or a long running gain.

Every football fan has either seen or heard of an NFL game that was decided by a penalty called by a game official. Even the most zealous football fanatic will agree that these calls—if they were indeed incorrect—were not nefarious. Most fans understand bad calls to be nothing more than honest mistakes.

During the latter part of the 1970s, several calls by NFL officials altered the course of the NFL playing seasons. However, none of these incidents was ever proven to have been the consequence of any form of bribery or fix. But they did serve as a prelude to an FBI investigation of possible game fixing by NFL officials.

• On December 7, 1975, a controversy over officiating in the NFL was touched off when the Buffalo Bills were knocked out of the AFC play-offs by their loss to the Miami Dolphins. Trailing 21–0 early in the game, the Bills battled back to within three points, 24–21, in the fourth quarter. With Miami in possession in its own territory, Dolphins running back Mercury Morris apparently fumbled. A Buffalo player recovered, but the play was blown dead by head linesman Jerry Bergman, who ruled that Morris had not fumbled. Immediately after the call, another Buffalo player brushed up against Bergman, who then threw another flag, penalizing the Bills fifteen yards for unsportsmanlike conduct. With possession and a fifteen-yard advantage, Miami drove downfield and scored, defeating the Bills, 31–21.

"It was a rotten call that cost our team a chance for the Super Bowl," Bills owner Ralph Wilson screamed after the game. "I will not again send my team out to play a game that he [Bergman] is working . . . The official who made that call should be barred from football. Anyone that incompetent should not be allowed to officiate."

Commissioner Rozelle immediately fined Wilson $5,000 for his remarks. Wilson angrily replied, "They can fine me $1,000, $5,000, or $10,000. I don't give a damn if they fine me $100,000. I'm sick of all this sportsmanship."

The following day, Rams owner Carroll Rosenbloom agreed

with Wilson and asked to pay half the fine. "When a man gets robbed like that, he must give me part of the action," Rosenbloom said defiantly. "I know the feeling. I have lost two major play-off games because of bad officiating. I suffered in silence, and wound up with a coronary."[1]

Rozelle fined Rosenbloom $5,000 too.

Soon after, Al Davis, the owner of the Oakland Raiders, complained, "We have to get rid of the incompetent officials in this league, and we will." Then Minnesota Vikings head coach Bud Grant added that the NFL was "a multimillion-dollar operation being handled by amateurs on Sunday afternoon." He suggested that the NFL hire full-time, instead of part-time, officials.

Both Davis and Grant were fined as well. Bergman was not charged by any party with any malicious intent.

• In a second incident, during a November 7, 1976, game between the Chicago Bears and the Oakland Raiders, referee Chuck Heberling, a respected, twelve-year veteran of NFL officiating, accidentally blew his whistle and nullified a Bears touchdown.

The Bears' defensive end, Roger Stillwell, had picked up a fumble by Raiders quarterback Ken Stabler and run thirty-nine yards in open field for the score in the fourth quarter of the game. Because of Heberling's whistle, which automatically blew the play dead, the Raiders did not bother to chase Stillwell. The four-point underdog Bears lost the game, 28–27.

"It was an inadvertent whistle," Heberling apologized after the game. "I blew it when I shouldn't have, so the only thing I could do was give Chicago the ball, and that's what I did."

The Bears found Heberling's apology difficult to accept. "When they're dreaming up stuff to call on you, then you know they're in trouble," Bears defensive lineman Wally Chambers said angrily after hearing Heberling's explanation. "After Stillwell was gone, I heard a whistle, but not until then."

• The following month, a third incident happened on December 18 during the AFC play-off game between the Raiders and the New England Patriots, who were seven-point underdogs. Another controversial, fourth quarter official's call helped Oakland win. With fifty-seven seconds remaining in the game—and New England leading, 21–17—Oakland had the ball, third down on the Patriots' twenty-eight yard line. Raiders quarterback Ken Stabler went back to pass and was hit by Patriots nose tackle Ray

Hamilton as Stabler released the ball for an apparent nine-yard loss. Head linesman Ben Dreith threw a questionable flag and charged Hamilton with roughing the passer. Instead of fourth down and a need to complete a desperation pass, the Raiders had the ball first-and-ten on the Patriots' thirteen yard line. Seconds later, the Raiders scored and defeated New England, 24–21.

"We took a screwing out there, and I don't care who knows it," barked Patriots defensive end Julius Adams. "What Ray Hamilton did . . . well, it was a legal hit. I'm not afraid to say it, either. They took the game away from us." Oakland advanced to the AFC championship game and then defeated the Minnesota Vikings, 32–14, in Super Bowl XI.

• A fourth controversy involving NFL officiating occurred on October 30, 1977, when Rozelle apologized to Houston Oilers head coach Bum Phillips for an official's call that cost the Oilers their game against the Cincinnati Bengals, who were a seven-point favorite, and ultimately a spot in the AFC play-offs. The dispute erupted after a kickoff was fumbled by Willie Shelby, the Bengals kick return man, and recovered by the Oilers in the end zone for a touchdown. However, game official Fred Silva made a questionable ruling that Shelby was on the sideline when he touched the football; thus, the touchdown was nullified, and the Bengals were given possession. Phillips complained to no avail and later said, "It frosted me that the referees would not discuss the play among themselves or even give me the time of day." The Oilers lost to the Bengals, 13–10, in overtime.

• A few weeks later, yet a fifth bad call was made on December 18 when a ruling, again by Fred Silva, cost the Miami Dolphins their spot in the AFC play-offs. Ironically, the Dolphins' loss and the bad call occurred in a game between the Patriots and the five-point-favorite Baltimore Colts.

Late in the Colts-Patriots game, Colts quarterback Bert Jones fumbled and the Patriots, who were ahead at the time, recovered on their own twelve yard line. However, Silva blew the play dead before Jones went down, and the Patriots player recovered the ball. Keeping possession, Baltimore went on to score and won the game, 30–24. Had New England won the game, the Dolphins, not the Colts, would have been in the AFC play-offs. Miami quarterback Don Strock said that his team expected an apology from Rozelle. "We got bummed . . . we got jobbed," Strock lamented. "I know what the officials were trying to do—protect Bert Jones. But he wasn't even close to being down."

• During the AFC play-offs on January 1, 1978, a sixth official's mistake cost a team the conference championship. This time, the team on the short end was the Oakland Raiders, who had won two games earlier on disputed calls by officials. In the championship game, Rob Lytle, a running back for the Denver Broncos, fumbled on the Raiders two yard line where the ball was recovered by the Raiders' nose tackle, Mike McCoy. But the officials missed it completely. Despite the Raiders' heated protests, Denver was given the ball and scored a touchdown on the next play. Denver won the game, 20–17. The Raiders had been three-and-a-half-point favorites.

Art McNally, the supervisor of NFL officials, announced a week later, "There's no question it was a fumble. We admit that. TV showed it. Coaches have told us that if we can't see a play, don't make a phantom call. The crew didn't see the fumble, and we know that if you don't see it, you don't give it to the other team."

To combat complaints about the poor officiating, the NFL added a seventh official, a side judge, to the on-field crew.[2] Carroll Rosenbloom opposed the idea, saying, "Let's go back to five officials so we can enjoy the game again." Also, the league began experimenting with the use of the televised instant replay to help settle certain controversial calls by officials. However, the idea was shelved for several years because of the long delays during replay reviews by officials.[3]

Oddsmaker Bobby Martin told me that during the late 1970s, he suspected one particular referee of being involved in gambling and influencing the outcomes of NFL games. "There was too much unnatural money showing up on the games he was officiating," Martin says. "So I put the word out on [the referee] to see what I could find out."

One of those whom Martin called was Las Vegas gambler Lem Banker, who told me, "Yeah, we had suspicions about certain games with some of the officials during the late 1970s. I remember Bob called me and wanted me to check out one particular referee. We watched some of the games, and a lot of unnatural money did show up. But we could never prove anything."

A third gambler told my associate, William Scott Malone, that two particular referees had been involved in game fixing since 1977. But the source refused to provide any details—because he was personally involved in the scheme. However, the same referee was named by Martin, Banker, and the confidential source, who also named the second referee.

In late 1979, the mere complaints and suspicions about NFL officials turned into a federal investigation. The Houston office of the FBI received information from a bureau underworld source that several NFL games had been fixed that year and in years past, including five 1979 *NFL Monday Night Football* games, which were broadcast on ABC-TV. In a memorandum to Anthony Vaccarino of the FBI's Organized Crime Division, special agents in Houston summarized their investigation regarding "allegations known concerning possible bribery of NFL officials in conjunction with eight NFL games played during the recent [*sic*] concluded season."

Those games listed in the FBI report were

- "Cleveland at Kansas City, September 9, 1979. Fixed for Cleveland. [Cleveland, a one-point favorite, won, 27–24.]
- "New York Giants at Washington Redskins, September 17, 1979 (Monday). Fixed for the Redskins. [Washington, a six-point favorite, won, 27–0.]
- "Seattle at Atlanta, [October] 29, 1979 (Monday). Fixed for Seattle. [Seattle, a one-point underdog, won, 31–28.]
- "Minnesota Vikings at New York Jets, October 15, 1979 (Monday). Fixed for the Jets. [New York, a five-point favorite, won, 14–7.]
- "Miami at Oakland, October 8, 1979 (Monday). Fixed for Oakland. [Oakland, a one-point underdog, won, 13–3.]
- "San Antonio [*sic*] at Oakland, October 25, 1979 (Thursday). Fixed for Oakland. [There is no San Antonio team. On October 25, 1979, Oakland, a one-point underdog, defeated the San Diego Chargers, 45–22, at Oakland.]
- "Dallas Cowboys at Cleveland Browns [September 24, 1979]. Fixed for Cleveland. [Cleveland, a three-point underdog, won, 26–7.]
- "Pittsburgh Steelers at Houston, December 10, 1979 (Monday). Fixed for Houston. [Houston, a three-point underdog, won, 20–17.]"

The FBI source had learned about the alleged fixes while playing in a high-stakes poker game in Houston. The table talk included a tip from one of the players to bet heavily on the Washington Redskins during their September 17 game with the New York Giants. The informant identified the source as a car dealer in the Houston area who also worked as a bookmaker. The informant told the FBI that the fixes had become known through a network of automobile dealers who were working in concert with an unnamed New York Mafia figure, who regularly bet $100,000 on a single NFL game.

"Specifically, regarding the bribery situation," the FBI report stated, "the $100,000 New York bettor allegedly has contact with two or three referees who are paid off by him and the initial information was that there would be four or five games fixed during the NFL season."

A second Texas bookmaker also told the informant that the payoff money for the referees came from the Galveston, Texas, vicinity. "Several million dollars had been placed on the Redskins throughout the U.S., especially in the Las Vegas area," the FBI report continued. By laying off the large bets around the country, the gamblers were able to avoid influencing the point spread and causing suspicion.

Game officials were expected to make an occasional call that would allow the gamblers to win their bets at the set point spread, the informant told the FBI.

The FBI decided not to contact NFL Security immediately, because notification "was judged as inappropriate due to the sensitivity and possible notoriety of such allegations. The plan was for Houston to continue contact with the source for any possible information that might develop into a more reliable case."

Information from the source on the Washington–New York game led to allegations about the other seven allegedly fixed games. The source gave specific details about bogus penalties called by game officials. The FBI reviewed game films of the Washington–New York game and found that certain disputed calls by game officials were clearly wrong.

In the midst of that investigation, a federal investigator received a call from a television reporter in Chicago who had received information from a source that certain NFL referees had received $100,000 each, per game, to fix games. Eight of the nine games the reporter listed were those originally supplied by the FBI's Houston source. The ninth was a college game between Notre Dame and Purdue.

Upon receiving that information, the FBI theorized that "the reporter's source and the former Chicago and Houston source were one in the same. It was the opinion of the Houston office," the FBI report continued, "that the source in this matter was motivated by money and saw an opportunity for sensationalism which he is attempting to capitalize on."

However, on February 4, 1980, the Houston source agreed to take a polygraph test, and he passed. He was specifically asked whether he had received information that NFL games were being fixed prior to the games being played.

The FBI report stated, "Due to sensitivity of this matter . . . all following requested investigations should be handled discreetly and on a need to know basis . . ."

Despite the apparent verification of the Houston informant's information, the FBI suddenly dropped the investigation.

The Houston informant told my associate, William Scott Malone, "I originally got these games from a major car dealer in Houston. In conversations with him, he told me that these games were coming from another major car dealer—but he never told me who. What was happening was this car dealer was giving it to these other car dealers on Tuesday and Wednesday to bet locally.

"If the FBI had wanted to they could have corroborated the information right away. The games were reported to the bureau in advance."

An IRS agent in Las Vegas told me that, indeed, several alleged fixed games had been given by the same informant to him in advance of the games. "The informant knew that there was betting on behalf of these guys in the legal sports books of Nevada. He [the informant] would wait around at the Barbary Coast [a hotel/casino in Las Vegas with a sports book]. Then a beard would come in and bet a bunch of money. He bet so much that the line would move. Then the informant called me at about nine-thirty in the morning, just before the ten o'clock games [Las Vegas time], and tell me about the bet. He'd say, 'So and so is refereeing such and such game.'

"But we never identified the beard at the Barbary Coast, and the informant didn't know him either. I wanted to do a whole surveillance, to follow the beard out, and get a tag number. I was told to go in there first, before I tied up a bunch of manpower, and check the informant out. I did it on two occasions. The informant was always right on the information. We verified it. But when we set up the full-scale surveillance, for some reason, the beard didn't show up again. I wish we had set it up earlier because there was something big going on. We just didn't have the guys to do it right."[4]

The IRS agent also told me that one Florida car dealer was also under investigation in the game-fixing case: former state senator Dick Fincher. However, neither Fincher nor anyone else was ever charged.

Another name mentioned prominently in the FBI internal report was that of Victor J. Weiss, a close associate of Carroll Rosenbloom. Federal agents had received information that "car dealers in several cities are involved with unnamed New York figures allegedly connected with organized crime in this scheme. Vic Weiss, a Los Angeles car dealer, was murdered six to eight months ago and was involved in the game-fixing scheme."

37 The Bagman

VICTOR J. WEISS, WHO had been implicated in the FBI/NFL referee game-fixing probe was also believed by the Los Angeles police to have been Carroll Rosenbloom's bagman. But before he could be questioned, Weiss was found murdered on Sunday, June 17, 1979. His badly decomposed body was discovered wrapped in a yellow blanket in the trunk of his maroon-and-white Rolls-Royce, which had been parked in the lot of MCA's Sheraton-Universal Hotel in North Hollywood. The fifty-one-year-old Weiss, who had been missing for four days, was found with his hands tied behind his back and shot twice in the head. His body was so badly decomposed that the police could identify him only by analyzing his fingerprints.

Weiss was last seen on Wednesday, June 13, at the Beverly Comstock Hotel in Los Angeles, meeting with Jack Kent Cooke, who was the owner of the Washington Redskins football team, and Jerry Buss, who was purchasing Cooke's California Sports Incorporated operations, which included the Los Angeles Lakers, the Los Angeles Kings hockey team, the Los Angeles Forum, and a thirteen-thousand-acre ranch. The total sale price was $67.5 million.[1]

Weiss had been serving as an agent for Jerry Tarkanian, the head basketball coach at the University of Nevada at Las Vegas, and had reached a tentative agreement with the Lakers for his client to replace head coach Jerry West. Weiss had the papers for the deal in his pocket when he was killed. Tarkanian and Weiss had been close friends since they were at Pasadena Junior College.[2] After Weiss's body was found, Tarkanian withdrew as a candidate for the coaching job; Jack McKinney, an assistant coach for the Portland Trail Blazers, was later selected.

Neither Tarkanian nor Cooke was under any suspicion and both cooperated fully with the murder investigation.

Born in Hamilton, Ontario, in 1912, Jack Kent Cooke had been brought up in a home of comfort and great wealth. However, after the stock market collapse in 1929, his life of leisure ended. With his family financially wiped out, Cooke quit school and went to work selling encyclopedias and soap. After buying into a chain of Canadian radio stations, which became the foundation of a communications empire, he again became wealthy and moved some of his operations to the United States.

Cooke bought his 25 percent interest in the Redskins for $350,000 from former Detroit Lions part owner Harry Wismer, who had been the longtime broadcast announcer for Redskins games, in 1960. Wismer had earlier become the majority owner of the New York Titans, later the New York Jets, in the AFL.

After buying the Lakers from Robert Short for over $5 million in 1965, Cooke was responsible for signing Wilt Chamberlain, who led the team to the 1972 NBA championship. The Lakers' owner later brought in Kareem Abdul-Jabbar to fill the large void left by Chamberlain when he left the NBA.

While Edward Bennett Williams was operating the Redskins as the executor of the estate of George Preston Marshall, who had died in 1969 after a long illness, Cooke, already a one-quarter minority owner of the club, bought an additional 60.3 percent of the team stock in 1974 and became its majority owner. Williams owned the remaining 14.7 percent.

Cooke was also a fight promoter. He had handled the 1971 brawl between Muhammad Ali and Joe Frazier, perhaps the greatest boxing match of all time, in which Ali lost his heavyweight crown. Cooke introduced the world to the concept of closed-circuit television; fans who could not be present at the fight could buy tickets and see it in their own towns at theaters licensed by Cooke's company. He also owned a minor-league baseball team and attempted but failed to buy the Detroit Tigers.

Cooke was also a horse-racing fan who patronized Hollywood Park in Los Angeles, which was directly across the street from the Forum. An accomplished yachtsman, "he was on one of his yachts in Havana Harbor when he heard what sounded like firecrackers but was in fact the beginning gunfire of Fidel Castro's revolution," according to reporter Robert Pack. Cooke was also deeply involved in California politics, with friends ranging from California governor Ronald Reagan, a conservative Republican, to former governor Pat Brown, a liberal Democrat.

Between 1976 and 1979—while Cooke attempted to salvage his troubled Teleprompter Corporation, a major cable television firm plagued by SEC investigations[3]—he lived in Las Vegas, reportedly in an effort to reduce his personal taxes and to avoid attempts by his estranged wife to serve him with papers for their divorce.[4] It was after the divorce from his first wife that Cooke sold his California holdings to Jerry Buss. That same year, Cooke bought the Chrysler Building in New York for a reported $90 million.

Cooke left Las Vegas and moved to Middleburg, Virginia, near Washington, after the sale of his Los Angeles sports interests. Cooke immediately began squeezing out Redskins president Williams, who, in late 1979, bought the Baltimore Orioles professional baseball team.[5] By the 1980 season, Cooke was in full control of the NFL team. However, Williams retained his financial interest in the Redskins.

During the investigation of Weiss's murder, Cooke, who had been a neighbor of Carroll Rosenbloom in Bel Air, told the police that he and Buss had met with Weiss for an hour. During their conversation, Weiss reportedly left the meeting to make a telephone call. He called a real estate agent who was selling a house he was supposedly interested in buying. Cooke said that he walked Weiss to his car in the parking lot of the hotel at a little after 5:00 P.M. on the day he disappeared.

Weiss mentioned that he was going home, would later have dinner with Tarkanian, and was expected in Las Vegas the following day to meet with Gerald Cutter, Weiss's partner in Gateway Ford and Riviera Rolls-Royce in Van Nuys, just north of Los Angeles. They also were reported to be partners in Prestige Motors in Las Vegas.

Married four times and the father of eight children, Weiss, at the time of his disappearance, was rumored to have been carrying as much as $38,000 in cash in a briefcase and was also wearing an expensive diamond pinkie ring and a $6,000 gold-

and-diamond-studded Rolex watch. No briefcase, no $38,000, and no Tarkanian contract were found when Weiss's body was discovered. But the ring was still on his finger and the watch was still on his wrist, causing the police to rule out the possibility that Weiss had been killed in the midst of a robbery. The police also noted that his address book was missing.

The friendly, round-faced, round-bellied, spectacled Vic Weiss was born in New Brighton, Pennsylvania, in 1928. He grew up in Beaver Falls, where he was a childhood friend of future NFL quarterback Babe Parilli. An avid, lifelong football and boxing fan, Weiss was a close friend of Sugar Ray Robinson and had purchased the contract of a young contender for the welterweight crown. He was known as an occasional gambler. When Weiss's body was found, the Los Angeles Police Department said publicly, "As far as we know, Weiss had no connections with organized crime . . . and he had no criminal record."

However, the LAPD questioned Weiss's widow about her husband's alleged association with Lefty Rosenthal and Tony Spilotro. She replied that her husband did not discuss his business dealings with her, and she had never heard of the two men. The police also discovered that Weiss had been arrested no fewer than three times from 1958 to 1964 for battery, petty theft, and auto theft.

Weiss's public image was that of the friendly, generous man-about-town who had plenty of money and threw it around. But, as the investigation proceeded, it became apparent that Weiss was leading a double life. He was hardly wealthy and heavily involved with the underworld and sports gambling.

In reality, Weiss owned only a vacant lot; his Encino house was owned by his "partner," millionaire Gerald Cutter; and his Rolls-Royce was a company car. Weiss owned no life insurance and had never bothered to draw up a will.

Like Weiss, Cutter had also been mentioned in the 1979 FBI internal report. "One car dealer in Las Vegas, Nevada, last name possibly Cutter, is also allegedly involved in this scheme . . . Cutter had a life insurance policy on Weiss' life and also held the mortgage on his house," the FBI report stated.

Also, instead of being Cutter's partner, Weiss had been only an employee of Cutter's agencies. Cutter had been the brains behind their string of car dealership operations, which had branched out to Honolulu and Las Vegas over the years.

Detective Leroy Orozco of the Los Angeles Police Department told me, "Weiss was just a front man. He was not financially in the company. His name would appear in documents, but he had no interest in any of the car dealerships. He was kept on because he had all the contacts with the Hollywood and sports crowds. He made the company look good."

When Cutter was interviewed by the police, he admitted that Weiss's interests had shifted to sports, but he was adamant that his employee had no association with the underworld. At the time of the Weiss murder, Cutter had been living in Las Vegas for six months. He had moved there just after his wife's bizarre accidental death at their house in the San Fernando Valley.[6]

The police linked Cutter to a major mob-controlled bookmaking operation in St. Louis. Police officials also did checks on Cutter's first cousin David Alexander Cutter, also from St. Louis, who had been identified as a key figure by the IRS in an illegal million-dollar sports-bookmaking ring in Las Vegas. David Cutter had been convicted of gambling and had been sentenced to fifteen months in prison in 1968 for federal gambling violations. In a search of his room at the Aladdin Hotel, a briefcase filled with cocaine was seized by federal agents.

Also, David Cutter's father, Michael Cutter, had been the onetime manager of the Stardust in Las Vegas. David Cutter had told the FBI "that he did not have a good credit rating and therefore had to put most of his assets in his father's name," according to an FBI document.

Gerald Cutter had been reportedly waiting for Weiss in Las Vegas on June 14, the day after he disappeared. He had expected to be at a meeting with Weiss at 9:00 A.M. Weiss was supposed to fly to Las Vegas with Cutter's son, Nick, and they were going to discuss a possible land development deal in Lake Tahoe.

For reasons unknown, James Henderson, the Los Angeles chief of the U.S. Strike Force Against Organized Crime, refused to allow the police to question protected federal witness Jimmy "the Weasel" Fratianno about the Weiss murder. The police had uncovered evidence of a relationship between Weiss and two of Fratianno's associates, San Diego mobster Frank Bompensiero and Los Angeles hit man Michael Rizzitello.

Although the Weiss murder remains officially unsolved and no arrests have been made, detective Orozco of the LAPD says that there were "reports that Weiss was involved in a major West

Coast layoff gambling operation, and that he had been placing large bets on NFL games."

Another law-enforcement official said, "In the evening hours at the auto shop where Weiss worked, an individual, unknown, would come in and leave a large brown paper bag filled with what an informant believed was money. This money was left for Vic. The next morning when Vic came in, he would take this bag and usually as near as everybody could tell, he would make a trip to Vegas. It was over to Vegas and then back the same day."

"Vic placed a lot of bets," says another LAPD official. "And we found some items in Vic's writing that indicated that he kept a record of NFL games, what the line would've been for the games, certain numbers and notations after the odds that would indicate that he is betting either for himself or for someone else. They were heavy wagers in sports bookmaking, particularly the NFL."

Orozco continues, "Weiss was definitely a bagman for some of the Vegas people. Weiss came up on some phone records at a place called the Gold Rush, a little jewelry shop in Circus Circus, a casino in Las Vegas. The Gold Rush was run by Tony Spilotro."

When I asked Orozco who Weiss's contact in the NFL was, the detective replied, "Weiss and Carroll Rosenbloom were definitely associated. Rosenbloom trusted Weiss, who had what appeared to be a close relationship with the Rams. He used to spend Sundays at the home games either with Rosenbloom or in the Rams press box. It was common knowledge that his wife's carrot cake was a favorite among the press members up in the box. We know Rosenbloom was gambling, and we believe that Weiss played some role in that."

Orozco added that several Rams games during the 1978 season were suspect. "We found that the Rams had very low-scoring games, which was an advantage to the bettor."

In fact, the Rams, which were 12–4 during the 1978 regular season, were 5–11 against the point spread, which was the worst in the NFL that year. Although the Rams were Western Division champions, the team lost the conference championship to the Dallas Cowboys, 28–0. The Rams had been only five-point underdogs.

A Chicago bookmaker, who is also a federal witness, says, "Weiss was Rosenbloom's bagman. He had held out some money on some games they were doing business on. He was $200,000 in debt from the previous year and was skimming. The problem was: Rosenbloom wasn't running the show. Other people were involved, too. And most of them were from Vegas."

When I gave that information to Orozco, he agreed, saying, "Weiss was skimming, was warned, and got hit."

The bagman was last seen near the hotel where his body was found in the company of two males. One was a large, six-feet-seven blond man, and the other was short, dark-haired, and much older. Both of them were dressed in three-piece suits and were wearing dark glasses. "We have been told that both these guys were killed," Orozco told me.

Carroll Rosenbloom couldn't be questioned either. Just two and a half months before the Weiss murder, the Rams' owner drowned in the Atlantic Ocean off the coast of Florida.

38 Rosenbloom's Fatal Swim

UNDER CARROLL ROSENBLOOM, THE Los Angeles Rams had won six consecutive NFC Western Division Championships—but they had lost four of the last five NFC title games and had never gone to a Super Bowl. To Rosenbloom, that was the prize, and he had been unable to grasp it—despite the fact that he had continued to have one of the biggest payrolls in the NFL.

Although he enjoyed calling the Rams "a family," it had been nearly torn apart by internal strife that he himself caused in his desperation to have another world championship team, just as he'd had with the Baltimore Colts in 1958, 1959, and in Super Bowl V in 1971.

Although Rosenbloom's oldest son, Steve, was running the team on the day-to-day basis, Carroll had become known as "the Godfather" and the "Great White Father" to those on the team. While some of his supporters viewed the descriptions as demonstrations of endearment, others saw them as being scornful slaps against the white-toupeed Rosenbloom who bullied his way through the Rams organization and the NFL. Suddenly, taking a hands-on approach to running his team, he often arrived at the Rams' practices in a helicopter and watched from the sidelines, sitting in a director's chair with his name printed on the back.

Watching Rosenbloom, according to his friends, was a déjà vu of his final days in Baltimore. He began having trouble with the local media and city officials. He again claimed a lack of fan support. He was irrational in his handling of his head coaches.[1]

He ran through a string of quarterbacks, all of whom he considered unworthy, until 1977 when Joe Namath came to the Rams to play his final season in the NFL. However, Namath was injured in the fourth game and spent the rest of the season on the bench.

Rosenbloom finally decided to leave the Los Angeles Coliseum to play in a newer stadium.[2] He had announced in July 1978 that he was planning to move the Rams nearly thirty miles south to Anaheim, where he had obtained almost a hundred acres of Orange County land with the right to develop parking lots adjacent to the stadium. He also had received a pledge from city officials prior to his real estate purchase to increase the seating capacity of its Big A Stadium, the home of the California Angels major-league baseball team, from forty-two thousand to seventy thousand.

When Rosenbloom made his decision to move, he called his old friend Howard Cosell for advice. Cosell, in one of the most vivid descriptions of Rosenbloom, testified before the U.S. Senate Judiciary Committee about this conversation he had had with the Boss Ram.

Cosell said, "I was on assignment one day in Los Angeles, and I got a call at the Beverly Wilshire Hotel from one of the most brilliant men I know . . . Carroll Rosenbloom, extraordinary businessman. And he asked me to come over to his home on [Bellagio Road] in the Bel-Air section of Greater Los Angeles. I went with my wife, and we sat at poolside with Carroll as he talked in those carefully muted measured tones wearing his great suede slippers, no socks. It was Hollywood. The manicured gabardine slacks, the proper suede belt, the carefully tailored suede sport shirt, the silk ascot to envelop the otherwise open neck. And he tried me on for media size, and he said, 'Howard, what would be your on-air position if I moved the Rams to Anaheim?' I said my position has never wavered . . . I believe that franchise removal should be countenanced, apart from abridgement [*sic*] of the lease or another extraordinary matter, to the detriment of the tenant, should be predicated only upon the ability to show continuity of economic distress.

" 'But, Howard, Walter O'Malley [who moved the Brooklyn Dodgers to Los Angeles] did it, [Wellington] Mara [who moved the New York Giants to New Jersey] did it. I can have the best of both worlds. I can have the land, indeed, options at a marvelous price for 95 acres, duly exercised, a subsequent deal with

Gannett Realty in Boston, and more than 110 luxury loges producing into the area of $2½ million a year.'

"I said, 'Carroll, this just is not right. You asked me my position; you know it. You know where I stand.'

" 'But, Howard, it is legal; is it not?'

" 'Yes; it is legal, because Los Angeles would take whatever they could get . . . Los Angeles had filthy hands. They had taken the Rams from Cleveland, the Dodgers from Brooklyn, the Lakers from Minneapolis. So they had to take another tack, steal another team . . .' "[3]

Cosell's advice might have had an impact on Rosenbloom's thinking, because Rosenbloom began speaking to Al Davis on a regular basis about moving the Oakland Raiders to the Los Angeles Coliseum. These conversations would result in Davis's antitrust suit against the NFL, which became Rosenbloom's final revenge against Pete Rozelle.

During the early spring of 1979, the Rosenblooms took a vacation in Golden Beach, Florida. In the early afternoon of Monday, April 2, after a week of vacationing, the seventy-two-year-old Carroll Rosenbloom returned from a telephone call with a Rams vice president, who later said that Rosenbloom's spirits were high and that he was feeling good. During their discussion, Rosenbloom also told him that the wind was too strong for tennis that day.

Rosenbloom was to have played with real estate developer Irving Cowan, the owner of Diplomat Hotel and Country Club in Hollywood, just north of Miami and near the Rosenblooms' Golden Beach vacation house.[4] However, Cowan was extremely busy that day and had to postpone. The night before, Cowan had given the Rosenblooms tickets to the Liza Minnelli concert in Miami Beach. "He was fine," Cowan told me. "We couldn't get tickets seated together, but we talked at intermission and after the concert. He didn't seem aggravated or agitated. I didn't see any perceptible problems. He was the old Carroll."

Instead of playing tennis, the Rosenblooms spent the day relaxing. Although the sun shone brightly, the wind was kicking up and gusting. The waves from the ocean were breaking heavily onto the beach, mixing a tremendous amount of sand with the surf and causing the clear blue Florida water to turn brownish-gray.

Just before 2:00 P.M., Carroll, wearing a blue-striped bathing suit, told Georgia, "I'm going to take a walk. I'll be back in a little while." The stretch of shoreline where Rosenbloom strolled was well known to him. He had lived at Golden Beach for nearly eight years until he sold his oceanfront house in 1972—when he swapped the Colts for the Rams. The sprawling beach house where the family was now staying was rented.

A few minutes later, at the Diplomat Hotel, Cowan was still working in his office. Cowan recalls, "I received a rather frantic call from Georgia, who told me that they were in the process of pulling Carroll from the water. Something terrible had happened. She cried, 'Please come down right away with a doctor.' There was a doctor/friend of mine with an office right across the street from my hotel. I told him that there was an emergency and asked him to do me a favor. He left a waiting room full of patients, and the two of us immediately went to the beach.

"When we arrived, Carroll was lying on the beach near the water's edge. He wasn't covered or anything. Georgia hadn't arrived yet, but the police were there. We knew right away that he was dead."

The police and the medical examiner's office concluded that Rosenbloom had drowned.

During my interview with then Golden Beach chief of police William Henrikson, he told me that he had heard a report over his police radio at the Golden Beach station that a man was drowning at the 100 block of Ocean Boulevard. He rushed out to respond to the call. "It was a rough day and the waves were high," Henrikson says. "Rosenbloom entered the water between two sandbars. He was caught in a washout, also known as a riptide—which is like a river running out to sea. Apparently, he tried to get in it, and that's when he ran into trouble."

Henrikson, who is six feet seven, had been a lifeguard for five years during his youth in New Hampshire. Seeing Rosenbloom and another man in the water, Henrikson and his deputy Ron Nasca, who had heard the radio report in his cruiser and arrived at the same time, stripped off their clothes and went in after Rosenbloom. Henrikson told me that the five-feet-eleven Rosenbloom was in water that was only a little over five feet deep. "But, even at my height, I had to swim to get out to him because of the washout. I could only wade for a short period of time. And deputy Nasca was swimming, too. I saw another man struggling in the water. He had tried to save Rosenbloom. I motioned to him to get back, and that I would take care of it.

"When I got to Rosenbloom, he was in a dead man's float position—in which his shoulders, arms, and head were on the surface but his face was down in the water. I turned him over, and I knew he was already dead.

"I used the typical rescue carry. My one arm was over his chest, and I swam with my other arm. The water was bad. A wave crashed, and I lost him for a minute—but I got him back."

The paramedics were just arriving as Henrikson, Nasca, and Rosenbloom reached the shore. Henrikson says, "We had been swept north about eighty to a hundred yards before we could get Rosenbloom out—because of the undertow. I had to walk down the beach in my underwear to get my pile of clothes."

Henrikson and Nasca then delivered Rosenbloom to the paramedics and then immediately left the scene. The investigation was handled by the Dade County Public Safety Department, which interviewed Raymond Tanguay, the other man in the water who had tried to save Rosenbloom. A French Canadian, Tanguay could speak only French to the police, causing an immediate communication problem. His wife, whose English wasn't much better, translated for the police.[5]

Georgia Rosenbloom was reportedly hysterical when she saw her dead husband on the beach. She pleaded with rescue workers to revive him. Their young son Chip also watched the scene in horror. After Rosenbloom was pronounced dead, she immediately called Tampa Bay Buccaneers owner Hugh Culverhouse, who then notified Pete Rozelle and the other NFL officials. Rosenbloom had been with Culverhouse earlier in the day and had talked to Rozelle on the telephone.

Rosenbloom's body was cremated on April 4, 1979. His wife, Georgia, was over an hour late for the private ceremony in Hollywood, Florida. When she did arrive, she reportedly was already talking about her husband's estate and how it was going to be divided up.

One week later, nearly nine hundred people attended Rosenbloom's memorial service at his Bel Air estate. His wife was an hour late for that too. Attending the hardly solemn extravaganza under a green-and-white tent were some of the biggest names in show business, politics, and sports: Warren Beatty, Mayor Tom Bradley, Jim Brown, Howard Cosell, Kirk Douglas,

Greer Garson, Cary Grant, Diane Keaton, Ethel Kennedy, Henry Mancini, Ricardo Montalban, George Peppard, Robert Stack, Rod Steiger, Jules Stein, Jimmy Stewart, Johnny Unitas, and Lew Wasserman, along with Pete Rozelle and half of the NFL team owners. Comedian Jonathan Winters was the master of ceremonies and a twelve-piece string orchestra played upbeat music.

Howard Cosell recalled, "The funeral was not exactly . . . well, funereal. In questionable taste, it was conducted as a celebration . . . Winters told jokes at which the audience uneasily laughed, brought on a couple of Carroll's favorite singers and a guitar player, and called upon a mix of Rosenbloom's friends to speak—as though it were a roast and toast."[6]

In the wake of Rosenbloom's funeral, numerous questions arose about the circumstances of his death, which have challenged the contention that he drowned by accident. It was suggested by some that Rosenbloom might have been murdered.

At the time of his death, Rosenbloom was still the second-largest individual stockholder in Warner Communications, owning 223,146 shares of stock worth nearly $11 million. However, in April 1979, the corporation was in the midst of its biggest crisis: Several of its top executives were being investigated for their ties to major East Coast Mafia figures.[7]

Also, Rosenbloom would later be cited by the LAPD as having been a possible link in a major West Coast sports-gambling operation with his bagman Victor Weiss, who was murdered two and a half months after Rosenbloom's death. And Weiss had been implicated with Tony Spilotro and the Stardust crowd in Las Vegas, as well as in reports of the mob's alleged fixing of referees—which was investigated by the FBI and the IRS in 1979—while Rosenbloom's football team was failing to cover the spread in two thirds of its 1978 games.

Could Rosenbloom's death have been anything but an accidental drowning? If it was not, there was a whole cast of characters who would have had the means, opportunity, and motive.

"I don't believe that his death was accidental," Rosenbloom's son Steve told my associate, William Scott Malone. "And I know other people in the family have discussed it with me and feel the same way, as do many other people who knew my father well. Why would a man who had a healthy respect for the water and never went in it by himself, go in on that day when the water was extremely rough with a strong undertow?"

However, regardless of Rosenbloom's son's suspicions, his father did go into the water despite the conditions that day.

Alexander Papp, a maintenance supervisor for Eastman-Kodak of New York, was the last-known person, other than Tanguay, to have seen Rosenbloom alive. Mary Papp, Alexander's widow, told me in 1988, "We had a place on Golden Beach about four doors down from where the man [Rosenbloom] and his family were staying. My husband was taking a walk on the beach when he saw this man going into the ocean. And it was a very, very bad morning. My husband yelled to him, 'Hey, mister, you better not go into that water because it's really bad.' The man said, 'Oh, don't worry about it. I'm a very good swimmer.' When my husband came back from his walk, the man was already dead on the beach, being attended to."

Nevertheless, the rumors of foul play persisted. The top individual stockholder in Warner Communications, Morris Mac Schwebel, told me, "I saw Carroll shortly before his death, and he was walking, running, and playing tennis. He was as healthy as any man could be." Schwebel adds that he, along with Rosenbloom's sister Mildred and Rosenbloom's personal accountant, believe that Rosenbloom was murdered.

San Diego Chargers owner Gene Klein agrees with Schwebel and told me, "Carroll had had open heart surgery and as part of his therapy he had to exercise. One of the best exercises is swimming. But Carroll was not a good swimmer, and I distinctly remember that he wanted somebody around when he went into the pool.

"I had used Carroll's home at Golden Beach when the Chargers played Miami. I spent a week there. So I am familiar with the neighborhood, and I am familiar with the beach and the water. I find it very difficult to believe that Carroll—who was walking on the beach or whatever—would go in the water when there were storm warnings out. I find it very difficult to believe that it was an accident."

Howard Cosell says, "Because everyone knew C.R. . . . would not have been foolhardy enough to risk his life, rumors began to circulate that indeed Rosenbloom was the victim of a foul act. Such an act, some whispered maliciously, was engineered by Georgia, the inheritor of her husband's fortune. Others focused on Rosenbloom's fondness for the heavy wager and theorized about alleged debts to the mob."[8]

Rosenbloom's close friend Senator Ted Kennedy—who had

come to Los Angeles to comfort the Rosenbloom family the day after Carroll's death—stood up during Senate proceedings in Washington and paid tribute to Rosenbloom. "He was familiar to generations of football players and lovers of the sport as a person with an extraordinary sense of excellence and leadership, and with a deep commitment and dedication to his teams and players."

There was irony that Rosenbloom had died in the sea. In 1976, he had told *Los Angeles Times* sportswriter Bob Oates, "The ocean does for me what the desert does for others. They like the stillness. I never tire of listening to the ocean or looking at it . . . I play those records that have nothing but the sound of the ocean washing up on the beach."

Rosenbloom left the bulk of his $300–$500 million estate, including 70 percent of the ownership of the Rams, to his fifty-one-year-old wife, Georgia. He was expected to have been succeeded as chief of the Rams by his thirty-three-year-old son Steve, who had been left 6 percent of the team, the same percentage that had been left to his other brothers and sisters.

Referring to his son in his will, the elder Rosenbloom stipulated, "I direct my Executor to retain my son, D. Stephen Rosenbloom, who I consider to be an outstanding football man, as Football Manager, for as long as my Executor, in his discretion, shall determine. The Football Manager shall have the power to make all managerial and operational decisions with respect to all football and football related activities carried on by the Los Angeles Rams Football Company . . ."

According to a codicil to Rosenbloom's will, filed six months before his death, Georgia and Hugh Culverhouse were named as two of the three executors of his estate. Rosenbloom's personal lawyer, E. Gregory Hookstratten, was the third. Hookstratten, described as "a kingmaker," had included among his clients Tom Brokaw, Bryant Gumbel, David Merrick, Elvis Presley, and Vin Scully.

However, within a week of her husband's death, Georgia Rosenbloom appointed herself the president of the Rams. And she soon became the queen of professional football.

39 Cobra in a Sunbonnet

IN JULY 1980, NFL Security chief Jack Danahy, after nearly twelve turbulent years with the league, retired from the NFL and soon after opened his own private security firm in Manhattan, Intercon Special Service, which he started with two other former FBI agents.[1]

Finding a replacement for Danahy was no small task. "They had a little problem finding a successor to me," Danahy told me. "The problem was age. We had two pension plans, and the insurer of the pension plan told the league after I retired that they had to find someone who was under age fifty to balance the books. There were a lot of FBI agents retiring, but they were retiring after age fifty. So Pete had a problem."

Eventually, he hired former FBI special agent Warren Welsh, who told me, "I was a brick agent in Miami who primarily worked on gambling—the Lefty Rosenthals, the Elliot Paul Prices, the Gil Beckleys. A friend of mine headed the Beckley investigations.

"In 1968, when I was still in the bureau, they [NFL Security] brought down Paul Hornung to appear secretly before the grand jury that was tied in with Beckley. They were going to introduce the commissioner and the owners to a new concept for security . . . They were going to regionalize the program. Evidently that didn't fly. And then Jack Danahy came aboard and pretty much started the system that other sports leagues have adopted: having security representatives in the league cities.

"When Jack started, [NFL Security reps] were, more often than not, retired FBI agents . . . Among the things we added were three former DEA agents to our cadre, which none of the other sports leagues had done. In addition, we had the traditional security rep network—twenty-eight teams in twenty-six cities.

"We have a very small staff. My title is director and then there is an assistant director, Charlie Jackson. He came aboard in 1975. He has worked drugs his entire law-enforcement life."

Welsh, who became the fourth and current head of NFL Security, immediately had his trial by fire.

Georgia Rosenbloom is a former Miss St. Louis, a former professional singer, and an ex-Las Vegas chorus girl. The five-feet-three beauty, a believer in astrology and numerology, had long been in show business. "I found that Georgia would perform anywhere, anytime," quipped Gene Klein. "When she opened the refrigerator and the light went on, she started singing."[2]

A busty blonde, she, accompanied by Rosenbloom, occasionally sang for Joseph P. Kennedy at the Kennedy family compound in Hyannis Port. When the elder Kennedy was ailing, she reportedly even cut a record for him. Rosenbloom was Georgia's sixth husband. Her first marriage was annulled. Her second husband was hit by a bus and killed. She left her third husband for the chorus girl job in Las Vegas. Her manager there became her fourth husband—in less than a week after her divorce from her previous husband. She divorced number four in 1958 because he could not support her financially. While she was working as a weather forecaster on a Miami television station, then hosting her own talk show, she met her fifth husband, who was also a Miami television personality. After a brief marriage and quick divorce, she moved to New York and began doing the weather report on NBC's "Today Show," then hosted by Dave Garroway. The weather gig lasted only two weeks.

In August 1979, four months after Carroll Rosenbloom's death, Georgia fired her stepson as the head of the Rams and also dismissed twenty-six other team employees, including Harold Guiver, a trusted associate of her husband.[3] She later gained full ownership of the Rams by buying out her children and stepchildren.

Steve Rosenbloom was bitter about his firing and became the general manager of the New Orleans Saints in December 1979.

He questioned the ethics of Hugh Culverhouse, the owner of the Tampa Bay NFL team, because as one of Rosenbloom's executors he was making managerial decisions about the Rams. Georgia said that the decision to fire her stepson had been made by all three of her husband's executors, including attorney E. Gregory Hookstratten, who pushed hard for the dismissal, and Culverhouse, who, in the end, spent fourteen months settling Rosenbloom's estate. Remarkably, the NFL saw no need for anything more than a *pro forma* investigation of Culverhouse's possible conflict of interest.

In early news releases, Georgia's public-relations flacks boasted that she had been her late husband's partner in running both the Colts and the Rams. However, in reality, he had always forbidden her to sit in the owner's box during either Colts or Rams games. Nevertheless, everyone who knew the Rosenblooms had confirmed that he was crazy about her and that their life together was idyllic.

Prior to her husband's death, Georgia Rosenbloom had become a close friend of musician Dominic Frontiere, a two-time Emmy Award-winning composer, whom she had hired as her "personal lyricist." He escorted her to Rams games, with the permission of Rosenbloom, who had reportedly invited Frontiere to accompany them on his fatal holiday at Golden Beach; Frontiere had decided not to go. Georgia later asked Frontiere to arrange the music for her husband's memorial service. Soon after, Georgia and Dominic began having frequent lunches, and then he moved into a guest house on the Rosenblooms' Bel Air property. Frontiere had divorced his second wife, Cicely, just the previous year.

On July 21, 1980, fifty-two-year-old, once-annulled, twice-widowed, thrice-divorced Georgia Rosenbloom married the forty-eight-year-old Frontiere in Jacksonville, Florida, at the home of Culverhouse—who, as a Florida notary, performed the ceremony. Among the sixty-two guests were Irv Cowan, Pete Rozelle, Art Modell, Tex Schramm, William Sullivan, Leonard Tose, and Max Winter. John Wayne's son Michael was the best man; Cowan's wife was a bridesmaid.

After their European honeymoon, the Frontieres participated in the gala opening of the Rams' new home at Big A Stadium in Anaheim in August.

But soon the honeymoon was over. A Los Angeles organized-crime figure, Jack Catain, had reportedly been trying to convince Georgia to sell the Rams to him, according to a police report of an LAPD surveillance at the Indian Wells Country Club in Palm Desert, California. Dominic reportedly told her, "You'd better listen to the man. He's connected." Both of the Frontieres have denied that this conversation ever took place. However, federal prosecutors told me that Dominic had personally known Catain long before his marriage to Georgia, and that Catain had a pretty unsavory reputation.

Gerald D. Petievich, a special Secret Service agent who was investigating a counterfeiting operation in which Catain was involved, wrote in an affidavit, "I have reviewed the official files of other law enforcement agencies which reflect that Jack Catain is a major organized crime figure and has been known in the past to deal in stolen securities as well as other various crimes."

The LAPD also was looking into murdered car dealer Vic Weiss's connection to a Super Bowl ticket-scalping scheme being operated by an associate of Catain. Investigated by federal law-enforcement agencies for his ties to Las Vegas mobster Tony Spilotro and the Chicago Mafia's underboss, Jackie Cerone, Catain was forced out as president of his business, Rusco Industries, by the Securities and Exchange Commission.

But, apparently, neither Catain's corrupt activities nor his associations repelled Georgia and Dominic Frontiere.

In December 1980, Catain and Georgia Frontiere were implicated in several California news reports in a Super Bowl XIV ticket-scalping operation from the previous January. Playing in the game at the Rose Bowl in Pasadena were the Rams and the Pittsburgh Steelers. The ten-point favorite Pittsburgh team won, 31–19.

According to NFL rules, the league office receives 15 percent of the total allotment of tickets for the Super Bowl. The competing teams split 45 percent, the team hosting the Super Bowl receives 10 percent, and the remaining NFL teams equally divide 30 percent. In 1980, the Rams Club, as player and host, received over 30 percent of the total allotment, twenty-seven thousand tickets for Georgia Frontiere.

Mrs. Frontiere had allegedly sold a thousand $30 tickets for the 1980 Super Bowl XIV for $100 each, but she insisted, "I have never scalped a ticket in my life." Yet, the charges of scalping were supported by depositions filed by Raiders owner Al Davis;

Mel Irwin, Carroll Rosenbloom's personal assistant; and Harold Guiver, a former Rams executive.

The ticket-scalping controversy began as a result of Al Davis's $160 million lawsuit against the NFL, which had prevented him from moving his Oakland team to Los Angeles.[4] The charges appeared in Davis's deposition taken in the midst of his antitrust suit against the NFL. He had wanted to move his Raiders team from Oakland to the Los Angeles Coliseum, which had been vacated by the Rams. Davis's move was being met with heavy resistance from Rozelle and other NFL owners, particularly Georgia Frontiere, who didn't want to share the local spotlight with Davis.

Davis said in his sworn statement that he was considering selling Super Bowl tickets to at least five casinos in Las Vegas: the Aladdin, Caesars Palace, the Hilton, the Riviera, and the Sands. "I called several other owners in the League and asked them what they thought about it, and they told me they were all doing it." Specifically, Davis fingered Carroll Rosenbloom, Max Winter of the Minnesota Vikings, Lamar Hunt of the Kansas City Chiefs, and John Mecom of the New Orleans Saints.[5] In return for the tickets, NFL players were "comped" and received complimentary rooms and meals at the Las Vegas hotels. "A lot of our players liked to go to Las Vegas," Davis said.

Davis explained that the issue of scalping Super Bowl tickets had been discussed since 1974. The owners complained that the price of the tickets was too low. Davis stated, "[T]he commissioner [Rozelle] would always give some far-out answer about 'We don't want to gouge. We don't want to give the country the feeling that we are trying to take advantage of them.' And then [owners would] stand up and say, 'Yes, but we are not gouging—but everyone else is making a fortune on the sale of these Super Bowl tickets from money above the face value of the tickets . . .' I remember Lamar Hunt standing up and saying we are selling a twenty-dollar ticket that should be fifty dollars. And I remember asking one owner in the League, 'Why the hell doesn't he [Hunt] do it?' And he made the statement to me, 'Are you kidding? That is how he makes his big score.' "

Davis continued that he had received a telephone call in 1976 from Rosenbloom who asked him what he was going to do with his Super Bowl tickets. Davis replied that he was going to sell them at face value. Rosenbloom said, "Look, I have a guy who knows how to . . . market these tickets, and we could make a fortune on the tickets above the face value." Davis insisted that he refused to get involved.

Davis discovered that Rosenbloom's "guy" was Harold Guiver, the Rams executive who was later fired by Georgia. There is no California law against ticket scalping—unless it is done on the premises where an event is taking place. According to Guiver's attorney, "At that time, he was actually an authorized ticket broker and authorized by law to sell tickets in excess of their value as long as it went with the travel package, etc."

Davis also added in his deposition that Pete Rozelle "knows what is going on. He knows about the scalping . . . He has never done a thing about it with all the security agents he has around the country, and with all the supposed investigations of irregularities and illegalities in the league."

Chuck Sullivan, the chief executive officer of the New England Patriots, joined the Davis-NFL fray by alleging that Davis's attorney, Joseph Alioto, had issued "threats of blackmail" against Rozelle and the NFL—if it did not permit the Raiders to move. "If you owners don't let Al move to Los Angeles," Sullivan quoted Alioto, who is also Sullivan's brother-in-law, "we are going to expose a Super Bowl ticket [scalping] conspiracy which could send Georgia to jail. We are going to involve Rozelle in this thing."

In denying Davis's charge and any knowledge of widespread ticket scalping in the NFL, Rozelle told Neil Amdur of *The New York Times,* "I think he [Davis] knows that the league as a whole does not like distasteful publicity. It's a form of intimidation. He figures that the league will get so tired they'll say, 'Al, you go to Los Angeles without a court case.' "[6]

However, former Rams employee Harold Guiver further added to the controversy by accusing Jack Catain of threatening him. Catain had apparently served as an envoy from the Rams' management to discuss Guiver's compensation upon leaving the team to become assistant general manager of the New Orleans Saints under Steve Rosenbloom.[7] According to Guiver's deposition, Catain, accompanied by one of his leg breakers, met with Guiver at the Los Angeles Hilton and instructed him to keep his "mouth shut about what [I] knew about the Los Angeles Rams." Catain also told Guiver to give the same message to Steve Rosenbloom.

Regarding the situation, Catain agreed to talk to Los Angeles attorney Carl A. "Tony" Capozzola, who represented Steve Rosenbloom, Guiver, and former Rams coach George Allen. Capozzola says, "Jack indicated that he was offered tickets in a lump sum. He was to take the tickets and distribute them to various brokers, and when he received the money on that, which would [include] money in excess of face value, he was then supposed to split that amount. Just consider ten thousand tickets for a Super Bowl. If those tickets are sold at a hundred dollars over face value, there's one million in cash.

"According to Mr. Catain," Capozzola continues, "Dominic had requested his services. Harold Guiver told me that Mr. Catain had made it very clear it was not in [Guiver's] best interest to say one more thing about the ticket scalping or any other derogatory thing about the Rams. And, in fact, not only Harold Guiver, but Steve Rosenbloom would be in some sort of jeopardy if they continued to say anything about that. And I think it was a huge concern, and that was what prompted me to notify the NFL top management. Mr. Rozelle expressed his concern, said that he would like to know if the matter was not resolved and that he planned to notify the appropriate people in the NFL Security, etc. I never heard from anybody from the NFL."

When asked in his deposition who had been making the profit from the scalped tickets, Guiver replied, "Georgia Rosenbloom." He added that she was responsible for setting the $100 price on the thousand $30 tickets. Guiver was to have sold the tickets because he knew how to market them.

After selling the tickets, Guiver gave Georgia Frontiere the $30,000 face value. However, when rumors about the ticket-scalping operation began, Guiver placed the remaining $70,000 in a trust account. Georgia denied any role in the scalping of Super Bowl tickets but admitted charging Guiver $100 for each of the thousand tickets she gave him. She insisted that Guiver owed the Rams organization, by coincidence, $70,000 for past expenses—which he claimed had been waived in writing by Carroll Rosenbloom before his death.[8]

With information that the total income from the sale of the tickets had not been reported, the IRS launched an investigation of the matter. Although it is also not against U.S. tax laws to scalp tickets, it is against the law not to report the income derived from the activity. The target of the investigation became the Rams' front office.

In December 1981—while the ticket-scalping matter

stewed—Catain was indicted for being involved in the counterfeiting scheme that the Secret Service had investigated. Catain described the charges against him as "total bullshit." He had been named in the crime by his unindicted coconspirator, Ray Cohen, already a convicted counterfeiter and the second man with Catain when they had visited and threatened Guiver.

Cohen, who turned state's evidence, also told investigators that he and a third coconspirator, Arthur Howard, had been given large blocks of Super Bowl tickets to sell to ticket brokers throughout Southern California. He reportedly sold the $30 tickets for between $180 to $200. The U.S. attorney's office in Los Angeles also entered the investigation because it had received information that the underworld, represented by Catain, had no fewer than three thousand Super Bowl tickets for sale—all received from the Los Angeles Rams.

Legal pressure then began to fall on the Frontieres, especially Dominic, who had begun to play a more prominent role in the operations of the Rams while the team's general manager, Don Klosterman, was being systematically stripped of his power.[9]

40 At War: Rosenthal and Spilotro

BY APRIL 1979, THE month Rosenbloom drowned, the investigation of Allen Glick and Argent had escalated dramatically. A year-long joint investigation by the FBI, IRS, OCRS and its Strike Forces, and the Kansas City Police Department had accumulated four thousand hours of court-authorized electronic surveillance. Federal agents alleged that $1,336,242 in revenues from Argent's sports-betting operation, as well as $7 million in slot-machine revenues, had been skimmed or embezzled under Rosenthal's management of the casino. There was also a separate investigation of the Las Vegas sports books amidst charges that they were serving as layoff operations for illegal bookmakers outside Nevada.[1]

Meantime, Tony Spilotro, who lived modestly with his family, had actually been conducting surveillance on FBI agents and various federal, state, and local law-enforcement officials. A raid on his house in 1978 yielded confidential FBI reports on him and Rosenthal as well as other sensitive documents. It turned out that Spilotro had a connection within the Las Vegas police who allegedly supplied him with a list of FBI informants and grand-jury transcripts, among other records.

The yield from the raid included stock certificates from Major Realty in Florida, as well as evidence that he was "a financial backer of a major bookmaking operation in Las Vegas, which was disseminating line information on sporting events to other parts of the country and which presently accepted bets and layoff wagers on college and professional football games," according to an FBI affidavit. Soon after, the state's gaming officials barred Spilotro from all Nevada casinos.

In July 1979, Allen Glick was stripped of his Nevada gaming license and fined over $500,000 for a variety of alleged improprieties. Soon after, Glick sold the Argent Corporation and his casinos for $70 million to Allan D. Sachs, the owner of Trans-Sterling, Inc. and the former president of the Stardust.

However, the FBI believes that Sachs and one of his partners were "figureheads for the Chicago mob responsible for providing skim monies" from Las Vegas casinos.[2] According to federal agents, the mob's skim of the Stardust continued under Sachs, who was a close friend of Rosenthal.

In June 1980, the SEC filed a complaint against Glick, on grounds he had allegedly filed false statements about his business activities at the time of his purchase of Recrion and his creation of Argent. Glick told me, "The SEC suit dealt with personal loans I had to help in the Saratoga bankruptcy and the method they were reported since the bonds of Recrion were publicly traded but my company was privately held."[3]

After taking the Fifth Amendment before three federal grand juries, Glick turned state's evidence against his onetime partners.[4] "I was never threatened with prosecution in any case," Glick told me, "nor did I fear it. I was a victim and ultimately the government was able to acquire credible evidence of its own and came to this conclusion. I refused to answer government questions on advice of counsel until it was clear the government had the correct facts, verified by others, that I was innocent."

However, Joe Yablonsky, the chief of the FBI office in Las Vegas at the time, had different feelings about Glick and told me, "He's a guy who rode the fence and came out looking like the victim."

The investigation of the Argent Corporation had caused chaos within the Chicago Mafia, particularly in its Las Vegas operations, where a power struggle was building between the brains and the muscle of the NFL's outlaw line: Lefty Rosenthal and Tony Spilotro.

According to federal prosecutors, in 1980 Spilotro began to exercise his independence from Rosenthal by having an affair with Rosenthal's wife, Geri, a former dancer and cocktail waitress at the Tropicana in Las Vegas. Just the previous year, Rosenthal had been placed in Nevada's "Black Book," the list of undesirable people forbidden to enter any casino in the state.

Spilotro appeared to use the affair as a show of power over Rosenthal, who had always been loyal to him. Despite the long friendship between the Rosenthals and the Spilotros, the affair was not kept secret—because Geri Rosenthal flaunted her relationship with Spilotro. The entire mess culminated on September 8, 1980, when an intoxicated Geri, who had been out all night, confronted her husband with a gun on the front lawn of their house. Although she was disarmed and no one was physically injured, Lefty filed for a divorce a few days later.

Soon after, Spilotro starting getting really crazy. According to statements made by one of his longtime associates, Frank Cullotta, Spilotro plotted in 1981 to murder an entire seventeen-member grand jury in Las Vegas that was investigating his activities. His method was to poison the food the grand jurors were to be served by a local caterer.

On October 4, 1982, at 8:30 P.M., fifty-three-year-old Lefty Rosenthal, who had begun to fear for his life, was having drinks with three old friends—Marty Kane, Sam Green, and Reuben Goldstein—at the Clint Murchison-owned Tony Roma's restaurant on East Sahara Avenue in Las Vegas.

After his meeting, Rosenthal, clad in a blue jogging suit, walked into the parking lot, stepped into his gold 1981 Cadillac Eldorado, sat down behind the wheel, and closed the door.[5] When he started the engine, a bomb exploded. The initial blast blew backward not forward, allowing Rosenthal a split second to force open his door with his left arm and leg.

After he tumbled out of the car, a second explosion blew a portion of the car's roof thirty feet into the air. The detonating device, which exploded first, had been placed under the gas tank between the rear tires. A specially made steel floor plate protected Rosenthal from being directly hit by the blast, and he escaped any serious injury when the gas tank exploded.

Marty Kane told me the events of that evening, "Lefty went on his way because the kids were coming home. We walked out of Tony Roma's. I went off to the right toward my car beside the building; his car was straight ahead by Maria Callender's restaurant. As I was walking toward my car, I heard this tremendous explosion. I had no idea what was happening. And then I heard another one. When I looked up, there were pieces of glass flying everywhere. So I opened my car door and got behind it. I still didn't know what had happened. And then I saw the black smoke. I ran around toward Marie Callender's, and I saw two guys leading Lefty away from his car. Those two guys were Secret Service agents, who were doing an advance."

The two Secret Service agents, who were scouting the area prior to a visit to Las Vegas by President Reagan, were eating at Maria Callender's restaurant at the moment of the blast. They were struck by flying glass and slightly injured. Both agents ran outside and found Rosenthal wandering around near his demolished car. The agents convinced Rosenthal to lie down until the ambulance arrived.

Kane continues, "When I saw Lefty walking around in a daze, I couldn't believe it. I mean, his car was totally demolished. It was one big pile of junk. I ran up to him, and I could see that his left arm and his left leg were burned. He was bleeding from the forehead and his hair was singed."

When the ambulance arrived, Ruby Goldstein climbed in the back with Rosenthal. Kane and Sam Green followed close behind in Kane's car.

Rosenthal was treated at the Teamsters-financed Sunrise Hospital for cracked ribs, shrapnel injuries, and burns on his legs, hands, and face. After Rosenthal was released two hours later, Kane, Green, and Goldstein took him home.

Rosenthal was later interviewed at his house "for several hours" by the FBI and the Clark County Metropolitan Police Department, which described Rosenthal as being "very, very, very cooperative. He signed a crime report and gave us a lengthy statement." Although the FBI did not have jurisdiction in the case, it offered intelligence information and its investigative facilities to the local police who were conducting the probe of the bombing. One of the police officers had told Rosenthal that he was "a walking dead man."

Two of the FBI agents who interviewed Rosenthal after the bombing were Joe Yablonsky and Charlie Parsons. Yablonsky, the chief of the Las Vegas office, told me, "We had a long talk with Lefty. We went for hours at his place. He wasn't going to tell us anything about the cause or his theories of it. But our basic purpose was to talk him into the witness program and to testify. But he wasn't a typical candidate for the program because he had plenty of his own money.

"Lefty said, 'What are my kids going to think if I become a snitch?' I told him, 'Don't you think your kids know what the fuck you are? Look at what the fucking Mafia did to you. You don't owe them anything.' But we couldn't budge him. He just wouldn't talk about what we wanted."

FBI special agent Charlie Parsons told me, "We never knew for sure who put the bomb in his car, but there isn't much question that the Chicago family was behind it. No one would dare do that without authority."[6]

Regardless of the lack of evidence, the bombing was immediately blamed on Spilotro, who was supposedly afraid that Rosenthal would become a government witness, as Glick had.

Within forty-eight hours of the explosion, Rosenthal held a press conference at his house. He told reporters that the FBI had "offered me fortresslike protection for an indefinite period of time . . . It was an invitation I thought to be honest and sincere. But I was not interested. I have nothing to offer and nothing to gain." He repeated that—although he had made several appearances before the federal grand jury investigating skimming at the Stardust—he had not become either a government witness or an informant.

When asked whether he thought he had been the target of a Chicago underworld contract, Rosenthal—who said that he viewed the bombing as "No message; No warning" but a straight-out effort to kill him—replied, "I know it didn't come from the Boy Scouts of America." Specifically asked about the likelihood of Spilotro's involvement, Rosenthal became deadpan serious and said that he would be "very, very unhappy and very, very angry" if he was behind it. "It would be a very unhealthy situation—for all of us."

Rosenthal added, "I just wanted to find out who did it, and make sure it doesn't happen again . . . I have no thoughts of revenge. If I say I'm looking for revenge, then I'm as low as they are."

On November 6, 1982, at 4:35 A.M., forty-six-year-old Geri Rosenthal, who had visited her estranged husband while he was recuperating from his superficial injuries, walked into the lobby of the Beverly Sunset Motel on Sunset Boulevard in Hollywood and started screaming before collapsing to the floor, according to eyewitnesses. Comatose, she was rushed to the nearby Cedar Sinai Hospital. Attempts to save her life were unsuccessful, and she died three days later without ever regaining consciousness.

The Los Angeles coroner's office determined that she was the victim of a drug and alcohol overdose, a lethal combination of cocaine, Valium, and Jack Daniel's whiskey. The coroner also noted a large bruise, the size of a football, on her right hip and concluded that "foul play is not ruled out." But foul play has never been proven. Lefty Rosenthal and the couple's two children did not attend the funeral.

In December 1982, Rosenthal and his children moved into a heavily secured $370,000 house in Laguna Niguel, a community south of Los Angeles. He insisted that he hadn't left Las Vegas because of the attempt on his life and considered his relationship with Spilotro "a private matter."

One problem that existed with regard to the pursuit of bookmakers and the national gambling syndicate was the refusal of the Reagan administration to prosecute. A top Justice Department official admitted, "We're no longer in the gambling business."

Despite the fact that organized crime was still controlling the major bookmaking and layoff operations, gambling became a low priority among the Reaganistas except when a major gambling network was discovered. Also, the President's Treasury Department was urging Congress to repeal two federal taxes on gamblers because they had not been effective deterrents to gambling and they were "wasteful and inefficient" to enforce. Significantly, in the past, government prosecutors had depended on tax evasion cases to try organized-crime figures who had managed to avoid prosecution for other, more serious crimes.[7]

Also, during the early months of President Reagan's first term, Nevada senator Paul Laxalt, Reagan's closest friend in Congress, met with Attorney General William French Smith no fewer than three times, specifically to discuss the possibility of minimizing the role of the Justice Department's Strike Force Against Organized Crime in Las Vegas.

Laxalt had been loudly complaining that Las Vegas was "infested" with pesky FBI and IRS agents, and he pledged to use his influence on the U.S. Senate Appropriations Committee to get federal investigators off the backs of Nevada's casino operators. Laxalt had taken the position that organized crime was no longer a factor in Nevada, which, he insisted, had established tight monitoring programs to keep out mobsters.

Joe Yablonsky, who headed the FBI's office in Las Vegas, told me, "Having the best friend of the President of the United States complaining about what I was doing had a chilling effect on the Justice Department's view of investigating Las Vegas."

Reagan took Laxalt's advice, and the President's first opportunity to revise the federal budget yielded a one-third cutback of the FBI's investigations of gambling, prostitution, arson-for-profit, gangland murders, and pornography—along with a hiring freeze and dramatic staff reductions within the FBI. Reagan also indicated that no new undercover operations would be authorized against organized crime or white-collar crime. Instead, the Reagan Justice Department wanted to concentrate on street crime and small-time drug use.[8]

41 Appearances and Realities

THE FINAL PRETRIAL HEARING before Al Davis's antitrust case to move his Oakland Raiders to Los Angeles was heard on May 7, 1981. During the hearing, NFL attorneys attempted to introduce as evidence Davis's relationship with Chicago Mafia "straw man" Allen Glick. The former mayor of San Francisco, Joseph Alioto, who was Davis's lawyer, agreed to permit the evidence as long as he could discuss the underworld contacts of Carroll Rosenbloom who "was much more involved than Mr. Davis." Alioto added, "Other NFL owners have ties to known gangsters far greater than Mr. Davis ever had . . . Mr. Davis will tell the whole story about Mr. Glick provided we are allowed to tell the whole truth about the other owners."[1]

The following day, to the relief of the NFL and several of its team owners, U.S. District Court Judge Harry Pregerson refused to admit testimony about the Glick-Davis relationship.[2]

The NFL players weren't so lucky because they became the new targets of public scrutiny.[3] Once again, when glimpses of organized crime's coziness with NFL owners appeared, new gambling scandals among the players hit the headlines, making the owners back-page news.

Like Joe Namath, Ken Stabler was a product of the University of Alabama. Coached by Paul "Bear" Bryant—who called him "the best quarterback I ever had at Alabama"—Stabler, nicknamed Snake, was among the most colorful players in the NFL. Drafted by the Oakland Raiders, Stabler played for Al Davis from 1970 to 1979, amassing an impressive list of statistics.[4]

After playing the 1980 season with the Houston Oilers, Stabler decided to retire. But he was lured back by the Oilers and a two-year $800,000 contract to play in the 1981 and 1982 seasons.

During the Oilers' summer training camp, a story by reporters John M. Crewdson and Wendell Rawls, Jr., broke in *The New York Times* on August 30, charging, in part, that Stabler had maintained a long relationship with sixty-three-year-old, twice-convicted bookmaker Nick Dudich, who had been linked to New Jersey's DeCavalcante crime family.[5]

An NFL investigation of Stabler, which had supposedly begun the previous March, was continuing but inconclusive by the time the story was published: There was no evidence that Stabler had gambled, shaved points, or fixed games.[6]

Years earlier, Al LoCasale, an assistant to Al Davis, had allegedly reported the association between Stabler and Dudich to NFL Security. Team officials, including Raiders head coach John Madden, had instructed Stabler to sever his ties with Dudich, but Stabler refused.

Bud Adams, the Oilers' owner and Stabler's new boss, charged that Davis had contrived the whole matter to embarrass Pete Rozelle and the NFL. Stabler agreed, and several former Raiders—Fred Biletnikoff, Pete Banaszak, and Phil Villapiano—told reporters that they had known Dudich as well. While insisting that Stabler had done nothing wrong, they all denied ever gambling or giving Dudich any inside information.

At the same time, the Raiders' head trainer, George Anderson, who had been with the Raiders since 1960, was also accused of gambling on NFL games and passing inside information to his bookmaker, Thomas "Whitey" Green, who was identified as the major layoff man in the Bay Area. Green, Dudich, and a third bookmaker, Samuel Reich, according to *The Times,* had tremendous access to Raiders players and staff.

The charges against Anderson had been made by bookmaker Gino Tropiano, a Green associate and check forger with a long arrest record, who was asked by the NFL to take a two-day polygraph examination about his charges—which included claims that Green had provided a bag of pills to Anderson. Although these allegations had been passed on to NFL Security as early as 1972, neither Tropiano nor Anderson was questioned by the league until September 1981.[7] Tropiano passed the examination. One answer was deemed as being "inconclusive."[8]

Whitey Green could not be interviewed. Just three months earlier, on June 3, 1981, Green and his wife were murdered. The forty-four-year-old, twice-convicted bookmaker was found bound with twine in the couple's bedroom; a single bullet from a small caliber gun had been fired into the top of his head. Nearby, his wife had been gagged and tied and was lying face-down on the bed with thirteen stab wounds in her body. Her head had also been struck three times with a claw hammer. There was no evidence of forced entry. Other than Green's wallet, nothing of value appeared to be missing from his $200,000 house in Livermore, a suburb of Oakland. Their bodies were discovered by their grandson, who became concerned when they didn't answer the door. The murder remains unsolved.

Tropiano said that four days before the murders, three men from Las Vegas had come to Green's house to collect on a $60,000 bet. Green had refused to pay them.

Meantime, after the Green murder, Stabler was questioned at length by Warren Welsh in 1981 about his relationship with Dudich. Anderson, who admitted making "a few small horse bets" with Green during the early 1970s, was also interviewed. The FBI reportedly received confirmation for Tropiano's earlier charges against Anderson from two confidential sources—whom the bureau refused to reveal to the Alameda County district attorney's office.

Although the D.A.'s office refused to reopen its investigation of Anderson, the NFL continued its probe. "Our role is different than that of the law-enforcement agencies who are looking for criminal violations," Rozelle said. "We have standards for the integrity of our sport, and our requirements for evidence are not as stringent as theirs. Still, we must have sufficient information to take action."

Surprisingly, the gambling community was cavalier about the entire Stabler incident. *The Gold Sheet,* in particular, wrote, "The Ken Stabler affair is just another example of irresponsible reporting. Using innuendos and inferences, two *New York Times* reporters intimated charges against Stabler that lacked any substance or evidence. They syllogized that because Stabler was seen associating with a known gambler—and that because a concurrent circumstance saw Stabler play below his capacity—therefore some hanky-panky might be suggested . . . If Stabler were indeed involved in some nefarious act, would he not have been more discreet about the company he kept? One would hardly be so blatant as to show off these associations in public places."[9]

In his 1986 autobiography, Stabler was brief and nonchalant about the whole Dudich matter. "What I had done was have a few drinks over the years with a nice old guy named Nick Dudich . . . If Al Davis really wanted me to stop my occasional beers with Dudich, he certainly could have forced me to. I worked for Al. And when Al said jump, you jumped."[10]

While the Stabler/Anderson investigations were up in the air, NFL legend Johnny Unitas became the focus of considerable controversy after sports reporter Frederick C. Klein of *The Wall Street Journal* received a notice of a new betting tip sheet coming out of Baltimore, the *John Unitas All-Pro Football Report.* After inquiring about the publication through its toll-free number, Klein then called Unitas. "I don't gamble, but I follow the games and enjoy making the picks," Unitas told the reporter. "As long as I'm doing it anyway, I may as well get paid for it, even though I don't need the money."[11]

In his promotional literature, Unitas was touted as a football handicapper by Mike Warren, who owned the sports service. Unitas wrote, "I'm invited everywhere. I get to see teams and players and game films other people don't see. Heck, there probably isn't an important person in this game I'm not on a first-name basis with. If I plugged up my ears, I couldn't stop getting information you never read in the newspapers." Unitas's service cost $125 a year, which the onetime star quarterback promised would be won "your very first weekend."

Unitas, who was listed as a "special consultant" for the Baltimore Colts, then felt the wrath of Pete Rozelle, who told Colts owner Robert Irsay, "It would not be appropriate for an employee of your club to be associated with this type of business." Reportedly, Rozelle had never called Unitas. Although not a salaried employee of the Colts, Unitas had been doing occasional public-relations work for the team and was paid on a case-by-case basis. His principal occupations were operating a Baltimore restaurant and an air-freight company.

A close friend of Unitas told me that "Johnny was paid a fee from a Baltimore handicapping firm to use his name. They asked for his picks once a week. He didn't start the business. He didn't organize it. Johnny never owned any part of it."

Unitas agrees with that and told me, "Mike [Warren] asked me if I would be willing to analyze two or three games a week. All I would do is, like, take Green Bay and Detroit, analyze the two different teams. And I'd say, 'On the whole, because of injuries, Detroit could win this ball game.' I never made any point spreads or picks or anything like that.

"Commissioner Rozelle came out and made a bold statement that no one in the National Football League was allowed to talk with me—or have anything to do with me from now on. What right did he have to say that to anybody about me? I wasn't under contract then to Rozelle or the NFL. He never even picked up the telephone and talked to me about it."

Unitas adds that he wasn't in the Colts organization at the time he was working with the handicapping service. "I had a contract [stipulating that] whenever I retired from the Colts, or retired from football, [that I would] go to work for the Colts for a ten-year period. But [Colts owner] Robert Irsay breached that contract. He traded me to San Diego [in 1973, Unitas's final season], and he never lived up to our agreement."

The Unitas tout sheet problem didn't end the troubles of past and present NFL players. In November 1981, two other players had trouble with associations with gamblers. Tommy Kramer, the star quarterback for the Minnesota Vikings, was admonished for demonstrating "poor judgment" but was not disciplined for making a $25.00 "friendly bet" with a local bartender on a game between the Pittsburgh Steelers and the Houston Oilers on Monday night, October 26.[12] Kramer had taken Pittsburgh and three points and won his bet. The Steelers beat the Oilers, 26–13.

Don Strock, the backup quarterback for the Miami Dolphins, was advised to sever his relationship with the management of Club Top Draw, a restaurant in North Bay Village, near Miami, which was known as a hangout for several top organized-crime figures. Strock and his wife had done television commercials on behalf of the restaurant. After the FBI and the NFL informed Strock about the reputation of the restaurant, he immediately asked that the commercials be pulled. Strock also returned the money he had made for his role in the advertising promotion.

* * *

Later, in February 1982, George Anderson was cleared by NFL Security but reprimanded by commissioner Rozelle for making "nonfootball events" wagers and "socializing" with bookmakers.

Bookmaker Gino Tropiano told my associate, William Scott Malone, that Anderson had "been betting with us since the late sixties and early seventies—and good size bets, betting for the Raiders and for himself." Speaking of Dudich, Tropiano added, "Nick Dudich had three or four beauty salons in Perth Amboy, New Jersey, and he used to lay off bets on the West Coast with us and other bookmakers. He would send his girls out, and someone would meet them at the airport and exchange envelopes. And that's the way they used to settle it."

In late August, the month after Stabler was waived by the Oilers, Rozelle cleared him of all charges, warning him to avoid "undesirable elements" in the future.[13] Stabler immediately signed a new contract with John Mecom and the New Orleans Saints.

42 Cranking Up the Drug Problem

DESPITE THE ORGANIZED-CRIME ties of so many NFL team owners during the 1980s, the sports media concentrated on the reporting of player drug use. And nothing gave the players and the NFL Players Association more public-relations problems—and the owners more public sympathy—than the growing pattern of drug abuse among the players.

In February 1981, all-pro linebacker Thomas "Hollywood" Henderson of the Dallas Cowboys went public with details of his cocaine habit. Henderson told *Los Angeles Herald-Examiner* columnist Doug Krikorian, "I started using coke in 1976. My paycheck was eight thousand dollars a week in my best days—and I used all the money to buy coke. I'd borrow the money. The dealers would give me credit. I even sold some to make ends meet."[1] Also that year, former Minnesota Vikings stars Carl Eller and Randy Holloway followed suit with their confessions of drug use.

And things got worse. Larry Csonka and Jim Kiick, formerly of the Miami Dolphins, who starred in Super Bowls VII and VIII, were investigated by a federal grand jury in New Orleans, which was probing marijuana smuggling in the Gulf states. Csonka reportedly took the Fifth;[2] Kiick was never subpoenaed.

The two former players had allegedly made plans to purchase a large shipment of marijuana from undercover federal agents involved in an investigation called Operation Grouper, a massive federal organized-crime drug probe that began in 1978 and had yielded 165 indictments and the seizure of 1.2 million pounds of marijuana, 831 pounds of cocaine, and three million Quaaludes. Wiretaps and videotape had been used in the Csonka-Kiick probe, but neither man was charged. Both men had reportedly backed out of the conspiracy before any crime was actually committed.[3]

Then, in April 1981, NFL Security announced that for nearly five months it had been investigating several members of the Denver Broncos for cocaine use.[4] Subsequently, more serious questions arose when the Colorado Organized Crime Strike Force revealed that "eight to ten" Broncos players had accepted the cocaine from known Denver gamblers and bookmakers. In return, according to law-enforcement authorities, the players supplied the dealers with inside information about Denver's games.

The Rocky Mountain News found the dealer who supplied the drugs to the players and interviewed him. He said that he had met several of the Broncos players during the pregame festivities to Super Bowl XII in January 1978, in which Denver, five-point underdogs, lost to Dallas, 27–10. The gambler/drug dealer became friendly and began meeting socially with the players. "I might get together with one or two on Monday and drink wine and snort some coke," the dealer/gambler said. "For the players, I think it was a way to escape reality. Those players weren't taking drugs to help them in a game. It was for relaxation. The pressure on them is so intense."[5] The gambler/drug dealer passed a polygraph test about his relationships with the Broncos players.

NFL Security chief Warren Welsh told me he was convinced, on the basis of his lengthy investigation, that no point shaving or game fixing had occurred. "The charges were never substantiated," Welsh said.

Five alleged cocaine dealers, two of whom were major gambling figures in the Denver area, were arrested and convicted in connection with the case. No one from the Broncos team was charged. However, three players—linebacker Tom Jackson, safety Billy Thompson, and return specialist Rick Upchurch—were reprimanded in a letter from commissioner Rozelle.

Within a year after the Colorado Organized Crime Strike Force uncovered the information, it was disbanded. Robert Cantwell, the coordinator of the strike force, told reporter Jim Herre of *The Denver Post,* "By [the NFL] not taking aggressive action . . . they are encouraging it [drug use]. I don't think the NFL has done enough homework, and they don't have the resources to investigate the many complaints they receive."

During the spring of 1981, while the investigation of the Broncos wound down, another investigation of the New Orleans Saints cranked up. A federal grand jury in New Orleans probed allegations that at least ten members of the Saints team were receiving drugs from suspected gamblers. George Rogers, the 1980 Heisman Trophy winner and a rookie running back for the Saints, told the grand jury that the price for his drug use during a single season was as high as $10,000. Also testifying was Rogers's teammate rookie quarterback David Wilson, who fingered former Saints running back Mike Strachan as the team's supplier.

Strachan had earlier been indicted for cocaine trafficking. He pleaded guilty and was sentenced to three years in prison. His customers were listed as Rogers, Chuck Muncie of the San Diego Chargers, and Saints defensive end Frank Warren, all of whom had cooperated with the grand-jury investigation and, thus, were not charged.

Strachan later testified before the grand jury, saying that his cocaine habit began after he became a friend of Chuck Muncie, a running back for the Saints until 1980 when he joined the Chargers. "When I got to Muncie and his life-style and his friends," Strachan told reporters, "it [cocaine] was so prevalent, I just started indulging as he did."

Strachan also charged that Rogers supplied the black players on the Saints team, while cornerback Dave Waymer supplied the white players. Like Rogers, Waymer was given immunity to testify against Strachan.

Strachan told me that there was never any attempt to compromise his on-field performance. However, he conceded that his drug suppliers did have "a power of blackmail" over him. "They did. But that power was never exercised. Gambling wasn't widespread then. I heard about a few players who were gambling, but it just wasn't in the picture. But, I guess, anyone who is that close to a player is going to know what's going on with the team."

San Diego Chargers owner Gene Klein told me about how he obtained Muncie from the Saints. "I walked into the office one day and someone says to me, 'We can get Chuck Muncie for a second-round pick.' I said, 'Go get him. Don't waste time.' He said, 'Our competition is the Raiders.' I said, 'Pick up the phone and close the deal.' He said, 'You know there's talk about Chuck having drug problems.' I said, 'That's talk; nothing's been proven.' And so we got Chuck for a second-round pick. He was a helluva football player. He also had a helluva drug habit, too."

At the time of the cocaine/gambling investigations of the Broncos, Chargers, and the Saints, no fewer than five other teams were being investigated on similar charges: the Cleveland Browns, Dallas Cowboys, Miami Dolphins, San Francisco 49ers, and Washington Redskins. Although a small number of players from these teams would be prosecuted, all these investigations eventually collapsed. A few law-enforcement officials have claimed that the NFL was more concerned with damage control than informing fans about this serious problem facing the game of professional football. Once again, it was the isolated cases that made the headlines.

- In April 1982, Kirby Criswell of the St. Louis Cardinals and an associate were accused of manufacturing and distributing amphetamines. Criswell was convicted and was sentenced to five years in prison. That same month, his teammate E. J. Junior was arrested for possession of cocaine and marijuana. Junior pleaded guilty.
- In the June 14, 1982, issue of *Sports Illustrated,* former Miami Dolphins, New Orleans Saints, and San Diego Chargers defensive player Don Reese, who had been busted and imprisoned for purchasing cocaine, wrote an explosive cover story confession. Reese told *SI* investigative reporter John Underwood, "What you see on the tube on Sunday afternoon is often a lie. When players are messed up, the game is messed up. The outcome of the game is dishonest when playing ability is impaired. You can forget about point spreads or anything else in that kind of atmosphere . . . I've seen dealers literally standing on the practice fields of the NFL, guys everybody knew. They're not there to make the game better. What they do, and what they know about the players, can't possibly be good for the game."[6]
- On August 18, 1982, former Miami Dolphins running sensation Mercury Morris was arrested with four others on cocaine charges. The police had raided the star's south Miami house, seizing more than a pound of cocaine, $124,000 in cash, and

several guns. He was convicted on one count of trafficking and sentenced to twenty years in prison.

"Cocaine certainly poses a possible threat to the integrity of the game," NFL Security's assistant director Charles S. Jackson told Ronald Sullivan of *The New York Times* in late June 1982. He added that forty to fifty players might have a "chemical dependency on the drug." Sullivan quoted Jackson as saying that "there was 'absolutely no evidence thus far' that gambling interests had succeeded in using cocaine to corrupt the game. But he also said that 'the longer the problem of cocaine continues to grow, the greater the chance of [corruption] occurring . . .' Other officials said it was only a question of how long it would take before an addicted player would be confronted with what the league fears most: a cocaine dealer with organized-crime connections, offering the drug free to a player with only one thing in mind—the opportunity to fix a game."

Minnesota Vikings star Carl Eller, an admitted drug user who had become an NFL consultant to deal with the problem, told reporter Sullivan that more than 40 percent of NFL players use cocaine.

To further complicate the NFL's problems, a new, rival league was founded on May 11, 1982. Unlike the defunct World Football League,[7] the new United States Football League (USFL) immediately received a two-year, $18 million contract with ABC-TV.[8] Also, in the first college draft in 1983, the USFL's New Jersey Generals, which were later bought by Manhattan real estate tycoon Donald Trump, signed 1982 Heisman Trophy winner Herschel Walker of Georgia.

The owner of the Pittsburgh Maulers in the new league was Edward J. DeBartolo, Sr., who was frequently under suspicion of having mob ties.[9]

For example, the U.S. Customs Service had received information from one of its special agents, William F. Burda, in January 1981 that the DeBartolo organization "through its control of particular state banks in the state of Florida is operating money-laundering schemes, realizing huge profits from narcotics, guns, skimming operations, and other organized-crime-related activities. This organization is reported to have ties to [Carlos] Marcello, [Santos] Trafficante, and [Meyer] Lansky and because of its enormous wealth and power has high-ranking political influence and affiliations."

In an earlier report, authored by Burda, the special agent wrote that he had developed source information indicating that "Meyer Lansky, the financial wizard of OC [organized crime], is now considered by most to be almost senile and getting out of the business. His successor and new financial wizard is recognized as Edward J. DeBartolo."

The DeBartolo organization was extremely concerned by the allegations made by special agent Burda after his reports began to surface in connection with DeBartolo's bid to be licensed in Oklahoma. DeBartolo's attorney, Charles Ruff, was asked to provide a legal opinion about the Burda report.

In a letter to the DeBartolo Corporation's general counsel, Ruff wrote in 1985, "The Burda report consists of statements attributed to unidentified persons and therefore its reliability cannot be confirmed without further investigation . . . In view of the time that has passed, some five years since the date of the Burda material, during which time Mr. DeBartolo has not been informed of any prosecutive steps by the Department of Justice, such as the convening of a grand jury, it is my opinion that the allegations contained in the Burda report were found by the Department either to be of no interest to it or an unreliable basis for concluding that possible criminal action was warranted . . . I have discussed the Burda report on an informal basis with officials in the Department of Justice, and although the Department's practice in matters such as this is not to comment formally, those discussions are not inconsistent with the opinion I have expressed in this letter."

DeBartolo denied any wrongdoing and has not been charged with any. When asked by Peter Phipps of the *Akron Beacon Journal* about the appearance of ties to the underworld, DeBartolo replied, "No one ever comes up with a thing, and still we have to hear about all these crazy innuendoes about us and the rackets. We're so clean it's amazing. I've never even gotten a union pension fund loan."[10]

DeBartolo had also acquired Louisiana Downs, a racetrack in Shreveport that became the target of an investigation by the Texas state legislature in 1983. Information submitted to the House committee that conducted the probe alleged that "reliable sources indicate that Mob money is being 'laundered' at

Louisiana Downs with the knowledge and complicity of Edward J. DeBartolo, Sr."

The information also alleged that DeBartolo and Carlos Marcello worked behind the scenes to defeat a pari-mutuel betting bill in Texas—which would have competed with the Louisiana track. The investigation of DeBartolo, who denied any wrongdoing, was later dropped. The Texas state legislature defeated the pari-mutuel bill, 75–73, just as DeBartolo had hoped.

The problems of DeBartolo Sr.'s owning a team in the USFL—in direct competition with the popular Rooney family and their Pittsburgh Steelers and DeBartolo Jr.'s owning the San Francisco 49ers in the NFL—were glaringly obvious, especially since both teams were subsidiaries of DeBartolo's parent company. Consequently, DeBartolo Jr. was confronted with the problem in March 1983 at the NFL owners' meeting. However, both DeBartolos brushed the whole issue off. They owned their teams. They were their properties. And no one could do anything about it.

"The League can't hurt me," DeBartolo Jr. said. "It's not big enough. They don't like it? That's the way it is. Nobody's going to take this team away from me, including the League. Because, I tell you, the League can't afford the lawsuit, I can. Enough of this bullshit about conflict of interest. That's ridiculous. They can't afford a lawsuit because I'll bury them."[11]

Like the American Football League nearly twenty years earlier, the USFL caused a dramatic escalation of salaries for the most-sought-after professional football players. The players, of course, loved it, but the team owners did not. USFL games were scheduled to begin during the NFL's off-season. The first game was played on March 6, 1983, almost six weeks after Super Bowl XVII.

In a move, aside from the ABC television contract, that seemed to ensure the USFL's success, the legal bookmakers in Las Vegas began accepting action on its games. "If somebody bets five dollars on a game, he's going to watch it on television," predicted Billy Kilmer in an interview with reporter Bob Sansevere. "That's what's going to make [the USFL] successful."

While the USFL was optimistic about its future, the NFL's growing problems seemed to culminate after only two weeks of games in the 1982 season. Unable to gain the owners' approval on a new contract, the NFL Players Association announced that its members were on strike. It was the first time that NFL regular season games had been canceled as a result of a dispute between the league's owners and players.

Ending in November, the strike lasted fifty-seven days and cost the NFL cities, owners, club staffs, players, concessionaires, and others dependent on the smooth operation of the sport—including gamblers and bookmakers—billions of dollars. The season resumed at the conclusion of the strike—which the players clearly won—with each NFL team playing a total of only nine games. Incredibly enough, the NFL owners enjoyed the universal support of professional football fans, who naïvely viewed the players as being drugged-up, overpaid, and underworked.

Ed Garvey, the executive director of the NFLPA, is proud of the 1982 settlement. "It was one of the most successful strikes in labor history in that we obtained guaranteed collective benefits of $1.4 billion over five years," Garvey told me. "We asked for fifty-five percent of the gross profits, and the players ended up with fifty-eight to sixty percent. We totally changed the way in which money is spent in the National Football League—with the union having an equal voice. Before, management could spend it any way it wanted. It was the only strike I know of in which people came off strike and received a bonus for the time they were on strike."

Although many fans did not share Garvey's enthusiasm, the average NFL player's salary was still only $95,000 a year. Meantime, professional hockey players were making $110,000 annually. NBA players were averaging $214,000. Major-league baseball players were receiving a whopping $220,000. While fans complained about the NFL players' salaries, the annual revenues of the NFL team owners and the sale values of their teams were skyrocketing.

With the NFL players strike, increasing drug problems in the league, the creation of the USFL, the ticket-scalping scandal among the NFL owners, and Al Davis's antitrust suit, 1982 had been a terrible year for Pete Rozelle and Warren Welsh.

Little did they know that in 1983 things were going to get much worse.

43 The *Frontline* Controversy

ON JANUARY 15, 1983, an era within the underworld ended with the death of Meyer Lansky, the last surviving dinosaur of the old mob, which had Americanized and organized disorganized crime in 1931. The syndicate's financial wizard died in Mount Sinai Hospital in Miami Beach after a long bout with cancer. Speaking of his crime empire, Lansky once said, "We're bigger than U.S. Steel." In his entire life, he had been imprisoned only once as an adult—serving two months in Saratoga Springs, New York, for local gambling violations.

Two days after Lansky's death, *Frontline,* a new weekly PBS production, presented its premier program, "An Unauthorized History of the NFL," which became the most-watched current-affairs program ever broadcast on public television. The one-hour program was moderated by NBC reporter Jessica Savitch, who was on loan to PBS.

The concept for the PBS program began after Tom Mechling, the chairman of the National Commission on Gambling Information, a nonprofit public-interest group, was approached by Ed Garvey, the executive director of the NFL Players Association, for the purpose of doing an investigation of the NFL owners on a consultancy basis. Mechling had come highly recommended after his work on an NBC "White Paper" on gambling which aired in December 1980.[1]

Mechling told me, "What I found out about many of the NFL teams after about six months of looking [on behalf of the NFLPA] was really more than I wanted to know about who really owns the Great American Game. The NFLPA locked up the research in their files and never used it in any fashion and/or never wanted to."

Garvey told me, "All we really had was rumors. Frankly, the battle with the owners was so great—through the National Labor Relations Board, the federal courts, collective bargaining, and just trying to hold the union together as a unit—that the rumors seemed to be the least of our problems. The union is not deputized by the U.S. marshal. It doesn't have any control over how management deals with its books. It doesn't have its own investigative arm."[2]

Mechling persisted. "Later," he says, "I boiled the material down to the TV program outline. I first took it to Tony Potter of NBC News Documentaries, whom I had worked with on the gambling 'White Paper' and other program subjects. At the time, NBC was in dire financial straits. But, regardless, Potter looked at the program idea, whistled, said it was a good program and that he would give his left nut to do it. But he also said, 'I'm not even going to send it upstairs,' meaning to the NBC News head. He explained that fully twenty-five percent of NBC's revenues then were coming from the NFL contract with the network for televising their games and selected college ones too."

Potter suggested that Mechling call executive producer David Fanning, who was starting the new *Frontline* series on PBS. Fanning had made his reputation with his production of the controversial "Death of a Princess" program and the *World* series. Fanning had received nearly $5 million from the Corporation for Public Broadcasting, the Chubb Insurance Group, and seven of the local PBS stations around the country to produce weekly news programs too hot for the networks.

Mechling met Fanning and his producer, director, and writer William Cran. They accepted Mechling's idea and hired him as a consultant. Also hired to do the reporting were reporters Ben Loeterman and my associate, William Scott Malone.

This fascinating show was critical of the close association between the worlds of professional football and syndicate gamblers and charged that inside information is regularly provided, points are occasionally shaved, and games are sometimes fixed. The program was dramatic and startling, discussing the dark side of the NFL that few fans ever hear about, particularly from network television—which enjoyed a cozy and lucrative sweetheart relationship with the NFL.

The most controversial portion of the PBS report was the claim by a bookmaker, John Charles "Butch" Piazza, that between 1968 and 1970 he had been involved in payoffs to a particular team's head coach, quarterback, and defensive captain.

"With the quarterback," Piazza said, "if he knew the perimeters of the score that we wanted to hold . . . he'd throw a bad pass or throw it out of bounds and only kick a field goal. We also bagged the defensive captain, a defensive back, so he could slip and fall down and let the other team score." The head coach was needed to guarantee that neither the quarterback nor the defensive back were pulled out of the game.

Piazza added that he had known of the fixing of four games in each of those years. He said that the players had received and split an average of $300,000 per game, plus 10 percent of what the fixers made gambling. Their biggest payoff, he claimed, was $795,000 for a single fixed game, which he had personally delivered. The money for the bets was laid off through the Beckley/Sklaroff national gambling syndicate.

Was Piazza credible? At the time of the program, he was awaiting sentencing on drug charges and for the illegal possession of a silencer. However, Piazza—who asked *Frontline* to pay his wife's moving expenses of $10,000 in return for his cooperation—did pass a voice stress evaluation test concerning his charges. Nevertheless, the program did not name the two players and the head coach Piazza had allegedly paid off.

The PBS report also raised questions about the investigation of the accidental drowning of Carroll Rosenbloom, suggesting that he might have been murdered.

William Scott Malone located Raymond Tanguay, the French Canadian citizen who had witnessed Rosenbloom's drowning and jumped in the water in an effort to save him. Malone was aided by Edward Noel, a former sergeant in the Royal Canadian Mounted Police. Both men talked to Tanguay at his home in a small town outside of Montreal.

Speaking in French, Tanguay, with the RCMP officer serving as interpreter, said that he had not had a decent night's sleep since Rosenbloom's death because he had desperately tried but failed to save Rosenbloom's life.

According to PBS, Tanguay's version of what happened that

afternoon on April 2, 1979, is at complete odds with the official police version, which probably resulted from the language barrier. Then thirty-six years old, Tanguay said that he was walking up the beach, collecting seashells, when he saw Rosenbloom crossing behind him and heading toward the ocean. As Tanguay came strolling back down the beach about ten to fifteen minutes later, he heard someone calling for help. He spotted Rosenbloom thrashing about in the water about a hundred yards from the shore. Tanguay said that he dove into the water with a piece of wood for buoyancy and went after Rosenbloom—who was slowly being taken out to sea.

"As [Tanguay] approached within fifty yards," the RCMP officer said, "he saw a black object in the water about a hundred yards from the victim. [Tanguay's] first impression was that he thought it was another person and that a boat had overturned. This object only appeared for a short period as the waves were breaking. He can only describe this object as being black, that it was partially submerged and that he thought that it was part of a person's body in a diver's suit or the bottom of a boat. One thing he is certain of is that he saw a black object." He also noted that the object was moving against the waves in a direction opposite Rosenbloom.

Rosenbloom was motionless and floating on the surface as Tanguay got close to him. The Rams owner was frothing at the mouth as Tanguay pushed the piece of wood under Rosenbloom's body and began dragging him back to shore. "On a couple of occasions, heavy swells broke [Tanguay] loose from the victim, and finally he had to let [Rosenbloom] go and drag himself to shore in a state of total exhaustion.

"Once he reached the shore, he saw two men run into the water and drag the victim to the beach and then walk away. He could only describe these individuals as being well-tanned men who looked like 'hoodlums.'

"Tanguay stated that the two policemen who arrived on the scene minutes later were not the persons who pulled the body out of the water. According to Tanguay, the only other witness on the beach at the time he came out of the water was a woman in her mid-fifties."[3]

During my interview with William Henrikson, who was the chief of the Golden Beach police at the time of Rosenbloom's death, this mystery about the two additional men on the scene was cleared up. Henrikson told me that he and his deputy Ron Nasca—both of whom were large and tanned men—had stipped off their clothes when they jumped into the ocean trying to save Rosenbloom. Both had passed Tanguay and instructed him to return to the shore. When the two officers recovered Rosenbloom's body and dragged him onto the beach, two paramedics arrived soon after. Both paramedics were dressed in gray uniforms.

Clearly, Tanguay, who was not familiar with the look of local police uniforms, mistook the two police officers as the well-tanned hoodlums and the two uniformed paramedics as the police. "I found no evidence of foul play," Henrikson told me. "And Tanguay never mentioned anything about the black object at the time the Dade County detectives interviewed him after Rosenbloom's death. I certainly never saw any other objects in the water."[4]

Also, during the research for this book, I found four additional photographs taken during Rosenbloom's autopsy, which had been reported to have been missing from the coroner's office. There has been considerable speculation that these four pictures may have been suppressed and would prove that Rosenbloom had been murdered.

I gave the photographs and accompanying official reports to several friends within the law-enforcement community for their analyses. Detective Joseph Quantrille of the Washington, D.C., Metropolitan Police Department's homicide division was among them. He told me that the pictures showed no evidence of foul play and confirmed the reports filed by the Dade County Department of Public Safety and the original autopsy report—although he noticed evidence of trauma on the right side of Rosenbloom's chest cavity. A small clot and stream of dark blood bordered the outside rim of Rosenbloom's lung and pancreas. However, this trauma could have easily occurred during the attempts either to rescue or revive him. Others who reviewed the material came to the same conclusion.

In short, the evidence appears to be clear that Rosenbloom died in a tragic accident and was not murdered.

The *Frontline* program on the NFL received mixed reviews. *The Chicago Tribune* described it as "one whale of a report. We can only wonder why it was so slow arriving and why it finally emerged on public TV rather than one of the big, football-wise commercial networks."

Variety wrote, "It's even more amazing that the newspapers—seemingly less needful of league goodwill—had devoted so little space to the subject. It isn't as if they were unaware of the matter; most papers carry a betting line on Sunday afternoon and Monday night games and many handicap the games for bettors on the basis of that line."

In the worst and most idiotic attack on the show, William Taaffe of *Sports Illustrated* wrote, "To say that PBS threw an incomplete pass with this program . . . isn't to say that all NFL owners have just come out of a monastery. It's also not to aver that no quarterback has ever intentionally thrown an interception or that no owner has ever bet on—or even against—his team. Betting exists. Not all mobsters sell tomatoes."

Rozelle, who predictably called the PBS program "cheap sensationalism," added, "The program presented by PBS Monday night was chiefly a rehash of press clippings, gossip, and rumor, some almost twenty-five years old." The show was also criticized because two of those who appeared on camera were paid—John Piazza and bookmaker Gino Tropiano—causing cries of "checkbook journalism" from those who could not attack the program for any other reason. At a press conference after the show, Rozelle told reporters, "We are looking into the possibility of bringing suit against PBS."

Rozelle added, "If the producers of the show and their paid informants are at all confident of their information, why don't they offer specific facts including the names of the players and the dates of the games? Without these facts, every player and coach of the period this show cited is subject to suspicion."

Sports columnist Dave Anderson of *The New York Times* wrote that PBS had "dug up no new cadavers, only a convict's allegation that an unidentified coach, an unidentified quarterback and an unidentified team captain on an unidentified team had fixed a total of 12 unidentified games during the 1968, 1969 and 1970 seasons."

According to the *Frontline* documents, as well as federal law-enforcement records, Piazza claimed to have seen and identified the two players who were present when the money was allegedly exchanged. His information about the head coach is secondhand.

Born in Atlanta in 1941, Piazza was known as a major bookmaker, like his father, and a drug dealer whose façade of legitimacy was his racehorse farm in Ocala, Florida, which he had purchased in 1975 for $1.5 million. Between 1959 and 1972, Piazza had been arrested no fewer than eight times for such crimes as disorderly conduct, AWOL while in the U.S. Navy, "betting or soliciting bets on athletic contests," conspiracy to smuggle marijuana, and aggravated assault, among other offenses. There is no record of conviction on any of these charges.

Piazza had spent much of his time in Miami during the 1970s. In 1977, he pleaded guilty to drug smuggling and was given immunity from further prosecution in return for his cooperation against his coconspirators. He was sentenced to twelve years in prison; he served only forty-two months. He was released in 1981 and placed in the Federal Witness Protection Program after he agreed to testify against Meyer Lansky, who had hatched an illegal gambling scheme. However, charges against Lansky were never brought. At that time, Piazza was living under the name "John Petracelli" in Dallas with his wife.

While in the witness program, Piazza was arrested in Miami on illegal narcotics and weapons charges. He was later convicted.

Frontline's concerns about Piazza revolved around his background and a diverse view of his credibility by law-enforcement officials. Some flat out didn't trust him, while others, especially those who had gained important convictions from his testimony, believed him to be "extremely credible."

During Piazza's 1980 testimony in a drug-smuggling case, Judge Norman Roettger said of Piazza, "He has admitted just about everything under the sun. I think his testimony is impeached."

However, FBI supervisor Ralph Hill, who specialized in sports gambling, disagrees. "I came in after a given game or after a given season, so what we saw were the results. Piazza was seeing it as it was going on. So I would state that what he says bears credence."

Between 1967 and 1970, Piazza was known by local, state, and federal officials as being heavily involved with sports gambling and bookmaking. His immediate supervisors were Atlanta's most active bookmakers, Elmer H. Dudley and Barney T. Berry, both of whom were top lieutenants to Gil Beckley in Georgia.

Dudley and Berry, who both had long police records, had been indicted along with Marty Sklaroff for federal gambling violations and forty-one counts of mail fraud in the fall of 1969, just a few months before Beckley disappeared.[5] Piazza was arrested in November 1969 in connection with that case. However, the charges against Piazza were eventually dropped. Piazza's attorney was Joe Salem, an Atlanta lawyer who had also represented Beckley on occasion.

When interviewed by *Frontline,* Piazza made the following charges:

1. That from 1968 to 1970 he was involved in the Beckley/Sklaroff bookmaking syndicate, operating under the direction of Dudley and Berry, as well as Sklaroff.

2. That he knew of numerous professional football games that had been "fixed" during those years in which his gambling syndicate worked in cooperation with players.

3. That—at the direction of Sklaroff—he had gone to Kansas City and personally delivered a $795,000 payoff which he believed was intended for three members of the Kansas City Chiefs: head coach Hank Stram, quarterback Len Dawson, and defensive cornerback Emmitt Thomas.[6]

4. That these people had been allegedly paid for their cooperation to "fix" the supposed last game of the 1969 regular season between the Kansas City Chiefs and the San Diego Chargers, in which the Chargers upset the Chiefs, 27–24.

5. That Piazza's gambling syndicate had made between $4.5 million and $5 million as a result of having the game ensured.

6. That another game between Kansas City and the Oakland Raiders earlier in the year had also been fixed.

A spokesman for the *Frontline* program said, "We had two different versions of the show ready for broadcast. One named the players Piazza mentioned and the other did not. We went with the latter because we had no evidence of gambling associations against the third man [Thomas]. And, in the end, we simply ran out of time."

What makes Piazza's allegations suspect is the fact that the Kansas City Chiefs did not lose the last game of the 1969 season to San Diego. In the history of the Kansas City–San Diego rivalry, there has never been a final score that ended up 27–24, regardless of who won.

In an attempt to verify Piazza's charges, *Frontline* hired the Philip Manuel Resource Group, a respected Washington consulting firm, to conduct an investigation.[7] The independent probe showed that

1. Any wiretaps supporting Piazza, particularly those targeting Sklaroff, would have already been destroyed. None of the prosecutors who was involved in the Sklaroff case could remember "any wiretapped conversation involving Sklaroff in which there was talk of a specific pro-football fix." The prosecutors—who did recall discussions about the Chiefs' being taken off the boards—could not rule out the possibility that a transcript of such a conversation might have existed at some point. However, Manuel's investigation showed that "to date there is no corroboration of the existence of wiretap information which bears on Piazza's alleged trip to Kansas City."

2. Piazza's description of himself as a key figure in the Beckley/Sklaroff–Dudley/Berry gambling syndicate was true, and that he was particularly active from 1967 to 1970. Also, Piazza was linked with John Owen Tyler, an Atlanta bookmaker, who "repeatedly took Kansas City off the boards in the late 60s."

During my interview with Len Dawson, I read him the official unedited transcript of the *Frontline* interview with Piazza and told him that Piazza had passed the voice stress evaluation test. Dawson replied, "You know, because of that program, not only did he [Piazza] take a test, but I had to take one, too. They [the NFL] did it just to clarify it. The NFL Security people and Warren Welsh flew into Kansas City and were out at the Marriott hotel by the airport. I had to clear myself all over again."

Once again, Dawson passed the test, proving his innocence. Dawson continued, "I'll tell you who was really hot when that PBS program came out: John Brodie [the star quarterback of the San Francisco 49ers from 1957 to 1973]. He wanted to sue them because it implicated all the starting quarterbacks in that era. He had gotten a tape [of the program] and looked it over and wanted all the quarterbacks of that era to see if we could get a lawsuit against public television."

Dawson said that it was laughable that Emmitt Thomas would be involved in anything like that. "Of all people, Emmitt Thomas, why, he's the most superstitious guy in the world. I was quiet my first few years of professional football; but Emmitt was that way all the way through. I never ran around with Emmitt or hung out with him, other than on the football field."

Stram, who was not polygraphed, laughed off Piazza's charges, repeating that he had never gambled on anything in his life. More concerned with the claim against his onetime defensive star, Stram told me, "I never heard Emmitt Thomas's name mentioned with a gambling issue. You'd have to know Emmitt to understand that he would never even consider anything like that."

When I contacted Thomas and told him what Piazza had said, he told me that he wanted to talk to Len Dawson first and would then get back to me—which he never did.

When I asked Dawson why he was the target of so many rumors over the years, particularly regarding his alleged relationship with a variety of bookmakers and even the Civella Mafia family in Kansas City, he said, "I don't know why they singled me out. Maybe it's because I'm the quarterback. In 1966, I started my career in broadcasting. Maybe that was it: because I was so visible. I had four radio shows a day, five days a week, and I was the sports director of the television station in Kansas City. I was doing the six o'clock and the ten o'clock sports, starting in 1966 and all through that period. So Monday through Friday, everybody knew where I was."

Len Dawson was inducted into the Pro Football Hall of Fame in 1987.

44 The Double Standard

ON JANUARY 20, 1983—just three days after the *Frontline* broadcast and five days after Lansky's death in bed—Allen Dorfman, the onetime fiduciary manager of the Teamsters' Central States Pension Fund, was murdered by three ski-masked gunmen who approached him while he was walking across a parking lot in Lincolnwood, a Chicago suburb. He had been prominently mentioned in the PBS story because of his loans to Las Vegas casinos. At the scene of his slaying, Dorfman was accompanied by an old friend Irwin Weiner, the longtime bail bondsman for the Teamsters Union, who also had ties to numerous organized-crime figures. Weiner, who was not a target, ducked behind a car and escaped uninjured.

In addition to his pension fund activities, Dorfman was also involved in sports-gambling operations. The names of several NFL owners, coaches, and players were in his address book: Dallas Cowboys owner Clint Murchison, former Chicago Bears quarterback Sid Luckman, former Washington Redskins president Edward Bennett Williams, and former Minnesota Vikings running back Ed Marinaro, who had become an actor with a role on NBC's *Hill Street Blues.*[1] No NFL member listed in Dorfman's address book was ever charged with any wrongdoing.

Just the previous month, Dorfman had been convicted of conspiring to bribe U.S. Senator Howard Cannon of Nevada, culminating the FBI's Pendorf—Penetrate Dorfman—investigation that had been initiated in 1979. In return for his influence to defeat a bill providing for the deregulation of the trucking industry on behalf of the Teamsters, Cannon, who was not indicted, was offered property owned by the union's pension fund. Evidence in the case had been accumulated with the help of court-authorized wiretaps. Four other men were convicted with Dorfman, including Teamsters general president Roy Williams and Chicago Mafia capo Joseph Lombardo, who was Tony Spilotro's immediate supervisor. The sixty-year-old Dorfman was facing a maximum fifty-five-year prison sentence.[2]

"There was a real fear among the Chicago mob that Dorfman was ready to talk to save himself," Patrick Healy, then head of the Chicago Crime Commission, told me. "And if Dorfman had decided to talk, he could have done some serious damage. The Mafia was well aware of that fact. They knew that he was not prepared to spend the rest of his life in jail. The murder was a blatant effort to silence him. And among the subjects Dorfman could have discussed was NFL football."

Spilotro was again the key suspect for being responsible for making the arrangements for the Dorfman hit.[3] Four alleged Chicago hit men—Anthony Panzica, Frank Schweihs, Ron DeAngeles, and former Chicago Cardinals defensive tackle Wayne Bock—were all called to testify before a federal grand jury in Chicago that was probing the Dorfman murder.

Two months after the airing of the *Frontline* documentary, twenty-three-year-old Art Schlichter, a reserve quarterback with the Baltimore Colts, admitted to having placed bets on sporting events with four Baltimore bookmakers. Schlichter's bookies had all been indicted by a federal grand jury in Columbus, Ohio—where Schlichter had starred at Ohio State University and became an all-American, and where his parents were active on the harness-racing circuit. Schlichter had aided the FBI in its investigation.

Schlichter—who had received a $145,000-a-year salary as well as a $350,000 signing bonus from the Colts in 1982—had gone into heavy debt to the bookmakers, reportedly betting mostly on basketball games. He lost as much as $700,000 in bets during a two-year period. Schlichter, who had also made wagers on no fewer than ten NFL games, denied ever placing a bet on a game in which the Colts played.[4]

When he was unable to pay his gambling debts, the bookmakers reportedly threatened to go to the Colts and tell the team that he had been calling them regularly from a pay telephone just prior to game time. Schlichter had spent so much time in a locker room phone booth that several of his teammates once placed his equipment in the booth as a prank. However, in response to the blackmail attempt, Schlichter went to the FBI. The FBI then monitored the telephone calls of the bookmakers, which served as the basis for their indictments.

On May 20, 1983, Pete Rozelle suspended Schlichter indefinitely for his gambling habits and his associations with bookmakers. At the time of the announcement, Schlichter was in a rehabilitation program being treated for compulsive gambling. Schlichter was the first player since Alex Karras and Paul Hornung to be suspended on charges of gambling and associating with gamblers. The only other players suspended for gambling associations had been Frank Filchock and Merle Hapes in 1946.

In his statement, Rozelle said, in part, "I accept [Schlichter's] statement that he has never bet on or against his own team, attempted to improperly affect the outcome of any game, or accepted money or anything of value from those who might have been interested in doing so."

Three of the four bookmakers with whom Schlichter had done business later pleaded guilty to lesser charges; those against the fourth man were dropped.[5] Like Karras and Hornung, Schlichter was reinstated after a one-year suspension.[6]

In an interview with Paul Attner of *The Washington Post,* Cleveland Browns owner Art Modell, commenting on the Schlichter case, used the age-old line: "I just don't believe there is a lot of this type of gambling activity going on in the league. You can't keep a secret that long in this business, mainly because [of] the bookmakers who would report any big swing in odds. I remember in 1964, I left one of our practices just as Frank Ryan twisted an ankle. Twelve minutes later, when I arrived at my office, I already had a call from the league. They wanted to know why our game that week had been taken off the boards."

Modell was not asked whether he conducted an investigation of who on his team or staff had leaked the inside information about Ryan's ankle to the bookmakers during those twelve minutes.

The Schlichter affair, coming on the heels of *Frontline,* seemed to cause another round of attempts to get at football's hidden cancer. Interestingly, just a few months earlier, on the day of the *Frontline* broadcast, the *Akron Beacon Journal* was in the midst of its three-part series about Art Modell. In part, news reporter Peter Phipps charged, "In New York, he [Modell] worked in an advertising firm with two clients linked to the underworld. In Cleveland, he raced horses with a man prominently mentioned in the Senate's Kefauver investigation into organized crime 30 years ago, despite an NFL prohibition against associating with gamblers . . . Modell, however, does not deny that his associates have included personalities ranging from professional gamblers to the country's most esteemed citizens."

Of course, only Schlichter was suspended because of his gambling connections. The NFL didn't give much thought to doing the same to Modell.

After the Modell series and Schlichter's suspension, the players, perhaps in self-defense, publicly complained about the NFL owners. Ed Garvey, the executive director of the NFL Players Association, told me, "You have the commissioner and his office, hired by management and serving at their pleasure. It's obvious that the servant is not going to rise up and slay the master. To suggest that there is a 'double standard' is to suggest that there is also a possibility of objectivity.

"It's like the old song, 'Whose Side Are You On?' If you have a bargaining table, Rozelle sits on the owners side. He is a part of them. So there can only be one standard. And that is: What management does through his office is to investigate players. Rozelle doesn't have the authority or the mandate for the owners to be looking at themselves."

Besides Modell, Garvey was also specifically referring to Leonard Tose, the owner of Philadelphia Eagles. Tose, an admitted gambler, who said that his favorite game was blackjack (he reputedly bet as much as $70,000 a hand), reportedly lost millions of dollars at gaming tables in Las Vegas and Atlantic City. "He's probably one of the worst blackjack players I've ever seen," a casino source told *The Philadelphia Inquirer.* "He was a sweetheart to deal with. He paid us like he was a man with no worries." But nothing could be further from the truth.

In 1980, when Tose needed relief from his debts, he received a $400,000 loan from Hugh Culverhouse, the owner of the Tampa Bay Buccaneers. Three years later, Culverhouse guaranteed a $3 million loan for Tose. By that time Tose was rumored to have at least $2 million in gambling debts. Another NFL owner financially helping out Tose was William Clay Ford of the Detroit Lions, who arranged for Tose to receive loans from a bank controlled by the Ford family.[7]

The NFL constitution prohibits owners from lending money to each other.

In January 1983, Rozelle commented defensively on Tose's behavior. "I would be a hell of a lot more concerned if I knew that [a player] had bet at the casinos," he said. "An owner doesn't control the outcome of a game. So when you talk about the credibility of the game, anyone close to football knows that an owner doesn't interfere with the coaches and players. He's not going to send in plays, except in infrequent situations. But he's not going to have a big effect."

In spite of all the gambling problems in professional sports and the disastrous Delaware NFL lottery, Governor Mario Cuomo of New York supported another state-run sports-gambling operation in the fall of 1983, which was expected to produce massive revenues "for education." Cuomo specifically wanted gambling on professional football, basketball, and baseball legalized via a state lottery, which he predicted would raise $100 million a year as an extension of New York's Off-Track Betting operation. New York's state attorney general Robert Abrams insisted the Cuomo plan violated state law "both through its specific bans on bookmaking and pool-selling and through its general ban on all forms of gambling not expressly authorized."

Soon after, the Cuomo plan collapsed and died.

Also, during the summer of 1984, former Washington Redskins quarterback Billy Kilmer took over Johnny Unitas's Baltimore-based handicapping business. Unitas, who had accepted a job with International Harvester, had quit the controversial enterprise under pressure from the NFL.

When asked who applied the pressure on Unitas to sell his interest in the tout sheet, NFL Security chief Warren Welsh told me, "That was done by the commissioner. Unitas, at that time, had a position with the Colts in an advisory capacity. It was distressing."[8]

Unitas told me, "I got out of it because I was getting so much abuse from sportswriters and people across the country that I was ruining my reputation—and I'm contributing to gambling. And

I said, 'Wait a minute, you people, as sportswriters, condone it in your newspapers by printing the line. The National Football League condones it because they allow the television networks to pick games with the point spreads. You guys are promoting it yourself. Every damn newspaper in this country has some writer on their staff making picks. And I was contributing to gambling? Come on. All I was doing was analyzing a couple of games."

The new service was called *The Billy Kilmer All-Pro Football Super Service,* which promised to pick almost nothing but winners and make all subscribers wealthy. His promotional literature read, "I'm Billy Kilmer and . . . I Have Started a Football Handicapping Service to Destroy the Las Vegas Spread!" Also like Unitas, Kilmer promised to deliver inside information. "As a former pro, I'm well known . . . Heck, when your name is Billy Kilmer you can't avoid finding out the important football information."

Washington Post columnist Ken Denlinger quoted Kilmer as saying, "I don't have any qualms about it. I've never been hypocritical in my life. The NFL was made strong by people betting all over the country . . . I don't care what Pete Rozelle says."

Kilmer might not have cared what Rozelle said, but his wife did. When I tried to interview Kilmer, it was his wife who called me back and responded on his behalf. "Billy was a consultant," Sandy Kilmer told me. "This service was not something that Billy started or that he ran. The man from Baltimore [handicapper Mike Warren] did. Mike called Billy and said that Johnny Unitas wasn't going to do it anymore, and how would he [Kilmer] like to do it. And Billy said, 'I'll try it for a while.' And that was the service. It was Mike Warren Sports. Billy had one sheet that they sent out, and they used Billy's name, of course. But it was a nine hundred number that you called to get his picks. Billy had nothing to do with any mailing lists or anything. There was a TV part of it too. They would tape him for cable, and they would have his picks, like Jimmy the Greek.

"Billy [later] got out of it, because it wasn't being run like he thought it ought to be. People would call him, and say that they were calling his number and not getting any response. So Billy called Mike and said, 'This is not what you said it would be.' And he got out of it."

Warren did not respond to my request for an interview.

Mrs. Kilmer insisted that her husband never made a bet on a game while he was an active player. Interestingly, just the previous year, several publications in the Washington area reported that Kilmer and another former Redskins quarterback Sonny Jurgensen had become partners in two Tony Roma's restaurant franchises in Washington suburbs and received a 12.5 percent interest at no cost to them. The majority owner of the franchise was Clint Murchison, who had had other business dealings with Kilmer.

Mrs. Kilmer also disputed these reports. "Billy and Sonny didn't have a percentage in Tony Roma's. When Tony Roma's opened up there, the business used their names. But they didn't get a piece of the action. Clint was sick at the time. So Clint's son ran it. They [the ex-players] never really did anything with it. They had very poor management in there. Billy and Sonny would go there, hang around there, and we'd all go to dinner there a lot. But they never had anything to do with the management of it. They never got anything out of it. There was some talk of them having a part of it after it got going. There was a discussion that they would have an option. But nothing ever came of it. They never owned any of it.

"Billy and Clint were not in business together at all. Clint and Billy were friends. Clint was one of the nicest people you'd ever want to meet in your life. He was a fantastic person who loved Billy to death. Billy worked for Clint in the Nevada National Bank [which Murchison bought in 1982]. They didn't have any business dealings."

With Allen Glick's cooperation, the FBI's Strawman/Argent operation climaxed. Federal investigators amassed a wealth of information, with the help of Glick and court-authorized wiretaps, about the Stardust and the sports-gambling scene in Las Vegas. On September 30, 1983—after a five-year investigation—the most sweeping indictment against organized-crime figures was handed up for their roles in a $1.6 million casino-skimming operation.[9] Glick was neither indicted nor named as an unindicted coconspirator. Former Cleveland Mafia boss Angelo Lonardo and former Teamsters general president Roy Williams, who had both been convicted in unrelated cases, testified as government witnesses, as did Glick.

Sheryle L. Jeans, one of the prosecutors in the case, said, "In short, the defendants are charged with conspiring to have a hidden interest in and receive skim money from particular Las Vegas casinos: the Stardust, the Fremont, the Hacienda, and the Marina."

"Just about everybody who was anybody in the underworld was involved," a top FBI agent involved in the case told me. "It's a devastating blow to them. Since 1974, these people had used their influence on Teamsters officials to receive multimillion-dollar loans for their front men, and then they skimmed the profits from these investments."

Glick told me, "None of the people indicted in [the Stardust case] were my associates. I testified as to what I believed to be the truth. I wanted the record set straight after years of untruths and unproven rumors, bad reporting and even bad work on the government's part—until they had clear and convincing outside evidence that I had done nothing wrong."

Unfortunately, little evidence from the Stardust case has been made public about the organized-crime syndicate's influence on professional sports, particularly on NFL football. "Those matters are peripheral to the focus of the case: hidden ownership and skimming at the Stardust," a Strike Force attorney told me. "Don't expect to ever see that other stuff [about the NFL] come out."

Interviewed by *The New York Times,* former NFL Security chief William Hundley's protégé, David Margolis, the head of the Justice Department's Organized Crime and Racketeering Section, said, "We're aware of the sizable amounts of money involved in illegal bookmaking. And we know that much of it comes through professional football. But at the moment, we don't see any organized-crime activity that threatens the integrity of the National Football League."

45 Gambling or Drugs?

IN THE WAKE OF the NFL ticket-scalping scandal, the *Frontline* presentation, widespread drug use, the Schlichter gambling probe, and Leonard Tose's bad luck at the blackjack tables in Atlantic City, most professional sports beefed up their security procedures. Like the NFL, Bowie Kuhn hired security agents in June 1983 in each of the cities that play major-league baseball, to "monitor gambling, scalping, and other matters."[1]

While the NFL was in the midst of its gambling and drugs scandals, Kuhn, who had been the commissioner of major-league baseball for fourteen years, was forced to resign by the team owners in August 1983. In a tribute to Kuhn, columnist Thomas Boswell of *The Washington Post* wrote, "At the simplest level, Kuhn really does love baseball and truly does believe that maintaining its public image of integrity is his central job as commissioner . . . What baseball needs is a person of ingrained moral sense who understands that gambling and drug-use among players, and racketeers in the boardroom, constitute the most fundamental concern of any pro sport."

The National Basketball Association, which has had its own internal security force since 1972, began a joint program with the U.S. Drug Enforcement Administration to educate players about the impact of narcotics on professional sports and the gambling and bribery that goes along with it. Also, the National Hockey League, which has had its own security unit since 1971, increased its forces.

Of course, Howard Cosell knew just what questions needed

to be asked. On that sports reporter's popular *SportsBeat* program, during a discussion about the Schlichter affair, Cosell asked commissioner Rozelle, "Do you think players other than Schlichter are gambling?"

"I don't think so," Rozelle replied. "I think it's a very isolated case . . . The players know that it strikes at the integrity of the game, and I don't think there's gambling in the National Football League . . . Gambling goes right to the heart of our sport's integrity . . ."

"But what about drug users? Carl Eller of Minnesota went bankrupt because of drugs. When a man gets into fiscal trouble because of the use of drugs, doesn't that, too, go right to the integrity of the game?"

"It could, it could. And it's a serious problem. I'm not attempting to play down the problem of drugs. I'm merely saying what gambling does directly, rather than indirectly, to the integrity of the game. And that's why it's such a problem for us, and a lot of players know that we will not tolerate it."[2]

Both men were right, because the problems of gambling and drugs were already dovetailing.

In June 1983, Tony Vaccarino, the FBI's national coordinator for gambling and sports-bribery investigations, stated during a seminar at the National Association of Collegiate Directors of Athletics convention that cocaine had become an epidemic in college and professional sports and could cause players to participate in fixed games. "I think there is a strong likelihood it does exist. It can be easily done—especially in the over-under where a bettor bets on the total points scored . . . We know many big-time athletes are involved in a very large scale of using cocaine." Vaccarino, who was involved in the Art Schlichter and 1979 referee-fixing investigations, added that despite the high salaries of the players, "the price of cocaine is very, very expensive."

Just a few months before the seminar, on March 4, 1983, former all-pro lineman John Niland of the Dallas Cowboys had been indicted for cocaine possession. Within the next few weeks, he was arrested again for driving while intoxicated. Also, Jim Clack, a former center for the New York Giants, was indicted for conspiracy to deliver cocaine. Both players were placed on probation.

That same month, Washington Redskins veteran running back Clarence Harmon was arrested for possession of cocaine in

Texarkana, Texas. Harmon, who pleaded guilty and was placed on probation, did not play the 1983 season in the NFL.

In July, the month after the seminar, Rozelle suspended, for all of the 1983 preseason play as well as the first four regular season games, four players for their drug abuse: Ross Browner and Pete Johnson of the Cincinnati Bengals, Greg Stemrick of the New Orleans Saints, and E. J. Junior of the St. Louis Cardinals. Both Junior and Stemrick had been arrested and pleaded no contest to possession charges in separate cases. Browner and Johnson, who had both admitted their cocaine use, had been given immunity as part of their plea-bargaining defense.

Soon after, Tony Peters, a star defensive back for the Washington Redskins, was arrested by DEA agents at the Redskins' training camp in Carlisle, Pennsylvania, for engaging in a coke deal with an undercover agent. He pleaded guilty and was also suspended from the NFL.

Rozelle's actions against the five players marked the first NFL front-office-imposed suspensions for illegal drug use. In announcing the suspensions, Rozelle said, "Involvement with illegal drugs poses numerous risks to the integrity of professional football and the public's confidence in it . . . Such involvement may also give rise to pressures on players to alter their performance on field in the interests of illegal gamblers."

The basic drug policy enforced by Rozelle and the NFL was a three-step process, which had been negotiated in the 1982 NFL Players Association contract:

Step 1: After a player tests positive in a drug test, he must voluntarily begin an approved drug-rehabilitation program.

Step 2: If the player tests positive a second time, he is immediately suspended for thirty days, placed on his team's non-playing reserve list, and must again enter a drug-rehabilitation program.

Step 3: If the player tests positive for a third time, he is automatically banned from the NFL; but he can appeal the suspension after one year.

Drug tests were permitted once in the preseason and once during the regular season—if "probable cause" could be demonstrated.

Also as part of the agreement, the league and the NFLPA jointly selected the Hazelden Foundation—a drug-rehabilitation program in Center City, Minnesota, which had been in operation since 1949—as the NFL's official treatment center.

The NFLPA responded to Rozelle's announced suspensions on August 4, 1983, in *The New York Times,* blaming Rozelle for not adopting a consistent antidrug policy. "Since Mr. Rozelle has not articulated a policy, players—not knowing what to expect—now will think twice before admitting a dependency," wrote Ed Garvey, who the previous month had been replaced by Gene Upshaw as the executive director of the NFLPA. "Is a player who admits a dependency subject to suspension? If a player is not dependent but is convicted, will he be suspended? If he is not convicted of a crime but aids in the prosecution of others and in the process admits having purchased drugs, is this enough to warrant suspension? . . . It is time to stop treating this as a public relations problem and to start treating it as one of the most serious problems in our society."

Soon after the five suspensions, five members of the Dallas Cowboys—Larry Bethea, Tony Dorsett, Tony Hill, Harvey Martin, and Ron Springs—were linked to federal cocaine investigations. The names of Bethea, Dorsett, Martin, and Springs had been picked up on federal wiretaps and all had been identified as cocaine users. Although these four players had denied it, they reportedly engaged in plea-bargaining sessions with federal prosecutors. Also Hill and Martin had been subpoenaed to testify as defense witnesses in the cocaine-smuggling case of Lauriberto Ignacio, a former professional soccer player who had tried out to be the Cowboys' placekicker but was cut. Although Ignacio was convicted, no member of the Cowboys was accused of any wrongdoing.[3]

On October 31, 1983, in the midst of all the turmoil within the NFL, league charter member George Halas died at age eighty-eight and was succeeded by his forty-two-year-old grandson Michael McCaskey—an ex–Peace Corps volunteer in Ethiopia. McCaskey also received his undergraduate degree from Yale and his doctorate in business from Case Western Reserve. The owner of a management consulting firm in Massachusetts, McCaskey also was a member of the faculty of the Harvard Business School.

With Halas's death, the old world of professional football officially came to an end. The new age was ascending.

46 The Computer Group

IN LAS VEGAS, A GROUP of gamblers who used computer technology to aid their handicapping and betting was creating a stir. Known by the local gaming community only as the Computer group, it was rumored to be backed by wealthy New York businessmen, probably from Wall Street, who were betting enormous sums of money on a variety of sporting events. Each week, the Computer group poured so much money into the betting pool that the line moved, causing the legal Vegas sports books and illegal bookmakers around the country to make adjustments.

On NFL games alone, the Computer group routinely bet as much as $250,000 a game. Wagers were placed with numerous bookmakers. Sophisticated gamblers outside the computer circle were so impressed with the group's record that they began to bet with it once they saw the line begin to change—to the chagrin of legal and illegal bookmakers, who occasionally could not lay off their bets because of the high, one-sided volume and the rapidly changing line.

The Computer group had begun during the late 1970s, primarily betting on horses. The bettors who were involved with the Computer operation allegedly had obtained inside information about fixed horse races on the East Coast. They would bet heavily on these races at the legal sports books in Las Vegas but cover their apparent knowledge of the fixed races by betting moderately on races that were not fixed. Consequently, the Computer group began destroying the legal books in Vegas.

"While I was running the Stardust sports book in 1978–79," Marty Kane told me, "I got so goddamn hot at the Computer guys that I told them to get the hell out of the Stardust. And if they didn't, I'd run their asses out. My responsibility was to make the Stardust win. And what they were doing was absolute dynamite.

"The Computer guys would play slow, and then they'd send their beards in and they'd play big. We got so jammed up with these horses that they could, in one day, take the profit away from the casino for three months. They'd come and bet twenty-five horses in a day; and they might have two or three races in which something was going on [that were fixed]. And they'd load you up with those, but they'd cover it up by giving you a lot of other horses, which came by way of the computer."

After several Boston-based bookmakers were indicted and convicted for fixing horse races, the Computer horse-betting operation ceased.

"So all of a sudden, they came along with football," Kane continues. "And they had two fabulous years. They won a lot of goddamn money. They drove bookmakers crazy all over the country. The Computer guys were handicappers and bettors. I know guys around here who made so much money with these goddamn guys, it was unbelievable."

An FBI investigation of the Computer group began in Las Vegas in early 1984. Through a succession of wiretaps authorized by U.S. District Judge Lloyd D. George, the FBI collected information that no fewer than eight people had been involved in the illegal gambling business, simply known as Computer. The mastermind of the group was Dr. Ivan Mindlin of Las Vegas, an orthopedic surgeon who was sidelined from his practice by a 1981 car accident after founding his gambling empire.

Las Vegas gambler Lem Banker told me, "Mindlin loved to gamble and was a very intelligent guy. I got to know him, and he asked me how to handicap. I showed him some basic things. Then he started getting into sports.

"After he had some personal problems during the late 1960s, Mindlin left Vegas for New Jersey. When he got there, he called me and asked if I knew any gamblers. I'm originally from Union City, New Jersey, so I went back and introduced him to a few friends of mine. Mindlin got into gambling there and was moving money for Gil Beckley.

"Mindlin later returned to Vegas in the early 1970s, and he met a guy named Johnny Bura, who was from Youngstown. They called him 'the Machine.' Bura was one of the first sports gamblers to use a computer, and he was a bookmaker who would only deal with professionals. Mindlin learned how to use Bura's computer, and then he put together a crew of computer specialists."

The FBI described Mindlin's Computer group as a highly sophisticated illegal bookmaking operation. "They are taking bets and laying them off with local, legal books [in Las Vegas]," an FBI affidavit asserted.

Mindlin, with houses in Las Vegas and Vail, Colorado, was accused by the FBI of directing his associate William Thurman Walters to place layoff bets for the Computer group. According to the FBI, "Walters operates a large bookmaking operation which he uses to place bets with legal and illegal bookmakers for the 'Computer' group. Walters will contact illegal bookmakers and place bets on desired games and point spreads or [Computer associate Glen Andrews] Walker will contact various bookmakers and 'beards' and instruct them on how to place certain bets for the 'Computer' group."

Illegal bookmakers around the country had grown suspicious of those associated with the Computer group—whom they learned to identify—and some refused to accept their bets. Consequently, the Computer group established a national network of beards, with no visible connection to the Computer group, to place its bets.

The FBI report continued, "Mindlin commonly gives Walters a 'Computer' order on a particular game at a particular point spread and tells Walters that the order is 'open.' This is believed to mean that the 'Computer' group will accept as much in wagers as can be obtained on the desired game and line."

The FBI chose the day before the 1985 Super Bowl to raid the group. As one agent explains, historically it is the day before Super Sunday when bookmakers receive their largest volume of bets from gamblers. Thus it was guaranteed that the Computer group would be active.[1]

The Computer group won an estimated 65 percent of its wagers. Its big betting money often forced the point spread of a sporting event to be dramatically altered. For instance, it bet so much on one team in a college football game that the point spread went from six to eight points for the other team. Then, minutes before the game, the Computer group doubled its bet on the opposing team—with the inflated eight-point handicap. The ideal situation was for the team it bet on first to win by seven points—thus allowing the group to catch a middle and win both bets, which it often did.

The biggest victims appeared to be the small-time, illegal bookmakers around the country who received the last-minute bets from the Computer group's beards and had no time to lay off these bets with bigger bookmakers.

Mindlin and Walters each received 7 percent of the profits, according to the FBI. Walters then paid off his staff with a share of his earnings. On a single day, Walters netted $100,000 and gave his associate Walker 2 percent of that amount. In 1984 alone, the Computer group netted $25 million. At the time of the January 19, 1985, raids, the Computer group was preparing to purchase a large business building in New York City.

After conducting successful raids on forty-five locations in twenty-three cities in sixteen states, federal officials described the Computer group as the largest sports-betting operation in history. More than fifty people were under investigation—but no indictments were ever brought.

However, the brains of the Computer group insisted that they were only handicappers and bettors and nothing more.

During my interview with Mindlin, he told me, "The FBI raided the Stardust because there was skimming going on. They just came in the middle of the day, closed it, and then reopened it with other people becoming the managers. The former people were barred from coming into the place. And the FBI used the opportunity to go through everything, the books and records. Well, one of the things that came under scrutiny was the sports book.

"So they called me in, and they wanted to know who I had given money to in the hotel organization. And I said, 'What are you talking about?' And the FBI agent said, 'We know as a fact that you have given over seventy thousand dollars to someone in this organization.' I asked, 'How did I do that?' He said, 'It was very clever of you. We happened to pick up on it, and when we added it up we figured out what happened. You see, every time you won a thousand dollars, they credited you with a thousand dollars. But every time you lost, you paid him eleven hundred dollars. So the plurality of the hundred dollars over the thousand dollars is the method you used to give the extra hundred dollars to someone.'

"I looked at the guy—this is the guy in charge of an FBI gambling investigation—and said, 'Do you know what eleven-ten is?' He said no. And that was the initial start of their investigation.

"When the raids took place, they claimed that it had become a layoff operation. It was totally ludicrous. You don't have to be a psychology Ph.D. to understand that if a person is a bettor and is doing well, the last thing in the world he is going to do is to change it and go into something illegal.

"Anyone who knows anything about gambling recognizes that if you have devised a way to beat a game—any game, whether it be commodities, the stock market, sports betting, casinos, anything—the last thing in the world you would do would be to change the rules that you have, with regard to bookie versus bettor. Because, as a bettor, you have the sense of what it is you want to do. A bookie has to be passive. And the bettor might end up doing what the bookie wanted to do. Plain, cold mathematical logic tells you that a guy who is a successful bettor is never going to become a bookmaker."

I asked Las Vegas oddsmaker Michael Roxborough about the Computer group and Mindlin. "I know who he is," Roxborough replied. "Nobody really knows what he was doing. And to this day I have trouble tracking [his operation]. I didn't really care where the money was coming from but if anybody asked me, 'Where was it coming from—from the guys booking or betting?' I really couldn't tell. Sometimes they would have a really big impact on the college games. Those games would really move. On the pros, there's so much money being bet, sometimes the games didn't move all that much."

Roxborough explains that the Computer group was destroying most of the oddsmakers and legal bookmakers in Las Vegas. "They drove us up a wall one year in colleges," he says. "They were betting early in the week and late in the week, and I could never figure out what they were doing. I remember that we had to beat them to win one season, and we didn't beat them. They were real good on colleges. And then the following year, they were real, real bad.

"But the year they had was real good. When the people know you're running real good, you get a lot of followers. A lot of people were tagging on to their games, and it was a bad year for the books."

Scott Schettler, the manager of the Stardust Sports Book since 1983, told me, "At the Stardust, I don't gamble. I book. Now the Computers had good years and bad years. To a bookmaker, that means nothing. Because all I'm doing is bringing the winners and the losers together in my sports book and hoping they both make a bet. Regardless of whether the Computers win or lose, I know how to maneuver the business to get money on the other side.

"I am a bookmaker. I do not know who is going to win or lose the games. I put the number up on the board, and then I change the point spread as the money comes in. So no matter who wins or loses, I don't care.

"Let's say that the Computer guys did win twenty-five million dollars. Theoretically, if you book your games right, you had twenty-five million bet on the other side. So for every big winner, there is a big loser. And all I want is the juice. That's just the basic theory of bookmaking."

47 Oddsmaker

MICHAEL ROXBOROUGH IS THE heir to Bobby Martin, the man who sets the line for Las Vegas on sporting events, mostly on NFL games.[1] Roxy went to high school in Vancouver, British Columbia, and became a student of political science at American University in Washington, D.C. He switched to psychology at the University of Nevada at Las Vegas.

Bringing an academic but extremely sophisticated approach to oddsmaking, Roxborough is the president of Las Vegas Sports Consultants, which he founded in 1981, and which has a staff of five full-time employees.[2]

Roxborough is anything but flashy. He dresses like an insurance agent, wearing dark suits, basic white shirts, and conservative ties. His wife teaches Sunday school in Las Vegas. He is an intense, no-nonsense man, who hardly drinks and never smokes. A vegetarian who swims a half mile four days a week, he is more like Charles McNeil, the University of Chicago mathematician who refined the point spread system, rather than a streetwise Bobby Martin or a flamboyant Kentucky gentleman like Ed Curd.

Roxborough's office is on the twelfth floor of the Valley Bank Center on Convention Center Drive, down the street from the Las Vegas Convention Center and up a few doors from the Stardust, just off the Strip. The main room where Roxborough's staff works is Spartan. There is no artwork, no football posters on the walls. There are three desks, five chairs, several wire machines, a large IBM computer, and a slew of pocket calculators.

There is a clutter of long sheets of paper from the wire services scattered about the room, mostly filled with general sporting news, and more important, results of the recent college and professional football games, including player injuries and other data. The sports sections of several daily newspapers and weekly and monthly sports magazines are piled atop the desks. They are creased, underlined, and marked up, highlighting bits of trivia, which might figure as variables in some oddsmaking equation.

Roxy's adjacent private office is equally unspectacular except when his window shades are open. He has a panoramic view of the Strip. The most sophisticated piece of equipment on his desk is a small fax machine.

"I got interested in oddsmaking because I liked to go to the racetrack, and I liked to gamble," Roxborough told me. "It's funny. I thought gambling was a good thing to do, and I thought it would be great to be a professional gambler. When I came to Las Vegas, I learned that it was different than I thought. I wanted to be a professional gambler to escape conventional work. What I found out was, yes, I was escaping conventional work, but it looked like I was going to have to work sixty hours a week to do it. I figured: It's not really glamorous, and it's a lot of work. And I also found that people don't make a lot of money by just going out and trying to pick winners. These gamblers are value people or arbitragers.

"It's like the stock market. The real money isn't being made by guys who are trying to pick stocks that are going up so much. It's being made by guys who can arbitrage, who can buy and sell at a profit, immediately. That's basically the way the game is here. I thought it would be great if you could sleep until noon, drink a few beers, pick a few games, and collect a few tickets. I think most people come to Vegas for that type of life-style, but it doesn't work that way. If you think it does work that way, well, there are some people who spend several years going broke and getting into money, and then going broke again—because they think that's the life-style. I just didn't think it was for me."

Roxborough's mentor is Herb Lambeck, better known in Vegas as Herbie Hoops, because he was to basketball oddsmaking what Bob Martin was to the football weekly line. "I wanted to learn how to make a line, but no one ever wanted to work with me," Roxborough says. "With Herb, it was a real close-knit thing. He listened to me. I used to try to do some work for him, so I wasn't just a guy taking up his time. There was no remuneration for it. I did it to try to keep me on top of the game, so that I would learn more about it. The first time I was paid for making a line was when I started my own business in 1981."

Although most people have been amazed at his rapid success, Roxborough is philosophical about it. "I think it was the type of thing where I was doing some work that was good. But, more important, I was in the right place at the right time. I think what happened was that I was providing a service that probably no one else was. In other words, I had made a business out of just line making. I had an office. I had a spot where you could actually reach me or somebody from six-thirty in the morning to seven at night. No one had ever thought of doing it that way.

"The [legal sports-gambling] business was exploding in Las Vegas, and there weren't a lot of managers to fill these new race and sports books. Because of that, people would call up who didn't have as much expertise as previous oddsmakers, and they needed people to help them. We had an office that was available that did that. And we were here and doing a pretty good job for the people we were servicing. And we got on a big wave.

"We provide services to licensed [casino] operators. What makes our service unique from others is that we are oddsmakers, so we are actually making the point spreads. We are not copying them from somebody else. The other thing that makes us unique is that we only deal with licensed operators. You have to be licensed by some governmental agency. We also do a place in the Caribbean and a place in England. So that makes us a little different too. In other words, we will not provide odds to private individuals. We will not go across state lines to other people.

"So we furnish casinos in Nevada with odds that they can post on betting events that we feel are going to get a good cross section of the betting public. We don't want to get too esoteric. I don't do something like a small-time fight or collegiate high-jumping contest. I deal with those sports that have broad public interest. And that is in the best interest of the casinos because they'll attract enough action to create a profit. The NFL has the broadest public interest by far."

Contrasting his operation to that of Bobby Martin, Roxborough continues, "We do it a little differently. The man-to-man betting was a good way to do it when the circle was smaller. But I don't have good contacts among the bettors. I don't know who they are. I follow the way the line goes, but I don't follow the people who are betting it. It doesn't make any difference to me whether Joe Blow makes the game move from three to four. I just know that it has moved from three to four. And that's my major concern. I really don't have contact with what's going on with the books and the people.

"In years past, when someone would make a line, like Bob Martin, who is the legendary oddsmaker, he would think about it, and then he would ask a couple of his associates what they thought of his line. And they would tell him by betting money into it—which is a great way to have an opinion. But times have changed.

"What I do now is have people working for me, and we all work independently of one another. When we create odds, my checks and balances are the people who work for me. And the idea is to get everybody to work independently, not sharing anybody else's work or power ratings. And that's how I come up with a diversified opinion—as opposed to the way Bob Martin did it. So, basically, the result is the same—we're getting different opinions. We're just going about it in different ways."

Roxborough says that history has no impact on the odds he posts. "I can't remember what happened last week. The way I see it is that the bettors are completely different than they were ten, fifteen years ago. Right now, we have all these guys in a stock-marketlike atmosphere where it's sort of an efficient market. If the spread is six and goes to seven and a half, there's a pretty good chance it's not going to go higher. A lot of people who lay the six, they're going to take the seven and a half back [on the other team, thus trying to middle]. So we actually see these efficiency markets within the betting. I think that's the new wave bettor. If you go down there and take a look at the bettors and these operations with walkie-talkies and clipboards and beepers, they're all more into arbitraging than they are in selecting winners."

Also, cutting against the traditional wisdom, player injuries don't receive much emphasis when Roxborough sets the line. "Injuries are generally overrated. I don't feel the need to go out and find this information. You can't have every injury. There're ninety-six college teams we follow. We're trying to get every injury we can. We're not going to have them all. Somebody may know someone in some region of the country who knows about an injury we don't know about."

When I asked him about his own inside information, he replied, "We don't talk to correspondents outside of town. We just talk to people here in town. One of the reasons I don't like to talk to people out of town is I don't know any gamblers outside of town. And unless a guy is a gambler, I don't think he really knows what we're interested in. A fan's scouting report is totally useless."

Roxborough posts his weekly line at the Stardust. "The Stardust traditionally has done this. There is no prize for going first [being the first sports book to post the line]. So it's not financially advantageous to go first because there may be some flaws in the line. But the Stardust creates a lot of publicity for itself and has made a name for itself this way. I think that's one of the reasons why they continue to go first. But it is risky."

When I asked Roxborough whether he or his oddsmaking operations have ever been influenced by the organized-crime gambling syndicate, he replied sharply, "No, and there are reasons. I don't see how, if you put out a bad line, it will help a team win or lose a game—if it's just a couple of points. Plus you have the public who is going to be betting into the line anyway. I think that since the hotel casinos have been involved in the sports-gambling business, there have been changes."

Roxborough says that he doesn't stay in touch with Warren Welsh of NFL Security directly. "Warren Welsh has a contact in Las Vegas, who is here full-time. I know him. His job is to inform Warren if there are any unusual line movements. I work with this guy."[3]

The oddsmaker added that he has taken NFL games off the boards—but has always put them back up by game time. "I didn't take them off because of injuries, unless it was a key player. I didn't take them off because of too much one-sided betting. Let's say Dan Marino [the star quarterback for the Miami Dolphins] hurts his elbow. And there was a fifty-fifty chance that he would play or not play. We don't know what to do. Between his playing and not playing might make a four-point difference in the line. If he's out, fine, we know what to do. If he's going to play, that's fine, we know what to do. But if we don't know whether he's going to play or not, that's a problem. And we might take the game off the boards until we get a further medical report."

Citing a specific incident that caused him to take an NFL game off the board, Roxborough remembers, "Somebody thought that Dan Marino [who was getting ready to play New

England in 1985] had been arrested for drunk driving the night before. The story was so unbelievable that I didn't want to give it any credence—except the number [the point spread] was moving all over town. So we ended up having to scratch the game.

"We hated to take it off, but it was Sunday morning, and we just didn't know what to do. So we started taking some bets on it, and it kept moving and moving. And it turned out that the rumor was totally unfounded, and the game went right back to the number it should have been. That was the craziest rumor I'd ever heard. I still don't know how it got started."

48 "I'm so fucking glad I'm out"

BY MID-1984, AFTER suffering two heart attacks in the past three years, San Diego Chargers owner Gene Klein was increasingly becoming involved in thoroughbred racing—and later built Del Rayo Stables in Rancho Santa Fe, just north of San Diego near the Del Mar racetrack.[1]

Klein told me that his wife, Joyce, was responsible for getting him interested in the business. "I went to the track, and I ran into [former Chicago Bears star linebacker] Dick Butkus, who owned a few horses. He said a guy named Wayne Lucas was his trainer. So one day, I said, 'Maybe I'll buy a racehorse.' So I called Wayne Lucas, and I said, 'Wayne, if you ever find a horse that you think is a decent racehorse, give me a call.'

"A couple of weeks later, he said he had a filly who had never run but he thought she'd be a winner. I told him to buy her. The first time out, she ran fifth. I thought, 'Oh shit.' He says, 'Whoa, whoa, this is just a break-in race.' The next time she won. I told him if he found any more to call me. One day, I saw him at the track. He was very down and I asked him what was wrong. He said one of his favorite clients had just died, and her kids wanted him to sell her stable of horses right away. I asked him for the number. He gave it to me, and I bought them. I started with two hundred horses."

Describing the difference between horse racing and the NFL, Klein said, "You've got stars and superstars in horse racing just as you do in football. I don't think the fans understand how hard you work to build a football team. You draft, you have training camp. It's a whole year's preparation. You blow one important game, and it's over. In horse racing, if you lose a big race, you have two more next week.

"But then only one of twenty-eight teams will win the Super Bowl every year. That's a lock. There are fifty thousand thoroughbreds born every year. Only twenty can run in the Derby and only one can win it. And you get one shot at it. I mean, what are the odds of winning the Kentucky Derby?"[2]

Weary of the headaches of professional football, Klein sold his interest in the Chargers to multimillionaire Alex G. Spanos in August 1984. Klein says that he doesn't miss football at all. "I am so fucking glad I'm out," he sighs with genuine relief and a broad smile. "I pick up the sports page every day, and there're two more guys getting suspended for cocaine use. Some of these players are assholes . . .

"It was a complicated deal with Alex. It was for somewhere between eighty million and eighty-five million dollars, based on a hundred percent of the club."

Spanos is the son of a Greek immigrant who came to this country and opened a bakery. Baking bread wasn't enough for young Spanos, so he set out on his own, building an empire worth nearly half a billion dollars.

Also a horse-racing enthusiast, Spanos is the owner of A. G. Spanos Construction—one of the largest construction firms in the United States with corporate headquarters in Stockton, California, and Las Vegas, where he owns a string of office buildings and apartment complexes. His company is the largest builder of federally subsidized housing in the country.

Claiming to travel an average of six thousand miles a week, Spanos flies around the United States in his nine-passenger Lockheed Jetstar, watching over his investments that stretch from Stockton to Tampa, Florida.[3] In whatever free time he has left, he plays golf with Bob Hope, Gerald Ford, and Telly Savalas.

Spanos and entertainer Pat Boone attempted but failed to purchase the Oakland franchise in the American Basketball Association in 1967. Earlier, Spanos was jilted in his effort to buy a minor-league baseball team. In 1974, he bid for the Tampa Bay Buccaneers but was outbid by Tom McCloskey and then Hugh Culverhouse, after McCloskey could not come up with the franchise fee. In 1977, Spanos made a strong push for the San Francisco 49ers but was outbid again by Culverhouse's business associate Edward J. DeBartolo.

Five years later, after considering the purchase of a USFL franchise, Spanos purchased 10 percent of the Chargers from Barron Hilton. Klein sold his controlling interest to Spanos two years later. Hilton still maintained a 10 percent interest in the San Diego team.

Meantime—despite his control of two major casinos in Las Vegas, the Las Vegas Hilton and the Flamingo Hilton—Barron Hilton was having troubles on the East Coast. In the midst of negotiations for the sale of a portion of his stock in the Chargers, Hilton had been making plans to build a $270 million hotel/casino in Atlantic City. While filing his application to the New Jersey Casino Control Commission for his casino license, state investigators discovered Hilton's links to labor lawyer Sidney Korshak, who had been identified as an organized-crime figure in 1978 by the California attorney general's office.[4]

"It is quite evident that over the years [Korshak] has made good contacts with very powerful politicians . . ." according to a commission staff report. "Korshak's list of past and present associates reads like a who's who of prominent Southern Californians."

The subsequent report also revealed that between 1971 and 1984 Korshak had made over $700,000 from Hilton alone. Korshak was chiefly responsible for handling some tax and real estate matters for Hilton, as well as a number of affirmative action cases.

Realizing that the Korshak connection could cause him severe licensing difficulties, Hilton suddenly fired the attorney. Hilton, through his legal counsel, sent Korshak a letter, stating: "I appreciate very much your understanding regarding the action we feel we're forced to take in dissolving the longstanding relationship between you and Hilton Hotels Corporation. As I stated in our telephone conversation, we very much regret this situation. We feel, however, that we cannot risk jeopardizing in any way the huge investment we have committed to New Jersey . . .

"You can rest assured that you continue to be held in high esteem and affection by those of us at Hilton who have had the privilege of having you as a friend and adviser."

In the midst of the opening round of testimony before the casino control commission in July 1984, Barron Hilton received a barrage of hostile questions about his association with Korshak.

Hilton said, "I wish the hell we would have never hired him, because I can see it's a very distinct problem here in the minds of you gentlemen about this fellow's integrity." In another round of questioning in November, Hilton again repudiated Korshak, who was furious.[5]

At the conclusion of the hearings, New Jersey gaming commissioner Joel R. Jacobson said, "In my judgment, the . . . relationship of the Hilton Hotels Corporation with Sidney Korshak is the fatal link upon which I primarily based the conclusion that this applicant has not established its suitability for licensure in New Jersey."

The commission rejected Hilton's bid on February 28, 1985. The refusal was based solely on Hilton's association with Korshak—whom the commission charged as being "a key actor in organized crime's unholy alliances with corrupt union officials and its pernicious efforts to frustrate the rights of working men and women by infecting legitimate unions, to rob their members' future by stealing the benefits they have earned in the past from honest labor."[6]

There was solace for Hilton. Even though he was viewed as unsuitable for ownership of a casino in Atlantic City by the New Jersey Casino Control Commission, he was still suitable enough to continue his minority interest in the San Diego Chargers. The NFL conducted neither a known investigation nor a hearing on Hilton's relationship with Korshak.

The NFL also did nothing to curtail Hilton's corporate sports-gambling activities, particularly the $17.5 million Hilton sports book at the Las Vegas Hilton.

In a promotional brochure, the Las Vegas Hilton boasts of its "magnificent new addition to the Hilton [that] dwarfs anything of its kind. Over thirty thousand square feet—nearly the size of a football gridiron—devoted exclusively to a lavish center for race handicapping and sports wagering.

"The visual display itself is breathtaking. A wall 35′ high and 230′ in length. Containing 30 giant projection screens and eight 46-inch television monitors for simultaneous viewing of all major sports events and racing from every major U.S. track. Including odds and up-to-the-minute sports handicapping information. There's comfortable seating for over 400 with over 60 seats intended exclusively for sports bettors . . .

"So whatever the season, whatever your game, you can bet

the action's at the Las Vegas Hilton Race and Sports Super-Book.

Barron Hilton
President, CEO
Chairman of the Board
Hilton Hotels Corp."

On the inside of the brochure, Hilton uses the team of which he is still part owner as an example for the novice about sports wagering. "You may wager on which team will win the game as adjusted by the stipulated pointspread. This is called a straight wager. In this example, the [San Diego] Chargers are a three-point favorite over the [Los Angeles] Rams. If you wish to wager on the Chargers, three points will be deducted from their final score. Therefore, you are wagering that the Chargers will win the game by *more* than three points. Conversely, if you wish to wager on the Rams, three points will be added to their final score. You are then wagering that the Rams will either win the game or lose by *less* than three points. Should the Chargers win by *exactly* three points, it's classified as a tie and all wagers would be refunded."

Here, Hilton is not only telling gamblers where to bet on NFL games but how to bet—using a team in which he still has a financial interest as his example. Predictably, the NFL remained silent.

While Hilton was busy institutionalizing his gambling empire, the United States Football League was busy folding up, unable to retain a high-priced television contract. The USFL had challenged the domination of the NFL over professional football—but only momentarily and rather meekly. It could never come up with and keep the biggest stars in the game either through the college draft or by raids on NFL teams. Frustrated by what it considered to be the excessive monopolistic practices of the NFL, the USFL filed an antitrust suit against the NFL in the fall of 1984.

On July 29, 1986, a federal jury in New York agreed with the USFL and found against the NFL. However, the jury awarded damages to the USFL of only $1—trebled to $3. A week later, on August 4, 1986, the USFL team owners, nearly $150 million in debt, suspended play.

In the wake of its guilty verdict, the unrepentant NFL owners continued to laugh all the way to the bank. Adding insult to injury, just seven months after the USFL called it quits, the NFL signed another astronomical television contract with all three major networks and, for the first time, cable television's ESPN, which had helped carry the USFL through its final season.

49 Trouble in Paradise

AS THE IRS INVESTIGATION began to zero in on Dominic Frontiere—two men, Daniel Whitman, a co-owner of Hollywood's popular Cyrano's restaurant, and cocaine dealer Robert Cohen—were arrested for conspiring to murder Raymond Cohen, no relation to Robert, allegedly to keep him from testifying in the NFL ticket-scalping investigation.[1]

Both Whitman, a close friend of the Frontieres, and Robert Cohen were associates of mobster Jack Catain. The murder plot was discovered when Robert Cohen gave an FBI informant $5,000 in cocaine to make the hit. Upon his arrest, Robert Cohen agreed to cooperate with the government. Federal investigators told Cohen to call Whitman and say that the murder of Raymond Cohen had been committed. The call was secretly tape-recorded by the government.

Included on the tape was Whitman's statement that Raymond Cohen had to be killed because he was informing on several "heavyweights out of Chicago" who were involved in Mafia activities on the West Coast. He said that Catain was among them. Believing that Raymond Cohen was dead, Whitman added, "If it means anything to you, let me tell you what was done was sanctioned . . . Those things [murders] don't just happen unless you get it cleared." Telling Robert Cohen on the telephone that he had been approached by federal agents, Whitman said he told them, "Do you want to talk to me about Dan Whitman, sit down. You want to talk about Ray Cohen, Jack

Catain, Dominic Frontiere . . . I don't want to talk to you guys about it."

"Whitman had a subhuman personality," Treasury agent Gerald Petievich, who headed the Secret Service's counterfeiting investigation of Jack Catain, told me.[2] "He was trying to make a reputation for himself with the underworld. He was talking tough, and this situation gave him the opportunity to do something that would get him respect. That was the reason for the murder contract.

"There was a meeting with the Strike Force [in Los Angeles]. My suggestion was to show that the murder was the intent. I wanted to show Whitman a picture of a dead body. So we took Ray Cohen over to a Burbank studio and had a makeup man make him up with a hole in his head. It looked so realistic. Then we drove up by Universal Studios and had him lie in the bushes up in the hills. And we took a picture of him lying there. Then, in case that didn't work, we took him down to the morgue and had him lie on a slab. We put a sheet over him.

"They were very realistic photos. They were shown to Whitman by [Robert Cohen], who said, 'Hey, I did it.' And he showed him the photograph [of Cohen's acting dead in the hills]. When he saw the photograph, Whitman said, 'Oh yeah, that's good.' And [Robert Cohen] was wired and got him on tape. The meeting was inside Whitman's restaurant, and the theme from *The Godfather* was playing in the background."

Would the murder of Ray Cohen have benefited Dominic Frontiere? Strike Force prosecutor Bruce Kelton of Los Angeles says, "I can't say that. What I can say is that the evidence in the case showed that Whitman had hired some people to kill Cohen. In cryptic conversation, he indicated that Cohen had been cooperating with Treasury agents. Our argument to the jury was that all this had happened after the Treasury agents had approached Whitman to question him. But as far as whether the murder would have helped Frontiere, I have no comment on that. I have no evidence that he was a part of any attempt to murder anybody."

The following year, on March 9, 1984, Raymond Cohen testified in court during Whitman's trial that he had given money from the ticket-scalping scheme he and Catain were operating to Dominic Frontiere, who was also the source of the tickets. Frontiere had repeatedly denied being involved in the ticket-scalping scam. Whitman was convicted of attempted murder and sentenced to eight years in prison.

By the end of the year, the screws began to tighten on Frontiere when a federal judge ordered Catain to appear before a grand jury investigating the ticket-scalping allegations. Catain—who, like Whitman, was given immunity from prosecution in the case—had earlier refused to talk because of a reported heart condition. Both Whitman and Catain finally testified, as did Pete Rozelle on behalf of the NFL. These testimonies remain sealed.

On June 19, 1986, Dominic Frontiere was indicted by the federal grand jury on three counts of failing to report over $500,000 in income he had received from the scalping of the 1980 Super Bowl tickets. He was described by a federal prosecutor as "a major white-collar criminal."

According to the indictment, Frontiere had failed to include on his and his wife's 1980 joint income-tax return their income from the sale of Super Bowl tickets above the $397,000 claimed. Instead of reporting their total profit from the sale of the tickets, the couple had taken a $116,335 deduction for supposedly giving them away.

Federal investigators had also learned that Georgia Frontiere had all twenty-seven thousand of the Rams' allocation of Super Bowl tickets delivered to her house. When it was discovered by team accountants that over thirty-two hundred tickets were missing, Mrs. Frontiere told them that she had given them to her friends at no charge. However, she could not produce a list of who those friends were, and prosecutors had evidence that she had specifically ordered that no complimentary tickets be given to anyone—even members of the Rams management staff.

Despite the fact that she was also implicated in the scheme in an affidavit by Jack Catain, Mrs. Frontiere was not indicted and insisted that she was completely unaware of her husband's activities—despite the fact that the deductions were listed on their signed, joint income-tax returns.

Catain's affidavit revealed that "Danny Whitman clearly stated that Dominic and Georgia Frontiere wished to have my assistance in scalping tickets for the Super Bowl on a yearly basis and preferred to have a lump sum payment from myself with me to be responsible for distributing them to ticket agencies and various other outlets." Catain, who refused to sign the affidavit unless he was given a deal by the government, added that it was

Dominic Frontiere who earlier instructed him and Raymond Cohen to muzzle Rams executive Harold Guiver.

Los Angeles attorney Tony Capozzola, who solicited Catain's statement, told me, "I am convinced that Jack Catain was telling the truth. But I also believe that many of the facts in this case will never be clarified because of the unbelievable twists and turns the investigation took. I know that there are a lot of people who are not satisfied by the explanations given to date."

Bruce Kelton told me, "The Frontiere tax case had nothing to do with who was giving us information. The reason Georgia Frontiere wasn't indicted was that the investigation was about knowingly making false statements on income-tax returns. And there was not sufficient evidence to indict her with respect to that particular charge. It was a different story with Dominic. He and Ray Cohen were going around selling Super Bowl tickets. In his case, there was clear intent.

"Don't think we didn't look at Georgia. We did. We looked at every angle of that case and spoke to almost every NFL owner of every team and to Pete Rozelle several times." All these statements by Rozelle and the NFL team owners also have been sealed.

Four months after his indictment, the fifty-five-year-old Frontiere pleaded guilty, insisting that he received only $88,000 of the money from the sale of the tickets. The rest, he claimed, was extorted by Catain and Ray Cohen, the chief witnesses against him.[3] In a plea-bargaining arrangement, Frontiere admitted to two counts of income-tax fraud. The third count for obstruction of justice was dropped. Facing a maximum eight-year jail term, he was sentenced to one year in prison and fined $15,000.

At his sentencing, Frontiere told the judge, "I swear to you, I didn't know what I was doing was illegal . . . It seemed like a way to make a lot of money that wasn't illegal." U.S. District Judge William D. Keller was skeptical and replied, "At best, it's a bizarre story. At worst, I'm not being told the truth."

Immediately after Frontiere copped his plea, the NFL announced that it was finally going to conduct an "administrative review" of the circumstances revolving around the ticket-scalping situation in the NFL. Predictably, nothing more was heard from the NFL on this subject.

The Frontieres were not the only NFL owners who were

having serious problems. Others were in such bad shape that they were being forced to sell or move their teams.

• Beset with financial difficulties resulting from the collapse of the world oil market, Clint Murchison, stricken with a degenerative disease that impaired his ability to walk and talk, sold his interest in the Dallas Cowboys and its stadium corporation in March 1984 to an eleven-member partnership headed by the chairman of Texas A & M's board of regents, Harvey R. "Bum" Bright—another right-wing, freewheeling but widely diversified Dallas oilman with a string of savings and loan banks—for $86 million.[4] Bright and his syndicate had outbid car dealer W. O. Bankston, a longtime friend of both the Cowboys and Murchison.

Because Bright had only a 17 percent interest in the team, his purchasing group had to receive special permission from the other NFL owners, who had earlier ruled that one person from each NFL team had to own 51 percent of the franchise. The NFL owners agreed to the deal—with the proviso that Tex Schramm remain as the team president.[5]

Murchison died at sixty-three, two years after the sale.

However, in late February 1989, Bright, who had lost $29 million in the October 1987 stock market crash, and his partners sold the Cowboys and the stadium for over $126 million to Arkansas oilman Jerry Jones, who immediately fired Tom Landry, the Cowboys' head coach for twenty-nine years. Landry was replaced by Jimmy Johnson, the head coach of the University of Miami. Both Jones and Johnson had been the co-captains of the 1964 national championship team at the University of Arkansas. Schramm resigned as the president of the franchise in April 1989 and was immediately appointed by the NFL owners to chair a newly conceived International Football League, which is expected to begin league play in April 1990.

• Also in March 1984, Edgar Kaiser sold the Denver Broncos to Denver real estate executive Patrick D. Bowlen for $73 million. Bowlen owned the Canadian-based Bowlen Holding, Ltd. in Edmonton. Later, Bowlen created a small stir when he made a statement, indicating that his team needed players who exhibited the toughness of prison inmates.

• That same month, the Baltimore Colts became the Indianapolis Colts as team owner Robert Irsay moved his team out of Baltimore in the middle of the night. Irsay had wanted the

Colts to play in a bigger stadium. The NFL owners decided not to interfere—since Al Davis had won his antitrust suit against the league on May 7, 1982.

In January 1985, while Irsay was driving his car on Chicago's North Side, it was hit with two bullets fired by persons unknown. The Colts owner was shaken up but unharmed.

• On April 29, 1985, Leonard Tose, wracked with gambling debts, sold the Philadelphia Eagles to Florida automobile dealer Norman Braman for $70 million.[6]

The fifty-two-year-old Braman, a native Philadelphian, was one of the largest car dealers in south Florida, with sixteen dealerships for his big-ticket automobiles: Rolls-Royces, Cadillacs, Porsches, and BMWs, among others. Because of his business savvy, Braman earned the title "the Baron of the Biscayne Boulevard Auto Dealers."

Heavy into Republican politics, Braman was nominated by President Reagan to be commissioner of the Immigration and Naturalization Service, but Braman withdrew his name from consideration. Braman had made his fortune while still in Philadelphia with his drug store franchise company, Rite Aid, which he sold in 1968. He moved to Florida, opened his first auto dealership in Miami, and then moved into Tampa as well.

• On June 3, 1985, John Mecom, who was in his fourth year as the chairman of the Houston-based John W. Mecom Company, sold the New Orleans Saints to another car dealer Tom Benson, who became the team's managing general partner. The sale price for the team was $70.2 million.

A native of New Orleans who also invested heavily in real estate and banking in Texas, Benson outbid the A. N. Pritzker family of Chicago, the owners of the Hyatt Hotel chain, which has also been represented by Sidney Korshak. However, Benson was not the majority owner of the Saints. He had eleven partners. As with the sale of the Cowboys by Bum Bright's group, the syndicate had to receive special permission from the NFL to purchase the team without a majority owner.

• Billy Bidwill, the son of Charles Bidwill who had bought the Chicago Cardinals in 1933, made his plans to move the St. Louis Cardinals to Phoenix after years of demands for a new stadium. He finally did so after the 1987 season and renamed his team the Phoenix Cardinals.

• In August 1988, the Seattle Seahawks franchise was purchased from the Nordstrom family by Ken Behring and Ken Hofmann, two east Bay Area developers in San Francisco, for $80 million. Another former car dealer and a native of Wisconsin, Behring controls 75 percent of the Seattle team and is worth an estimated $600 million. He was featured on a segment of Robin Leach's *Lifestyles of the Rich and Famous.*

Behring owns one of the largest car collections in the world. It includes Adolf Hitler's limousine. The University of California at Berkeley created a controversial tax-exempt charity, the Behring Educational Institute, to help obtain tax exemptions for Behring's car museum. Consequently, Behring's tax write-offs were in the millions of dollars. As part of the arrangement, the university agreed to purchase the collection after Behring's death. The institute had been created by the university's vice chancellor, who was also a director of the museum, and who had purchased two houses in one of Behring's developments—with the help of a Behring loan.

Hofmann, who specializes in building huge moderate-income housing projects and owns 25 percent of the Seahawks, was investigated by state law-enforcement agencies after he engaged in a local shopping center partnership with a state assemblyman who received $300,000 worth of stock for only $24,000. Citizens groups charged that Hofmann had made the deal because he needed the legislator to help rezone the land. No wrongdoing was ever proven. Hofmann is said to be worth over $500 million.

• In another team purchase, financially strapped Billy Sullivan,[7] after watching seventeen offers come and go, sold the majority control of the New England Patriots to Victor Kiam, who since 1979 has owned Remington Products, Inc., the Bridgeport-based electric shaver company. Sullivan retained a small percentage of the team while Kiam's partner, Philadelphia businessman Fran Murray, also became a minority owner. The sale price was $85 million.

50 Rozelle Gets Tough on Players

IN MID-DECEMBER 1985 six unnamed New England Patriots players were described by *The Boston Globe* as having drug problems. The disclosure about the six players came after a December 16, 1985, team party in Miami. According to team officials, it had been suspected that the players had been regularly using cocaine for over a year. Nevertheless, the team was 11–5 for the 1985 regular season and heading for the Super Bowl.

With the drama building for Super Bowl XX on January 26, 1986, the Patriots brushed off reporters questions about cocaine abuse and appeared to be fired up for the big game. The ten-point-underdog New England team came out swinging, scoring first on a thirty-six-yard field goal. But then that was it. After that, the Bears defense demolished the Patriots offense, forcing a safety and six turnovers, including a twenty-eight-yard interception streak for a touchdown. At halftime, the score was 23–3; when it was all over the Patriots had been fried, 46–10.

While the Bears' quarterback Jim McMahon, the game's most valuable player, began collecting his $3 million for endorsing everything from tacos to motor scooters, the Patriots returned to Foxboro, Massachusetts, to deal with their drug problems.

New England head coach Raymond Berry threatened to quit his job if the team did not agree to a voluntary drug-testing program, which would have established a precedent in the NFL. Team members agreed to go along with the program in a vote by secret ballot, with the proviso that the names of those with the drug problems not be revealed—unless they became repeat offenders. Agreements made, the Patriots' front office announced the historic deal to the public without mentioning any names.

Ron Borges, the *Globe* reporter who had broken the original story in December, had already obtained the names of the six players during an off-the-record interview with a member of the Patriots staff. After the Super Bowl loss, Borges looked for a second source to confirm the identities of the six players. He went to Patrick Sullivan, the club's general manager, and recited the list to him. Sullivan had already confirmed the names before the team vote was taken.

On January 29, 1986, the *Globe* published the names of the six players: Raymond Clayborn, Tony Collins, Irving Fryar, Roland James, Kenneth Sims, and Stephen Starring.

As soon as the names were released, the Patriots players, feeling double-crossed, canceled their participation in the voluntary drug-testing program. The NFLPA immediately filed an unfair labor practice complaint with the National Labor Relations Board on behalf of the Patriots players.

Soon after, in response to yet another *Globe* story, the NFL confirmed that Fryar, an all-pro wide receiver, was also under investigation for gambling on NFL games during the 1985 season. Several of his teammates were also suspected of gambling, but Fryar was the only player named. The Patriots' front office, already dealing with an avalanche of press inquiries about the team's drug problems, replied curtly, "There is and continues to be no hard evidence that Irving Fryar has gambled on a pro football game. The only fact is that the league is checking out this unsubstantiated rumor, as we asked them to do."[1]

The results of Fryar's polygraph test—in which he was asked whether he was gambling on NFL games—were not made public. However, Warren Welsh told me that Fryar is still under investigation.

The NFL had taken action against the league's mounting drug problems after the 1983 suspensions of five players. Stanley Wilson of the Cincinnati Bengals was suspended by his own team in 1984, reinstated in 1986, and then suspended again in 1987 indefinitely until being reinstated in April 1988. Chuck Muncie of the Minnesota Vikings, who had had previous bouts with cocaine while with the New Orleans Saints and the San Diego

Chargers, became the seventh player suspended over illegal drugs in 1985, his final season.[2]

Rozelle suspended Muncie for one game after he missed drug-counseling sessions. Muncie was later indicted for and pleaded innocent to selling cocaine to undercover agents. In unrelated cases, Mike Bell of the Kansas City Chiefs and New Orleans Saints running back Barry Word were also disciplined.[3]

In May 1988, Pete Rozelle personally assumed control over the monitoring of the NFL's drug epidemic because the team owners were not properly monitoring and disciplining their players.[4] Jan Van Duser, the NFL's director of operations told *Washington Post* reporter Bill Brubaker, "There were clubs that did not address their drug problems as well as they might have, either through putting football considerations first or just not knowing enough about the problem.

"What we heard from some clubs was this: 'We would be happy to do everything that's needed in a drug program provided we know that the team we're playing next week is doing the same thing.' "

Few believed that the drug problem within the NFL had truly subsided. According to Brubaker, Rozelle had held a "closed-door hearing" in New York on reports "that as many as 40 percent of the players on some NFL teams were using illegal drugs." Hearing testimony from Dr. Forest Tennant, the NFL's drug adviser, Rozelle learned that "half of the NFL's twenty-eight franchises had told him [Tennant] that between five and twenty players on each of their teams were 'known drug users.'

"Tennant went on to testify that some clubs had 'swept' their drug problems 'under the carpet' and that one player had informed him that cocaine was being sold in his team's training room."

Consequently, Rozelle augmented the NFL's drug program with a new $1.5 million random drug-testing program, which was administered by the league office.

Mike Strachan, formerly of the New Orleans Saints, whose cocaine use and 1981 conviction cost him his professional football career, told me, "Cocaine takes a toll on you, and you really can't perform when you're strung out. The game is so intense and so competitive that you can't stay up all night doing cocaine and then expect to get up and perform well. You're just going to point a finger at yourself.

"Random drug testing will change the complexion of the

game. The guys I know who are still in the league are scared of getting caught and won't do drugs. That's the deterrent. If the NFL strictly enforces its drug-testing program, there won't be a drug problem in the league.

"If they had had that kind of program when I was in the NFL, I probably never would have gotten into the trouble I got into. Back then, it just got out of hand, and there was nothing to stop it."

During the 1988 preseason, the NFL finally got tough—in accordance with the league's three-step policy. Several NFL players were suspended for violating the league's substance-abuse policy, including: Dexter Manley of the Washington Redskins, Doug DuBose of the San Francisco 49ers, Kevin Gogan of the Dallas Cowboys, Richard Reed of the Denver Broncos, Robb Riddick of the Buffalo Bills, Pat Saindon of the Atlanta Falcons, Greg Townsend of the Los Angeles Raiders, and Tony Collins of the Indianapolis Colts. All received thirty-day suspensions except former Patriots player Collins, who was suspended indefinitely after his third violation.

The NFLPA complained that Rozelle and the NFL did not have the right to suspend players without a collective-bargaining agreement between the players' union and NFL's management council. The three-step league policy had resulted from the 1982 contract, which had since expired. The NFLPA threatened to take the NFL to court if the suspensions did not cease.[5]

Ignoring the union the week before the beginning of the 1988 season, Rozelle suspended Lawrence Taylor of the New York Giants for thirty days after his second offense. Also suspended were Terry Taylor of the Seattle Seahawks, Emanuel King and Darryl Smith of the Cincinnati Bengals, Bruce Smith of the Buffalo Bills, and John Taylor of the San Francisco 49ers.

On September 7, two Chicago bears were suspended: Richard Dent, who refused to take the drug test and was later reinstated in the midst of a lawsuit challenging the suspension; and Calvin Thomas, who claimed that he had never been informed of failing a first test; as well as Charles White of the Los Angeles Rams, who was nailed for alcohol abuse, which can be used against a player when it occurs as a step-two offense. White, the 1979 Heisman Trophy winner, had been arrested the previous summer for being under the influence of a controlled substance which was believed to be cocaine.

On September 13, Antonio Gibson of the New Orleans Saints and Leonard Mitchell of the Atlanta Falcons were also suspended for substance abuse. Soon after, Mike Bell of the Kansas City Chiefs was also suspended.

In the wake of the 1988 Olympic Games and the controversy over the use of steroids by participating athletes, particularly Ben Johnson who was stripped of his gold medal after his world-record time in the hundred meters, the NFL announced that it would punish league players who tested positive for steroids. The penalties for steroid use, including a thirty-day suspension for first-time offenders, were to go into effect in the summer of 1989. Rozelle said that 6 percent of all NFL players had tested positive for steroids in 1987.

On November 9, there were two more players suspended for thirty days for drug use: Doug Smith of the Houston Oilers and Hal Garner of the Buffalo Bills. And, on November 30, Mark Duper of the Miami Dolphins[6] and Victor Scott of the Dallas Cowboys were suspended for substance abuse as well.

Just the previous month, on October 10, twenty-nine-year-old David Croudip, a reserve cornerback in his fourth season with the Atlanta Falcons, died at his home in Lawrenceville, Georgia, after he drank a concoction of fruit juice with a load of cocaine mixed in. During his college career at San Diego State, Croudip had acknowledged a cocaine problem and sought counseling. His death is still under investigation.

On the night before Super Bowl XXIII between the Cincinnati Bengals and the seven-point-favorite San Francisco 49ers on January 22, 1989, Bengals running back Stanley Wilson, who had already been suspended twice for cocaine use and was being tested three times a week, was found in the bathroom of his hotel room in a "disoriented state" by a team official. Cocaine was reportedly found nearby. While Wilson was being taken to a hospital, he bolted from members of the Bengals management and ran down a fire escape and into the night. Wilson, who missed the Super Bowl, did not resurface until the following Tuesday.

After the Wilson situation became public, questions were raised as to the whereabouts of the proof of drug use found in Wilson's hotel room. Soon after, it was discovered that all the evidence at the scene had been confiscated by Cincinnati chief of police Lawrence Whalen, who also headed the Bengals' security team during the week of the Super Bowl. However, instead of turning the evidence over to a law-enforcement agency, Whalen gave it to NFL Security. Whalen was reprimanded for his actions by Cincinnati officials.

For years, suspicions had abounded and charges made that NFL players' agents were supplying their clients with drugs. Pete Rozelle made such a charge during his testimony before a committee of the New York state legislature in May 1984. "We have information that leads us to believe agents are involved in the problem." Rozelle did not get specific and the issue passed.

As the Screen Actors Guild does in Hollywood, the NFL Players Association establishes guidelines for agents representing its membership. The NFLPA's oversight of players' agents was contained in the collective-bargaining agreement negotiated at the conclusion of the fifty-seven-day NFL players strike in 1982. Anyone wishing to represent a player coming into the pros or negotiating a veteran's contract must be approved and certified by the union. A newly certified agent is automatically subjected to a one-year probationary period.

Consequently, Ed Garvey, the union's former executive director, had been accused by the players' agents of initiating a "system of socialism." Garvey had described agents as "a group of people who have no ethical standards," who operated "for the total exploitation of young men." A natural alliance between some agents and some NFL team owners resulted, with both attempting to break the back of the NFLPA.[7] In one instance, players' agent Jerry Argovitz, a former Houston dentist, had openly tried to have Garvey ousted as the union's leader. In 1984, Argovitz became a co-owner of the Houston Gamblers of the USFL.

Two other agents, fifty-eight-year-old Norby Walters and twenty-nine-year-old Lloyd Bloom, were even greedier. Indicted in Chicago on August 24, 1988, under the RICO statute for racketeering, mail and wire fraud, and extortion after a seventeen-month investigation, the two New York sports agents, according to federal prosecutors, had offered cash, cars, and other gifts to star college athletes in return for exclusive representation contracts, some of which were postdated. Walters and Bloom pleaded not guilty.

Forty-three players had signed up with these agents, who

operated Walters' World Sports & Entertainment, Inc. of New York. They included, among others, John Clay of the San Diego Chargers, Doug DuBose of the San Francisco 49ers (who was among those players suspended during the 1988 preseason for substance abuse), Chuck Faucette of the San Diego Chargers, Terrance Flagler of the San Francisco 49ers, Brent Fullwood of the Green Bay Packers, Everett Gay of the Dallas Cowboys, Ronnie Harmon of the Buffalo Bills, Mark Ingram of the New York Giants, Tim McGee of the Cincinnati Bengals, Devon Mitchell of the Detroit Lions, Ron Morris of the Chicago Bears, Paul Palmer of the Kansas City Chiefs,[8] Robert Perryman of the New England Patriots, Tim Smith of the Washington Redskins, George Swarn of the St. Louis Cardinals, Tony Woods of the Seattle Seahawks, and Rod Woodson of the Pittsburgh Steelers.

Some players who considered breaking their contracts with Walters and Bloom, the government says, were threatened with a visit by New York Colombo crime family member Michael Franzese, who was later convicted of RICO violations in a separate case and is serving a ten-year sentence.[9] Franzese had allegedly given Walters $50,000 to start up his sports agency. The mobster was named as an unindicted coconspirator and cooperated with federal prosecutors.

Franzese, in an interview with Bruce Selcraig, a reporter with *Sports Illustrated,*[10] said, "Look, we were business associates. I'm not going to lie and say we weren't. But to say I had anything to do with his sports business, that I controlled it or called the shots, is ridiculous. If I gave it [the $50,000] to him I don't see a problem in telling you. There's nothing illegal about it. But at this point I'm not going to confirm it . . . Truthfully, it wasn't a whole lot of money to me, but that's beside the point."

Franzese, along with Walters and Bloom, was also charged with using threats while attempting to obtain a representation contract for Michael Jackson's Victory Tour in 1984—which was being operated by Chuck Sullivan of the New England Patriots. Franzese later testified that he had tried to muscle the Jackson's manager, Ronald Weisner. "We decided that Norby would make it known who I was and who I was associated with . . . and I would do my best to convince them that they should do the tour with Norby.

"I explained to him [Weisner] that if Norby wasn't involved in the tour in some manner there wasn't going to be a tour."

The forty-three players who cooperated agreed to be available to testify against Walters and Bloom, a former bouncer at New York's Studio 54 discotheque, who has been rumored to be associated with drug dealers. The government agreed to clear the players' records—if they made restitution to their schools for their scholarship violations, performed community service work, and generally stayed out of trouble.

A third man indicted was former Heisman Trophy candidate Cris Carter of the Philadelphia Eagles, the all-time leading receiver at Ohio State, who had accepted $5,000 to sign with another agent, Dave Lueddeke of Pro-Line Sports of Sherman Oaks, California. Lueddeke also was indicted for perjury and obstruction of justice and pleaded guilty. He also cooperated with the prosecution.

Among the players, Carter was singled out for indictment because he had concealed the payment from the federal grand jury investigating the case. Three weeks after his indictment, Carter pleaded guilty and agreed to cooperate with the prosecution. He told the court, "I am cooperating fully . . . and can only say that I regret my past mistakes." He had been facing ten years in prison and a $500,000 fine.

Harry Gamble, the president of the Eagles, issued a statement after Carter's plea, saying, "[The] Philadelphia Eagles firmly believe that Cris was one of many college athletes who were victimized by a system that permitted unscrupulous agents to take advantage of young men." Carter went on to star for the Eagles during the 1988 season.

During the trial of Walters and Bloom, the prosecutor told the jury, "I want to be blunt. The student athletes that we asked to testify in the case are not heroes . . . Norby Walters and Lloyd Bloom have no record of any of the cash paid to [them]. It's not surprising . . . when you take the mob's money . . . you don't give and you don't get receipts."

On April 13, 1989, the jury found Walters and Bloom guilty of racketeering and conspiracy.

51 Crime and Punishment

AN IMPORTANT THIRTY-TWO-PAGE special report on gambling was featured in the March 10, 1986, issue of *Sports Illustrated.*

The report made several specific disclosures about NFL personnel, which included

- charges that John Shaw, the vice president of finance of the Los Angeles Rams and a close confidant of Georgia Frontiere, had "gambled excessively over the last several years" with major Southern California bookmakers. This statement was corroborated by other sources. But Shaw denied any wrongdoing, and no action against him was taken by the NFL.[1]
- a statement from a former NFL Security consultant that "several Cleveland Browns players received drugs in the early 1980s from Frank Sumpter and his son Michael. Frank, who died in 1983, was . . . a major bookmaker and gambler. Michael is now serving a thirty-year federal prison sentence for drug trafficking. He is also said by authorities to have been a heavy gambler."
- a confession from former Miami Dolphins defensive back Lloyd Mumphord, who revealed that while he was an active player during the 1970s he established a relationship with a convicted felon Raymond L. Capri. Mumphord told *SI* that he and several other Dolphins "partied at Capri's house and that they were supplied cocaine by Capri. [Mumphord said] that Capri

listened to the players discuss team injuries and that [Mumphord] believed that Capri passed this information along to gamblers." Confronted by *SI,* Capri admitted giving coke to the players and listening to their injury reports; however, he denied ever using the information for gambling purposes.

The *SI* story even ran a short sidebar about the Computer group. Thomas Noble of Las Vegas, the FBI's agent in charge of the Computer investigation, said that the case "is not going to go away. It's big and the federal government moves slowly." However, after the *SI* piece ran, the Computer group investigation began to go awry. Noble was reassigned to Chicago. The slowness of the government had turned into total paralysis.

Special agent Charlie Parsons, formerly of the Las Vegas office, told me, "Noble was right out of Quantico [the FBI academy]. He was a brand-new agent. Because of the [Computer case], the normal rotation was held up for Tom until he could bring that case to its conclusion."

However, another source close to the investigation says that the case was nowhere near completion when Noble was transferred. "This whole thing started out as being an investigation of some computer guys making some bets on some college and professional football games," the Justice Department source told me. "The problem is that the Justice Department knows it's an organized-crime operation, with some embarrassing links to major celebrities in the worlds of sports, politics, and entertainment. This whole investigation has been stalled for political reasons."

Morris Golding of Boston—the attorney for the Computer group's mastermind, Dr. Mindlin—denied that the case was organized-crime-connected or dropped for political reasons; but Golding refused to comment about what celebrities were involved in the Computer operation. "We were hopeful that the case was going to be dropped," he told me, "because we persuaded the government that there was no crime. Gambling is a very widely accepted pastime that involves a lot of people."

Among those investigated for alleged involvement in the Computer group was Mervyn Adelson, the head of Lorimar-Telepictures Corporation, which has produced such television programs as *Eight Is Enough, The Waltons, Dallas, Knott's Landing,* and *Falcon Crest,* among other popular shows.[2] Adelson is also the husband of ABC News reporter Barbara Walters.

Adelson, a longtime business associate and friend of Moe Dalitz and other underworld figures, was the former co-owner of the Colonial House casino in Las Vegas, along with his partner, Irwin A. Molasky, a vice president at Lorimar. The two men had met soon after Adelson moved to Las Vegas in 1953. They were introduced to Dalitz by Allard Roen, who was then the manager of the Desert Inn, which at that time was owned by Dalitz and the Mayfield Road Gang.

Adelson also has the distinction of being the signator for receipt of one of the first loans from the Teamsters' Central States Pension Fund in 1959, specifically for the Sunrise Hospital, near the Strip. The $1 million loan was made through A & M Enterprises, which was owned by Adelson, Molasky, Dalitz, and four of their business associates who also had alleged ties to Meyer Lansky. Another partner in Sunrise was New York attorney Roy Cohn, who also did some of its legal work. The hospital was managed by Nathan Adelson, Mervyn's father. Through Dalitz, Adelson had met on several occasions with Jimmy Hoffa to discuss the loans. Adelson has insisted that he was unaware of Hoffa's criminal associations at the time.

La Costa Country Club of Carlsbad, California, which has often been referred to as "the playground for the mob," had been owned by Dalitz, Adelson,[3] Irwin Molasky, and others. Adelson had also developed the property, and, in 1968, he hired Wallace Groves of the Bahamas to handle La Costa's land sales. An FBI report had previously alleged that La Costa "is used as a clearinghouse for bookie operations. The phones are used to receive the incoming lay-off bets." Neither Adelson nor any of his partners was accused of any wrongdoing. Also, La Costa has since been sold to a Japanese business concern.

Neither Adelson nor Molasky has criminal records. However, government records show that both have close personal and business ties to major organized-crime figures.

A top gambling figure in Las Vegas told me, "Adelson and Molasky became beards. They were moving money for the Computer guys. Instead of betting themselves, the Computers went to guys like Adelson and Molasky and said, 'We have some great games to bet on.' " Attempts to interview Adelson for this book were unsuccessful.

In my February 1988 story, "The NFL and the Mob: Pro Football's Dirty Secret," in *Regardie's,* a Washington-based business magazine, I charged that "the inquiry into the Computer group has stalled. More than 50 people were investigated, but no indictments were brought. The FBI agent who was running the investigation has been reassigned . . . This is pretty much the way that investigations of gambling in the NFL tend to go; just as the connections begin to be made and the picture begins to take shape, the inquiry is abruptly called off. There's always a 'good' reason for it."

The Computer group investigation was under the jurisdiction of Michael DeFeo, the chief of the Strike Force's Western Division and OCRS chief Dave Margolis's top deputy. DeFeo—nicknamed Iron Mike because of his toughness as an organized-crime prosecutor—had been in charge of the Justice Department's investigations during the 1970s of corruption in the Bahamas and the Caribbean gambling industries in Operation Croupier. Further, he was responsible for the prosecution of those involved with skimming at the Stardust in the Operation Strawman/Argent case—for which he received rave reviews.[4]

However, his handling of the Computer case has gone unexplained by the OCRS, which refused comment officially about the matter.

Further, the OCRS's handling of the latter stages of the Dominic Frontiere case has also raised legitimate suspicions that the federal government pulled its punch. The Frontiere case is among the most recent illustrations of what has happened to so many government investigations involving corruption in the NFL.

Frontiere began serving his sentence at the federal minimum-security prison in Lompoc, California, on January 5, 1987. He was released in September 1987, five months early. Law-enforcement officials in Los Angeles told me that federal prosecutors were considering giving Frontiere immunity from prosecution before his release and forcing him to testify on a case involving the NFL. But the immunity question, too, became a political football among federal law-enforcement agencies.

During my interview with Salvatore Pisello—who has been identified in court as a Mafia soldier but vehemently denies it—he said that he had known Frontiere at Lompoc. "Dominic told me that he was a victim and was innocent," said Pisello, who was also serving time for income-tax evasion in connection with a case involving MCA, the Hollywood conglomerate. "When he said that, I said, 'Then why are you here?' " Pisello added that

Frontiere received everything he wanted in prison and had easy jobs. Pisello also said that he never heard Frontiere complain about government pressure on him to turn state's evidence.

"It's something that's been debated behind the scenes by the IRS, the FBI, the Strike Force, and just about every other law-enforcement agency," a top Justice Department official told me. "I think the punch was pulled after Dominic alone was indicted. If he was going to get immunity, he should have received it before he copped his plea. There are a lot of people who are afraid of what he could've said, and whom he could implicate. And the politics that have been played with this decision are making the whole system look bad."

Richard J. Leon, prosecutor in the Frontiere case, told me, "Indictments in criminal tax cases are reviewed up the line—within the tax division and in the U.S. attorneys offices, as well as the Justice Department. At the tax division, you have assistant chiefs, section chiefs; then at Justice you have deputy assistant attorney generals, and assistant attorney generals. And then on the U.S. attorneys' side, you have the chief of the criminal section, the first assistant, and the U.S. attorney himself. There are all kinds of people who were involved in the Frontiere case."

Georgia Frontiere still owns the Rams but divorced her husband after his release from prison. According to several sources close to the Frontieres, Dominic received a settlement of between $2 million and $4 million from his wife. If he did take a fall, she made it worth his while.

Another case may have been spiked by Margolis and DeFeo.[5] This investigation concentrated on MCA, which had permitted Sal Pisello to become a top executive in the company's record division. "In the end," Pisello told me, "I took the fall for the whole company. I was prosecuted and convicted twice for income-tax evasion while MCA got off scott-free."

The president of MCA's record division is Irving Azoff, who also manages special events at the Los Angeles Coliseum, the home of the Los Angeles Raiders. The chairman of the board of MCA is Lew Wasserman, a close friend of Rozelle. Wasserman had served as Ronald Reagan's Hollywood talent agent.

A familiar name was responsible for helping to get MCA off the hook: William Hundley, the former director of NFL Security. In September 1987, Hundley and his law partner since 1969, Plato Cacheris, dissolved their partnership. Hundley then joined the Washington, D.C., law firm—Akin Gump Strauss Hauer & Feld. This firm, which includes former Democratic National Committee chairman and MCA board member Robert S. Strauss of Texas, has been on the NFL's payroll for years and coordinated the league's lobbying efforts on Capitol Hill. Hundley was also involved in the defense of Drexel Burnham Lambert, which had retained the firm, during the 1988 federal investigation of the brokerage house.

Hundley told me that soon after joining Akin Gump and taking the MCA case, he had a meeting with Margolis, who has a picture of Hundley hanging in his office. "I said, 'Look, we're going to cooperate in any organized-crime investigation,'" Hundley explained to me. "'Whatever you want from the corporation: You want to talk to people? You want documents? Get in touch with me. I'll see you get them in a hurry.'"

It was the same "we're open, we're honest" strategy Hundley had used with investigators while he was with NFL Security.[6]

Immediately after Hundley met with Margolis, the Los Angeles Strike Force office issued a letter informing MCA that it was not a target of the federal government's investigation of Pisello. However, Marvin Rudnick, the Strike Force attorney—who had prosecuted Pisello—refused to relent and continued to pursue MCA as the target of his investigation. Soon after, Rudnick was summoned to Washington and met with Margolis and DeFeo. A Justice Department official told me that at that meeting Rudnick was ordered to confine his case to Pisello and not cause MCA "any embarrassment." During the meeting, Margolis pointed to Hundley's picture and told Rudnick, "That's Bill Hundley. If he starts complaining about you, you've got problems." Later, DeFeo recommended Rudnick's dismissal from the Strike Force.[7]

On March 30, 1989, Rudnick was suspended after nearly eleven years as a trial attorney with the Justice Department. At the time of his dismissal, Rudnick was trying to convince Dominic Frontiere's friend, the imprisoned Daniel Whitman, to turn state's evidence in return for a reduction in sentence.

The evidence is clear that there has been a cabal among some past and present officials of the Justice Department's Organized Crime and Racketeering Section and some of its Strike Force offices. And the NFL, through its long-term sweetheart relationship with a variety of law-enforcement agencies, particularly the OCRS, has been a direct beneficiary of this situation—which raises serious questions about possible conflicts of interest, as well as activities that border on sheer political corruption.

However, the problem of the OCRS and the Strike Forces is a two-headed monster. In fact, over the years, since its creation under the OCRS during the mid-1960s, the Strike Force program, conceived by Attorney General Robert Kennedy, has compiled an extremely impressive record in combatting organized crime. Its top prosecutors have been men of high integrity who were given, by law, the independence to conduct their investigations and prosecutions. They have been protected public servants, and their jobs are not contingent upon who is in the White House.

During the mid-1970s, there was a serious effort to eliminate the Strike Forces, which was led by Richard Thornburgh, the chief of the Justice Department's criminal division under President Gerald Ford's attorney general Edward Levi. Thornburgh's actions were supposedly based on the resentment of the Strike Force concept by U.S. attorneys—who are political animals and nominated by the incumbent president. These political appointees were threatened by the fact that the Strike Force could drop an indictment in their laps and ask for their signatures—without the U.S. attorneys being a part of their investigations. Strike Force advocates charged that decisions made by U.S. attorneys regarding its investigations were sometimes determined on political grounds rather than on the merits of the cases.

At first, Thornburgh, a former U.S. attorney in Pittsburgh who had chaired a department committee to investigate the matter, had advocated that Strike Force offices around the country be accountable to the U.S. attorneys in their jurisdictions. But after becoming the chief of the criminal division in 1975, Thornburgh actually began dismantling several Strike Force offices, starting with Baltimore and San Diego, and ran squarely into a confrontation with William S. Lynch, then head of the OCRS and director of Operation Anvil during the early 1970s. However, Lynch lacked the political clout to stop Thornburgh. Soon after, Lynch was removed as the head of the section and replaced by Kurt Muellenberg, who didn't want the job under those circumstances—but was encouraged by Lynch to accept it.

Muellenberg told Thornburgh that he would agree to take the job if the Strike Forces were preserved. Thornburgh agreed, according to Muellenberg. "Three days later," Muellenberg told me, "he came along and shut down the Strike Forces in St. Louis and New Orleans. That son of a bitch lied to me. It was not something that was decided overnight." Soon after, Thornburgh merged the Manhattan Strike Force into the U.S. attorney's office in New York's Southern District and then wiped out the Strike Force office in Pittsburgh.

Muellenberg continued, "At that time, Thornburgh already had political ambitions about being the governor of Pennsylvania. The thing about Thornburgh is that he caves in under political pressure. When the U.S. attorneys told him, 'Look at this Strike Force shit. We really don't need them. We can do it ourselves,' you knew it was going to go. He will kiss the asses of the U.S. attorneys because they will always have some kind of political power. That's much more important to him.

"Thornburgh always has his eye on the next thing he wants to do. And to piss off a few career prosecutors? So what? What can they do to him?"

When the bloodbath was completed, only fourteen of the original Strike Force offices remained in the major cities, along with a dozen suboffices in smaller cities.

Aaron Kohn, the managing director of the Metropolitan Crime Commission of New Orleans, told me, "We had to save the Strike Force here. Thornburgh had wiped it out, and then we revived it after about a year by lobbying with Congress and the Carter White House."

However, only the New Orleans office remained open; the others boarded up by Thornburgh remained closed. More cuts would have occurred had Ford defeated Jimmy Carter in the 1976 presidential election. It was understood that Ford planned to retain Thornburgh, who did return to Pennsylvania and was elected governor of the state. The Carter administration saved the Strike Forces, and the war on organized crime continued—then under Carter appointees Benjamin Civiletti as attorney general, William Webster as director of the FBI, and Margolis, who replaced Muellenberg as OCRS chief. All three of these appointments were made in 1978. With these three men, the mob was again under a genuine siege by the federal government for the first time since the Kennedy administration.

When Ronald Reagan defeated Carter in 1980—the Republicans ludicrously charged that Carter was soft on crime—the war against syndicate crime ended. The victories against organized crime claimed by the Reaganistas—like Operation Strawman/Argent, Brilab, Pendorf, and the prosecution of Tony Salerno and the heads of the other four crime families in New York,[8] among many other cases—had been initiated during the previous administration or by individual state agencies, like the New York Task Force Against Organized Crime, which was headed by Ronald Goldstock. Nevertheless, Reagan and his two attorney generals, William French Smith and Edwin Meese, shamefully took the credit.

On January 20, 1988, Attorney General Meese sent a memorandum—entitled "New and Expanded Initiatives in the Federal Organized Crime Effort"—to the OCRS, all U.S. attorneys, and Strike Force chiefs. In this letter, Meese wrote: "In order to maximize the benefits to be derived from a close working relationship and coordination between the United States Attorney as the chief federal prosecutor in each District and the Organized Crime Strike Force Chief, and in order to capitalize on our recent successes against organized crime, the Department will implement the following initiatives . . ."

Despite Meese's attempt to sugarcoat the bad news, the action was nothing more than a sleight-of-hand move. Essentially, Meese reinstituted the policy, previously advocated by Thornburgh, to compromise the independence of the Strike Forces. By again attempting to make the career prosecutors of the Strike Force accountable to the politically appointed U.S. attorneys, dissension was renewed within the Justice Department.

Immediately after Meese released his memo, Margolis threatened to resign.

Comparing the Meese action with that of Thornburgh over a decade earlier, the chief of the criminal division under Meese, William Weld, who later resigned in protest of Meese's overall pattern of unethical behavior, told me, "It was almost much worse. I threw my body in the middle [of Meese and Margolis] to prevent the total merger of the Strike Forces into the U.S. attorney's offices."

Weld said that a compromise was finally reached when it was decided that the U.S. attorneys would be the rating officials in personnel terms for the Strike Force chiefs—but that the chief of the criminal division would become the reviewing official with the power to overrule decisions by the U.S. attorneys.[9]

In August 1988, Meese resigned as attorney general. For his successor, Reagan appointed Richard Thornburgh, who was later retained by President George Bush.

Predictably, in mid-March 1989, Thornburgh announced that all of the Strike Force offices would be disbanded.

Later that same week, on March 22 at the NFL owners' meeting in Palm Desert, sixty-three-year-old Pete Rozelle, with two years left on his contract, resigned as NFL commissioner. While leaving the room after telling the owners of his decision, Rozelle was embraced by Al Davis. Later, at a press conference, Rozelle told reporters, "You go through life once . . . I wanted more free time . . . time to travel and do other things."

In a moving tribute to Rozelle, Joe Gergen, a columnist for *The Sporting News,* wrote, "Perhaps Rozelle should have taken his leave when he was still trim and full of what Kennedy called vigah. But say this about Rozelle: He was a man for his age. The NFL was no Camelot. Don't let it be forgotten, however, that once it was a mighty little kingdom governed by a wise man."

Earlier, on August 13, 1988, Edward Bennett Williams, the former president of the Washington Redskins and the owner of the Baltimore Orioles baseball team, died after an eleven-year bout with cancer. He was sixty-eight years old and took numerous secrets about the sweetheart relationship between the federal government and the NFL to the grave with him.[10]

Twelve days after Williams's death, eighty-seven-year-old Art Rooney, the patriarch of the Pittsburgh Steelers, died at Mercy Hospital in his hometown after suffering a stroke in his office at Three Rivers Stadium. The funeral mass was held at his 150-year-old parish church, St. Peter's on Arch Street, near Allegheny Center and the stadium on the city's north side. The church was also a short walk from his Victorian house, which he and his wife had purchased in 1933 for $5,000. He had spent half that much for the Steelers that same year. At the time of his death, Rooney was the only owner to have won four Super Bowl championships.[11]

Eleven hundred mourners attended the services to honor Rooney. Those who could not get into the church watched on closed-circuit televisions set up in the nearby church hall. Overshadowed by the solemnness of the funeral mass were rare handshakes between Pete Rozelle and Al Davis, as well as between members of the NFL Management Council and the NFL Players Association. Nearly every NFL owner was in attendance at the church, as well as numerous players and Jimmy "the Greek" Snyder,[12] who said that he had known Rooney for fifty-three years. Also in attendance was former Pennsylvania governor Richard Thornburgh, who had replaced Meese as attorney general earlier in the month.

"He [Rooney] was a man who belonged to the entire world of sports," Rozelle told reporters. "It is questionable whether any sports figure was more universally loved and respected."

Bishop Vincent Leonard, a longtime friend of Rooney, delivered the eulogy, telling the crowd that there was no public clamor to have the Steelers' owner canonized. If they tried, the bishop said, "the devil's advocates would have a field day for the likes of a man who, on his honeymoon, took his wife to the racetrack."

Rooney was buried in a Catholic cemetery next to his wife, who had died six years earlier. As his body was being lowered into his grave, his beloved Steelers players were preparing for a preseason game with the New Orleans Saints in Louisiana.

The bet was even-money that Art Rooney was there in spirit, cheering them on.

52 The Las Vegas and Outlaw Lines Today

ON JUNE 23, 1986—the same day as he was scheduled to stand trial for conspiracy and racketeering—forty-eight-year-old Tony Spilotro, the enforcer of the outlaw line, was found buried in a shallow grave in a Newton County cornfield in northwestern Indiana. Planted along with Spilotro was his younger brother, Michael, who was also under indictment in Chicago for extortion. Both men, who were reported missing on June 14, were found dressed only in their underwear. They had been beaten to death and placed in the ground several days earlier. Their bodies were so badly decomposed that an immediate identification could not be made. Fingerprints and dental records obtained by the FBI were used for positive makes. The murder remains officially unsolved—although law-enforcement officials say that it was probably ordered by Joe Ferriola, also known as Joe Nagall, who had become the new boss of the Chicago Mafia in 1986. Nagall had made his reputation as an enforcer under Sam Giancana and later Joey Aiuppa, who was convicted in the Stardust skimming trial and sentenced to prison.

According to federal investigators, Spilotro was upset when Nagall was named as Aiuppa's successor. Spilotro was planning to mount a challenge against him. "Aiuppa, along with Tony Accardo,[1] remained as Nagall's advisers and probably approved of Nagall's decision to take out Tony Spilotro," a top FBI official told me. "Michael Spilotro was killed along with him to prevent any act of vengeance, which could have caused a serious problem within the Chicago mob."

Among those suspected for being involved in the Spilotro murder was Frank Schweihs, who was also a top suspect in the murder of Allen Dorfman. In September 1988, the FBI revealed that it had taped Schweihs bragging about some of his jobs, but no specifics have been released. The investigation of Schweihs's roles in a variety of crimes, including the murders of Dorfman and the Spilotro brothers, is continuing. Soon after the existence of the tapes was revealed, Schweihs was arrested for extortion.

Also during the fall of 1988, with Accardo in retirement and Aiuppa in prison, another dramatic change within the top leadership of the Chicago Mafia occurred. Sam Carlisi of Elmhurst, Illinois, a longtime associate of Aiuppa and Nagall, became the acting boss of the Chicago Mafia. After just two years in power, Nagall had stepped aside because of his failing health and finally died in March 1989. Born in December 1921, Carlisi is the brother of Buffalo Mafia figure Roy Carlisi, who was arrested at the 1957 Apalachin Conference. Another Carlisi brother, Alphonso, owned a bar, which was a front for layoff sports-bookmaking activity in Chicago.

Meantime, even after the murders of the Spilotro brothers, Lefty Rosenthal, the brains of the outlaw line, continued his self-imposed exile—but moved from Laguna Niguel in Southern California to Boca Raton, Florida. During the fall of 1988, soon after his move to Florida, Rosenthal attempted but failed to have his name removed from the Nevada Black Book and to obtain a gaming license.

The new brain behind the outlaw line, according to law-enforcement authorities, is Chicago mobster Don Angelini, who, like Carlisi, is also from Elmhurst and has become known as the newest "Wizard of Odds." Angelini has been involved in the underworld's oddsmaking operations since 1957 when he and Bill Kaplan operated Angel-Kaplan Sports News, which had employed Lefty Rosenthal during his game-fixing days. At that time, Angelini was Rosenthal's immediate supervisor.

The five-feet-ten, medium-built Angelini, who has brilliant white hair, brown eyes, and wears glasses, is directed by Dominic Cortina, Nagall's and Carlisi's chief gambling lieutenant and a close associate of Angelini since the mid-1950s. Angelini and Cortina were convicted of federal gambling violations in 1970 and sentenced to five years in prison. In February 1979, Angelini and Cortina, along with five others, pleaded guilty and were sentenced to three years in prison for running a $1.5-million-a-month sports-betting business. Among those convicted was Joseph Spadavecchio, another close associate of Rosenthal.

Upon being sentenced, Angelini told the judge, "I've never used threats to collect a debt. I am not now and have never been a member of the Chicago crime syndicate."

Joe Yablonsky, the former head of the FBI's Las Vegas office, told me, "Angelini used to be a messenger, which is a trusted job. He delivered messages for the Chicago mob to Rosenthal in Vegas. They were paranoid about the telephone, so Angelini would actually fly to Nevada. They would meet at the airport and talk. And then Angelini would just get another flight and return to Chicago."

When I asked Angelini in late 1988 whether he had indeed become the new executive of the outlaw line, based upon his success as an oddsmaker during his days with the Angel-Kaplan line, he replied, "That's ancient history. That was twenty years ago. We went out of business in 1968, and I couldn't tell you anything about the gambling business since then. I'm out of it, and I have nothing to do with it anymore. I don't even have any interest in football anymore. I don't even watch the games. I'm far from a wizard. I'm an old man. Bill [Kaplan] died an old man. It's all over. I'm out of the business."

Ernest "Rocco" Infelise, Nagall's former driver, is Carlisi's and Cortina's chief enforcer—although he has yet to earn the awesome and brutal reputation achieved by Spilotro. A horse-racing enthusiast, the six-feet, 240-pound Infelise has a criminal record back to 1952 with arrests for murder, burglary, and robbery. He was also convicted for firearms violations and the theft of $1 million in silver bullion.

One of Infelise's top henchmen was Wayne Bock, a former player with the Chicago Cardinals of the NFL and a driver for Carlisi, who, along with Schweihs, is another top suspect in the 1983 Dorfman murder. Bock also spent a great deal of time at a second house in Hollywood, Florida.

Through these men, the Chicago Mafia continues to finance, distribute, and enforce the nation's principal outlaw line on all NFL games.

Today, the sports book at the Stardust, the onetime home of the outlaw line, is under new management but still resembles the bar scene in the movie *Star Wars* on Sunday afternoons during the football season. Some patrons wear suits and ties, while others are more relaxed, donning jerseys, T-shirts, hats, and headgear from their favorite NFL team. Other sports gamblers look as though they live in the street but appear to be regulars at the payout window.

Although the Stardust lacks the glamour and sophistication of the newer, state-of-the-art sports books at Caesars Palace and the Las Vegas Hilton, the Stardust is still the place to be before and during NFL games. On the large, glitzy marquee rotating outside the hotel, the Stardust boasts that its sports book is "the Home of the Official Las Vegas Line."

One of oddsmaker Michael Roxborough's top clients is the Stardust. Explaining the process, Roxy told me, "The whole thing begins on Saturday. We can't make a line until we see some college results. With the NFL, it starts right after the Sunday games. We're looking for injuries to skilled players, and anything else we can discover from the results of the games. Basically, it's a real crunch period between noon on Sunday and five P.M., when I phone my numbers into the Stardust. They take my line. On that basis the Stardust supervisors decide which way they want to go."[2]

The director of the Stardust sports book who takes and adjusts Roxy's numbers is Scott Schettler, who was born in Pennsylvania and has been in Las Vegas since 1968. By 1971, he was working at Bobby Martin's old haunt, the Churchill Downs Sports Book, writing betting tickets, handling the board, and giving out scores over the telephone. He remained at Churchill until 1977. Then he opened the sports book at the Royal Casino, leaving that job in 1978 to open another in Reno at the Club Cal-Neva. Schettler returned home to western Pennsylvania for a year before going back to Vegas in 1981 and becoming a clerk at the Stardust. He stayed at the Stardust for eighteen months before leaving to open another sports book at Jerry's Nugget, a casino in North Las Vegas.

In December 1983, with the Stardust in receivership by the state after the federal skimming indictments, Schettler was selected by gaming officials to operate the casino's sports book as part of the state-appointed management team. He has run the Stardust Sports Book ever since under the Stardust's owner, Sam Boyd, who purchased the hotel/casino from Al Sachs.

"At the Stardust," Schettler told me, "we open the line up first. Our line is based on Roxy's numbers and those of my guys who work here.[3] There are about four or five opinions that go into this. Then we take bets and move the line. When the line has flattened out, the other books will follow our lead. By putting my line up first, I have a chance to get two-way business. The other books are basically gambling. They are giving one-way business because they wait to put up the line. We strictly book here. We don't gamble. Right now, at the major hotels, we're doing forty-four percent of the business. Caesars and Hilton are the glamour places, but we're actually a book joint."

When I asked Schettler about today's outlaw line, he replied, "The whole world doesn't hinge on the Stardust line. There're guys who put lines up around the country before the Stardust. I'm talking about the outlaw bookmakers. They still have their own man-to-man betting system. They take bets and move their line. But we don't care what the outlaws have. We make our own line no matter what anybody else thinks. We put our own numbers up. We get no opinions from the outlaws."

In fact, today the first gamblers to have the opportunity to bet into the Stardust line are from the general betting public. By the time the Stardust opens its line on the NFL and college games at 6:00 P.M. every Sunday of the football season, a lottery to determine who bets first has already been conducted. Anyone who wants to bet into the initial line signs his name on a list, which is available at the front of the sports book throughout the day. When the list is picked up by the Stardust staff at 5:50, those who have signed it will have their names called.

They then draw cards to determine the order of gamblers who are each assigned to a specific cashier's window. The bettors quietly get in line. They understand that their minimum bet has to be at least $200. The most they can bet on an NFL game is $50,000; the limit on a major college game is $10,000.[4]

"In other words," says Roxborough, "everything has changed since the days of the old outlaw line. The public now has the opportunity to bet on the Stardust line before any of the so-called inside professionals."

When I asked Schettler why he created the lottery system, he replied, "It was out of necessity. The way it used to be done was a few wise guys bet the line first. Then the line would flatten out and all the bargains would be gone. We put the line up for the public. It's never been bet into. It's a virgin line.

"Before the lottery, guys were coming in here two days

before Sunday. And then it got to be so bad that they would come in a week ahead of time. People would pay guys five or six dollars an hour to stand in line twenty-four hours a day. I got so sick of seeing these people. Finally, I came in one day and some guy had left his place in line to get a cup of coffee and when he came back there was a guy in his place. And he told the new guy, 'You took my spot, and I want it back.' And the guy who took the spot opened his coat, and there was a gun. That's when I created the lottery.

"At first, we just opened the telephones, just so people wouldn't have to come in here and kill each other just to stand in line to give us their money. But the reason why we're in this business is to get people to come to this hotel and its casino. Hey, the guy who is sitting at his house is not going to come here and blow his money on something else.

"So then we came up with the lottery system. The government should come in here and watch how we do this—because it is a model of true democracy. The system couldn't be fairer. The gamblers police themselves. We put the list there. If you're first or second in line, you have to make a bet. You can't come in here with ten guys and whoever gets the best number will cause the other nine to drop out of line. So by forcing these guys to make a bet eliminates guys coming in here and clogging up the lines. If you get drawn and don't make a bet, you're out of the lottery forever.

"Also, once we draw the cards, there is no talking. The reason for that is, say, if you draw number seven and another guy draws number one, you could go up to him and say, 'Hey, make this bet for me.' And then the system would be useless. And, again, the gamblers actually police each other. Also, if you talk in line after the lottery, you're history. If one guy in line hands another guy in line a piece of paper with a bet on it, the gamblers will tell on him in a second. And then the guy who handed the paper is history. The system is for them and for us. And it's the only way it can work."

At 6:00 P.M. a Stardust employee who is standing in front of a microphone begins to read off only the favorite college teams along with the number of points in which they are favored. The opposing, underdog team is not mentioned. There is total silence in the large room as the thirty favored college teams and their lines are read off.

"Notre Dame minus twenty-one and a half . . . Duke and six and a half . . . Pittsburgh minus two . . . Iowa and twenty-four . . ."

After the college games are finished, the pros are read off. Twelve games are mentioned—"Chicago plus five . . . Minnesota and six and a half . . . Houston minus three and a half . . . New Orleans and thirteen . . ."

The thirteenth and fourteenth games to be played the next week involving the two teams playing each other the following night on *Monday Night Football* are not included. The line on their games will depend on their performances and casualties on Monday night.

After the pro games have been read off, those who have signed the list and drawn cards step up to the window and begin rattling off their bets. As the bets are being made, the line begins to move—with a Stardust employee calling out the shifts in the point spreads. No computer is computing the changing odds; in fact, the computer is ignored when the betting opens. The Stardust bookmaker, without the benefit of the computer, makes his own personal calculations to move the line, strictly based upon his own experience and his estimate of the money being bet. The computer is simply a bookkeeping device after the initial, frantic wave of action has been completed.

The first man in the lottery on September 18, 1988—who was wearing a blue jogging suit, carrying a clipboard, and bearding for persons unknown—told me, "We have a pretty good idea of what the numbers are going to be before they're read off. After I write them down while they're reading them off, I go down both lists and bet the games I want to bet. If something unexpected has happened, I'll take that into consideration too. Money is no object. My job is to take the lead. Our people will try to middle later on in the week."

Although reforms are evident on the Las Vegas sports-gambling scene, it would be naïve to think that the underworld has no further interest in Nevada—or that the state's gaming industry will never again be confronted with charges of penetration by the mob. But the key to the continued smooth and honest functioning of the legal Nevada sports books—as well as to the integrity of the NFL—will be keeping the organized-crime gambling syndicate's influence over professional sports in check. This means strong and vigilant law enforcement and surveillance in Nevada and within the NFL. And that demands public officials who are more sensitive to the problem of organized crime in America, and members of the sports media who are more willing to report it.

Epilogue: On Legalizing Sports Gambling

> If once a government indulges itself with organized crime, very soon it comes to think little of political corruption; and from this corruption it next comes to bingo, state lotteries, offtrack betting, and casinos; and from there to legalizing team sports gambling, drug dealing, and murder—while its people grow fearful and selfish, prone to incivility and procrastination. Inevitably, the government, itself, becomes organized crime.
>
> —The author, with an apology to Thomas De Quincey

Each year, gambling on professional football reaches new heights. Mobsters, gamblers, and drug dealers use their contacts in the NFL to obtain inside information that will help them cover the spread. Games are occasionally thought to be fixed; points are sometimes suspected to have been shaved. Betting lines are printed in the major newspapers around the country. Television oddsmakers are paid by the networks to make their picks, which occasionally do nothing more than mislead viewers and help bookmakers to balance their books. Consequently, sports fans outside of Nevada who reject man-to-man betting and bet illegally with bookmakers are exploited by the entire process.

Sports gambling, particularly on NFL games, is widespread and virtually out of control in America, and no reasonable law appears to dissuade the public from gambling illegally. Meantime, public officials are trying to quench the public's thirst for gambling while being responsive to increasing budgetary demands on local, state, and federal governments. Since 1987, several states have passed laws providing for offtrack betting—upscale versions of the OTB operation in New York.

Unavoidably, the question of whether or not team sports gambling should be legalized, regulated, and taxed by responsible government agencies will soon become a major public-policy issue.

Advocates of legalization adhere to the argument that gambling is going to continue regardless of laws they consider to be archaic and essentially unenforceable. They also express deeper, more fundamental questions about whether the government should be legislating personal morality—while insisting that legalization would drive organized crime out of the sports-gambling business.

Opponents charge that legalizing sports gambling will have a broad and serious impact on society. They contend that this system—in which the state assumes the role as bookmaker—will particularly harm lower-income people. They also cite an increase in political payoffs, loan-sharking, street violence, and other crimes that have traditionally accompanied legal and illegal gambling operations. And they add that legalization will give the American public an even higher toleration for other forms of organized-crime activities, such as drug trafficking—which has also become a subject of debate for possible legalization, because that problem, too, is growing uncontrollable.

Most people directly involved in sports, professional gambling, or law enforcement have strong feelings about the issue of legalizing sports gambling. And their opinions, in view of their professions, are not as predictable as one might think.

Pete Rozelle and NFL Security were consistent in their position against legalization, contending that it would impact on "the integrity of the game." Of course, the NFL has never publicly challenged the sports media on the ethics of printing the line or hiring handicappers to discuss point spreads. Rozelle and the NFL owners, like the television networks, understood that a betting public means higher revenues. Perhaps this is the best indication that the antigambling stance by the NFL has been hypocritical and nothing more than a public-relations charade that is certainly not rooted in principle.

Former San Diego Chargers owner Gene Klein, who has become a giant in the thoroughbred-racing world, told me in September 1988, "I firmly believe that people are going to gamble. I now bet, but I won't bet with [an illegal] bookie. I'm going to Vegas tomorrow. I've got five horses running around the country. I'm going to sit there, and I'm going to watch those five horses. I'm going to bet on them, and any other horse I want to bet on. And I'm going to watch UCLA play Nebraska, and I'm going to bet on that fucking game. And I'm going to see what the odds are, and I'll bet five or six pro games. Perfectly legal. I'll hand them the money, and I'll get my slips.

"I go to the races a lot. Three weekends ago the offtrack betting and the handle at Del Mar was $9.2 million. And on one Sunday it was $9.8 million. People are going to gamble.

"In England, you can pick up the phone, call your bookie, make a bet, and watch the race. One day, you will go to a baseball game or a football game and there will be betting booths. You'll have all kinds of exotic bets. You'll pay your money, you'll get a receipt, and you'll win or lose."

When I asked Klein about the impact that legalization will have on fans who then expect their teams to cover the spread, he replied, "In last week's Charger-Raiders game, the Chargers were five-point underdogs. I gave the five points. The Raiders were leading by three with thirty seconds to go. The Raiders had the ball on the Chargers one yard line. They took the ball and the quarterback got down on one knee. Game's over, right? Except the Chargers called time out. Why would they call time out? The next play they [Raiders] went over for a touchdown. Draw whatever conclusion you want to draw."

Predictably, former national oddsmaker Bobby Martin also supports legalization and told me, "The NFL says that it can live with illegal gambling, but it cannot live with legal gambling. I think Rozelle said that, which is ridiculous. Legalizing gambling is better than what you have now. It's not a hundred percent. It's not going to change everything overnight. But it's an improvement over the present conditions. It'll create quite a few jobs. The government will realize some revenue. It will have its drawbacks along the way. People may bet what they can't afford, which you have in the lottery. But it's better than what exists at the moment: an underground gambling network spread over the United States—from which the government gets nothing."

Las Vegas gambler Lem Banker disagrees with his old friend Bob Martin. "I'm against it," Banker says. "Most people can't control themselves. The average guy who likes to watch football and gamble will just bury himself. It's a scary thing. It's not like betting on a horse for five or ten dollars. The guy who bets fifty dollars cash on a football game will bet five hundred dollars over the telephone. But if it is legalized and if anybody does start booking, it should be the insurance companies. They're the best pricemakers in the world. And they'd make a ton of money."

Marty Kane, the former manager of the Stardust Sports Book, told me, "It's wrong for the state to gamble. But sports gambling will work if the state licenses independent contractors to bankroll the operations and allows them to take their percentage. In other words, just do it the way they do it in Nevada."

Kane's successor, Scott Schettler, who has operated the Stardust Sports Book since 1983, agrees with Kane, adding, "People have been contacting me all over the country, asking me how the states could operate a sports book. But the government could never, ever run a book—because the margin of profit is so small. They'd only make about two and a half percent. Can you imagine the bureaucracy? The only way it would work is if it is done like it's done here in Nevada: private industry which is regulated and taxed by the state."

When I asked Schettler whether legalized sports gambling outside of Nevada would hurt his business at the Stardust, Schettler replied, "I really don't think so. The more sports books that open up, the more business I'm going to do. When I came here to the Stardust, there were no books at this end of the Strip. Now, we're surrounded by seven books. Between now and then, the hotels saw people coming over to the Stardust to make a bet. And so the hotels decided, 'Well, let's put a book of our own in.' I do even more business now because gamblers shop for numbers. In other words, if I have a game at seven and across the street the same game is six and a half, that is going to create business."

Surprisingly, oddsmaker Michael Roxborough, Bob Martin's successor, is skeptical of widespread state-controlled sports gambling and told me, "There are a lot of reasons why I don't think you're going to see legalization. The main reason is that there's no revenue in it. You go to sports books here in Las Vegas, and they're jammed. But they're holding only two and a half percent. That's their win for the year. Look at the gross win in the business. It's not very high. In fact, it's incredibly low.

"Suppose a state goes to legalizing sports gambling. There's only one reason that they're going to do it: so that they can extract revenue from it. If they want to be competitive, they are going to have to go out and get independent operators to run the business for them. And if they do, all they can do is tax part of their gross win. If they do it like they do in Nevada where they tax six percent of the gross win, there wouldn't be enough money in there at the end of the year to pay for their regulation. If they go out and try to run it themselves, à la pari-mutuel—and they extract eighteen to twenty percent out, like they do at the horses—then they're not going to be able to compete with the illegal bookmakers.

"Suppose that a state decides that in order to make any money on it, it will go with six to five on football or even thirteen to ten. That's the way the state mentality works. If you take a look at the lottery, they're only returning about forty percent of the money to the winners. Suppose they charge thirteen to ten on a football game instead of eleven to ten. What they're going to do is whet the appetite of a lot of people who want to bet football. And after a while they're going to learn how to bet football, and they'll discover that thirteen to ten isn't so good—and that an illegal bookmaker will give them credit and eleven to ten.

"I think another dilemma with it is that you have to consider that if every state has sports wagering you'll literally have some people betting a million dollars on a game. And then you just have to ask: How will this affect the integrity of the game?

"You know, I'm not against it. I just don't think it would work."

Handicapper Mort Olshan of *The Gold Sheet* told me, "Gambling has been going on for five thousand years. We're the only Western industrial society that has this Puritan, Calvinist attitude toward gambling. But it seems to be changing. There are so many inconsistencies in the law right now. The media has created the stereotype of the gambler and bookmaker as shady characters with fedoras and big cigars, the Edward G. Robinson type. But everyone is betting with bookmakers who are just guys who wear suits and sports coats. The average gambler is a professional man. To have a law that is not respected is like having no law at all. The government is making lawbreakers out of the forty million Americans who bet. England is very civilized about it. They have gambling controlled by the state, and the system works. It is integrated into their society. It adds some fun and excitement to their lives."

But Karl Ersin, Olshan's onetime associate at the Minneapolis *Green Sheet*, disagrees. "No, I don't support legalizing gambling. There are too many things that get into it. There are too many crooks. They do a lot of things with these games. They try to fix them. If sports gambling were legalized, you'd find a lot more of that."

Jack Danahy, who has spent a distinguished career in law enforcement and as the head of NFL Security, is also against legalization. "They tried it in Delaware, and the state nearly welshed. In legalized sports gambling, you proliferate. You attract more people into gambling on that particular sport. Our feeling at the NFL was that gambling is inherent to horse racing. But gambling has never been inherent to football. It never has been. Nor is it to baseball or any of the team sports.

"If state officials want to legalize gambling for the sole purpose to make money for the state, I feel that this would be dangerous to the sport because you're going to introduce more people to gambling on football. I'm not naïve enough to think that a lot of people don't bet on football. It's become a popular pastime, but let's not encourage or enhance it more."

Ralph Salerno, who as both a law-enforcement official and private citizen has waged a one-man campaign against organized crime, favors legalizing sports gambling and told me, "Pete Rozelle [had] always been violently against sports betting. That is going to continue until the owners decide that they want some of the income and will take the bets at the stadium or elsewhere. The TV money isn't going to pay for everything forever. They're going to be looking for additional revenue.

"Absolutely, gambling on NFL games should be legalized—for the same reason you need offtrack betting. I don't think that gambling is evil. I just don't like the current management and how they use their money. I don't like the bookmakers of America—the gambling community or whatever you want to call them—and what they do with their profits. We long ago proved that you don't have to be a wizard bookmaker to be a successful bookmaker. That's the shit they threw at us when we opened OTB. They said, 'You're going to have to go out and hire Frank Costello.' Bullshit! At that time, in 1971, when OTB was created, the most sophisticated equipment I'd ever seen in a bookmaking operation was a hand-cranked adding machine.

"The government or the private sector can use IBM or Honeywell or anybody else that makes computer hardware and software. Why can't we do what any bookmaker already does? You get someone who knows how to program computers. Then you get someone from Merrill Lynch or Dean Witter. They've been running gambling operations for years—they call it the stock market.

"In the stock market, the numbers are changing by the second. The theory here is that you can change the line by the second—to ensure that you stay within the ten percent vigorish—with a computer. The computer balances your book. As long as it keeps the difference within the vig, then the government will make money."

When I asked Salerno about the disastrous sports lottery in Delaware, he replied, "I don't think Delaware was a real attempt. If you want to make a real attempt, you don't start in Delaware. If you could put together a national operation, then the individual states could legalize sports gambling and make money. The main problem is going to be the layoff. But if you organize it in, say, the private sector, then it can be done—with operations in several states that lay off with each other. If you keep your book close to balance, there is a ten percent fee, just like with a bookmaker. The only difference is that you have to put your money up front. There is no credit.

"If you play it right, the public will have less of a toleration for other forms of organized-crime activity. We haven't put bookmakers in jail for many years—but if it is legal, then the illegal bookmaker who operates in competition with the state should be sentenced and fined. He becomes a threat to the government—which is using the money for public needs.

"People who try to cheat the sports-gambling operation should be prosecuted just like an insider trader. It won't affect the integrity of the game. It becomes the responsibility of investigative agencies to enforce to law.

"It all just depends on who is running it. How honest are they? How closely do they watch the operation?" Former Senate investigator Phil Manuel disagrees with Salerno and told me, "Most forms of gambling, especially lotteries or numbers games, are a type of consumer fraud. Over the long haul, the sucker who bets money on lotteries, sporting events, or against the house cannot win. Many more people will lose than will win, and the only people who will reap profits are the people who control the game—whether they are part of the gambling syndicates or the political system. To raise revenue by legalizing sports gambling and other forms of gambling is to take money from those who can least afford it."

Aaron Kohn is the most vehement opponent of legalizing sports gambling I talked to and says, "Again, I get down to the character of our country. Our politicians are under tremendous pressure from their constituencies to provide public services in a way that the voters don't have to pay for them. And what we find is that the politicians, by reason of that imbalance between demand and responsibility, in order to satisfy the demand for services, are turning to trickery in order to provide the financing. That is exactly what legalized gambling is. Legalized gambling is saying to the people that in order to have greater services the society must be induced and provided the opportunity to gamble.

"Legalized gambling is a con game. You induce people to lose their money in order to make them believe that they can be enriched."

Gambling is indeed inevitable. And to create a complete prohibition against all forms of betting is as unrealistic as to assume that every NFL player performs at his peak level at every moment of every game. Passes will be dropped. Field goals will go awry. Blocks will be missed. But the problem for the NFL and for its fans is to ensure that when seemingly innocent on-field mistakes do occur that something nefarious hasn't actually happened. But the broader the base of legal and illegal sports gambling, the more suspicions will be raised when these errors are made and the greater the temptation for team members to fix games in order to make fast bucks.

To date, it is obvious that the NFL's public-relations machine has managed to allay the fears of football fans about threats to the integrity of the game. However, the evidence is also clear that the NFL has been more interested in covering up abuses within its system, particularly with regard to the relationships between certain team owners and a variety of underworld figures. Considering that the organized-crime gambling syndicate has always controlled the bulk of illegal sports betting, the NFL's response to this problem is sporadic and at times, deceptive.

Organized crime has not completely corrupted the NFL. However, if the situation remains consistent with the NFL's history, professional football will inevitably come helmet to helmet with a scandal of epic proportions—a scandal that will probably involve organized crime, drugs, and gambling and spell disaster for the league. Contrary to the popular wisdom, the threat to the league doesn't come from the Big Fix. The danger is far more insidious and is built on personal relations and casual contacts, as well as on business ties and friendly betting.

"There is no room for gambling in professional football," Gene Upshaw of the NFLPA told me. "We have to protect the integrity of the game. We don't want any doubts about why a receiver dropped a ball, a kicker missed a field goal, a lineman missed a block, or anything else that might affect the outcome of a game. We don't need that. NFL Security polices the players quite heavily, and I don't object to that. But I would also like to see that same type of enforcement and treatment of the owners."

History has repeatedly proven that the consequences of gambling and organized crime have had a significant impact on America and its institutions, particularly in the areas of drug trafficking and political corruption. And the time has come for the American public, its elected officials, the law-enforcement community, and the media to become realistic about the problem of organized crime in America.

Unfortunately, the public has been shown little evidence of organized crime's influence on professional sports, particularly the NFL. And fans who believe that they're placing harmless and innocent bets on NFL games with their friendly local bookmakers at their corner bars should know where a portion of their money will end up after it's been laid off: in the pockets of organized-crime figures who will continue to corrupt America.

Meyer Lansky, the financial wizard of organized crime, knew perhaps better than anyone else that the successful annihilation of organized crime's subculture in America would rock the "legitimate" world's entire foundation, which would ultimately force fundamental social changes and redistributions of wealth and power in this country. Lansky's dream was to bond the two worlds together so that one could not survive without the other. Those of us who recognize the vast power of the underworld in our nation today also understand how close Lansky's dream—and our nightmare—is to coming true.

Notes

PROLOGUE

1. Grantland Rice often told a story about an incident that occurred during halftime of a 1920 game, just before Gipp's death. Rice reported that he had been told by an assistant coach for the Irish, "Being behind by three points, Rock was really laying into the boys. He had about finished and Gipp, standing nearby, asked me for a drag of my cigarette. Rock looked up and spotted Gipp leaning against the door, his helmet on the back of his head, puffing the cigarette.

"Rock exploded, 'As for you, Gipp, I suppose you haven't any interest in this game . . . ?'

" 'Listen, Rock,' replied Gipp, 'I've got five hundred dollars bet on this game; I don't aim to blow any five hundred!' "

Rockne said nothing and never disciplined his player who had been gambling on the outcome of his own games.

2. "Page Six," *New York Post,* 9 January 1989.

CHAPTER 1

1. Deposition of Allen Davis, Los Angeles Memorial Coliseum Commission v. National Football League, U.S. District Court, Central District of California, Civil Action No. 78–3523-HP.

2. In the standard NFL players' contract, there is a section entitled "Integrity of Game" that reads: "Player recognizes the detriment to the League and professional football that would result from impairment of public confidence in the honest and orderly conduct of NFL games or the integrity and good character of NFL players. Player therefore acknowledges his awareness that if he accepts a bribe or agrees to throw or fix an NFL game; fails to promptly report a bribe offer or an attempt to throw or fix an NFL game; bets on an NFL game; knowingly associates with gamblers or gambling activity; uses

or provides other players with stimulants or other drugs for the purpose of attempting to enhance on-field performance; or is guilty of any other form of conduct reasonably judged by the League Commissioner to be detrimental to the League of professional football, the Commissioner will have the right, but only after giving Player the opportunity for a hearing at which he may be represented by counsel of his choice, to fine Player in a reasonable amount; to suspend Player for a period certain or indefinitely; and/or to terminate this contract."

CHAPTER 2

1. There is some confusion over the actual founding date of the APFC. Most of the old-timers, including George Halas, claimed that it was created on September 17, the first meeting Halas attended. However, NFL records show that the initial meeting was on August 20 in Hay's auto showroom. The charter teams were the Akron Professionals, Buffalo All-Americans, Canton Bulldogs, Cleveland Indians, Dayton Triangles, Hammond Pros, and Rochester Jeffersons. The teams from Buffalo, Hammond, and Rochester were not present at the first meeting but formally applied for membership in writing. Most reports also include the Massillon Tigers as a charter member, but no team from Massillon, a powerhouse in pre-1920 play, was entered.

At the second meeting in Hay's showroom on September 17, the original seven teams were joined by the Racine [Chicago] Cardinals, Halas's Decatur Staleys, Muncie Flyers, and Rock Island Independents. Three additional teams participated in the 1920 season: the Chicago Tigers, Columbus Panhandles, and Detroit Heralds.

The Akron Professionals finished the 1920 season in first place with an 8–0–3 record.

2. Myron Cope, *The Game That Was: The Early Days of Pro Football* (New York: World Publishing Co., 1970), p. 41.

3. Carr instituted the college draft in 1936.

4. In 1925, the Milwaukee Badgers Club placed four high school players on its roster. When Carr discovered this blatant violation, he forced the Badgers' owner, Ambrose McGurk, to sell his franchise and banned for life a member of the team who had recruited the four youngsters.

5. George Halas with Gwen Morgan and Arthur Veysey, *Halas by Halas: The Autobiography of George Halas* (New York: McGraw-Hill Book Co., 1979), pp. 62–63.

CHAPTER 3

1. *The New York Times,* 17 February 1959.

2. Halas had actually violated the NFL's rules by signing Grange before he had graduated from the University of Illinois. However, considering the revenues produced by Grange, an exception was made. Halas made his deal with Grange through the player's agent, C. C. "Cash 'n' Carry" Pyle.

Grange's "barnstorming" across the country provided the impetus for the big cities with major colleges and big-time college sports to accept professional football.

However, professional football was still not receiving respect. When Halas and Grange were introduced as members of the Chicago Bears to President Calvin Coolidge, the President replied, "I've always enjoyed animal acts." Coolidge thought that these Bears were part of the circus.

3. The Chicago Cardinals became the St. Louis Cardinals in 1960 and the Phoenix Cardinals in 1988.

4. In 1938, Rooney hired his first, big star player, Byron "Whizzer" White, an all-American halfback from the University of Colorado. White was later appointed as an associate justice on the U.S. Supreme Court by President John Kennedy.

5. Red Smith, *The Red Smith Reader* (New York: Random House, Inc., 1982), p. 107.

6. Myron Cope, *The Game That Was: The Early Days of Pro Football* (New York: World Publishing Co., 1970), p. 122.

7. Regarding Capone, Upton Bell told me, "When the Lindbergh baby was kidnapped, Bert Bell was one of the people the police talked to to see if he could go to Sing Sing and talk to Capone to find out if it was an underworld murder. The story is my father did go and talk to Capone. And within twenty-four hours, without ever removing himself from prison, Capone found out that the Mafia was not involved."

8. Harry Wismer, *The Public Calls It Sport* (Englewood Cliffs, N.J.: Prentice-Hall, Inc., 1965), pp. 25–26. The college roommate of future Florida senator George Smathers and *Washington Post* publisher Phil Graham, Wismer was principally a sports broadcaster. His first wife was Betty Bryant, the niece of Henry Ford; and Wismer's second wife was Mary Zwillman, the widow of New Jersey Mafia figure, Abner "Longy" Zwillman—who had been part of a conspiracy in the 1930s to take over the International Alliance of Theatrical Stage Employees union, which became the largest union in Hollywood. Zwillman had also bankrolled studio mogul Harry Cohn in his takeover of Columbia Pictures. The mobster was later found hanging from a water pipe in his basement. Zwillman's widow's lawyer was Sidney Korshak, the Chicago Mafia's liaison to the Hollywood film industry.

9. Cope, *Game That Was,* pp. 91–92.

10. Reeves's other partners were Fred Levy, Edwin W. Pauley, and Hal Seley. Levy had bought the Rams with Reeves in 1941 but sold his interest to his partner two years later.

11. The Philadelphia Eagles regrouped in 1944 and resumed play under Thompson. However, Pittsburgh merged with the Chicago Cardinals for the 1944 season, forming Card-Pitt. After a 0–10 year, both teams went back on their own in 1945.

CHAPTER 4

1. NFL president Joe Carr had died in 1939. Bert Bell was one of the few NFL owners who had objected to Elmer Layden's appointment as NFL commissioner.

CHAPTER 5

1. See William Barry Furlong's article "Of 'lines,' 'point spreads' and 'middles,'" *The New York Times Magazine,* 2 January 1977. Furlong also quotes oddsmaker Jimmy the Greek as saying, "I used to go to Chicago just to watch him [McNeil] work." Also, the March 10, 1986, issue of *Sports Illustrated* featured a special report on gambling, which included a sidebar story, "The Brain That Gave Us the Point Spread," that gave McNeil the credit.

"In 1950, McNeil suddenly quit bookmaking," reported *SI*'s Robert H. Boyle. "He later told a friend he did so because the Mob wanted 'to go partners with my brain.'"

2. Olshan peeled off from *The Green Sheet* in 1952 and began his own publication. In 1957, he founded *Nation-Wide Football,* a six-panel publication that covered college and professional football games. In 1966, *Nation-Wide Football* became known as *The Gold Sheet,* with Olshan as its publisher. It has become the premier handicapping service in the United States.

3. David Leon Chandler, *Brothers in Blood: The Rise of the Criminal Brotherhoods* (New York: E.P. Dutton & Co., 1975), pp. 181–82. Carolla, who was deported to Sicily in April 1947, was succeeded as the boss of the New Orleans Mafia by Carlos Marcello.

4. According to the FBI, through Curd, Costello won a traceable $26,000 on football games in 1950 alone.

During the Kefauver Committee hearings, Costello slipped up and identified Curd as the bookmaker who handled his bets on football games. Curd, who owned a large horse-breeding farm in Lexington and was viewed by all who knew him as a genuine "Southern gentleman," sold his house and fled the country before being indicted for federal tax evasion. Curd first went to Montreal but was expelled by the Canadian government. He later surrendered to authorities in Detroit, pleaded guilty, and was sentenced to a year in prison and fined $400,000. After being released from prison in 1959, Curd moved to the Bahamas.

Curd told me that he has forgiven Costello for fingering him. "I was really upset at the time, but he never dreamed that anything would come of it."

5. Other AAFC owners were baseball legend Branch Rickey and publisher Gerald Smith of the Brooklyn Dodgers, oil company executives James Brueil and Will Bennett of the Buffalo Bisons (the Buffalo Bills in 1947), Harvey Hester of the Miami Seahawks, and lumber company executive Tony Morabito of the San Francisco 49ers. After the 1946 season, the Miami team was replaced by the Baltimore Colts, owned by Washington businessman Robert H. Rodenberg. James Crowley was selected as the first AAFC commissioner but later resigned to take over the Chicago Rockets.

6. Hoffa became an international vice president of the union in 1952 under Teamsters president Dave Beck. In 1957, after Beck's indictment for theft, Hoffa was elected general president. Hoffa's election contributed to the decision to expel the Teamsters from the AFL–CIO.

7. Ryan also had some oil investments with oddsmaker Jimmy "the Greek" Snyder.

8. Ben Lindheimer's daughter is Marjorie Everett, who took over his racing empire after his death in 1960. She blamed Korshak for her father's fatal heart attack because the attorney had failed to head off a strike at one of Lindheimer's Illinois racetracks. State attorney general Otto Kerner, who later became Illinois' governor, was convicted on bribery, perjury, tax evasion, and mail fraud charges after he received stock at a cut-rate price from Everett's racetracks in return for favorable treatment. Everett was not charged with any wrongdoing.

CHAPTER 6

1. The Kefauver Committee began its investigation on May 26, 1950, and held hearings in fifteen U.S. cities.

2. Reserve players for the Cleveland Browns, who were waiting to join the team roster, were offered jobs with McBride's cab company; thus the term *taxi squad* was born.

3. John Cooney, *The Annenbergs: The Salvaging of a Tainted Dynasty* (New York: Simon & Schuster, Inc., 1982), p. 21.

4. Also the owner of *TV Guide* and *Seventeen,* Walter Annenberg was appointed the ambassador to Great Britain in 1969 by President Richard Nixon and was awarded the Presidential Medal of Freedom, along with Frank Sinatra, by President Ronald Reagan. In 1981, Reagan appointed Annenberg's wife, Leonore, as the White House chief of protocol. Mrs. Annenberg, the niece of movie mogul Harry Cohn, had been previously married to Beldon Katleman, the owner of El Rancho Vegas hotel/casino in Las Vegas, and Lewis Rosenstiel, the head of Schenley Industries, the liquor distributors. Annenberg sold his publishing empire to Australian tycoon Rupert Murdoch in 1988.

5. Among those indicted was Chicago mob leader Frank Nitti, the heir to Al Capone. Nitti committed suicide on the day the indictments were handed up. He was replaced as the head of the Chicago Capone underworld by Anthony Accardo.

For more information about the Hollywood extortion scheme, see my book *Dark Victory: Ronald Reagan, MCA and the Mob* (New York: Viking Press, 1986).

6. The police captain who headed the investigation of the Ragen murder was found slain in his garage, with his jaw torn off by a .45 caliber bullet.

7. After Bidwill's death, the Chicago Cardinals were inherited by his widow and their two sons, William V. and Charles Jr., also known as Stormy. Mrs. Bidwill, who had married St. Louis businessman Walter Wolfner in 1949, died in 1962. The two sons then took over the team. William bought out Stormy in 1972 after a turbulent partnership.

Charles Bidwill's brother Arthur J. Bidwill was an Illinois state senator at the time of Charles's death.

8. Erickson's partner, Frank Costello, also fell on hard times. During his fifth appearance before the Kefauver Committee, he angrily walked out of the hearing. Cited for contempt of Congress, Costello was found guilty in 1952 and sentenced to eighteen months in prison. The following year, Costello was in-

dicted again—this time for tax evasion. He was found guilty on three counts and sentenced to another five years in prison.

While fighting his convictions, Costello retained a young Washington attorney Edward Bennett Williams, who soon after became a part owner and president of the Washington Redskins. In 1955, while the federal government was attempting to deport Costello, Williams successfully engineered the dismissal of the deportation case because of illegal wiretaps used by the government. However, Williams was unable to overturn Costello's income-tax conviction, and in 1958, Costello was sent back to prison.

A year earlier, in May 1957, an assassin Vincent Gigante tried to kill Costello—but his bullet only grazed the mobster's head. Costello got the message and retired as the head of his crime family. He was replaced by Vito Genovese.

9. During the late 1940s and early 1950s, the sports world had been rocked by point-shaving and game-fixing scandals in college basketball. Seven schools and thirty-two players were involved, including Manhattan College, Kentucky, City College of New York (which won the national championship in 1950), Bradley, New York University, and Long Island University.

"All of these fixes were set up in the Catskill Mountains," Ralph Salerno told me. "The way it worked was that if you were a good basketball player, someone would come to you and say they could get you a cushy job at some Catskill resort—and just play basketball for the summer. And the hotels formed a basketball league—the Catskill Mountain League. People who vacationed up there would see some top basketball by players like Bob Cousy of Holy Cross. And there were a lot of New York bookmakers who went there for their vacations. Even though it was just a small summer league, the bookmakers would wine them and dine them [the players] and throw them a few bucks when they shaved points. What difference did it make to the kid? These games didn't count.

"But that's when they conditioned the kids. There were only seven colleges implicated—but there were many more involved. Frank Hogan, the D.A. in New York County, was a gentleman. Way back then, Bob Cousy was among those brought in for interrogation. But Hogan's policy was 'While we're still investigating, bring these college kids in late at night after the New York press has gone home. I don't want to see the name of a single college player in the paper until he's indicted. Then he gets his name in the paper.' "

One of those players implicated in the point-shaving scheme, Dale Bonstable of the University of Kentucky, said that, at first, he couldn't tell the gamblers from the average fan. "Those guys were smooth talkers. They should have been salesmen. They took us out for a stroll, treated us to a meal, and before we knew anything we were right in the middle of it. They said that we didn't have to dump a game."

Earlier, in 1948, two players in the National Hockey League—Don Galinger of the Boston Bruins and Billy Taylor of the Detroit Red Wings—were suspended for life because they had placed bets with a Detroit bookmaker. Galinger confessed that he had placed his money against his own team.

In the midst of these sports scandals, the Harry Gross police corruption case in New York also erupted. A top bookmaker in the Erickson sphere of influence, Brooklyn-based Gross had been paying off police officers in return for protection. After being arrested for gambling and imprisoned for a year, Gross turned state's evidence against his silent partners. Twenty-three officers, including five captains, were convicted and dismissed from the department. The fact that law-enforcement officials were accepting money to protect bookmaking operations was proven to be widespread.

The Gross case served as the impetus to expand the college basketball point-fixing investigation.

10. Harry Wismer, *The Public Calls It Sport* (Englewood Cliffs, N.J.: Prentice-Hall, Inc., 1965), pp. 54–55.

11. In 1950, the Los Angeles Rams became the first professional football team to sell its exclusive television rights and have all its games broadcast. The following year, in order to increase home attendance, the Rams permitted only the televising of road games.

CHAPTER 7

1. Briefly, after the AAFC–NFL merger, which was announced on December 11, 1949, the joint league was called The National-American League. That lasted just over two months.

2. Gene Klein and David Fisher, *First Down and a Billion: The Funny Business of Pro Football* (New York: William Morrow and Co., 1987), pp. 75–76.

3. The boys in the Rosenbloom family were Isadore, Hess, Ben, Leon, Harry, and Carroll; the girls were Rose, Ethel, and Mildred.

4. In May 1949, Blue Ridge moved its executive offices to Lynchburg, Virginia, about thirty-five miles east of Roanoke. At the time, Blue Ridge and its subsidiaries had twenty-four manufacturing plants in twelve states, including Alabama, Delaware, Georgia, Kentucky, Maryland, Mississippi, New York, Pennsylvania, Tennessee, Texas, Virginia, and West Virginia. In 1952, Blue Ridge purchased another large overalls firm, Big Jack Manufacturing Company of Bristol, Virginia, for $3 million. The purchase of Big Jack increased Blue Ridge's annual revenues to nearly $70 million. Blue Ridge continued to do work for the United States government and received a huge contract from the Armed Services Textile and Procurement Agency the following year. The order was for 1,424,120 pairs of U.S. Navy dungarees.

5. Rosenbloom was named as the president of the Colts on February 4, 1957.

6. Rosenbloom's partners were former Colts directors, local businessmen, and racehorse owners, including Zanvyl Krieger, Bill Hilgenberg, Tom Mullan, and R. Bruce Livie.

CHAPTER 8

1. Paul Brown with Jack Clary, *PB: The Paul Brown Story* (New York: Atheneum Pubs., 1979), p. 232.

2. Bernie Parrish, *They Call It a Game* (New York: Dial Press, Inc., 1971), p. 186.

3. Speaking of fixing games during the 1950s, Don Dawson told me, "In those days, maybe you'd find a couple of bookmakers in Cleveland or Detroit or Buffalo or Cincinnati or Miami or Dallas or Houston or L.A., wherever it was. Most of them were regular guys, not mob guys. But in order to move any big money, they'd have to go to the mob to get it approved."

4. On August 12, 1957, just prior to the opening of the NFL season, the Lions' head coach Raymond "Buddy" Parker suddenly resigned, saying, "I'm quitting. I can no longer control this team. And when I can't control it, I can't coach it. I don't want to get involved in another losing season, so I'm leaving Detroit." Parker was replaced by assistant coach George Wilson.

Piersante, who says he had heard about the alleged fixes, told me, "The Detroit team management broke up the operation. The way it was broken up was Bobby Layne was sold to the Pittsburgh Steelers in 1958 during midseason."

5. Layne died of cardiac arrest on December 1, 1986, in Lubbock, Texas. Dawson told me that he decided to reveal his on-field business relationship with Layne because, "Bobby got to be a bad boy. There were people back in Detroit that he owed. He'd borrow money and would not pay it back. He didn't have any regard for anybody. When he died, he owed me money—money I bet for him on games, even after he quit football."

CHAPTER 9

1. Baltimore, in 1958, had the second worst field goal percentage in the NFL, 35.7 percent, making five of fourteen attempts. On the other hand, Unitas, in 1958, had thrown 263 passes but had only 7 intercepted for a 2.7 percent interception rate, the best in the NFL. And Alan Ameche, in 1958, had fumbled only once in 171 carries; he was second in NFL rushing that year with 791 yards and a 4.6 average per carry. However, during the third quarter of the championship game—with the Colts leading 14–3, and on the Giants one yard line and fourth down—Ameche, after two previous carries on first and second downs, was thrown for a four-yard loss, allowing the Giants to roar back into the game and take the lead, later forcing Myhra to send the game into sudden death.

2. Kay Iselin Gilman, *Inside the Pressure Cooker: A Season in the Life of the New York Jets* (New York: G.P. Putnam's Sons, 1974) p. 29. Gilman also is the daughter of Phil Iselin, who later became the president of the New York Jets.

3. Courtney's real name is Morris Schmertzler and Ritter's alias is Red Reed.

4. The three communities were Port Charlotte, Port Malabar, and Port St. Lucie.

5. The syndicate later purchased the pre-1948 film library of Twentieth Century-Fox. Along with the Warner Brothers deal, the Chesler-Rosenbloom-Schwebel group owned 340 motion pictures.

6. In 1956, Adams became locked in a scandal involving Bernard Goldfine, a close friend, and was forced to resign from his post. A wealthy industrial-

ist from Boston, who had major ties to organized-crime figures and their racetracks, Goldfine had operated a political slush fund and was caught paying off Adams and a U.S. senator. After refusing to testify about his activities, Goldfine was indicted for contempt of Congress and pleaded guilty. Soon after, he was charged with income-tax evasion. In that trial, he was represented by attorney Edward Bennett Williams, who successfully had Goldfine ruled to be mentally incompetent to stand trial. Later, when the court ruled him competent, he pleaded guilty to the tax charge but received a suspended sentence because of his physical health. Goldfine died from a heart attack in 1967.

Raab later became the chairman of the board of the International Airport Hotel Systems, Inc., in which Meyer Lansky was a major stockholder. Under President Ronald Reagan, Raab was appointed as the U.S. ambassador to Italy.

7. In 1948, Dalitz left Cleveland and, after a brief stay in Newport, Kentucky, moved to Nevada, where gambling had been legal since 1931. The earliest Nevada casinos appeared in Reno. Dalitz and several members of the Mayfield Road Gang bought the controlling interest in Las Vegas' Desert Inn hotel/casino, which opened in April 1950.

In 1959, the Teamsters Union, headed by general president Jimmy Hoffa of Detroit, began making huge loans from its Central States, Southeast and Southwest Areas Pension Fund to several Nevada casinos. Among the biggest beneficiaries was the Desert Inn. In all, for the Desert Inn, the Sunrise Hospital in Las Vegas, and his La Costa Country Club in Carlsbad, California, Dalitz, a longtime ally of Hoffa from their early days in Detroit, received well over $200 million from the fund.

8. Chesler's bookmakers—Courtney, Ritter, and Brudner—were also employees of the Havana casinos.

9. Charles Luciano, Meyer Lansky, and Vito Genovese, among other mobsters, had cooperated with the Office of Strategic Services (OSS) and the U.S. Navy in World War II—after the war began to turn against the Axis powers, which the Mafia had initially supported. Luciano, who was in prison during the war, received a pardon in 1946 in return for his cooperation. However, he was immediately deported to Sicily. He and another deported mobster, Frank Coppola of Detroit, a top ally of Jimmy Hoffa, began manufacturing heroin in Sicily and exporting it to Montreal, through a gang of French Corsicans, who then distributed it to their underworld contacts in New York and Detroit. This was the earliest version of the *French Connection.*

Needing a southern route into the United States, Luciano went to Cuba in or about 1947 and created a major narcotics ring on the island. Lansky moved his operations from New York to Miami to oversee the Cuban operations, which also included gambling. Lansky was also responsible for greasing Cuban political leaders whose job was to protect the underworld's interests.

By the mid-1950s, Lansky's protégé, Santos Trafficante, the Mafia boss of Tampa, and Carlos Marcello, the Mafia boss of New Orleans, were running, respectively, the bulk of the mob's gambling and narcotics businesses, in concert with other crime families, that had invested in Cuba.

10. The Castro betrayal led to the CIA/Mafia plots to assassinate the Cuban leader, which were arranged as early as December 1959 and were well under way during the summer of 1960.

11. After the sale of Blue Ridge, Rosenbloom continued as the chairman and president of Blue Ridge and of Imperial Shirt Company. The following year, he yielded the presidencies of both companies—but continued to serve on their corporate boards. Another member of the Philadelphia & Reading board of directors was Laurence A. Tisch, who later became the chairman of the board of the Columbia Broadcasting System.

CHAPTER 10

1. Wismer hired Sammy Baugh as the first head coach of the New York Titans.

2. Harry Wismer, *The Public Calls It Sport* (Englewood Cliffs, N.J.: Prentice-Hall, Inc., 1965), p. 66. H. L. Hunt died in November 1974.

3. Don Kowet, *The Rich Who Own Sports* (New York: Random House, Inc., 1977), p. 81.

4. Conrad Hilton died in 1979 at age ninety-one. He had named Barron Hilton the chief executive officer of the hotel chain in 1966.

5. Nicky Hilton died of cardiac arrest at age forty-two in February 1969.

6. Casino gambling would later account for 40 percent of the Hilton empire's operating income. By 1972, Hilton had the controlling interest in two Las Vegas hotel/casinos, which later became the Las Vegas Hilton and the Flamingo Hilton.

7. *The Wall Street Journal,* 27 March 1987.

8. Involved with the major players in the extortion of Hollywood's motion picture studios during the late 1930s and early 1940s, Korshak had been described by Chicago Mafia figure Charles "Cherry Nose" Gioe as "our man." Gioe, who was among the six Chicago mobsters indicted, told a corrupt Hollywood union official, "I want you to do what he [Korshak] tells you. He's not just another lawyer but knows our gang and figures our best interest. Pay attention to him, and remember, any message he may deliver to you is a message from us."

9. Howsam lasted only one year. After a 4–9–1 premier season, he sold his interest in the Broncos to Cal Kunz and Gerald Phipps. Phipps, the son of a wealthy and respected Denver family, bought out Kunz in 1965. After a 3–11 sequel in year two, Filchock was gone, as well.

10. The Boston Patriots became the New England Patriots in 1971.

11. Jack Mara died in 1965, leaving his interest in the Giants to his own son but granting the operation of the team to Wellington.

12. Bell's heir apparent going into the first ballot was Marshall Leahy, a San Francisco attorney who wanted the NFL headquarters to be in his hometown. Leahy had to have eight votes among the twelve NFL teams to be elected but could never muster up more than seven. He was opposed by interim commissioner Austin Gunsel, who had received his support from the older owners but could not get as many votes as Leahy could. Wellington Mara asked Dan Reeves of the Rams if he would be interested in the job. He replied that he wasn't—but that his general manager, Pete Rozelle, might be. Mara and Paul Brown then went to Rozelle.

13. Reeves won the long ownership battle and bought full control of the Rams. For what had been a $4 total investment by his partners in 1947, Reeves paid them $4.8 million in 1962.

14. William Henry Paul, *The Gray-Flannel Pigskin: Movers and Shakers of Pro Football* (Philadelphia: J. B. Lippincott Co., 1974), p. 274.

15. NFL owners were not forced to split revenues derived from parking and concessions, among other stadium moneymaking enterprises. Therefore, it was in the owners' best interests to seek out new stadiums with more lucrative facilities.

16. Soda and four other partners sold their interests in the Raiders to the remaining partners—Ed McGah, Wayne Valley, and Robert Osborne—in January 1961. Osborne was bought out by his partners the following year. The Oakland Raiders became the Los Angeles Raiders in 1982.

CHAPTER 11

1. Nixon's purchase of his house in Trousdale Estates was first reported by *Los Angeles Times* reporters Gene Blake and Jack Tobin on May 17, 1962.

2. This comment from Hoover was made during an interview with Oscar Otis of *The Morning Telegram* and is quoted in Hank Messick, *John Edgar Hoover* (New York: David McKay Co., 1972), p. 147–48.

3. According to federal agents, evidence produced by government wiretaps in the FBI's Brilab sting operation in 1978 showed a clear and direct long-term business relationship between Marcello and Murchison. The two men had engaged in negotiations after Murchison had expressed an interest in buying a portion of Marcello's Churchill Farms estate in New Orleans.

4. Appendix to the Select Committee on Assassinations, U.S. Congress, House of Representatives, 95th Cong., 2d sess., March 1979, vol. 9, p. 335. Campisi was also known as being a friend of Jack Ruby, the murderer of John Kennedy's assassin. Ruby had dinner at Campisi's restaurant the night before the President's murder. Also, five days after Ruby killed Lee Harvey Oswald, he called Campisi and asked to see him. Campisi, his wife, and Ruby met privately in the Dallas County Jail on November 30, 1963.

5. Davidson told me that he had been first introduced to Marcello during the early 1950s by attorney Jack Wasserman, who represented the mob boss during the federal government's attempts to deport him.

Davidson also admitted that he was a major gunrunner to dictator Fulgencio Batista prior to the Cuban Revolution. "I sold a tremendous amount of tanks and whatnot to Batista in 1958," Davidson told me. "About two months before Batista fell, I delivered a big package to him." Earlier, Davidson had arranged for Murchison's principal corporation, Tecon Corporation, to construct several large military housing projects in Cuba.

6. When Wexler attempted to obtain a horse-racing license, he was rejected by the Ohio Racing Commission—because of his association with gamblers and underworld figures. Interestingly, accompanying Wexler's application for the license were the names of three people who could vouch for his character, one of whom was Modell's longtime friend George M. Steinbren-

ner III of Cleveland, the president of American Ship Building Company and later the owner of the New York Yankees major-league baseball team. Dan Topping and Del Webb sold their interests in the New York Yankees to the Columbia Broadcasting System in 1964. In 1973, Steinbrenner and his "committee of fifteen" purchased the team from CBS. Among Steinbrenner's partners in the Yankees were auto executive John DeLorean, Nelson Bunker Hunt, and Ohio real estate tycoon Marvin Warner.

After Wexler's application was rejected, Steinbrenner, who admitted knowing Wexler, insisted that he had not given Wexler permission to use his name as a character reference.

Wexler had also been banned from racing in Maryland in 1945 when one of his horses was found to be drugged. In 1958, he was denied a racing license in Florida because of his "close contact and relationship with bookmakers and gamblers." However, a Florida court overturned the state racing commission's decision and granted him the license.

7. Bernie Parrish, *They Call It a Game* (New York: Dial Press, Inc., 1971), pp. 209–14.

8. For more specific details about Modell's complicated financing of the Browns, see Parrish, *A Game.* Parrish is a former defensive back for the Browns, and the team's onetime player representative to the NFL Players Association. Also, see Peter Phipps's fascinating series in the *Akron Beacon Journal,* 16–18 January 1983, and David Harris's outstanding book *The League: The Rise and Decline of the NFL* (Toronto: Bantam Books, 1986).

9. The elder Ford had operated union-busting activities in Detroit, particularly against Walter Reuther and the United Auto Workers, with the help of the Detroit Mafia. The chief strike-breaker in Detroit was Santo Perrone, a feared and ruthless mobster who was born in Alcamo, Sicily, and later became one of Jimmy Hoffa's top henchmen. When Perrone went to court for assaulting Reuther and other trade unionists during the infamous "Battle of the Overpass" at Ford's River Rouge Plant in 1937, Perrone was represented by Ford legal counsel, Louis J. Columbo, Sr. Law-enforcement officials allege that Perrone also was behind the 1948 shooting of Reuther.

As part payment for their goon-squad activities, Perrone, who later went to prison for liquor law violations, and the Detroit Mafia received a major share of business in Detroit's trucking industry in concert with Hoffa and the local Teamsters, particularly its steel-hauling operations, which did considerable subcontracting with Ford. Perrone's work in the steel-hauling business netted him $4,000 a month, even while he was in jail. "Perrone's steel-hauling interests were handled by his wife while he was in prison," Vince Piersante told me. "She probably got some kind of break with the [Teamsters]—like it left the business alone. We also know that other crime families started getting into the trucking business during this period of time."

Ironically, it was Perrone and his underworld associates Angelo Meli and Frank Coppola whom Jimmy Hoffa turned to after Hoffa's Teamsters' turf was threatened by John L. Lewis and a raiding CIO local. Hoffa made a pact with these underworld figures and former Ford union busters—in return for driving the CIO out of Detroit. This deal became the major turning point in Hoffa's plunge from union reformer to labor racketeer. The myth has always been that Hoffa turned to organized crime in order to unionize stubborn employers. In fact, he had used the mob to run a rival union out of town.

Another Detroit mobster who worked with Ford was Anthony D'Anna, who received a half interest in a Ford dealership in return for his "cooperation." And yet another Mafia figure, Joe Adonis, had the controlling interest in a New Jersey firm that received Ford's regional distributorship.

The Kefauver Committee noted that "[o]n some occasions organized gamblers would throw very large funds into union elections in major locals in the Detroit area in the hopes of securing the election of officials who would tolerate in-plant gambling."

10. Vince Piersante vouched for Ford, saying, "Bill Ford's clean, and he runs a stable ownership structure."

Detroit bookmaker Don Dawson, who was well informed about the Lions' betting habits, agreed with Piersante, telling me that although Henry Ford II was a gambler, Bill Ford was not.

CHAPTER 12

1. The Universal film library had been purchased by MCA, the Hollywood entertainment conglomerate, in 1962 after MCA bought out Decca Records, the parent company of Universal Pictures. The U.S. Justice Department, which had filed an antitrust action against MCA, forced the Hollywood company, among other demands, to sell the entire Universal library, with the exception of fourteen movies that MCA was permitted to keep.

2. Doris Kearns Goodwin, *The Fitzgeralds and the Kennedys: An American Saga* (New York: Simon & Schuster, Inc., 1987), p. 804.

3. Gene Miller, a reporter for *The Miami Herald,* also obtained the Benton package and was the first to report its contents.

4. McLaney had originally testified, erroneously, that Rosenbloom had bet on the Colts, whom he claimed had won the game. He also erroneously stated that the opposing team was the Pittsburgh Steelers. Explaining these discrepancies, McLaney's attorney simply said, "He had the wrong game. It was a different one."

5. Taliaferro told me that he was so badly hurt he required surgery. The orthopedic surgeon who handled the knee operation was Danny Fortmann, a former guard with the Chicago Bears.

The Colts lost that final game with the Rams of the 1953 season, 45–2.

6. The *Tribune* story also included a quote from Rozelle—a quote that had been apparently fabricated. Rozelle had supposedly said, "Halas has asked me to track down the validity of these rumors. This we are now doing. We are always alert to protect the honesty of professional football. As of the moment, the investigation continues. There now is nothing to report. When there is, we will make public immediately all the facts." Rozelle denied ever being interviewed by the *Tribune* and was reportedly upset with Halas's statement because it violated the league's rule that forbid NFL personnel from commenting on internal investigations in progress.

7. Bob Curran, *The $400,000 Quarterback Or: The League That Came in from the Cold* (New York: Macmillan Co., 1965), p. 42.

CHAPTER 13

1. In 1968, John Gordy became the president of the NFL Players Association.

2. In 1986, Hornung told *Sports Illustrated* "that there were 10 or 12 other Green Bay Packer players who regularly wagered on NFL games in the team's glory days . . . betting on games by players was rampant throughout the league." See *Sports Illustrated,* 10 March 1986. Hornung refused to be interviewed for this book. He told me, "I feel like if I do it for one person, I should do it for everybody."

3. Rozelle had also received a character reference for Rosenbloom from New York attorney Roy M. Cohn, Senator Joseph McCarthy's right-hand man.

In September 1963, Cohn was indicted for perjury in connection with a Desert Inn stock deal he had with Morris Dalitz and the Mayfield Road Gang. Rosenbloom, Chesler, and McLaney had purchased the Hotel Nacional in Cuba from Dalitz and his partners. Cohn's first trial ended in a hung jury, but he was acquitted of the charge in July 1964.

CHAPTER 14

1. McCrary, who had handled public relations for Richard Nixon and Bernard Goldfine, was in charge of publicity for both Chesler and his Bahamian casino operations. He had also been named as Seven Arts' vice president for public relations. Another public-relations man, William Safire, became McCrary's partner, handling publicity for the Bahamian government. Safire left the following year to join the presidential campaign staff of Richard Nixon. After's Nixon's election, Safire became his top speech writer. Safire later became a columnist for *The New York Times.*

2. By 1960, the General Development Corporation was worth over $50 million. Among Chesler's other partners in Devco were Eliot Hyman and Ray Stark, who had founded Seven Arts. Devco's banker was Boston financier Serge Semenenko, who, along with with New York businessman Charles Allen, had negotiated the sale of Warner Brothers' film library to Associated Artists, which was soon bought by Seven Arts.

Allen had helped Wallace Groves arrange his financing for the creation of the Grand Bahama Port Authority. Semenenko was also directly involved in the $2 million payoff to Sands and arranged for Seven Arts' purchase of its 21 percent of Devco. Chesler's attorney, Morris Mac Schwebel, told me, "Allen originally brought the Bahamas deal to Chesler, who became fascinated with the islands. Then, Chesler got Seven Arts to put the $12 million into developing the islands."

3. Hank Messick, *Syndicate Abroad* (London: Collier-Macmillan Co., 1969), p. 70.

4. Orovitz had been Chesler's chief executive officer in General Development since 1956. Plans for the Bahamian casino were made in Orovitz's Miami office in 1962. Both Lansky and Chesler were present at the meeting. Others

known to have been included in the decision-making process were mobsters Mike Coppola, Charles Tourine, and Dino Cellini, as well as bookmakers Frank Ritter, Max Courtney, and Charles Brudner.

5. Since 1956, Schwebel had served on the board of directors of all Chesler's companies and was the vice president of Associated Artists before it was merged into Seven Arts. In 1958, Schwebel had been named the president of Universal Controls.

6. Lansky's associates in the skimming operation comprised some of the top Mafia figures in the United States, including Angelo Bruno of Philadelphia, Carlo Gambino of New York, Sam Giancana of Chicago, Steffano Maggadino of Buffalo, and Joseph Zerilli of Detroit.

7. *Report of the Commission of Inquiry into the Operation of the Business of Casinos in Freeport and in Nassau,* 31 October 1967, p. 54.

8. Bernie Parrish, *They Call It a Game* (New York: Dial Press, Inc., 1971), p. 209.

9. Bob Curran, *The $400,000 Quarterback Or: The League That Came in from the Cold* (New York: Macmillan Co., 1965), p. 45.

Chesler's ultimate demise resulted from actions by his own attorney Morris Mac Schwebel and other stockholders in Seven Arts, the company that owned 21 percent of the hotel/casino in Freeport. The stockholders were hoping to have their company traded on the American Stock Exchange, and Chesler's detractors believed that the SEC would block the move with Chesler in control—because of his public ties to the underworld. At the time of Chesler's ouster, Seven Arts stock was being traded only on the Canadian exchange.

The only two stockholders to support Chesler were Seven Arts directors Carroll Rosenbloom and Maxwell Raab.

Chesler's May 1964 ouster was engineered by Serge Semenenko and Charles Allen. Essentially, Chesler's position in Devco was contingent on his continued control of Seven Arts. With his grip on the film company loosening, Chesler attempted to borrow money from Semenenko's Boston bank in order to buy more stock in the company. But, instead, Semenenko loaned enough money to Seven Arts' other dissident stockholders to squeeze out Chesler.

Under new leadership, Seven Arts then put its stock in Devco on sale. Chesler desperately tried to raise enough money to buy it but failed. Groves bought Seven Arts' stock in the Bahamas and gained total control of Devco. Chesler's seat on the Devco board was filled by Lansky associate Max Orovitz, who began operating the casino.

10. For years, Hamilton was the nemesis of Southern California Mafia leader Jimmy Fratianno. He had been responsible for publicly naming Fratianno as the "Mafia's Executioner on the West Coast."

Hamilton also headed the LAPD's 1962 investigation of the suicide of Marilyn Monroe.

CHAPTER 15

1. Werblin's partners were New Jersey investment banker Townsend B. Martin; Leon Hess, the owner of Hess Oil and Chemical Company; Wall

Street broker Donald Lillis, the president of Bowie Race Course in Maryland; and Phil Iselin, the president of Korell Company, a New York textile firm and dress company. Martin, Hess, and Iselin were directors of Monmouth Park along with Werblin. Iselin was also Monmouth's vice president and treasurer.

2. During the 1961–62 MCA antitrust investigation, witnesses surfaced who stated that Kintner, in the presence of NBC board chairman Robert Sarnoff, told Werblin, "Sonny, look at the [NBC] schedule for the next season; here are the empty slots, you fill them in." Werblin did so, rearranging the NBC prime-time schedule and replacing set programming with MCA productions while the NBC programmers watched with their hats in their hands. When Werblin finished, MCA had fourteen shows on the air—eight and a half hours of MCA-produced programs on prime-time television. Soon after, Kintner was named the president of NBC.

In a Justice Department memorandum, attorneys wrote that "NBC is completely 'snowed under' by CBS in the program ratings . . . NBC's personnel are far inferior to CBS's in caliber and cannot turn out the quality product. Because of this, NBC is forced to rely on MCA's stable of stars and upon MCA's show production facilities. Hence NBC sticks close to MCA."

Prosecutors under Attorney General Kennedy who pursued the 1962 case against MCA described NBC's relationship with MCA as "a conspiracy" and considered naming NBC as a coconspirator in the litigation, according to Justice Department documents.

Kintner became the chairman of NBC's board of directors in 1965—but was squeezed out within a year.

For details of the MCA antitrust case and the sweetheart relationship between MCA and NBC, see my book *Dark Victory: Ronald Reagan, MCA and the Mob* (New York: Viking Press, 1986).

3. George Halas with Gwen Morgan and Arthur Veysey, *Halas by Halas: The Autobiography of George Halas* (New York: McGraw-Hill Book Co., 1979), p. 269.

4. In November 1976, Smith was fired as the chairman of his insurance company by its board of directors "because of the time required by his other business interests." There was no further explanation. Interestingly, company earnings had been up at the time of Smith's dismissal. Smith remained as a director and continued to hold nearly a twelfth of the company's stock.

5. Thomas sold his interest in the Dolphins at the end of the team's first season, in which it posted a 3–11 record. Robbie had sold 10 percent of the Dolphins to Miami businessman John O'Neil; another chunk was sold to George Hamid, who operated the Hamid-Morton Circus and the Atlantic City Pier Company. In 1967, land developer Willard "Bud" Keland bought out Thomas and Hamid. Trouble developed between Robbie and Keland over control of the team. The matter went to Pete Rozelle, who ruled in Robbie's favor and ordered Keland to sell his interest in 1969. Within ninety days, five members of the Miami community came up with the cash to buy out Keland. Robbie emerged as the majority partner.

6. Joe Namath with Dick Schaap, *I Can't Wait Until Tomorrow . . . 'Cause*

I Get Better Looking Every Day (New York: Random House, Inc., 1969), p. 153.

7. Halas, *Halas by Halas,* p. 270.

Interestingly, Rosenbloom also recalled that after the merger had been sealed, several owners from the meeting went to a local restaurant where they ran into New York Senator Robert Kennedy. Seeing Rozelle and the AFL and NFL owners dining together, Kennedy joked, "What's going on? This looks like an antitrust conspiracy."

8. In the first NFL–AFL championship game in January 1967, the NFL's Green Bay Packers defeated Hunt's AFL Kansas City Chiefs, 35–10.

9. David Harris, *The League: The Rise and Decline of the NFL* (Toronto: Bantam Books, 1986), pp. 91–92.

10. McLaney left Las Vegas when the Carousel Club was bought by Salvatore A. Rizzo, a partner with Frank Sinatra in the Berkshire Downs racetrack. New England mob boss Raymond Patriarca was suspected to have had a hidden interest in the racetrack.

McLaney was later indicted by the IRS for criminal tax fraud. An investigation showed that he had reported no taxable income during the years 1963 to 1966, the exact period that he spent running casinos in the Bahamas and in Las Vegas. He was convicted and served eighty-three days in jail.

11. Bernie Parrish, *They Call It a Game* (New York: Dial Press, Inc., 1971), p. 196.

12. Rosenbloom's daughter from his first marriage, Suzanne, later married Georgia's younger brother, Kenneth Irwin. Thus, Irwin became both Rosenbloom's brother-in-law and son-in-law.

CHAPTER 16

1. Paul Brown with Jack Clary, *PB: The Paul Brown Story* (New York: Atheneum Pubs., 1979), p. 284.

Brown's book so enraged Pete Rozelle, who is a close friend of Modell, that he fined Brown $10,000. It is a violation of NFL rules for one team owner to publicly make derogatory remarks about another NFL owner.

2. Jonathan Kwitny, *The Mullendore Murder Case* (New York: Farrar, Straus & Giroux, Inc., 1974), p. 96.

3. For additional details about Carlos Marcello's empire, see *Life,* 8 and 29 September 1967. Also see David Leon Chandler, *Brothers in Blood: The Rise of Criminal Brotherhoods* (New York: E.P. Dutton & Co., 1975); and Michael Dorman, *Payoff: The Role of Organized Crime in American Politics* (New York: David McKay Co., 1972). Both books are excellent. Also see: U.S. House Select Committee on Assassinations, vol. 9.

There is considerable evidence that Marcello, along with Santos Trafficante and Jimmy Hoffa, arranged and executed the 1963 murder of President John Kennedy. See my book *The Hoffa Wars* (New York: Paddington Press, 1978).

4. From 1967 to 1985, while Mecom owned the team, the Saints never had more wins than losses in a single season. The team had eight wins and eight losses in 1979 and 1983.

CHAPTER 17

1. Also in 1961, Kennedy was furious when another point-shaving scandal had broken out in college basketball, implicating twenty-two schools and thirty-seven players who were paid between $750 to $4,500 a game not to cover the spread.

2. The Kennedy Justice Department's biggest law-enforcement disaster was due to a series of illegal wiretaps conducted by the FBI, most of which were targeted at Las Vegas casino operators. For fifteen months, secret FBI wiretaps that had been placed on the business telephones of five major casinos yielded an astonishing history of syndicate involvement in Las Vegas, including hidden ownerships and massive skimming operations that were being funneled into other underworld-backed activities, such as narcotics and payoffs to politicians. The intelligence was so impressive that J. Edgar Hoover, who had denied throughout his career that the national crime syndicate existed, finally agreed that it did.

However, all the taps had been installed illegally—without court authorization—and none of the data obtained could be used in court. In fact, when the wiretaps were discovered by the casino operators in Las Vegas, they filed a massive civil suit against the federal government. The suit was dropped after the government agreed to quash an IRS investigation of skimming in the casinos.

Like the Kefauver Committee a decade earlier, the Kennedy Justice Department tried but failed to legalize court-authorized federal wiretapping and electronic surveillance in 1962.

3. The Sports Bribery Act says, "Whoever carries into effect, attempts to carry into effect, or conspires with any other person to carry into effect any scheme in commerce to influence, in any way, by bribery any sporting contest, with knowledge that the purpose of such scheme is to influence by bribery that contest, shall be fined not more than $10,000 or imprisoned not more than five years or both." Title 18 USC, Section 224.

4. Some bookmakers, to increase their earnings, have moved from the 11–10 payoff to a more lucrative 6–5, which is obviously less popular among the betting public.

There are numerous complex variations of gambling, bookmaking, and the layoff. Because this is not a gambling how-to book, I refer readers to other books on these subjects, including: Mort Olshan, *Winning Theories of Sports Handicapping* (New York: Simon & Schuster, Inc., 1975); Lem Banker and Frederick C. Klein, *Book of Sports Betting* (New York: E.P. Dutton & Co., 1986); Larry Merchant, *The National Football Lottery* (New York: Holt, Rinehart & Winston, Inc., 1973); Gerald Strine and Neil D. Isaacs, *Covering the Spread: How to Bet Pro Football* (New York: Random House, Inc., 1978); Bob McCune, *The Gambling Times Guide to Football Handicapping* (Secaucus, N.J.: Gambling Times, Inc., 1984); Kelso Sturgeon, *Guide to Sports Betting* (New York: Harper & Row, Inc., 1974); and Richard Sasuly, *Bookies and Bettors: Two Hundred Years of Gambling* (New York: Holt, Rinehart & Winston, Inc., 1982). Also see *FBI Law Enforcement Bulletin,* November 1977 and September 1978.

5. Erickson died in 1968 at age seventy-two.

6. There were two major layoff centers for the underworld during the late 1950s and early 1960s. One was Newport/Covington and the other was Biloxi, Mississippi. Combined, they handled over 90 percent of the bookmaking traffic in America.

7. The five-feet-five Coppola was the quintessential mob torpedo. A syndicate killer since New York's Castellammarese War in 1931, he was a top associate and trusted friend of Charles "Lucky" Luciano, Frank Costello, and Vito Genovese. For years, he ran the numbers rackets in Harlem. After his wife—who had been indicted for perjury—died while giving birth to their daughter, Coppola moved to Miami Beach. At his height, Coppola had jurisdiction over sixty family "soldiers."

Coppola's second wife, whom he had met through Beckley, informed to IRS officials about his criminal tax fraud activities and then committed suicide. Beside her dead body was a note to Robert Kennedy, which said, "Please do not lose the courage of your convictions . . . In my wildest dreams, I can't imagine how Washington can allow people working for cities, states, and Washington to play both ends to the middle by accepting money to uphold the law and then accepting money from gangsters to break the law. Please, Mr. Kennedy, stop this. Don't give up." (The letter is from Hank Messich's *Syndicate Wife* (New York: Macmillan Co., 1968), p. 2.)

8. A close associate of the Beckley/Coppola operation was Alfred Mones, another top layoff bookmaker who operated the Metro Mortgage Company, a Miami business that fronted for his gambling activities. Mones and New York Mafia figure Charles "the Blade" Tourine had been partners in the Capri hotel/casino in pre-Castro Cuba.

9. D'Agostino and the Cotronis were the underworld figures contacted by Charles Luciano and Frank Coppola during the aftermath of World War II while the two deported mobsters were creating their heroin network into the United States via Montreal.

10. Beckley had also been using a system of "blue boxes," an electronic device that, when installed, can distort the telephone signal and bypass the phone company on long-distance telephone calls. The "blue box" network covered fifteen cities. One location had placed a hundred long-distance calls in a single day and not been charged for any. Beckley's gambling syndicate had used the devices as a means of illegally transmitting wagering information.

11. Blanda retired from the NFL after the 1975 season after scoring 2,002 points in his career.

CHAPTER 18

1. A Nassau County wiretap picked up one Miami bookmaker telling his New York layoff contact, "Lay the eighteen, all you can."

"What is it all about?" the layoff man replied.

"The college coach is putting up his own stuff."

2. Hundley was succeeded as head of the OCRS by Henry Petersen.

3. In a separate memorandum on the layoff bookmaking syndicate, filed

by the FBI in Atlanta, Beckley was described as "the key figure in this organized crime operation."

Coppola, Vito Genovese's heir apparent, had died of natural causes on October 1, 1966, in a Boston hospital.

4. In May 1967, a New York City police detective was dismissed for his "dealings with known criminals," according to an NYPD report. The officer, a twelve-year veteran of the department, also had been "providing his criminal associates with "a quantity of police records." Named by police officials as the officer's underworld contact was Gil Beckley.

5. *Life,* 8 September 1967.

6. Tameleo had also been linked by a congressional committee to Bob Cousy and Gene Conley of the Boston Celtics of the National Basketball Association. Cousy and Conley, along with Parilli, often patronized Arthur's Farm and another gamblers hangout, the Ebb Tide.

7. Williams later bought a total 14.7 percent interest in the Redskins. For an excellent biography of Williams, see Robert Pack's, *Edward Bennett Williams for the Defense* (New York: Harper & Row, Inc., 1983).

8. Williams's firm also represented Carlos Marcello after he slapped an FBI special agent who had been tailing him. Marcello was convicted and sentenced to six months in a prison hospital.

9. Peloquin had been the first head of the U.S. Strike Force Against Organized Crime in Buffalo. (The Strike Forces are the field offices under the Organized Crime and Racketeering Section of the Justice Department.) The Strike Force concept was established to coordinate all federal agencies involved in the war against organized crime and to cut the red tape when attempting to gain authorizations from the top levels of the Justice Department. The Buffalo Strike Force was created in 1966; a second was created in Detroit the following year. In 1968, Strike Force offices were established in Brooklyn, Philadelphia, and Chicago. Soon after, two more Strike Force offices were placed in Newark and Miami. In 1969, more were added in Boston, Manhattan, and Cleveland. In 1970, the Strike Force was expanded to include Los Angeles, St. Louis, New Orleans, Pittsburgh, Baltimore, and San Francisco. In 1971, a Kansas City office was added followed by one in Las Vegas.

10. Promuto was the target of a subsequent investigation in early 1975 when the U.S. Senate Permanent Subcommittee on Investigations opened hearings into the conduct of former Newark Strike Force chief John Bartels, Jr., the Harvard-educated administrator of the Drug Enforcement Administration, which had been created by President Nixon in July 1973 as a means to coordinate the ten federal antidrug agencies. Bartels was appointed by Nixon as the agency's first chief upon the recommendation of Henry Petersen, then the head of the Nixon Justice Department's criminal division and later Hundley's law partner.

DEA public affairs specialist Promuto, an attorney who had been with the agency since 1972, was accused of compromising DEA investigations via his links to Washington gamblers and bookmakers, specifically McCaleb, McGowan, and Corsi, among others. He was also linked to Gerald LeCompte, a Maryland-based gambler and narcotics dealer, who, according to a confidential 1971 Prince George's County police report, "provided prostitutes . . . to professional football players." Promuto vehemently denied such associations or that he compromised any law-enforcement investigations.

Promuto told me, "Edward Bennett Williams talked me into going to law school. When I graduated, I went to work for the government. There, I infuriated a lot of people. I was kind of a maverick. I'm not a perfect person, but I never did anything wrong. I never leaked any information about gambling or that kind of stuff. Hey, they called me a $500-a-day gambler. I still don't bet five cents. I laugh at my wife when she goes to bingo. I'm really proud that I worked as hard as I did in the government. I would do the whole thing over again."

A Justice Department investigation also looked into the charges against Bartels and Promuto. That probe was conducted by a three-man team headed by government attorney Michael DeFeo, one of Hundley's protégés and later a top official with the OCRS.

Bartels, who had attempted to quash the Promuto probe, resigned under pressure from Attorney General Edward Levi in May 1975. Promuto was reassigned to the DEA's New York office. Neither Bartels nor Promuto was charged with any crime.

CHAPTER 19

1. Klein adds that he had not yet met Carroll Rosenbloom at the time of his attempt to purchase Warner Brothers-Seven Arts.

2. Kinney's chief executive officer was Caesar P. Kimmel, whose father, Emmanuel Kimmel, was a major syndicate gambler. A former FBI special agent says of Kimmel's business, "At one time, it was a front and the bankroll of one of the biggest sports books in the country." Another law-enforcement official alleges, "National Kinney was mob-linked. Fat Tony Salerno laundered money from one of his sports-bookmaking fronts through Kinney."

However, when Kinney purchased the film company, Caesar Kimmel made a strong denial during an interview with *Forbes* that his company had any ties to the underworld. "I've lived with this over the years—the charge that we are run by the Mafia. It just isn't true. We don't wear shoulder holsters. We've never been under the influence of any underworld group . . . To put it bluntly: I am not my father's keeper. He has his world—he was born about 1898—and I have mine." *Forbes* added that it had "been unable to find a shred of solid evidence to support [the charges linking Kinney to the Mafia]."

3. Another new member of the Seven Arts board of directors was Alfred Bloomingdale, who was the grandson of the founder of Bloomingdale's department stores and a member of Ronald Reagan's "kitchen cabinet." Reagan had been elected governor of California in 1966. Bloomingdale later was placed on the board of the Los Angeles Rams by Carroll Rosenbloom.

4. During the Watergate investigation, Murchison was accused of personally delivering a $5,000 campaign contribution to President Nixon's personal secretary, Rose Mary Woods, and then left without getting a receipt. In 1968 alone, Murchison and his brother contributed $50,000 to Nixon's presidential campaign. After the election, Nixon and Murchison remained close friends. At the Washington Redskins–Dallas Cowboys game in November 1969, Nixon sat

with Murchison in seats provided by General Dynamics, the military hardware firm with which Murchison did business.

5. The Mary Carter Paint Company became the new power in the Bahamas gambling operations in 1967. The origins of the paint firm—which was based in Tampa but had its factory in New Jersey—are fuzzy, but it was taken over in October 1958 by the Crosby-Miller Corporation. The company had been formed by businessmen James Crosby and Jack Miller earlier in the year. Among the investors was former New York governor and defeated presidential candidate Thomas E. Dewey. Another investor was author and television personality Lowell Thomas.

In 1960, Crosby's brother Peter was convicted in New York of securities fraud in a case involving stock in the Texas Adams Oil Company, which was owned by the family of Houston Oilers owner, Bud Adams.

6. Specifically, Hartford told me that financier Robert Vesco later laundered $250,000 from the Castle Bank through a casino on Paradise Island and then gave the money to Nixon's political fixer, Murray Chotiner. Hartford also alleges that Nixon had made three deposits totaling $35,883,070, between October 21, 1971, and June 11, 1972, in the Cosmos Bank in Zurich, Switzerland. Hartford says that Nixon's account was under the name of the Zephyr Group, #47932608ZRA. Attempts to confirm Hartford's claims have been unsuccessful.

7. At the time of Groves's deal with Mary Carter, he was working for the CIA. The April 18, 1980, issue of *The Wall Street Journal* quotes a "Secret" memorandum from Covert Security Approval, dated December 30, 1965. The memo stated that Groves "will be used as an advisor and possible officer for one of [the CIA's unidentified] Project entitles . . ."

8. On January 18, 1966, Bob Peloquin and David P. Bancroft, U.S. Strike Force attorneys, wrote a memorandum to Bill Hundley, who was in his final days as the chief of the Organized Crime and Racketeering Section before becoming the head of NFL Security. Peloquin had been working with the IRS in Operation Tradewinds, a highly secret probe that concentrated on illegal money-laundering operations in the Bahamas. The memorandum to Hundley was based on an interview the two attorneys had had with Huntington Hartford in Nassau.

Peloquin and Bancroft concluded in their memorandum to Hundley that Hartford could be "easily [developed] into a good informant who would be in a position to supply accurate information as to the Lansky-Groves-Chesler gambling operations . . . Mary Carter Paints will be in control of Paradise Island with the exception of the Casino which Groves will control.

"The atmosphere seems ripe for a Lansky skim."

9. Mastriana also charged that he had been approached by McLaney and Elliot Roosevelt, the former mayor of Miami Beach and the son of the late president Franklin D. Roosevelt, and "asked if I would take a contract on Lyndon O. Pindling, and I said I would if the price was right. I was asked what I wanted and I said $10,000 in advance and $100,000 when the hit was completed." Mastriana added that he received the $10,000 but never did the job. Another underworld figure, Patsy Lepera, confirmed Mastriana's story. Both Mastriana and Lepere were convicted stock swindlers. Both Roosevelt and McLaney denied the charges.

10. McLaney lost his libel suit against *Life.* He had denied being "in business" with Lansky. However, he did admit contributing the use of three airplanes, a boat, and a helicopter to Pindling's campaign. The estimiated worth of these contributions was $60,000.

In 1980, McLaney chartered one of his planes, usually used for gambling junkets, to Ronald Reagan's 1980 presidential campaign staff.

11. McLaney was ordered to leave the Bahamas. He then moved his gambling operations to Haiti, where he operated with the cooperation of the country's dictator, François "Papa Doc" Duvalier, to reopen the Casino International in the Royal Haitian Hotel in Port-au-Prince.

12. Commission report, p. 92.

13. Among the guests at the 1967 opening of Mary Carter's first casino was Richard Nixon, who soon after announced his candidacy for the Republican presidential nomination. Mary Carter chief James Crosby did much of his banking with Nixon's closest friend, Bebe Rebozo, who introduced Crosby to Nixon earlier in the year. Crosby became a close friend of Nixon and contributed no less than $100,000 to Nixon's 1968 campaign.

Also in 1968, Bebe Rebozo, the president of the Key Biscayne Bank, was asked to arrange a loan on behalf of an Atlanta businessman, who put up nine hundred shares of IBM stock as collateral. In the midst of a background check of the applicant, Rebozo called on Crosby, the chairman of the board of Resorts International, based on Paradise Island in the Bahamas. After the loan was granted, the stock was identified as being stolen. Rebozo claimed to have no knowledge about the matter, according to a sworn deposition he filed.

Later indicted for the theft were Gil Beckley, who was then operating out of Atlanta, and Beckley's banker, Tony Salerno.

14. On June 5, after winning the California primary for the Democratic nomination for president, Senator Robert Kennedy was gunned down after his victory speech at the Ambassador Hotel in Los Angeles. His murderer, Sirhan Sirhan, was a hot walker at Santa Anita and Del Mar racetracks—with ties to a New Jersey organized-crime figure Henry Ramistella, who had a criminal record in Florida. Kennedy's assassin lived on a horse farm in Southern California with Ramistella until shortly before the murder.

15. Intertel was responsible for Hughes's midnight departure from his Desert Inn hotel/casino in Las Vegas in late November 1970. Hughes, who was carried out by stretcher down the back stairs of the hotel, was immediately flown to the Bahamas and placed in the Britannia Beach Hotel. This incident caused Hughes's final break with his longtime confidant, Robert Maheu. Hughes died on April 5, 1976. Intertel continued to handle security for his company's casinos.

16. In February 1978, Peloquin was forced to respond to charges by Boston-mobster-turned-government-witness Vincent Teresa that he had attempted to bribe Teresa in 1972. Teresa alleged that Peloquin wanted him to recant his testimony against Resorts International in return for a $100-a-day job with the company. Peloquin admitted meeting with Teresa and offering to help find him employment, but "at no time did I in any manner indicate to Teresa that I desired him to change any testimony he might have given or planned to give. At no time did I tell Teresa that I would give him a job if he perjured

himself. I did indicate to Teresa that if I learned of any job opportunities I would communicate same to him."

17. Both the Omnibus Crime Control Act of 1968 and the Organized Crime Control Act of 1970 resulted from the work of the 1967 President's Commission on Law Enforcement and Administration of Justice.

CHAPTER 20

1. Jimmy the Greek with the editorial assistance of Mickey Herskowitz and Steve Perkins, *Jimmy the Greek by Himself* (New York: Playboy Press, 1975), pp. 145–46.

Snyder, whose real name is Dimetrios Georgos Synodinos, is a tenth grade dropout from Steubenville, Ohio, and the son of a grocer in a local ma-and-pa store. The Synodinos family had been victimized by a severe act of violence. Snyder's uncle murdered Snyder's mother, his estranged wife, and then himself during a shooting rampage when Snyder was only nine.

Snyder pleaded no contest to interstate transportation of bets and wagering information in 1963. He was fined $10,000 and placed on probation for five years. He received a full and unconditional pardon from President Gerald Ford in December 1974. In his autobiography, Snyder wrote that he had met Ford while he was still a congressman, at the home of Robert Maheu, the liaison between the CIA and the Mafia in the Castro assassination plots (p. 238).

Snyder insisted that he had not made a bet on any sport, other than horse racing, since 1961.

2. Larry Merchant, *The National Football Lottery* (New York: Holt, Rinehart & Winston, Inc., 1973), pp. 265–66.

3. Dawson finished his nineteen-year career, still with the Kansas City Chiefs, in 1975. At the time of his retirement, he had earned an 82.6 passing rating—which, according to the NFL, "is based on performance standards established for completion percentage, interception percentage, touchdown percentage, and average gain. Passers are allocated points according to how their marks compare with those standards." Only one NFL quarterback had done as well by 1975: Sonny Jurgensen, who also had an 82.6 rating and had retired in 1974.

4. Kemp left the Steelers at the end of the 1957 season and joined the Los Angeles Chargers in the first AFL season in 1960. He went to the Buffalo Bills in 1962 and played there until 1969.

5. As Kansas City had in Super Bowl I, the Oakland Raiders lost to the Green Bay Packers, 33–14, in the second AFL–NFL World Championship Game. The game produced a $3 million gate, which was then the largest in sports history.

6. Nolan was sentenced to prison in October 1970. He fled the country the following month and lived in fifteen countries. Finally, after fifteen months on the run, Nolan surrendered and went to jail. There, he told me, he later became a good friend of convicted former U.S. attorney general John Mitchell. Nolan was released in August 1978.

7. The four games were LSU vs. South Carolina, September 17, 1966; LSU

vs. Texas A & M, October 8, 1966; LSU vs. Kentucky, October 15, 1966; and LSU vs. Florida, October 22, 1966.

8. Nolan—through one of his younger brothers Charles—had become a friend of several other local sports stars, including fullback Jim Taylor, who later played for the Green Bay Packers; halfback Billy Cannon, who later played for the Houston Oilers; and basketball player Bob Petitt, who later played for the Boston Celtics.

"I used to keep away from Bob," Nolan says. "He never had a shadow on him. He's the all-American-type. And I like him. But I used to stay on the other side of the room if we were in the same place—because I gambled and he was a professional athlete.

"One time, Jimmy Taylor came up to me and grabbed me around the neck and said, 'What's the matter with you? Why aren't you speaking to me?' And I said, 'Oh, Jimmy, I'm gambling, and you're playing football.' He said, 'I've known you all my life. You mean we can't even talk?' " Nolan described Taylor as "the cleanest man I ever knew." He added that Billy Cannon was "lily-white."

Cannon completed his career with the Kansas City Chiefs in 1970. In 1983, Cannon, by then a successful Baton Rouge dentist, pleaded guilty for his role in a $6 million counterfeiting scheme. He was sentenced to five years in prison. Earlier in the year, Cannon had been selected to be enshrined in the Pro Football Hall of Fame in Canton, Ohio. However, his induction was withdrawn after his conviction.

9. Responsible for arranging the loan was Kansas City Teamsters official Roy Williams, who was owned by the Civellas. Williams later became general president of the union. Also, six years before the pension fund loan, both Nick and Carl Civella, along with Motel Grezebrenacy of Kansas City, were listed in the original 1960 Las Vegas "Black Book," a distinction for those who are forbidden to enter a Nevada casino. Other charter members include John Battaglia, Tom Dragna, Bobby Garcia, and Joe Sica of Los Angeles; Marshall Caifano, Sam Giancana, and Murray Humphreys of Chicago; and Mike Coppola of Miami and New York.

10. Coincidentally, in the midst of the NFL investigation of Dawson and Robinson, the league suspended six game officials in December 1968 for the remainder of the season after they made a serious mistake that cost the Los Angeles Rams a down during the final seconds of their game against the Chicago Bears. The Bears won, 17–16. The error occurred while the game clock was running down and after a Rams lineman was cited for holding during a first-down play that resulted in an incomplete pass. The Rams were penalized ten yards. At the time of the penalty, the Rams were on the Bears thirty-two yard line.

When play resumed, the Rams should have had the ball first down and twenty-five on the forty-seven. Instead, the referee said it was second down and twenty-five. Rams quarterback Roman Gabriel then threw three more incomplete passes. Out of downs, according to the officials, the ball was turned over to the Bears with five seconds left in the game. The 10–2–1 Rams immediately lost the divisional championship to the 12–1 Baltimore Colts, whom the Rams played the following week in what would have been the decisive game.

The suspended officials were referee Norm Schachter, umpire Joe Connell, head linesman Burl Toler, line judge Jack Fette, back judge Adrian Burk, and field judge George Ellis. Toler received the blame for the mistake. However, all game officials are equally responsible for keeping track of the downs in a game.

There was no evidence of any wrongdoing among the officiating crew, which was considered among the best in the league.

11. The polygraph examinations were conducted by former FBI special agent Tom McShane. The fact that Dawson had taken the test was not revealed until January 1970.

12. One of the biggest problems faced by NFL Security is impersonations, people impersonating NFL players. "They were often involved in fraud and passing bad checks," Danahy says. "Every year when the training camps were being conducted, we would get a rash of impersonators in the areas of the training camps. Some guy who looked and smelled like a football player would walk into a local bar with a couple of friends who would drop the word that he was Joe Schmoe, the new prized draftee of the local team. The next thing, he'd be writing a check to buy his friends a few drinks and whatever. Then two or three days later, we'd start getting calls from the owners of the bars, who were complaining that our ballplayers' checks had bounced. Of course, the ballplayers had been nowhere near the places. It was the impersonators."

CHAPTER 21

1. The illegal device was a so-called spike mike, a microphone that contains a special crystal which, when slightly compressed, produces an electrical signal. In this particular case, the spike mike was placed on an eleven-inch rod drilled from the next-door row house and through the common wall between the two houses. The crystal was compressed against an air duct in the wall, which immediately turned into a huge receiver that monitored everything discussed in that room.

2. "Man-to-man" betting is straight up—with no 11–10 skim for the person booking the bet.

3. Handicappers, like Mort Olshan, who owns *The Gold Sheet,* have a different job than Martin does but do use his numbers. Olshan told me, "Bobby and I are really adversaries in this business. He puts up the line to attract public betting, and then I try to find the soft spots in his line." Personally, Martin and Olshan are close friends, according to both men.

4. There had been trouble for Werblin over his handling of quarterback Joe Namath. When Namath walked out of practice, Ewbank fined him—but Werblin paid Namath's fine, saying, "Joe is a star. What applies to others doesn't necessarily apply to him." During the 1967 exhibition season, Namath was discovered to have been out all night on New York's Upper East Side. When Jets head coach Weeb Ewbank ordered that he be fined again, Werblin replied, "I do not believe any player should be fined for such a thing. But Weeb runs the club."

Later, during the 1967 regular season, the night before a game between the Jets and the Denver Broncos, Werblin kept Namath out partying until 7:00 A.M. During the game later that day, Namath threw four interceptions and blew the Jets' chance for their first divisional championship. The Broncos won, 33–24.

The coup de grace was when Werblin signed Namath to a second three-year contract—without notifying his partners. Werblin was then given the "You buy us out or we buy you out" ultimatum. Werblin reportedly couldn't get the money together and sold his interest.

After leaving the Jets, Werblin became involved in horse racing and bought a yearling named Silent Screen for $39,000. In its third start, it won the $366,000 Arlington-Washington Futurity, which was sponsored by Marjorie Everett. From that win alone, Werblin won over $200,000. Werblin told reporter John Crittenden: "In football your inventory can cause you trouble overnight. Players can have a fight with their wives or girlfriends. They can stay out late drinking. They can feud with each other. They can pop off and make controversial headlines. Silent Screen, he gets to bed early, gets up early, drinks water, keeps his mouth shut, and does his work. Of course, I'm only kidding."

Iselin died in December 1976, and Hess bought his interest in the team. In 1984, Hess became the sole owner of the Jets.

5. Bubba Smith of Michigan State had been the first college player selected in the first joint NFL–AFL draft in March 1967.

6. Bubba Smith and Hal DeWindt, *Kill, Bubba, Kill!* (New York: Wallaby, 1983), p. 130.

7. After a seven-year, 71–23–4 record with Baltimore, Shula left the Colts after the 1969 season. He was replaced by Don McCafferty. Shula had been courted by Joe Robbie and the Miami Dolphins, who offered him 10 percent of the team. Although Robbie signed Shula, the Dolphins' owner violated NFL rules in doing so, causing a personal dispute with Carroll Rosenbloom. Rozelle intervened and fined Robbie his team's 1971 first-round draft pick, giving it to the Colts as compensation under the Rozelle Rule. After a 3–10–1 season in 1969 under fired head coach George Wilson, who was formerly with the Detroit Lions, Shula led Miami to a 10–4 record and a spot in the play-offs. However, Rosenbloom culminated the 1970 season with the Colts defeating the Dallas Cowboys, 16–13, in Super Bowl V in January 1971.

8. Bernie Parrish, *They Call It a Game* (New York: Dial Press, Inc., 1971), p. 190.

9. Also, Colts quarterback Earl Morrall had played sensationally during the 1968 season and had been named the NFL's Most Valuable Player. In the 1969 Super Bowl, he completed only six passes in seventeen attempts for seventy-one yards and had three interceptions. He was replaced by Johnny Unitas in the third quarter of the game.

10. Joe Namath with Dick Schaap, *I Can't Wait Until Tomorrow . . . 'Cause I Get Better Looking Every Day* (New York: Random House, Inc., 1969), p. 54.

11. Lou Sahadi, *The Long Pass* (New York: World Publishing Co., 1969), p. 16.

12. Namath, *Can't Wait,* p. 65.

13. Lou Michaels and Frank Namath, Joe's brother, had been roommates at the University of Kentucky.

14. Michaels played for the Los Angeles Rams from 1958 to 1960, the

Pittsburgh Steelers from 1961 to 1963, the Colts from 1964 to 1969, and he finished his distinguished career with the Green Bay Packers at the end of the 1971 season. As of 1988, he ranked fourteenth on the all-time list for career field goals, making 187 in 341 attempts. Also, during his thirteen-year career, he made 386 of 402 extra-point attempts, which is fifteenth on the all-time list. He is also seventeenth on the all-time scoring list with 955 points.

CHAPTER 22

1. Joe Namath with Dick Schaap, *I Can't Wait Until Tomorrow . . . 'Cause I Get Better Looking Every Day* (New York: Random House, Inc., 1969), p. 13.

2. Ray Abruzzese had played his college football with Namath at Alabama where they were close friends. He was a defensive back with the Buffalo Bills from 1962 to 1964.

3. Carmine Trumanti was later convicted of narcotics trafficking and sentenced to fifteen years in prison.

4. The night before his meeting with Rozelle, Namath attended the opening of a restaurant owned by another member of the Jets, Gerry Philbin, a defensive end and later a member of the All-Time AFL Team. While celebrating with Philbin, Namath told several of his teammates that he was planning to quit football the following day.

5. Namath, *Can't Wait,* p. 15.

6. *Ibid.,* pp. 31–32.

7. During a 1981 deposition for Rancho La Costa's 1981 libel suit against *Penthouse,* Meyer Lansky twice took the Fifth Amendment when asked about his alleged relationship with Namath.

8. Because of Wolman's troubled financial condition, which resulted from a disastrous construction project in Chicago, the NFL had considered taking over the administration of the franchise in October 1968. Upon the advice of the NFL, Wolman hired Bert Rose, the former general manager of the Minnesota Vikings, as an adviser. Wolman had also built the Spectrum arena in Philadelphia and owned Connie Mack Stadium and the Yellow Cab Company of Philadelphia and Camden, New Jersey. Wolman had bought the Eagles for $5.5 million in December 1963.

9. Tose sold K. S. Canning to Walter Kidde and Company in 1969 for over two hundred thousand shares of Kidde stock, worth nearly $8 million.

10. David Harris, *The League: The Rise and Decline of the NFL* (Toronto: Bantam Books, 1986), p. 118.

CHAPTER 23

1. The Chiefs games taken off the boards in 1969 were the September 14 game against the San Diego Chargers, which the Chiefs won, 27–9; the September 21 game against the Boston Patriots, which the Chiefs won, 31–0; the September 28 game against the Cincinnati Bengals, which the Chiefs lost, 24–19; and the October 5 game against the Denver Broncos, which the Chiefs

won, 26–13. After the Denver game, the Chiefs remained on the boards for the rest of the season.

2. The IRS used the "pen register," a device that is attached to a telephone line and then maintains a record of each number dialed.

3. I asked Don Dawson whether he had any knowledge about the inability of the IRS to receive wiretap authorization. Dawson replied, "I had called [attorney and Redskins president] Ed Williams up, and Ed said, 'I'll get to John Mitchell and see what the story is.' Williams told me that Mitchell said, 'It's too hot to handle. I can't touch it, Eddie.' And it was too hot to handle because there were players involved, and nobody wanted to mess with the NFL."

Also, at the time of the investigation, legislation authorizing an intense crackdown on organized crime's involvement in professional and college sports by the IRS was also stalled in the Senate Judiciary Committee.

4. When the gambling investigation became public, Joe Namath—who had been forced by the NFL to sell Bachelors III just the previous year—was named as being among those players involved with Don Dawson. However, Namath denied knowing Dawson.

Supporting Namath, a top IRS official involved in the investigation told me that "Namath was never a target of the investigation. We had no idea where the media came up with his name. We had nothing on him at all."

Another Jets player named in news reports was tight end Pete Lammons.

Dawson told me that he didn't know either Namath or Lammons. However, Dawson added, "Joe bet pretty good." He claims that he knew a bookmaker in Miami with whom Namath did business.

5. Nick Civella was convicted for running an interstate sports-bookmaking operation in 1970.

6. Len Dawson's father died in November 1969, the day before a game between Kansas City and the New York Jets. Dawson played in that game and won it for his dad, 34–16. Dawson told me that after the game, he flew home to Alliance, Ohio, for the funeral. Don Dawson called him at his parents' home.

7. Stram had been an assistant coach at Purdue, his own alma mater, for part of the time that Dawson had played his college ball there; the two men had developed a close friendship as well as a player/coach relationship.

8. Marty Ralbovsky, *Super Bowl: Of Men, Myths and Moments* (New York: Hawthorn Books, Inc., 1972), p. 113.

9. In lieu of taking the game off the boards, the oddsmakers simply allowed the line to skyrocket. Initially, Minnesota was considered a three-point favorite. When Len Dawson was named as a possible target of the grand-jury investigation, the line jumped to nine and then to thirteen by kickoff. The ten-point variance in the spread indicated that gamblers believed that Kansas City would be slaughtered in anticipation of Dawson's collapse under the extreme pressure he was under.

10. Just the previous week, Detroit Tigers pitching star Denny McLain had been hauled before a federal grand jury in Detroit investigating his relationship with a Michigan bookmaker since 1967. He was also implicated with Detroit Mafia figures Tony and Vito Giacalone, both of whom figured prominently in the 1963 Detroit Lions betting scandal. McLain, who was suspended

by baseball commissioner Bowie Kuhn, was later indicted and convicted of racketeering and narcotics trafficking.

Ironically, McLain was the first pitcher to win thirty games in a single season since it had been done in 1934—by Dizzy Dean.

CHAPTER 24

1. Osadchey was fingered by the Kefauver Committee as being closely associated with Kansas City's "Five Iron Men," who were five of the most vicious racketeers in the region and controlled gambling operations in Iowa, Kansas, Missouri, and Nebraska.

2. Klein had also been part owner of the Seattle SuperSonics of the NBA, along with Sam Schulman, his onetime partner in the San Diego Chargers.

3. Lansky offered $1 million to any country that would give him sanctuary. No one would, so, in November 1972, he returned to the United States where he was arrested and charged with federal income-tax violations, conspiracy, and skimming. U.S. District Judge Roger Foley later ruled that Lansky was too ill to stand trial, and the charges against him were dropped.

Marjorie Everett—the daughter of Chicago racetrack overlord Ben Lindheimer, who once owned the Los Angeles Dons of the AAFC—was responsible for exposing the underworld links to Acapulco Towers. Philip Levin had given her a long-term contract to remain as the executive director of the two racetracks. However, Levin squeezed her out early in the contract period. She was so angry that she hired a private investigator to investigate Levin, a partner in Acapulco Towers.

4. Aside from Klein, Korshak, Levin, and Morton, the other partners in Acapulco Towers were Hollywood attorney Greg Bautzer; Parvin-Dohrmann chief Delbert Coleman; City National Bank of Beverly Hills president Alfred Hart; businessman Gerald Herzfeld, who had considerable interests in hotels and casinos; investor Alfred Lushing; Helen Morton, Moe's wife; actress Donna Reed's husband, Tony Owen; and Bautzer's law partner, Eugene Wyman, a top official in California's Democratic party.

5. Levin had been the largest stockholder in Metro-Goldwyn-Mayer studios. Levin had sold his stock in the film company in 1968 and invested it in Gulf & Western. G & W founder and chairman Charles Bluhdorn, who also purchased Paramount Pictures in 1966, then named Levin as president of G & W real estate.

Levin's first purchases were the two racetracks owned by Marjorie Everett. He merged these two tracks with the Madison Square Garden Corporation, another G & W subsidiary. Levin, who purchased Acapulco Towers on behalf of G & W in 1970, immediately appointed Korshak as house counsel.

Korshak had personally engineered a $16 million loan for Levin and his new company, Transnation Development Corporation, from the Teamsters' Central States Pension Fund for a construction project that was owned by G & W's Madison Square Garden Corporation. Through his holdings, Levin exercised considerable control over the New York Knickerbockers of the NBA, the New York Rangers hockey team, and Roosevelt Raceway on Long Island.

Sonny Werblin, the former owner of the New York Jets, took over the Madison Square Garden Corporation in 1978.

CHAPTER 25

1. The legislation permitting the wiretaps was Title III of the June 1968 Omnibus Crime Control and Safe Streets Act, which permitted court-authorized electronic surveillance *if* the alleged crime, the targets, the location of the taps, and an explanation of what types of discussions are expected accompany the request. Also, law-enforcement agencies must show that all other means of investigative procedures have been exhausted. However, federal authorities could not place bugging equipment in bedrooms or record conversations between targets and their attorneys. As a result, whenever possible, mobsters began holding business meetings in their bedrooms or in their attorneys' offices.

2. Clark Mollenhoff, *Strike Force: Organized Crime and Government* (Englewood Cliffs, N.J.: Prentice-Hall, Inc., 1972), p. 184.

3. Ironically, also in April 1971, while Sklaroff was having all his legal difficulties, the New York City Off-Track Betting Corporation, which had been promoted by Governor Nelson Rockefeller, went into business and began accepting bets. All wagers were limited to horse racing and had been legalized by the state legislature the previous year. Connecticut followed suit in May 1976.

Also in 1971, Jimmy "the Greek" Snyder began syndicating his line in daily newspapers through Field Enterprises. He was given his first column by Hank Greenspun, the editor of *The Las Vegas Sun.* By 1978, Snyder was appearing in over 150 newspapers, including *The Atlanta Constitution, The Miami News,* and *The Washington Post.*

4. Goldstein pleaded guilty to federal gambling violations in 1972.

5. In the midst of the grand-jury investigation, a new book *They Call It a Game* was published by former defensive back Bernie Parrish of the Cleveland Browns. A stunning but sometimes acrimonious indictment against the professional football establishment, the book was Parrish's effort to take off the gloves and examine the league as no one had ever done before. In his preface, Parrish writes, "This book is intended to drive Pete Rozelle, Arthur Modell, Carroll Rosenbloom, Tex Schramm, Clint Murchison . . . and the other so-called sportsmen-owners out of professional football. They are my enemies and they know it." Parrish was among the first witnesses to testify before the grand jury.

6. The committee's focus had concentrated on corruption in the racing industry. The principal target was the Buffalo-based Sportservice Corporation, aka Emprise, a nationwide sports concession conglomerate, which had been convicted in 1972 of racketeering and serving as a front for several Mafia families in their hidden ownership of the Frontier hotel/casino in Las Vegas.

7. The first story of the attempted fix with no names mentioned was reported by Clark Hoyt of *The Miami Herald* on December 2, 1972. Sturm was first identified as the player who received the bribe offer in a story by Dave Brady of *The Washington Post* on July 5, 1973. Donnie Stone was first

identified as the man who had allegedly approached Sturm in an article by Bill Guthrie, the sports editor of *The New Haven Register* in Connecticut on July 8, 1973.

CHAPTER 26

1. U.S. Congress, House of Representatives, Testimony of Aaron Kohn, "Organized Crime in Sports (Racing)," Hearings before the U.S. House Select Committee on Crime, 92d Cong., 2d sess., 1972, pt. 2, p. 956.

2. *Ibid.*, pp. 893–94.

3. Sarkowsky was replaced by Nordstrom's son John as managing general partner in 1982.

4. Irsay remained with his company until 1978 when he organized Colt Construction and Development Company.

5. Rosenbloom accepted personal responsibility for paying Unitas $250,000 in retirement benefits. Unitas left the Colts at the end of the 1972 season and played his final season with the San Diego Chargers in 1973.

6. In 1972, Warner Communications purchased the New York Cosmos of the North American Soccer League (NASL) for $25,000. Warner's chairman, Steven Ross, reportedly had wanted his company to buy an NFL team—but was prevented from doing so because of NFL rules that forbid corporations from becoming team owners.

Although Rosenbloom wasn't affected by Warner's ownership of the NASL team, Rozelle was already on record in his opposition to cross ownership of professional sports teams. On May 25, 1972, the NFL adopted a policy stating that no NFL owner could have a majority interest in another major sport team. However, instead of requiring those who did to divest themselves, it simply asked that their present interests not be increased.

Among other owners in violation of the resolution, Lamar Hunt of the Kansas City Chiefs owned the majority interest in the Dallas Tornado of the NASL and was half owner of the World Championship Tennis tour, which he founded. He also owned an 11 percent share of the Chicago Bulls of the National Basketball Association.

It was an easy problem to get around. The NFL owners who engaged in cross ownership simply could place the majority of shares in their other sports ventures in the names of members of their families.

7. Carroll Rosenbloom had toyed with the idea of giving the Colts to his son Steve and buying the Rams for himself. However, Pete Rozelle quickly scotched that idea because of the inherent conflicts of interest.

8. *The Gold Sheet,* 2 November 1974.

CHAPTER 27

1. Although, at the time, gambling was the underworld's biggest revenue-producing operation, by 1982 its biggest money-maker clearly and indisputably had become drugs, particularly cocaine.

Interestingly, in the midst of Operation Anvil, several states began to debate the pros and cons of legalizing professional football lotteries. Among these states were Connecticut, Iowa, Massachusetts, Montana, New York, Rhode Island, and Wisconsin. Montana was the only state where the issue made significant progress. The NFL appeared to be adamant in its opposition.

2. Sklaroff was again indicted for nine counts of interstate gambling in April 1974 and again pleaded not guilty. On March 12, 1975, Sklaroff was convicted on all nine counts. He was sentenced to four years in prison.

Later in 1975, all questions about Sklaroff became moot when the forty-three-year-old bookmaker died suddenly of natural causes in jail after being asked to testify against Salerno during a federal grand-jury investigation. According to a confidential Justice Department memorandum, just before his death, "Sklaroff had been offered the opportunity to cooperate with the Government and testify against Salerno and in turn he would be relocated with a new identity. However, Sklaroff is so scared of Salerno that he has refused to cooperate."

3. It is also important to note that during the Nixon administration, particularly in its second term, the sincere crime-fighting prosecutors and investigators had been totally demoralized by the behavior of two attorney generals—John Mitchell and Richard Kleindienst—both of whom had broken the law and were later convicted; and by the White House, which, during the Watergate cover-up, had engaged in a sweetheart relationship with the Teamsters Union that resulted in dramatic punch pulling in the federal government's war against labor racketeering and organized crime.

In addition, Nixon had been employing the traditional tools used against organized crime, such as wiretapping, not against the mob but against his political enemies.

4. Rosenthal had attracted the attention of Meyer Lansky. As an indication of how well Lansky liked Rosenthal, the mobster tried to interest Rosenthal in marrying his niece—but Lefty declined.

5. The hidden owners of Caesars Palace included Tony Accardo and Sam Giancana of Chicago, Raymond Patriarca of Boston, and Genovese members Vincent "Jimmy Blue Eyes" Alo, Gerardo Catena, and Tony Salerno. All these mobsters participated in the casino's illegal skimming operations.

6. The SEC filed a complaint against Lum's in 1971, charging that the company had provided false information to potential investors in an effort to manipulate the price of its stock. Among the executives named in the action by the SEC was William Weinberger, one of Art Modell's closest friends. Without being forced to admit or deny guilt by the SEC, Caesars executives were slapped on the wrist and ordered never to violate securities laws in the future. The consent decree forced settlement of Lum's stockholder suits.

In addition, Zarowitz was found to have owned 2 percent of the stock in the Golden Nugget in 1972. Also, Price was convicted in 1979 of fixing no fewer than twenty races between August 1974 and August 1975 at tracks in Massachusetts, New Hampshire, New Jersey, Pennsylvania, and Rhode Island.

7. In July 1970, just five months before the raids, the Nixon administration—through Attorney General Mitchell, who had been pressured by an Ital-

ian defamation group—ordered that the words *Mafia* and *La Cosa Nostra* be stricken from the vocabulary of all federal employees.

8. The circumstances revolving around the wiretap authorization remain a mystery. What is known is that in 1972 a Florida defense attorney spotted two different signatures for the Justice Department official who had authorized the electronic surveillance. A check of Attorney General Mitchell's public schedule showed that he had not been available to initial the authorizations—a procedure that is required under Title III. As a consequence, nearly seven hundred federal indictments, which had been based on wiretaps, were summarily dismissed. It was one of the worst setbacks ever in the history of the war against organized crime.

Without the wiretaps, Judge Foley said, "The government represents it does not have sufficient evidence to proceed." Foley had previously attempted to dismiss the case on the basis of other issues regarding the wiretaps in May 1973—but was overturned by the U.S. court of appeals.

9. Don Kowet, *The Rich Who Own Sports* (New York: Random House, Inc., 1977), pp. 175–76.

CHAPTER 28

1. Glick would later receive a $7 million loan (at an incredible 4 percent interest rate) from the Teamsters' pension fund for the purchase of the 375-acre Beverly Ridge Estates, which was a real estate development in Los Angeles. The previous owners of Beverly Ridge had received a $13.5 million loan from the union but defaulted in 1970 when the company folded. Several executives of the company were indicted and convicted for bankruptcy fraud, including Irving Davidson, Carlos Marcello's front man. Upon acquiring the property, Glick changed the development's name to Beverly Summitt.

2. At the time, Hughes owned the Desert Inn, Sands, Castaways, Frontier, Silver Slipper, and Landmark in Las Vegas and Harold's Club in Reno.

Also, in 1973, the year before Glick's purchase of the four casinos, Las Vegas's gaming industry reported net profits totaling over $761 million.

3. Spilotro, using the alias Anthony Stuart, also ran the Gold Rush jewelry store at Jay Sarno's Circus Circus casino. Spilotro's small business served as a fencing operation for stolen goods. Circus Circus had received $20 million in loans from the Teamsters' pension fund. Spilotro also had operations at the Dunes, which was owned by Morris Shenker, one of Jimmy Hoffa's attorneys. Spilotro was a close friend of several celebrities, including Robert Conrad and Barbara McNair. Spilotro was suspected of engineering the 1976 murder of McNair's husband, Rick Manzie, a small-time Chicago hood.

At the time of Glick's purchase of Argent, Spilotro was still reporting to Chicago Mafia capo Joseph Lombardo.

4. Glick responded to my written questions in writing—via his attorney, Louis R. "Skip" Miller of Christensen, White, Miller, Fink & Jacobs of Los Angeles.

5. In May 1975, in a Las Vegas parking lot, Buccieri was found behind the wheel of his car with five bullets in his head. Buccieri, the former partner

of Tito Carinci in Newport, Kentucky, had also been a close associate of Gil Beckley.

6. Derlachter, formerly of St. Louis, was the executive vice president of the Sargent-Fletcher Corporation, formerly known as Fletcher Aviation, a major aerospace company owned by Wendell S. Fletcher, who owned a 15 percent interest in the Dunes hotel/casino in Las Vegas. Because of his job, Derlachter, who also worked at the Dunes part-time, had received a high-level security clearance from the Department of Defense.

7. Parvin-Dohrmann Company had been owned by Albert Parvin, who had been accused of being a front man for Meyer Lansky. One of Parvin's employees was Edward Levinson, who had been implicated in the Bobby Baker scandal and was identified as Lansky's bagman in Las Vegas. Parvin had purchased the Stardust from Cleveland mobster Morris Dalitz.

Parvin became embroiled in a massive federal investigation in 1966 after it was discovered that U.S. Supreme Court Associate Justice William O. Douglas had received $12,000 a year since 1962 from the Albert Parvin Foundation, which was funded by the Flamingo hotel/casino.

In the wake of the Douglas scandal, Parvin sold his casino interests in 1969 to businessman Delbert Coleman, reputed to be a front man for Los Angeles attorney/organized-crime figure Sidney Korshak. It was Korshak who had received a $500,000 finder's fee for his role in Dalitz's sale of the Stardust to Parvin.

Through a complex—and illegal—series of manipulations, the stock of the company suddenly became hugely inflated. But, before the SEC stepped in to investigate, the Coleman/Korshak group attempted but failed to sell the company to San Diego Chargers owner Gene Klein, who told me that he canned the deal because he didn't trust Coleman.

Subsequently, Denny's Restaurants purchased Parvin-Dohrman, just before the company's stock collapsed and its trading was suspended by the SEC on the American Stock Exchange. Coleman desperately tried to lift the suspension—which led to an alleged attempt to bribe U.S. Speaker of the House John McCormick through a Washington lobbyist who later pleaded guilty to influence peddling.

Questioned by the SEC, Korshak, a target of the SEC complaint, told investigators that he also represented Gulf & Western, the Hyatt Hotel Corporation, and Hilton Hotels, owned by Barron Hilton, who at the time still owned 30 percent of Klein's Chargers.

An eventual settlement was reached with the SEC, which forced Coleman to resign as the head of the company. Parvin regained control of the corporation and changed its name to Recrion. He gave Korshak another $500,000 finder's fee for making the arrangements.

8. Regarding the purchase of insurance, Glick told me, "Dorfman was head of an insurance company that provided insurance to Recrion before I bought it, and we continued the policy and renewals."

9. Glick's Hacienda also came under the Argent umbrella, as did the Marina Hotel in 1975.

10. Prior to the creation of the Stardust Sports Book, there were sixteen such wagering parlors in Nevada. In 1975, the Nevada Gaming Com-

mission permitted the state's hotels to open legal sports-bookmaking operations.

11. Explaining the collapse of the company, Glick told me, "Saratoga was a highly leveraged real estate company with good property, but the real estate recession in Southern California in 1973 forced it into a cash flow crisis and ultimately bankruptcy. I had personal guarantees that were called on and to protect creditors and some of the very good properties, I had to get involved again and pledge money to make a plan of arrangement. Wittman left when the largest lenders and the creditors committee forced him to resign on the eve of the filing. Prior to the filing, the creditors had a committee to see what was happening, and they and Wittman could not work together."

12. Investigative reporter Jeff Morgan of *The Oakland Tribune* first broke the story about the Glick-Davis business partnership in the Eastmont Mall on June 1, 1975.

13. Deposition of Allen Davis, Los Angeles Memorial Coliseum Commission v. National Football League, U.S. District Court, Central District of California, Civil Action No. 78–3523–HP.

CHAPTER 29

1. Tony Salerno, the top capo in the Genovese crime family, was still running the group's bookmaking operations.

2. *The New York Times,* 22 August 1974.

3. A similar suit was filed at the same time by all-pro guard Ken Gray of the St. Louis Cardinals. He won in an out-of-court settlement with undisclosed terms.

4. The eight Chargers players were Deacon Jones, Tim Rossovich, Coy Bacon, Dave Costa, Jerry LeVias, Rick Redman, Walt Sweeney, and Bob Thomas.

5. Arnold J. Mandell, *The Nightmare Season* (New York: Random House, Inc., 1976), p. 50.

6. Klein remained with National General as a paid consultant until 1980.

7. La Costa was owned by Cleveland/Las Vegas mobster Morris Dalitz and his partners. The development received nearly $100 million in loans from the Teamsters' pension fund.

8. Looney was killed in a motorcycle accident on September 24, 1988, in southwest Texas.

9. Over the next six years, Herron was arrested four more times for drug-related offenses. In 1978, he was arrested in Atlanta after receiving a package containing half a pound of 60 percent pure cocaine. He was later convicted and sentenced to five years in prison.

10. Bernie Jackson later became a New York state supreme court judge.

11. In 1978, Werblin left the New Jersey Sports and Exposition Authority to become head of Gulf & Western's Madison Square Garden Corporation. At the time of Werblin's move, G & W also owned and operated Roosevelt Raceway in Long Island and Arlington Park in Chicago as well as New York's Madison Square Garden.

CHAPTER 30

1. In New Jersey, voters approved casino gambling in Atlantic City in a November 1976 referendum. Resorts International became the first corporation to apply for a gaming license the following year. The Resorts casino opened over the Memorial Day holiday in 1978. Six months later, Florida voters decisively rejected an attempt to establish casino gambling in that state.

A movement for state-run casinos was also being conducted in New York. The principal spokesman for the drive was Robert Tisch, the president of Loews Hotels and the chairman of the New York City Convention and Visitors Bureau. Loews already had casino holdings in Aruba, Monaco, and Puerto Rico. It also owned a hotel on Paradise Island. Its casino was operated by Resorts International.

In 1987, Loews purchased the Columbia Broadcasting System.

2. The Commission on the Review of the National Policy Toward Gambling's tainted work was the last federal effort to examine sports gambling in America. In 1974, the Justice Department estimated that the volume of illegal sports gambling was between $29 billion and $39 billion annually. Most experts on gambling disagreed with those figures, insisting that they were too low.

3. *The Washington Post,* 5 February 1978.

4. *The Gold Sheet,* 11 September 1976.

5. In 1974, Snyder served as spokesman for Dell O. Gustavson, the owner of the Tropicana hotel/casino in Las Vegas, which was under siege by the Nevada Gaming Control Board because of questionable credit operations involving the Detroit Mafia. Earlier, Snyder, who had owned a public-relations firm, had been placed on a $7,500-a-month retainer by Howard Hughes. Snyder's company was implicated in the illegal 1968 takeover of Air West by Hughes and was enjoined with others in litigation by the SEC—because of acts of fraud and financial manipulation revolving around the Air West sale. Snyder did not contest the decision.

6. Jimmy the Greek with the editorial assistance of Mickey Herskowitz and Steve Perkins, *Jimmy the Greek by Himself* (New York: Playboy Press, 1975), p. 149.

7. *Ibid.,* p. 217. Specifically, Snyder wrote, "I never subscribed to the theory that the casinos were linked, or backed, by a national syndicate, what conspiracy fans have sometimes called 'The Organization'... Crime has always struck me, an observer of the passing scene, as notoriously disorganized. If it were not, if there really was such a thing as 'Organized Crime,' it would run the country."

CHAPTER 31

1. Glick had been hoping for another $40 million from the Teamsters' pension fund to remodel his casinos. All hopes for that were dashed after Glick's chilly meeting with Civella.

Civella was sentenced to prison again after his conviction for operating an interstate sports-bookmaking operation in July 1975.

2. It was difficult for law-enforcement officials not to notice that onetime Chicago Mafia boss Sam Giancana had been murdered in an almost identical manner in June 1975—just before he was to have testified before a U.S. Senate select committee investigation on the CIA/Mafia plots to assassinate Fidel Castro. Giancana was shot by the same type of weapon that killed Rand. He was hit in the neck and the mouth, and five times through the head. Although the murder remains unsolved, law-enforcement officials believe that Giancana had been taken out by his bodyguard Butch Blasi.

Chicago mobster Johnny Rosselli, who did testify before the Senate select committee, was found murdered, dismembered, and decomposed in a fifty-five-gallon drum floating in Biscayne Bay—in August 1976. He was last seen on a boat owned by Santos Trafficante.

3. Federal investigators believe that one of Spilotro's two possible accomplices in the Rand slaying was William "Butch" Petrocelli, a low-level Chicago underworld figure. Thought to have killed another possible federal informant, Chicago restaurant owner Nick Yalentzas, in 1980, Petrocelli was known to have been in a San Diego motel near the Rand house on the day of the murder. His longtime partner, Harry "the Hook" Aleman, was suspected as being the second man. Aleman was convicted of racketeering charges in 1978 and imprisoned. Petrocelli was found dead in early 1981 in his car with his throat cut, his body partially burned, and his mouth taped shut.

4. Deposition of Allen Davis, Los Angeles Memorial Coliseum Commission v. National Football League, U.S. District Court, Central District of California, Civil Action No. 78–3523–HP.

5. Rozelle also had been critical of Davis's friendship with oddsmaker Jimmy "the Greek" Snyder. In a sworn deposition, when Rozelle was asked whether he had ordered Davis to sever his ties with the gambler, Rozelle replied, "I did not order him to. I told him I thought, because of the publicity he was getting at that time by being seen with Jimmy, it would be probably better if he wasn't seen with him a lot." Rozelle added that he relented after Snyder was hired as a commentator by CBS. After that, "I didn't see any more criticism that I can recall of Al's being seen with him."

6. Rosenthal appealed the commission's decision, charging that his constitutional rights had been impinged upon. Clark County Judge Joseph Pavlikowski overturned the decision in November 1976, saying that many of Nevada's gaming laws were unconstitutional and that the state legislature had given the state's gaming commission too much power. "The absence of standards," the judge said, "creates a void in which malice, vindictiveness, intolerance, and prejudice can fester." Pavlikowski ordered Rosenthal reinstated.

Immediately, Rosenthal returned to Argent, officially as a "low-level employee," specifically under the guise of the Stardust's director of food and beverages. However, regardless of his position, he resumed his duties as the key operator of the company's casino holdings, replacing Carl Thomas.

The Nevada Gaming Commission immediately appealed to the Nevada Supreme Court in Carson City, which overturned the lower court decision in February 1977, citing that qualifying for a gaming license was a matter for the state, not the federal government, to decide. Essentially, the court ruled that possession of a gaming license was a privilege, not a right.

Rosenthal was ousted from the Stardust again.

7. Federal officials believe that Hoffa was killed by longtime underworld associates. Government investigators believe that Hoffa was murdered by Salvatore Briguglio, a top associate of Genovese capo Anthony Provenzano. They also suspect that Provenzano had acted on orders from eastern Pennsylvania/upstate New York crime boss Russell Bufalino, who was serving as the interim head of the Genovese family. Like Sam Giancana, Hoffa was murdered in the midst of the investigation of the plots to kill Castro. Bufalino, a close associate of Carlos Marcello and Santos Trafficante, had been brought into the plots, along with four other mobsters, by Hoffa in the spring of 1960.

For details on the murder of Hoffa, the events leading up to it, and its aftermath—including my interview with Briguglio and his alleged accomplices—see my book *The Hoffa Wars: Teamsters, Rebels, Politicians and the Mob* (New York: Paddington Press, 1978).

8. The principal targets of the federal investigations were the Teamsters, the Laborers International Union, the Hotel and Restaurant Workers International Union, and the International Longshoremen's Association. All had documented ties with organized crime. However, federal prosecutors determined that only three hundred union locals of seventy-five thousand nationwide were corrupt—one half of 1 percent.

9. In June 1976, the IRS revoked the tax-exempt status of the Teamsters' pension fund, which had loaned over $230 million to Las Vegas casinos. Soon after, control of the $2 billion fund was given to outside fiduciary management, Equitable Life Assurance and the Victor Palmieri Corporation, a consulting firm.

Three years later, the FBI taped a conversation in which Chicago Mafia capo Joseph Lombardo told Kansas City mob boss Nick Civella, "The old man [Chicago Mafia chief Joseph Aiuppa] wanted me to come and see you. We have to get things running smooth again like they used to be." Lombardo went on to say that they had to rid themselves of the independent pension fund managers and bring back their own people.

CHAPTER 32

1. The decision in *Mackey* v. *NFL* was announced in December 1975. The judge ruled that the Rozelle Rule "is so clearly contrary to public policy it is illegal under the Sherman [Antitrust] Act. It is also an unreasonable restraint of trade at common law." However, the appeals court watered down the decision considerably, saying that the Rozelle Rule should be the subject of collective bargaining. The compromise struck was a new free agency system, in which the team losing the veteran player would gain one or more college draft picks from the team signing him. The number of picks would be based upon the free agent's negotiated salary. However, there was little reform with this system—since NFL team owners became reluctant to sign free agents for fear of losing their college prospects.

However, on February 16, 1977, as a direct result of the *Mackey* decision, the NFL owners agreed to recognize the NFLPA as a closed shop. All NFL players' dues to the union were checked off, whether they considered themselves members of the NFLPA or not.

2. David Harris, *The League: The Rise and Decline of the NFL* (Toronto: Bantam Books, 1986), p. 219.

3. *Ibid.*, pp. 233–34.

Later, as an extension of Rosenbloom's war against Rozelle, he accused the commissioner of being anti-Semitic for scheduling a Rams–Miami Dolphins game on October 3, 1976, the beginning of the sacred Yom Kippur holiday. Rosenbloom, who was not at all religious, charged, "[Rozelle] goes out of his way to play a Jewish owner in Miami, which is heavily Jewish, on a holy day. It is a punishment and a warning to other team owners that if they criticize Pete Rozelle, they also will be punished."

4. Including interest, Culverhouse's price for the team was $17.2 million. To help him acquire the Tampa Bay franchise, Culverhouse allowed his friend since childhood, banking tycoon Marvin Warner, to purchase 48 percent of the franchise. Later, Warner sold his interest in the team to Culverhouse and invested his money in the Birmingham franchise of the short-lived United States Football League.

Warner made his fortune as a housing developer in Cincinnati. He was also a minority owner of the New York Yankees and the owner of two large horse-breeding farms in Kentucky and Ohio. Appointed by President Jimmy Carter as the ambassador to Switzerland, he also later became the owner of the Great American Bank, which was indicted in 1982 for laundering $96 million in drug money. Warner was not personally charged with any wrongdoing. However, in 1987, he was convicted for securities violations, stemming from the collapse of his savings and loan empire in Ohio.

Another part owner of the Tampa Bay team was Hulsey S. Lokey, the chairman of the board of Host International. Lokey's commanding officer in World War II had been Culverhouse, whom Lokey appointed to Host's board of directors. Lokey was appointed vice chairman of the team. He died on September 29, 1980.

Culverhouse was also selected to the board of directors of American Financial Corporation, which had bought out Gene Klein's National General in 1974.

5. Seventy-two-year-old Trafficante died in March 1987 in Houston—soon after a federal judge dismissed racketeering and conspiracy charges against him developed during a 1980 FBI sting operation. Also at the time of his death, he was suspected as being the principal receiver of illegal drugs from Central America during the Iran/Contra scandal. There is considerable evidence showing that top officials of the Reagan administration were also involved in the drug-smuggling operation.

6. Smathers, known as "the Senator from Cuba" because of his unconditional support for Fulgencio Batista, also had ties to numerous organized-crime associates, including Meyer Lansky, Jimmy Hoffa, and Tatum Wofford. An October 11, 1971, *Newsday* report noted that Smathers, whose family owned the Flagship Banks in Florida, "owned no Major [Realty] stock when named as a director, but as of May 1971, a report filed by Major with the Securities and

Exchange Commission reflects that he owned 94,000 shares valued at more than $940,000. The circumstances of his stock acquisitions are not indicated by public records."

CHAPTER 33

1. DeBartolo was baptized Anthony Paonessa. His father, Anthony Paonessa, an Italian immigrant, died just before his birth. His mother remarried when he was one. His stepfather was Michael DeBartolo, who adopted him. DeBartolo also took the first name of his uncle, Edward. However, DeBartolo didn't get around to changing his name legally until he was thirty-four.

2. Interestingly, at the same time baseball players Mickey Mantle and Willie Mays were having troubles with baseball commissioner Bowie Kuhn because of their casino connections in Atlantic City, former Cleveland Browns superstar Jimmy Brown was busy working on his two-hour, semiweekly radio show, "The Stardust Line," live from the Stardust hotel/casino in Las Vegas.

An FBI report, dated April 17, 1965, alleged that Brown, one of the greatest runners in the history of football, had been associating with a top Cleveland underworld figure and gambling with him. According to the report, James "Jack White" Licavoli, a major sports gambler who later became the boss of the Cleveland Mafia, had boasted of his golf matches with the Browns star. The report indicated "that there is heavy betting on these golf matches with Brown, and that on a certain day he [lost] as much as $700. On another day Brown lost $600, then on another day Brown won $800." According to the report, Licavoli conceded that "Brown never plays these fellows even and must give them strokes because he shoots a game in the low 70s."

There was no known investigation of the matter by the NFL. Brown, who began his career with the Cleveland team in 1957, retired from professional football at the conclusion of the 1965 season and has never been accused of any wrongdoing in this matter.

3. The founder of the 49ers, Anthony J. Morabito, had a heart attack while seated in his owner's box at Kezar Stadium—just before halftime in the 49ers game against the Chicago Bears in October 1957. His brother, Victor Morabito, took control of the team until 1964 when he, too, died of a heart attack. The team was then inherited by the widows of the two brothers, Josephine and Jane Morabito. They authorized Lou Spadia to run the team for them. Jane Morabito retained 5 percent of the stock of the 49ers after the DeBartolo purchase.

4. Mieuli was also the owner of the Golden State Warriors of the NBA. Like Morabito, he kept 5 percent of the stock in the 49ers.

Mieuli had attempted to purchase the 49ers in December 1976, along with Spadia, former San Francisco mayor Joseph Alioto, and Libero P. Balderelli. However, on December 9, Denny Walsh, a Pulitzer Prize-winning reporter with *The Sacramento Bee,* broke a story, saying that Balderelli, the owner of a tax consulting firm and the foreman of the Nevada County Grand Jury, had been accused by the IRS of failing "to report income, file a return and pay taxes for various periods in the last 12 years." He had also established lines of credit at a dozen casinos in Las Vegas and Lake Tahoe. Balderelli was to have owned 11 percent of the 49ers.

The day after Walsh's story appeared, the syndicate's negotiations for the purchase of the team were terminated.

5. Deposition of Allen Davis, Los Angeles Memorial Coliseum Commission v. National Football League, U.S. District Court, Central District of California, Civil Action No. 78–3523–HP.

6. Davis had other motives for greasing the sale of the 49ers for the DeBartolos, namely, his ex-partner in the Raiders, Wayne Valley, had indicated an interest in buying the team. Davis did not relish the thought of a hostile owner operating across the San Francisco Bay.

Hired as the DeBartolos' general manager was Joe Thomas, who had been a top executive with the Miami Dolphins from 1965 to 1972 and then also helped engineer the 1972 swap of the Baltimore Colts for the Los Angeles Rams. In the wake of that deal, he became the general manager of the Colts under Robert Irsay.

7. Carabbia was later convicted of murdering Cleveland's Irish mob leader Danny Greene in 1977 on behalf of the top brass of the Cleveland Mafia. Carabbia had planted and detonated a bomb in Greene's car. The murder was handled so sloppily that Carabbia's accomplice, who was not a made-Mafia figure and thus not subject to *omertà,* turned state's evidence when apprehended. In the end, the entire hierarchy of the Cleveland Mafia was indicted in the conspiracy and convicted for its role in the Greene murder.

8. The president of Yonkers Raceway was Art Rooney's son Timothy J. Rooney, whose daughter Kathleen married Tim Mara's grandson and Wellington Mara's son, Timothy Christopher Mara, thus linking the heirs of two of the NFL teams: the Maras of the New York Giants and the Rooneys of the Pittsburgh Steelers.

9. William Henry Paul, *The Gray-Flannel Pigskin: Movers and Shakers of Pro Football* (Philadelphia: J. B. Lippincott Co., 1974), p. 267.

10. Patriarca was the target of illegal federal wiretaps from 1962 to 1965, which showed his hidden interests in a number of racetracks, including Green Mountain, as well as his association with other top members of the national crime syndicate.

CHAPTER 34

1. McLaney was convicted of securities fraud in 1970. At the time, he was still the owner of the Royal Haitian and the International Casino in Haiti.

2. When Tito Carinci of Newport, Kentucky, fame, who pleaded guilty to placing interstate bets for Beckley, was placed on probation in 1968, he became a car salesman for Fincher.

Also, one of Fincher's businesses, an auto parts company, became the target of federal wiretaps in 1970. However, whatever case had been made by government investigators was immediately dismissed when Fincher wiretaps were among those deemed illegal in 1975 because of the signature problems within Attorney General John Mitchell's office at the Justice Department. Others who had charges dropped in these cases included Lefty Rosenthal, Elliot Paul Price, and Jerome Zarowitz.

3. Brown, a Democrat who became Kentucky governor in 1979 and had been a gambling associate of McLaney, is married to the 1971 Miss America, Phyllis George, who did a television duet with Jimmy "the Greek" Snyder prior to NFL games on CBS. A federal grand jury later investigated Brown's banking and gambling activities, but no charges were ever filed. In one transaction, Brown had reportedly withdrawn $1.3 million in cash from a Florida bank to pay off, for the most part, a gambling debt.

4. Hornung was described in the report by law-enforcement agents as "an associate of Luther Albert James who is reputed to be a non-member associate of organized crime. Hornung and James at one time flew gambling junkets to Las Vegas (Riviera Hotel)."

5. DeBartolo, who bought Metropolitan in 1975, owned 227,000 shares of stock in the bank. His position was so strong at the Metropolitan Bank that he, unilaterally, forced the bank's president to resign in 1981. Other board members had no say in the matter. Metropolitan collapsed in 1982. It was the largest bank failure in Florida history. Federal bank examiners discovered as much as $50 million of questionable loans due. DeBartolo was not accused of any wrongdoing. Hugh Culverhouse's business partner, Marvin Warner, and Warner's Great American Bank immediately bought Metropolitan, paying its eight thousand depositors/investors $18.3 million.

CHAPTER 35

1. Just the previous year, defensive back Steve Tannen of the New York Jets, who had been out for the season with a dislocated shoulder, was linked to Florida bookmaker Ira Vernon, who had been arrested on December 7, 1975, with five others for his role in a major interstate sports-gambling and layoff operation. Tannen was a limited partner in a Gainesville boutique near the University of Florida campus. Although Tannen was not implicated in the gambling probe—which included a wiretap on the boutique's telephone—the NFL launched an investigation. "Trusting people has always been a bad trait of mine," Tannen told *New York Times* reporter Gerald Eskenazi. "I'd like to sell out my interest in it, but now I wonder whether I can."

A similar situation arose with Jim Bertlesen, a running back for the Los Angeles Rams. His partner in a restaurant had been booking bets for customers. Bertlesen was not accused of any wrongdoing.

Both Tannen and Bertlesen sold their interests in their respective businesses and were then cleared by the NFL. The case against Vernon and his associates was dismissed when the evidence acquired through the wiretaps was ruled as inadmissible.

2. Morton's partner in the restaurant was Billy Bob Harris, with whom Morton shared an apartment. In 1984, Harris, who had become a stockbroker, was charged in an SEC insider-trading case. Harris was accused of receiving $1.9 million as a result of illegal inside information provided him by Paul Thayer, then the deputy secretary of defense under President Reagan. Harris

had met Thayer through Morton, who had been dating Thayer's daughter. Others named in the SEC complaint along with Harris and Thayer were convicted gambler Malcolm B. Davis and Atlanta stockbroker William Mathis, a former fullback with the New York Jets.

Both Thayer and Harris were convicted.

3. The story about Scott's and Hertwig's presence in Fuqua's house was first published by M. Anthony Lednovich and Dan Christensen of *The Fort Lauderdale News/Sun-Sentinel* on August 22, 1982. The reporters wrote in a subsequent story that Jack Danahy of NFL Security had been notified of Scott's and Hertwig's association with Fuqua. They quoted Georgia Bureau of Investigation agent Gary Garner as saying, "We contacted the proper authorities in the NFL and they didn't seem to care."

In January 1973, Scott was named the Most Valuable Player in Super Bowl VII while he was with the Miami Dolphins, which defeated the Washington Redskins, 14–7.

CHAPTER 36

1. There was no particular loyalty between Rosenbloom and Wilson—from whom Rosenbloom later tried to steal the Bills' superstar O. J. Simpson. Rosenbloom's outburst appeared to be nothing more than just another act in defiance of Rozelle, with whom he was still warring.

2. Also, in 1978, the NFL went to a sixteen-game schedule.

3. In March 1985, the NFL decided to experiment again with the instant replay on controversial calls by game officials. The trial period was to extend over the 1985 preseason and to be used in nine, nationally televised exhibition games. This action was prompted after the Los Angeles Raiders were credited with a touchdown—in which the receiver who scored was clearly out of bounds—during their 1984 13–7 loss against the Pittsburgh Steelers. The instant replay went into effect for the 1986 regular season.

The fledgling United States Football League had been first to institutionalize the instant replay on controversial calls.

Those NFL teams voting against the use of the replay were the Houston Oilers, Kansas City Chiefs, Los Angeles Raiders, New York Giants, and New York Jets.

4. One reason for the delay in the surveillance was that the informant was trying to be paid for his information from at least two federal agencies: the FBI and the IRS. The IRS agent told me, "We paid him some pretty good bucks, but we told him that he wasn't entitled to two payments. We got together with the FBI and ironed that out really quick."

CHAPTER 37

1. With the sale of his other sports teams, Cooke became the first NFL owner to comply with the NFL's rules prohibiting cross ownerships.

Cooke later bought the Los Angeles *Daily News*.

2. Tarkanian became the head coach at Long Beach State University in 1968 and then landed the same job at the University of Nevada at Las Vegas in 1973. In the latter position, he received a $22,000 salary, plus $10,000 for his participation in a television program on basketball, $15,000 from Caesars Palace for some public-relations appearances, two new cars, a $100,000 house at cost, and many other benefits. Twice disciplined for NCAA recruiting violations, Tarkanian had also received $45,000 a year for other promotional activities from David Bliss, the president of Las Vegas ticket-selling firm Royal Reservations, who had been linked to a federal extortion and bribery case. Tony Spilotro, who was a target in that probe, was heard on FBI wiretaps telling an associate to "take care" of Bliss, who had received immunity from prosecution and could incriminate Spilotro.

Weiss had been implicated in a 1972 recruiting violation investigation at Long Beach State, where Tarkanian was in his final year as head coach. Weiss allegedly offered $150 cash to a high school player. The player reportedly refused the money but later played for Tarkanian at UNLV.

For an excellent background story on Tarkanian, see Mary Neiswender and Mark Gladstone, *Sunday Independent Press-Telegram* (Long Beach, California), 29 July 1979.

3. Cooke had merged Teleprompter, which had a legacy of scandal, with his H & B American Cable Television Company in 1971. By 1973, according to reporter Bob Pack, the SEC "had halted trading in Teleprompter stock, amid allegations that the company had defrauded its stockholders and the public by failing to disclose that it had a cash-flow problem, that it had been denied additional loans by its banks, and that it had to cancel an expansion program for lack of funds."

Cooke, as chairman of the board, then removed Teleprompter's president Raymond P. Shafer, the former governor of Pennsylvania. After the collapse of the company's stock, Cooke began to rebuild Teleprompter. Cooke finally sold the company to Westinghouse in 1980, after yet another suspension of trading by the SEC in 1977.

4. While living in Las Vegas, Cooke met and fell in love with Jeanne Williams Wilson, an employee of the Sands hotel/casino on the Strip. They were married in late October 1980 but were divorced within ten months.

Also, there was no great love between Cooke and Pete Rozelle, who had married Carrie Cooke, the ex-wife of Cooke's son Ralph Cooke, in 1973. Rozelle and his second wife had been married at the New York home of Herbert J. Siegel, the owner of Chris-Craft Industries. Rozelle was a member of Siegel's board of directors. Like Gene Klein's National General Corporation, Chris-Craft had attempted but failed to take over Warner Brothers-Seven Arts in 1968, losing out to National Kinney.

In 1984, Siegel became a major stockholder in Warner Communications and a member of its board of directors.

5. Williams had actually begun negotiating the purchase of the Orioles on behalf of a syndicate of prospective buyers headed by former treasury secretary William Simon in 1978. When the two sides could not come to terms and the negotiations collapsed, Williams stepped into the breach the following year and bought the Orioles for a mere $12 million. The move proved to be a face-saving

device for Williams, who realized that he was being moved out as president of the Redskins by Cooke. After his purchase of the Orioles, he resigned as president of the football team, claiming that he was obeying the NFL's rarely enforced rules prohibiting cross ownership of professional sports teams.

Williams's Orioles won the 1983 World Series, defeating the Philadelphia Phillies in five games, the same year that the Redskins, in which Williams had retained his 14.7 percent interest, defeated the Miami Dolphins, 27–17, in Super Bowl XVII.

6. Fifty-seven-year-old Geraldine Cutter was killed when her new Thunderbird rolled from their driveway through a twelve-foot retaining wall and over a seventy-five-foot cliff. She was found dead, barefoot, and in her housecoat. Soon after his wife's death, Cutter reportedly began driving in a bulletproof car and traveled with bodyguards. Cutter married a Las Vegas show girl at Caesars Palace in February 1980.

CHAPTER 38

1. Rosenbloom's biggest coaching dispute was with Chuck Knox, an outstanding head coach who had achieved a phenomenal record while with the Rams. In 1973, he was 12–2, 10–4 in 1974, 12–2 in 1975, 10–3–1 in 1976, and 10–4 in 1977. After the falling out, Knox, who went with the Buffalo Bills, was replaced by George Allen, who only lasted a few months, reportedly because of problems with Rosenbloom and his son Steve. The head coach during the Rams' 1978 season, Rosenbloom's last, was Ray Malavasi, whom Rosenbloom had lured away from Al Davis and the Oakland Raiders. Malavasi finished the season 12–4 and won the NFC West but lost the divisional play-off. Rosenbloom had also earlier caused friction with Cleveland Browns owner Art Modell after he "stole" a Browns assistant coach, Ray Prochaska.

2. At first, Rosenbloom wanted to move to Inglewood, just south of Los Angeles, and build a stadium in cooperation with the owners of the Hollywood Park racetrack.

3. U.S. Congress, Senate, Testimony of Howard Cosell, "Professional Sports Antitrust Immunity," Hearings before the Committee on the Judiciary on S. 2784 and S. 2821, United States Senate, 97th Cong., 2d sess., September 16, 1982, pp. 235–36.

4. In August 1976, Cowan had been subpoenaed to testify before a Florida grand jury in Dade County, which was investigating a major statewide gambling operation. Cowan was never charged with any wrongdoing. During my interview with him, Cowan said, "I appeared once in my life before a grand jury. I don't think they asked me any questions about gambling. And if it had anything to do with gambling, I wouldn't have known about it. The only questions I recall were about who may or may not have frequented my hotel."

5. There were four other people who were near the scene at the time of Rosenbloom's drowning: Rosa Lee Scott, Grace Rotelli, Theresa Politzer, and her husband Hugo Politzer. None of them saw any evidence of foul play. After seeing Rosenbloom struggling in the water, Scott called the rescue squad.

6. Howard Cosell with Peter Bonventre, *I Never Played the Game* (New York: William Morrow and Co., Inc., 1985), p. 22.

7. The federal investigation of Warner stemmed from an earlier probe of an extortion scheme in Las Vegas—in which an underworld figure was picked up on a legal wiretap discussing a plan "to siphon off money from an upcoming Frank Sinatra appearance at the Westchester Theatre in New York to keep the money from bankruptcy officials," according to an FBI affidavit.

Solomon Weiss, Warner's assistant treasurer, and Jay Emmett, a top assistant to Warner boss Steven J. Ross, were both indicted and accused of accepting bribes from the theater's management, hoping to influence Warner Communications to buy Westchester stock in 1973. Soon after, Warner bought $250,000 of stock in the theater. Emmett was represented by attorney Edward Bennett Williams. Emmett later pleaded guilty to reduced charges of signing false invoices. Weiss pleaded not guilty and was later convicted.

8. Cosell, *I Never Played,* p. 27.

CHAPTER 39

1. Within a year after leaving NFL Security, Danahy experienced an act of violence on a New York street. He told me, "In 1981, I was with Intercon. We were doing a survey for a client. I went into the office on a Sunday morning to get some paperwork done. While I was walking up Madison Avenue, I got rapped from behind by a guy with a little zippered ditty bag in which he had a can of shaving cream inside. It was like a blackjack. He hit me with that. It damn near killed me. He broke my arm, knocked me down, and he had me up against the wheel of a car. And he was kicking me—preparatory to fleece me. And so I decided that I wasn't going to be able to get up off the ground to square this guy. So I happened to be carrying a gun, and I shot him and killed him."

2. Gene Klein and David Fisher, *First Down and a Billion: The Funny Business of Pro Football* (New York: William Morrow and Co., 1987), p. 77.

3. Georgia replaced Steve Rosenbloom with longtime Carroll Rosenbloom aide Don Klosterman as the Rams' general manager. Klosterman, a childhood friend of Pete Rozelle and a former Rams quarterback who played behind Bob Waterfield and Norm Van Brocklin for part of the 1952 season. Klosterman had also been with the Kansas City Chiefs during the mid-1960s before joining Rosenbloom and the Colts.

4. According to Article IV, Section 4.3, of the NFL's constitution, "[N]o member shall have any right to transfer its club or franchise to a different city outside its home territory except with the prior approval of the members of the League." Approval required support from three quarters of the owners or twenty-one votes.

In October 1978, the NFL owners—with two owners absent from the vote—had voted unanimously to allow Rosenbloom to move the Rams thirty miles south to Anaheim. Instead of renewing the Oakland Raiders' lease with the Oakland-Alameda County Coliseum Commission, Davis signed an agreement with the ninety-two-thousand-seat Los Angeles Coliseum and announced that he was moving his team to L.A. In March 1980, the NFL owners voted against Davis's move four hundred miles south to Los Angeles. With Davis choosing to leave the room for the vote, there were zero votes for, twenty-two votes against, and five abstentions. Davis decided to move anyway, forcing the

NFL to file an injunction against him. Davis countered with a $213 million antitrust suit against the league.

5. Davis charged that Mecom and Rosenbloom had met in Los Angeles in early 1978, ostensibly to discuss a coaching situation. In fact, according to Davis, they had agreed to meet to discuss the scalping of Super Bowl tickets.

6. Because of the bad blood between Rozelle and Davis, high drama was present in the locker room of the Oakland Raiders after Super Bowl XV in January 1981 when Rozelle presented the Vince Lombardi Trophy to Davis. The Raiders had defeated the Philadelphia Eagles, 27–10, for the NFL championship. It was the first time that a wild card team had won the Super Bowl. During the brief presentation ceremony, the two adversaries remained civilized to the chagrin of those hungry for a memorable confrontation. The scene was repeated in January 1984 after the Los Angeles Raiders defeated the Washington Redskins, 38–9, in Super Bowl XVIII.

7. Steve Rosenbloom resigned as the general manager of the New Orleans Saints in January 1981.

8. Carroll Rosenbloom was reportedly very fond of Guiver and helped him gain financing for a shopping center. According to court documents, Rosenbloom had wanted Guiver with the Rams. To facilitate that, he wrote off the $140,000 debt Guiver owed to him. Rosenbloom also gave him a new Mercedes and the promise of a thousand Super Bowl tickets whenever the game was played in Los Angeles, regardless of whether the Rams were participating.

Also, during the dispute between Georgia Frontiere and Guiver, she had been routinely tape-recording conversations with everyone from Guiver and Steve Rosenbloom to Pete Rozelle, according to a sworn statement by Mel Irwin, an employee of Frontiere. Reportedly, Frontiere had elaborate taping systems hooked up to her telephones and meeting rooms, as well as one in her purse. She claimed under oath, "I didn't tape phone conversations unless it was something I had to remember."

9. The morale of the team remained low after its 31–9 loss to the Pittsburgh Steelers in Super Bowl XIV in 1980. The Rams came back the following season with an 11–5 season but lost to the Dallas Cowboys, 34–13, in the wild card game. However, in 1981, the Rams slipped to a dismal 6–10 and 2–7 in the strike-shortened 1982 season. The Rams did bounce back in 1983 with a 9–7 record, led by their new head coach, John Robinson, who had won 81 percent of his games and a national championship while being the longtime head coach at the University of Southern California.

CHAPTER 40

1. In 1978, Nevada gaming officials had fined the Union Plaza Sports Book $80,000 for accepting thirty-seven illegal bets from outside Nevada during a one-month period in the fall of 1977.

2. Simultaneously, the Aladdin, Dunes, Riviera, and Tropicana hotel/casinos in Las Vegas came under siege by the Justice Department's Strike Force Against Organized Crime, which also charged in federal corruption cases that these companies were concealing skimming operations and hidden ownerships by major organized-crime figures.

3. A federal court later ruled against the SEC and in favor of Argent.

4. Glick's cooperation was secured after the FBI conducted a search of mob boss Frank Balistrieri's safe in his Milwaukee office. One of the documents recovered was an agreement for an interest in the Argent Corporation. "The agreement, this option," said federal prosecutor Sheryle Jeans, "was between Glick, on the one hand, and defendants John and Joseph Balistrieri on the other hand . . . The option provided that for the payment of $25,000 they could purchase half interest in the Argent Corporation." The FBI also found $200,000 in cash and Frank Balistrieri's address book.

5. Rosenthal is known for having his own unique ways of doing things. He wasn't even predictable in the manner in which he started his car. Sometimes he would stand outside the open door and start the car from that position. At other times, he would leave the door open and keep his left foot on the ground as he started it.

6. In April 1984, an affidavit filed in federal court by FBI agent Michael DeMarco alleged that Milwaukee crime boss Frank Balistrieri was involved in the Rosenthal bombing. The affidavit stated that Balistrieri had been picked up in a telephone conversation with his two sons angrily charging that Rosenthal "fingered us and he fingered the Argent Corporation." The Milwaukee mobster pledged to "get full satisfaction." The FBI also accused Balistrieri of ordering the murder of a local rival and then placing bombs in the cars of two others. One of the targets was killed in the explosion. The other man discovered the bomb—which had failed to detonate; he later became a government witness.

7. A 2 percent federal tax on wagers made on sporting events and other forms of nonstate gambling operations had long been imposed on those booking the bets, who also were required to pay an occupational tax of $500 a year. Prior to December 1974, the excise tax was 10 percent, with the occupational tax at $50. The federal government estimated that, ideally, its income from these post-1974 taxes were close to $100 million annually.

The Treasury Department's position on the repeal of the taxes came in the midst of hearings on a bill proposal by Nevada Senator Howard Cannon to exempt legal gambling from taxes.

8. For details that the Reagan administration's war on organized crime and drugs was nothing more than a charade and a public-relations campaign, see my book *Dark Victory: Ronald Reagan, MCA and the Mob* (New York: Viking Press, 1986).

CHAPTER 41

1. At the time of the hearing, Alioto was having his own problems fighting off allegations of mob ties. In 1969, *Look* magazine charged that he had associations with six major underworld figures. Earlier, Alioto had been seriously considered as Democratic presidential nominee Hubert Humphrey's running mate in 1968. Alioto filed a libel suit against *Look* and eventually was awarded $350,000 in damages. The charges were rekindled in 1981 with the release of Southern California mob boss James Fratianno's book, written by Ovid Demaris, *The Last Mafioso* (New York: Times Books, 1981). Fratianno contradicted Alioto's claims that the former mayor had no ties to the underworld.

Alioto is the son-in-law of Billy Sullivan, the owner of the New England Patriots. Alioto had previously defended the NFL against an antitrust suit that challenged the NFL players' basic contract filed by Joe Kapp of the Minnesota Vikings. Kapp won his case in April 1976 but received no damages. The ruling was upheld by the court of appeals two years later.

2. On May 11, 1981, the jury in Davis's antitrust suit against the NFL was hopelessly deadlocked. A mistrial was declared. Finally, a year later, on May 7, the federal court ruled in favor of Davis, finding that the NFL had violated U.S. antitrust laws. Davis then moved his Raiders to Los Angeles. In March 1989, just before Rozelle's resignation, Davis settled with the NFL for $18 million.

3. In July 1981, college basketball was rocked by another point-shaving scheme as former Boston College star Richard Kuhn was indicted by a federal grand jury in Brooklyn. He was promised $2,500 a game, as well as "drugs, women, and cars . . . just to see to it that the games would never go beyond the point spread." Also indicted as his coconspirators were four others, including a major organized-crime figure. All five had cooperated in a conspiracy to fix the final point spreads of several BC games. Kuhn, who had solicited the cooperation of other players, had begun his involvement with the gamblers by providing them with inside information.

Kuhn and three others were convicted and sentenced to prison. Kuhn, sentenced to ten years, was released after serving twenty-eight months.

The prosecutor in the case, Edward McDonald of the Brooklyn Strike Force, said in 1985, "We have found in two of the four sports corruption cases that we have had in my office that cocaine was offered as an inducement to the [athletes]. We are not talking about a situation where there was an addiction, but simply that cocaine was offered as an inducement to the sports participants to get them to go along with the fix. I think that in . . . the last few years . . . cocaine use has become much more widespread throughout the country and especially among athletes, both on a professional and amateur college level. So I think that the likelihood of the offer of narcotics, primarily cocaine, is much greater now than it was in 1978 when Mr. Kuhn was approached."

4. When he retired from football in 1984, Stabler had played in 184 games, attempted 3,793 passes, completing 2,270 for a 59.85 percentage and 194 touchdowns. When he joined the Oilers, Stabler was the most accurate passer in the history of the NFL. He was a three-time selection to the Pro Bowl and, in 1974, was picked for the NFL's all-pro team. He also led the Raiders to the team's first Super Bowl win in 1977. Oakland defeated the Minnesota Vikings, 32–14. In the game, Stabler completed 12 of 19 passes for 180 yards, one touchdown, and no interceptions.

5. On September 7, 1981, *The New York Times* published another story about Stabler's business relationship with Anthony James Romano, a member of the Stefano Magaddino crime family in Buffalo, New York. Reporters Crewdson and Rawls charged that the NFL had approved of the partnership between the two men—without a thorough background check on Romano, who had been convicted of wire fraud and criminal tax fraud and had served two years at Lewisburg Penitentiary.

6. After *The New York Times* story, *NBC Nightly News* alleged that Stabler had left Shea Stadium with Dudich after a November 23, 1980, game with

the New York Jets. The six-point-favorite Oilers lost the game, 31–28, in overtime. During the game, Stabler had thrown four interceptions.

At halftime, the Jets were leading the Oilers 21–0. But Stabler and the Houston team, in front of the partisan New York crowd, battled back in the second half—despite the fact that the Oilers' top runner, Earl Campbell, had been injured in the third quarter. With the score 28–21 late in the fourth quarter, Stabler threw his fourth touchdown pass to tie the score and send the game into overtime. However, the Jets ended the game in overtime with a field goal, winning, 31–28.

Bookmakers around the country say that no unnatural money was detected on the game. The Oilers opened as six-point favorites; the line did not change at all during the week before the game.

7. The Alameda County district attorney, Lowell Jensen, believed that there was no evidence to support the charges against Anderson or Stabler. Jensen was later appointed by President Reagan as the head of the criminal division in the U.S. Justice Department and later to a federal judgeship.

8. When informed of the results of Tropiano's lie detector test, Rozelle said, "A lie detector test, for one thing, does not stand up in court." And Warren Welsh cautioned, "I think it's important to note that a polygraph is really a detector of emotions," and placed little faith in the test. Significantly, during previous discussions about polygraph tests of NFL personnel who reportedly passed them—such as those of NFL owners, as well as players Rick Casares, Len Dawson, Johnny Robinson, and Babe Parilli, among others—the NFL viewed those tests as being definitive.

9. *The Gold Sheet,* September 1981.

10. Ken Stabler and Berry Stainback, *Snake* (Garden City, N.Y.: Doubleday & Co., Inc., 1986), pp. 210–11.

11. Unitas had retired from the NFL after the 1973 season, playing from 1955 to 1972 in Baltimore and finishing his career with San Diego. Named by the Pro Football Hall of Fame selection committee as the all-time greatest quarterback to ever play the game, Unitas, at the time of his retirement, held NFL career records for most passing attempts, most completions, most yardage, most three-hundred-yard games, and most touchdown passes. He also threw at least one touchdown pass in forty-seven consecutive games, another NFL record. Unitas was also known for his clean-cut image and his tremendous poise under incredible pressure on the football field. He was inducted into the Pro Football Hall of Fame in Canton, Ohio, in 1979.

12. The NFL has yet to establish guidelines regarding with whom a bet may be made or how much that bet may be in order for it to be considered a "friendly bet."

13. Stabler filed a libel suit against *The New York Times* and *NBC News* for their stories linking him to Dudich. The specific reason for the NBC suit resulted from the network's distribution "to its affiliated stations a videotape which suggested Stabler threw or deliberately lost football games or shaved points in football games so that gamblers might prevail or win bets . . ." In his autobiography, *Snake,* Stabler writes, "some viewers may well have been led to believe that I had thrown the game. NBC settled with us out of court. All I cared about was clearing my name completely" (p. 243).

Stabler later dropped his suit against the *Times.* In reporting Stabler's decision, the *Times* wrote, "[L]aw enforcement officials said such associations [with gamblers] were not in themselves illegal, but could be considered in violation of the N.F.L. constitution which provides penalties for a player who knowingly associates with gamblers."

CHAPTER 42

1. In 1984, Henderson was sentenced to fifty-six months in prison after he pleaded no contest to charges of forcible oral copulation, sexual assault and battery. According to testimony at a preliminary court hearing, Henderson had attacked two teenage girls in his apartment and forced them, at gunpoint, to perform oral sex. One of the girls was a paraplegic who was confined to a wheelchair. Henderson later reportedly offered them $10,000 not to testify against him.

2. In 1975, Csonka was also one of nineteen investors in a Connecticut corporation that was investigated by the U.S. Strike Force for its alleged role in a jai-alai-financing scandal. Csonka was not charged with any wrongdoing.

3. The Csonka-Kiick story, first reported by WVUE-TV in New Orleans, was advanced by M. Anthony Lednovich and Dan Christensen of *The Fort Lauderdale News and Sun-Sentinel.*

4. On February 26, 1981, just prior to the eruption of the Broncos drug scandal, team owners Allan and Gerry Phipps sold their interests in the team for $35 million to Edgar F. Kaiser, Jr., the chairman and chief executive officer of Kaiser Resources, Ltd., an international coal, oil, and gas company headquartered in Denver. A Harvard M.B.A. and a former AID employee stationed in Vietnam, Kaiser kept the team for only three years, selling out to forty-year-old real estate executive Patrick Dennis Bowlen. Denver industrialist John Adams became a minority owner.

5. At the same time of the Broncos investigation, NBA star David Thompson of the Denver Nuggets was traded to the Seattle SuperSonics after having admitted to the local police about his personal drug problems. Three members of the professional basketball team were also targets of the same investigation as the Broncos were.

6. Reese also credited Saints owner John Mecom with doing everything he could to get his player cleaned up by paying him enough money to clear up his debts after his drug habit became known and providing him with invaluable moral support.

7. The World Football League operated only in 1974 and for half of the 1975 season. Without a network television contract, it lost $20 million and quietly faded away. The league's only big score came early when its Toronto franchise signed Larry Csonka, Jim Kiick, and Paul Warfield of the Miami Dolphins in a $3 million package. Although a trickle of other NFL stars followed, they were not enough to save the league.

8. In 1982, the NFL signed over its television rights with the three major networks for over $2 billion during the five-year-contract period. Each NFL owner received over an incredible $14 million a year.

9. In addition to Trump and DeBartolo, other USFL owners in 1984 included Edward B. Diethrich of the Arizona Wranglers, Marvin L. Warner of the Birmingham Stallions, James F. Hoffman of the Chicago Blitz, Ron Blanding of the Denver Gold, Jerry Argovitz of the Houston Gamblers, Fred B. Bullard of the Jacksonville Bulls, J. William Oldenburg of the Los Angeles Express (which was later operated by General Manager Don Klosterman, who had grown disenchanted with the Los Angeles Rams), Billy Dunavent of the Memphis Showboats, A. Alfred Taubman of the Michigan Panthers, Joseph C. Canizaro of the New Orleans Breakers, Ted Taube of the Oakland Invaders, William R. Tatham of the Oklahoma Outlaws, Myles H. Tanenbaum of the Philadelphia Stars, Clinton Manges of the San Antonio Gunslingers, John Bassett of the Tampa Bay Bandits, and Berl Bernhard of the Washington Federals.

Four of the original owners sold their teams in 1983.

USFL head coaches included Craig Morton of the Gold, John Hadl of the Express, and John Ralston of the Invaders.

10. See Peter Phipps's story on DeBartolo in the *Akron Beacon Journal Magazine,* 27 November 1983.

11. David Harris, *The League: The Rise and Decline of the NFL* (Toronto: Bantam Books, 1986), p. 588.

CHAPTER 43

1. Mechling, also an author and investigative reporter, had won the Democratic nomination in Nevada, for the U.S. Senate, defeating Alan Bible and the Pat McCarran political machine in 1952. Running on an anti-organized-crime platform in the heart of casino country and refusing to accept *any* political contributions, Mechling was found to have been cheated of several thousand votes in the general election—during which the Democratic McCarran machine supported Mechling's Republican opponent, George Malone. With the election hopelessly corrupted, the contest was handed over to the U.S. Senate for its decision on who would be the next Nevada senator. However, the Senate vote ended in a tie. The deadlock was officially broken by the new U.S. vice president and president pro tem of the Senate, Richard Nixon. There, Mechling ran out of luck.

2. Garvey told me that during the 1982 collective-bargaining negotiations there was an attempt by the NFLPA to gain access to NFL Security. Garvey added, "We tried to make it a joint operation, and we failed. We made a demand that NFL Security respond to both the union and management. But we knew we weren't going to get it."

3. In fact, Tanguay did *not* conclude that Rosenbloom was the victim of foul play. And four witnesses, who had claimed to see Rosenbloom drown and saw no evidence of it either, described the black object near Rosenbloom as sea debris.

4. There was also some suspicion about a possible cover-up by the Golden Beach police, particularly after Henrikson resigned as sheriff the month after Rosenbloom drowned. However, Henrikson told me that he had been trying to get a job as the director of security of Federal Express's international opera-

tion, which is based in Memphis, Tennessee. "In fact," Henrikson says, "I received my formal offer in the mail from Federal Express earlier in the day before Rosenbloom drowned."

5. At the time these charges were being filed against Dudley, Berry, and Sklaroff, Beckley was under indictment for running an illegal lottery in Atlanta.

6. Thomas spent his entire professional football career from 1966 to 1978 with the Kansas City Chiefs. A graduate of Bishop College, Thomas twice led the NFL for most interceptions in a season. Selected four times to play in the NFL's Pro Bowl, Thomas made a key interception in the 1970 Super Bowl, in which the Chiefs defeated the Minnesota Vikings. Thomas later became an assistant coach with the Washington Redskins.

7. Phil Manuel is one of the most respected organized-crime investigators ever to work on Capitol Hill. For years, he was the chief investigator for the U.S. Senate's Permanent Subcommittee on Investigations. He headed many inquiries into financial manipulations by organized crime groups, including traffic in stolen and counterfeit securities and similar frauds.

CHAPTER 44

1. Government investigators refused to confirm or deny reports that a second address book was found on Dorfman, which supposedly included the names and telephone numbers of five additional NFL owners.

2. Just weeks before Dorfman's murder, an FBI report had been filed, accusing him of skimming in Las Vegas, which added to the increasing pressure on him. "Dorfman represents the Chicago and Kansas City organized crime groups dealing with Central States, Southeast and Southwest Areas Pension Fund (CSPF)," the report read. "For many years he has arranged for and continues to control all loans made to organized crime entities from CSPF. Also, he controls organized crime investments in various Las Vegas, Nevada, casinos out of which these organized crime groups derive 'skim' money . . . Dorfman currently has a hidden ownership interest in the Slots-A-Fun Casino in Las Vegas. 'Skimming' of monies from this and other casinos goes back to the Chicago organized crime group utilizing Dorfman as a conduit."

Thirteen days before he was shot to death, Dorfman took the Fifth Amendment thirty times in a Chicago federal court, refusing to answer questions about his business ties with the Teamsters' Central States Pension Fund.

3. In early 1974, Spilotro and Dorfman were indicted in Chicago, along with five others, including Irwin Weiner, by federal attorneys for bilking the Teamsters' pension fund of $1.4 million. Among the witnesses called to testify against them was Daniel Seifert, who was shotgunned to death by three ski-masked assailants in front of his family. After Seifert's brutal murder, the charges against Spilotro were dropped. Dorfman and the others were later acquitted. Spilotro is widely reputed to have arranged the murder.

I attended Dorfman's trial in April 1975. During a recess, I saw Dorfman and Weiner sitting on a bench outside the courtroom. I walked up and introduced myself. During our conversation, I asked Dorfman whether he was as bad as everyone was claiming. He insisted that he was "no different and no worse" than anyone else in a position to manipulate money and power.

4. Schlichter played in only three Colts games during the 1982 season under Colts head coach Frank Kush. Without starting a single game, Schlichter completed seventeen of thirty-seven passes for 197 yards. He threw no touchdown passes and had two interceptions.

5. The bookmakers were Samuel R. Alascia, Harold E. Brooks, Joseph A. Serio, and Charles T. Swift. The charges against Swift were dismissed.

6. In early May 1982, just two weeks before the Schlichter suspension, *The Cleveland Plain Dealer* reported that similar gambling charges against no fewer than a dozen other NFL players had been uncovered by NFL Security as a result of the Schlichter investigation. Although the report was confirmed by other sources, no other player was named or disciplined for gambling.

7. Tose admitted that he lobbied on Ford's behalf to bring Super Bowl XVI to the Lions' Pontiac Silverdome in January 1982, in which the San Francisco 49ers defeated the Cincinnati Bengals, 26–21.

8. Welsh added that the NFL was faced with a similar situation with former New York Jets head coach Walt Michaels who also became involved in a tout sheet.

9. Among those indicted were Chicago mobsters Joe Aiuppa, Jackie Cerone, Joseph Lombardo, and Angelo LaPietra; former Chicago police officers Tony Chiavola, Sr., and Tony Chiavola, Jr.; Kansas City mobsters Carl DeLuna and Carl Civella; Milwaukee mobsters Frank Balistrieri, John Philip Balistrieri, and John Joseph Balistrieri; Las Vegas mobster Tony Spilotro; Rosenthal's replacement at Argent, Carl Thomas; and Cleveland mobster Milton Rockman. Thomas was the only defendant licensed by the Nevada Gaming Commission. He was accused of skimming at the Stardust and the Tropicana. Nick Civella, who had been named as a coconspirator, later died before the case went to trial.

The indictments were based upon wiretaps, as well as on even more controversial devices of intelligence gathering, including court-authorized "surreptitious entry" into the houses, offices, and cars. Authorization was given in May 1978 after information was received that a contract killing was about to occur in the midst of a labor dispute in Kansas City. The victim, Mike Spero, was shot and killed in a bar and two of his brothers were seriously wounded. One of the brothers recovered and swore revenge, but he, too, was killed.

Also, in July 1983, seven men were convicted of skimming and having hidden interests at the Tropicana. The key government witness in the trial was Joseph Agosto, who had supervised the skimming operation. Agosto died of a heart attack soon after the trial ended.

CHAPTER 45

1. Eight months earlier, Warner Communications, which had bought a 48 percent interest in the Pittsburgh Pirates in 1979, named Caesar Kimmel, a longtime National Kinney executive, as the team's executive vice president. However, after Kuhn left as commissioner, reporter Gregory B. Hladky of *The New Haven Journal-Courier* reported that Kimmel was also the chairman of the board of a gambling casino in Antigua, which he had co-founded in 1979 and opened in 1981. Warner had sold its 57 percent interest in Kimmel's National Kinney in 1978 for $8.2 million.

Kimmel told Hladky, "I don't think I've violated any of the rules of baseball . . . It certainly doesn't have any impact on baseball in the United States. I'm not actively engaged in any part of the casino. I really don't know anything about running a casino."

When reminded of Kuhn's declaration that "baseball and casino employment are incompatible," Kimmel replied that Kuhn's prohibition was "outdated and outmoded."

In October 1984, Kimmel was ordered by Kuhn's successor, Peter Ueberroth, to sell his casino holdings or leave baseball. Kimmel resigned from the Pirates, denying that he had done so because of the controversy.

2. Howard Cosell with Peter Bonventre, *I Never Played the Game* (New York: William Morrow and Co., Inc., 1985), pp. 111–12.

3. The NFL also investigated charges that the five players were allegedly involved in a point-shaving scheme during the early 1980s in return for the cocaine, according to *The Miami News,* which first broke the story. The allegations were made by Daniel Anthony Mitrione, Jr., a former FBI special agent who was involved in Operation Airlift, a south Florida-based, FBI sting operation. Mitrione, who had pleaded guilty in March 1985 to cocaine trafficking, based his charges on a 1983 conversation he had had with two Dallas narcotics dealers. An FBI supervisor described Mitrione's claims as being "unsubstantiated."

CHAPTER 46

1. In March 1985, in the midst of the Computer group investigation, another point-shaving scandal broke out in college basketball. At Tulane University in New Orleans, several arrests were made, including three Tulane players and a Louisiana bookmaker Roland Ruiz, who had a long arrest and conviction record for gambling violations. Law-enforcement officials alleged that two games had been fixed by Ruiz, who had sought and received the cooperation of the three players. Ruiz allegedly used two students as intermediaries for the payoffs. In one of the games against Southern Mississippi, Tulane, favored to win by ten and a half points, won only 64–63. In the other game against Memphis State, Tulane, then four-point underdogs, lost, 60–49.

Through Ruiz and his middlemen, the players were given cocaine and cash in return for their point-shaving efforts.

CHAPTER 47

1. In 1980, popular oddsmaker Bobby Martin was indicted in Rhode Island for his role in a six-state gambling operation, specifically for illegally transmitting betting information across state lines. Martin had been picked up on federal wiretaps, supplying the point spreads on sporting events to a Rhode Island bookmaker.

The indictments of Martin and fifteen others culminated a two-year investigation by the FBI, the U.S. Strike Force, and the Rhode Island State Police.

Martin, who told me that he was fingerprinted by a police officer who had just lost a bet using the oddsmaker's line, was later convicted and served thirteen months in the federal minimum-security penitentiary in Boron, California. He was released in March 1984.

2. Roxborough is also the coauthor, along with Mike Rhoden, of *Race and Sports Book Management,* which is a 1988, self-published, 128-page handbook. It is used by Roxy in a course he teaches on the sports book business at Clark County Community College in North Las Vegas.

3. Speaking of watching the line move on the basis of the money bet, Roxborough told me, "We monitor the line during the week. In fact, we monitor it by the minute. We have runners in the books who are monitoring the line to see which way it moves. It's very important. That's part of our service."

CHAPTER 48

1. Del Rayo Stables won $5.4 million in purses in 1985, shattering the moneymaking record for a single stable.

Another NFL owner to purchase a thoroughbred horse farm was Jack Kent Cooke of the Washington Redskins. In December 1984, he, along with four partners, bought the 525-acre, 250-horse Elmendorf Farm in Lexington, Kentucky, for a reported $43.32 million. His entire empire is estimated to be worth over $2 billion.

In 1984, Cooke led the first serious effort to oust Pete Rozelle as NFL commissioner. Rozelle's ten-year contract, which gave him a $700,000-a-year salary, was to expire in 1991. Cooke's attempted purge failed.

2. Klein's prized horse, Winning Colors, won the 1988 Kentucky Derby. He told me, "What ran through me when my horse won the Kentucky Derby never ran through me when I owned the Chargers. It was one of the greatest thrills I've ever had."

3. During the early 1970s, Spanos, then a harness-racing promoter as well as a developer, purchased the controlling interest in the California Capital Trotting Association. Almost single-handedly, he was responsible for bringing night harness racing to California, increasing the pari-mutuel handle as well as attendance. Intrigued by the success of Cal-Cap, Spanos was contacted by other harness-racing operators all over the country, including the Art Rooney family of the Pittsburgh Steelers.

Asked by *Sacramento Bee* sports columnist Marco Smolich his views on sports gambling in 1971, after the state approved night racing, Spanos replied, "I've got nothing against gambling, you know. In fact, I've done a bit, only it hasn't been on horses . . . I'm interested in sports, all sports."

4. Korshak was the target of a four-part series, written by Seymour M. Hersh of *The New York Times* from June 27 to June 30, 1976. For more on Korshak, see my book *Dark Victory: Ronald Reagan, MCA and the Mob* (New York: Viking Press, 1986).

In 1983, Los Angeles Dodgers manager Tommy Lasorda caused a stir when he was seen having dinner at a Chicago restaurant with Korshak. For years, Korshak had been the baseball team's attorney on labor matters and had maintained a long, personal relationship with team owner Walter O'Malley. Korshak owned a portion of the Dodgers' parking lot concession.

5. Attorney Korshak was so bitter after Hilton's repudiation of him that he angrily sent off a letter to Hilton, dated November 29, 1984. Korshak wrote, in part, "I read with interest your disparaging remarks about me to the New Jersey Gaming Commission. When did you discover that I was unworthy of being an attorney or that I was associated with characters that shocked your most decent sensibilities?

"I have in my possession a number of letters from your staff extolling my virtues as an attorney and telling me how happy the hotels were with my representation of your corporation. Those letters were also sent to your office for your personal perusal."

Korshak then launched into a brief litany of personal favors he had done for Hilton over the years. Korshak concluded, "You have caused me irreparable harm, and as long as I live I will never forget that. When did I become a shady character? I imagine when you were having difficulty getting a license in Atlantic City."

6. State of New Jersey Casino Control Commission, "Plenary Licensing Hearing of Hilton New Jersey Corporation—Volume XIV: Decision," February 28, 1985.

CHAPTER 49

1. According to a government prosecutor, "On Easter Sunday 1983, Mr. Frontiere met with Raymond Cohen, who he knew was a potential witness in the IRS investigation, and corruptly endeavored to influence, impede and obstruct the investigation by counseling, advising and suggesting to Raymond Cohen that he give fictitious, fraudulent, false and manufactured information and testimony to IRS agents."

2. Petievich left the Treasury Department in 1985. He is now a novelist who has written, among other works, *To Live and Die in L.A.,* which was made into a major motion picture.

3. Jack Catain died in February 1987 in an Encino hospital.

4. The Bright syndicate outbid longtime Cowboys backer W. O. Bankston, who owned the largest Lincoln-Mercury dealership in the country. Bright held only 17 percent of the team—but the NFL waived its rule insisting on a 51 percent owner.

Bright is remembered for having purchased the full-page ad, "Welcome Mr. President" in *The Dallas Morning News* on the day President Kennedy was murdered in Dallas. In the ad, Bright had accused the President and his attorney general of being soft on communism. Sharing Bright's expenses for the ad was Nelson Bunker Hunt, the brother of Kansas City Chiefs owner Lamar Hunt. Both Bright and Bunker Hunt were active in the John Birch Society.

5. Soon after the sale to Bright and his syndicate, there was an unsuccessful attempt to buy the Cowboys from the new owners. This time it was by Marvin Davis, who had tried to purchase other NFL teams, including the Denver Broncos and the Los Angeles Rams, as well as the Oakland Athletics

major-league baseball team. Davis bought the controlling interest in Twentieth Century-Fox in 1981 and later sold the company to Rupert Murdoch.

6. Braman created a political stir when he gave Republican presidential candidate Jack Kemp, a former star quarterback with the Buffalo Bills, several hundred complimentary tickets to the 1988 Super Bowl, which Congressman Kemp then used to attract $1,000 contributors to his campaign.

7. Harvard-trained attorney Chuck Sullivan, team owner Billy Sullivan's oldest son and the executive vice president of the team, had invested much of the family fortune in rock star Michael Jackson's Victory Tour. The total ticket for the Sullivans was $21 million with no less than a $4 million loss assured.

In May 1984, the same month that Sullivan purchased the rights to the Jackson tour, he also leased the Foxboro Raceway, the racetrack near Sullivan Stadium. However, by the end of its first year of operations under the Sullivans, the racetrack had lost nearly $2 million. Consequently, the state's racing commission denied the track any racing dates and declared it "financially insolvent." Both investments had seriously impaired the Sullivan family's ability to keep the Patriots.

CHAPTER 50

1. The Patriots had learned of the gambling allegations against Fryar from *Boston Herald* staff writer Lynne Snierson, who had received information and was following leads. When the leads led to dead ends, the reporter went to the Patriots for comment. Head coach Ray Berry then reported Snierson's information to Warren Welsh and NFL Security.

Fryar, a first-round draft pick from the University of Nebraska in 1984, had scored the Patriots' only touchdown in the fourth quarter of Super Bowl XX.

Aside from drug and gambling charges, Fryar was knifed and the tendon in his finger was cut, reportedly during an argument with his wife. Fryar insisted that he had accidentally done it to himself. In February 1988, he was arrested in New Jersey for the unlawful possession of a .38 caliber revolver and hollow-point bullets, as well as a loaded shotgun. After his arrest, Fryar said, "I didn't know those things were against the law."

2. Also in 1985, two players, linebacker Mike Green of San Diego and nose tackle Tim Newton of Minnesota, pleaded guilty to possession of illegal drugs in separate cases. Both were slapped on the wrist. Green was sentenced to a drug program for first-time offenders; Newton paid a $50 fine.

On June 27, 1986, Don Rogers, a safety with the Cleveland Browns, died of a cocaine overdose.

3. Mike Bell had been arrested in November 1985 for cocaine possession and was later convicted; Barry Word was signed to a three-year contract in April 1987 after doing five months in the wake of his drug conviction.

Also in April 1987, three players for the Phoenix Suns of the NBA were indicted by a Maricopa County grand jury for cocaine trafficking. The players were James Edwards, Grant Gondrezick, and Jay Humphries. Also indicted were former players Mike Bratz and Garfield Heard. Other past and present members of the Suns were also present when the deal came down, according to the indictments, but were not involved in the sale. Two of these bystanders had been given immunity and testified at the grand jury against those later indicted.

In the NBA, a drug conviction or a guilty plea can result in suspension for life.

The investigation began after *The Arizona Republic* reported that a member of the Suns and two other NBA players had discussed the "over the total" line with a gambler in a February 1987 game between the Suns and the Milwaukee Bucks. The newspaper quoted the Suns player saying the total points of both teams would not go over 226 points. Only 222 points were scored in the game won by the Bucks, 115–107. The gambler reportedly won over $100,000 betting under the total.

4. The NFL teams were not getting much encouragement from the Reagan White House to take the national drug problem very seriously. After Ronald and Nancy Reagan appeared on national television in September 1986 to declare its politically popular "Drug-Free America" program and "Just Say No" campaign, the President—in his January 1987 federal budget proposal—cut over $913 million out of a $1.7 billion antidrug package. The following month, he selected Attorney General Edwin Meese to coordinate budget priorities for the administration's war-on-drugs charade.

5. Another major NFL Players Association strike began on September 22, 1987, canceling the third week of games. The NFL owners then introduced the controversial concept of "replacement players" for the next three games. The replacement games—which featured mostly an array of players who had not made the cut of an NFL team—secured at least a portion of the television revenues of the owners.

On October 15, after twenty-four days, the NFLPA returned without a contract. The players' union filed an antitrust suit against the NFL owners, again challenging the restrictions on players who wish to move from team to team. A year later, there was still no contract and no resolution in the antitrust case, even though the owners implemented on February 1, 1989 a scheme known as "Plan B," under which clubs could protect thirty-seven of their players while all the rest were unrestricted free agents, for a two-month period. Of the 619 "Plan B" players in 1989, 229 signed contracts with new teams. However, no player under the old restrictions continued under "Plan B" moved.

Although the volume of betting was down during the strike, the betting line from Las Vegas was still produced, distributed, and printed in newspapers around the country. Universally, weekend gamblers were at a loss about the talent accumulated by the owners for the replacement teams and found it difficult to determine how to bet. "It was like flipping a coin," one gambler told me. "We were betting on players we had never seen play before. Most of us just bet on our favorite teams out of some weird form of blind loyalty. The professionals with the real inside information on those games must have really kicked ass."

Warren Welsh told me that betting on the replacement games "caused a few problems" for NFL Security. He did not elaborate.

6. Duper, who had refused to appear for two drug tests, allegedly re-

ceived cocaine from John Rafael Gomez, who had been regularly seen on the Dolphins' practice field. Gomez, who was arrested in early December 1988 for his alleged role in a $3 million drug deal, admitted that he was a friend of Duper, who supplied him with free tickets to Dolphins games. In a related drug case, a police search yielded photographs of Duper and other members of the Miami team in the company of two convicted cocaine dealers, Nelson Aguilar and Timothy Taylor. Aguilar had also described Duper as a close friend.

Because of Duper's associations with drug dealers, the NFL claimed to have been "watching" the star receiver since 1986.

However, *Sports Illustrated,* which first reported the Duper story, charged that "NFL investigators had ignored evidence that . . . Duper had consorted with drug dealers as far back as 1986." *SI* also received information from former Florida assistant state attorney Herbert H. Cohen that "an NFL investigator showed little interest in information offered by the lawyer regarding cocaine use in the league."

7. Citing an example of the merging interest of agents and team owners, Garvey told me, "The owners sometimes want to sign players to long-term, nonguaranteed contracts. And the agents want long-term contracts because their bonuses are based on the total amount of the contract signed. It's in their interests to work together."

8. Palmer was suspended by the Chiefs on November 28, 1988, after he was quoted by an assistant coach and other players as saying that by "dropping a few balls on the carpet" he could help get head coach Frank Gansz fired. The remark was made prior to the Chiefs game with the Pittsburgh Steelers. He was immediately sent back to Kansas City. However, after the one-game suspension, he was reinstated after apologizing to all concerned.

9. Considered by law-enforcement officials as among the Mafia's new breed, Franzese was convicted in a criminal conspiracy to infiltrate numerous legitimate businesses, including Beneficial Finance, Chemical Bank, the Chevrolet division of General Motors, Mazda Motors, and Mobil Oil, as well as the Allied International Union, which organizes security guards.

Franzese is also the son of John "Sonny" Franzese, a top capo in the Colombo crime group.

10. Selcraig and Jill Lieber were part of a team of *SI* reporters who worked on a Craig Neff-bylined story about the Walters/Bloom case over a year before the indictments were handed up.

CHAPTER 51

1. Shaw was apparently not harmed by the publicity. In 1988, he became Georgia Frontiere's most trusted adviser on Rams football matters and the second most powerful executive on the management team.

2. Warner Communications officially acquired Lorimar in January 1989; Adelson became the vice chairman of Warner and a member of its board of directors. The merger had been jeopardized as a result of a power struggle and litigation between Warner chairman Steven Ross and former Hollywood talent agent Herbert J. Siegel, the chairman of Chris-Craft Industries. Siegel, encour-

aged by attorney Arthur L. Liman, had aided Ross during a hostile takeover bid of Warner Communications by Australian publishing tycoon Rupert Murdoch in 1984. In the process, Siegel bought a chunk of Warner. Soon after, a shooting war began between Ross and Siegel after Siegel filed suit to gain access to an internal Warner report about the indictments and convictions of three Warner executives, including Ross's two top assistants, Jay Emmett and Solomon Weiss.

Sitting on the Warner board of directors with Ross and Siegel was Hugh Culverhouse, the owner of the Tampa Bay Buccaneers.

On March 4, 1989, Warner and Time, Inc. announced the plan to merge and form Time Warner, Inc. Warner's stockholders will reportedly own 60 percent of the new company.

3. In May 1987, Adelson and Walters hosted a weekend celebrity tennis and golf charity affair at La Costa. Among the three hundred guests in attendance at the Adelson and Walters party were Irwin Molasky, former RCA corporate chief and MacArthur Foundation head Thorton Bradshaw, Twentieth Century-Fox head Barry Diller, Reagan's former ambassador to Mexico John Gavin, attorney and civil rights activist Vernon Jordan, talent agent Swifty Lazar, *New York Times* associate editor A. M. Rosenthal, attorney Mickey Rudin, developer Donald Trump, and publisher Mort Zuckerman, as well as a list of Lorimar's top stars, including Larry Hagman and Linda Gray.

In 1986, Adelson, Molasky, and company made a deal to purchase nine television stations, including six network affiliates. According to Jonathan Kwitny of *The Wall Street Journal,* Lorimar had to "borrow possibly as much as $2 billion, mostly in high-yield bonds to be sold to investors via Drexel Burnham Lambert."

4. On January 21, 1986, in Kansas City, five top underworld figures were convicted for conspiracy in the Stardust case. Among those found guilty were Joey Aiuppa, Jackie Cerone, Joseph Lombardo, Angelo LaPietra, and Milton Rockman. Frank Balistrieri had pleaded guilty earlier.

A total of seventeen organized-crime figures and their associates were convicted in three separate federal trials in Kansas City as part of the FBI's Strawman investigation.

5. See my story "MCA and the Mob" in the June 1988 issue of *Regardie's.*

6. During my interview with Hundley about the 1968 grand-jury investigation of the Washington Redskins, he told me that he had gone to Henry Petersen, Hundley's immediate successor as the head of the Organized Crime and Racketeering Section, to find out whether anyone involved in professional football was a target of the grand-jury investigation. Using almost the exact same words as in the MCA case with Margolis and DeFeo, Hundley told me, "I told him [Petersen] that if the department needed anything, I would supply it. If they need information from anyone, I would deliver them." (See ch. 18.)

7. Although the MCA case was killed, the Computer group case was renewed suddenly during the summer of 1988—within months after I had charged that the case had been stalled. Noble was reassigned again and returned to the FBI's office in Las Vegas to resume his investigation of the Computer group.

When I interviewed Mindlin in September 1988, he appeared to be lethargic over the case. He told me, "One of our former members, out of jealousy, went to them [the FBI] and tried to reawaken the case. But I've retired from the wars. I've undergone severe personal tragedy with the loss of my son and wife [in 1987–88]. It's been a very devastating period of my life. All I do is trade commodities, which is very much like sports. I stay by myself. I'm on a ranch, which is very isolated. My only link to the world are the phone lines and a satellite dish."

8. By the efforts of Ronald Goldstock and the New York Organized Crime Task Force, the heads of three of the five crime families in New York—Tony Salerno of the Genovese group, Anthony Corallo of the Lucchese group, and Carmine Persico of the Columbo group—and two underbosses were convicted of RICO violations. Each received a hundred years in prison and was fined $240,000 at their sentencing on January 13, 1987.

With Salerno's conviction, the acting head of the Genovese family became Vincent Gigante, who in 1957 had shot and wounded Frank Costello, forcing the old mobster into retirement.

9. Weld added, "Just one personnel rating was given to the U.S. attorneys. Other than that, the system was maintained, pretty much, status quo. The only other change was that the U.S. attorneys' initials are required on all case initiation reports. But if ten days go by and the U.S. attorney hasn't initialed them by then, then it is deemed initialed."

10. Less than a week before Williams's death, the *Legal Times* reported, "Court records . . . show that in 1986, before her marriage to [Jack Kent Cooke], Suzanne Martin had retained Edward Bennett Williams and three of his partners to negotiate a $2-million settlement with Jack Kent Cooke for mental anguish arising from her two abortions during their courtship.

"According to a Dec. 19, 1986, letter from Williams & Connolly to Suzanne Martin, the firm agreed to represent her in settlement talks for a 25-percent contingency fee." Martin's attorney was Williams's associate Brendan Sullivan, Jr., who later became famous as "the potted plant" while serving as Lieutenant Colonel Oliver North's lawyer during his testimony before the Iran/Contra committee and at his subsequent trial.

Martin dropped her claim against Cooke, whom she later married in July 1987. Soon after, they separated when he discovered that she was pregnant and would refuse to have another abortion.

Many believe that Williams's readiness to take Martin's case was an indication of the bitter rivalry that had developed between Williams and Cooke.

11. After forty-two years without an NFL crown, the Steelers won Super Bowl IX in 1975, defeating the Minnesota Vikings, 16–6. They repeated as NFL champions the following year, beating the Dallas Cowboys, 21–17. In Super Bowl XIII, the Steelers won their third championship, again downing Dallas, 35–31. And the year after that, Rooney's team defeated the Los Angeles Rams, 31–19.

12. In January 1988, Snyder told a WRC-TV film crew in Washington, D.C., that blacks were better athletes than whites because they were "bred" to be. He also insisted "there's not going to be anything left for the white people" because of increased jobs for blacks in sports. For these and other racial comments, Snyder was fired by CBS after twelve years with the network's sports division.

CHAPTER 52

1. Tony Accardo's son-in-law Ernest Kumerow had become the head of Laborers Local 1001. Kumerow's son and Accardo's grandson is Eric Kumerow, a defensive end-linebacker from Ohio State, who was the Miami Dolphins' number one draft pick in the 1988 college draft.

2. Roxborough's company, Las Vegas Sports Consultants, now offers casinos and sports books a computerized service that transmits up-to-the-minute line changes, weather conditions, and significant injuries, as well as future book prices and proposition wagers.

3. Another top Las Vegas oddsmaker who was paid to supply his numbers to the Stardust, forty-six-year-old Gerald "Jerry the Hat" Taffel, died from a heart attack on January 5, 1989.

4. Las Vegas gambler Gene Maday—who owns and operates Little Caesars, a small, independent sports book on the Strip in Las Vegas—has made his reputation for accepting the largest sports bets in Nevada. In the 1985 Super Bowl XIX between the San Francisco 49ers and the Miami Dolphins, Maday accepted a $500,000 bet on the 49ers, who were favored by three points and lost. He also reportedly accepted a $1.05 million bet from Bob Stupak, the owner of Vegas World, on the Cincinnati Bengals, who were seven-point underdogs in the 1989 Super Bowl XXIII, and lost that bet as well. Although considerable suspicion revolves around the actual circumstances of the Maday-Stupak bet, Maday, formerly of Detroit, has earned the reputation as the boldest sports gambler in the country.

Index

Page numbers above 436 refer to notes.